Texas Quails

Texas Quails

Edited by
Leonard A. Brennan

Ecology and Management

Texas A&M University Press COLLEGE STATION

The paper used in this book meets the minimum requirements
of the American National Standard for Permanence
of Paper for Printed Library Materials, Z39.48-1984.
Binding materials have been chosen for durability.

Publication of this book was assisted by generous support from the South Texas
Chapter and Texas State Council of Quail Unlimited, the Texas Cooperative Extension
Quail Decline Initiative, the Caesar Kleberg Wildlife Research Institute, and the
Richard M. Kleberg Jr. Center for Quail Research.

Library of Congress Cataloging-in-Publication Data

Texas quails : ecology and management / edited by Leonard A. Brennan. —
1st ed.
p. cm.
Includes index.
ISBN-13: 978-1-58544-503-5 (cloth : alk. paper)
1. Odontophoridae—Texas. 2. Game bird management—Texas. I. Brennan,
Leonard A. (Leonard Alfred)
QL696.G259T49 2007
598.6'2709764—dc22
2006011359

To R. J. Gutiérrez,
mentor, colleague, sportsman,
and friend

Contents

Section I:
*Ecology and Life History of Texas
Quails*

Section II:
*Quail Populations
in the Ecoregions of Texas:
Management Opportunities
and Research Challenges*

Foreword

One of my earliest memories while growing up on the family ranch in South Texas is the cheerful whistle of the bobwhite. I still recall those special times when the calls of bobwhites at daybreak were so frequent and loud that they often drowned out the other songbirds in the brush. South Texas remains a stronghold for quails in the United States. Sadly, there are signs that these once-strong populations of quails are following a trend similar to that of their cohorts in the southeastern United States.

There are many half-truths, speculations, and plain old wives' tales regarding quails and quail populations. Many years spent on the ranch, as well as many days in the field pursuing the wily bird, have led me to conclude that habitat and weather conditions are the most important factors influencing quail populations. Practices such as supplemental feeding have been shown, through research, to be neutral population management practices at best. However, feeding birds can concentrate them into smaller areas, reducing hunting time and making location of birds more predictable. Feeding often gives hunters and managers an upwardly biased view of quail population levels on their properties or leases. The bottom line is that quails are losing suitable habitat at an alarming rate. Increasing human populations and changing uses of the Texas landscape are slowly, but steadily reducing the amount of contiguous habitat once available for quails.

Texas Quails: Ecology and Management takes an important step in addressing the quail situation in Texas. Before we can move forward in a productive manner, as it relates to quails in Texas, we need to know and understand where we have been. There has been a lot of quail research conducted in Texas, but no one has ever compiled all of the information we know about quails into one comprehensive volume. This book does exactly that.

Some of the best quail experts in Texas and Oklahoma have contributed their work and insights in this book. I am proud to say that Texas and Oklahoma currently have the finest group of quail specialists in the world. We have fantastic quail researchers at our universities, one of the best Cooperative Extension programs in the country, and super staff with extensive quail knowledge and experience working at the Texas Parks and Wildlife Department. Perhaps most important, we have thousands of landowners and hunters who are keenly interested in doing what they can to put this information to work on the ground.

Quails and quail hunting are an important tradition in Texas. Cool winter days, shotguns, bird dogs, covey rises, friends, and family all are part of the tradition and what many of us look forward to each fall and winter. There are many facets of quail hunting that make it special. No two covey rises are exactly the same; no two points and no two hunts are ever the same. Watching good dogs working the grassy cover, interspersed with mottes of low-growing brush, is similar to watching a form of ballet and can be appreciated by the dedicated quail hunter and novice alike.

Anyone with an interest in Texas quails—hunter, landowner, manager, researcher, or biologist—should have a copy of this book. It is an essential addition to any wildlife library.

Katharine Armstrong, Chair
Texas Parks and Wildlife Commission, 2001–2003

Preface

Álvar Núñez Cabeza de Vaca's mention of "quails" appears to be the first record of birds seen within the territory that now comprises the state of Texas.
Oberholser (1974)

The previous quotation is from Harry C. Oberholser's monumental *Bird Life of Texas*. Assuming Oberholser's scholarship is correct—and there is no reason to think otherwise—this means that quails are at the very heart of Texas ornithology.

Quails also have a place in the hearts of many Texans. Hunting Texas quails is serious business to many Texans and to many people who visit Texas. More and more, quail hunting in Texas is a magnet that attracts dollars from wealthy urban economies to struggling rural communities. Although cattle have been king in Texas for more than 150 years, people are finding that these little birds may bring as much as, or more than, cattle when it comes to economic returns. Quail populations, and the habitat that supports them, can become potential income streams that keep family lands in the family and prevent large ranches from being sold, fragmented, or developed into subdivisions and shopping centers. We have enough subdivisions and shopping centers. What we do not have enough of is wild quails.

One of my early visits to Texas was in response to an invitation to hunt on the Norias Division of King Ranch during January 1992. This was a legendary boom year for quails in the state. Seeing quails flush one, two, or even three "new" coveys as they landed after the initial covey rise completely changed my perspective of quail populations and habitat. Seeing such a density of birds—at least seven birds per hectare (about three birds per acre)—left an impression that is still with me today. It illustrated, among other things, how productive the Texas landscape can be when all the right habitat components are managed to capture the benefits of precipitation when it finally does rain. It also illustrated the lucrative sums that people are willing to pay to enjoy hunting what Aldo Leopold once called "grand-opera game."

Despite the fact that quails in Texas usually have two or maybe three boom years per decade, there may be some serious storm clouds for quails on the horizon. Huntable populations of bobwhites have been all but gone from the East Texas landscape for nearly three decades. This past year, quail numbers in the Cross Timbers failed to increase, even though rainfall was abundant. Long-term data show that quail numbers—and quail hunters—are declining at about 3–4 percent per year, depending on the region of the state. The regionwide declines that have devastated quail numbers in the southeastern states are moving west.

Fortunately, Texas is one of the few states taking quail conservation and restoration seriously. Virtually all of the people who wrote the chapters in this book are involved with the new Texas Quail Conservation Initiative (TQCI). With many other colleagues, they have helped develop a plan to stem the declines and restore quail populations in

Texas. The compilation and production of this book are but one small part of the TQCI.

If this book does nothing else, I hope that it helps raise awareness about the plight wild quails are facing in Texas. Each year, less and less of the Texas landscape is hospitable to quails. The grasses that cattle prefer to eat are the same grasses quails need for nesting. The ever-burgeoning urban centers are inexorably creeping into, and taking over, wild quail habitat. Resource agencies and extension services are promoting quail conservation and restoration at the same time they are encouraging people to convert native grasslands to "improved" pastures. Modern agricultural landscapes are now essentially moonscapes when it comes to quail and grassland bird habitat.

Until recently, people more or less accepted the philosophy that wild quails were an automatic by-product of land use in Texas. I hope that the people of Texas, after reading these chapters, will realize that we can no longer embrace this philosophy and expect to sustain wild populations of quails and the dozens of other species of grassland birds and vertebrates that share their habitat. Proactive management, policy incentives, and the adoption of a stewardship philosophy hold the solutions to this problem.

Leonard A. Brennan
Corpus Christi, Texas

Acknowledgments

Even if someone had a photographic capacity to capture the scientific literature on quails in Texas and the surrounding states, the Texas landscape is so vast—and diverse—that it would take a career lifetime to master the nuances of all factors that influence wild quail populations throughout the state. For this reason, I am indebted to the 24 people who contributed their time—and endured my nagging and cajoling—to write this book.

My colleagues at the Caesar Kleberg Wildlife Research Institute helped in various ways, both directly and indirectly, to produce this book. I owe my supervisor, Fred Bryant, thanks for developing the Endowed Chair for Quail Research that brought me to Texas. Such a position is a great opportunity that allowed me the time and space to work on this project.

Shannon Davies of Texas A&M University Press was an enthusiastic supporter of this project from the beginning. Her encouragement was especially helpful while I was struggling with assembling the photos and graphs for the initial draft.

I must thank Bill Kuvlesky and Steve DeMaso for their encouragement when I first started thinking out loud about compiling and editing a comprehensive volume on Texas quails. Bill and Steve provided excellent counsel by recommending potential authors and by making motivational recommendations when the inevitable deadlines came and went.

The South Texas Chapter and Texas State Council of Quail Unlimited provided a significant grant that helped defray publication costs. Tim Connolly, Ronnie Howard, and Chip Martin are to be thanked for this generous contribution. The Texas Cooperative Extension Service, on the recommendation of Dale Rollins, helped significantly with the costs of publication, as did Fred Bryant and the Caesar Kleberg Wildlife Research Institute.

Section I
Ecology and
Life History of
Texas Quails

Introduction   1

Leonard A. Brennan, Fidel Hernández, and Fred C. Bryant

> The landscape of any farm [or ranch] is the owner's portrait of himself.
> A. Leopold (1939)

Wild quails, and the opportunities to hunt, photograph, or simply
watch them, are among the most important wildlife resources in Texas.
During the past 20–30 years, as bobwhite populations have declined
in East Texas and elsewhere throughout the coastal plain of the southeastern United States, quail hunters have gravitated toward South and
West Texas in search of quail hunting.

Parts of Texas have the reputation of being some of the last great
places for wild quails in North America. The reputation Texas enjoys as
a mecca for quail hunting draws millions of dollars from wealthy urban
areas to struggling rural economies. The current importance of quails
in Texas points to a new era of wildlife management in which game
animals are a cultural and economic resource equal to traditional agricultural commodities such as livestock and timber.

Texas quails have been the focus of a rich legacy of creative and vi-
sionary wildlife research (Lehmann 1984; Hellickson and Radomski
1999; Guthery 2000, 2002; Hernández, Guthery, and Kuvlesky 2002).
We know a great deal about the basic biology, physiology, and natural
history of quails in Texas and elsewhere. We also have pillars of knowledge about the basics of quail management (chapter 24). Nevertheless,
numerous questions remain about factors that limit quail populations
and how these limiting factors can be mitigated through management,
especially during times of drought.

Land-Use Lessons from the Southeastern United States

The declines that have been so pervasive across vast areas of the eastern
part of the geographic range of the northern bobwhite (*Colinus virginianus*) are a direct function of habitat loss in relation to changing land uses
in agriculture, forestry, and urban-suburban development encroaching
into rural areas. From the late nineteenth century through the 1970s,
a "quail wave" rolled through the southeastern United States (Rollins
2002). This widespread abundance of northern bobwhites was largely
an accidental function of primitive agriculture and an entrenched rural
culture of woods burning in the southern states (Leopold 1929). Over
time, modern, clean-farming methods dominated the agricultural landscape, and the widespread use of fire became less prevalent. Concomi-
tant with the decline in use of fire was the development of high-density
planted-pine silviculture (primarily loblolly pine, *Pinus taeda*). Neither
of these modern agricultural or silvicultural landscapes provides much
in the way of habitat space for quails. When the inexorable losses from
urban-suburban encroachment into once-rural areas were added to the
losses from changing agricultural and silvicultural land uses, it was
inevitable that extensive areas of the early-successional grassland and

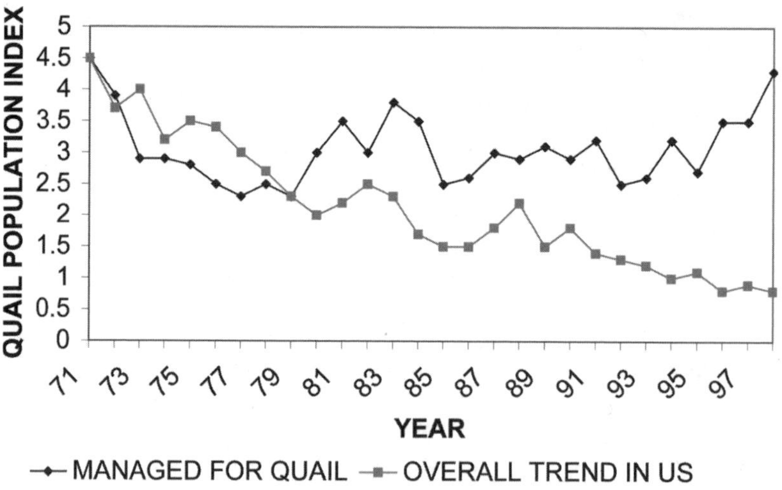

Figure 1.1.
Two wild northern bobwhite population trends. The "managed for quail" data are from a 4,050-hectare (10,000-acre) quail plantation in the southeastern United States. The overall trend in the United States data are from the National Audubon Society Christmas Bird Counts.

open forest habitats that supported vast numbers of quails would be negatively impacted (Peterson, Wu, and Rho 2002).

Despite the widespread declines and local extinctions of quail populations throughout the Southeast, remnant, scattered populations of relatively abundant bobwhites (with densities often greater than 2.5 birds per acre, or a bird per acre) can be found in various places throughout Coastal Plain states such as Mississippi, Alabama, Georgia, and Florida. Aggressive habitat management is responsible for maintaining these remnant populations of quails in what is otherwise a large region of unsuitable habitat. Where people manage quail habitat on areas where the minimum area is between 400 and 2,000 hectares (1,000 and 5,000 acres), wild populations of quails can, and do, persist despite the broad-scale declines (figure 1.1). The concept of using management strategies that provide habitat space is the foundation of effective quail management anywhere, including Texas.

Texas Quails: From Accident to Management

A number of accidental cultural and land-use factors have occurred to make parts of Texas one of the last great places for quails. For more than a century, the presence of large, private landholdings such as King Ranch, Kenedy Ranch, and other parcels that range from tens to hundreds of thousands of acres, formed the backbone of quail habitat across large regions of Texas (Lehmann 1984). Unlike the quail plantations of southern Georgia and northern Florida, where intensive management is used to maintain usable habitat space for quails, these birds have been a by-product of range management for livestock in South Texas (Guthery 1986). Sustainable management techniques that produce habitat space for quails will be the primary strategy for perpetuating huntable populations of wild quails across the Texas landscape.

Raising the Stakes

Many quail populations in Texas are declining. Some declines have been severe and prolonged, such as in the East Texas Piney Woods. Although other declines are not nearly as severe, such as in South Texas, they are worrisome.

Fee-lease hunting in Texas started in the 1930s and during the past three decades has developed into a lucrative economy on many Texas ranches. Monies generated from hunting leases are an important source of income for supplementing eroding returns from livestock and declining revenues from oil and gas leases. The combination of fee-lease hunting on the large, historic ranches and the direct purchase of rangelands for private hunting are now major factors in the Texas economy, especially in the southern and western regions of the state. It is obvious that revenues from hunting represent a new, significant economic factor in the South Texas economy. The resources that attract these revenues, specifically opportunities to hunt white-tailed deer (*Odocoileus virginianus*) and quails, have reached such a level of economic significance that many people are now motivated to identify strategies for sustaining populations of these wildlife resources through management.

Challenges and Opportunities

The diverse ecological regions of Texas contain dramatic gradients of rainfall, humidity, and vegetation. This presents both a challenge and an opportunity for quail managers and researchers. It is a daunting task for even the most creative wildlife scientists to design studies that will result in a unified understanding of the factors that limit quail populations. To date, wildlife scientists have not been able to develop a single set of objective management decision rules that can be applied across the state to enhance quail populations. However, broad, and in some cases, unifying management concepts and philosophies can be used to stabilize and increase quail numbers (chapter 24).

Purpose, Goal, and Organization

The purpose of this book is to make the knowledge generated from past quail research available to anyone interested in quails and quail management in Texas. A large number of research publications have addressed various aspects of quail populations, habitat, and related management issues in Texas. The most cohesive, modern body of research on Texas quails has focused on northern bobwhites in South Texas (Hernández, Guthery, and Kuvlesky 2002). Dan Lay in East Texas and A. S. Jackson in the Rolling Plains conducted other significant quail research initiatives. There is a diverse body of research that covers various aspects of quail ecology and management throughout the rest of Texas. The references section of this book aptly illustrates this point.

The goal of this book is to summarize and synthesize the existing literature on quail ecology and management in Texas. With four species of native quails and 10 diverse ecoregions in Texas, such a compendium is long overdue.

This book is organized into three broad sections. Section I, chapters 2–5, describes, reviews, and summarizes the life history of the four quails that are native to Texas. Chapter 6 presents the first published overview of diseases and parasites of Texas quails. Section II, chapters 7–16, describes how quail populations have fluctuated and how quail management has—or has not—been conducted in the 10 ecological regions of the state. Section III, chapters 17–25, addresses various issues that pertain to the culture and heritage of wild Texas quails.

2 Gambel's Quail Ecology and Life History

William P. Kuvlesky Jr., Stephen J. DeMaso,
and Michael D. Hobson

> The Gambels [*sic*] are a hardy bird,
> and under ordinary conditions multiply rapidly.
> H. Brown (1900)

6 The Gambel's quail (*Callipepla gambelii*) is named after William Gambel, a naturalist employed by the Philadelphia Academy of Sciences who collected specimens along the Santa Fe Trail in 1841 (Brown 1989). Gambel's quail are most common in the Sonoran Desert and associated semiarid ecosystems of Arizona and Sonora, Mexico (Brown et al. 1998). They are often called desert quail. The birds are gregarious and emit a distinctive gathering call that makes them easy to identify. This distinctive assembly call is the vocalization that most people associate with Gambel's quail because the birds produce the call throughout the year.

The Texas subspecies of Gambel's quail (*C. g. ignoscens*) (Johnsgard 1975) has received little attention from biologists, managers, and researchers in Texas because the species has such a limited distribution in the state (figure 2.1). Most of the information we have regarding this bird is from research conducted in Arizona and New Mexico. Many Texas quail hunters are not aware that Gambel's quail occur in Texas and can be hunted here.

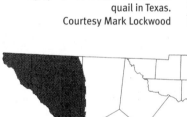

Figure 2.1.
Geographic distribution of Gambel's quail in Texas.
Courtesy Mark Lockwood

This chapter provides information about what is known about Gambel's quail in Texas as well as some basic guidelines for conservation, habitat management, and research. However, because Gambel's quail have been largely ignored by researchers in Texas, little information specific to these quail is available. Consequently, we have relied on information from other states where Gambel's quail occur in habitats similar to those where they occur in Texas to describe their life history and ecology in Texas.

Distribution

Brown and Gutiérrez (1980) hypothesized that Gambel's quail evolved in mild climates where annual rainfall peaks during winter and where the spring and summer are dry. Hot summer temperatures, low humidity, and high evaporation rates characterize these regions. The center of Gambel's quail distribution in North America is the Sonoran and Chihuahuan deserts of south-central Arizona, northwestern Sonora, and south to northern Sinaloa, Mexico (Brown 1989). The species occurs from this region west into arid and semiarid areas of California along the Colorado River and north into arid areas of southern Nevada, southern Utah, and isolated locales in southwestern Colorado. From southern Arizona, Gambel's quail are also distributed to the south and east into the Chihuahuan Desert in New Mexico and northern Coahuila and Chihuahua, Mexico (Brown et al. 1998). The species range is gradually reduced to arid riparian areas of southeastern New Mexico and West Texas, and the populations are eventually restricted to the Rio Grande.

Gambel's quail distribution continues into Texas but is limited to the upper Rio Grande Valley from El Paso to southeastern Terrell County at elevations ranging from 790 to 1,190 meters (2,500 to 3,900 feet) (Texas Game, Fish and Oyster Commission 1945; Oberholser 1974). The species probably extends less than 64.4 kilometers (less than 40 miles) inland from the river, where it is closely associated with the floodplains and bottoms of Rio Grande tributaries and numerous intermittent streams.

Annual Cycle and Life History

Understanding the annual cycle and life history of any animal is essential for effective management. This section presents an overview of these topics as they relate to Gambel's quail.

Behaviors and Vocalizations

Gambel's quail tend to run and hide in dense, desert vegetation rather than fly. They flush more readily than scaled quail (*C. squamata*) if a predator or hunter surprises them or if they are persistently pursued. They are among the most gregarious of quail species in North America, as indicated by their diverse vocal behavior and the large feeding concentrations that form during winter. They use woody vegetation for cover, food, and roosts (Brown 1989), which are all important adaptations in environments where herbaceous plants may be available for only a few weeks each year.

Appearance

Perhaps the most distinctive physical feature of Gambel's quail is the black, teardrop-shaped plume on the top of the head that occurs in both sexes. The upper bodies and backs of both sexes are blue gray, leading some people to refer to them as blue quail, according to Brown (1989). However, unlike scaled quail, which are sometimes referred to as blue quail in Texas, the feathers on the chest of Gambel's quail do not have a scalelike pattern but are instead a uniform cream color (Brown et al. 1998). The upper wing surfaces are olive gray with a distinctive cream margin on the bottom edge of the secondary feathers, and the yellow brown tail coverts are streaked with rust (Brown 1989). Flanks of both sexes are rich, reddish brown and are visible from considerable distances. Heads of males have a bright rusty crown, with a black face and bib outlined in white; their cream-colored chests have a horseshoe-shaped black splotch (Brown 1989). Females have a smaller black plume on their heads and are less brilliantly colored than the males. They lack the rusty cap and black faces, bibs, and smudge on the chest (figure 2.2).

Gambel's quail chicks are covered with a reddish brown down and have a cinnamon stripe running down their heads and backs (Brown 1989). They typically resemble the young chicks of other quail species until four to six weeks of age, when pinfeathers begin to appear. Johnsgard (1975) reported that juveniles then begin to closely resemble adult females, though he believed that juveniles have dull brown crests and

Figure 2.2.
Male (left) and female (right)
Gambel's quail.
Photos by Charles W. Melton

broad bands of cinnamon buff above their eyes, which females lack. Juvenile Gambel's quail can be readily distinguished from adults because the tips of primary covert feathers on the wings of juveniles have distinctive buff tips, whereas the secondary feathers of adults are a uniform olive gray (Leopold 1939).

Size

Gambel's quail are larger than northern bobwhites (*Colinus virginianus*) but smaller than scaled and Montezuma quails (*Cyrtonyx montezumae*). Johnsgard (1975) reported that wing lengths ranged from 105 to 120 millimeters (4.1 to 4.7 inches) and tail lengths ranged from 80 to 107 millimeters (3.1 to 4.2 inches). In Arizona and New Mexico, Gambel's quail generally weigh between 160 and 180 grams (5.6 and 6.3 ounces), with males and adults being slightly heavier than females and juveniles (Gorsuch 1934).

Pair Formation and Breeding

The onset of Gambel's quail breeding activity is largely determined by photoperiod but is also influenced by mid- to late-winter precipitation (Swank and Gallizioli 1954; Heffelfinger et al. 1999) and temperature (Heffelfinger et al. 1999). Presumably, rainfall determines the abundance of important foods (Brown 1989). Hungerford (1964) hypothesized that breeding behavior is influenced by the quantity of green feed available to the birds because consumption of forbs and, to a lesser extent, grasses may, along with increasing photoperiod, stimulate the development of reproductive organs. Furthermore, Hungerford noted that breeding condition is correlated with the quantity of vitamin A or closely related substances in livers.

Heffelfinger et al. (1999) found that Gambel's quail productivity responded positively to increasing precipitation and negatively to increasing temperatures. High productivity was associated with cool annual temperatures and high rainfall; and poor productivity, with annual hot temperatures and low rainfall. Breeding may begin as early as mid- to late February during cool, wet years or be delayed during hot, dry years (Hungerford 1964; Brown 1989).

If breeding is delayed, Gambel's quail remain in coveys until environmental conditions improve, at which time coveys disintegrate into pairs. Coveys aggregate again if dry conditions continue during spring

(Brown et al. 1998). Breeding activity can be significantly reduced if drought persists into summer (MacGregor and Inlay 1951).

Pairs begin to form within winter coveys (Brown et al. 1998). According to Raitt and Ohmart (1966), the sexual organs of males develop about two weeks prior to those of females, and juvenile males reach sexual maturity about two weeks before females. When males enter reproductive condition, they begin emitting a single-note "cow" call, often from an elevated perch (Brown 1989). Johnsgard (1973) reported that pair formation is a subtle process that requires repeated contact between males and females over an indeterminate time period. Males initiate breeding behavior by chasing and nudging females and performing a behavioral ritual called "tidbitting," which can best be described as a downward head movement in which males simulate placement of a small quantity of food in front of hens (Brown 1989). In addition to tidbitting, males stand directly in front of females with their legs fully extended, the feathers on their flanks fluffed, and their tails fanned in a sloping posture with their heads close to the ground (Brown et al. 1998). Ellis and Stokes (1966) reported that while a male is performing the head-bobbing ritual, it often emits a "wit wit" call. They also state that females and possibly males produce a series of short squeaks during copulation.

Brown (1989) reported that peak calling activity in Arizona coincides closely with the peak of the breeding season, which, in years of adequate precipitation, occurs between mid-April and early May. Raitt and Ohmart (1966), however, indicated that peak calling activity in New Mexico may not occur until mid-June if rain has been poor the previous winter. Calling activity diminishes through early and midsummer and then terminates by the beginning of August. Brown et al. (1998) noted that the peak of the breeding season depends on temperature and plant phenology more than on the actual location of a quail population. Hungerford (1960a) reported that in breeding populations, 25 to 75 percent are calling males, depending on breeding habitat conditions and quail density. Ellis and Stokes (1966) and Raitt and Ohmart (1966) stated that only unmated males deliver breeding calls, but Brown (1989) reported that when pairs are separated, males with mates will also emit the breeding call. Therefore, Gambel's quail breeding surveys may not reflect the numbers of unmated males in a population.

Nesting
Gambel's quail are claimed to be strongly monogamous (Brown et al. 1998), but this remains an open question until definitive studies are conducted using radiotelemetry. Once pair bonds have formed, the pair usually remains together throughout the breeding season. Raitt and Ohmart (1966), however, reported that two hens in their New Mexico study abandoned their mates and broods and nested again. They assumed that these hens had found and mated with another male. Most Gambel's quail biologists believe that polyandry is rare among these quail, though it can occur, particularly during years when breeding densities are high (Brown et al. 1998). If one member of a pair dies, particularly early in the breeding season, the other pair member may attempt to mate again. When pairs become separated, one mate will emit

a location or assembly call, which Brown (1989) described as a three- or four-note "ka-KAA-ka-ka."

Brown et al. (1998) stated that significant intraspecific variation exists for each distinctive vocalization emitted by Gambel's quail. Furthermore, they added that members of pairs can recognize the distinctive assembly calls of their mates when the two birds are separated. When alarmed, both sexes emit a "chip-chip-chip" whistle to warn one another and their broods when they are raising chicks.

According to Brown et al. (1998) neither male nor female Gambel's quail defend territories. A few wildlife biologists have calculated crude estimates of breeding-pair home ranges. Hensley (1954) reported 1 pair/7 hectares (18 acres) on one of his Arizona study areas, 1 pair/3 hectares (8 acres) on another study area, and 1 pair/1.6 hectares (4 acres) on a third study area. The area used by a breeding pair of Gambel's quail likely varies considerably from year to year and area to area, depending on food, cover, and water resources.

Females select nest sites, construct nests, and evidently incubate eggs, because males do not have a brood patch (Brown et al. 1998). Nevertheless, males seem to maintain a strong interest in the nest and incubating hen because they often remain close and guard the nest from potential predators (Brown 1989). Gorsuch (1934) believed that nest-site selection and construction are generally accomplished in about 10 days. Brown et al. (1998) reported that eggs are deposited in the nest about every 25–28 hours, and when 4–6 eggs have been produced, hens cease egg production for a day before resuming another egg-laying cycle. Three cycles generally occur before egg production is complete. Gorsuch (1934) estimated that a hen requires more than 30 days to complete a clutch. Clutch sizes average between 10 and 14 eggs (Gorsuch 1934; Brown 1989), though Gorsuch reported clutch sizes approaching 20 eggs in Arizona. According to Bent (1932), clutch size ranges from less than 5 eggs in dry years to 20 during years with adequate rainfall. However, clutches exceeding 15 are usually the result of more than one female using a nest; such "dump nests" are not uncommon.

Eggs weigh approximately 10 grams (0.35 ounce), are white to cream colored, and are covered with irregularly distributed brown splotches (Bent 1932).

Brooding

Gambel's chicks begin communicating with conspecifics or adults before they hatch, by emitting "peeps" through eggshells (Brown et al. 1998), and synchronous hatching occurs after an incubation period that ranges from 21 to 23 days (Bent 1932). Hatching can occur as early as March and even into July (Raitt and Ohmart 1966; Hungerford 1960a), though peak hatching generally occurs between late April to mid-May in Arizona (Hungerford 1960a; Brown 1989), Nevada (Gullion 1960), and New Mexico (Raitt and Ohmart 1966).

Chicks are precocial. The female may lead her brood away from the nest (Brown 1989). Sex ratios for Gambel's quail after hatching are basically equitable between sexes. However, sex ratios begin to favor males as the summer progresses into fall and winter (Brown et al. 1998).

Gambel's quail broods seem to be attended by both parents; however, a single adult will raise a brood if a mate is killed or when an unmated bird adopts chicks. Though Gambel's quail brood size averages about 10–12 chicks, very large broods consisting of up to 40 chicks are sometimes observed. Brown et al. (1998) described these very large broods as mixed broods because they typically consist of chicks of a variety of ages that become separated from the parents and are apparently adopted by another pair, or perhaps unmated adults. Brown et al. (1998) also described some large broods observed in Arizona as communal broods because they are composed of several adults and chicks of similar age and basically represent the amalgamation of two groups.

Gambel's quail chicks are physiologically incapable of thermoregulation during the first three weeks after they hatch; therefore, both the male and female brood chicks during this time period (Brown 1989). Brooding behavior consists of an adult squatting on the ground and allowing chicks to nestle in between the feathers on its back and along its flanks. Soon after chicks are capable of thermoregulation, they begin roosting with adults in small shrubs (Brown et al. 1998).

The chicks remain dependent on adults until the chicks are about three months old. Brown (1989) reported that during these periods of dependency, adults spend an average day leading chicks to sources of water; favored foraging areas; and loafing, dusting, and roost sites. Females generally encourage feeding among chicks when they are a day old by engaging in tidbitting behavior, which stimulates chicks to rush toward a hen and attempt to consume a food item. Chicks therefore gradually learn to identify suitable foods. Chick mortality is high during the first three months; perhaps 50 percent or more of the members of a brood do not survive to become members of a covey (Sowls 1960).

Coveys

Covey formation for Gambel's quail typically begins in late August or September. The basic covey unit is a mated pair of adults and their brood and consists of 5 to 7 birds, or aggregates of several family groups that can range from 9 to 22 individuals (Gullion 1962). Gorsuch (1934) reported a sex ratio of 51 males to 49 females; Sowls (1960) reported a winter adult sex ratio of 56 males to 44 females and a juvenile sex ratio of 53 males to 47 females.

Covey fidelity is strong, though individuals leave coveys and new members join occasionally throughout fall and winter (Brown et al. 1998). Coveys do not defend winter territories (Brown 1989). The sizes of Gambel's quail covey home ranges vary considerably, depending on annual production and habitat quality, and adjacent home ranges may sometimes overlap to some degree. Brown stated that home ranges vary from 19 to 95 hectares (47 to 235 acres). Gullion (1962) reported that the average home range on his desert study area in Nevada was 14 hectares (35 acres). Similarly, Goodwin and Hungerford (1977) found that Gambel's quail had a home range of about 15 hectares (37 acres) on their shrub-invaded grassland study area in Arizona.

Gullion (1962) reported a tendency for covey movements to increase as winter progressed. Daily movements on his Nevada study averaged about 100 meters (110 yards) during fall but increased to almost 1,000 meters (1,110 yards) during March. Brown et al. (1998) indicated that coveys do not move a great deal during winter, although they mentioned that there is a general trend for coveys to move uphill as the winter progresses. Similarly, Goodwin and Hungerford (1977) estimated that more than 60 percent of the Gambel's quail on their study area migrated when temperatures began decreasing to near-freezing levels during late fall. They moved along washes to higher elevations in a mountain range adjacent to the uplands that they occupied during the spring and summer. Birds began to descend in early March to the spring and summer habitats occupied during the previous year.

Large coveys of Gambel's quail numbering more than 100 birds are often observed during winter. Brown (1989) indicated that because of the gregarious nature of Gambel's quail, these groups are probably large aggregations of several coveys that congregate where food concentrations occur.

Covey members maintain contact with one another while feeding by emitting several vocalizations. Brown et al. (1998) stated that assembly calls associated with an "UT err" growl are commonly produced when a covey is feeding. A trill is sometimes added to the growl when food or water is located. They also described a rising "took" call that can be heard throughout the day when Gambel's quail are feeding, preening, loafing, and roosting.

Males and juveniles begin to leave coveys during late winter when pair formation recommences, and aggressive behavior between males becomes more common (Raitt and Ohmart 1966). Brown et al. (1998) reported that large aggregations of quail also begin to disintegrate during late winter, and individuals reconstitute themselves into smaller coveys. Membership within these coveys is very similar to that of the previous fall, though sufficient membership interchanges occur between coveys during winter to assure maintenance of genetic heterozygosity within the quail population. Pair bonds are established between members of these smaller coveys.

Habitat Use

Little information is available about Gambel's quail habitat use in Texas. Most of what is known comes from research conducted elsewhere within their distribution areas, particularly in Arizona, southern New Mexico, and southeastern California. Consequently, we must rely on information from these studies to a large extent to discuss habitat use of Gambel's quail in Texas.

General Habitat Relationships

The Sonoran Desert where Gambel's quail evolved is a shrub and succulent plant community (figure 2.3). Most herbaceous plant species are desert annuals present only for a few weeks each year if adequate winter rainfall has occurred. Consequently, in the absence of adequate ground cover, and unlike most other North American quail species, Gambel's quail roost aboveground in shrubs (Goodwin and Hungerford 1977; Brown 1989; Brown et al. 1998). Another adaptation to life in a habitat dominated by shrubs and cactus is that mast (nuts and berries) constitutes a higher proportion of the diet of Gambel's quail than of other western quail species (Brown 1989). Consequently, Gambel's quail populations must have adequate woody vegetation to persist in an area.

Coues (1874) recognized the importance of woody vegetation to Gambel's quail during his visits to Arizona almost 150 years ago. He noted that although they occur in every kind of cover, they prefer habitats consisting of low, tangled brush. Goodwin and Hungerford (1977) believed that the availability of suitable roost sites could significantly limit the distribution of Gambel's quail. Brown (1989) also recognized the importance of woody vegetation to Gambel's quail by stating that they are a scrub-adapted bird. Furthermore, he believed that the most productive habitats are characterized by almost any brush locale composed of thorny woody legumes, cactus, and other leaf-succulent plant species. However, Brown (1989) and Brown et al. (1998) emphasized that mesquites (*Prosopis* spp.) are more closely associated than any other woody species with the presence of Gambel's quail, though this association might be more a function of range overlap between the two species than a dependence of the quail on mesquite. Nevertheless, Brown et al. observed that in Arizona and Sonora, Mexico, the banks of rivers, creeks, and arroyos dominated by mesquite below an elevation of 1,650 meters (5,400 feet) support abundant Gambel's quail populations.

Bajadas, or the slopes of desert mountains intersected by washes, as well as outwash plains are also attractive Gambel's quail habitats (Brown 1989). Additionally, Gambel's quail frequent seeps, springs, and stock tanks some distance from favored brushy washes and arroyos in upland plant communities if these water sources are surrounded by mesquite thickets (Brown et al. 1998). However, good populations can be found in habitats where mesquite is not prevalent. Coues (1874) and Bent (1932) observed an abundance of Gambel's quail in willow (*Salix* spp.) thickets along the banks of rivers and creeks. Below elevations of 1,000 meters (3,300 feet), saltbush (*Atriplex* spp.) communities are important habitat

Figure 2.3.
Gambel's quail habitat north of the Rio Grande River in Texas.
Top left: dry washes;
Top right and bottom left: shrubby cover with interspersed openings;
Bottom right: native bunchgrasses interspersed with woody shrubs.
Photos by Michael D. Hobson

(Brown 1989). Gambel's quail can also be found where agricultural production is a major land use if sufficient woody cover remains available to them. Shrubby cover adjacent to fencerows and irrigation canals and rivers lined with woody plants such as tamarisk (*Tamarix* spp.) all support farmland Gambel's quail populations (Brown 1989).

Additionally, Engel-Wilson and Kuvlesky (2002) and Kuvlesky, Fulbright, and Engel-Wilson (2002) noted that viable populations of Gambel's quail currently exist in Phoenix and Tucson, where suburban sprawl has replaced traditional Sonoran Desert native habitat, largely because xeric landscaping typically features drought-tolerant shrubs and cacti, which represent key habitat elements. Coues (1874) reported seeing Gambel's quail in areas devoid of vegetation, such as granite boulder fields and masses of lava.

Woody species that are key Gambel's quail habitat indicators include velvet mesquite (*P. juiliflora*), honey mesquite (*P. velutina*), desert hackberry (*Celtis pallida*), ironwood (*Olneya tesota*), catclaw acacia (*Acacia greggii*), saguaro cactus (*Carnegiea gigantea*), jojoba (*Simmondsia chinensis*), allthorn (*Castela* spp.), scrub oak (*Quercus turbinella*), and prickly pear and cholla cactus species (*Opuntia* spp.). Important understory species include shrubby buckwheat (*Erigonum wrightii*), snakeweed (*Gutierrezia sarothrae*), burroweed (*Haplopappus tenuisectus*), turpentine bush (*H. laricifolius*), and brittlebush (*Encelia farinosa*).

Guthery, King, Kuvlesky, et al. (2001) believed that Gambel's quail's preference for high woody canopy cover represents not only an evolutionary adaptation to reduce exposure to aerial predators but also a behavioral mechanism to avoid high operative temperatures. They further hypothesized that these habitat preferences increased fitness by reducing exposure to aerial predators and by reducing the risks of hyperthermia. Similarly, Goldstein and Nagy (1985) noted that the habitat preferences in the Mojave Desert of California reflected an adaptation to reduce hyperthermia risks. As a result of their study, they learned that Gambel's quail have evolved specific physiological adaptations that permit them to survive ground-surface temperatures sometimes exceeding 67°C (150°F). Goldstein and Nagy found that costs of thermoregulation for Gambel's were negligible, but not only because they exhibited specific energy-conservation behavior patterns, such as long periods of inactivity and a reluctance to fly. Goldstein and Nagy (1985) determined that the reason for the low energy costs of thermoregulation was also related to the resting metabolic rates (RMRs) of Gambel's quail, which were substantially lower than predicted basal metabolic rates (BMRs), ranging from 51 to 70 percent during the two years of the study.

Clearly, Gambel's quail have wide habitat tolerances and can adapt to significant alterations of the native plant communities they inhabit. Though they evolved in the Sonoran Desert where perennial herbaceous vegetation density and cover were often reduced, Brown (1989) argued that the highest Gambel's quail densities today might be sustained not in desert habitats but in shrub-invaded, semiarid grasslands. Shrub invasions have transformed semiarid grasslands from habitats largely occupied by only scaled quail, and to a lesser extent Montezuma quail, to habitats more conducive to Gambel's quail production. For example, many overgrazed, shrub-invaded grasslands in Arizona and New Mexico are now excellent Gambel's quail habitat because decades of overgrazing, together with periodic droughts, have transformed savannas to shrublands where herbaceous species are often restricted to places inaccessible to cattle. Even on the Sonoran savanna grasslands of Buenos Aires National Wildlife Refuge in southeastern Arizona—which has not been grazed by livestock for almost 15 years—Guthery, Land, and Hall (2001) noted the affinity that Gambel's quail have for shrublands. Though Gambel's quail were often observed in extensive open areas dominated by tall, luxuriant grass species, Guthery, King, Kuvlesky, et al. (2001) found that they remained associated with habitats that had high canopy coverage of woody plants and high exposure of bare ground.

The exotic grass invasions that are occurring throughout the Southwest probably do not degrade Gambel's quail habitat to the same extent as these invasions do for other quail species. The reason is that herbaceous vegetation is not as important to Gambel's quail as shrubs are. For example, high Gambel's quail densities were recorded on ranches in northwestern Sonora, Mexico, despite extensive buffelgrass (*Pennisetum ciliare*) infestations because shrubland was a prominent landscape feature.

Diet

Gambel's quail diets vary seasonally and are composed of mainly plant material. Seeds constitute a major part of their diets (Brown 1989; Brown et al. 1998; table 2.1). Gorsuch (1934) reported that more than 90 percent of the Gambel's quail diet on his Arizona study area consisted of plants. Leafy material and the seeds of a variety of plant species dominated diets, although legumes were favored items. He found little mast and few cultivated grains in the diet of Gambel's quail on his study areas in Arizona and Utah. However, Campbell (1957) stated that all of the Gambel's quail crops on his New Mexico study area contained mast. He also indicated that the quail consumed mainly legume seeds and that crops contained remnants of at least 87 plant species, although 22 plants species composed 90 percent of their diets. Similarly, Gullion (1960) reported that Gambel's quail in Nevada consumed a wide variety of plant foods but that deervetch (*Lotus* spp.), filaree (*Erodium* spp.), locoweed (*Astralagus* spp.), and lupine (*Lupinus* spp.) were the most important food items. Hungerford (1962) reported that vetches (*L. humistratus* and *L. tomentillis*), filaree, and lupines were important foods of Gambel's quail in southern Arizona; but he also determined that velvet mesquite, whitethorn acacia (*Acacia constricta*), catclaw acacia, blue palo verde (*Ceridium floridum*), mustard (*Descurinia* spp.), mistletoe (*Phoradendron* spp.), wait-a-minute bush (*Mimosa biuncifera*), and saguaro fruit were important food items.

More recently, a comprehensive food habit study for Gambel's quail in New Mexico revealed that annual and perennial forb seeds, mast, and green vegetation were the major food items consumed (Schemnitz, Dye, and Cardenas 1997). Major plant species consumed included Russian thistle (*Salsola kali*), grain sorghum (*Sorghum vulgare*), crownbeard (*Verbesina enceliode*), and kochia (*Kochia scoparia*). Gambel's quail also consumed snakeweed, honey mesquite, screwbean mesquite (*Prosopis pubescens*), pigweed (*Amaranthus* spp.), brown dalea (*Psorothammus scoparia*), desert willow (*Chiliopsis linearis*), sumac (*Rhus* spp.), and

Table 2.1.
Plants and Animals Consumed by Gambel's Quail in Arizona, New Mexico, and Nevada

Food item	Scientific name	State	Source
Plants			
Bignonia	*Bignonia* spp.	Arizona	Gorsuch (1934)
Bindweed	*Convolvulus* spp.	Arizona	Gorsuch (1934)
Blue palo verde	*Cercidium floridanum*	Arizona	Hungerford (1962)
Brown dalea	*Dalea* spp.	Arizona, New Mexico	Campbell (1957); Schemnitz et al. (1997); Gorsuch (1934)
Buckthorn	*Rhamnus* spp.	Arizona	Gorsuch (1934)
Carpetweed	*Mollugo* spp.	Arizona	Gorsuch (1934)
Catclaw acacia	*Acacia greggii*	Arizona	Hungerford (1962); Gorsuch (1934)
Desert hackberry	*Celtis pallida*	Arizona	Brown (1989); Gorsuch (1934)
Desert willow	*Chiliopsis linearis*	New Mexico	Schemnitz, Dye, and Cardenas (1997)
Elm	*Ulmus* spp.	Arizona	Gorsuch (1934)
Filaree	*Erodium cicutarium*	Arizona	Hungerford (1962); Brown (1989)
Geranium	*Geranium* spp.	Arizona	Gorsuch (1934)
Goosefoot	*Chenopodium* spp.	Arizona	Gorsuch (1934)
Grain sorghum	*Sorghum vulgare*	New Mexico	Schemnitz et al. (1997)
Grasses	*Graminae*	Arizona	Gorsuch (1934); Brown (1989)
Horse purslane	*Portulaca* spp.	Arizona, New Mexico	Gorsuch (1934); Schemnitz et al. (1997)
Jojoba	*Simmondsia* spp.	Arizona	Brown et al. (1998)
Kochia	*Kochia scoparia*	New Mexico	Schemnitz et al. (1997)
Locoweed	*Astralagus* spp.	Nevada	Gullion (1962)
Lupines	*Lupinus* spp.	Arizona, New Mexico, Nevada	Gullion (1960); Hungerford (1962); Schemnitz et al. (1997)
Mallow	*Malva* spp.	Arizona	Gorsuch (1934)
Mesquite	*Prosopis* spp.	Arizona	Brown (1989); Gorsuch (1934)
Mistletoe	*Phoradendron* spp.	Arizona	Hungerford (1962); Gorsuch (1934)
Mustard	*Descurinia* spp.	Arizona	Hungerford (1962)
Phlox	*Phlox* spp.	Arizona	Gorsuch (1934)
Pigweed	*Amaranthus* spp.	New Mexico	Schemnitz et al. (1997)
Potato	*Solanum* spp.	Arizona	Gorsuch (1934)
Prickly pear	*Opuntia* spp.	Arizona	Brown (1989); Gorsuch (1934)
Ragweed	*Ambrosia* spp.	Arizona	Gorsuch (1934)
Russian thistle	*Salsola kali*	New Mexico	Schemnitz et al. (1997)
Saguaro	*Carnegiea gigantea*	Arizona	Hungerford (1962)
Snakeweed	*Gutierrezia* spp.	New Mexico	Schemnitz et al. (1997)
Spurge	*Euphorbia* spp.	Arizona	Gorsuch (1934)
Sumac	*Rhus* spp.	New Mexico	Schemnitz et al. (1997)
Sunflower	*Helianthus* spp.	Arizona	Gorsuch (1934)
Trailing allionia	*Allionia* spp.	Arizona	Gorsuch (1934)
Vetches	*Lotus* spp.	Arizona, Nevada	Gullion (1960); Hungerford (1962); Brown (1989)
Wait-a-minute bush	*Mimosa biuncifera*	Arizona	Hungerford (1962)
Whitethorn acacia	*Acacia constricta*	Arizona, New Mexico	Hungerford (1962); Schemnitz et al. (1997)
Wolfberry	*Lycium* spp.	Arizona	Brown et al. (1998)
Animals			
Ants	Hymenoptera	Arizona	Brown (1989); Gorsuch (1934)
Beetles	Coleoptera	Arizona	Brown (1989); Gorsuch (1934)
Flies	Diptera	Arizona	Gorsuch (1934)
Grasshoppers	Orthoptera	Arizona	Brown (1989); Gorsuch (1934)
Leafhoppers	Homoptera	Arizona	Brown (1989); Gorsuch (1934)
Moth caterpillars	Lepidoptera	Arizona	Brown (1989); Gorsuch (1934)
Spiders	Arachnida	Arizona	Gorsuch (1934)
Termites	Isoptera	Arizona	Gorsuch (1934)

pecan (*Carya illinoinensis*). Brown et al. (1998) took data from Gorsuch (1934) and developed a list of foods consumed by Gambel's quail. Many of the plant species previously identified in this section are provided in this list; however, Brown et al. also noted that jojoba seeds, prickly pear fruit, and wolfberry (*Lycium* spp.) seeds were consumed. Brown (1989) and Brown et al. (1998) emphasized that mesquite is a very important food item in Arizona because Gambel's quail rely heavily on the seeds, leaves, and flowers as staples throughout the year.

Gambel's quail consume invertebrates in addition to plant material (table 2.1). Ants and grasshoppers are favored food items (Gorsuch 1934; Hungerford 1962; Brown 1989) along with beetles, moth caterpillars, small worms, termites, and spiders (Gorsuch 1934; Brown 1989).

Several biologists have reported that invertebrates compose only a small percentage of Gambel's quail diets. Johnsgard (1975) concluded after reviewing numerous field studies that invertebrates rarely exceed

13 percent of the total diet during spring and summer. Furthermore, Gorsuch (1934) found that invertebrates typically make up less than 10 percent of the diet and, together with Brown (1989), stated that invertebrates are consumed primarily during the breeding season, when they are an essential component of adult and young chick diets. Invertebrates are, however, important components of Gambel's quail diets because invertebrates provide essential amino acids and provide more energy/unit weight than plants do.

Water

Many people continue to believe that sources of water such as rivers, stock tanks, or seeps and springs are important components of Gambel's quail habitat because the quail are frequently observed in the vicinity of these water sources. Gambel's quail will drink water if it is available. However, free sources of water are not necessary for the quail's survival, according to early research by naturalists and biologists who studied Gambel's quail in their desert habitats (Vorhies 1928; Leopold 1933; Gorsuch 1934). Nevertheless, during the 1940s and 1950s in Arizona, quail hunters were convinced that water catchments placed in the desert—gallinaceous guzzlers—provided water critical to the maintenance of healthy Gambel's quail populations. However, a study conducted by the Arizona Game and Fish Department during the 1950s indicated that water catchments seemed to have little influence on Gambel's quail densities because quail numbers harvested by hunters and breeding-season male call counts on areas where quail were provided with water did not differ from those obtained on areas where water was not provided (Smith and Gallizioli 1965).

Like bobwhites in Texas, Gambel's quail generally meet their water requirements from the foods they consume (Hungerford 1960b). However, Goldstein and Nagy (1985) stated that forb and grass seeds alone do not provide sufficient water to meet the daily requirements of Gambel's quail during summer. They believed that the quail must incorporate moist food items in their diets or drink free water to survive summer. Preformed water from moist dietary items and metabolic water produced during digestion, as well as free water when dew is deposited on vegetation or the soil surface, are probably sufficient to meet the daily requirements of Gambel's quail throughout the year.

Nesting Habitat

Adequate amounts of forbs are probably the most important habitat component required by Gambel's quail for nesting activity. If cool-season forb populations are reduced because of drought, Gambel's quail reproductive activity is reduced and nesting activity can be delayed and/or decline. Moreover, forb and annual grass communities also provide important habitat for invertebrates, which are essential components of hen diets when they are producing eggs (Brown 1989). In fact, the high Gambel's quail densities that Brown reported for some shrub-invaded semiarid grasslands may be due in part to the high abundance and diversity of invertebrates supported by the herbaceous plant community that is absent in traditional desert habitats.

Herbaceous material appears to be unimportant to Gambel's quail for nest construction. Unlike bobwhites, Gambel's quail do not require grass cover to build nests. Johnsgard (1975) described nests as generally no more than a shallow depression about 10 centimeters (4 inches) deep and 60 centimeters (24 inches) in diameter excavated on bare ground. However, Bent (1932) and Thompson (1993) reported finding nests in shrubs in Arizona and New Mexico, respectively. Nest interiors are sometimes insulated with a small amount of plant material, and feathers and twigs are usually placed around the perimeter. Brown (1989) observed that nests are often located in litter beneath a shrub or subshrub such as snakeweed, or next to and under a clump of prickly pear. It appears that Gambel's quail expend little effort camouflaging or otherwise attempting to hide clutches. Instead, the cryptic coloration pattern of eggs serves to decrease the probability that potential predators will detect them. The egg color of Gambel's quail represents an elegant adaptation to an environment generally devoid of herbaceous material and its associated detritus. The cool-season forbs of February and March desiccate rapidly and literally dissolve into dust during the hot dry months of April, May, and June, when most nesting activity occurs.

Though locating nests under some kind of structure hides eggs from predators, adults also construct nests under structures because of the thermoregulatory advantages provided by shade. Because Gambel's quail inhabit the warm deserts of North America and most of their nesting and incubating activity occurs during hot and dry weather, constructing nests in the shade of a shrub or rock prevents desiccation of unattended eggs and helps incubating adults maintain thermoneutrality during the heat of the day.

Brood Habitat

Brooding habitat probably differs little from nesting habitat. Suitable roosts remain important because at least one of the adults must roost aboveground at night. Annual grass and forb cover that occurs in response to winter precipitation may be important escape cover for chicks. However, the presence of herbaceous cover is probably not an essential habitat requirement, because as previously mentioned, Gambel's quail evolved in the shrub- and cacti-dominated Sonoran Desert where herbaceous cover was limited. The soil may provide adequate cover, because the cryptic coloration of 1- to 14-day-old chicks allows them to mimic clods of earth, permitting very young chicks to escape detection by predators. Cacti, subshrubs, and low-growing shrubs seem to fulfill the cover requirements of broods and parents. When adults are brooding young chicks, they typically do so under or within protective cover. Brooding cover both shields adults from predators and provides shade while brooding adults are thermoregulating.

Brown (1989) stated that brush-lined washes and arroyos are important brooding habitats because adults and brood seem to restrict their activities to these habitat types. Again, the dense shrub and tree growth that typically occurs on the banks of washes and arroyos provides Gambel's quail family units with escape and thermal cover. Mast produced by various shrubs and cacti also provides food. In the arid Sonoran Desert, where herbaceous cover may be very limited when adults are caring for broods, woody plants and cacti furnish habitat for invertebrates, which are essential dietary items to rapidly growing chicks. Brown et al.

(1998) observed that when Gambel's quail with broods leave roost sites early in the morning, they typically lead chicks down washes to water or a favored feeding area, where they remain for most of the day. They may drink water if it is available, but it seems likely that daily visits to water are important for food procurement too. Water sources in arid areas attract invertebrates and also may provide forbs that are able to germinate and survive in the moist soil on the margins of stock tanks, seeps, or ponds. Gambel's quail may be able to fulfill their daily moisture requirements during their morning visits to water sources by consuming invertebrates and moist plant material.

Shrub-invaded semiarid grasslands probably provide excellent brooding habitat, and as a result Gambel's quail production may be higher in these grasslands than in deserts and may contribute to the high quail densities that are said to occur in these vegetative communities (Brown 1989). The brushy fencerows and brush-lined irrigation canals of agricultural fields in the river floodplains of arid regions probably also meet all of the habitat requirements of brooding Gambel's quail.

Habitat Used by Winter Coveys

As it does for nesting and brooding habitats, woody cover remains an essential habitat requirement for coveys. Goodwin and Hungerford (1977) reported that winter coveys continued to be closely associated with the mesquite-hackberry plant communities along washes on their southern Arizona study area as the quail migrated to higher elevations where they again frequented the brushy habitat along washes. Goodwin and Hungerford speculated that cold air moving from the mountain down to the valley at night made higher elevations warmer and thus more attractive to the coveys. Quail began to descend to lower elevations during the breeding season in March, again following washes, and by April most Gambel's quail had abandoned higher elevations for nesting habitat at lower elevations. The shrubs and trees associated with washes and draws apparently continue to provide adequate food and cover during winter, just as these habitat types do during the nesting and brood-rearing seasons.

Demography and Populations

Birds hatched in one year do not breed until the spring of the following year (Gullion 1960; Raitt and Ohmart 1966). Young birds appear to form pair bonds and breed later than older birds (Brown et al. 1998).

Annual Reproductive Success

Fall age ratios are measures of breeding success, that is, the percentage of young in the hunting bag (Smith and Gallizioli 1965). In Arizona, age ratios of Gambel's quail varied by year and area, ranging from less than 10 percent to greater than 80 percent young in fall populations (Brown 1989). Egg and chick depredation appears higher in dry years than in wet years (Sowls 1960). In Nevada and Arizona, breeding success is positively correlated with preceding winter-spring precipitation (Gullion 1954; Hungerford 1960b; Raitt and Ohmart 1966). Heffelfinger et al. (1999) reported that in Arizona, December and January precipitation invoked a stronger calling response than October–November or February–March precipitation. Reproductive failure (less than one juvenile/adult) was associated with low rainfall in October–March and high mean daily temperatures during June–July. For any rainfall pattern, lower age ratios were associated with higher July temperatures (Heffelfinger et al. 1999). Quail in riparian and irrigated farming areas do not experience the almost total reproductive failure caused by the absence of rain-induced green feed in desert areas (Gullion 1958; Brown 1968).

Number of Broods Raised per Year
Gullion (1956, 1960) believed that Gambel's quail were capable of producing more than one brood per year, especially during good, wet years, because his Nevada study population consisted of 88 percent juveniles during a fall that was preceded by a very mild, wet winter. He observed that most of the broods he saw in late June already appeared to be independent of adults, and later in the summer he saw two age classes of chicks. He also observed males with broods, probably abandoned by a hen that was perhaps incubating a second clutch of eggs. Like bobwhites in Texas, Gambel's quail have a long reproductive season. Their reproductive potential is tremendous during good years, so it is entirely possible that Gambel's quail are capable of "double-clutching," although it is probably a rare event.

Life Span and Survivorship
Juvenile mortality is usually higher than adult mortality, which is about 40 percent per year, and juveniles and adult males are more vulnerable to trapping and shooting (Gallizioli 1967; Raitt and Ohmart 1968). Life expectancy based on an annual mortality rate of 40 percent would be about 2.5 years. A 60 percent annual survival rate would require an age ratio of 1 adult to 1.5 juveniles to sustain that population. Lawson (1950) and Swank and Gallizioli (1954) reported high mortality of juveniles from July to September; however, Brown (1989) found juvenile-to-adult ratios in fall samples to equal or exceed those from July brood counts.

Causes of Mortality
Depredation is a large cause of mortality in Gambel's quail populations. Predators of adult Gambel's quail include bobcats (*Lynx rufus*), Cooper's hawks (*Accipiter cooperii*), and Harris's hawks (*Parabuteo unicinctus*) (Brown et al. 1998). Nest and egg predators include cotton rats (*Sigmodon* spp.), round-tailed ground squirrels (*Citellus tereticaudus*), coachwhips (*Masticophis flagellum*), king snakes (*Lampropeltis getulus*), gopher snakes (*Pituophis melanoleucus*), and Gila monsters (*Heloderma suspectum*) (Brown and Carmony 1991; Brown et al. 1998).

Recreational hunting is the only mortality source to receive serious study. Hunting mortality ranges from about 4 percent in low-population years to about 31 percent in high-population years (Gullion 1954; Gallizioli and Webb 1958). However, a recent analysis of Arizona Gambel's quail-harvest and population-trend data showed that harvest rates increased as population trends decreased (Guthery et al. 2004). Gallizioli and Webb (1961) reported similar quail populations on adjacent study areas in Arizona, following high hunter numbers and trapping removal on one area and none on the other.

Gambel's Quail Population Trends in Texas

Although Texas Parks and Wildlife Department conducts quail surveys in counties that have Gambel's quail, its limited distribution results in few observations during these surveys. Likewise, few hunters pursue Gambel's quail in Texas because the majority of these quail occur on private property and gaining access can be difficult. Therefore, acquiring sample sizes to reliably estimate Gambel's quail harvest and number of hunters is difficult.

Long-term population trends from 1942 to present from the Audubon Society's Christmas Bird Count data set indicate that Gambel's quail may have been more abundant in Texas 50 years ago (http://www .audubon.org/bird/cbc/; figure 2.4). Populations apparently began to decline during the late 1940s and into the 1950s, though they seem to have remained relatively stable, but at low levels, for at least the past 40 years. However, Gambel's quail population trends based on the Breeding Bird Survey (BBS) show an increasing trend from the early 1990s to the present (http://www-pwrc.usgs.gov/bbs/; figure 2.5). Nonetheless, caution should be used when interpreting these results because of small sample

Number of Gambel's Quail Observations/Party Hour in Arizona and Texas, 1917-2002

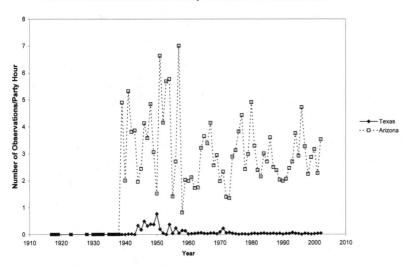

Figure 2.4.
Gambel's quail population trends in Texas and Arizona, Christmas Bird Count Survey, 1917–2000.

Gambel's Quail Breeding Bird Survey Population Trend in Texas

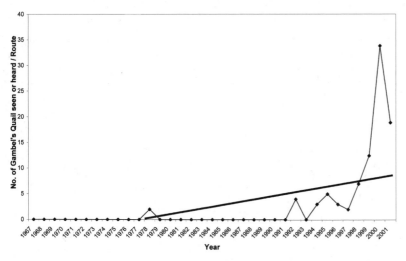

Figure 2.5.
Gambel's quail population trend in Texas, Breeding Bird Survey, 1967–2001.

sizes and the distribution of survey routes in counties with Gambel's quail. Some survey routes may not be surveyed every year, thus leading to incomplete population-trend data. Clearly, however, Gambel's quail populations in Texas are substantially lower than those in Arizona and have been for at least 60 years. This is probably a reflection of the greater abundance of quality habitat (e.g., usable space) that exists in the core area of their geographic range in Arizona. Texas represents a peripheral area of their geographic range and has less usable space.

Conservation and Management

Because of the limited distribution of Gambel's quail in Texas, only minor conservation and management efforts have been devoted to the species. Habitat conditions and weather are the two greatest factors influencing Gambel's quail populations. The largest threat to this species and other quail species is the loss and/or degradation of suitable habitat. Good habitat conditions with good weather conditions will maximize quail production and fall populations. Good habitat conditions with bad weather conditions will provide some production and suitable fall populations. However, poor habitat conditions with bad weather conditions provide minimal production and low fall populations.

Overgrazing by livestock causes a reduction of ground cover and loss of suitable nesting cover. In areas of the state with varying, sporadic rainfall patterns and amounts, landowners should use conservative stocking rates for livestock if quail are a priority.

As pointed out earlier, most of what we know about Gambel's quail in Texas comes from research conducted in other states. Some of the information priorities for Gambel's quail include the following:

1. Updated distribution map
2. Surveys of population trends, harvest, and hunter numbers
3. General life history information, such as cause-specific mortality, seasonal food habits, habitat use and description of that habitat, and nesting chronology
4. General population ecology information, such as age ratios, annual and seasonal mortality rates by age and sex, and annual and seasonal survival rates by age and sex
5. Information on habitat, weather, and population relationships

Despite having a relatively limited distribution in Texas, Gambel's quail represent a significant avian resource to hunters, birders, and photographers. They are an important component of the biodiversity of arid and semiarid rangelands, and they are an indicator of the condition and ecological health of these landscapes.

Montezuma Quail Ecology and Life History   3

Louis A. Harveson, Ty H. Allen, Froylan Hernández,
Dave A. Holdermann, James M. Mueller, and
M. Shawn Whitley

> Without bulbs, the Montezuma quail disappears,
> for from them the bird obtains not only food but water.
> Leopold (1959)

Montezuma quail (*Cyrtonyx montezumae*), or Mearns' quail, are
unique birds found in the pine-oak woodlands of Mexico and
the southwestern United States, with limited occurrence in Texas
(figure 3.1). Their strange appearance and behavior have earned
them numerous colloquial names, including harlequin quail,
black quail, Massena, painted quail, crazy quail, fool's quail, and
codorniz pinta. They differ from other Texas quails
in many respects, including foraging behavior, diet,
habitats, defense mechanisms, clutch size, covey size,
and covey dynamics.

Four subspecies of Montezuma quail are recognized.
Cyrtonyx montezumae mearnsi occurs in the southwestern
United States and northern Mexico, whereas, *C. m. montezu-
mae*, *C. m. rowleyi*, and *C. m. sallei* occur exclusively in Mexico. Montezuma quail are sister species to ocellated quail (*C. ocellatus*) of southern
Mexico and Central America and are thought to be closely related to
wood quail (*Odontophorus* spp.) and singing quail (*Dactylortyx thoraci-
cus*) (Holman 1961; Johnsgard 1973; Stromberg 2000).

Montezuma quail are sexually dimorphic, with males being more
ornate and larger (195 grams, or 6.9 ounces) than females (176 grams,
or 6.2 ounces) (Brown 1989; figures 3.2, 3.3, and 3.4). Males are strik-
ing and have a distinct black-and-white harlequin face mask and dark
charcoal contour feathers with white spots along the breast, sides, and
flanks (figure 3.5). Females are a duller version of the male but with buff
and chestnut colors replacing the black-and-white patterns of the males.
Both sexes have a slight crest that extends to the nape, bluish mandibles,
short tails, and a "bug-eyed" appearance. Montezuma quail possess
strong legs and large feet with long claws that are used for scratching
and digging for subterranean plant foods (Fuertes 1903; Miller 1943;
figure 3.6).

Figure 3.1.
Geographic distribution of
Montezuma quail in Texas.
Courtesy Mark Lockwood

Figure 3.2.
Female (left) and male (right)
Montezuma quail.
Photos courtesy Larry Ditto/
KAC Productions

Figure 3.3.
A male Montezuma quail sits atop
a small rock that is surrounded
by herbaceous cover.
Photo by Louis A. Harveson

Figure 3.4.
A radio-marked female Montezuma
quail being aged using the presence
(juvenile) or absence (adult) of buffy
coloration on the primary wing coverts.
Photo by Louis A. Harveson

Figure 3.5.
Male Montezuma are ornately colored
with a harlequin mask, white spots
down their flanks, and a bluish bill.
Photo by Louis A. Harveson

Figure 3.6.
Montezuma quail are well equipped for
digging for tubers and seed, as noted
by the abnormally long claws.
Photo by Louis A. Harveson

Figure 3.7.
A male Montezuma quail with radio transmitter and band in a holding box prior to being released by researchers at Sul Ross State University.
Photo by Louis A. Harveson

In Arizona and New Mexico, Montezuma quail are game birds. However, in Texas, Montezuma quail are classified by Texas Parks and Wildlife Department (TPWD) as a game bird with no open season.

The life history and ecology of this quail are known primarily from widely scattered field observations (e.g., Fuertes 1903; Ligon 1927; Bent 1932; Miller 1943; Wallmo 1954) and relatively few dedicated studies (Leopold and McCabe 1957; Bishop and Hungerford 1965; Brown 1978; Albers and Gehlbach 1990; Stromberg 1990). Stromberg provides a detailed review on the life history of Montezuma quail; however, most of the literature (i.e., nesting, habitat requirements, food preferences) regarding Montezuma quail is based on natural history observations. Further, other than Stromberg's, no data have been collected on Montezuma quail using contemporary methods (i.e., radiotelemetry, mark-recapture) (figure 3.7).

This chapter is an overview of the life history and ecology of Montezuma quail in Texas. Because almost no data exist on the ecology of Montezuma quail in Texas (Hernández, Harveson, and Brewer 2002a), we draw upon literature from other regions of their distribution.

Distribution in Texas

Historically (pre-1950), Montezuma quail have been reported from the Edwards Plateau and Trans-Pecos regions of Texas (Oberholser 1974); both regions connect biogeographically with the Sierra Madre in Mexico. The Trans-Pecos range minimally included portions of the following counties: Brewster (Chisos, Del Norte, and Glass mountains), Culberson (Guadalupe Mountains), El Paso (Franklin Mountains), Jeff Davis (Davis Mountains), Presidio (Chinati Mountains and Sierra Vieja), and Reeves (Barilla Mountains) (figure 3.8; table 3.1). The Edwards Plateau range of Montezuma quail was bounded on the west by Crockett and Val Verde counties, on the east by Burnet and Bexar counties, and on the south by Kinney and Uvalde counties. The Edwards Plateau range extended beyond the plateau region northward into Tom Green, Concho, and Nolan counties and southward to Maverick County. Trans-Pecos and Edwards Plateau populations may have connected across the Stockton Plateau of Pecos and Terrell counties, although no documented records of Montezuma quail exist from this area.

Bryan (2002) considered Montezuma quail to be a rare and localized breeder in the Trans-Pecos. Montezuma quail are known to reside in suitable habitat in the following Trans-Pecos counties and mountain

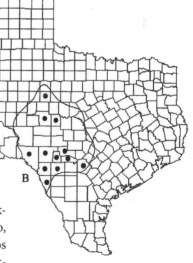

Figure 3.8.
Approximate historic distributions (pre-1950) of Montezuma quail in the Trans-Pecos (A) and Edwards Plateau (B) ecoregions of Texas. Black dots represent county records.

Table 3.1.
Records of Montezuma Quail in the Trans-Pecos and Edwards Plateau Ecoregions of Texas

Ecoregion (county)	Historic (pre-1950)		Contemporary (post-1950)	
	Record type	Source	Record type	Source
Trans-Pecos				
Brewster	V, S	Fuertes (1903); Strecker (1930); Van Tyne and Sutton (1937); O'Connor (1945)	V	Sorola (1986); Hughes (1993); Wauer (1996)
Culberson	S	Oberholser (1974)	V	F. Armstrong (National Park Service, unpublished data)
El Paso	S	Oberholser (1974)	—	
Hudspeth	—	—	V	J. A. Foster (TPWD, unpublished data)
Jeff Davis	V, S	Smith (1917); Oberholser (1974)	V	Sorola (1986)
Presidio	S	Oberholser (1974)	V	J. Miller (C. E. Miller Ranch, unpublished data)
Reeves	S	Oberholser (1974)	—	—
Edwards Plateau				
Bandera	S	Oberholser (1974)	—	—
Bexar	V, S	Oberholser (1974)	—	—
Burnet	V[a], S[a]	Oberholser (1974)	—	—
Concho	V[a]	Oberholser (1974)	—	—
Crockett	V[a], S[a]	Lloyd (1887); Strecker (1912); Oberholser (1974)	—	—
Edwards	S	Lloyd (1887); Oberholser (1974)	V	Sorola (1986); Albers and Gehlbach (1990); J. W. Thomas, TPWD (unpublished data)
Kerr	S	Oberholser (1974)	—	—
Kimble	V[a], S[a]	Oberholser (1974)	—	—
Kinney	S[a]	Oberholser (1974)	V	Sorola (1986); Albers and Gehlbach (1990)
Maverick	V	Oberholser (1974)	—	—
Nolan	S	Oberholser (1974)	—	—
Real	V	Oberholser (1974)	V	Sorola (1986)
Schleicher	V[a], S[a]	Oberholser (1974)	—	—
Sutton	V[a], S[a]	Oberholser (1974)	—	—
Tom Green	V	Lloyd (1887)	—	—
Uvalde	V	Oberholser (1974)	V	Sorola (1986)
Val Verde	V	Oberholser (1974)	V	Sorola (1986)

Note: V = sight record; S = specimen.
[a]County listed in Oberholser (1974) with no supporting documentation.

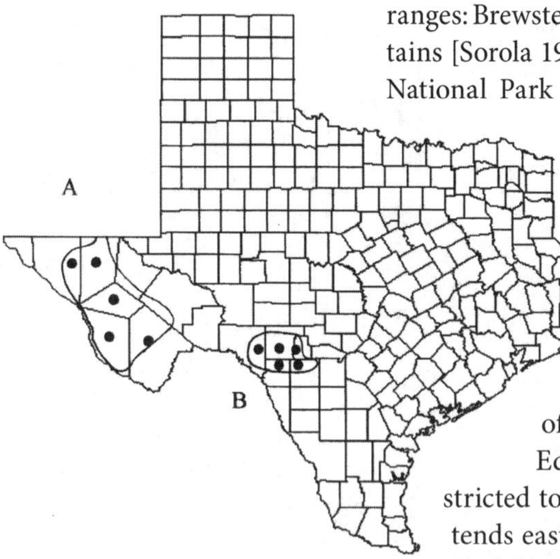

Figure 3.9.
Approximate contemporary distributions (post-1950) of Montezuma quail in the Trans-Pecos (A) and Edwards Plateau (B) ecoregions of Texas. Black dots represent county records.

ranges: Brewster (Del Norte [Sorola 1986; Hughes 1993] and Glass mountains [Sorola 1986]), Culberson (Guadalupe Mountains [F. Armstrong, National Park Service, unpublished data]), Hudspeth (Sierra Diablo [J. Foster, TPWD, unpublished data]), Jeff Davis (Davis Mountains [Sorola 1986; Bryan 2002]), and Presidio (Chinati Mountains and Sierra Vieja [J. Miller, C. E. Miller Ranch, unpublished data]) (figure 3.9). However, because of limited access to private lands and the bird's secretive nature, Montezuma quail may be more widespread throughout the Trans-Pecos in montane woodlands and adjacent desert grasslands of upper elevations than is currently reported.

Edwards Plateau populations of Montezuma quail are restricted to a small area in east-central Val Verde County that extends eastward through Edwards County to the western edge of Real County and southward into the northern portions of Kinney and Uvalde counties (Sorola 1986; Albers and Gehlbach 1990).

Changes

Montezuma quail appear to have retained much of their historic range in the Trans-Pecos, with several exceptions. Oberholser (1974) reported that Montezuma quail were last collected near El Paso in 1883, presumably from the Franklin Mountains. There are no known subsequent reports of them from El Paso County. Fuertes (1903), Strecker (1930), Van Tyne and Sutton (1937), and O'Connor (1945) provided early accounts of Montezuma quail in the Chisos Mountains. Wauer (1996) stated that the Chisos Mountains population (Big Bend National Park) declined dramatically between the 1940s and 1960s and that the last confirmed sighting was made in 1983, despite an effort to reintroduce the quail in 1973.

Montezuma quail have undergone their greatest range constriction in the Edwards Plateau. Oberholser (1974) noted that by 1940 the Edwards Plateau distribution had been reduced to populations centered where Val Verde, Edwards, and Kinney counties join and another in the vicinity of Concan in the Frio River drainage, Uvalde County. Subsequently, Sorola (1986) documented a similar, but slightly larger, distribution in this region.

Annual Cycle and Life History

In this section we address pair formation and breeding, nesting and incubation, and other key aspects of Montezuma quail life history.

Pair Formation and Breeding

In preparation for breeding, coveys disassemble (Bristow and Ockenfels 2000) and males and females spend the next few weeks searching for mates and nesting areas (Leopold and McCabe 1957). Like other quail, male Montezuma quail begin calling from elevated perches (e.g., rocks) and pursuing females. They may be paired as early as February and March (Wallmo 1954; Bishop 1964; Sorola 1986; figure 3.10). Precipitation in the Edwards Plateau is bimodal, with peaks in May–June and September–October (figure 3.11). In the Trans-Pecos, precipitation peaks in midsummer (National Oceanic and Atmospheric Administration 2003a). Because Montezuma quail vary their nesting date based on the patterns of spring-summer rainfall and conditions of the surrounding habitat, they may nest earlier in the Edwards Plateau than in the Trans-Pecos.

Despite early pairing by Montezuma quail, breeding does not occur

Figure 3.10.
A female Montezuma quail photographed during the breeding season while she forages in the desert grassland habitats of Brewster County, Texas.
Photo by Louis A. Harveson

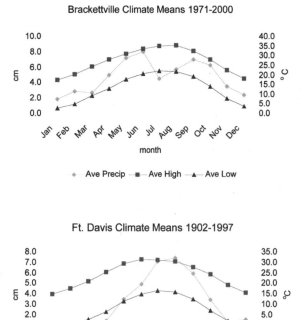

Brackettville Climate Means 1971-2000

◆ Ave Precip ■ Ave High ▲ Ave Low

Ft. Davis Climate Means 1902-1997

◆ Ave Precip ■ Ave High ▲ Ave Low

Figure 3.11.
Average monthly precipitation and temperature for Brackettville (1971–2000) and Fort Davis (1902–97), Texas.

until after the peak of summer rains (Stromberg 2000). The extended pair bonding that occurs well ahead of the onset of breeding (July–September) is unique among quails in Texas and may represent an adaptation that allows Montezuma quail to prepare for specific breeding habitat conditions that occur after the onset of summer rains. Drought can negatively impact Montezuma quail populations. Smith (1917) noted that Montezuma quail were common until a string of dry years in the Davis Mountains diminished the local population. Because rainfall during the summer months ultimately influences the amount of available plant foods in the fall (Bishop and Hungerford 1965), a prolonged period of insufficient rainfall decreases plant foods, vegetation used for cover and nesting, and insect abundance. However, the specific mechanisms (i.e., reproductive failure, nest failure, or chick survival) of failed Montezuma quail populations associated with drought are unknown.

Nesting and Incubation

Nests in the wild are typically found at bases of perennial bunchgrasses on rocky slopes (Owen, cited in Bent 1932). Dead trees or rock outcrops may also provide adequate nesting sites. Montezuma quail top their nests with a grass-domed roof (Leopold and McCabe 1957). Todd (cited in Bent 1932:86) described the grass-lined interior of a nest as "5 inches [12.7 centimeters] in diameter and 2 inches [5 centimeters] deep." Grass stems, leaves, and feathers may be used in nest construction. Clutch size averages 11 eggs/nest and ranges between 6 and 16 (Leopold and McCabe 1957). Eggs are 33.0 × 25.0 millimeters (1.3 × 1.0 inches), slightly glossy, unblemished, and white (Bent 1932; Oberholser 1974; Leopold and McCabe 1957).

Female Montezuma quail have the predominant role in incubation, which lasts 24–26 days (Wallmo 1954). Although no definitive studies have revealed the reproductive strategies of Montezuma quail, Stromberg (2000) noted recent accounts of males tending nests. Falvey (1936) suggested that a second clutch may occur in favorable conditions. Hatching dates have been recorded from the beginning of July through October (Leopold and McCabe 1957; Bristow and Ockenfels 2000).

Brooding

Female and male Montezuma quail share parental responsibilities (Leopold and McCabe 1957; Ligon 1961). The chicks grow rapidly after they hatch and do not immediately resemble adults. The overall presence of brownish red natal down on chicks may last for a few weeks, but juvenile quills begin to emerge within a few days of hatching. During the juvenile period, both sexes resemble the adult female pattern. The juvenile male plumage appears more cinnamon above and gray below, whereas the female is more uniformly gray. The postjuvenile molt may happen as late as November, depending on the hatch date (Bent 1932). Except for its outer primary feathers, a 16-week-old juvenile should have its first full adult winter plumage (Leopold and McCabe 1957) and resemble adults.

Like many bird species, a pair of Montezuma quail will attempt to distract intruders from finding their brood. Henshaw (1875) witnessed a hen with a young brood flying up and acting hurt while falling to the ground. She did this several times, avoiding capture, while the brood hid in surrounding cover. Leopold and McCabe (1957) flushed a pair with young chicks; the male feigned injury while the female hovered around their horses. These distractions allowed the brood to escape.

Coveys

Ligon (1961:98–99) claimed that "none has a stronger covey attachment" than Montezuma quail. During the fall and winter months they are found in coveys containing young of the year and adult birds (Bristow and Ockenfels 2000). Montezuma quail average 6.4 birds/covey and are noted for not making large aggregations (Leopold and McCabe 1957; Oberholser 1974; Stromberg 1990). However, larger groups have been reported by O'Connor (1936), who observed coveys with more than 20 individuals. These larger congregations will live together throughout the winter until adults disperse during early spring in search of mates.

Awareness is an important survival factor in winter months as food becomes scarce and predation continues. Coveys spend the night roosting in a tight circle, rump to rump, in flat, lower areas. Most daylight hours are spent foraging for underground food sources. Stromberg (1990) reported that Montezuma quail in Arizona forage on north-facing slopes. Although this pattern has not been confirmed in Texas populations, it is suspected that daily activities are dependent on the abundance and spatial distribution of food sources. Daytime activities may include foraging in one area with abundant foods until the source becomes scarce and then moving to a different area with sufficient foods. Knowing that these quail did not travel very far from day to day, Huggler (1987) used fresh food diggings to find them in Arizona. Stromberg (1990) noted that movements to new foraging areas occur more often in winter when plant foods are less available; Montezuma quail had small home ranges of 1–5 hectares (2.47–12.4 acres) during fall and winter seasons and up to 50 hectares (124 acres) during spring.

Compared to other Texas quails, Montezuma quail rely more on cryptic coloring than on flying or running from danger (O'Connor 1936; Oberholser 1974). When encountered in the field, covey members frequently crouch and freeze in an attempt to blend into their surroundings. Hiding birds remain motionless until they are nearly stepped on. They explode from underfoot and fly to a safe distance (Stromberg 1990). Fuertes (1903) expressed his frustration in trying to locate Montezuma quail in the rough habitat of the Chisos Mountains in the Texas Big Bend even as they called nearby. In unnatural habitats, such as roadways, birds have been killed by unsuspecting car traffic while attempting to blend with their surroundings. T. H. Allen (unpublished data) watched a Montezuma quail covey take cover at the overhead approach of a turkey vulture (*Cathartes aura*), suggesting that the "crouch-and-freeze" response is used to avoid detection and capture by avian predators.

Montezuma quail are less likely to flush than other quails in Texas.

Of 19 coveys observed by Leopold and McCabe (1957), the flushing distance of 18 coveys was less than 46 meters (50 yards). Longer flush distances may occur when the quail are able to glide down a slope. After rapid flight to a safe distance, or a distance at which the breast muscles become fatigued, the Montezuma quail falls to the ground seemingly out of control (Fuertes 1903; Leopold and McCabe 1957). Upon returning to the ground, the quail attempts to hide by running into surrounding cover, then rests and begins to locate the covey with vocalizations.

Vocalizations

Unsuspecting persons in the field may become startled when a covey of Montezuma quail flushes. Not only do the birds erupt from underfoot but they also emit a soft cry to confuse an intruder. By the time the person realizes what is happening, the birds are long gone.

Montezuma quail often use what can be termed an assembly call. This call resembles a slowed canyon wren's (*Catherpes mexicanus*) call in that it descends the pitch scale. Usually there are about nine notes followed by a nearly inaudible ending (Bent 1932; Levy, Levy, and Bishop 1966). This call may be heard shortly after a flushed covey settles as the birds attempt to regroup. The quail will respond to this call when imitated by a person. Leopold and McCabe (1957) reported that both sexes of adults and chicks use this call. Bailey (1928) and Oberholser (1974) noted that the assembly call is "ventriloquial" because the location of the bird was difficult to determine from the direction of the call.

Another common call heard in the field is made by the male during the breeding season when searching for other quail. The sound is a high-pitched buzz-shrill sound (Brown 1976) that can be easily mimicked. Beginning after winter coveys disassemble, unpaired males will reply to this call and begin searching for the source. The male never walks directly to the source. Rather, he walks a semicircular pattern until the source is in sight. When he stops replying to the call, he is either in viewing distance of the caller or may perceive his calling has put him in danger. This call can be heard in the field until late autumn when winter coveys form (T. H. Allen, unpublished data).

When quail are foraging together, they cluck, which was described by McCall (1852) as a "social cluck" and by Leopold and McCabe (1957) as a "low chitter." It promptly ceases when the covey is alerted to possible threats.

Habitat Use and Diet

Information gathered from several different sources provides a limited view of Montezuma quail habitat requirements. In comparison to other North American quail species, Montezuma quail are considered habitat specialists. They subsist on food and water found in the underground corms of wood sorrel (*Oxalis* spp.) and tubers and rhizomes of sedges (*Cyperus* spp.) and onions (*Allium* spp.) that are most frequently associated with habitats of pine (*Pinus* spp.) and oak (*Quercus* spp.) (Ligon 1927; Bishop and Hungerford 1965; Albers and Gehlbach 1990; Holdermann and Holdermann 1998; figure 3.12). Leopold and McCabe (1957) noted that the combination of pine, oak, and adequate understory made the proper habitat for Montezuma quail; however, they are not exclusively limited to pine-oak woodlands (Stromberg 2000). Montezuma

Figure 3.12.
The pine-oak-juniper complex in the Davis Mountains of Texas is thought to contain some of the best Montezuma habitat in the state.
Photo by Louis A. Harveson

quail have also been found in association with pine-juniper (*Juniperus* spp.) woodlands, montane meadows, and desert grasslands (Holdermann 1992; Holdermann and Holdermann 1998; Brown 1982; Hernández 2004).

Montezuma quail are typically associated with wooded, mountainous terrain with a prominent grassy understory at elevations greater than 1,500 meters (about 5,000 feet) (Leopold and McCabe 1957; Brown 1989; Holdermann 1992). However, lower elevations are used in the Edwards Plateau portion of the Texas range (approximately 500 meters, or 1,600 feet) (Sorola 1986; Albers and Gehlbach 1990); and birds have been found in subalpine environments (greater than 2,500 meters, or about 8,200 feet) in Arizona and New Mexico (Swarth 1909; Ligon 1927). At higher elevations, Montezuma quail were associated with alpine meadows and parklands of ponderosa pine (*P. ponderosa*) (Ligon 1961; Brown 1989; Holdermann 1992). At lower elevations, riparian corridors, desert washes, and mixed-oak woodlands were used (Wallmo 1954; Holdermann 1992; Hernández 2004; Albers and Gehlbach 1990). Regardless of plant community, the common structural elements that tie together all Montezuma quail habitats are adequate grass cover (e.g., bunchgrasses) and forbs and grasses that support subterranean foods.

Nesting and Brooding Habitat

There are few documented accounts of Montezuma quail nests, thus making it difficult to characterize nesting habitat. Documented nests occur in various types of habitats (Stromberg 2000). Wallmo (1954) encountered nests in dense understory of Rocky Mountain maple (*Acer glabrum*) and Arizona white oak (*Q. arizonica*) and in hot arid slopes dominated by mountain mahogany (*Cercocarpus montanus*), sotol (*Dasylirion wheeleri*), agave, and bunchgrasses. Site characteristics included level ground, hillsides, and sometimes adjacency to a large rock or tree trunk (Stromberg 2000).

There is general consensus that the late-nesting strategy of Montezuma quail is timed to coincide with the summer rains (Miller 1943; Wallmo 1954; Leopold and McCabe 1957). Miller hypothesized that this strategy enabled quail broods to benefit from the greater production of plant and animal foods associated with the summer rainy season. Adequate levels of food and cover resources are essential for raising chicks. Although adult quail are able to survive temporary habitat degradation, the same habitat would be inadequate for raising chicks (Texas Game, Fish and Oyster Commission 1945).

Montezuma quail brooding habitat was characterized by Bristow and Ockenfels (2002) and had greater grass canopy cover, less woody canopy cover, and greater visual obstruction than random locations. Brooding habitat also had a diversity of vegetation forms, including bunchgrasses, forbs, and trees. In general, it provided more cover (vertical and horizontal) than unused sites did.

Covey and Roosting Habitat

Adequate grass cover is critical to Montezuma quail defense and escape strategies (Brown 1982; figure 3.13). Perennial bunchgrasses are essential not only for cover but also for nest building and concealment (Brown 1979). Brown (1982) suggested that Montezuma quail do not inhabit areas that lack ample ground cover even if sufficient food supplies are available. In Arizona, heavily grazed lands produced an abundant supply of Montezuma quail food but lacked protective ground cover. This lack of protective cover renders habitats virtually useless to quail (Heffelfinger and Olding 2000). Albers and Gehlbach (1990) noted 40–50 percent grass cover removal by grazing had detrimental impacts on quail survival in the Edwards Plateau of Texas.

Stromberg (1990) characterized roost sites used by Montezuma quail in Arizona. Roost sites were aggregated and used repeatedly. Most were found at the base of rocks with overhanging tall grass (e.g., tanglehead [*Heteropogon contortus*]). Roost sites faced southeast with a mean aspect of 138° and had a mean slope of 15 percent. In contrast, day-use sites were typically on north-facing hillsides with more woody cover.

Diet

Montezuma quail feed exclusively on the ground of hillsides, gullies, and creek beds and under trees and shrubs, at the base of rocks, and in clumps of grass (Leopold and McCabe 1957). Grass cover taller

Figure 3.13.
A male Montezuma quail in characteristic habitat consisting of abundant screening cover provided by herbaceous vegetation.
Photo by Louis A. Harveson

Figure 3.14.
Remnants of a Montezuma quail dig
with bulb removed.
Photo by Ty H. Allen

than 0.3 meter (1 foot) typifies their feeding habitat (Albers and Gehlbach 1990). Montezuma quail dig for soft bulbs, sedge tubers, and seeds
(Bishop and Hungerford 1965). Quail diggings are evident by the remains (e.g., onion hulls) surrounding the dig (figure 3.14) and vary in
size and shape. Bishop and Hungerford (1965) reported diggings as cone-
shaped holes 1–3 centimeters (0.39–1.18 inches) deep; whereas Leopold
and McCabe (1957) described diggings as 5 centimeters (2 inches) long,
2.5 centimeters (1 inch) wide, and 5–8 centimeters (2–3.2 inches) deep.

Plant foods represent almost 80 percent of diet year-round (Judd
1905; Brown 1978; Stromberg 2000). Bishop and Hungerford (1965)
found that in June–August, insects and acorns made up about 50 percent and 37 percent of quail diet in Arizona, respectively. Insects found
in the diet included grasshoppers (Orthoptera), beetles (Coleoptera),
and ants (Hymenoptera). The shift to an animal diet coincided with
both the nesting season and the summer rains. It is during this time
that insects are most abundant and readily eaten by adults and chicks
alike.

Demography and Populations

Data on the demographics and population ecology of Montezuma quail
are lacking. In fact, only Stromberg (1990) reported population demography of Montezuma quail using contemporary techniques (e.g., radiotelemetry, mark-recapture methods). Data are even more restricted on
population ecology and demographics of Montezuma quail in Texas
(Sorola 1986; Albers and Gehlbach 1990; Hernández 2004). However,
more information on the population characteristics of Montezuma
quail is available from other regions of the Southwest.

Population Dynamics, Trends, and Monitoring

Montezuma quail, like other gallinaceous birds of the Southwest, are
subject to the "boom-and-bust" phenomenon associated with fluctuating precipitation levels (Serventy 1971). Brown (1979) found that boom
years in Montezuma quail were correlated with the summer rainfall of
the preceding year. Although double brooding and reproductive strategies have not been confirmed, Brown (1989) suggested that Montezuma

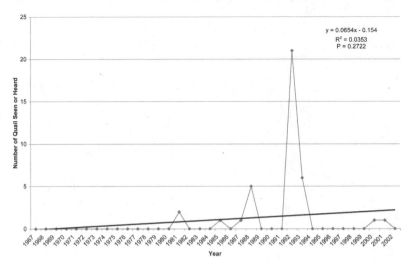

Montezuma Quail Population Trend in Texas from the Breeding Bird Survey

$y = 0.0654x - 0.154$
$R^2 = 0.0353$
$P = 0.2722$

Figure 3.15.
Mean number of Montezuma quail observed during North American Breeding Bird Surveys in Texas, 1967–2002 (Sauer, Hines, and Fallon 2002).

quail have the highest reproductive success of southwestern quail, thus allowing for rapid population growth. Severe drought or overgrazing can lead to drastic declines and even local extirpation of Montezuma quail populations (Brown 1979; Brown 1982).

Because of their unique status, limited distribution, and cryptic nature, Montezuma quail may be the most difficult game bird in North America to survey. The TPWD does not conduct surveys of Montezuma quail as part of its annual quail surveys. Sauer, Hines, and Fallon (2002) found that data from the Breeding Bird Surveys (BBS) have detected Montezuma quail in Texas, but there is no apparent trend in these data (figure 3.15). For the period 1967–2002, Montezuma quail were not detected in 20 of 28 years by the BBS in Texas, supporting the notion that they are difficult to monitor.

Several investigators have attempted to establish a monitoring technique for Montezuma quail (Brown 1976; Bristow and Ockenfels 2000; Hernández, Harveson, and Brewer 2002b; Robles et al. 2002). Techniques to monitor populations based on call counts, dig counts, maps of foraging signs, and line drives have all proven futile. Population indices derived by working trained bird dogs along established transects (Brown 1976; Holdermann 1992; Bristow and Ockenfels 2000) and using line transect methodology (Robles et al. 2002) appear to be the only valid methods for this elusive quail.

Survival Rates and Mortality Factors

Little information is available regarding annual survival rates of Montezuma quail. For example, mark-recapture data to estimate survival rates have not been published on Montezuma quail, and only one radiotelemetry study has been reported (Stromberg 1990). However, the sample size ($n = 8$) in Stromberg (2000) was too small to calculate survival estimates. Brown (1979) provided the only survival estimates on Montezuma quail based on hunter surveys; annual survival ranged from 0.18 to 0.59.

Historically, hunting mortality in Montezuma quail has been considered compensatory to other mortality factors (Leopold and McCabe 1957; Brown 1979; Bristow and Ockenfels 2000); however, Stromberg

(2000) felt that it may lead to local extirpation. Additionally, populations of Montezuma quail appear to be vulnerable to drastic changes in herbaceous cover (Brown 1982; Albers and Gehlbach 1990). When their primary defense mechanisms, camouflage and crouching, are jeopardized, Montezuma quail appear susceptible to avian predation (Hernández 2004; figure 3.16). Various researchers have documented raptor predation, for example, Cooper's hawk (*Accipiter cooperii*), sharp-shinned hawk (*A. striatus*), great horned owl (*Bubo virginianus*), and red-tailed hawk (*Buteo jamaicensis*) (Ligon 1927; Leopold and McCabe 1957; Brown 1982; Stromberg 1990; Holdermann and Holdermann 1993; Hernández 2004). Other mortality factors for Montezuma quail include canids, vehicular collisions, and inclement weather, such as hard freezes (Stromberg 2000).

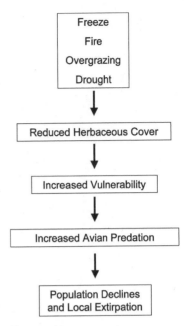

Figure 3.16.
Relationship between disturbances to Montezuma quail habitat and subsequent population declines.

Sex and Age Ratios
Male-to-female sex ratios (M:F) of Montezuma quail approximate 60:40 (Brown and Gutiérrez 1980) and are thought to be the most highly skewed sex ratios of all birds in North America (Stromberg 2000). Although age structure of Montezuma quail varies annually with precipitation, data from hunter-shot and flush counts suggest that juveniles represent 64–80 percent of fall populations (Brown 1978).

Movements and Density
Immigration and emigration rates for Montezuma quail have not been documented. Stromberg (2000) reported that Montezuma quail densities ranged from 0.7 to 1.3 birds/hectare (0.28–0.5/acre) with up to 1.82/hectare (0.7/acre) occurring in good habitat. Using line transects, Robles et al. (2002) reported Montezuma densities in Mexico ranging from 0 to 0.27/hectare (0.10/acre), with an average density of 0.18/hectare (0.07/acre). Albers and Gehlbach (1990) reported 0.09/hectare (0.04/acre) in the Edwards Plateau. Sorola (1986) estimated densities in the Trans-Pecos (Brewster and Jeff Davis counties) and Edwards Plateau (Edwards, Kinney, Real, Uvalde, and Val Verde counties) ecoregions, based on an average covey size of 7.77 birds, at 0.009/hectare and 0.007/hectare (0.004 and 0.003/acre), respectively.

Conservation and Management
The geographic range of Montezuma quail has decreased dramatically in Texas during the last 150 years. Densities and trends of the remaining populations are unknown. Development of a conservation and management strategy for Montezuma quail in Texas will require initiatives to (1) learn more about their life history, (2) identify and monitor populations, and (3) conduct basic research on population dynamics and habitat relationships.

One of the first challenges that must be addressed in the conservation of Montezuma quail in Texas is evaluating the potential of habitat throughout the former range of the species for reintroductions. The TPWD has attempted one reintroduction of Montezuma quail in the Edwards Plateau, and the National Park Service has attempted two reintroductions in the Trans-Pecos ecoregion.

During January 1991, TPWD obtained 22 Montezuma quail from Buenos Aires National Wildlife Refuge and released them on the Kerr

Wildlife Management Area, Kerr County, Texas (M. J. Peterson, Texas A&M University, pers. comm.). Since the release, no reports of signs, calls, or visual documentations have been made.

Montezuma quail were apparently common in the Chisos Mountains at the beginning of the twentieth century (Fuertes 1903). Three decades later, Van Tyne and Sutton (1937) noted a great decrease in their numbers and stated that overgrazing was surely a factor. Wauer (1973) suggested that the combination of severe drought following overgrazing by livestock likely resulted in the extirpation of Montezuma quail from the Chisos Mountains. In 1973, the National Park Service attempted to restock Big Bend National Park with Montezuma quail from the Davis Mountains but was unable to capture any birds for release. In January 1973, Roland Wauer (National Park Service) and David Brown (Arizona Game and Fish Department) succeeded in netting 26 Montezuma quail near Nogales, Arizona (Wauer 1973). The quail were released in Pine Canyon at Big Bend National Park and were sighted in 1973 and 1974, but not in 1975 or 1976. In 1977, an attempt was made to locate Montezuma quail in the Chisos Mountains using a bird dog. Although two areas were found with scratchings attributed to Montezuma quail, no birds were found (Brown 1977). Brown reported a few observations during the 1980s, suggesting the population persisted at least until that time. The lack of sightings and signs of Montezuma quail suggests that the population may have been extirpated. However, no surveys using bird dogs or callback tapes have been conducted since 1977.

Montezuma quail were last seen in the Guadalupe Mountains in the 1960s. During 1984 and 1985, 54 Montezuma quail were captured from Unit 36 in Arizona and released in Dog Canyon. The first 24 birds were subject to a hard release in November 1984. The remaining 30 birds were released following 3–4 weeks of acclimatization and ad libitum feed and water in a holding pen. Four of the birds were radio-marked and briefly monitored. Although Montezuma chicks were recorded in 1986, sightings were sporadic during the late 1980s and were not recorded from 1991 to 1996. More recently, Montezuma quail were detected using callback surveys in 2001 in Dog Canyon, and they were observed on Frijole Peak and Hunter Peak (F. Armstrong, National Park Service, unpublished data). It is unknown whether original Montezuma quail populations persisted, reintroduction efforts succeeded, or adjacent populations from the Sacramento Mountains recolonized.

The identification of potential reintroduction sites will involve an assessment of key habitat components previously described. It is possible for Montezuma quail to persist in an area for an extended time undetected by humans when the population is at a low density. Thus, when a suitable area is identified, multiple surveys of the locale should be conducted using trained dogs. These surveys should be conducted following at least one year of weather conducive to good reproduction. If a suitable area is identified and found to have no sign of Montezuma quail, the potential for natural recolonization of the area should be assessed. At present, little is known about dispersal of Montezuma quail. Observations suggest that the species is philopatric. However, occasionally Montezuma quail are reported in uncharacteristic habitats (e.g., scrublands, desert grasslands), suggesting that dispersal might be over greater distances than expected, especially when rainfall is sufficient to allow the birds to use areas outside their core ranges.

Conservation Genetics

Releasing animals into areas where they are nearly or totally extirpated can be a double-edged sword for the conservation of a species. New populations can increase the long-term survival of a species by reducing the chance of extinction due to a random event, such as a prolonged drought. Also, very small populations may be vulnerable to a genetic bottleneck. Introducing individuals into the population can improve the genetic variability, resulting in a population that can better adapt to changes.

However, the release of animals into areas can also have negative consequences, including the introduction of new diseases and the elimination of genetically distinct populations. Unfortunately, the potential genetic uniqueness of isolated populations is often given little consideration when the animal is a game species. For example, the genotype of white-tailed deer (*Odocoileus virginianus*) and bighorn sheep (*Ovis canadensis*) in the mountains of West Texas today is not the same type that occurred there 100 years ago. The same might be true for Montezuma quail.

Whether Montezuma quail from Texas and Arizona are genetically distinct is unknown. If Montezuma quail from Arizona could be distinguished from those in Texas based on genetics, an interesting question could be addressed. Montezuma quail from the Guadalupe Mountains could be tested to determine if they descended from birds reintroduced using stock from Arizona or had recolonized from adjacent habitats. This would confirm that the original population was, indeed, extirpated and that the current population is completely a result of reintroductions by the National Park Service. Additionally, if Montezuma quail from Arizona differ genetically from those in Texas, future reintroductions should not use stock from Arizona if the Texas strain is to be preserved.

The current range for Montezuma quail shows that the distance between populations in Arizona and Texas is much greater than the straight-line distance if you follow the contiguous range of the species from Texas, south into the Sierra Madre of Mexico, and north into Arizona. The shape of this range has almost certainly changed dramatically during the last 100 years. Currently, there is no evidence to support or refute a genetic distinction between Montezuma quail in Arizona and Texas. Further, genetic analysis could help determine effective population size, determine how long the relict population in the Edwards Plateau has been isolated, and elucidate dispersal strategies used by Montezuma quail in island habitats.

Management

The exotic beauty of Montezuma quail makes this species a favorite among birders. It is a popular draw for Davis Mountains State Park, near Fort Davis. A viewing station at the park attracts about a dozen people per day to watch for Montezuma quail at a feeding station (J. Holland, Davis Mountains State Park, pers. comm.; figure 3.17). The

Figure 3.17.
Bird enthusiasts watch as a male Montezuma quail forages on commercial seed at the bird-viewing site at Davis Mountains State Park, Jeff Davis County, Texas. Photo by Louis A. Harveson

Davis Mountains State Park has been successful in marketing Montezuma quail watching. It is the only public area in Texas where this species can be regularly seen. The popularity of the species among birders suggests that it could be used as a centerpiece for ecotourism on public and private lands in West Texas.

Although Montezuma quail are hunted in Arizona and New Mexico, Texas has a closed season. During 2003, the TPWD proposed opening a Montezuma quail hunting season with a two-bird bag limit. Public comments from local ranchers, bird-watchers, and biologists were decidedly against the proposal and the lack of data to support it. The proposal was eventually withdrawn. Bristow and Ockenfels (2000) reported that Montezuma quail hunting mortality was compensatory to other natural sources of mortality in Arizona. However, Stromberg (2000) questioned this conclusion and suggested that Montezuma quail might be locally vulnerable to overharvesting. Future crafting of Montezuma quail hunting recreation in Texas should consider the species' life history characteristics, overall population status, and the security of existing habitats to sustain healthy populations at local and regional levels.

Historically, hunters have championed the conservation of species, and the case of the Montezuma quail will be no different. The plight of the Montezuma quail in Texas during the last 100 years must be communicated to hunters. Perhaps areas in Texas exist where some harvest of Montezuma quail can be made on a sustainable basis, as appear to exist in Arizona and New Mexico. However, no data exist today to support that position.

One of the biggest incentives for land managers to invest in habitat improvements for a species is their ability to recoup the investment. A hunting season for Montezuma quail might allow that possibility for private landowners. Davis Mountains State Park has a visitor base who demand that the park be managed for Montezuma quail. However, little is known about effective habitat management strategies for Montezuma quail.

The first lesson from the history of Montezuma quail in Texas is that overgrazing is the number-one sin of past land management. Removal of 40–50 percent or more of the tall grasses in an area was correlated with extirpation of Montezuma quail in Arizona and Texas (Brown 1982; Albers and Gehlbach 1990); thus, tall-grass cover is imperative for good habitat. Woody cover is also typically associated with Montezuma quail habitat. Throughout the range of Montezuma quail in Texas, woody cover has increased during the last 100 years, primarily due to the virtual elimination of wildfires (Warnock and Loomis 2002). Like Montezuma quail, range fires require grass cover. These three entities—grass cover, range fire, and Montezuma quail—have obviously coevolved. Although prescribed range fire is one tool that can be used to maintain grass cover and reduce excessive woody encroachment, it is not known whether the quail derive other benefits from fire, such as enhancement or growth stimulation of plants used for food. This will be an important question for future research because of the difficulty and risk associated with implementing prescribed burns in mountainous terrain. If land managers could get the same benefit for Montezuma quail by hand clearing excessive woody cover as with removing woody cover by prescribed burns, many who own small tracts would opt for hand clearing.

Summary

For the most part, Montezuma quail populations in Texas have never been managed. During this period of neglect, the range of the species has contracted and local populations have been extirpated. Overgrazing by livestock was probably the most significant factor causing these declines. Thirty years ago marked the beginning of efforts to restore the Montezuma quail to parts of its historic geographic range. Many questions remain regarding the basic biology of this species in Texas, but enough is known to manage land for key habitat components. Perhaps in the future, hunters will be able to try to bag Montezuma quail and tell stories similar to those told by Fuertes (1903) during his adventures in the Chisos and Guadalupe mountains. However, for the present, much needs to be learned about this unique quail of Texas.

4 Northern Bobwhite Ecology and Life History

Fidel Hernández and Markus J. Peterson

> Primarily east of the 102nd meridian, *Colinus virginianus* resides virtually everywhere—from sandy, semi-arid mesquite country and open pine-oak woodlands to upland coastal prairie.
>
> Oberholser (1974)

40   Northern bobwhites (*Colinus virginianus*) have captured the public's interest for many years. Part of this interest can be attributed to the favorable impact that bobwhite hunting has on local economies. Landowners can supplement their income via fee-lease hunting, while local merchants benefit from the increased business caused by the influx of hunters. Interest in bobwhites, however, does not accrue solely from a consumptive perspective. These birds also are popular in the nonconsumptive realm among photographers, artists, and birders.

In many ways, bobwhites are one of the most studied wildlife species in the world. Thousands of articles have been published addressing various aspects of ecology, management, and conservation (Scott 1985). The intent of this chapter is not to summarize all this material but rather to provide a general overview of the life history and ecology of bobwhites in Texas. For a detailed description of the life history and ecology of bobwhites, we refer the reader to Stoddard (1931), Rosene (1969), Lehmann (1984), Roseberry and Klimstra (1984), and Brennan (1999).

Distribution in Texas

Texas lies on the western fringe of the geographic distribution of bobwhites (figure 4.1), although the masked bobwhite (*C. v. ridgwayi*), an endangered subspecies, can be found farther west in southeastern Arizona and northern Sonora, Mexico. Winter cold probably determines the northern limit of bobwhites' range, whereas the western limit is probably determined by lack of precipitation (Rosene 1969). Bobwhites can be found in all 10 ecoregions of Texas (Gould 1975b). They occur only in the drainages of the eastern edge of the Trans-Pecos, Mountains and Basins. Although bobwhites may be present within an ecoregion, they never are evenly distributed across the entire region because unsuitable conditions limit their range in some portions of each region (e.g., urban areas, large areas of agricultural fields, juniper breaks [*Juniperus* spp.]). Thus, the precise boundary of the geographic distribution of bobwhites is dynamic and is influenced by factors such as weather and availability of suitable habitat.

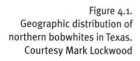

Figure 4.1.
Geographic distribution of
northern bobwhites in Texas.
Courtesy Mark Lockwood

Annual Cycle and Life History

In this section we describe the following aspects of bobwhite life history: vocalizations, covey breakup, pair formation and breeding, nest construction, and other important events in their annual cycle in Texas.

Vocalizations

Bobwhites are highly social organisms. They live in social units (e.g., pair, brood, or covey) most of their lives (figures 4.2 and 4.3). As such, they have evolved a wide repertoire of calls for communication (Stoddard 1931:97–111; Stokes 1967). We discuss only the most familiar calls that loosely can be categorized as those used to attract mates, reunite a scattered covey, alert covey mates of approaching danger, or warn a hen of a distressed brood. In terms of Collias's (1960) taxonomy of calls, these can be classified as reproduction, group movement, and avoidance of enemies, respectively.

Reproduction Call

Perhaps the most well-known call of the species is the "ah, bob-white." Males issue this call during the breeding season in an attempt to attract a female (figure 4.4). It was believed that unmated males primarily issued this call; however, mated males have also been known to issue the breeding call when separated from their mate (Kabat and Thompson 1963), but females rarely give this call (Stokes 1967; F. Hernández, personal observation). In Texas, the first "bob-white" call can be heard beginning approximately in March, with a peak calling period dur-

Figure 4.2.
Female (A) and male (B) northern bobwhites.
Photos by Charles W. Melton

Figure 4.3.
A pair of northern bobwhites. Mated pairs were originally thought to be monogamous during the breeding season. However, radiotelemetry studies show that bobwhites exhibit a wide repertoire of mating strategies during the course of a reproductive season.
Photo by Fidel Hernández

ing May through June. The timing of the first "bob-white" calls varies by latitude (Rosene 1969:58–59). Although this call is heard primarily during the breeding season, it has been documented during the nonbreeding season. Bobwhite calling during the nonbreeding season has been documented in January and February on plantations located between Georgia and Florida (Rosene 1969:58–59). In southern Texas (Brooks County), a bobwhite emitted two "bob-white" calls following a light shower in early December 2001 (F. Hernández, personal observation). These observations probably represent exceptions rather than the rule, however.

Group-Movement Call

The separation call, "koi-lee" or "hoyee," emitted by either males or females, is used to reunite a scattered covey. This call is also referred to as the scatter call or covey call and can be heard moments after a covey has been flushed or just prior to sunrise as coveys begin to leave their roost site. It is speculated that this call also might be used in various situations as a spacing mechanism (Stokes 1967); however, this is speculation that lacks empirical documentation.

Avoidance-of-Enemies Call

Bobwhites emit an alarm call, "toil-ick, ick, ick," when predators approach (Stoddard 1931:109). This nervous chatter escalates and becomes especially evident whenever a bird cannot escape, such as when approaching a covey trapped within a funnel trap. Young chicks also emit a lisping alarm call, "t-s-I-e-u, t-s-I-e-u, t-s-I-e-u," when disturbed (Stoddard 1931:107). This call often elicits a defense response from the attending adult birds, resulting in either direct attacks against the intruder or "broken-wing" displays to distract the apparent danger.

Annual Cycle

Although most data on bobwhite life history are relevant across the species' geographic range, some aspects differ through space and time (e.g., length of nesting season). We discuss the life history of bobwhites primarily as it pertains to populations in Texas, only highlighting notable exceptions that occur elsewhere.

Covey Breakup

The breakup of coveys generally begins in February and early March in South Texas (Lehmann 1984:67–69). Bobwhite pairs often are observed in February in southern Texas and the Rolling Plains (F. Hernández, personal observation). Large coveys will begin to subdivide into smaller coveys during this period. However, cold weather, rain, and late cold fronts may cause bobwhites to regroup in coveys (Lehmann 1984:67–69). Independent pairs generally do not become common until mid-March and are especially numerous by April throughout Texas.

Pair Formation and Breeding

Male sexual behavior may include lateral displays and bowing, whereas females exhibit wing quivering and presentation (Stokes 1967). Lateral displays are characterized by males walking slowly toward the

Figure 4.4.
A male bobwhite making a "bob-bob-white" call from a fence post during the reproductive season. Calling from an exposed location represents a trade-off between the benefits of attracting a mate and the risk of being killed by an avian predator.
Photo by Dale Rollins

female with a fanned tail and slightly lowered head. Lateral displays are strongly sexual in function, and the female usually responds by crouching to the male during or shortly after the display. As such, lateral displays by a subordinate male often provoke attacks by a dominant male if one is present. In the bowing display, a male moves about the female with his body oriented horizontally, feathers fluffed, and legs somewhat extended. This display resembles a male that is pecking at food without the beak ever touching the ground. The wing-quivering display involves a female approaching a male while rapidly lifting and settling her partially opened wings that are held away from her body. Several quivers may occur within a second. In most cases, the female approaches a male from about 2 meters (6 feet) away and passes by him in a straight line. It is believed that only females receptive to copulation give the quivering display. Females then initiate copulation by the solicitation crouch. The male approaches the crouching female from behind and mounts her while grabbing the back of her neck feathers with his beak. The male holds his tail up while the female everts her cloaca. The male then lowers his tail, pressing it firmly against her body. Copulation lasts about 10 seconds, after which the male dismounts. There is no postcopulatory display.

The mating system of bobwhites originally was thought to be monogamous, with hens renesting if their original nests failed (Stoddard 1931). Recent research using radiotelemetry (figure 4.5) has documented that bobwhites actually employ polygamous mating systems (i.e., rapid multiclutch and ambisexual) (Curtis et al. 1993; Burger, Dailey, et al. 1995). Rapid multiclutch polygamy is characterized by both the female and male simultaneously incubating two clutches (Persson and Ohrstrom 1989). A female laying a first clutch that is incubated by the male and a second clutch that is incubated by the female accomplishes this. Either the same or a different male may fertilize the second clutch. Both males and females having more than one mate during the breeding season characterize ambisexual polygamy. It differs from rapid multiclutch polygamy in that only a limited proportion of females

Figure 4.5.
Radiotelemetry has revolutionized our understanding of bobwhite reproductive ecology, movements, and habitat use. However, the extent to which being radio-marked lowers survival or adds stress to the birds, initially thought to be minimal, may be biologically significant.
Photo by Dale Rollins

lays multiple clutches and only a limited proportion of the males incubates nests. The proportion of bobwhites that exhibit monogamy, rapid multiclutch polygamy, and ambisexual polygamy is unknown (Burger, Dailey, et al. 1995).

Nest Construction

The nesting season in Texas may last from mid-April to early October; the peak nesting months are June–August (Lehmann 1984:84–29; Carter 1995; Hernández 1999). Late hatches (October–November, or even December) can happen in southern Texas, especially if rains occur in September (F. Hernández, unpublished data). Interestingly, evidence of egg laying has been obtained for all months of the year in South Texas (Lehmann 1984:84).

The length of the nesting season is strongly influenced by weather. It can be shortened by drought or intense heat, or lengthened by rainfall and relatively cool weather, especially in South Texas. Klimstra and Roseberry (1975) documented a negative correlation with ending dates of the nesting season and average maximum daily temperature during July and August in Illinois. In southern Texas, Guthery, Koerth, and Smith (1988) also found a shorter nesting season (i.e., three months versus five months) in the arid western region than in the more mesic eastern Rio Grande Plains (Gould 1975b).

Bobwhites are ground nesters. They generally construct nests in residual cover of perennial bunchgrasses, although other substrates such as forbs and shrubs are often used. Both male and female bobwhites participate in the nest-site selection and nest building and apparently construct more nests than are used. Stoddard maintained that the expected ratio of unused to used nests was 2:1 (cited in Lehmann 1984:80). In Shackelford County, Texas, bobwhites also have been observed constructing extra nests (F. Hernández, personal observation). Stoddard (1931:24) speculated that they represented nests the pair found unsatisfactory. Klimstra and Roseberry (1975) found that bobwhites were more inclined to build extra nests in areas having abundant, as opposed to limited, nesting cover but offered no explanation for their observation. The significance of unused nests is unknown, although hormones influencing incubating behavior may be involved (Vleck 2002).

A bobwhite nest consists of a nest bowl, which may include a roof (Lehmann 1984:82). The nest bowl is constructed by bobwhites scratching the ground and forming a slight depression about 12 centimeters (about 5 inches) wide and 6 centimeters (2.5 inches) deep. The depression then is lined with vegetation litter, such as grass blades or leaves. Much of the actual nest material consists of dead, residual grass that was produced during the previous year.

Laying, Incubation, and Nesting Success

Upon nest completion, the female lays the first egg within 1–7 days, then lays approximately one egg per day, occasionally skipping a day, until the clutch is complete (Rosene 1969:67–69; Lehmann 1984:86). Average initial clutch size is about 12–15 eggs. Egg laying spans 18–20 days (Stoddard 1931:26–28; Lehmann 1984:84–90). During the egg-laying stage, the nest remains unattended except when the female is depositing an egg. When the clutch has been completed, incubation begins and is accomplished primarily by one parent. Females incubate most of the nests, although males incubate about 20 percent (Burger, Dailey, et al. 1995; Carter 1995; Hernández 1999). The incubation period lasts 23 days. Approximately 85 percent of eggs in successful nests hatch within two to four hours. Therefore, the time dedicated to nesting spans about 47–55 days when one accounts for nest construction (5 days), egg laying (18–20 days), time to onset of incubation (1–7 days), and incubation (23 days; Rosene 1969:71).

Individual nests have a relatively low probability of success. Klimstra and Roseberry (1975) reported that of 863 nests in Illinois, 34 percent were successful. Causes of nest failure were depredation (55 percent), human activities (22 percent), abandonment (16 percent), weather (5 percent), and miscellaneous (2 percent). In southern Texas, Lehmann (1984:91) documented that 45 percent of 532 nests were successful, with predators accounting for 84 percent of nest failures. Other causes of nest failure included farming (9 percent), weather (5 percent), and abandonment (2 percent).

Despite these high rates of nest failure, bobwhites are capable of maintaining adequate reproduction for population persistence through renesting and, in some cases, producing multiple broods. Bobwhites are likely to renest regardless of the reason their initial nests failed, with some hens exhibiting two to three attempts (Roseberry and Klimstra 1984:83). Mean clutch size decreases, however, as the nesting season progresses and hens renest (Lehmann 1984:86; Hernández 1999). Although biologists traditionally believed that bobwhites rarely if ever raised more than one brood per season (Stoddard 1931:492; Rosene 1969:73–75), research using radiotelemetry has commonly documented multiple brooding (Sermons and Speake 1987; Taylor 1991; Curtis et al. 1993; Carter 1995; Hernández 1999).

Brooding

Toward the end of incubation, embryos develop an egg tooth for pipping the shell (Rosene 1969:71). Embryos begin pipping a small hole near the large end of the egg and continue along the circumference. During pipping, embryos squirm about in an effort to exit the eggshell until hatching is successful. The newly emerged chicks are brooded by the parental adult. The parental adult and chicks leave the nest typically within one day of hatching. Chicks drop their egg tooth within the next two to three days.

The growth and development of bobwhite chicks are rapid (Stoddard 1931:79–83; Rosene 1969:44–56; Lehmann 1984:106–16). Chicks are hatched with natal down that does not provide efficient protection from the elements. They are also poor thermoregulators. Thus, chicks must be brooded intensively until they are capable of thermoregulation. Chicks less than a week of age are brooded for the majority of the day, with only short periods for foraging. Primary feathers develop within 3–4 days, and by 14 days chicks are able capable of short flights of 12–15 meters (13–16 yards).

Juvenile plumage begins to predominate by week 3, and by week 5 only traces of natal down remain. By about 5 weeks of age, chicks no longer require intensive brooding by adults and are capable of living without parental care. In captive propagation experiments, Stoddard (1931:80) found that 5-week-old chicks survived heavy rains (5 centimeters, or 2 inches) at night without brooding. Juvenile plumage is complete by about 8 weeks of age, with sex of the chicks becoming recognizable at 8–10 weeks. Adult plumage predominates by weeks 12–13. Bobwhites are considered mature based on plumage and size at 15 weeks of age.

Habitat Use and Diet

In this section we emphasize how bobwhite habitat use and diet vary across the Texas landscape. We also point out the common elements of habitat use and diet throughout bobwhite distribution in the state.

Nesting

Bunchgrasses are common nesting substrates for bobwhites in Texas (Lehmann 1946; Lay 1954; Jackson 1969; figure 4.6). Warm-season, perennial, native bunchgrasses provide excellent nesting cover. Lehmann reported that bobwhites in South Texas nested in six genera of grasses, including bluestems (*Andropogon* spp.), threeawns (*Aristida* spp.), balsamscales (*Elyonurus* spp.), paspalums (*Paspalum* spp.), panicums (*Panicum* spp.), and lovegrasses (*Eragrostis* spp.), with 97 percent of nests (*n* = 189) situated in only three of these genera (*Andropogon, Aristida,* and *Elyonurus*). Studies in other parts of bobwhite range also support the importance of bunchgrasses as nesting cover (Stoddard 1931:20–26; Klimstra and Roseberry 1975). Similarly, Peoples et al. (1996) reported that 98 percent of bobwhite nests (*n* = 161) were in little bluestem (*Schizachyrium scoparium*) in Oklahoma.

Bobwhites, however, often nest in a variety of other substrates, including forbs and shrubs (Lehmann 1984:81; Carter, Rollins, and Scott 2002; Hernández et al. 2003). In the Rolling Plains ecoregion of Texas, bobwhites commonly nest in sand sagebrush (*Artemisia filifolia*) (F. S. Guthery, Oklahoma State University, pers. comm.). Further, recent research indicates that prickly pear cactus (*Opuntia* spp.) may represent an important nesting substrate in addition to bunchgrasses, particu-

Figure 4.6.
Native, warm-season perennial bunchgrasses provide excellent nesting habitat for bobwhites.
Photo by Fidel Hernández

larly in the Rolling Plains of Texas. Carter, Rollins, and Scott (2002) reported that 57 percent of 21 bobwhite nests were found in prickly pear instead of traditional bunchgrass habitat. Hernández et al. also found moderate use (31 percent of 81 nests) of prickly pear as a nesting substrate despite adequate bunchgrass cover (greater than 1,000 potential nest sites/hectare). Bent (1932:35) provided an anecdotal statement dating to 1925 that mentioned prickly pear as a nesting substrate used by bobwhites. Lehmann (1984:81) found only 1 of 189 bobwhite nests in prickly pear during 1946–70 in South Texas. Hernández et al. speculated that the recent documentation of bobwhites nesting in prickly pear might be an artifact of recent research being conducted in a region within the bobwhite's range where prickly pear grows in a form favorable for bobwhite nesting (e.g., Carter 1995; Hernández 1999).

Brood-Rearing Habitat
Lehmann (1984:106–10) described brood-rearing habitat as consisting of three components: shade, open herbaceous cover, and green, growing vegetation. He observed that broods often used shade provided by shrubs and tall weeds. Taylor and Guthery (1994) provided data demonstrating the importance of shade; broods in southern Texas used microsites with higher brush canopy during midday for loafing sites (approximately 30 percent brush canopy cover) compared to feeding (approximately 5 percent brush canopy cover) or roosting sites (approximately 15 percent brush canopy cover). However, Taylor, Church, and Rusch (1999) did not find differences in selection of habitat structure by broods in Kansas for different diurnal periods (i.e., sunrise–11:00 A.M., 11:01 A.M.–4:00 P.M., 4:01 P.M.–sunset, and sunset–sunrise). They hypothesized that the cooler, more mesic climate of their study area accounted for the difference between Texas and Kansas broods in this aspect of habitat selection.

Lehmann (1984:107) also speculated that open, herbaceous cover facilitated brood movement while offering good visibility for the attending adults. Taylor and Guthery (1994) did not find differences in habitat structure among foraging, loafing, or roosting sites used by broods. However, they speculated that brood selection for habitat structure might have been difficult to discern in their study because drought and brush management before and during the study provided uniformly open herbaceous structure over much of their study area. Taylor, Church, and Rusch (1999) documented that broods in Kansas selected habitat patches based on ground-cover components (i.e., percentage of bare ground, litter, grass, and forb cover) but selected sites within patches based on vegetation height and structure. They reported that broods preferred patches with relatively high exposure of bare ground (14.8 percent) and forb cover (29.9 percent) and sites with tall vegetation (39.8 centimeters, or about 15 inches). Taylor and Guthery (1994) found that moisture content of vegetation was higher at foraging sites (approximately 140 grams/square meter, or 5 ounces/square yard) used by broods than at loafing (approximately 40 grams/square meter, or 1.4 ounces/square yard) and roosting sites (approximately 60 grams/square meter, or 2.1 ounces/square yard). They speculated that succulent vegetation provided a higher relative abundance of insects. Hurst (1972), working in Mississippi, also suggested that invertebrate density was influenced by the quantity of succulent vegetation. Vegetation succulence has been shown to be an important element of the nutritional ecology of herbivorous arthropods (Scriber and Slansky 1981). Because invertebrates are the primary component in the diet of bobwhite chicks, the availability and abundance of insects often are regarded to be a major consideration for brood habitat (Stoddard 1931:159–64; Hurst 1972).

Few studies have described the roosting habitat of bobwhites (Stoddard 1931:1953–55; Rosene 1969), and even fewer have quantified roosting habitat specifically for either adults (Klimstra and Ziccardi 1963; Chamberlain, Drobney, and Dailey 2002) or broods (Taylor and Guthery 1994; Taylor, Church, and Rusch 1999). Taylor, Church, and Rusch found that broods selected roost sites with taller vegetation (44.8 centimeters, or about 18 inches) and greater visual obstruction (defined as the lowermost strata on a visual obstruction pole that was ≥50 percent visible; 5.1 decimeters, or 20 inches) than available within habitat patches (36.3 centimeters, or 14 inches; 3.8 decimeters, or 15 inches), respectively. They hypothesized that these characteristics might have provided favorable nighttime microclimates for chicks that had not yet reached thermal independence. In southern Texas, vegetation height and visual obstruction at roost sites decrease with increasing age of fall broods (i.e., hatched during September–October), with broods initially roosting in tall, dense vegetation such as shrubs, but then progressively roosting in more open habitats such as grasslands as they mature (F. Hernández, unpublished data). However, summer broods hatched during May–August do not exhibit this phenomenon but instead commonly roost in open habitats throughout their life, regardless of age.

Covey Habitat

Defining bobwhite habitat in terms of specific characteristics is difficult. Bobwhites select for habitat features over a wide range of values (Hammerquist-Wilson and Crawford 1987; Kopp et al. 1998). Further, it is possible for different configurations of habitat patches to result in fully usable habitat (Guthery 1999a). Given this caveat, we present a general description of what characterizes suitable bobwhite habitat.

Bobwhite habitat often has been described in terms of specific component features, such as percentage of bare ground, herbaceous cover, and woody cover (Edminster 1954; Schroeder 1985; Bidwell et al. 1991; Rice et al. 1993). Jackson (1969) stated that bobwhites required nesting cover, screening cover, loafing coverts, and woody thickets (dense patches of coarse weeds and grasses). Bare ground facilitates foraging, whereas screening cover provides overhead concealment during feeding and movement. Loafing coverts provide cover for resting, dusting, and thermal protection during the midday inactive period (Johnson and Guthery 1988). Woody and dense herbaceous cover provides protection against predators and heat. In southern Texas, bobwhites selected for dense herbaceous cover (Hammerquist-Wilson and Crawford 1987) and habitat patches with woody cover at a greater frequency than what is available at the landscape (Kopp et al. 1998). Kopp et al. summarized this relationship by presenting hypothetical properties of ideal landscapes for bobwhites; these landscapes should contain approximately 44 ± 23.8 percent bare ground ($x \pm$ SD), 38 ± 29.3 percent herbaceous cover, and 53 ± 26.6 percent woody cover. However, Guthery (2002) concluded that ideal landscapes (i.e., perfect habitat) could not be explicitly defined but can be recognized and confirmed.

Bobwhites generally have been thought of as a lower successional species (e.g., adapted to early seral stages) (Rosene 1969:11). In semiarid rangelands, however, this concept is insufficient (Spears et al. 1993). For example, in xeric habitats within the Rio Grande Plains of Texas, sites with more perennial grass cover had higher densities of bobwhites than sites with less grass cover (Campbell-Kissock, Blankenship, and White 1984). In more mesic habitats, however, bobwhites selected sites with greater coverage of bare ground and forbs and lesser coverage by grasses (Hammerquist-Wilson and Crawford 1981; Wilkins 1987). The optimum seral stage for bobwhites therefore appears to vary inversely with site productivity and precipitation in southwestern rangeland (Spears et al. 1993). Thus, bobwhites require early seral stages (more open ground, less grass cover) in sites of high productivity and precipitation, but later seral stages (less open ground, more grass cover) in sites with lower productivity and precipitation.

Diet

Adult bobwhites are largely granivorous (seed eating), with a diet consisting primarily of seeds produced by forbs and grasses. However, bobwhites also consume green vegetation, mast (i.e., seeds and fruits of trees and shrubs), and insects. During the fall and winter, bobwhites feed on seeds produced during the previous growing season. Jackson (1969:9–15) reported that seeds of forbs, grasses, and woody plants composed about 90 percent of the fall-winter diet in the Rolling Plains of Texas, with insects accounting for the remaining 10 percent. He found that as spring approached and vegetation began growing, bobwhites switched from a diet primarily of seeds to one consisting of green shoots and insects. Insects became increasingly important in the bobwhite diet during spring and summer because of the nutritional demands associated with reproduction. Breeding bobwhite females have higher nutritional demands (e.g., protein, calcium, and phosphorus) relative to those of nonbreeding hens (National Research Council 1977). Insects help meet this increased protein requirement because they are high in digestible protein.

Bobwhites eat seeds and other parts of more than 1,000 plant species (Stoddard 1931:113–65; Rosene 1969:102–20; Lehmann 1984:165–76; Guthery 1986:10). However, on a given pasture and during a given season, 5–10 species of plants generally constitute more than 75 percent of the food eaten (Guthery 1986:10). The important food plants for bobwhites in Texas therefore vary by locality and season (Jackson 1969:9–15; Guthery 1986:10–16). Generally speaking, important forbs include western ragweed (*Ambrosia psilostachya*), croton (*Croton* spp.), sunflower (*Helianthus* spp.), and legumes such as snoutbeans (*Rhynchosia* spp.) and bundleflowers (*Desmanthus virgatus*). Hard-seeded grasses such as bristlegrasses (*Setaria* spp.), panicums, and paspalums often constitute staple items in the bobwhite diet. Important shrubs providing mast include chittam (*Bumelia lanuginosa*), mesquite (*Prosopis glandulosa*), hackberry (*Celtis* spp.), and agarito (*Berberis trifoliata*). Important insects include grasshoppers, beetles, crickets, ants, termites, and spiders.

Demography and Populations

Northern bobwhites are short-lived. The average life span of an individual bobwhite is six months, and annual mortality—from all sources—can be as high as 80 percent (Brennan 1999). This trait is so well recognized that numerous adages, such as "bobwhites spend their lives looking for a place to die" and "everything eats bobwhites," have arisen in reference to it. As detailed earlier, nests have a relatively low probability of surviving until incubation is complete. Although little reliable data exist, it appears that less than 40 percent of chicks survive two to three weeks posthatch (DeVos and Mueller 1993; DeMaso et al. 1997). The daily probability of survival then begins to approximate that of adults (DeMaso et al. 1997).

The range of survival values for adult bobwhites is more difficult to acquire than one might expect. One might assume that studies employing radiotelemetry would have addressed this question long ago. Interestingly, these studies often report bobwhite survival rates so low that the populations would have gone extinct during the study or shortly thereafter (Curtis et al. 1988; Pollock, Winterstein, et al. 1989; Burger, Ryan, et al. 1995; Taylor et al. 1999; Townsend et al. 1999; Liu et al. 2000; Sisson, Speake, and Stribling 2000; Suchy and Munkel 2000; Taylor et al. 2000; Williams, Lutz, et al. 2000). This obviously did not occur, because bobwhites are still present on the areas used for these studies. Therefore, survival rates observed during radiotelemetry studies apply only to those bobwhites in the study populations marked with radios and only during the period the study was conducted. Research indicates that radio transmitters handicap bobwhites (Osborne, Frawley, and Weeks 1997; Guthery and Lusk 2004).

Based on the unrealistically low survival values reported in the literature and cited earlier, this handicap apparently is not trivial. Therefore, research designed to quantify the negative effects of various types of telemetry packages for wild quail is needed. Although radiotelemetry has been instrumental for documenting important life-history traits, such as double brooding, mortality-survival data derived from such studies must be interpreted with caution.

One way to address this problem is to determine the rate of bobwhite senescence in environments where all adults die of old age. Using longevity data from captive bobwhite populations, Guthery (2002:49–50) estimated that the annual probability of survival under ideal conditions would be approximately 56 percent. Stated another way, one should expect about 44 percent of bobwhites to die annually in the absence of predation, disease, resource limitations, inclement weather, or any other vagary of the natural environment. This is an important and almost always overlooked reason why management strategies designed to reverse broadscale declines in bobwhite abundance typically have been unsuccessful (see Brennan 1991a; Peterson, Wu, and Rho 2002). A large proportion of bobwhites in a population will die each year as a result of genetically programmed causes that are beyond the control of even the best-intentioned wildlife manager. Worse, if managers successfully reduce mortality from one source—such as predators—mortality due to another is likely to increase (Guthery 2002:45–67). Guthery put it this way: "From a management standpoint, meddling with survival-mortality schedules in a bobwhite population may be like walking up a steep sand dune: the gain is not commensurate with the effort" (51).

When sources of mortality in addition to senescence are considered for free-roaming bobwhite populations, adult survival is approximately halved and estimated mortality doubled; annual adult survival typically falls between 18 and 30 percent (Jackson 1969; Rosene 1969:385–86; Lehmann 1984:133; Roseberry and Klimstra 1984:218). Thus, 70–82 percent of bobwhites live less than one year, given that a bird has reached adult size. It is rare indeed for a bobwhite to live more than five years in the wild (Marsden and Baskett 1958; Marsden 1961). More specifically, adult survival is distributed clinally, with highest values at lower (warmer) and lowest values at higher (colder) latitudes (Guthery et al. 2000; Guthery 2002:45–67). Conversely, population productivity, as measured by juvenile/adult ratios in the fall hunter bag, is lesser at lower and greater at higher latitudes. On average, in warmer (southern) climates adult bobwhite survival is about 30 percent, with net production of 2.7 juveniles per adult; whereas adult survivorship in colder (northern) climates is less than 20 percent with more than 5 juveniles produced per adult (Rosene 1969:385–86; Lehmann 1984:133; Roseberry and Klimstra 1984:218; Guthery et al. 2000; Guthery 2002:45–67). Because of the latitudinal distance within Texas, these clines are obvious within the state as well. Long-term mean juvenile/adult ratios in hunter bags were 3.9:1 in the northern Rolling Plains ($n = 15$ years and 42,460 bobwhites) (Jackson 1969:9), 3.5:1 in the Piney Woods ($n = 10$ years and 14,910 bobwhites) (Rosene 1969:385), and 2.7:1 in the South Texas Plains ($n = 28$ years and 131,833 bobwhites) (Lehmann 1984:133). Finally, adult females appear to survive at a lower rate than males, resulting in the proportion of hens in the breeding population being approximately 44–47 percent (females per male = 0.78–0.89) (Roseberry 1974; Pollock, Moore, et al. 1989; Curtis et al. 1993; Burger, Ryan, et al. 1995).

In sum, regardless of nesting success, renesting, double brooding, latitudinal gradients, or other reproductive characteristics of bobwhites, the number of females that go into reproductive condition and the length of time they stay reproductively active are the key demographic variables of bobwhite populations (Guthery, Koerth, and Smith 1988; Guthery and Kuvlesky 1998; Peterson 2001; Guthery 2002:69–94). Stated another way, despite all the interesting reproductive adaptations of bobwhites, only hens lay eggs—everything else cascades one way or another from this event.

Mortality Factors

What variables, beyond senescence, limit bobwhite survival in Texas? A number of factors kill bobwhites either outright or in conjunction with other agents or lead to impaired reproduction. These include catastrophic weather events, such as wind and deluges associated with hurricanes (Lehmann 1984:153; Hernández, Harveson, and Brewer 2002a); extreme cold, freezing rain, or long-term snow cover that leads to starvation and hypothermia (Roseberry and Klimstra 1984:56–64; Lehmann 1984:147–50; Guthery 2002:15–16); and periods of drought, extremely hot weather, and associated hyperthermia (Forrester et al. 1998; Guthery et al. 2000; Guthery, King, Kuvlesky, et al. 2001; Guthery, Land, and Hall 2001; Guthery 2002:16–21).

Several population interactions directly or indirectly lead to bobwhite mortality. These include parasites, predators, and lack of sufficient nutrients (starvation). The parasites, infectious diseases, and selected toxic diseases of bobwhites in Texas are detailed in chapter 6. Finally, although it is rarely discussed, bobwhites, like many other species, and their nests are subject to trauma-induced losses.

Nutrition

Although many bobwhite biologists and hunters have assumed that food commonly limits populations—hence supplementary feeding and food-plot programs—there are no studies that unequivocally demonstrate that lack of food quantity or quality limits survival of wild adult or juvenile bobwhites in Texas or other western bobwhite ranges (Guthery 1997, 2002:148–49). Management strategies designed to produce more food for adult quail, however, might still benefit the population, regardless of whether food is limiting, if more habitable area—usable space available through time—is inadvertently developed during attempts to produce more food (Guthery 1997).

The situation with newly hatched chicks is less clear. The diet of chicks typically consists of greater than 80 percent arthropods during the first two weeks of life to obtain sufficient protein for growth (Handley 1931). In field situations, the proportion of chicks that die of starvation or other nutritional deficiencies before they mature to the age where they can obtain required nutrition primarily from vegetation (six to eight weeks of age) is unknown, but may be substantial.

Nest Predation

As detailed previously, nonhuman predation is the largest proximate cause of nest loss. The relative impact of specific nest predators undoubtedly differs by Texas physiographic region. Some of the most important predators of bobwhite nests can include coyotes (*Canis latrans*), raccoons (*Procyon lotor*), stripped skunks (*Mephitis mephitis*), and snakes (Lehmann 1946a, 1984:90–102; Jackson 1969:70–72; Hernández, Rollins, and Cantu 1997; figure 4.7).

Recently, it has become popular to assume that the crash of the fur market during the late 1980s led to decreased harvest of fur-bearing animals in Texas, which in turn led to increased numbers of these predators, resulting in increased nest predation, thence decreased quail abundance. Silvy et al. (2000) addressed these hypotheses for the Rolling Plains, Edwards Plateau, and South Texas Plains physiographic regions. They found that decreasing fur prices were indeed associated with decreasing furbearer harvest. Conversely, however, there was no increase in the abundance of fur-bearing animals during this period, and fur prices, furbearer harvest, and abundance of fur-bearing animals were not correlated with bobwhite abundance.

Three points concerning nest predation and long-term trends in bobwhite abundance in Texas are relevant for understanding how the process of nest predation influences population abundance. First, although many animals depredate bobwhite nests, because of this species' propensity to renest, the probability of producing more than one successful nest annually allows bobwhites to persist despite substantial nest losses. Therefore, the fact that predators are the largest cause of nest loss does not necessarily imply that nest losses ultimately are responsible for broadscale declines in bobwhite abundance—there is nothing alarming about 30 percent nest loss. Second, there is no evidence that fur markets are responsible for declining bobwhite abundance. Finally, even if it were determined that nest predation now is a much greater problem than previously thought, this would not necessarily imply that nest predation was the ultimate cause of declining bobwhite numbers. Rather, it would be much more likely that habitat conditions had changed in such a way that nests became more prone to predation. In other words, if nest predation now is far more important to bobwhite populations than it was previously, then the proportion of the area of interest where bobwhites could successfully fulfill their life requisites (including nesting) throughout the year (including the nesting season) must have decreased (Guthery 1997, 2002:163–87). Nest predators, in such a scenario, simply would serve as a proximate manifestation of this ultimate problem.

Bobwhite Predation

Wild bobwhites, be they chicks, juveniles, or adults, are subject to an array of predators. Most quail biologists assume that predation is the primary cause of the high mortality typically documented for bobwhite chicks. Although both mammalian and avian predators are certain to be important, because of logistical constraints and lack of creativity, researchers have not been able to meaningfully evaluate the influence of these predators on chick survival in Texas.

Figure 4.7.
Infrared videography now provides an opportunity to obtain a complete inventory of bobwhite—and other quail—nest predators. By filming a radio-marked hen returning to her nest, a small camera records behavioral data and documents predation events by badgers (top), bobcats (middle), coyotes (bottom), and many other nest predators.
Photos by Michael Rader

As the range of the red imported fire ant (*Solenopsis invicta*) has expanded in Texas and polygynous colonies have developed, these predators have increasingly concerned bobwhite aficionados. It has long been recognized that native fire ants (*S. geminate*) sometimes prey on quail chicks in Texas, particularly during and shortly after hatching (Lehmann 1946a). Red imported fire ants can also negatively influence chicks with nonlethal stings (Giuliano et al. 1996; Pedersen, Grant, and Longnecker 1996; Mueller et al. 1999). Giuliano et al. found that survival of two-day-old bobwhite chicks was reduced when they were exposed to more than 50 or more than 200 red imported fire ants in large beakers for 60 and 15 seconds, respectively. In an experiment more analogous to field conditions, Pedersen et al. found that chicks spent considerable time responding to fire ants, and much less time moving about, sleeping, and eating, when temporarily released in an area of southeastern Texas where red imported fire ants occurred, compared to an adjacent site where fire ants had been removed. These behavioral changes could result in reduced growth and, consequentially, reduced avoidance of mammalian or avian predators. Further, Mueller et al. (1999) found that red imported fire ants reduced survival of bobwhite chicks under field conditions in Refugio County. The mechanisms accounting for such reductions in survival are unclear. Possible explanations include direct chick mortality, decreased insects available for chicks to eat, and behavioral alterations caused by red imported fire ants. Red imported fire ants certainly prey on bobwhite chicks, alter their behavior, and reduce insect resources (Porter and Savignano 1990; Allen et al. 2001). Insect availability did not appear to be a problem during a short-term study conducted in Refugio County (Mueller et al. 1999), but definitive experiments that directly tie any of these three explanations to chick survival have yet to be conducted.

Although it was interesting to learn that red imported fire ants sometimes kill or alter the behavior of bobwhite chicks, whether they influence the dynamics of bobwhite populations is more relevant to wildlife managers. After all, the list of species that kill or aggravate bobwhite chicks is long, and increased nesting or brood-rearing success does not necessarily translate into increased recruitment of newly hatched birds into the breeding population. It is extraordinarily difficult to unequivocally determine whether *any* species of predator actually regulates or limits numbers of a prey species over time. The bobwhite–red imported fire ant interaction is no exception. In order to adequately address this question, researchers will need to conduct replicated field experiments over multiple years to determine whether polygynous red imported fire ants reduce the number of female bobwhites recruited into breeding populations in Texas, and if they do, in which life-history stage(s) this reduction primarily occurs.

Surprisingly, few studies have addressed which nonhuman predators most influence survival of juvenile and adult bobwhites in Texas. Coyotes sometimes depredate grown bobwhites in South Texas (Lehmann 1946a, 1984:190–96). Avian predators known to take grown bobwhites include the northern harrier (*Circus cyaneus*), sharp-shinned hawk (*Accipiter striatus*), Cooper's hawk (*A. cooperi*), several buteos, and large owls (Jackson 1947; Parmalee 1954). The abundance of these raptors has increased since at least the late 1960s (Sauer, Hines, and Fallon 2002).

Finally, we should not overlook that humans may well be the most significant predator of adult bobwhites in Texas (Guthery et al. 2000; Peterson and Perez 2000; Peterson 2001; Guthery 2002:95–114). Without doubt, harvest typically is to some degree additive (which means more than zero birds are subtracted from the breeding population for each bird harvested) to other forms of bobwhite mortality (Roseberry and Klimstra 1984:139–50; Guthery 2002:95–114; figure 4.8). In southern Illinois, at least, the degree of additivity increases as the hunting season progresses (Roseberry and Klimstra 1984:143). This fact does not imply that quail cannot be harvested without jeopardizing the population. As Guthery et al. (2000) found, however, it should call into question the assumption that hunters can remove more than 30 or 40 percent of

Figure 4.8.
Hunting bobwhites may result in additive mortality to the population, especially if heavy losses are inflicted in the population late in the hunting season. Photo by Dale Rollins

bobwhite populations annually in southern and northern populations, respectively, without biological repercussions. Unfortunately, harvest rates of 45, 50, 55, and even 70 percent have been recommended (respectively, Rosene 1969:206; Stoddard 1931:341; Roseberry and Klimstra 1984:148; Vance and Ellis 1972). The higher rates, particularly, are untenable over the long term.

Population Dynamics

Considering the low survival of bobwhite nests, chicks, juveniles, and adults, one might wonder how this species persists. Clearly, their reproductive potential must be enormous. This is due primarily to the large array of reproductive strategies bobwhites can employ (see the section on life history). Contrary to urban legend, there is no evidence that bobwhites hatched early in the reproductive season attempt to breed later in this same season (Peebles et al. 1996), even in South Texas, where nesting often begins in March (Lehmann 1984:84–89). Both males and females that survive until the subsequent breeding season attempt to breed at about the same rates as older age classes (Brennan 1999:13).

As with other ground-nesting galliformes, most female bobwhites attempt to lay a clutch if environmental conditions are suitable (for contrary examples, see Guthery, Koerth, and Smith 1988), clutch size is large, and egg hatchability is high in nests that survive incubation (Roseberry 1974; Suchy and Munkel 1993). As already detailed, although a large proportion of initial nests is lost, bobwhites exhibit a marked tendency to renest if conditions are still appropriate. Some hens exhibit between two and four nesting attempts per reproductive season (Rosene 1969:73–74; Roseberry and Klimstra 1984:83; Carter 1995; Hernández 1999). Burger, Dailey, et al. (1995) and Burger, Ryan, et al. (1995) found a mean of 19.5 days (range = 5–67) between nest failure and renesting. Even though clutch size decreases somewhat during subsequent nesting attempts (Stoddard 1931:28–29; Klimstra and Roseberry 1975:19–21; Lehmann 1984:86–87), simple mathematical models support the contention that persistent renesting largely accounts for the tremendous reproductive potential of northern bobwhites as compared to other galliformes, such as tetranids and wild turkeys (Guthery and Kuvlesky 1998; Guthery 2002:69–94).

Recognition of multiple brooding in bobwhite populations forced wildlife ecologists to reconsider production in this species (see previous discussions on life history, laying, incubation, and nesting success). It appears that up to 30 percent of at least some populations attempt a second brood (Burger, Ryan, et al. 1995). Similarly, under typical probabilities of producing a successful nest (e.g., 30 percent), contributions of second broods to autumn juvenile/adult ratios might be about 24 percent, whereas contributions of third broods would be trifling (Guthery and Kuvlesky 1998; Guthery 2002:74). Multiple brooding probably should be perceived as a special case of renesting. Guthery and Kuvlesky (1998) found that with typical nest success, fall age ratios would be little different whether hens quit nesting after their first successful attempt—given three possible attempts—or whether they used all three attempts to produce broods. This occurred because of the low probability of success on any nesting attempt and diminished time available for renesting as the laying season progresses. As Guthery (2002:87) put it, "The phrases 'up to three' and 'all three' mean about the same thing biologically because of the effects of time." At any rate, managers attempting to increase production should attempt to maximize the proportion of hens that lay, the probability of nest success, and the number of days in the laying season (Guthery and Kuvlesky 1998).

Variation in Production

Bobwhite populations in most Texas physiographic regions exhibit marked variations in abundance among years—a boom-and-bust phenomenon (Peterson 2001). Ultimately, weather probably drives these fluctuations in most regions of Texas. Biologists have long maintained that precipitation is the dominant factor that influences bobwhite population dynamics in certain parts of the Lone Star State (Lehmann 1946a, 1953; Jackson 1947). Subsequent researchers determined that the amount of precipitation during the reproductive season was correlated with the ratio of juveniles/adult in the South Texas hunting bag during 1968–74 (Kiel 1976), as well as the number of bobwhites observed on August roadside surveys conducted by Texas Parks and Wildlife Department (TPWD) biologists across several physiographic regions during 1976–91 (Giuliano, Lutz, and Patiño 1999). Rice et al. (1993) found that Thornthwaite's (1948) index of precipitation effectiveness (12 months) was correlated with bobwhite abundance in semiarid South Texas and the Rolling Plains, but not in the more mesic Gulf Prairies and Marshes. This study also indicated there was no single relationship between precipitation and bobwhite abundance that was universally applicable throughout the state.

Recently, three detailed evaluations of interaction among weather variables and bobwhite production were completed. Bridges et al. (2001) found that each of the Palmer suite of drought indices (12-month sum), as well as annual precipitation, was sufficient to account for the mean number of bobwhites observed in the TPWD August roadside surveys in the South Texas Plains (1978–98). The Palmer drought indices use precipitation, temperature, Thornthwaite's (1948) evapotranspiration index, runoff, soil recharge, and average regional weather conditions to quantitatively evaluate the long-term impacts of departures from normal weather conditions on an ecosystem (Palmer 1965; Alley 1984; http://www.ncdc.noaa.gov). The Modified Palmer Drought Severity Index (MPDI) also could account for bobwhite production in the Rolling Plains, Edwards Plateau, and Cross Timbers and Prairies, but annual raw precipitation could not during 1978–98 (Bridges et al. 2001). Neither index was associated with variation in bobwhite abundance among years in the Gulf Prairies and Marshes. The strength of these relationships was directly related to the relative aridity of the ecological region, a result that contextualizes the findings of Rice et al. (1993).

Bridges et al. (2001) also found that several monthly MPDI values were related to bobwhite production in physiographic regions where the annual MPDI was correlated with production. From least to most arid region, monthly MPDIs were sufficient to explain the mean number of bobwhites observed in August roadside surveys in the Cross Timbers and Prairies (November–February), Edwards Plateau (September–November), Rolling Plains (September–February, April, June), and South Texas Plains (October–July). February raw precipitation was correlated with bobwhite production only in the South Texas Plains.

Monthly and annual MPDIs were correlated with bobwhite production in the South Texas Plains, Rolling Plains, Edwards Plateau, and Cross Timbers and Prairies, yet monthly and annual precipitation were correlated with these changes only in semiarid South Texas (Bridges et al. 2001). This should give researchers pause. Clearly, precipitation alone cannot adequately explain bobwhite production in Texas, yet the MPDI could. What other variables included in MPDI might be important? Guthery, Land, and Hall (2001) provided compelling evidence that heat loads, at least in South Texas, had the potential to limit reproductive performance (see next section). Thus, temperature might explain why the MPDI performed better than raw precipitation.

Lusk et al. (2002) addressed this issue by explicitly representing both precipitation and temperature variables in a neural network model designed to predict bobwhite abundance for six Texas ecological regions evaluated together during 1978–97. Fall precipitation was an important factor relevant to the number of bobwhites observed during August roadside counts conducted by TPWD. These results were quite similar to those of Bridges et al. (2001). Maximum daily July temperature was also important, but the relationship was opposite of that anticipated; predicted bobwhite numbers increased with increasing July temperatures (Lusk et al. 2002). Guthery et al. (2002) used a similar analytic approach to evaluate how these variables might predict the ratio of juveniles/adult in hunter bags in South Texas during 1940–97. Ratios increased in an asymptotic manner with fall (September–November), spring (March–May), and summer (June–August) precipitation; they were least sensitive to fall and most sensitive to spring precipitation. Further, juvenile/adult ratios were insensitive to maximum daily July temperature up to 36°C (97°F), when they began to rapidly decline as predicted by the stress hypothesis. Therefore, the results of Guthery et al. (2002) support the hypothesis that heat loading is detrimental to bobwhite production, whereas those of Lusk et al. (2002) do not. Further field research will be needed to clarify this relationship.

Mechanisms Accounting for Variation in Production

Although weather ultimately controls much of the variation in bob-white production in semiarid regions of Texas (Bridges et al. 2001; Lusk et al. 2002), the proximate processes governing resulting population booms and busts remain unclear (Guthery et al. 2002; Hernández, Guthery, and Kuvlesky 2002; Lusk et al. 2002). A number of hypotheses have been proposed to explain this phenomenon, and some have been critically evaluated. Although the history of these explanations is interesting, it is beyond the scope of this chapter to do more than provide a brief summary. For detailed reviews, see Guthery (2002:39–94) and Hernández, Guthery, and Kuvlesky (2002). Explanatory hypotheses fall into three classes: those based on nutrients, nonspecific stress, or heat stress. Weather could drive all three of these explanations.

One group of nutrition-based hypotheses holds that reproductive inhibitors in foods limit reproduction during years when reproduction fails, yet are essentially absent in years characterized by high reproductive success. Leopold, Erwin, and Browning (1976) proposed that plant hormones called phytoestrogens could inhibit egg production in California quail (*Callipepla californica*). Cain, Lien, and Beasom (1987), however, found that the phytoestrogens they studied did not impair reproductive success of scaled quail (*C. squamata*) at levels expected in the field.

A second class of nutrition-based hypotheses postulates that key nutrients are present in sufficient quantities during boom years but are insufficient during bust years. Nutrients that have been considered important include vitamin A, phosphorous, macronutrients (e.g., energy, protein), and water. Nestler (1946) found that increased levels of vitamin A in the diet of pen-reared bobwhites increased reproductive productivity in an asymptotic fashion (about 3,000 IU), although females still laid at low rates even when levels of vitamin A approached zero. Working in South Texas, Lehmann (1953) reported that vitamin A levels varied substantially between age classes and among individuals in the same covey during drought years when reproduction failed. So far, there is not a clear link between vitamin A and variation in bobwhite production in Texas (Guthery 2002:82).

Because phosphorous can influence egg production in birds and South Texas is known for phosphorous-deficient soils and plants, Cain et al. (1982) hypothesized that deficiencies might account for the booms and busts characteristic of bobwhite populations in this region. Their laboratory experiments suggested that females on diets with essentially no phosphorus might produce half as many chicks as those on phosphorous-rich diets. Based on the totality of their laboratory results, Cain et al. maintained that even though variation in phosphorus intake between wet and dry years might contribute to variations in productivity, it probably was not the primary factor. Moreover, Wood, Guthery, and Koerth (1986) found that even when wild bobwhites in South Texas consumed 75 percent less phosphorus than recommended for poultry, reproductive failure still did not occur.

Female game birds require higher levels of protein, energy, calcium, and other nutrients during the reproductive season than at other times of the year (National Research Council 1977). For this reason, Wood,

Guthery, and Koerth (1986) speculated that macronutrient intake might be insufficient during drought (bust) years. They found that protein and energy consumption was sufficient for reproductive needs but that calcium and phosphorous were low during their study period (precipitation ≥40 centimeters, or about 16 inches). Despite these mineral deficiencies, an average of 1.8 juveniles/adult was recorded in autumn samples, so reproductive failure did not occur. Harveson (1995) was unable to find differences in macronutrient consumption between areas with large differences in the availability of protein and energy in the form of invertebrates. Moreover, if foods rich in protein, for example, are unavailable, bobwhites still might obtain adequate protein by consuming larger quantities of less-ideal foods.

In a laboratory setting, bobwhites are sensitive to water stress during reproduction (Koerth and Guthery 1991). Water deprivation led to failure to lay eggs or reduced laying rates. Guthery and Koerth (1992) tested the water-deprivation hypothesis in the field. They found that preformed water in plants during dry years was much greater than needed by reproducing bobwhites and that reproductive success was not different between study areas with and without supplemental water. Guthery (1999b) reached a similar conclusion in his review of bobwhite water ecology. Curiously, Lehmann (1953:243) speculated that during droughts, bobwhites might increase egg hatchability by carrying moisture back to the nest after bathing in water holes during the afternoon. This premise is unlikely (Guthery 2000:199–200). Because of the hours spent feeding after bathing and their water-repellent feathers, bobwhites are unlikely to carry water to the nest. Moreover, there are no experimental data demonstrating that moisture beyond that available at the nest site is needed to promote incubation of bobwhite nests.

The nonspecific-stress hypothesis holds that during drought (bust) years, hens somehow react to adverse conditions for laying and brood rearing by producing stress hormones (corticosterones) that inhibit reproductive organs (Cain and Lien 1985). Cain and Lien found that administration of corticosterones inhibited development of reproductive organs in both sexes. Although this is a plausible physiological explanation for the boom-bust phenomenon, it does not address what these stressors might be. This hypothesis is not necessarily independent of the nutritional explanations discussed earlier—after all, less-than-ideal nutrition could be a stressor. Harveson (1995:40–44) was unable to detect differences in corticosterone levels among reproductively active or inactive females and reproductively active males in the Gulf Prairies and Marshes or South Texas Plains. Unfortunately, drought conditions did not occur during his study, so Harveson could not test the nonspecific-stress hypothesis. Radomski (1999) tested the nonspecific-stress hypothesis using a laboratory experiment. Both male and female bobwhites were fed one of six diets having three levels of protein (8, 15, and 24 percent) and two levels of metabolizable energy (8.37 and 12.22 kilojoules/gram). Plasma corticosterone concentrations were elevated for females fed the low-protein diet. No other abnormalities were noted. In a second experiment, Radomski (1999) measured responses to three levels of exogenous adrenocorticotropic hormone. He found that chronic stress probably would not include long-term elevation in corticosterone necessary to depress reproductive function in bobwhites. Radomski concluded that protein deficiency might contribute to reproductive failure in female bobwhites but rejected the hypothesis that changes in plasma corticosterone concentrations because of macronutrient deficiencies resulted in decreased reproductive performance.

Klimstra and Roseberry (1975) found that ending dates of the bobwhite nesting season were negatively correlated with maximum daily temperature during July and August. Roseberry and Klimstra (1984:75–76) linked embryonic death to high temperatures and seasonal decline in egg fertility. Guthery, Koerth, and Smith (1988) documented lower temperatures and evaporation rates, and a longer reproductive season, in the eastern versus western Rio Grande Plains. They also found that high temperatures were associated with reduced proportions of hens laying eggs and males producing sperm. Based on the assumption that bobwhites could tolerate areas with operative temperatures of less than 39°C (103°F) (Forrester et al. 1998), Guthery, Land, and Hall (2001) provided compelling evidence that heat in South Texas was sufficient to kill embryos, chicks, and adults; cause premature incubation, resulting in staggered hatching; reduce the length of the laying season, thus inhibiting renesting and multiple brooding; and cause both males and females to go out of reproduction condition. To date, work by Heffelfinger et al. (1999) in Arizona; Lusk, Guthery, and DeMaso (2002) in Oklahoma; and Guthery et al. (2002) in South Texas supports the heat-stress hypothesis, whereas a study by Lusk et al. (2002) does not. Critical tests of this hypothesis are still required.

Finally, regardless of the hypotheses just discussed, variation in the percentage of hens that lay eggs probably influences bobwhite production profoundly in semiarid regions of Texas. Guthery et al. (1988) found that only 41 percent of female bobwhites were in laying condition during April–August 1981–83 in the comparatively hot and dry western Rio Grande Plains, whereas 65 percent were reproductively active during this period in the eastern Rio Grande Plains. Further, the effective reproductive season ended approximately two months earlier in the hotter and drier region. Using an ecological model, Guthery and Kuvlesky (1998) found that increasing the proportion of hens laying from 50 percent to 100 percent might be expected to increase the autumn juvenile/adult ratio from about 1.5 to 3.0, given two nesting attempts and typical clutch size, proportion of females in the population, and probability of nest success. This alone could account for the difference between a fair- and high-production year. Moreover, because the probability of producing more than one brood per season is key to bobwhite population dynamics, decreasing the length of the laying season by 60 days (Guthery et al. 1988) greatly reduces the opportunity for multiple brooding or for subsequent nesting attempts should initial nests fail (Guthery and Kuvlesky 1998; Guthery 2002:69–94). Guthery (2002:86) found that for a 150-day nesting season, if all hens began laying within 30 days and 30 percent of nests were successful, a mean of 3.4 nesting attempts and age ratios of 4 juveniles/adult would be expected. If the nesting season were decreased to 90 days and all other variables held constant, 1.8 nesting attempts and 2.8 juveniles/adult would be expected. Clearly, variation in the proportion of hens laying eggs as well as the length of the egg-laying season could account for much of the variation in bobwhite production among years. More work is needed to delineate the mechanisms controlling these variations.

Despite the studies reviewed in this section, we still do not understand *exactly* how weather influences the booms and busts characteristic of bobwhite populations in semiarid regions. Most hypotheses that seemed reasonable based on laboratory research were not supported by empirical data in the field, although the heat-stress hypothesis may still have merit. Compelling field data are needed to explain why fewer females come into reproductive condition in hot, dry areas and why the laying season is shortened under these conditions. In the final analysis, the overall relationship accounting for the boom-bust phenomenon in arid-land quail probably will prove complex. It seems likely that the influence of precipitation, temperature, and soil moisture on vegetation and possibly on bobwhites themselves, as mediated by an array of land-use practices such as livestock grazing, ultimately accounts for the boom-bust dynamics of bobwhite populations in semiarid regions.

Land Use

In a state such as Texas that is almost entirely privately owned, wildlife biologists have been understandably reluctant to explicitly identify land-use practices that negatively influence bobwhite abundance. Whether we wish to admit it or not, what land managers do with landscapes influences bobwhite population dynamics and long-term trends in abundance. Obviously, urban sprawl and landscapes saturated with cotton fields, for example, do not bode well for bobwhites. Probably less clear is exactly what the trends in Texas land use and land cover have been and how these changes influenced bobwhite populations at different spatial scales.

Peterson, Wu, and Rho (2002) illustrated trends in cropland, rangeland, woodland, and Conservation and Wetland Reserve Program cover as well as average farm or ranch size across the range of the northern bobwhite in the United States for the period 1979–97. All these variables were associated to some degree with spatially explicit changes in bobwhite abundance, but no single, universal land-use-based explanation for trends in bobwhite abundance was suitable throughout the range of this species.

At a finer spatial scale, Bridges et al. (2002) compared the land-cover changes associated with TPWD quail survey routes in the Rolling and South Texas Plains between 1976 and 1998. During this period, there was a loss of savanna and shrubland and a large increase in types of parkland cover in the Rolling Plains. In the South Texas Plains, woodland and shrubland decreased, whereas types of parkland cover increased. These parkland increases typically were greater than 200 percent. Although there was no long-term trend in bobwhite abundance in these regions during this period, possibly due to slack in habitat configurations that bobwhites can use (Guthery 1999a), scaled quail nearly disappeared from the Rolling Plains yet were unaffected in the South Texas Plains. If current trends in land-cover changes continue, however, there eventually would be a threshold beyond which bobwhites are not well adapted.

It has long been recognized that a certain amount of cropland interspersed in a region sometimes benefited bobwhites, whereas too much was detrimental (e.g., Leopold 1931:24–32; Stoddard 1931:5–6; Texas Game, Fish and Oyster Commission 1945:47–48). More specifically, Roseberry and Sudkamp (1998) reported that optimal levels of row crops for bobwhites in Illinois counties were 30–65 percent, whereas Lusk, Guthery, and DeMaso (2002) found 40–50 percent cultivation optimal in Oklahoma. Lusk et al. (2002) determined that bobwhite abundance varied in a curvilinear manner with the proportion of a county in cultivation for six western physiographic regions of Texas. Bobwhite abundance increased by 25 percent with increasing cultivation until about 20 percent of county area was under the plow. Further increases in cultivation then reduced bobwhite abundance by 43.8 percent at about 48 percent cultivation. Finally, robust bobwhite populations occur in portions of the South Texas and Rolling Plains in the absence of cropland. Based on these studies, it appears that interspersion of cropland can be beneficial in mesic systems, but less so in semiarid environments.

We can no longer afford to ignore the influence of livestock grazing on bobwhite populations in Texas (figure 4.9). Actually, quail biologists have long warned that sheep and goat grazing was incompatible with abundant quail in the Lone Star State (e.g., Lehmann 1937:21–23; Baker 1940) and that cattle grazing must be well regulated to be tolerable. Lusk et al. (2002) found that the mean number of livestock (primarily cattle) per area of rangeland was an important determinant of bobwhite abundance for the six Texas ecoregions. Bobwhite abundance rapidly dropped 39 percent as livestock density increased from 0.15 to 0.4 head/hectare (0.06 to 0.16 head/acre). Bobwhite abundance continued to decline (another 50 percent) at a decelerating rate as livestock densities increased to 1.2 head/hectare (0.5 head/acre) of rangeland in a county. Therefore, bobwhite abundance in Texas decreases in a nonlinear, monotonic fashion with increasing livestock density over the entire range of values existing in these ecoregions. Do these data suggest that cattle grazing is incompatible with high bobwhite densities? Not necessarily. However, if land managers wish to maintain robust bobwhite

Figure 4.9.
Good quail hunting can occur on grazed rangelands, if stocking rates and duration are strictly and conservatively regulated and if adequate habitat and cover are allowed to remain for the birds.
Photo by Dale Rollins

populations during hot, dry years, they must have the ability to greatly reduce and even eliminate livestock grazing if need be.

Interactions
In some ways, the influence of factors limiting bobwhite abundance could be perceived as greater than the sum of the parts. These variables are not independent. For example, a hot, dry year does not bode well for bobwhite production in the South Texas or Rolling Plains—one would expect fewer females to come into reproductive condition and the nesting season to be shorter. However, it would be substantially worse if high livestock densities occurred on these properties. Lack of cover caused by drought and heavy grazing, along with extremely hot weather, could devastate reproductive output—the probability of an individual nest or brood being depredated probably would be higher under these conditions. Just as one-size-fits-all generalizations regarding the importance of nest predators should not be made, a given number of cattle per hectare will not influence bobwhite production identically under all climatic and edaphic conditions in Texas. Researchers are only now beginning to explore how myriad interactions among these variables influence bobwhite population dynamics.

Conservation and Management

As with all wildlife populations, the conservation of a species ultimately depends on the conservation of suitable habitat areas of sufficient size to allow for population persistence. Bobwhites are no exception. Loss and fragmentation of bobwhite habitat have occurred primarily through urbanization and agricultural development. These are the primary factors that have caused widespread declines in bobwhite numbers across Texas. Further, factors operating at a regional scale, such as overgrazing, conversion of native rangeland into improved pastures, and brush encroachment, exacerbate the problem of habitat loss by transforming previously suitable habitat into unusable space. How much area is needed to ensure persistence of bobwhite populations? Both spatial and temporal scales must be considered when addressing this question. The quantity of suitable habitat necessary for population persistence will depend on the conservation goal. For example, is the goal to ensure persistence of the population across the entire geographic range of the species, over the range of a particular subspecies, for a state of interest, or at the physiographic region or ranch scale? Similarly, for how many years must the population persist? Clearly, each goal will require a different amount of suitable habitat.

Guthery et al. (2000) provided some insight into these questions by conducting viability analyses of bobwhite populations. Under a criterion of quasi extinction at less than 14 bobwhites, they estimated that an autumn population of 700 bobwhites would be required to ensure at least a 95 percent probability of persistence for 100 years in southern latitudes. This estimate represented a population subjected to both summer weather catastrophes (e.g., droughts, heat waves) and a 30 percent winter harvest. From these results, Guthery et al. estimated that bobwhites would require about 700–1,400 hectares (1,700–3,400 acres) of usable space by assuming that bobwhite populations required 1–2 hectares (2–5 acres) per individual. This estimate undoubtedly underestimates what most quail hunters or wildlife managers would consider to be the entire spatial area required for the population under consideration. Guthery et al. presented their estimate in terms of usable space through time, which is different than mere acreage. Guthery (1997) defined *usable space* as that area of habitat compatible with all behavioral, physical, and physiological adaptations of bobwhites throughout the year. It is likely that pastures or ranches of interest to wildlife managers may not be able to provide 100 percent usable space every day of the year (i.e., usable space saturation), although near saturation (95 percent) has been reported (see Guthery 2000:102). Thus, space that bobwhites can actually use throughout the year composes some proportion of the entire area typically perceived by humans to be bobwhite habitat. Nevertheless, the estimate of Guthery et al. provides a theoretical basis for practical bobwhite conservation, and methodologies exist for estimating the proportion of an area of interest that bobwhites can use through time (Kopp et al. 1998; Guthery 2002:163–87).

Scaled Quail Ecology and Life History   5

Nova J. Silvy, Dale Rollins, and Shane W. Whisenant

> The scaled quail is a fine game species, although hunters find it
> rather exasperating at times when trying to run down a covey
> and force it to fly and scatter.
>
> Leopold (1959)

The scaled quail (*Callipepla squamata*), also known as blue quail or   65
cottontops, is the second most abundant quail found in Texas. Scaled
quail provide hunters with a challenging and unique hunting experience because they prefer to run rather than fly. There are quail hunters
who prefer pursuing scaled quail to the more popular northern bobwhite (*Colinus virginianus*) because of this challenge (Wallmo and Uzzell 1958). Although scaled quail are not as well studied as the northern
bobwhite, there is considerable scientific literature on them. Until recently, only meager research attention has been directed at scaled quail
in Texas.

This chapter provides a general overview of the life history and
ecology of scaled quail in Texas. Although much of the information is
based on scaled quail research in adjacent states, such as Oklahoma and
New Mexico, it has implications for the management of this species in
Texas.

Distribution in Texas

Scaled quail are distributed throughout the western half of Texas
(figure 5.1). According to Texas Game, Fish and Oyster Commission (1945) and Oberholser (1974), the geographic range of scaled
quail has contracted in Texas during the past century. Historic
specimens have been collected as far east as Wichita, Young,
Colman, and Gillespie counties, where they are not found today
(Oberholser 1974).

There are two subspecies of scaled quail in Texas:
the Arizona scaled quail (*C. s. pallida*) and the
chestnut-bellied scaled quail (*C. s. castanogastris*).
Chestnut-bellied scaled quail have a patch of chestnut-
colored plumage on their abdomen and are about 3.4 percent smaller and slightly darker than Arizona scaled quail.
The two subspecies have affinities for different types of habitats. Chestnut-bellied scaled quail are typically found in thorn-scrub vegetation
on well-drained caliche ridges or in lowlands along creeks and rivers,
whereas Arizona scaled quail are most abundant in open grassland with
less than 10–15 percent shrub cover.

In West Texas, scaled quail are distributed over the arid and semiarid vegetation (figure 5.2) (Tharp 1971). They can be found at elevations from about 30 meters (100 feet) to 1,676 meters (5,500 feet) and,
rarely, to 2,377 meters (7,800 feet) (Oberholser 1974). Reid, Grue, and
Silvy (1993) documented scaled quail in the Trans-Pecos, Mountains
and Basins; High Plains; Rolling Plains; Edwards Plateau; and South
Texas Plains ecoregions of Texas.

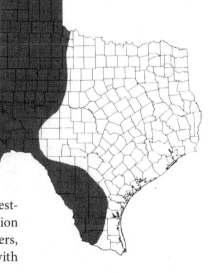

Figure 5.1.
Geographic distribution of scaled quail
in Texas.
Courtesy Mark Lockwood

Scaled quail are found west of the 100th meridian in the western portions of the Rolling Plains, Edwards Plateau, and South Texas Plains ecoregions; they overlap northern bobwhites on the eastern boundary of scaled quail distribution. On the Rolling Plains, Edwards Plateau, and South Texas Plains, where the two species also are sympatric, they appeared to use separate habitats (Reid, Grue, and Silvy 1979), an observation corroborated in South Texas by Wilson and Crawford (1987).

Unlike the northern bobwhite, the western boundary for scaled quail does not appear to depend on rainfall (Tharp 1971). Scaled quail usually inhabit arid to semiarid areas that average 10–61 centimeters (4–24 inches) of annual precipitation (Giuliano, Patiño, and Lutz 1998). Oberholser (1974) noted that Texas counties with greater than 76 centimeters (27 inches) of annual rainfall do not support scaled quail populations. Giuliano and Lutz (1993) observed that northern bobwhite numbers increased with increased rainfall in the South Texas Plains, whereas scaled quail numbers decreased. Periodic scaled quail range expansions and restrictions also apparently occur within the Rolling Plains (Rollins 2000).

Cold climates may limit the northern range of scaled quail. Although unproven, competition with other quail species and/or availability of suitable habitat may limit their western and eastern distributions. Wallmo (1956) noted that continuous prairies apparently limit the northeastern distribution of chestnut-bellied scaled quail, whereas high temperatures and/or dry climate may limit their western distribution. Wallmo also suggested that cold climate limited their northwestern distribution and woodlands limited the eastern edge of their range.

Status of Populations

Scaled quail populations are declining throughout much of their range in Texas (Church, Sauer, and Droege 1993; Bridges et al. 2001; Rollins and Carroll 2001; figure 5.3). The magnitude of scaled quail declines varies across the different regions where they are found in Texas (see chapters 7, 11, 12, and 13).

The most likely of the various hypotheses proposed to explain scaled quail declines in Texas is a confused combination of rangeland deterioration from overgrazing in conjunction with changing land use

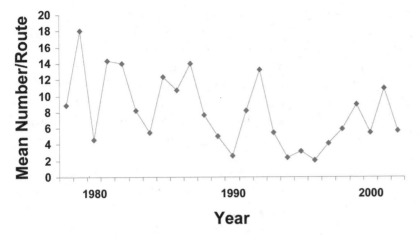

Figure 5.3.
Mean number of scaled quail found along TPWD roadside routes, 1978–2002. Points for 1988–92 do not include information from the High Plains ecoregion (not collected); therefore, means presented for this period may be higher than they should be because the High Plains ecoregion usually had the lowest means of all ecoregions.

(Bridges et al. 2002). Rho (2003) hypothesized that the decline of scaled quail in the Rolling Plains was related to a decrease of grassland/herbaceous and aggregation of cropland/pasture landscape patterns. In West Texas, the Arizona subspecies has strong affinities for large (greater than 250 hectares, or about 100 acres) areas dominated by grasses and low (less than 10–15 percent) shrub coverage. Excessive grazing has caused woody cover to increase over vast areas at the expense of scaled quail habitat. There is little evidence to support other hypotheses concerning scaled quail declines, such as changing precipitation patterns and epizootic disease.

Weather drives annual quail population changes (Bridges et al. 2001; Engel-Wilson and Kuvlesky 2002). Annual and regional differences in scaled quail abundance are associated with rainfall during the breeding season (Wallmo and Uzzell 1958; Schemnitz 1961; Brown 1969; Campbell et al. 1973; Giuliano and Lutz 1993). Campbell (1968) concluded that scaled quail populations in New Mexico were controlled by spring-summer rainfall, but fall-winter precipitation did not seem to have a major influence on the population.

Annual Cycle and Life History

In this section we summarize key aspects of scaled quail annual cycle and life history. The topics covered include vocalizations, breeding behaviors, nesting success, brooding, and covey formation.

Vocalizations

Wallmo (1956) divided scaled quail vocalizations into those associated with reproduction and those associated with nonreproduction. In the breeding season, he noted there were calls associated with mate attraction, care of young, and behavior of young. In the nonreproductive season, he noted four principal calls: gathering call, group alarm cry, individual fright cry, and conversation notes.

Calls Associated with Reproduction
The call of an unmated scaled quail male in the breeding season is a nasal whistle, called a "cree" by Russell (1932), a "squawk" or "kwook" by Wallmo (1956), or a "whock" whistle by Schemnitz (1961). This call is usually made from an elevated, visible position and probably

only by unmated males as long as they are in reproductive condition. Wallmo noted that the call was first heard in early spring prior to covey breakup.

MALE AGGRESSIVE CALLS

Johnsgard (1973) documented a call between aggressive males in the laboratory and noted the call in retreating quail, with some individuals also giving "chip" or "chipeee" calls. Anderson (1974, 1978) recorded a "squeel" call associated with the male tossing its head upward and backward vigorously. He stated that the call had several functions depending on its context, but usually occurred in agonistic encounters between two males.

CARE-OF-YOUNG CALLS

When flushing a pair of scaled quail with a brood, Wallmo (1956) noted that the female acted crippled (broken-wing act) and then began to call in a high, metallic, resonant "ping-g-g, ping-g-g" sound. The male ran and flew and gave a "chip" sound. Russell (1932), referring to disturbed brood calls, described the male call as "ptrack" and the female call as a sharp "tweet."

Calls Not Associated with Reproduction

There are several important scaled quail vocalizations not associated with reproduction. These calls are summarized and described in the following sections.

GATHERING CALL

This call is the one most frequently heard from scaled quail and is a means by which birds announce their locations to other quail, provoking a reply from nearby quail. It is given by both sexes to reunite a covey. Bendire (1892) described the call as "chip-churr, chip-churr"; Wallmo (1956), as "ching-tang, ching-tang" and "chuk-ching, chuk-ching." Johnsgard (1973) described it as a separation call used by individuals separated from their covey as well as by both sexes when visually separated from their mates, sounding like a two-syllable, nasal "pe-cos?" or "pey-cos?" Brown (1989) described the disturbance call as a two-note "chu-ching" or "ping," and their separation call as a two-syllable "chuck-churr." Males are known to respond to a playback of a female "pey-cos?" call by approaching the recorder during the breeding season. Anderson (1974, 1978) described two variations of the "chekar" call, a low-volume "wip-woo" sound and a high-volume "chekar" call and noted that the low-volume call could also end as it started ("wip-wip"). Anderson stated that unmated males interspersed "chekars" and "shrieks," "advertising the single status of such birds," and that when a female left a nest to feed, she would give the "chekar" call and her mate would run or fly to join her.

GROUP ALARM CRY

Scaled quail emit an alarm cry, "chink-chank?-a, chink-chank?-a," when a threat is perceived (Wallmo 1956). Anderson (1978) described the call as "CHUPuh." Although a single bird first gives the call, most, if not all, birds cry out until the perceived threat is gone. Anderson (1974, 1978) observed an "aerial alarm response," "TiCHUNK" call when scaled quail were chased by a hawk.

INDIVIDUAL FRIGHT CRY
Under extreme fright or stress, scaled quail gave a single metallic note described as "tsinggg" (Wallmo 1956). This call was usually heard when Wallmo removed birds from traps and when a bird was attacked by a hawk. Anderson (1978) described the call as "tsing."

CONVERSATION NOTES
Wallmo (1956) described the normal cluckings and chirpings of undisturbed scaled quail as conversation notes. A feeding group made quiet, low "clung" (or clucking), and "chirp, chirp" sounds. Anderson (1974, 1978) noted that when a bird found a large or attractive food source, it uttered a low, rapid series of "cut" syllables. He often observed a male scaled quail uttering a soft "cut cut" to attract his mate when he located a choice food item, especially an insect.

Chick Calls

Wallmo (1956) also noted that scaled quail chicks incessantly uttered a "peep, peep" call. He thought this was a "food clamor" to which the parents responded. He never detected a distress call from young chicks but observed that at the appearance of danger, they silently ran for cover. He also observed a soft "clerk" call by chicks that he thought was comparable to the "pleasure notes" described for domestic chickens. Adult quail respond quickly with wings aflutter to a distressed chick's "tseep, tseep, tseep" call.

Reproductive Pairs and Coveys
The annual cycle of scaled quail can be divided into two six-month periods (Wallmo 1956): reproductive period (April–September) and social aggregations (October–March). Although Wallmo recognized that the correlations of behavior to calendar dates were not exact, covey behavior fits closely with fall and winter (September 21–March 20), and reproductive behavior corresponds more or less with spring and summer (March 21–September 20).

Covey Breakup
Time and duration of winter covey breakup varies from year to year, depending on weather (early breakup during wet winters and late breakup during dry winters) and range conditions (Wallmo 1956). By May, Wallmo observed only pairs in Texas. The large winter coveys of scaled quail begin to break up about March 1–April 15 in Oklahoma (Schemnitz 1961), and breakup is complete in New Mexico by April (Banks 1970). However, Campbell (1968) observed coveys in late July in Lea County, New Mexico. Covey breakup did not occur until April in Arizona (Anderson 1974).

Pair Formation and Breeding
Pairing probably occurs when birds are still within coveys (figure 5.4). Brown (1989) observed that some birds begin forming pair bonds as early as late February and early March, and by late March most hens

Figure 5.4.
A pair of scaled quail.
Photo by Charles W. Melton

had selected a mate. Tharp (1971) noted that pairing began in late April, but complete covey breakup was not terminated until late May in Texas. Mating apparently occurs occasionally within the covey before pair bonds are definitely established, and penned birds were observed to mate as early as January 17 in West Texas (Wallmo 1956). Anderson (1974) observed copulation on February 23 within a covey of 30 quail. The earliest copulation observed by Schemnitz (1961) in Oklahoma was April 5.

Courtship behavior usually includes the male fluffing feathers, calling softly, and occasionally giving the "cree" call (Russell 1932). Brown (1989) stated that during courtship, the male fed the female "tidbits" and engaged in ritual chasing. Wallmo (1956) observed courtship behavior prior to mating only twice. On one occasion, he saw a male quietly step up on the female while she was feeding. She crouched with elevated tail prior to copulation. In the second case, within a covey during the breeding season, copulation followed a brief chase.

It is typical for a bachelor scaled quail cock to call from an elevated perch (tree or shrub) and then move on to other perches in an attempt to locate unattached females (Wallmo 1956; Anderson 1974). Anderson found that both sexes reach reproductive maturity by the breeding season following their first winter. Males are very protective of their mates (Evans 1997).

Nest Construction

The nesting season may last from April through September (Bent 1932). Wallmo (1956) found nests in West Texas only during June, but nests have been observed in New Mexico from April 15 (Russell 1931) to September 22 (Jensen 1925). In Oklahoma, Schemnitz (1961) first observed nests in early May and observed a chick, about 75 percent fully grown, with two adults on December 25. Lerich (2002) recorded a nest with 11 eggs on May 1 and suggested it had been initiated about April 15. Wallmo (1956) and Tharp (1971) indicated that hatching occurred from early May to late August. The extended nesting season tends to increase the opportunities for successful nesting despite temporarily adverse weather conditions (Schemnitz 1961). Brown (1989) observed that dur-

Figure 5.5.
Common nest sites for scaled quail in West Texas include tobosa grass (left) and yucca (right).
Photos by Dale Rollins

ing dry springs, scaled quail might delay nesting activity until the onset of summer rains in late June, July, or even August.

The location and structure of scaled quail nests are extremely variable. Most commonly, the nest is located in a shallow depression in the ground, usually lined with grass or other stems and leaves, and under some kind of cover for shade. Brown (1989) found that nests were located on the ground, usually on a flat or open ridge, and commonly placed at the base of a cactus or clump of dense vegetation. Nests are commonly placed under plants such as tobosa grass (*Hilaria mutica*), prickly pear (*Opuntia* spp.), and yucca (*Yucca* spp.) in Texas (Rollins 2000; Lerich 2002; figure 5.5). Both males and females have been observed bringing soft, dead grass to line the bowl (Evans 1997). Nests normally do not have a canopy, but Bent (1932) observed at least one nest arched over with grass. Wallmo (1956) also observed a nest that had a complete canopy of growing grass with no apparent entranceway, although a bird had been flushed from it. Lerich (2002) found that 6 of 11 nests in Brewster County, Texas, were associated with javelina bush (*Condalia ericoides*).

Laying, Incubation, and Nesting Success

Eggs are cream colored and about 30–33 millimeters (1.2–1.3 inches) in length, with a breadth of about 24–25 millimeters (0.9–1.0 inch) (Schemnitz 1994). Average egg mass is 11 grams (0.38 ounce) (Johnsgard 1973). Giuliano, Patiño, and Lutz (1998) noted that scaled quail eggs are larger than northern bobwhite eggs; larger eggs produce larger chicks, perhaps making them more adaptable to survival in unpredictable environments. A scaled quail egg has a mass of about 11 grams (0.4 ounce). Scaled quail are thought to be more drought tolerant than northern bobwhites (Schemnitz 1964; Giuliano, Lutz, and Patiño 1999). Giuliano, Patiño, and Lutz (1998) found that scaled quail required less water and food (relative to body mass) than northern bobwhites to successfully reproduce. A year with an unusually wet breeding season resulted in either a high population of northern bobwhites or a low population of scaled quail (Hatch 1975).

Wallmo (1957) in Texas, Schemnitz (1961) in Oklahoma, and Anderson (1974) in Arizona emphasized that the lack of summer rains restricts the range of scaled quail. No research has shown conclusively that water development has increased scaled quail populations (Wallmo and Uzzell 1958; Evans 1997).

Wallmo (1956) reported an average (based on 42 nests) of 14 eggs/clutch from several literature sources. Average clutch size was 13 eggs, with a range of 5–16, in Pecos County, Texas (R. J. Buntyn, Texas Agricultural Experiment Station, unpublished data). Tharp (1971), also in Texas, found an average size of completed clutches to be 13.0 eggs (4 nests), with a range of 11–14. The average (39 nests) size of completed scaled quail clutches in Oklahoma was 12.7 eggs, with a range of 5–22 (Schemnitz 1961). In Texas, the average (4 nests) size of completed clutches was 13.0 eggs, with a range of 11–14 (Tharp 1971). Scaled quail lay one egg/day (Evans 1997), each an hour later in the day, until the clutch is complete. If the time for laying an egg approaches late afternoon, a day is usually skipped, with the egg laid early the next morning.

Incubation for scaled quail requires 22–23 days (Johnsgard 1973; Evans 1997). The female has a brood patch (Evans 1997), which aids in regulating egg temperature during incubation.

Scaled quail males often stay near a nest with an incubating female and attempt to divert predators by chirping loudly and flying short distances. The males apparently share in incubation to an unknown extent. Both Russell (1932) and Schemnitz (1961) observed one male sharing incubation with a female. Evans (1997) observed only one male incubating eggs and only after the hen had been killed by a great horned owl (*Bubo virginianus*) while she was off the nest feeding in the morning. He successfully hatched all 10 eggs, and six chicks survived to at least three months of age.

During a seven-year study in New Mexico, Campbell (1968) reported June 10 as the earliest date that broods were seen. Chicks have been observed in late April in Crane County, Texas (D. Rollins, unpublished data), and by May 1 in Brewster County, Texas (Lerich 2002). Tharp (1971), in Texas, observed the first scaled quail brood on June 6, 1969, and June 8, 1970; and juvenile birds one to two days old were observed during the last week in August. Campbell et al. (1973) reported that during three of eight years, the peak of hatch probably occurred in May, and one year the peak occurred in July; however, these inferences were based on primary feather replacement and may bias hatching distributions toward later dates. During the other four years, the peak of hatch occurred in June. Brown (1989) reported that downy young were observed as late as October.

Schemnitz (1961) observed that about 90 percent of eggs in successful nests hatch (based on 6 nests). Tharp (1971) observed that 100 percent of eggs hatched in 2 successful nests, and Pleasant (2003) documented hatchability of 95 percent for 51 nests in the High Plains of Texas.

Nest success for scaled quail has typically been observed to be low (table 5.1). However, because of the high rate of abandonment as a result of human disturbances (plowing, mowing, irrigation flooding, etc.), data on nest success summarized by Schemnitz (1961) may not be indicative of nest success in areas undisturbed by humans. Causes of nest failure, according to Schemnitz, were depredation (25.0 percent), human activities (38.9 percent), abandonment (19.4 percent), weather (2.8 percent), and unknown (13.9 percent).

Despite these high rates of nest failure reported in the literature, scaled quail are capable of maintaining populations through renesting, even though subsequent nests are smaller. Evans (1997) observed two pairs of scaled quail that had lost their first nests in June, but

Table 5.1.
Average Success of Scaled Quail Nests

Source	State	Nest success (%)	Comments
Wallmo (1957)	Texas	<25	Summarized data
Schemnitz (1961)	Several	16	Summarized all available studies
Evans (1997)	Arizona	83	18 nests
R. J. Buntyn (unpublished data)	Texas	71	73 nests
Pleasant (2003)	Texas	44	50 nests in 1999 15% for subadults 56% for adults
		64	55 nests in 2000 67% for subadults 63% for adults

they renested within five weeks and hatched 10 eggs in August (41 and 50 days, respectively, after the first nests had been destroyed). Another pair that had lost a nest on June 14 started a second nest on July 1. Wallmo (1956) reported that renesting was probably common in scaled quail because of the common occurrence of late broods with hatching dates in late August and early September. These late dates provide indirect evidence of renesting, based on the assumption that earlier nesting attempts had occurred between April and August. An alternative hypothesis could be that the first nests occurred late in the breeding season. Wallmo noted that second nesting (starting a second nest after successfully bringing off a first brood) was probably less common. However, Wallmo observed a case in which a pair raised one brood tended by the male, while the female, identified by a deformity, started laying a second clutch. Second nesting has been observed in Irion and Pecos counties, Texas, using radio-marked scaled quail (Carter 1995; Rollins 2000). Evans (1997) observed no second nesting in a two-year radiotelemetry study. However, both years of the study were drought years. Pleasant (2003) observed 31 hens that produced 50 nests in 1999, of which 11 hens produced 2 nests and 4 hens produced 3 nests. In 2000, he observed 38 hens that produced 56 nests, of which 14 hens produced 2 nests and 2 hens produced 3 nests. In addition, he noted that during both years, all renesting occurred after loss of a previous nest or loss of young prior to 21 days of age.

Brooding

Brood sizes from different studies are difficult to interpret because the approximate ages of the young birds are usually not provided (table 5.2).

Table 5.2.
Average Size of Scaled Quail Broods by State

Source	State	No. of young	Comment
Schemnitz (1961)	Oklahoma	10.0/pair	3-year study
Hoffman (1965)	Colorado	8.7/pair	6-year study
Banks (1970); Griffing (1972); Borden (1973)	New Mexico	7.5/pair	Mean/3 studies
Tharp (1971)	Texas	13.0/pair 10.2/pair 3.2/adult	Nonflying Flying In July

However, the average brood size appears to quickly decrease within a few weeks after broods leave the nest (Tharp 1971).

Young quail are capable of short flight at about 14 days of age and can fly well by 4 weeks of age. Adult weight was attained in 22–28 weeks, and beyond this age, males continued to be slightly larger than females (Wallmo 1956). However, subadults were indistinguishable from adults by 12 weeks (Cain and Beasom 1983). The loss of family behavior and the beginning of covey behavior occurred when young were 12–20 weeks old (Wallmo 1956).

Coveys

As chicks mature, broods become organized into larger groups, or coveys. The formation of coveys is a prolonged process resulting from the progressive decomposition of family groups through the summer and fall and from the incorporation of adults that are unpaired or without broods (Wallmo 1956).

In Oklahoma, Schemnitz (1961) never observed breeding-season coveys, but Bendire (1892) saw flocks of scaled quail in southwestern New Mexico during late summer 1886, and Wallmo (1956) commonly noted groups of 4–8 adult scaled quail in Texas during the dry summer of 1953. Lehmann (1984) reported an average (based on 500 coveys) covey size of 15.0 birds in South Texas. Tharp (1971) observed an average covey size of 24.5 birds (based on 37 coveys) during August in Texas and first saw a covey on June 25 that consisted of 4 adults and 22 juveniles. Campbell (1968) reported coveys as late as the first week in July in New Mexico. Banks (1970) observed a group of 4 birds on April 26 and another group of 4 birds on May 4 but noted that covey breakup was apparently complete by April.

Large nonbreeding-season coveys are typical for scaled quail (Lehmann 1984). In Texas, the largest covey size observed by Wallmo (1956) was 150 birds, but most winter coveys were between 20 and 50 birds. Schemnitz (1961) observed 9 coveys over two years in Oklahoma and found that size of coveys ranged from 16 to 127 individuals (average = 65.2). Borden (1973) found coveys to range between 8 and 25 individuals (average = 13.4) in New Mexico, and Evans (1997) observed 1 winter covey of 70 birds in Arizona.

Habitat Use and Diet

Scaled quail nests are usually located under shrubs or some other protected site (table 5.3). Nests were closer to water sources during dry years than during years of normal rainfall (Evans 1997).

Carter (1995) found that sympatric northern bobwhites and scaled quail selected prickly pear for nesting sites. Eight of 12 scaled quail nests and 12 of 21 bobwhite nests were situated in prickly pear. Subsequently, Slater et al. (2001) documented that nests situated in prickly pear survived at about twice the rate of more conventional nest sites (i.e., bunchgrasses). Thus, prickly pear appeared to provide some measure of protection against nest predators.

Tharp (1971) observed a mixed clutch of scaled quail eggs (10) and northern bobwhite eggs (3) being incubated by a scaled quail hen. Davis (1979) also observed a mixed clutch of eggs in a nest in buffalograss (*Buchloe dactyloides*) at the base of a dead mesquite tree.

Table 5.3.
Predominant Substrates for Scaled Quail Nests

Nest substrates	Source
Grass	Russell (1932); Wallmo (1956); Schemnitz (1961,1964); Tharp (1971); Brown (1989); Carter (1995); Rollins (2000); Slater et al. (2001); Lerich (2002)
Junk areas	Schemnitz (1961)
Forbs	Russell (1932); Jackson (1942); Lehmann (1984); Schemnitz (1961)
Prickly pear	Tharp (1971); Brown (1989); Ligon (1961); Carter (1995); Slater et al. (2001)
Yucca or small bushes	Russell (1932); Jackson (1942); Wallmo (1956); Ligon (1961); Schemnitz (1961); Sawyer (1973); Wilson (1984); Evans (1997); Rollins (2000); Lerich (2002)
Hay fields	Bendire (1892); Schemnitz (1961)
Grain fields	Bendire (1892); Schemnitz (1961)
Overhanging rocks	Schemnitz (1961)
Potato fields	Bendire (1892)
Mesquite (*Prosopis* spp.)	Sawyer (1973); Davis (1979); Evans (1997)
Packrat (*Neotoma* sp.) mounds	Evans (1997)
Vines	Ligon (1961); Schemnitz (1961)

75

Scaled Quail Ecology and Life History

Brood-Rearing Habitat

Habitat preferred by scaled quail broods includes rough broken habitat and shallow soil habitat with low grass cover (Tharp 1971). Scaled quail move their broods to water sources within a few days of hatching (Evans 1997).

Covey Habitat: Chestnut-Bellied Scaled Quail

In the South Texas Plains, chestnut-bellied scaled quail use areas with sparse ground vegetation and a shrub overstory (Reid, Grue, and Silvy 1979, 1993; Lehmann 1984; Wilson and Crawford 1987). The habitat patches average greater than 35 percent canopy cover of woody plants (Wilson and Crawford 1987; Hall 1998). However, Campbell-Kissock et al. (1985) noted limited use of dense shrubland habitats in South Texas. In addition to using dense shrub overstory, scaled quail in the South Texas Plains also use areas of scattered shrubs (Reid, Grue, and Silvy 1979). Hall (1998) reported that scaled quail use roosting locations having about 45 percent grass cover (0.1–0.4 meters tall, or 4–16 inches). It appears that cover can be either grass or brush, but the grass must be of sufficient height to provide protection from the elements and predators.

Covey Habitat: Arizona Scaled Quail

Breeding and nonbreeding habitat of Arizona scaled quail is generally similar (Schemnitz 1994) in that the birds have a strong affinity for large areas of grassland with relatively few shrubs. Numerous studies support this observation.

Campbell et al. (1973) found that areas with a dense understory of forbs and shrubs were not optimal scaled quail habitat, and Brown (1989:145) advocated clearing dense brush on hilltops to improve habitat. Schemnitz (1964) and Wilson and Crawford (1987) observed that scaled quail preferred less dense cover than northern bobwhites did.

Reid, Grue, and Silvy (1979) noted that scaled quail selected shorter shrub types with more closed canopies, and northern bobwhites chose taller, more open, and diverse shrub types.

Where northern bobwhites and Arizona scaled quail are sympatric, Arizona scaled quail tend to prefer more open sites (lower grass height, more bare ground) (Rollins 1980; Lehmann 1984:229). Brown (1989) reported that in Arizona, scaled quail were not fond of steep slopes and rugged country but preferred open plains, rolling hills, low ridges, and mesas. The birds used scattered shrubs under 0.9 meter tall (3 feet) but avoided dense thickets, tall brush, and tree-lined washes. Guthery, King, Kuvlesky, et al. (2001) observed scaled quail in Arizona using patches with low amounts of woody cover.

In Arizona, King (1998) found that scaled quail preferred open grassland dominated by perennial bunchgrasses with about 10 percent woody cover, and Anderson (1974) documented their preference for areas with calcareous soils. According to Goodwin and Hungerford (1977), scaled quail in Arizona preferred low-growing grasses, forbs, and shrubs with 10–50 percent ground cover. Medina (1988) observed that scaled quail in Arizona were most abundant in habitat with low perennial grass cover but high forb cover.

In north-central Texas, Reid, Grue, and Silvy (1979) found that scaled quail use dry mesquite habitats, and shrubland is a key breeding habitat as long as it is not too dense. Areas with large areas of cropland are avoided.

In New Mexico, Banks (1970) noted that scaled quail preferred mesquite grasslands, and Campbell et al. (1973) reported limited use of dense vegetation types. According to Saiwana et al. (1998), areas with a mixture of late- and midseral plant communities provided the best available habitat for scaled quail in the Chihuahuan Desert in New Mexico. The availability of food sources and protective cover were primary determinants of habitat use. There were more sightings of scaled quail in early-seral stage shrubland than in climax-grassland communities. Smith et al. (1996) reported no scaled quail on a climax Chihuahuan Desert site dominated by black grama. Saiwana (1990) indicated that shrub-grass habitat was important to maintain scaled quail populations in New Mexico, also noting that grassland communities near the climax provided less suitable habitat than early-seral communities dominated by shrubs and forbs. Germano, Hungerford, and Martin (1983) observed more scaled quail on areas with mesquite than on mesquite-free sites. Campbell et al. (1973) reported that scaled quail used moderately grazed ranges, which supported a variety of forb species for food and a moderate amount of brush for cover. Dense, unbroken stands of grass or brush with abundant forbs were less likely to be used.

Scaled quail are usually found in xeric uplands, tributary canyons, and mesa slopes above river bottoms in the Oklahoma Panhandle (Schemnitz 1964). Schemnitz (1961) observed that the habitat of scaled quail in this region was composed of shrubs and certain kinds of artifacts found around farmsteads. Hatch (1975) documented scaled quail in Oklahoma in a great variety of areas, but always in open country. They avoided groves of trees but fed and rested in dense thickets of skunkbush (*Rhus trilobata*) in which some of the shrubs were more than

1.8 meters tall (5.9 feet). He noted that the typical habitat had sandsage, skunkbush, and rock rubble. Scaled quail tend to use pastures that are more heavily grazed than bobwhites do (Rollins 1980).

Cropland interspersed with rangelands provides suitable scaled quail habitat (Schemnitz 1961; Snyder 1967; Rollins 1980), and abandoned homesteads often served as covey headquarters (Schemnitz 1961). In Colorado, scaled quail preferred sandsage grasslands interspersed with agricultural crops (Andrews and Righter 1992).

Roosting Cover

Scaled quail roost on the ground in groups of 2–5 birds, with heads pointing outward (Wallmo 1956). Roosting cover consists of shrubs with a canopy of about 35 percent mixed with grasses (10–40 centimeters tall, or 4–16 inches) covering 45 percent of the ground (Stormer 1984). Roosting cover contains well-spaced low brush 30–122 centimeters tall (12–48 inches). Sawyer (1973) noted that roosting cover consisted primarily of grasses and shrubs, but grasses were favored when available. Hall (1998) showed that scaled quail used different roosting locations, perhaps reducing losses to predators, and that habitat should contain a minimum of 1 percent roosting cover containing shrubs about 10–40 centimeters tall (4–16 inches). Units of cover should have patches with 35 percent shrub cover surrounded by shrubs of lower density (Hall 1998). A typical patch for roosting should also support grasses 0.1–0.4 meters tall (0.3–1.3 feet) with about 45 percent cover; and a 0.3-hectare (0.74-acre) patch of roosting cover per 23 hectares (about 50 acres) should be adequate.

Loafing Cover

Loafing (i.e., resting) coverts are key components of scaled quail habitat (figure 5.6). Desirable loafing coverts should be at least 1 meter tall (3 feet) and be dense above, yet open at ground level (Schemnitz 1994; Rollins 2000). In West Texas, preferred loafing coverts include lotebush

Figure 5.6.
Loafing coverts such as this lotebush often function as the headquarters of a covey.
Photo by Dale Rollins

(*Ziziphus obtusifolia*), sandplum (*Prunus angustifolia*) thickets, and catclaw mimosa (*Mimosa biunciferae*) (Rollins 2000). Cover that provided shade and security from avian predators was excellent resting cover. Cholla cactus (*O. imbricate*) was used as resting cover during spring and winter in the Texas Panhandle (Stormer 1981). Schemnitz (1961, 1964, 1994) and Snyder (1967) found that scaled quail used numerous human structures (e.g., corrals, feedlots, buildings, farm machinery, old car bodies, post and board piles, cattle guards, windmills, and culverts) as loafing cover when natural habitats were limited. Mesquite provided 90 percent of the loafing cover for scaled quail in New Mexico (Sawyer 1973). They were observed resting in patches averaging about 4.5 meters (15 feet) in width and 2 meters (6 feet) in height, but the quail used some patches as small as 1.4 meters (about 3.5 feet) in width and 0.4 meter (2.6 feet) in height.

Escape Cover

In heavy cover, scaled quail tend to form a tight group and freeze until the perceived danger is close; then they burst into flight, a behavior similar to that of northern bobwhites. Although the majority (70 percent) of scaled quail escape predators by flying, some (30 percent) prefer to run (Hatch 1975). Griffing (1972) noted that when running, birds (based on 314 observations) ran to mesquite (59 percent) or nonshrub cover (31 percent). Sawyer (1973) found that they used shrubs and forbs as escape cover in 70 percent of the escape observations. According to Schemnitz (1961), some scaled quail in Oklahoma used human structures as escape cover. Hatch (1975) observed that scaled quail coveys that were flushed along rivers in Oklahoma primarily used dense thickets of skunkbush, patches of soapweed (*Yucca glauca*), and boulders as escape cover.

Diet

Scaled quail usually feed before midmorning and again before dark, although Schemnitz (1994) documented that during snowstorms, feeding usually ceased and quail remained in dense cover. If the snowfall stopped during daylight, quail resumed feeding. Hunt and Best (2001) reported that scaled quail consumed more insects in the morning and more seeds in the afternoon, and there was no difference in foods selected by sex or age (subadult and adult). Coveys foraged as a loose group or as scattered individuals (Russell 1932; Barkley 1972).

Foods primarily eaten by scaled quail include seeds, herbaceous vegetation, and grains, with seeds and grains a main fall and winter food (Schemnitz 1994; Rollins 2000; table 5.4). Cain et al. (1982) determined that at least 26 percent crude protein is required for scaled quail growth. As is the case with other galliformes, abundant fat deposits around the crop area are an indication that nutritional needs are being met or exceeded.

Rollins (1981) observed that scaled quail consumed about four times more green vegetation by volume than did northern bobwhites on the same range. Scaled quail also utilize a larger proportion of insects in their diet than other quail do (Kelso 1937). Scaled quail in Duval County, Texas, consumed more greens and fewer grass seeds than bobwhites did

Table 5.4.
Primary Foods of Scaled Quail

Source	State	Food items
Judd (1905)	Arizona, New Mexico, Texas	29.6% animal matter (15.9% grasshoppers, 10.4% beetles, 3.3% other, but largely ants) 70.4% plant matter
Kelso (1937)	Arizona	22% animal matter (19.5%–48.5% from March to September)
Lehmann and Ward (1941)	Texas	Elbowbush (*Forestiera angustifolia*), catclaw acacia (*Acacia roemeriana*), bluebonnet (*Lupinus subcarnosus*)
Wallmo (1956)	Texas	70% seeds (October–February); 15%–32% seeds (March–June); 9% animal matter (34% in June and 27% in September); greens (most eaten March–May)
Schemnitz (1961)	Oklahoma	Russian thistle seeds
Banks (1970)	New Mexico	62.6% seeds, 4.8% greens, 30.7% insects, 2.3% unknown (April–August); 73.0% seeds, 16.4% insects, 1.0% greens, 7.4% unknown (September–March); pigweed (*Amaranthus graecizans*) 20% by weight (seed most eaten)
Barkley (1972)	New Mexico	Mesquite seeds, plains bristlegrass (*Setaria macrostachya*), greens, *Coleoptera* (summer and winter foods); sandsage, winged pigweed (*Cycloloma atriplicifolium*), crownbeard (*Verbenia* sp.), *Hemiptera* (winter foods)
Campbell et al. (1973)	New Mexico	Snakeweed (stable winter food)
Haussamen (1974)	New Mexico	Mesquite seeds
Davis, Barkley, and Haussamen (1975)	New Mexico	Snakeweed (stable winter food); mesquite seeds
Howard (1981)	Texas	Greens (December–March); algarita berries (*Berberis trifoliolata*) (March–June); sumac (*Rhus* sp.) (July); beetles (August); spurges (*Euphorbia* spp.) (September); doveweeds (*Croton* spp.) (November)
Rollins (1981)	Oklahoma	Russian thistle seeds, mesquite seeds, dove-weeds, spurges, common broomweed (*Xanthocephalum dracunculoides*) (winter foods)
Best and Smart (1985)	New Mexico	Mesquite seeds
Campbell-Kissock, Blankenship, and Stewart (1985)	Texas	Termites during droughts
Medina (1988)	Arizona	57% seeds, 39% forb seeds, 16% greens (February–June); 12%–57% grass seeds (September–November); insects (March–August)
Brown (1989)	Arizona	Cactus seeds and fruit
Hunt and Best (2001)	New Mexico	Sunflower (*Helianthus* sp.), spurges, croton
Rollins (2000)	Texas	Filaree (*Erodium* sp.) (January)

on the same range (Lehmann 1984). However, most food items eaten by scaled quail were also eaten by northern bobwhites (Schemnitz 1964).

Many of the same foods were used by scaled quail throughout their range. However, snakeweed (*Guterrezia* spp.), which was a staple winter food in New Mexico, was ignored by scaled quail in West Texas. Russian thistle (*Salsola tragus*) seeds were important in the diet of scaled quail in western Oklahoma, but were only a minor part of the diet in northwestern Texas (Ault and Stormer 1983).

Little is known about the diet of scaled quail chicks. Howard (1981) examined 21 chicks, aged 1–13 weeks, and compared foods they had eaten to those eaten by adults. Chicks at 1 week of age had a high-animal–low-seed diet and gradually changed to a low-animal–high-seed diet by 13 weeks of age.

Demography and Populations

Understanding demographics is the key to population management. In this section we address scaled quail survival, fall age ratios, and several other key elements of their demography.

Survival

Until recently, there were few band-recovery or radiotelemetry studies to estimate scaled quail survival (figure 5.7). The results from these studies have not been published as of this writing.

Brood Survival

Little is known about scaled quail brood survival. Attempts to quantify chick survival at different time intervals by direct observation are hampered by the propensity of the birds to scatter (R. J. Buntyn, Texas Agricultural Experiment Station, unpublished data) and by the tendency of young chicks to remain motionless (N. Silvy, unpublished data). Chick mortality appears to be highest just after hatching and before young are able to fly (Tharp 1971). Tharp observed an 18.5 percent reduction in number of young within broods from the time before they could fly to after they could fly, but this did not take into account the situation in which all young were lost from a brood. Pleasant (2003) reported that 46 percent of 33 hens in 2000, and only 10 percent of 21 hens during 1999, had chicks present with them 3 weeks after hatch. Of the seven broods tracked by Evans (1997) in 1994, only 5 percent of the chicks were alive after 10 days, and none were alive after 16 days. In 1994, chick mortality was 100 percent, and in 1995, chick mortality for eight broods tracked was 50.4 percent for chicks up to 3–4 months of age.

No juvenile quail were trapped in 1995, indicating little production in 1994 (Evans and Schemnitz 2000). If all 183 eggs (Evans 1997) hatched from the 15 nests observed for both years, then the two-year calculated combined survival for chicks up to 3–4 months of age would be 18.6 percent.

Figure 5.7.
Scaled quail with radio transmitter.
Photo by Scott P. Lerich

Adult Survival

Like other quail, scaled quail are short-lived. There is a rapid turnover in wild populations (Schemnitz 1994). Survival of subadult birds from hunted sites in New Mexico based on ban recoveries was estimated to be 14 percent, with a mean annual survival of 17 percent for the entire population. Females survived at a lower rate than males, and this held for both young (females 10.9 percent and males 17.6 percent) and adult birds (females 25.0 percent and males 36.4 percent) (Campbell et al. 1973).

Survival of radio-marked scaled quail hens from April to August in Pecos County, Texas, was high (averaged 80 percent in 1999 and 69 percent in 2000) (R. J. Buntyn, unpublished data). Lerich (2002) reported that survival rates (February–August) of both male and female scaled quail ranged from 50 to 64 percent. Pleasant (2003) found that survival was not different between subadults and adults, and hen survival from February 18 until August 15 was about 75 percent in 2000 but only about 35 percent in 1999.

Fall Age Ratios as Indicators of Annual Production

Age ratios are an important source of information because young-to-adult ratios may be used as a measure of natality and rearing success of a population. However, age ratios cannot be interpreted, even in a general way, without additional demographic data. Hunters frequently provide large samples for determining age-ratio data, but there are potential biases in such data because young birds are more susceptible to harvest. Therefore, the harvest age-ratio data reported for scaled quail in table 5.5 should be viewed with caution. Age-ratio data taken from collected or trapped birds also have biases. If birds are collected immediately after broods hatch, the ratio will reflect more juvenile birds; if birds are collected or trapped closer to the hunting season, the ratio may parallel data from hunter bags.

Weather Influences on Annual Production

Bridges (1999) used a 21-year Texas Parks and Wildlife Department data set (1978–98) to analyze the influence of weather (rainfall and drought index) on the abundance of scaled quail within three ecological regions of Texas. He concluded that wet weather conditions generally resulted in increased abundance of scaled quail. The correlations between scaled

Table 5.5.
Juvenile:Adult Age Ratios of Scaled Quail

Source	State	Young:adult	Comments
Wallmo (1956)	Texas	1.6:1	Hunter bag
Gallizioli and Swank (1958)	Arizona	1.5:1	Hunter bag
Schemnitz (1961)	Oklahoma	2.9:1	Hunter bag
Hoffman (1965)	Colorado	2.9:1	Hunter bag
Snyder (1967)	Colorado	1.7–2.5:1	Hunter bag
Banks (1970)	New Mexico	2.3:1	Collected
Borden (1973)	New Mexico	3.8:1	Collected summer
Campbell et al. (1973)	New Mexico	2.8:1	Collected and trapped
Davis (1979)	Texas	1.3–10.4:1	Trapped and hunter bag
Pleasant (2003)	Texas	0.4:1	Trapped in 1999
		2.3:1	Trapped in 2000

quail abundance and weather conditions were stronger in drier than in wetter ecological regions. Brown, Cochran, and Waddell (1978) observed a significant correlation between the October–August precipitation of the previous year and hunting success. Leyva-Espinosa (2000) found that precipitation occurring in July–September played an important role in scaled quail populations located in the Rolling Plains and in the distributional range for the species. She suggested that in general, precipitation was the variable that best described scaled quail population changes in Texas.

Scaled quail are thought to be more drought tolerant than northern bobwhites (Schemnitz 1964; Giuliano, Lutz, and Patiño 1999; Rollins 2000). In areas where their ranges overlap, scaled quail typically do not "boom" as greatly during good years nor "bust" as badly during dry years as bobwhites (Rollins 2000), although there are counterexamples to this alleged phenomenon, but none to our knowledge in the literature.

Evans (1997) observed that incubating female scaled quail spread their wings over the nest in an apparent effort to try to cool eggs when ambient temperature was 33.3°C (92°F). When the ambient humidity averaged 8 percent during the course of her study (except during rainfall), hens kept the nest humidity at 19 percent. Hens were always observed on the nests during the hottest part of the day.

Mortality Factors

Probably few scaled quail die of old age. Campbell et al. (1973) estimated that only 0.1 percent of scaled quail were still alive at the start of their fifth year of life. They die from various natural causes, including malnutrition, parasites, disease, toxic substances, weather events, predators, hunters, and other human-related causes. Many of these mortality factors are interrelated (e.g., quail weakened because of lack of food may by more likely to die from extreme weather conditions or predators).

Nutrition

In most cases the specific nutritional requirements of scaled quail are unknown but are thought to be similar to those of northern bobwhites. Cain et al. (1982) suggested that scaled quail could increase food consumption to compensate for dietary energy deficiencies. Giuliano et al. (1996) argued that protein deficiencies could not be compensated for by increased food consumption. Such deficiencies could cause growth depression, mass loss, and reduced egg production and mass. Using captive-reared scaled quail, they found that protein and energy deficiencies led to declines in body and ovary mass and egg production but did not affect egg mass. Although body mass and reproduction were affected by protein and energy deficiencies, scaled quail were less affected by such deficiencies than northern bobwhites were.

During drought, moisture-stressed plants produce estrogenic compounds (phytoestrogens), which have been shown to affect the reproductive capabilities of some mammals (Labov 1977). Relatively high levels of phytoestrogens were postulated by Leopold et al. (1976) to inhibit reproduction of California quail (*Callipepla californica*); however, this relationship remains unproven. In dietary studies on captive scaled quail, Cain, Lien, and Beasom (1987) observed no significant role (either inhibitory or stimulatory) of phytoestrogens on their reproductive success.

There are limited published data on the diet of scaled quail chicks (Howard 1981). Most quail chicks feed on arthropods during the first weeks of life. It is theoretically possible that during drought, when green vegetation and insects are less abundant, scaled quail chicks may die of starvation.

Predation

Predators can adversely affect scaled quail populations in two direct ways: they can feed on eggs, and they can prey on young and adult quail (Silvy 1999). Indirectly, they can affect quail populations by preying (or not preying) on species that may be in competition with scaled quail for limited resources.

Predation is the largest proximate cause of nest loss. Important predators of scaled quail nests include coyotes (*Canis latrans*), raccoons (*Procyon lotor*), striped skunks (*Mephitis mephitis*), domestic cats, and snakes (Schemnitz 1961; Tharp 1971; Evans 1997; Rollins 1999a, 2000; Rollins and Carroll 2001). Other common nest predators include gray foxes (*Urocyon cinereoargenteus*), corvids (Slater 1996), and feral hogs (*Sus scrofa*) (Tolleson et al. 1995). Pleasant (2003) reported one nest depredated by a badger (*Taxidea taxus*). Of 26 depredated nests where Pleasant (2003) indicated cause, snakes had depredated 19.

Predation is the proximate cause of most scaled quail mortalities (Rollins and Carroll 2001). Neither Wallmo (1957), Schemnitz (1961), nor Campbell et al. (1973) cited predation as a management concern; in fact, predation was hardly mentioned as a source of mortality. The only mention of predation in Wallmo were events that occurred at quail-trapping sites; the species involved were gray fox, striped skunks, ringtails (*Bassaricus astutus*), raccoons, and Cooper's hawks (*Accipiter cooperii*).

Rollins and Carroll (2001) reasoned that mortality rates of scaled quail from predation have been poorly documented because of the paucity of telemetry studies, even though use of telemetry may exacerbate mortality in scaled quail. Earlier investigations of scaled quail (Wallmo 1957; Schemnitz 1961; Campbell et al. 1973) were either unaware of, or dismissed, the incidence of predation because they lacked the technology to study it (i.e., radiotelemetry). More comprehensive studies involving radio-tagged scaled quail are needed to assess cause-specific mortality patterns.

Anecdotal Observations of Scaled Quail Predation

Pleasant (2003) noted from his study of scaled quail in the High Plains of Texas that his data did not support the moisture-facilitated nest depredation hypothesis for scaled quail. This hypothesis infers that nests are more likely to be found by predators during wet periods because predators are better able to "scent" nests during wet periods than dry periods. However, Pleasant observed just the opposite during his study: wet days were not a good predictor of nest predation.

Jackson (1947) reported that evidence of predation on scaled quail was light and that they were apparently less vulnerable to avian predation than were bobwhites. Evans (1997) noted that a female scaled quail was killed by a great horned owl while the quail was foraging off the nest in the early morning, and raptor kills may have accounted for 8 percent of monitored adult females killed. She also observed prairie falcons (*Falco mexicanus*) taking two male scaled quail at dusk.

Tewes, Mock, and Young (2002) reviewed 54 scientific articles about the food habits of bobcats (*Lynx rufus*) and found that quail (including scaled quail) were taken in 9 of 35 (25.9 percent) of studies that were within quail range.

According to Lerich (2002), predation accounted for 29 of 32 (91 percent) scaled quail mortalities in Brewster County, Texas. Of those, mammals accounted for 14 kills; raptors, for 4; and unknown predators, for 10. P. S. Carter (Angelo State University, unpublished data) radio-marked 27 scaled quail in west-central Texas (Irion County) and documented 9 scaled quail mortalities; 5 by mammals, 2 by raptors (1 by a great horned owl), and 1 by a western diamondback rattlesnake (*Crotalus atrox*).

The fact that predators account for most of the mortality of chicks and adults and the preponderance of disrupted nests is indisputable. But is predation a management concern? What are the impacts of predation on scaled quail abundance? The former is easy to document; the latter is inherently more difficult to assess.

Predation on quail nests has been proposed as a factor limiting quail abundance (Rollins 1999a). There has been much speculation that predator communities have changed over the last 20 years as a result of the demise of the fur market in the 1980s (Rollins 1999a; Rollins and Carroll 2001). Under this hypothesis, the collapse of the fur market has led to high predator densities and thus to decreased quail numbers. Silvy et al. (2000) addressed these hypotheses for the Rolling Plains, Edwards Plateau, and South Texas Plains ecological regions. They found that decreasing fur prices were indeed associated with decreasing furbearer harvest. However, they found no increase in the abundance of fur-bearing animals during this period, and fur prices, furbearer harvest, and abundance of fur-bearing animals were not correlated with scaled quail abundance.

The potential role of predation as a suppressing agent in quail populations needs additional study (Rollins and Carroll 2001). It is crucial to understand how landscape-level changes in land use might influence relationships between quail and their predators, as well as change both predator and prey communities. Experimental research is needed to define more clearly the relationships between quail and their predators within the context of current land use and habitat management. Specifically, the relationships among precipitation, vegetation dynamics (including nest site availability [i.e., thresholds]), land management (e.g., livestock grazing, brush control), predator searching effectiveness, and consequent nesting success and recruitment need additional investigation (Schemnitz 1994).

Hunting

Wallmo and Uzzell (1958) noted that scaled quail were probably the most difficult of all quail to hunt. Restricted and closed hunting seasons during low population levels have not been recommended, as hunting apparently has little effect on populations of scaled quail (Wallmo and

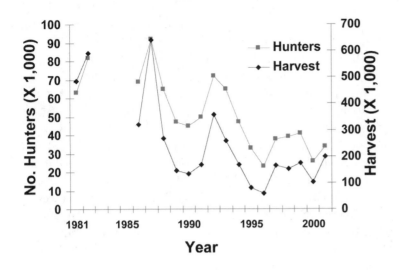

Figure 5.8.
Number of scaled quail hunters and
the number of scaled quail harvested
in Texas, 1981–2002
(TPWD, unpublished data).

85
*Scaled Quail Ecology
and Life History*

Uzzell 1958; Hoffman 1965; Campbell et al. 1973); however, harvest rate
was not considered in relation to these conclusions. Brown, Cochran,
and Waddell (1977, 1978) and Brown (1989) observed a linear relationship between the number of scaled quail calling in the spring and the
hunter success in the fall. Quail harvest at broad spatial scales is probably self-regulating (Peterson and Perez 2000). As Texas scaled quail
populations increase, hunter numbers also increase (figure 5.8). Peterson and Perez found that about twice as many hunters hunted quail in
Texas during boom years than in bust years. They also determined that
summer production could account for 77–87 percent of scaled quail
harvested annually.

According to DeMaso et al. (2002), the roadside surveys carried out
by Texas Parks and Wildlife Department were more closely related to
estimated statewide harvest of scaled quail than those by the North
American Breeding Bird Survey. A nine-year investigation (Campbell et al. 1973) of the effects of hunting on scaled quail populations on
hunted and nonhunted areas concluded that hunting was independent
of scaled quail densities, a finding that is quite different from that of
Peterson and Perez (2000).

Wallmo and Uzzell (1958) estimated that 90 percent of scaled quail
in their study probably never saw a hunter. Campbell et al. (1973) noted
that few hunters ever achieved a daily bag limit, even when birds were
plentiful, and the average season take per hunter was less than the al-
lowable daily bag limit. Peterson (2001) found that reducing the daily
bag limit from 15 to 8 would impact only 7 percent of scaled quail hunters in Texas. This reduction would reduce scaled quail harvest by only
about 15 percent; whereas a bag limit of 6 quail would reduce the harvest by 35 percent. Reducing the season length would have little effect,
as few hunters spent more than 10 days hunting quail.

Other Human-Related Mortality

Evans (1997) found three 1-day-old chicks drowned in cattle water
troughs, and Lerich (2002) found three radio-tagged scaled quail hens
drowned in the same water trough in Brewster County, Texas. Campbell (1960) indicated that water developments had little value for scaled
quail.

Campbell (1950) found a dead scaled quail with lead shot in the gizzard, and Campbell et al. (1973) noted that about 3 percent of fall-winter scaled quail crops contained lead shot. Best, Garrison, and Schmitt (1992) found lead in only 1 of 226 gizzards examined, and lead content of the liver was less than 8 parts per million for all but 3 birds sampled. Twelve of 101 scaled quail gizzards from Harmon County, Oklahoma, contained spent shot (D. Rollins, unpublished data). Although Campbell et al. (1973) noted that the ingested lead shot could cause quail mortality, they believed this was rare for scaled quail in New Mexico. Accumulations of spent shot would most likely be encountered around ponds that were the focus of waterfowl and dove hunting.

Scaled quail have died from flying into human structures (e.g., fences) and have been hit by vehicles on roads (N. Silvy, unpublished data). The impact of these human-related deaths on scaled quail populations is unknown.

Population Dynamics

In spite of the low survival of nests, chicks, and adults, scaled quail continue to maintain huntable populations in Texas. To sustain their populations, scaled quail have evolved several reproductive strategies. Scaled quail breed at an early age (one year of age). Clutch sizes are large and egg hatchability high (see previous discussion), and if the first nest is lost, renesting is common (Evans 1997; Rollins 2000). Evans observed an average of 45.5 days between the loss of a first nest and the start of second nests. Therefore, if initial nests are lost, scaled quail can readily compensate through renesting attempts, especially given that the nesting season normally runs from May to August. Even though clutch size decreases with subsequent nesting attempts, persistent renesting probably accounts for the tremendous reproductive potential of scaled quail.

Few data are available on multiple brooding in scaled quail populations. Multiple brooding has been documented (Rollins 2000), but we do not know how frequently it occurs.

Conservation and Management

More than 97 percent of the Texas landscape is privately owned. Therefore, land use and land-use practices by private landowners can greatly influence scaled quail densities. There are no studies that have estimated or determined the minimum population size or quantified the minimum area necessary to sustain scaled quail populations.

Rho (2003) observed a negative correlation between human population density and scaled quail abundance for both the South Texas Plains and the Rolling Plains. In the South Texas Plains, scaled quail were rarely observed in an area of more than 0.2 person/hectare (about 0.2/2.5 acres) but were relatively abundant in lightly populated areas (less than 0.2 person/hectare). Road density was also negatively correlated with scaled quail abundance in the South Texas Plains. The quail were most abundant in areas with less than 5 meters of road/hectare (2.2 yards/2.5 acres); few birds were observed in areas with road density greater than 10 meters/hectare (4.4 yards/2.5 acres). These findings suggest a threshold of human population density of less than 20 persons/100 hectares (245 acres) for maintaining high densities of scaled quail.

Grazing

It is clear that livestock grazing influences scaled quail populations in Texas. The old adage "to take half and leave half" of the annual production of vegetation has probably caused considerable damage to scaled quail populations. What is important for quail production is not how much grass gets eaten by cows but how much grass is left. There must be enough cover left during all periods of the year, even during time of drought, to meet all life requisites of scaled quail if they are to prosper.

Heavily grazed early-seral rangelands and lightly or ungrazed climax Chihuahuan Desert rangelands support fewer scaled quail than those grazed moderately and maintained in mid- or late-seral condition (Smith, Holechek, and Cardenas 1996; Nelson et al. 1997; Saiwana et al. 1998; Joseph et al. 2003). Moderately grazed pastures contain areas with a mix of grazing intensities ranging from ungrazed to heavily grazed areas.

Little consensus exists in the literature about which grazing methods are best for scaled quail management (Ligon 1927; Wallmo 1957; Campbell et al. 1973; Davis 1979; Campbell-Kissock, Blankenship, and White 1984). Campbell-Kissock, Blankenship, and White found higher densities of scaled quail on areas under a short-duration grazing system than on a continuously grazed site in the South Texas Plains. Rollins (2000) suggested using moderate to light stocking rates (15 hectares, or 37 acres/animal-unit [one cow and her calf]; and greater than 30 hectares, or about 75 acres/animal-unit, respectively) as one goes from east to west to improve range condition. Saiwana (1990) noted that moderate grazing by cattle (30–40 percent use of grasses) benefited scaled quail and that high-fair to low-good range condition (45–55 percent of climax) provided optimum habitat on upland sandy areas in south-central New Mexico. Pleasant (2003) concluded that preventing overgrazing in scaled quail habitat was probably the single most important thing a manager could do to help this species.

Management Strategies

Wallmo (1956, 1957), Wallmo and Uzzell (1958), and Campbell (1960) summarized their efforts on enhancing scaled quail range with guzzlers and concluded that there was no relationship between water availability and population size.

Campbell (1959) speculated that supplemental feeding was ineffective, but his study was confounded with availability of water, which may also have concentrated the birds. Rollins (2000) observed that scaled quail readily use quail feeders and, therefore, become more available to hunters. He also photographed scaled quail chicks less than three weeks old at feeders and noted that adult quail frequently used deer feeders during fall and winter months.

Jackson (1969) suggested that in areas with a high percentage of grass, fallow disking of strips should increase scaled quail habitat. Jackson observed and Rollins (2000) promoted the concept that soil disturbance caused by winter disking and livestock grazing would stimulate early-successional plant species (e.g., buffalobur [*Solanum rostratum*]) and provide the bulk of the scaled quail diet. They suggested that disking should be done December–February in proximity to suitable woody cover.

Snyder (1967) observed considerable use of brush shelters by scaled quail during summer, fall, and winter months. They can benefit from brush piles and by half-cutting mesquite trees to provide cover (Rollins 1997).

Rollins (2000) suggested that managers should learn to recognize the structure and places that support high densities of scaled quail and seek to maintain the integrity of these sites. He recommended leaving at least 10 percent of the brush canopy intact and suggested that mechanical control methods are preferred over chemical methods because of the forbs produced by soil disturbance. Mechanical methods also offer greater selectivity concerning which individual plants should be killed. Tharp (1971) recommended not chaining large areas, as scaled quail were observed to use only the edges of these areas, and leaving brush strips through the center of such areas would increase quail use. Tharp also noted that the effects of herbicide spraying on scaled quail was dependent on the type of brush canopy remaining after treatment.

Predator Control

Rollins (2000) stated that for predator control to be effective, it should be directed at nest predators. However, predator control remains an unproven management technique for increasing scaled quail numbers. Guthery and Beasom (1977) conducted intensive removal of mammalian predators (e.g., coyotes and striped skunks) in the western Rio Grande Plains of Texas but did not find a treatment effect on either scaled quail or northern bobwhite populations. Their conclusion was that if predator removal was effective at all, it would be by allowing quail populations on poorer areas to be similar to those in better habitats.

Economics

Unlike conditions observed decades earlier by Wallmo and Uzzell (1958), today the economics of leasing scaled quail hunting opportunities should provide landowners an incentive to manage their lands for scaled quail. However, Wallmo and Uzzell noted (and it holds true today) that we do not understand the consumers (hunters) and the producers (landowners) well enough to make use of our knowledge of scaled quail ecology.

A comprehensive research program that examines the economic aspects of effective scaled quail management and the way that scaled quail habitat management impacts other arid land wildlife would be a fundamental contribution to wildlife science in Texas.

Diseases and Parasites of Texas Quails   6

Markus J. Peterson

> The rôle of disease in wild-life conservation has probably been radically
> underestimated. The long-prevailing under-valuation of the disease fac-
> tor may be definitely associated with the limitation of the observational
> method of studying natural history.
> Leopold (1933)

The mammoth work *The Grouse in Health and Disease* (Committee of
Inquiry on Grouse Disease 1911), among other things, argued that the
cecal worm *Trichostrongylus tenuis* (= *T. pergracilis*) was the primary
cause of "the Grouse Disease" in red grouse (*Lagopus lagopus scoticus*)
in the British Isles. The principal impetus for this study was to determine whether infectious agents controlled variation in grouse abundance among years. This publication undoubtedly stimulated North
American game-bird researchers not only to attempt similarly massive
studies (e.g., Stoddard 1931; Bump et al. 1947) but also to search for their
own version of "the Grouse Disease" (Gross 1925:424; Lack 1954:164),
"the quail disease" (Bass 1939, 1940; Durant and Doll 1941), and the
parasites of northern bobwhites (*Colinus virginianus*) in general (e.g.,
Cram 1930; Cram, Jones, and Allen 1931). Leopold (1933:325), in his
influential *Game Management,* maintained that "density fluctuations,
such as cycles and irruptions, are almost certainly due to fluctuations
in the prevalence of, virulence of, or resistance to [infectious] diseases."
Thus, Leopold placed host-parasite interactions on par with other important interspecific relationships, such as predator-prey interactions.
He did not, however, offer any empirical or experimental evidence to
support his suppositions.

About 1950, many influential wildlife scientists began to assume that
infectious agents of free-roaming wildlife were ecologically unimportant, except as almost inanimate extensions of poor habitat conditions
or as natural disasters (Trippensee 1948:369–84; Taylor 1956:581–83;
Lack 1954:161–69). Herman (1969:325) ended his review of how diseases influence wildlife populations by stating that there was only "limited documentation that disease, as an individual factor, can drastically
affect population fluctuations" and that "it is imperative that we recognize the dependency of the occurrence of disease in wildlife on habitat
conditions." Herman (1963) pointed out elsewhere, however, that few
studies had been conducted in such a manner that the population-level
effects of infectious agents could be documented, even if they occurred.
This criticism still holds (Peterson 1996; Tompkins et al. 2002). At any
rate, perceiving bacterial or viral diseases as simply extensions of poor
habitat conditions or as natural disasters where management could not
reasonably be brought to bear—much like hurricanes or volcanic erup-
tions—led North American wildlife ecologists and managers to neglect
these important interspecific relationships (Peterson 1991a).

Conversely, since the early part of the twentieth century, those interested in parasite systematics continued to study their favorite taxa
in wild hosts, including northern bobwhites and other quails. Such

efforts tended to emphasize host lists, parasite descriptions, and revisions of taxonomic relationships. Similarly, those interested in the diseases of pen-reared bobwhites continued to publish case reports and study diseases important to these poultry operations. These articles, however, often were cataloged under key words related to particular, often now obsolete, parasite taxonomic names rather than terms transparent to wildlife scientists (e.g., "disease" or "parasite"). This renders comprehensive literature searches difficult for many interested in the infectious agents of quails.

Host-Parasite Ecology

Although others previously addressed host-parasite interactions from an ecological perspective, Anderson and May (1978) and May and Anderson (1978) provided the basic theoretical framework still used for evaluating host-parasite interactions ecologically. They demonstrated how parasites could, under certain circumstances, not only cause disease in individual animals but also regulate host populations. Probably in part because of May's stature as a leading theoretical ecologist of this period, studying host-parasite ecology in wild populations suddenly was again orthodox, and numerous theoretical and a few applied publications grounded in these ideas soon followed. These included the well-known studies demonstrating that *T. tenuis* could regulate red grouse populations under certain circumstances (e.g., Hudson 1986; Dobson and Hudson 1992; Hudson, Dobson, and Newborn 1992, 1998; Hudson, Newborn, and Dobson 1992). This renewed interest in the relationship between parasites and wild hosts eventually spread to North America, although few studies based on this theoretical foundation specifically addressed the infectious agents of northern bobwhites, let alone other quails occurring in Texas.

Ecologically, parasites are organisms that meet the following three conditions: utilizing their hosts as habitat, depending nutritionally on the hosts, and causing some sort of harm to the hosts during their life cycle (Anderson and May 1978). Anderson and May (1979) also offered an ecologically based categorization of parasites that is directly relevant to those concerned with wildlife conservation. Macroparasites (parasitic arthropods and helminths) tend to have longer generation times than microparasites (e.g., parasitic protozoans, fungi, bacteria, viruses); direct multiplication in or on the host is either absent or occurs at a low rate; and the immune response elicited by these metazoans depends on the number present and typically is of short duration. For these reasons, macroparasites generally occur as endemic host infections that are more likely to cause morbidity than mortality. Conversely, microparasites are characterized by small size, short generation times, high rates of direct reproduction on or within the host, and a tendency to induce long-lasting immunity to reinfection. Microparasitic infection typically is short relative to the expected life span of the host. For this reason, microparasitic diseases often occur as epidemics in which the pathogen apparently disappears as susceptive hosts die or become immune, only to reappear when sufficient densities of susceptible hosts are again available in the population. Parasites can complete their life cycles either directly by contact between hosts, inhalation, ingestion, or skin penetration; or indirectly via biting vectors, penetration by free-living larva produced in an intermediate host, or ingestion by the host of an intermediate host. One of the primary approaches to controlling infectious diseases in wildlife is to interrupt parasite life cycles, so understanding how these agents are transmitted is important to wildlife managers. Parasites potentially can influence host population dynamics by regulating host numbers (Tompkins et al. 2002); markedly reducing host abundance during epizootics characterized by high host mortality (Friend, McLean, and Dein 2001); or extirpating small, isolated populations (Peterson et al. 1998; Cleaveland et al. 2002). All three of these effects could be applicable to Texas quail populations.

Parasites and Texas Quails

Not surprisingly, research addressing the parasites of Texas quails has generally paralleled that occurring elsewhere in North America. Several comprehensive studies addressing the macro- and microparasites of bobwhites were conducted in Texas during the 1940s and early 1950s (tables 6.1, 6.2, and 6.3). Only sporadic efforts have been made since. So far, the resurgence in research directed toward the infectious agents of bobwhites that began in the mid-1980s elsewhere has not occurred in Texas. Less effort has been expended studying the parasites of scaled quail (*Callipepla squamata*) in Texas, and almost no research has addressed the infectious agents of Gambel's (*C. gambelii*) or Montezuma quail (*Cyrtonyx montezumae*) in the Lone Star State. This probably reflects the historical popularity of bobwhites compared to that of the three other Texas quails.

This chapter addresses macroparasites, microparasites, and a few toxic diseases of Texas quails and then provides a brief integration and synthesis of what this information means. For each category of parasite, the northern bobwhite is discussed first, because much more is known about the parasites of this species; then, what is known for the scaled, Gambel's, and Montezuma quails in Texas is contextualized. Results from studies bordering Texas and elsewhere sometimes are included, but there is no attempt to comprehensively summarize what is known about the infectious agents of the northern bobwhite throughout its geographic range. For those interested in this material, biologists affiliated with the Southeastern Cooperative Wildlife Disease Study unit have provided reasonably comprehensive parasite lists and reviewed what was known about the infectious agents of bobwhites in the southeastern United States (e.g., Kellogg and Prestwood 1968; Kellogg and Calpin 1971; Kellogg and Doster 1972; Doster, Wilson, and Kellogg 1980; Davidson, Kellogg, and Doster 1982a). Comparable lists and reviews are not available for the scaled, Gambel's, or Montezuma quail. *The Birds of North America* accounts for these species address this void to varying degrees (Schemnitz 1994; Brown et al. 1998; Stromberg 2000). For this reason, this chapter provides a more comprehensive summary of this material.

Macroparasites

Macroparasites can be found in and on all species of Texas quails. They are organisms that can typically be seen by the naked eye—such as flies, ticks, intestinal worms—as opposed to pathogenic protozoa, bacteria, and so on, which require microscopes for identification.

Table 6.1.
Parasitic Arthropods Found on Northern Bobwhites in Texas

Arthropods	Year(s)	Texas county or region	Prevalence	Source
Fleas				
Echidnophaga gallinacea	1951	Kleberg		Hightower, Lehmann, and Eads (1953)
Orchopeas howardi	1951–52	Brazos, Grimes, Robertson	0.9 (1/109)	Parmalee (1952b)
Lice				
Brüellia illustris	1951–52	Brazos, Grimes, Robertson	1.9 (1/53)	Parmalee (1952b); Parmalee and Price (1953)
Colinicola numidianus	1917	Near Eagle Pass		McGregor (1917)
	1951	Kleberg		Hightower, Lehmann, and Eads (1953)
	1951–52	Brazos, Grimes, Robertson	39.6 (21/53)	Parmalee (1952b)
		Bexar		Wiseman (1959:215)
	1961–62	Cottle	32.7 (17/52)	Wiseman (1968)
	1985–86	Goliad, Refugio	5.9 (1/17)	Teel et al. (1998)
Goniodes ortygis	1951	Kleberg		Hightower, Lehmann, and Eads (1953)
	1951–52	Brazos, Grimes, Robertson	45.3 (24/53)	Parmalee (1952b)
	1961–62	Cottle	76.9 (40/52)	Wiseman (1968)
	1985–86	Goliad, Refugio	58.8 (10/17)	Teel et al. (1998)
Menacanthus pricei	1951	Kleberg		Hightower, Lehmann, and Eads (1953)
	1951–52	Brazos, Grimes, Robertson	13.2 (7/53)	Parmalee (1952b)
	1961–62	Cottle	40.4 (21/52)	Wiseman (1968)
	1985–86	Goliad, Refugio	35.3 (6/17)	Teel et al. (1998)
Oxylipeurus clavatus	1951	Kleberg		Hightower, Lehmann, and Eads (1953)
	1951–52	Brazos, Grimes, Robertson	37.7 (20/53)	Parmalee (1952b)
	1961–62	Cottle	63.5 (33/52)	Wiseman (1968)
	1985–86	Goliad, Refugio	82.4 (14/17)	Teel et al. (1998)
Unidentified	1951–52	Brazos, Grimes, Robertson	3.8 (2/53)[a]	Parmalee (1952b)
	1993	Colorado	100.0 (41/41)	Purvis (1995:26–27)
Mites				
Boydaia colini		Lubbock		Clark (1958)
Unidentified	1993	Colorado	87.8 (36/41)	Purvis (1995:26–27)
Ticks				
Amblyomma americanum	1943–44	Bexar, Comal	100.0 (38/38)	Brennan (1945a, 1945b)
	1951–52	Brazos, Grimes, Robertson		Parmalee (1952b)
A. cajennense	1951	Kleberg		Hightower, Lehmann, and Eads (1953)
A. maculatum	1951	Kleberg		Hightower, Lehmann, and Eads (1953)
	1985–86	Goliad, Refugio	76.5 (13/17)	Teel et al. (1998)
Haemaphysalis chordeilis	1907	Cameron	100.0 (1/1)	Hooker (1909)
	1907	Victoria	100.0 (12/12)	Hooker (1909)
H. leporispalustris	1950	Kleberg	93.5 (43/46)	Hightower, Lehmann, and Eads (1953)
	1951	Kleberg		Hightower, Lehmann, and Eads (1953)
	1951–52	Brazos, Grimes, Robertson		Parmalee (1952b)
Unidentified	1993	Colorado	2.4 (1/41)	Purvis (1995:26–27)
Hippoboscid fly				
Microlynchia pusilla	1951	Kleberg		Hightower, Lehmann, and Eads (1953)
	1951–52	Brazos, Grimes, Robertson	5.5 (6/109)	Parmalee (1952b)

Note: Prevalence (%; *n* positive/*n* examined) included where these data were available.
[a] Thought to be three different species.

Parasitic Arthropods

Hippoboscid flies (louse flies) and fleas rarely were reported for bobwhites in Texas (see table 6.1 for the parasitic arthropods found on northern bobwhites in Texas). The primary significance of hippoboscid flies is that they serve as vectors for avian malarial organisms. Because

Table 6.2.
Prevalence of Enteric Nematodes Found on Northern Bobwhites in Texas

Texas ecoregion and county	n ex.	Aulono- cephalus lindquisti		Heterakis gallinarum		Stron- gyloides avium		Subulura brumpti		Syn- gamus trachea		Tricho- strongylus cramae		Other nematodes		Reference
		n	%	n	%	n	%	n	%	n	%	n	%	n	%	
Piney Woods																
Bowie	13			10	76.9											Parmalee (1952b)
Gulf Prairies and Marshes																
Refugio	109	7	6.4									28	25.7			Demarais, Everett, and Pons (1987)
Colorado	62					20	32.3			2	3.2	60	96.8	3[a]	4.8	Purvis et al. (1998)
Post Oak Savannah																
Multiple	717			34	4.7											Parmalee (1952b)
South Texas Plains																
Duval, Jim Hogg, Jim Wells, Zapata	270	248	91.9							2	0.7			1[b]	0.4	Webster and Addis (1945)
Kleberg	300	265	88.3													Webster (1947)
Dimmit, Duval	239	231	96.7													Lehmann (1984:206–14)
Dimmit, Duval	113	109	96.4													Lehmann (1984:206–14)
Brooks	372	174	46.8													Demarais, Everett, and Pons (1987)
Rolling Plains																
Shackelford	6							6								Parmalee (1952b)
Cottle[c]	54							46	85.2					8[d]	14.8	Jackson (1969)
Cottle	61							36	59.0							Jackson (1969)
Multiple regions																
Coleman, Harris, Trinity, Colorado	14	1	7.1													Webster and Addis (1945)
Total	2,330	1,035	44.4	44	1.9	20	0.9	88	3.8	4	0.2	88	3.8	12	0.5	

Note: Prevalence by study, Texas ecoregion (figure 7.1, Gould 1962) and county, and number of quail examined (n ex.).
[a] Dispharynx nasuta.
[b] Cyrnea sp.
[c] Ascaridia galli (=A. lineata), S. avium, and Tetrameres sp. were found for 5.0% of quail examined.
[d] Cheilospirura spinosa.

many birds examined during ectoparasite surveys were collected for other purposes, they were not immediately placed in individual bags. Thus, it is unclear whether these parasites actually were rare or simply left cooling carcasses and were not observed. Further research could clarify this point. Hightower, Lehmann, and Eads (1953) found 57 *Echidnophaga gallinacea* and 11 *Microlynchia pusilla* for 20 bobwhites collected in Kleberg County. Parmalee (1952b) found 1 *Orchopeas howardi* and 6 *M. pusilla,* respectively, on 1 and 6 of 109 bobwhites examined in the Post Oak Savannah.

Howard (1981:52–73) found 22.5 percent of 240 scaled quail collected in Pecos County infested with the hippoboscid fly *Pseudolynchia canariensis* (see table 6.4 for the prevalence of parasitic arthropods, nematodes, and cestodes found on scaled quail in Pecos County). Prevalence, or the percentage of quail harboring the parasite, was higher during summer and fall than winter and spring; infestation intensity (mean number of parasites per infested individual) was low during all seasons. I found no reports of hippoboscid flies for Gambel's or Montezuma quail in Texas. The hippoboscid fly *Stilbometopa impressa,* however, was recovered from scaled quail in Arizona and Nevada, as well as from Gambel's quail in Arizona, Nevada, and New Mexico (Gorsuch 1934:55–57; Campbell and Lee 1953:48–52; Gullion 1957; Hungerford 1955). The hippoboscid flies *M. pusilla* and *Ornithoica vicina* also were found on scaled and Gambel's quail, respectively, in New Mexico (Campbell and Lee 1953:48–52). I found no records of fleas for scaled,

Table 6.3.
Prevalence of Cestodes Found on Northern Bobwhites in Texas

Texas ecoregion and county	n ex.	Hymenolepis sp. n	%	Raillietina cesticillus n	%	Raillietina klebergi n	%	Raillietina minuta n	%	Raillietina tetragona n	%	Raillietina spp. n	%	Rhabdometra odiosa n	%	Other cestodes n	%	Unidentified cestodes n	%	Reference
Piney Woods																				
Trinity	1			1								1[a]								Webster (1944)
Gulf Prairies and Marshes																				
Refugio	109																	14	12.8	Demarais, Everett, and Pons (1987)
Colorado	62											27[b]	43.5							Purvis et al. (1998)
Post Oak Savannah																				
Multiple	717	3	0.4							[c]								[c]		Parmalee (1952b)
South Texas Plains																				
Duval, Jim Hogg, Jim Wells, Zapata	270													14	5.2	1[d]	0.4			Webster and Addis (1945)
Kleberg	300					21	7.0	4	1.3									3	1.0	Webster (1947)
Kleberg	38					3	7.9	1	2.6									3	7.9	Webster (1951)
Brooks	372									1	0.3			3	1.0	1[e]	0.3	45	12.1	Parmalee (1952b)
Dimmit, Duval	97																	4	4.1	Lehmann (1984:206–14)
Dimmit, Duval	113			12	10.6	1	0.9	2	1.8			5[b]	4.4			1[e]	0.9	8[f]	7.1	Lehmann (1984:206–14)
Rolling Plains																				
Cottle	54	6	11.1																	Jackson (1969)
Total	2,133	9	0.4	13	0.6	25	1.2	7	0.3	1	0.1	33	1.5	17	0.8	7	0.3	77	3.6	

Note: Prevalence by study, Texas ecoregion (figure 7.1, Gould 1962) and county, and number of quail examined (n ex.).
[a] R. colinia was recovered from the same bobwhite.
[b] Raillietina sp.
[c] Both R. tetragona and Raillietina sp. were identified for 7 bobwhites.
[d] Polycercus sp.
[e] Darvinea sp. (Lehmann 1984:359).
[f] Unidentified larval cestodes.

Gambel's, or Montezuma quail in Texas. The fleas *Oropsylla* sp. and *Hoplopsyllus* sp. were recovered from Gambel's quail in Arizona (Gorsuch 1934:55–57), and *E. gallinacea* were found on scaled quail in New Mexico (Campbell and Lee 1953:53–56).

I obtained only two reports documenting mites for bobwhites in Texas, although Lehmann (1984:201) mentioned he had observed a few mites on bobwhites in unrecorded regions of the state (table 6.1). Purvis (1995:28–32) found a mean of 30.7 (±34.4; range = 1–135) unidentified mites per bobwhite in Colorado County. Mite intensity was not related to host age, sex, or body mass. Mites similar to *Boydaia sturni* were taken from scaled quail in Lubbock County (Clark 1958). No mites were reported from Gambel's or Montezuma quail in Texas, but *Neoschongastia americana* was recovered from Gambel's quail in Arizona (Gorsuch 1934:55–57). Because of the methods used during most ectoparasite surveys, mites probably would not have been detected even if they were present. It is reasonable to assume that mites of various species probably occur at some level in most quail populations.

Conversely, chewing lice (Mallophaga) of at least five species commonly were observed on bobwhites collected in Texas, and prevalence sometimes exceeded 80 percent. The intensity of these infestations varied considerably. For example, working in Cottle County, Wiseman (1968) found means of 4.6, 3.5, 3.2, and 1.2 *Oxylipeurus clavatus*, *Goniodes ortygis*, *Colinicola numidianus* (= *C. numidiana*, = *Lagopoecus numidianus*, = *Lipeurus aberrans*), and *Menacanthus pricei*, respectively, for 33, 40, 17, and 21 infested bobwhites. In the Post Oak Savannah, means of 15.8, 11.6, 7.0, 5.0, and 4.1 *G. ortygis*, *O. clavatus*, *Brüellia illustris*, *M. pricei*, and *C. numidianus*, respectively, were removed from 20, 24, 1, 21, and 7 individuals (Parmalee 1952b; Parmalee and Price 1953; Wiseman 1968). Purvis (1995:28–32) found a mean of 48.8 (ISD = 54.0; range = 2–256) unclassified lice per bobwhite in Colorado County; intensity was not related to host age, sex, or body mass. Working in Goliad and Refugio counties, Teel et al. (1998) found mean infestations of 4.9 (range = 1–13), 4.2 (range = 1–8), 1.8 (range =

Table 6.4.
Prevalence of Parasitic Arthropods, Nematodes, and Cestodes Found on Scaled Quail in Pecos County, Texas

Class, order, or superfamily Genus and species	Prevalence				Intensity			
	Winter	Spring	Summer	Fall	Winter	Spring	Summer	Fall
Lice								
Colinicola pallida	98.3 (59)	91.6 (55)	55.0 (33)	100 (60)	20.4	25.9	93.6	18.3
Goniodes squamatus	90.0 (54)	91.6 (55)	38.3 (23)	90.0 (54)	18.2	37.3	13.7	9.7
Oxylipeurus callipeplus	93.3 (56)	88.3 (53)	63.3 (38)	95.0 (57)	23.1	26.2	17.4	25.4
Tick								
Haemaphysalis leporispalustris	96.7 (58)	78.3 (47)	75.0 (45)	91.6 (55)	15.0	3.6	12.4	36.6
Hippoboscid fly								
Pseudolynchia canariensis	10.0 (6)	13.3 (8)	31.7 (19)	35.0 (21)	1.2	1.3	2.8	1.5
Nematode [a]								
Aulonocephalus lindquisti	100 (60)	100 (60)	100 (60)	100 (60)	153.7	130.4	117.2	198.9
Cestode [b]								
Raillietina sp.	13.3 (8)	51.7 (31)	23.3 (14)	8.3 (5)	1.8	6.0	3.3	2.0

Note: Prevalence (%; *n* positive) and intensity (mean number per infested bird) of parasitic arthropods (lice, ticks, hippoboscid flies), nematodes, and cestodes recovered from 60 scaled quail collected by season (winter = Dec.–Feb.; spring = Mar.–May; summer = June–Aug.; fall = Sep.–Nov.), Dec. 1977–Nov. 1978; data from Howard (1981:52–73).
[a] *Tetrameres americana* and *Oxyspirura mansoni* (probably *O. petrowi*) were recovered from an unrecorded proportion of hosts; *Procyrnea* sp. was identified in 2 hosts.
[b] An unidentified tapeworm was recovered from 4 quail.

1–3), and 3 for 14, 10, 6, and 1 bobwhite(s) harboring *O. clavatus, G. ortygis, M. pricei,* and *C. numidianus,* respectively. Finally, Hightower, Lehmann, and Eads (1953) examined 20 bobwhites captured in Kleberg County and found 290 *G. ortygis,* 151 *C. numidianus,* 139 *O. clavatus,* and 117 *M. pricei.* Intensities of infestations were much higher in mid-February than early January.

Emerson (1949a, 1950) described *C. pallida* (= *Lagopoecus pallidus*) and *G. squamatus* from scaled quail collected in Pecos County, Texas, and Arizona. Wallmo (1956:113) reported the mallophagans *G. squamatus, Menacanthus* sp., and *Lagopoecus* sp. (probably now *C. numidianus*) from scaled quail collected from the Trans-Pecos, Mountains and Basins (primarily Brewster County). Wiseman (1959:228) recovered *O. callipeplus* from scaled quail collected in Tom Green County. None of these authors provided data on prevalence or infestation intensity of these mallophagans.

Howard (1981:52–73), working in Pecos County, completed the only study of Mallophaga prevalence and intensity in scaled quail in the Lone Star State (table 6.4). He recovered *C. pallida* from 86.3 percent of 240 quail examined. Prevalence was lowest, and infestation intensity highest, during the summer. He also obtained *G. squamatus* from 77.5 percent of these quail. Prevalence was much lower during the summer than other seasons, whereas intensity was highest during the spring. Howard recovered *O. callipeplus* from 85.0 percent of the 240 scaled quail. Prevalence and intensity were somewhat lower during the summer than in other seasons.

Although I found no reports of chewing lice from Gambel's or Montezuma quail in Texas, these hosts undoubtedly harbor these macroparasites to some extent. For example, chewing lice were observed on Gambel's quail in Nevada (Gullion 1957), *L. gambelii* described for Gambel's quail collected in Arizona (Emerson 1949b), and *Goniodes* sp. and *Colinicola* sp. recovered from Gambel's quail in Arizona (Gorsuch 1934:55–57). Emerson (1948, 1949b, 1950) described *C. mearnsi, G. submamillatus,* and *O. montezumae* for Montezuma quail collected in Arizona.

Ticks of at least five species commonly were found on bobwhites in Texas, with prevalences sometimes reaching 100 percent and infestation intensity varying considerably (table 6.1). Parmalee (1952b) reported that 11 of 53 bobwhites collected in Brazos, Grimes, and Robertson counties harbored from 1 to 19 ticks. These included the lone star (*Amblyomma americanum*) and rabbit ticks (*Haemaphysalis leporispalustris,* = *H. leporis-palustris*), with the latter being most numerous. In Colorado County, Purvis (1995:28–32) found only a single tick on 1 bobwhite. Teel et al. (1998) found means of 10.4 *A. maculatum* larvae (range = 6–48) and 2.7 nymphs (range = 1–7) for 13 and 9 bobwhites, respectively, collected in Goliad and Refugio counties. Hooker (1909) found more than 1,000 *H. chordeilis* on 12 bobwhites collected in Victoria County, and Brennan (1945b) documented a mean of 4.7 and 87.8 *A. americanum* nymphs and larvae for 38 northern bobwhites collected in Bexar and Comal counties. Working in Kleberg County, Hightower, Lehmann, and Eads (1953) found a total of 370 *H. leporispalustris,* 4 *A. maculatum,* and 4 *A. cajennense* for 20 bobwhites examined for ectoparasites. There is anecdotal evidence, however, suggesting that ticks typically are found on bobwhites much less frequently once red imported fire ants (*Solenopsis invicta*) invade an area. For this reason, it is possible that tick prevalence and intensity may now be much lower than when most studies listed in table 6.1 were completed. Controlled experiments could be designed to evaluate this hypothesis.

Wallmo (1956:113) reported *H. leporispalustris* from scaled quail from the Trans-Pecos but provided no information regarding rates of infestation. Howard (1981:52–73) recovered *H. leporispalustris* from 85.4 percent of 240 scaled quail collected in Pecos County (table 6.4). Prevalence was highest during fall and winter, and intensity was highest in fall and lowest in spring. There are no published reports of ticks infesting Gambel's or Montezuma quail in Texas, but infestations undoubtedly occur. For Gambel's quail, *Argas persicus* and *H. leporispalustris* were recovered in Arizona (Gorsuch 1934:55–57), and *A. persicus* and larval *Ixodes* sp. were documented in Nevada (Gullion 1957).

Although some authors (table 6.1) thought ectoparasites might be detrimental to the health of individual bobwhites, none attempted to determine whether these macroparasites influenced bobwhite population dynamics. There are also vast regions of quail range in Texas where no surveys have been conducted. In sum, although we know which parasitic arthropods might be expected to occur in certain regions of Texas, we know next to nothing about whether these macroparasites influence the health of individual birds, let alone the dynamics of quail populations in the Lone Star State.

Enteric Nematodes

The roundworms typically found in the intestinal tracts of northern bobwhites in Texas depend upon where the birds were collected (see table 6.2 for the prevalence of enteric nematodes found on northern bobwhites in Texas). For example, the most prevalent nematode in the Rolling Plains, *Subulura brumpti* (72.7 percent of 121 bobwhites), was not found during studies conducted elsewhere in the state. Similarly, *Aulonocephalus lindquisti* was documented for 79.4 percent of 1,294 bobwhites collected between 1941 and 1975 in the South Texas Plains. Despite this large sample size, only two other species of enteric nematodes were recovered in this physiographic region. In contrast, although bobwhites collected in the southern Gulf Prairies and Marshes sometimes harbor *A. lindquisti*, nematodes such as *Trichostrongylus cramae* (= *T. tenuis*), which are more typical in the remainder of the southeastern United States, were more prevalent. Climatic factors can account for the helminthic endoparasite communities of prairie grouse across their range (Pence and Sell 1979; Peterson 1996). Geographic relationships among bobwhites and their parasitic helminths have yet to be thoroughly evaluated in Texas. Except for the fact that most scaled quail apparently harbor *A. lindquisti*, too little data exist to form hypotheses regarding typical patterns of nematode prevalence for other Texas quails.

Ascaridia galli (= *A. lineata*), *Heterakis gallinarum*, *Strongyloides avium*, and *T. cramae* all have direct life cycles. Most authorities maintain that the intestinal nematodes *A. galli* and *S. avium* and the cecal worm *T. cramae* are not particularly pathogenic in adult bobwhites (Davidson, Kellogg, and Doster 1982a; Freehling and Moore 1993). The primary significance of the cecal threadworm *H. gallinarum* is that it can transmit the protozoan *Histomonas meleagridis,* the etiologic agent of histomoniasis, or blackhead disease. Most early studies did not evaluate prevalence by season or parasite intensity. Demarais, Everett, and Pons (1987), however, found that *T. cramae* prevalence and intensity were higher during spring-summer than fall-winter in Refugio County. Mean annual prevalence and intensity of *T. cramae* were 25.7 percent and 19 (ISE = 6; range = 1–131). They found no relationship among host age or sex and *T. cramae* prevalence or intensity. In Colorado County, Purvis et al. (1998) found mean annual prevalence and intensity of *S. avium* and *T. cramae* to be 32.3 and 96.8 percent and 31 (ISD = 46; range = 1–162) and 27 (ISD = 41; range = 1–286) nematodes, respectively. More adult females and juvenile males than adult males and juvenile females were parasitized with *S. avium*. Adult females had higher intensities of all nematodes identified, taken collectively, than did males. Directly transmitted enteric nematodes have not been documented for scaled, Gambel's, or Montezuma quail in Texas and apparently are quite rare in these species elsewhere. Whether directly transmitted nematodes influence the health of individual bobwhites or bobwhite populations in Texas is unknown.

The life cycles of *Cheilospirura spinosa, Cyrnea* sp., *Tetrameres* sp., *Dispharynx nasuta,* and *S. brumpti* are indirect. The intermediate hosts for the gizzard nematode *C. spinosa* and the proventricular worms *Cyrnea* sp. and *Tetrameras* sp. are grasshoppers (*Melanoplus* spp.) and/or cockroaches (*Blattella germanica*) (Cram 1929, 1931, 1933). Webster and Addis (1945) recovered two male *Cyrnea* sp. from a single bobwhite in South Texas. Jackson (1969:69) did not record the intensity of *C. spinosa* or *Tetrameres* sp. infections. The proventricular nematode *D. nasuta* uses sowbugs (*Porcellio scaber*) and pillbugs (*Armadillidium vulgare*), as well as three other genera of isopods (*Chaetophiloscia, Oscelloscia, Venezillo*) as intermediate hosts (Cram 1931; Hon, Forrester, and Williams 1978; Rickard 1985). Purvis et al. (1998) found a mean of two (ISD = 1; range = 1–3) *D. nasuta* for five infected bobwhites. The cecal worm *S. brumpti* uses various grasshoppers, cockroaches, and the beetle *Alphitobius diaperinus* as intermediate hosts (Cuckler and Alicata 1944; Baruš 1970; Karunamoorthy, Chellapa, and Anandan 1994). Although Jackson (1969:69) commonly found this parasite in bobwhites collected in the Rolling Plains, he did not provide data on intensity of infection. Rollins (1980:20–31) also recovered *S. brumpti* from numerous bobwhites collected in the Rolling Plains of Oklahoma near the Texas border (prevalence and intensity not provided). The cosmopolitan gapeworm, *Syngamus trachea,* is a somewhat special case in that it can be transmitted both directly and indirectly via the earthworms *Eisenia foetidus* and *Allolobophora caliginosus* (Ruff and Norton 1997). Purvis et al. (1998) found 1 *S. trachea* in an infected bobwhite and 2 in another; Webster and Addis (1945) did not provide the number of *S. trachea* per infected host.

Howard (1981:52–73) recovered *T. americana* in high but unrecorded intensities from an unreported number of scaled quail collected in Pecos County (table 6.4). He also found 23 nematodes identified as *Procyrnea* sp. in a scaled quail and 1 in another quail collected during May. Rollins (1980:20–31) recovered *S. brumpti* for scaled quail obtained from Harmon, Tillman, and Comanche counties, Oklahoma, and Eddy County, New Mexico. These study areas were ecologically similar to nearby Texas quail habitats. No data on *S. brumpti* prevalence or intensity were provided. No indirectly transmitted nematodes have been documented for Gambel's or Montezuma quail in Texas. *Subulura strongylina,* however, was documented for scaled quail in New Mexico and Gambel's quail in both Arizona and Nevada (Gorsuch 1934:57–59; Campbell and Lee 1953:53–56; Gullion 1957). *Habronema incertum* (= *H. incerta*) was recovered from the proventriculus of Gambel's quail in Arizona (Gorsuch 1934:57–59).

Most authorities maintain that *C. spinosa, Cyrnea* sp., and *S. brumpti* precipitate few pathological changes in galliform hosts, although *Cheilospirura spinosa* can cause disease and mortality when intensities are high for extended periods (Cram 1930, 1931; Cram, Jones, and Allen 1931; Cuckler and Alicata 1944; Davidson, Kellogg, and Doster 1982a; Davidson et al. 1991; Ruff and Norton 1997). In infected galliformes, *D. nasuta* typically are found buried deep in the mucosa of the proventriculus and can lead to considerable tissue damage. In fact, many researchers have contended that *D. nasuta* is "the chief cause of 'grouse disease' in the northeastern United States" (Ruff and Norton 1997:821–22). Kellogg and Prestwood (1968) reported that *D. nasuta* sometimes causes substantial mortality in immature pen-reared bobwhites, but few cases of serious disease have been reported for free-roaming adults (Davidson, Kellogg, and Doster 1982a; Davidson et al. 1991). *Tetrameres americana* apparently causes little disease in northern bobwhites (Cram, Jones, and Allen 1931), but *T. pattersoni* is more pathogenic (Davidson, Kellogg, and Doster 1982a; Davidson et al. 1991; Ruff and Norton 1997). For this reason it would be useful to determine which species of *Tetrameres* is harbored by bobwhites in the Rolling Plains. "Gapes," or labored breathing, caused by *S. trachea* often results in bacterial pneumonia and death of young poultry of several species (Ruff and Norton 1997). The pathogenicity of these organisms for bobwhites is unclear. The population-level significance, if any, of these indirectly transmitted nematodes for Texas quails is unknown.

The life cycle of *Aulonocephalus lindquisti* has yet to be worked out but probably has an arthropod, most likely insect, as an intermediate host (table 6.2). It is surprising that so little is known about this nematode considering its prevalence in northern bobwhite populations in the South Texas Plains and how much revenue landowners in this region generate from bobwhite hunting. Bobwhites in South Texas sometimes carry considerable *A. lindquisti* burdens. Webster and Addis (1945) reported infestations as high as 315 parasites per bird, with 15–40 most common (average = 30.4) (Lehmann 1953), and Webster (1947) found a mean of 15.3 *A. lindquisti* per infested bird (range = 1–143) (Lehmann 1953). Working in Dimmit and Duval counties during 1950–55 and 1975, Lehmann (1984:207–209) found mean infestations of 51.4 and 62.4 worms per bobwhite, respectively (range = 1–353 and 1–270). He also reported means of 54.0 and 21.8 *A. lindquisti* for 52 juvenile and 8 adult bobwhites and speculated that drought led to higher *A. lindquisti* burdens. Demarais, Everett, and Pons (1987), however, found no differences in *A. lindquisti* prevalence and intensity by bobwhite age in Brooks County, and precipitation could not account for variation in monthly parasite intensity. They did find that *A. lindquisti* prevalence and intensity were much lower in Refugio than in Brooks County. Moreover, this parasite was not found any farther northeast during studies conducted in Colorado County, the Post Oak Savannah, or the Piney Woods. It was documented, however, in semi-arid regions of the Oklahoma Rolling Plains bordering Texas (Rollins 1980:20–31). The pathogenicity of *A. lindquisti* for individual bobwhites and its population-level consequences, if any, are unknown.

Both the genus *Aulonocephalus* and the species *A. lindquisti* were first described from specimens taken from a scaled quail in Uvalde County (Chandler 1935). Since then, this parasite routinely was found during surveys for helminths of scaled quail. Wallmo (1956:112) identified *A. lindquisti* from 45 of 48 (93.8 percent) scaled quail collected in the Trans-Pecos. Dancak et al. (1982) recovered *A. lindquisti* from 77 of 104 (74.0 percent) scaled quail obtained primarily in the High Plains. A mean of 40 (range = 1–263) *A. lindquisti* was found per infected host, and there was no differences in prevalence or intensity by host sex or age. Howard (1981:52–73) recovered *A. lindquisti* from all 240 scaled quail collected in Pecos County, with high intensity observed year-round. Rollins (1980:20–31) also found this parasite in scaled quail collected in Oklahoma and New Mexico study areas ecologically similar to nearby regions of Texas. *Aulonocephalus lindquisti* has not been documented for Gambel's or Montezuma quail in Texas but occurs in Gambel's quail in Nevada (Gullion 1957). Even though *A. lindquisti* is an extraordinarily common parasite of scaled quail in Texas, its pathogenicity to individual hosts and population-level significance, if any, are unknown.

Other Nematodes

Jackson (1969:69–70) found eyeworms identified as *Oxyspirura sygmoidea* under the nictitating membranes of 30 of 61 (49.2 percent) bobwhites from Cottle County (range = 0–15 worms per host). About the same proportion of hosts were infected during the next four years. Jackson (1969:70) speculated that the vision of some bobwhites might have been impaired by eyeworms, but most authorities maintain that these parasites typically cause mild if any clinical signs (e.g., Pence 1972; Ruff and Norton 1997). Identification of this eyeworm as *O. sygmoidea* is somewhat puzzling—this species previously had been described only from corvids in Austria during the nineteenth century (Addison and Anderson 1969). Further, in their revision of the genus *Oxyspirura*, Addison and Anderson considered *O. sygmoidea* as a *species inquirendae*, meaning they found *all* existing descriptions inadequate for identification. It is probable that these nematodes actually were *O. petrowi*, the eyeworm routinely recovered from other quail, ring-necked pheasants (*Phasianus colchicus*), and lesser prairie-chickens (*Tympanuchus pallidicinctus*) in Texas (Pence 1975; Pence and Sell 1979; Pence, Young, and Guthery 1980; Dancak et al. 1982; Pence et al. 1983).

Wallmo (1956:112–13) recovered *Oxyspirura* sp. from 14 of 42 (33.3 percent) scaled quail collected in Brewster County. Howard (1981:52–73) recovered 1 to 9 eyeworms identified as *O. mansoni* from an unrecorded proportion of scaled quail collected in Pecos County.

It is likely that the eyeworms recovered by Wallmo and Howard were *O. petrowi*. Pence (1975) documented *O. petrowi* for 2 of 7 scaled quail collected in Presidio County, whereas Dancak et al. (1982) recovered this parasite from only 2 of 104 (1.9 percent) scaled quail collected primarily in the High Plains. Pence also recovered *O. petrowi* from 2 of 3 Montezuma quail from Jeff Davis County.

Although the life history of *O. petrowi* has yet to be detailed, it is assumed to have an arthropod, probably insect, intermediate host (Pence 1972). The fact that *Oxyspirura* sp. was found during only one bobwhite study probably has more to do with how many researchers examined the eyes of bobwhites than the prevalence of this parasite. The same probably is true for most parasite surveys of scaled, Gambel's, and Montezuma quails in other states (however, see Campbell and Lee 1953:52–56). Definitive experiments designed to determine the significance of *O. petrowi* for individual quail or their populations have yet to be completed.

Jackson (1969:69–70) recovered encysted *Physaloptera* sp. (= *Skrjabinoptera* sp.) larvae from the breast muscles of 9 of 61 (14.8 percent) bobwhites collected in Cottle County (figure 6.1). Prevalence appeared to decrease with declining bobwhite density during the next four years. Similarly, Boggs et al. (1990) identified *Physaloptera* sp. larvae for 5 of 6 bobwhites examined in western Oklahoma. *Physaloptera* sp. was also documented for 2 of 6 scaled quail in New Mexico (Campbell and Lee 1953). Quail presumably acquire larval *Physaloptera* sp. by ingesting infected arthropods. Although it is typically assumed that these parasites are of little consequence to quails or their populations, no definitive studies have been completed.

Cestodes

Cestodes commonly were encountered during surveys for parasitic helminths of northern bobwhites in Texas, but prevalences and intensities were low (see table 6.3 for prevalence of cestodes found on northern bobwhites in Texas). Tapeworms of the genus *Raillietina* were recovered from bobwhites in all physiographic regions where helminth surveys were completed. Of the tapeworms identified, *R. cesticillus* and *R. tetragona* are cosmopolitan parasites of domestic poultry and might in some cases represent spillover from these hosts. Because the species of *Hymenolepis*, *Polycercus* (= *Paricterotaenia*), and *Davainea* were not determined, they may be unique to bobwhites or identical to parasites of domestic galliformes. *Rhabdometra odiosa,* a parasite seen in many species of game birds, was recovered from bobwhites only in southern Texas.

Because avian tapeworms use arthropod or isopod intermediate hosts, prevalence and intensity should be expected to vary by season. Further, because arthropods and isopods constitute a larger proportion of the diet in young birds, they might be expected to have higher cestode prevalence and intensity than adults. Unfortunately, most studies included in table 6.3 were not conducted in a manner that could elucidate these ecological relationships. In South Texas, however, Webster and Addis (1945) found higher *R. odiosa* prevalence during May–August (19.1 percent; 9 of 47) than December–January (2.0 percent; 4 of 205). Lehmann (1984:206–207) reported that mean tapeworm intensity for 51 infected bobwhites collected in South Texas during the 1940s and 1950s was 2.5 (range = 1–15). Lehmann (1984:208) also found that the number of *R. cesticillus, Raillietina* sp., and range of larval tapeworms was 0–160, 0–60, and 0–19, respectively, in Dimmit and Duval counties during 1975. Although Demarais, Everett, and Pons (1987) did not identify the cestodes recovered, they noted that tapeworm prevalence was highest during March–August. Purvis et al. (1998) found *Raillietina* sp. prevalence and intensity to be 52 and 39 percent, and 56 (ISD = 90; range = 1–250) and 22 (ISD = 39; range = 1–153) worms for juvenile and adult bobwhites, respectively. Juvenile males had greater numbers of *Raillietina* sp. than adult males. Although available data are limited, they tend to support the hypothesis that tapeworm prevalence and intensity are associated with insect availability and bobwhite age.

Wallmo (1953:112–13) found *R. odiosa* and/or *Raillietina* sp. in the small intestines of 11 of 48 (22.9 percent) scaled quail collected in the Trans-Pecos. Similarly, Howard (1981:52–73) recovered *Raillietina* sp. from 24.2 percent of 240 scaled quail collected in Pecos County. Prevalence and intensity were highest during the spring, as expected with a parasite requiring an insect intermediate host (table 6.4). Dancak et al. (1982) described *R. odiosa* for 12 of 104 (11.5 percent) scaled quail taken primarily in the High Plains. Cestodes have not yet been documented for Gambel's or Montezuma quail in Texas, but *R. odiosa* was recovered from Gambel's quail collected in Arizona and Nevada (Gorsuch 1934:57–59; Gullion 1957).

Davidson, Kellogg, and Doster (1982a) found that *Hymenolepis* sp. occasionally caused mild disease in bobwhites, and *R. cesticillus, R. colinia,* and *R. odiosa* sometimes led to intestinal obstruction. In domestic galliformes, including pen-reared bobwhites, *R. tetragona* causes moderate to severe disease. Although numerous authors have voiced the opinion that cestodes are of little consequence to quail populations, definitive studies designed to address this issue have yet to be conducted.

Acanthocephalans

Webster (1947) found 3 acanthocephalan parasites in the small intestines of one bobwhite and 1 in another of 300 (0.7 percent) collected in Kleberg County. Webster (1948) later identified these thorny-headed worms as *Mediorhynchus papillosus* (= *M. colini,* = *Disteganius colini*) (Schmidt and Kuntz 1977). Parmalee (1952b) also observed *Mediorhynchus* sp. in 11 of 717 (1.5 percent) bobwhites from the Post Oak Savannah; Lehmann (1984:208) found 1 *M. papillosus* for 3 and 1 *Mediorhynchus* sp. for 4 of 133 (2.7 and 3.5 percent, respectively) bobwhites collected in Dimmit and Duval counties. Demarais, Everett, and Pons (1987) reported *M. papillosus* from 1 of 109 (0.9 percent) and 1 of 203 (0.5 percent) bobwhites collected in Brooks and Refugio counties, respectively. The intermediate hosts of *M. papillosus* in the United States are unknown but probably include several species of arthropods (Amin and Dailey 1998). I found no records of acanthocephalans for scaled, Gambel's, or Montezuma quail. The significance of these parasites, if any, to bobwhites or their populations is unknown.

Trematodes

Trematodes, which use gastropods or bivalves as intermediate hosts, apparently are rather rare in Texas quails. Considering the semiarid environments inhabited by these species, this is not surprising. Craig et al. (1980), however, diagnosed schistosomiasis for two clinically ill scaled quail. They found numerous eggs containing active *Gigantobilharzia* sp. miracidia in intestinal scrapings but were unable to obtain adult schistosomes from the mesenteric blood vessels. Intermediate hosts for *Gigantobilharzia* sp. include several species of snails. These quail had been held in a captive flock near Tyler, Texas, where climatic conditions ensured that freshwater snails were much more common than in native scaled quail habitats. The prevalence and significance of schistosomes for free-roaming quails in Texas or elsewhere are unknown.

Microparasites

Only limited research has addressed the microparasites of Texas quails. This is unfortunate because some pathogenic protozoa, bacteria, viruses, and fungi have the potential to significantly influence quail population dynamics (Tompkins et al. 2002). The renewed interest in factors influencing bobwhite populations in Texas should be expanded to include microparasites. Similarly, initial surveys for key microparasites of scaled, Gambel's, and Montezuma quails in Texas are needed.

Hematozoa

Parmalee (1952b), Lehmann (1953), and Purvis (1995:32) found no hematozoa on blood films taken from 73, 75, and 46 bobwhites collected in Brazos and Robertson, Kleberg, and Colorado counties, respectively. I found no records of surveys for blood parasites of scaled, Gambel's, or Montezuma quail in Texas. As discussed in the section on parasitic arthropods, suitable vectors for hematozoa are known to occur in bobwhites and presumably the other three Texas quails.

Plasmodium spp. and *Haemoproteus* spp., etiologic agents of avian malaria, have long been recognized in free-roaming northern bobwhites from across their range. For example, *Plasmodium* sp. was reported from Maryland (Wetmore 1941), *P. relictum* (= *P. praecox*) from Georgia (Cram, Jones, and Allen 1931), *P. pedioecetii* from Colorado (Stabler, Kitzmiller, and Braun 1974; Stabler and Kitzmiller 1976), and *P. hermai* from Florida (Forrester, Nayar, and Young 1987). *Haemoproteus* sp. also was obtained from a bobwhite in Maryland (Wetmore 1941). Either *H. lophortyx* or *Plasmodium* sp. was documented for 11 of 689 (1.6 percent) adult scaled quail, and 517 of 1,207 (42.8 percent) adult Gambel's quail collected across New Mexico (Campbell and Lee 1953:22–24), including Quay County, which borders Texas. Wood and Herman (1943) found 13 of 24 (54.2 percent) Gambel's quail collected during the late 1930s near Phoenix, Arizona, positive for *H. lophortyx*. Also working in southern Arizona, Hungerford (1955) found 31 of 111 (27.9 percent) scaled quail and 830 of 881 (94.2 percent) Gambel's quail collected between 1952 and 1955 to be infected with *H. lophortyx*. In Colorado, 1 of 2 Gambel's quail were positive for *Haemoproteus* sp. and *P. pedioecetii* (Stabler, Kitzmiller, and Braun 1974; Stabler and Kitzmiller 1976). Gullion (1957) found 62 of 110 (56.4 percent) samples taken from Gambel's quail in southern Nevada positive for *H. lophortyx*. Of these samples,

60 were collected from a markedly declining population in which 95 percent were positive. These data suggest that *H. lophortyx* infection might have contributed to declining quail abundance in this population.

Because hematozoa require arthropod vectors, quail malaria tends to occur seasonally. Hematozoa possess the characteristics necessary to regulate quail populations and justifiably concern wildlife managers in areas where these organisms are sometimes prevalent. Studies designed to rigorously evaluate the population-level significance of these microparasites have yet to be completed.

Other Protozoa

Parmalee (1952b) failed to find intestinal coccidia in fecal samples taken from 36 bobwhites collected in Brazos and Robertson counties. I found no other surveys for coccidia, but these microparasites are certain to occur in Texas quails. *Eimeria* spp. have been recovered from free-living bobwhites in several states since the 1930s. These reports include *Eimeria* spp. from Florida, Georgia, Kansas, Mississippi, North Carolina, Ohio, South Carolina, and Tennessee (Cram, Jones, and Allen 1931; Ward 1945; Wickliff 1932; Venard 1933; Williams, Davidson, et al. 2000), *E. dispersa* from Ohio and Oklahoma (Wickliff 1932; Venard 1933; Sneed and Jones 1950), and *E. lettyae* from Florida and Pennsylvania (Ruff 1985). Duszynski and Gutiérrez (1981) found no evidence of *Eimeria* sp. for 12 scaled quail from Roosevelt County, New Mexico (which borders Texas), nor 20 Montezuma quail collected in Arizona. They did, however, find 3 of 15 Gambel's quail taken in southeastern New Mexico positive for low numbers of coccidia resembling *E. lophortygis*. *Cryptosporidium* sp. is an important disease of young pen-reared bobwhites (Ritter et al. 1986; Fischer 1997), but I found no records of this microparasite in free-roaming quail. Most intestinal coccidia have complex but direct life cycles. Although these coccidia theoretically have the potential to regulate quail populations, their actual significance to free-roaming quails or quail populations in Texas is unknown.

Histomoniasis (blackhead disease), caused by *Histomonas meleagridis,* has long concerned those interested in northern bobwhites. Cram, Jones, and Allen (1931) found lesions consistent with histomoniasis in bobwhites collected from northern Florida and southern Georgia but were unable to isolate *H. meleagridis*. Histomoniasis is a serious threat to pen-reared bobwhites, where morbidity and mortality, respectively, can exceed 75 and 50 percent (Davidson, Doster, and Kellogg 1982a; Davidson and Nettles 1997:294–95). Histomoniasis is much less prevalent in free-roaming bobwhites. It is likely that this difference occurs primarily for two reasons: crowding associated with captive propagation and vector availability. Captive bobwhites tend to be infected with *Heterakis gallinarum,* an excellent vector for *Histomonas meleagridis,* whereas wild bobwhites more often harbor *H. isolonche* (= *H. bonasae*)—a relatively poor vector for this microparasite (Davidson, Doster, and McGhee 1978). Because *Heterakis gallinarum* occurs in bobwhite populations in eastern Texas, histomoniasis might occur more often in this region than elsewhere in the state. The population-level significance of histomoniasis for free-roaming bobwhites or other Texas quails is not known.

Another flagellated protozoan, the directly transmitted *Trichomonas* sp., has been isolated from the ceca of pen-reared and free-roaming bobwhites in the southeastern United States (Allen 1930; Cram, Jones, and Allen 1931). This is probably the most important disease of mourning doves (*Zenaida macroura*). *Trichomonas* sp. can cause serious disease in captive situations, but its significance to free-living bobwhites, if any, is unknown.

Bacteria and Similar Organisms

Few studies have evaluated whether bobwhites in Texas have been exposed to pathogenic bacteria or related organisms. These agents are primarily transmitted directly. During a bobwhite die-off in South Texas during 1950–51, Lehmann (1984:211) reported culturing actinomycetes, a group of bacteria that in many ways resemble fungi, from the lungs of affected bobwhites. Hightower, Lehmann, and Eads (1953) failed to culture *Francisella tularensis* (= *Pasteurella tularensis*), the etiological agent of tularemia, from 66 bobwhites collected in Kleberg County. Lehmann (1953) found all 8 bobwhites from the same county serologically negative for antibodies against *F. tularensis* and *Coxiella burnetii*—the causative agent of Q fever. Purvis et al. (1998) found all bobwhite plasma samples collected in Colorado County serologically negative for specific antibodies against *Mycoplasma gallisepticum*, *M. synoviae*, *Salmonella pullorum*, *S. typhimurium* ($n = 53$), and *Chlamydophila psittaci* (= *Chlamydia psittaci*; $n = 49$). However, they found 3 of 53 (5.6 percent) individuals seropositive for *Pasteurella multocida*, the causative agent of avian cholera. An avian cholera epizootic in waterfowl had recently occurred on this study area. Bobwhites are quite susceptible to *P. multocida*. Avian cholera can cause 99 percent mortality in captive bobwhites within a six-day period (Bermudez, Munger, and Ley 1991). Moreover, Dabbert, Lochmiller, Morton, and Powell (1996) found that a strain of *P. multocida* avirulent to domestic chickens—and used as a commercial vaccine (Avichol®)—resulted in 30–75 percent mortality in bobwhites when injected intramuscularly at a dose lower than that recommended for vaccinating chickens. When the occurrence of avian cholera outbreaks across Texas is considered, a better understanding of how *P. multocida* might influence bobwhite populations is needed. I found no published reports of bacterial diseases for the scaled, Gambel's, or Montezuma quail in Texas.

Most publications discussing bacterial diseases of bobwhites address pen-reared birds (see references listed in Kellogg and Calpin [1971] and Kellogg and Doster [1972]). Ulcerative enteritis, caused by *Clostridium colinum*, is probably the most important disease of captive bobwhites (Berkhoff 1985; Davidson and Nettles 1997:293) but has not been documented in free-living individuals. Williams, Davidson, et al. (2000), in a survey similar to that of Purvis et al. (1998), found all 25 free-roaming bobwhites collected in Kansas seronegative for *M. gallisepticum*, *M. synoviae*, *S. pullorum*, *S. typhimurium*, and *P. multocida*. Gullion (1957) provided anecdotal evidence of bacterial disease for Gambel's quail in Nevada.

Texas quails probably would succumb to most galliform diseases caused by bacteria and similar organisms having broad host ranges. The influence of these agents on free-roaming quail populations, however, has yet to be explored.

Viruses

Wilson and Crawford (1988) found no lesions resembling those caused by avian poxvirus on 177 northern bobwhites examined in San Patricio County during 1976–77 (figure 6.2). In 1980–81, however, 5 of 66 (7.6 percent) bobwhites collected at this location had poxvirus-like lesions. Lesions were also found primarily on the wings of 28 of 124 (22.6 percent) bobwhites taken at various locations in Kinney, Maverick, Webb, and Zavala counties. Probably because mosquitoes are important mechanical vectors of the avian poxvirus, prevalence was greatest during late spring and early summer but did not vary by host sex or age. Leg lesions typically cause birds few problems (figure 6.2B), but lesions around the eyes and nares (figure 6.2A) or in the oral cavity can lead to emaciation and death (figure 6.2C). Lehmann (1953) and Jackson (1969:69) found no serologic evidence of exposure to the Rocky Mountain spotted fever virus or encephalitis viruses (names not provided) for 8 and 19 bobwhites, respectively, sampled in Kleberg and Cottle counties. Similarly, Purvis et al. (1998), working in Colorado County, found all bobwhites serologically negative for antibodies against the avian influenza, Newcastle, and infectious bronchitis viruses ($n = 53, 53,$ and 46, respectively). Drew et al. (1998) found no serologic evidence of reticuloendotheliosis virus (REV) exposure for 45 of these same samples. Unfortunately, because cellular material was unavailable, the more definitive polymerase chain reaction (PCR) could not be used.

Wilson and Crawford (1988) noted poxvirus-like lesions on 13 of 24 (54.1 percent) scaled quail captured in Val Verde County during 1979. Poxviruses were observed via electron microscopy for 2 of these quail. In 1980–81, poxlike lesions were noted for 36 of 105 (34.3 percent) scaled quail collected in Kinney, Maverick, Webb, and Zavala counties. As with bobwhites collected at these locations, most lesions were on the wings (42 of 49 positive birds; 85.7 percent), and prevalence was greatest during late spring and early summer but did not vary by host sex or age. I found no published reports of viral diseases for Gambel's or Montezuma quail in Texas.

As with the bacterial diseases of bobwhites, most reports of viral infections in this species addressed pen-reared birds (Kellogg and Calpin 1971; Kellogg and Doster 1972). The reports on avian poxvirus are an exception. Gallagher (1916) observed avian pox lesions on numerous wild bobwhites being translocated from undisclosed locations in Mexico to Missouri. Stoddard (1931:326–27) observed lesions on a small percentage of Georgia and South Carolina bobwhites. Davidson, Kellogg, and Doster (1980) described an epornitic (outbreak of a disease in a bird population) of avian pox in bobwhites inhabiting north-central Florida and southwestern Georgia; and Davidson, Kellogg, and Doster (1982b) documented additional cases in wild bobwhites collected in Arkansas, Florida, Georgia, Louisiana, North Carolina, South Carolina, Tennessee, and Virginia. Avian pox was also reported for 11 of 66 (16.7 percent) Gambel's quail trapped in Arizona (Blankenship, Reed, and Irby 1966). Although Mueller, Davidson, and Atkinson (1993) found that

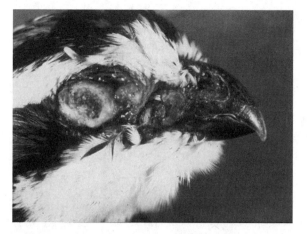

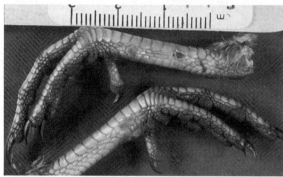

bobwhites with the wet form of pox had lower survival than birds with either dry pox or no lesions in southwestern Georgia, the significance of avian poxvirus to the population dynamics of quails is unclear, but might be significant.

Quail bronchitis, an important disease of young pen-reared bobwhites, is caused by an adenovirus (Jack and Reed 1994; Davidson and Nettles 1997:293–94). Although inclusion bodies and antibodies against this virus have been detected in free-living bobwhites in the southeastern United States (King, Pursglove, and Davidson 1981; Davidson, Kellogg, and Doster 1982a), clinical disease has not been documented in the wild. Avian adenoviruses also cause inclusion body ventriculitis and hepatitis in captive bobwhites and Gambel's quail (Goodwin 1993; Bradley et al. 1994). Williams, Davidson, et al. (2000) found all 25 bobwhites they collected in Kansas seronegative for avian adenoviruses.

Reisen et al. (2000) found 27 and 6 of 1,471 (1.8 and 0.4 percent) Gambel's quail sampled from the Coachella Valley of southeastern California seropositive for specific antibodies against the western equine encephalomyelitis (WEE) and St. Louis encephalitis (SLE) viruses, respectively, during 1996–98. Mean seroprevalence of SLE-specific antibody in Gambel's quail increased at this location to 2.4 percent, then 7.4 percent in 2000 and 2001 (9 of 373 and 22 of 297, respectively) (Reisen et al. 2002). WEE, SLE, and other viral encephalitides are important zoonotic diseases. Most researchers contend that native quails do not develop clinical illness when exposed to these mosquito-borne viruses.

Northern bobwhites developed viremia when experimentally challenged with West Nile virus (Komar et al. 2003). No deaths were noted,

Figure 6.2.
Northern bobwhites with (counterclockwise from top left) proliferative lesions associated with avian pox around the eye and bill, avian pox lesions on the legs, and emaciation caused by avian pox lesions on the eyes and nares (compare with normal bobwhite on left).
Photos from the Southeastern Cooperative Wildlife Disease Study

few individuals shed the virus, and the virus was not transmitted to cage mates. The proportion of Texas quails typically exposed to West Nile virus is not yet available. Similarly, too little is known about West Nile virus in quails to speculate about whether or how this virus might influence quail populations.

It is reasonable to assume that viruses known to cause disease in a broad array of galliformes, such as Newcastle disease, avian influenza, and REV, would be pathogenic to Texas quails as well. The population-level significance of these or other viruses for Texas quails is unknown.

Fungi and Mycotoxins

Fungal diseases rarely have been documented for northern bobwhites in Texas (Lehmann 1984:211), but there is no reason to assume they do not occur there at rates similar to those seen in ecologically similar areas elsewhere in the United States. *Aspergillus fumigatus* and *Candida albicans* are ubiquitous in the southeastern United States and sometimes cause primary disease in wild bobwhites (Davidson, Kellogg, and Doster 1982a). Fowl favus ("ringworm"), caused by the ubiquitous *Trichophyton gallinae* (= *Achorion gallinae*), has been reported in Gambel's quail in Nevada (Gullion 1957). Although pulmonary aspergillosis, for example, undoubtedly is a serious disease, the importance of fungal infections to Texas quails or their populations has not been evaluated.

Recently, mycotoxins, toxic metabolites produced by various species of fungi, have peaked the interest of quail biologists working in Texas. Because feeding and baiting many wild species are not only legal but common in Texas, quail biologists and hunters have become increasingly concerned that bobwhites could be exposed to dangerous levels of mycotoxins in contaminated grains used as feed or bait. So far, most efforts have addressed aflatoxins, a group of highly toxic, carcinogenic mycotoxins produced by *Aspergillus flavus, A. parasiticus,* and *Penicilium puberulum* (Hoerr 1997:958–62). Oberheu and Dabbert (2001b) found that aflatoxin levels increased from presample to one month after filling feeders in Wheeler County, Texas, and Roger Mills County, Oklahoma. They found no pattern in aflatoxin concentration in feeders among months or between years, but concentrations were related to the highly variable relative humidity on their study areas. Similar results were found for ochratoxin A (Oberheu and Dabbert 2001c), a nephrotoxic mycotoxin produced by *A. ochraceous* and *P. viridicatum* (Hoerr 1997:962–64). Oberheu and Dabbert (2001a) also determined that bobwhites on these same study areas obtained higher concentrations of aflatoxin in native ($n = 11$) as compared to supplemental ($n = 21$) or mixed ($n = 18$) foods. In all three cases, however, aflatoxin levels were extraordinarily low. Ochratoxin A concentrations were below levels shown to be dangerous to game birds in the laboratory (Oberheu and Dabbert 2001c). Some individuals have argued that bobwhites can detect and avoid grains high in aflatoxins, thus rendering aflatoxin levels irrelevant. Using a cafeteria trial, Perez, Henke, and Fedynich (2001) tested this hypothesis and found that bobwhites did not avoid aflatoxin-contaminated feed. Because of the widespread feeding and baiting occurring in Texas quail range, much better data are needed regarding the effects of low levels (less than 200 parts per billion) of aflatoxin and other dangerous mycotoxins on northern bobwhite reproduction, growth, and chick survival. If these levels are shown to be detrimental, the Texas Parks and Wildlife Commission might need to revisit the issue of baiting and feeding quails and other wildlife.

Do Parasites Matter?

In recent years, it again has become popular to assume that predators markedly influence the dynamics of northern bobwhite and scaled quail populations. If it is reasonable to think that predators influence quail populations in Texas, it is at least as reasonable to assume that macro- and microparasites also have this potential. Unfortunately, few researchers have addressed deductively derived hypotheses related to the parasites of Texas quails, and no one has attempted to determine whether any of the macro- or microparasites discussed previously regulate or otherwise influence quail population dynamics in Texas. In essence, although certain classes of bobwhite parasites have been cataloged for some areas of Texas, we know almost nothing about whether these agents are important to bobwhite populations. Much less has been learned regarding the parasites of scaled quail in Texas, and next to nothing is known about the parasites of Gambel's and Montezuma quails in the Lone Star State. This glaring intellectual void extends well beyond the borders of Texas, and as Robel (1993) and Brennan (2002b) maintained, should embarrass those considering themselves quail experts.

This call for experimental studies designed to determine the population-level significance of the macro- and microparasites of Texas quails should not be construed as a prohibition of further cataloging of the infectious agents associated with these species. This review also demonstrated how few comprehensive surveys of bobwhite parasites have been conducted in Texas and that even the most basic information is unavailable for the scaled, Gambel's, and Montezuma quails. Rather, we should welcome additional parasite surveys of the sort typically published in the *Journal of Wildlife Diseases, Avian Diseases,* or *The Journal of Parasitology,* but must recognize that those interested in quail conservation desperately need ecologically based studies that address the potential significance of infectious agents to quail populations.

Evaluating Potential Influences on Populations

How does one approach determining whether a parasite regulates or otherwise influences populations of Texas quails? As I have argued elsewhere (Peterson et al. 1998), research addressing *T. tenuis* and red grouse populations in northern England and Scotland offers a useful point of departure for such endeavors. For example, it was determined long ago that *T. tenuis* could cause cecal lesions and inflammation in free-roaming red grouse (Shipley 1911; Wilson and Leslie 1911; Watson, Lee, and Hudson 1987). High *T. tenuis* intensities then were shown to be associated with reduced host fecundity and survival of wild red grouse (Wilson and Leslie 1911; Potts, Tapper, and Hudson 1984; Hudson 1986; Hudson, Newborn, and Dobson 1992). Experimental reductions in parasite intensities in free-living red grouse demonstrated that increased *T. tenuis* intensities were associated with decreased body weight, adult survival, clutch size, egg hatchability, nesting success, and brood-rearing success in red grouse (Hudson 1986; Shaw 1990; Hudson, Dobson, and Newborn 1992; Hudson, Newborn, and Dobson 1992), including rendering laying and incubating hens and their nests far more vulnerable to predation (Hudson, Newborn, and Dobson 1992). This research theme then led to a definitive experimental field study (Hudson, Dobson, and Newborn 1998). Using data collected earlier (Potts, Tapper, and Hudson 1984; Hudson, Dobson, and Newborn 1985; Hudson 1992), Hudson, Dobson, and Newborn (1998) documented cyclic fluctuations in red grouse abundance during a period of four to eight years for 77 percent of 175 grouse moors evaluated. They used long-term data from 6 of these moorlands to predict the next two crashes in grouse numbers at these sites. Red grouse in four of the six populations were captured and treated with an oral anthelmintic prior to the first predicted crash, grouse at 2 of these 4 sites were treated again before the second predicted crash, and the remaining two populations were used as untreated controls throughout. With this replicated field experiment, Hudson, Dobson, and Newborn (1998) demonstrated that anthelmintic application markedly reduced the tendency of all six treated populations to cycle, as compared to the control moors, thus unambiguously demonstrating that *T. tenuis* was the driving force behind cycles in these populations. The mechanism accounting for this observation was identified earlier, via modeling and empirical data, as primarily a density-dependent reduction in host fecundity (Dobson and Hudson 1992).

Moss, Watson, and Parr (1996) also were able to prevent a population cycle on a study area in Scotland by removing territorial cocks from the population. They maintained that in this case, changes in food availability, nitrogen metabolism, and *T. tenuis* intensity could not explain their results. This study illustrates another strength of the *T. tenuis*–red grouse model—one should not necessarily expect *T. tenuis* to regulate red grouse numbers everywhere within the range of this host and under all conditions. For this same reason, we would not know whether *T. tenuis* regulated populations of the conspecific willow ptarmigan (*L. lagopus*) in North America without further research. In sum, one should expect climatic, edaphic, and vegetative factors to be involved not only with where specific parasitic helminths occur but also with how hosts and parasites interact.

Although it is not particularly difficult to determine whether parasites reduce fecundity and survival of wild hosts, it is a different matter entirely to demonstrate that a parasite regulates host populations. In addition to the example cited concerning *T. tenuis* and red grouse, Tompkins and Begon (1999) and Tompkins et al. (2002:50–53) outlined useful criteria for this purpose. At any rate, correlative studies relating quail nesting success or juvenile/adult ratios to parasite burdens are insufficient to demonstrate population-level influences of a parasite, even if they occur, let alone rule them out if they do not. It seems certain that integrative research approaches combining laboratory studies, retrospective analyses of field data, and field experiments will be necessary to determine whether a specific parasite regulates populations of Texas quails and to describe the mechanisms accounting for such relationships (Peterson 1991b, 1996; Peterson et al. 1998; Peterson, Ferro, et al. 2002).

Research Needs

There are two major areas in which further research is needed on the infectious agents of Texas quails. The first deals with surveys. Studies designed to document the macroparasites of Gambel's and Montezuma quails in Texas have yet to be completed. Similarly, macroparasite surveys have not been conducted in some physiographic regions where bobwhites and scaled quail are important game species. Probably more important, little effort has been expended to determine which microparasites occur for any of the four species of quails across Texas. Second, researchers must begin to determine whether specific macro- and microparasites influence populations of Texas quails. A logical place to begin this task is with the infectious agents delineated earlier in this chapter as worthy of further research. One should be aware, however, that systematic survey efforts might suggest other candidate species.

Before delineating specific infectious agents where further research might be most fruitful, two fundamental, but often overlooked issues must be addressed. First, although high parasite-induced mortality might be necessary to quickly extirpate a small, isolated quail population, obvious disease outbreaks are not required for a parasite to regulate its host population (Tompkins et al. 2002). Thus, a macroparasite that appears innocuous still could profoundly influence quail population dynamics under certain conditions. Second, as discussed earlier, not all the parasitic helminths listed in tables 6.2 and 6.3, for example, should be expected in all bobwhite populations in Texas. Thus, a specific nematode might regulate bobwhite populations in one physiographic region, yet not even occur in another. For this reason, one must be cautious regarding generalizations.

Macroparasites

Although most macroparasites found in Texas quails have the potential to regulate populations (Tompkins et al. 2002), at least four species require further consideration. As discussed previously, *A. lindquisti* is extraordinarily prevalent in South Texas bobwhite populations and is the dominant macroparasite of scaled quail. The life cycle, pathological effects, and population-level relevance of this parasite are unknown. These deficiencies should be remedied. Although *H. gallinarum* is not particularly pathogenic in quails, because of the potential importance of blackhead disease, better data on the distribution of this vector in Texas are needed. Similarly, because of the pathogenicity of *T. pattersoni* versus *T. americana*, we should determine the species of *Tetrameras* occurring in bobwhites in the Rolling Plains. Because *D. nasuta* causes significant disease in bobwhite chicks, it has the potential to regulate quail populations. This parasite was implicated in the demise of the heath hen (*T. cupido cupido*) (Gross 1928:526–27) and caused significant disease and mortality in young ruffed grouse (*Bonasa umbellus*) (Gross 1925, 1931; Levine and Goble 1947; Ruff and Norton 1997). It also was an important cause of mortality in blue grouse (*Dendragapus obscurus*) chicks and appeared to regulate a blue grouse population on Vancouver Island, Canada (Bendell 1955). The distribution of *D. nasuta* in Texas quail populations and the population-level significance of this parasite require further clarification.

Currently, there are insufficient data to develop informed judgments regarding many other macroparasites of Texas quails. Ecologically grounded surveys as well as laboratory and field experiments will be needed to clarify which macroparasites influence the dynamics of Texas quail populations.

Microparasites

Endemic microparasitic diseases that reduce fecundity or recruitment of young into the breeding population in a density-dependent fashion could regulate quail populations (Tompkins et al. 2002). Coccidia such as *Eimeria* spp. typically cause decreased growth rates and significant mortality in young birds (Ruff and Wilkins 1987; Friend and Franson 1999), thus potentially limiting recruitment. Agents causing avian malaria (e.g., *Plasmodium* spp., *Haemoproteus* spp.) also could regulate quail populations because they can cause severe anemia, weight loss, and mortality, particularly in chicks (Atkinson 1999). Another microparasite that might regulate quail populations is REV. This retrovirus causes immunosuppression and an overall disease syndrome in captive greater and Attwater's prairie-chickens (*T. c. pinnatus, T. c. attwateri*) (Drew et al. 1998) that is not unlike that induced by the human immunodeficiency virus (HIV), also a retrovirus. The HIV has caused negative human population growth in vast regions of the world (Hudson et al. 2002) and might regulate these populations. The REV is known to occur in free-roaming Attwater's prairie-chickens and Rio Grande wild turkeys (*Meleagris gallopavo intermedia*) sympatric with Texas quails (Drew et al. 1998; Peterson, Aguirre, et al. 2002). Future surveys for microparasites of Texas quails should employ a PCR to search REV proviral DNA. Finally, avian poxvirus might also play a regulatory role. Mosquitoes probably introduce the poxvirus to naïve bobwhite populations (Davidson, Kellogg, and Doster 1982). Once quail become infected, however, the virus can also be transmitted by inhalation of infected dander, ingestion of scabs containing poxvirus, and contact with abraded skin or mucous membranes (Davidson, Kellogg, and Doster 1982; Tripathy and Reed 1997). This density-dependent transmission probably explains the high morbidity and mortality sometimes seen in captive propagation facilities. Further research is needed to determine how transmission varies with host density in the wild. By delineating these microparasites as possible regulatory candidates, I am not ruling out other agents.

Unlike the situation with waterfowl (Friend, McLean, and Dein 2001), there is little evidence of large-scale epizootics characterized by high mortality that are limited to wild quails. Although it would be foolish to assume that such epizootics could never happen, if a disease outbreak did occur, it seems likely that it would involve primarily other wild or domestic avian species and would simply spill over into quail populations. There are many microparasites of quails that sometimes occur epizootically, cause significant mortality, and could possibly extirpate small, isolated quail populations. As detailed earlier, *H. meleagridis* could lead to substantial morbidity and mortality (70 and 50 percent, respectively) in pen-reared bobwhites, particularly if effective vectors are available (Davidson, Kellogg, and Doster 1982a; Davidson and Nettles 1997:294–95). Histomoniasis was the second most common infectious disease of free-roaming wild turkeys observed during a 12-year period in the southeastern United States (Davidson et al. 1985), with mortality greater than 75 percent of infected birds common (Davidson and Nettles 1997). Although bobwhites are somewhat less susceptible to histomoniasis than wild turkeys are, mortality approaching even 50 percent during an epizootic could have profound effects on quail populations. Moreover, *H. meleagridis* and *H. gallinarum* probably have been associated with ring-necked pheasants since the late Cenozoic (Lund and Chute 1974). Because ring-necked pheasants serve as nearly ideal hosts for these parasites (Lund and Chute 1972), wildlife managers might question the wisdom of perpetuating this species in areas where bobwhite populations are a priority.

Avian cholera is another potential threat to quail populations in areas where epizootics commonly occur in waterfowl or other species. There are areas in the Texas Panhandle and coastal prairies where avian cholera epizootics frequently occur. For example, those managing the Attwater Prairie Chicken National Wildlife Refuge in Colorado County take the threat of interspecific transmission of *P. multocida* seriously; they routinely collect and incinerate carcasses of waterfowl that have succumbed to avian cholera to prevent this disease in Attwater's prairie-chickens (Peterson et al. 1998). As discussed previously, bobwhites at this refuge also have been exposed to *P. multocida* (Purvis et al. 1998).

There are insufficient data to develop informed judgments regarding many other microparasitic diseases of galliformes that occur epizootically. For example, although avian influenza, Newcastle disease, and salmonellosis have not been reported in Texas quails, there is no reason to assume that these agents would not cause significant mortality if epizootics occurred. There is also no clearly discernible line between parasites that regulate and those that might extirpate tenuous host populations. By way of illustration, although I discussed coccidia under population regulation, *Eimeria* sp. killed approximately 400 juvenile greater sage-grouse (*Centrocercus urophasianus*) in Wyoming out of a total population of about 2,000 (Simon 1940). Likewise, coccidiosis in quail not only might be regulatory but also could threaten small, isolated populations.

Mycotoxins

Although mycotoxins are not parasites, the potential for disease caused by these biotoxins requires further investigation. Mycotoxins can lead to immunosuppression and decreased reproductive success, growth, and survival of bobwhites (Hoerr 1997). Even though regulations are in place limiting aflatoxin levels in wildlife feed sold in Texas, as long as feeding and baiting remain legal in areas inhabited by quails, these agencies will find it difficult to control aflatoxin levels in wildlife feeds after these products leave retailers' shelves. Laboratory experiments designed to determine mycotoxin LD-50s for Texas quails would be useful. Data on the effects of low levels (less than 200 ppb) of aflatoxins and other dangerous mycotoxins on Texas quail reproduction, growth, and chick survival are probably even more important. Quist et al. (2000) found that eastern wild turkey (*M. g. silvestris*) poults fed even low levels of aflatoxin had markedly decreased food consumption and weight gains when compared with control poults. Because body size (time to flight) is the primary factor influencing predation rates of ground-nesting galliformes after hatching, decreased growth induced by mycotoxins could substantively reduce recruitment. Even though wild turkeys might be more susceptible to aflatoxins than bobwhites are (Hoerr 1997), experimental studies are still needed to determine how low levels of mycotoxins influence Texas quails. If these levels are found detrimental, the Texas Parks and Wildlife Commission could address the problem.

Implications

Natural resource policy makers must become aware that macro- and microparasites of wildlife are not something they can safely ignore. For example, administrators of several North American wildlife agencies recently came face-to-face with the ecological and political morass associated with chronic wasting disease in free-living cervids (Williams et al. 2002). I expect that only a few years ago most would never have guessed that a controversy of this magnitude caused by an infectious agent was even a remote possibility. There is no reason to believe that avian species, including quails occurring in Texas, are exempt from such ecological and political conundrums. When one considers long-term trends in the abundance for Texas quails, it seems obvious that infectious agents having the potential to regulate host abundance or extirpate small, isolated populations should be taken into consideration during the formation and implementation of wildlife management plans.

This task will not be easily accomplished. Wildlife scientists are not accustomed to addressing host-parasite interactions in the systematic way they do other interspecific relationships, such as predator-prey interactions (Peterson 1991a). Probably for this reason, North American wildlife scientists rarely have designed, let alone conducted, studies that directly tested hypotheses pertinent to those formulating and implementing wildlife disease management policy (Peterson 1991b). More typically, wildlife disease researchers have evaluated wild species as potential reservoirs for diseases of humans or domestic animals, as elements of host lists for parasite taxa of interest to systematists, as limiting factors for captive production, or for other reasons. This situation must be rectified. Wildlife administrators could go a long way toward this goal by funding research designed to clarify the influence of specific parasites on quail populations. If requests for research proposals of this type were produced, researchers with the requisite expertise in ecological approaches to host-parasite interactions would answer the call. Similarly, parasitologists and other wildlife disease researchers might consider integrating studies that address how macro- or microparasites influence *populations* of Texas quails with their more customary investigations of parasite systematics, pathogenesis, vaccine development, or diagnostic and monitoring techniques. In the end, integrative research approaches using expertise from multiple academic disciplines will be needed if answers to questions about the importance of parasites to populations of Texas quails are to be found.

Section II
Quail Populations
in the Ecoregions
of Texas:
Management
Opportunities
and Research
Challenges

Quails on the Rolling Plains

Dale Rollins

While South Texas may raise more quail year in and year out,
there is no better place to *hunt* quail than in the Rolling Plains.
A. V. Jones, Albany, Texas

The Rolling Plains have historically provided some of the best opportunities to hunt northern bobwhite (*Colinus virginianus*) populations
anywhere. Historically, scaled quail (*Callipepla squamata*) have been
common to abundant over much of the Rolling Plains, but the populations decreased dramatically in the late 1980s and have been slow to
reclaim their historic range.

Rainfall and rangeland management for livestock are the primary
factors that affect quail habitat in the Rolling Plains. Range management practices (e.g., brush management, grazing management) can be
prescribed to benefit quail habitat, but a large part of potential quail
range in the Rolling Plains suffers from overgrazing and excessive brush
control. Farm Bill policies have had a major impact on dryland agriculture in this region, but the impacts of these policies on bobwhites are
mostly undocumented. Income generated from quail hunting in this region currently rivals or exceeds income generated from grazing leases.
Accordingly, more landowners are beginning to temper traditional
land management goals and incorporate more quail-friendly practices,
such as brush sculpting and reducing the stocking rates. Educational
efforts aimed at landowners should strive to implement existing knowledge and develop informed decision makers. The current demand for
quail hunting provides an excellent opportunity to promote—and subsequently adopt—management practices that will sustain the heritage
of quail hunting in this region for the future. The purpose of this chapter is to provide a description of the Rolling Plains ecological region in
the context of quail management.

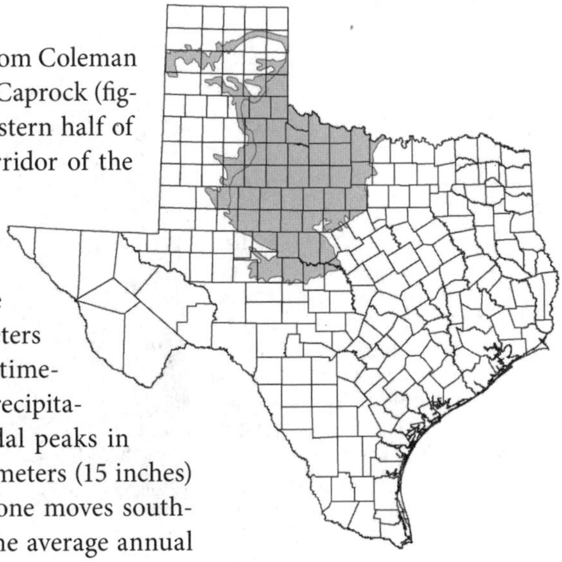

Description of the Rolling Plains

The Rolling Plains at the southeastern point stretch from Coleman
County, north to the Red River, and then west to the Caprock (figure 7.1; Gould 1975b; Bailey 1995). It includes the eastern half of
the Texas Panhandle and western Oklahoma. A corridor of the
Rolling Plains bisects the Panhandle along the Canadian River basin. This ecoregion grades into the
Cross Timbers on the east, the Edwards Plateau on
the south, and the High Plains on the west. Average
annual precipitation varies from about 40 centimeters
(16 inches) along the westward edge to about 75 centimeters (30 inches) along the eastern periphery. Most precipitation occurs during spring and summer, with bimodal peaks in
May and September. Snowfall ranges about 40 centimeters (15 inches)
annually in northwestern portions and declines as one moves south-
eastward. Summers are hot and winters are mild. The average annual

Figure 7.1.
The Rolling Plains ecoregion of Texas.
Courtesy Caesar Kleberg Wildlife
Research Institute (CKWRI) GIS
Laboratory

frost-free growing season ranges from 190 to 230 days. Elevation ranges from about 450 to 900 meters (1,500 to 3,000 feet).

Soils

The major soils are Ustolls, Ustalfs, and Ochrepts. The nearly level to gently sloping, well-drained, and moderately well-drained, deep Argiustolls (Abilene, Carey, and St. Paul series), Paleustolls (Hollister, Rotan, Sagerton, and Tillman series), and Natrustolls (Foard series) are on uplands (Soil Survey Staff 1981). The Ustalfs mainly are deep and sandy or loamy and have a loamy subsoil. The nearly level to undulating or rolling, well-drained, deep Haplustalfs (Devol and Grandfield series) and Paleustalfs (Miles, Springer, Wichita, Winters, and Nobscot series) are on uplands. The gently sloping to moderately steep Ustochrepts (Dill, Enterprise, Hardeman, Obaro, Quinlan, Vernon, and Woodward series) are on uplands.

Land Uses

Rangelands compose about 65 percent of the Rolling Plains; and croplands, about 30 percent. The major land uses are ranching (beef cattle) and farming (mostly dryland wheat and cotton). Vegetation within this region varies from moderately dense to sparse, grading from short grasses in the west to relatively taller grasses in the eastern sections. The landscape of the Rolling Plains has changed greatly over the last century. Mesquite (*Prosopis glandulosa*) savannas have become increasingly dense because of the lack of prescribed fire and regrowth from chemical and mechanical brush-control methods. In general mesquite, junipers (mostly *Juniperus pinchotii*), and prickly pear (*Opuntia* spp.) have become increasingly common and are often the focus of control efforts by ranchers.

Mesquite-dominated grasslands are the characteristic vegetation throughout the region. Other codominant woody species include lotebush (*Ziziphus obtusifolia*), prickly pear, and redberry juniper, especially along drainages and areas with more topographic relief. Other important woody plants for quails that occur in the region include

Figure 7.2. Rolling topography, low brush, cooler temperatures, and abundant quail make the Rolling Plains a popular destination for Texas quail hunters. This site in Fisher County contains a desirable diversity of woody plants, including mesquite, catclaw mimosa, littleleaf sumac, lotebush, and prickly pear. Photo by Dale Rollins

netleaf hackberry (*Celtis reticulatus*), sand shinnery oak (*Quercus havardii*), sandplum (*Prunus angustifolia*), chittam (*Bumelia lanuginosa*), sumacs (notably *Rhus aromatica* and *R. microphylla*), catclaw (*Acacia* sp., *Mimosa biunciferae*), sandsage (*Artemisia filifolia*), and wolfberry (*Lycium berlandieri*) (figure 7.2).

Grassland communities have shifted more toward mid- and short-grass species, including a greater proportion of increasers, such as silver bluestem (*Bothriochloa saccharoides*), and invaders, such as threeawns (*Aristida* spp.). Grasses are most often short (e.g., buffalograss [*Buchloe dactyloides*]) or midstature (e.g., sideoats grama [*Bouteloua curtipendula*]), especially on finer-textured soils. Taller grasses, such as sand bluestem (*Andropogon gerardii* var. *paucipilus*), are often found on sandy soils or on subirrigated sites, especially along the eastern half of the Panhandle. Taller bunchgrasses, such as little bluestem, are often restricted to areas where good grazing management has been practiced.

Range management for steers, deer, cattle or quails boils down to two essential items: knowing plants and knowing how to manipulate them. Competent wildlife managers should know which plants are important for their key species of interest (in this case, quails). They also need to know which management practices, such as disking or burning, foster a specific suite of plants. Plants important to bobwhite and scaled quail in this region are listed in table 7.1. Management practices recommended for promoting these plants are the same as the methods championed by Leopold (1933): ax, plow, cow, and fire. Modifications of these practices in the context for quail management in the Rolling Plains are discussed later.

Foundations to Build Upon

Despite its popularity—and hence importance—as a quail area, the Rolling Plains has not received the level of research attention that has been focused on South Texas. Accordingly, South Texas biologists have extensive information and experience regarding quail management (Lehmann 1984; Guthery 1986; Hernández, Guthery, and Kuvlesky 2002), but few management treatises exist for the Rolling Plains. The most intensive effort was published as *A Handbook for Bobwhite Quail Management in the West Texas Rolling Plains* (Jackson 1969), commonly referred to as "Bulletin 48." This handy reference is out of print but is available online at the TeamQuail Web site (http://teamquail.tamu.edu).

Jackson, a long-time biologist for Texas Parks and Wildlife Department (TPWD), was a naturalist who was especially fond of bobwhites. His contributions to our understanding of bobwhite natural history in this region are notable (Jackson 1947, 1952, 1962). Bulletin 48 was his magnum opus. In it, Jackson identified several key principles for quail managers in this region: (1) bobwhite habitat falls into one of three main types: bottomlands, which he considered key survival habitats; cropland/rangeland ecotones; and rangelands; (2) plant succession is a powerful tool for manipulating plant communities favorable for bobwhite food and cover situations; and (3) the variability of quail populations can be tied to cover situations that fluctuate with weather patterns.

The TPWD has Wildlife Management Areas (WMAs) located in

Table 7.1.
Plants Important to Bobwhites and Scaled Quail on the Rolling Plains of Texas

Common name	Scientific name	Importance to Quails			
		Food	Nesting	Loafing	Escape
Woody plants					
Algarita	*Mahonia trifoliolata*	X			X
Catclaw acacia	*Acacia* sp.	X		X	X
Catclaw mimosa	*Mimosa biunciferae*	X		X	X
Chittam	*Bumelia lanuginosa*	X		X	X
Elbowbush	*Forestiera pubescens*				X
Hackberry	*Celtis reticulata*	X		X	
Littleleaf sumac	*Rhus microphylla*			X	X
Lotebush	*Ziziphus obtusifolia*	X			
Mesquite	*Prosopis glandulosa*	X		X	X
Pricklyash	*Xanthoxylum hirsutum*	X		X	X
Redberry juniper	*Juniperus pinchotii*				X
Sand sagebrush	*Artemisia filifolia*	X	X		X
Sandplum	*Prunus angustifolia*			X	X
Shinoak	*Quercus havardii*	X		X	X
Skunkbush	*Rhus aromatica*	X		X	X
Whitebrush	*Aloysia gratissima*			X	X
Wolfberry	*Lycium berlandieri*	X			X
Succulents					
Cholla	*Opuntia imbricata*			X	X
Prickly pear	*O.* spp.	X	X	X	X
Tasajillo	*O. leptocaulis*	X			
Grasses					
Fringed signalgrass	*Brachiaria ciliatissima*	X			
Johnsongrass	*Sorghum halepense*	X			X
Little bluestem	*Schizachyrium scoparium*		X		X
Panicgrass	*Panicum* spp.	X			
Paspalums	*Paspalum* spp.	X			
Plains bristlegrass	*Setaria macrostachya*	X			
Rescuegrass	*Bromus* spp.	X[a]			
Silver bluestem	*Bothriochloa saccharoides*		X		X
Threeawn	*Aristida* spp.		X		
Tobosa	*Hilaria mutica*		X		X
Forbs					
Basketflower	*Centaurea americana*	X			
Broomweed	*Xanthocephalum dracunculoides*	X			X
Buffalobur	*Solanum rostratum*	X			
Cowpen daisy	*Verbesina encelioides*	X			
Curlycup gumweed	*Grindelia squarrosa*	X			
Dayflower	*Commelina erecta*	X			
Dotted gayfeather	*Liatris squarrosa*	X			
Doveweed	*Croton* spp.	X			
Filaree	*Erodium* spp.	X[a]			
Fireweed	*Kochia scoparium*	X[b]			
Illinois bundleflower	*Desmanthus illinoensis*	X			
Milkvetch	*Astragalus* spp.	X			
Pigweed	*Amaranthus* spp.	X			
Pricklypoppy	*Argemone* spp.	X			
Russian thistle	*Salsola iberica*	X			
Sandlily	*Mentzelia* spp.	X			
Sawleaf daisy	*Prionopsis ciliata*	X			
Snow-on-the-mountain	*Euphorbia marginata*	X			
Spurge	*Euphorbia* spp.	X			
Sunflower	*Helianthus* spp.	X			
Texas bullnettle	*Cnidoscolus texanus*	X			
Western ragweed	*Ambrosia cumanensis*	X			
Wildbean	*Strophostyles* spp.	X			
Crops					
Cotton		X[b]			
Peas		X			
Sorghum		X			
Wheat		X			

Note: Plant names follow Gould (1972).
[a] Primarily for greens.
[b] Primarily for its production of insects.

Cottle County (Matador WMA) and Hemphill County (Gene Howe WMA). However, few studies on quails have been conducted on these areas to date. The Packsaddle WMA, operated by the Oklahoma Department of Wildlife Conservation, is located just across the Oklahoma line east of Wheeler County and enjoyed a surge of quail research in the

1990s. The Packsaddle WMA studies (Townsend et al. 1999; Townsend et al. 2001; DeMaso et al. 2002) resulted in the following conclusions:

1. Quail feeders did not increase bobwhite density but may increase quail survival during severe winters.
2. Avian predation was the highest cause of quail mortality (40 percent), followed by mammalian predation (26 percent) and hunting (15 percent).
3. Avian predation was slightly higher on the portion of the study area that contained feeders.
4. No mortality over the five-year study was determined to be the direct result of disease.
5. About 25 percent of nests were incubated by males.
6. One-fourth of female bobwhites attempted second nests.
7. Chick survival from hatching to 39 days averaged 37 percent.
8. Almost 20 percent of bobwhite broods ended up with more chicks than were hatched from the nest.

Population Trends

Trend lines of bobwhite and scaled quail abundance as estimated by the Breeding Bird Survey (BBS) indicate a decline, especially since 1980 (Sauer, Hines, and Fallon 2002; figure 7.3). Bobwhite declines have been less drastic in the Rolling Plains (identified as Rolling Red Plains by BBS) than in the South Texas Plains (referred to as South Texas Brushlands in BBS). However, bobwhite and scaled quail trends in these areas can be difficult to assess in the short term (e.g., over a 10-year period), as both species exhibit irruptive population growth (Jackson 1962).

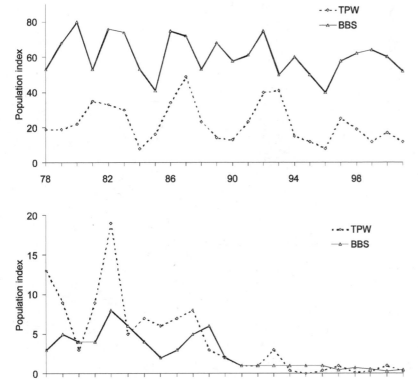

Figure 7.3.
Population trends of bobwhite (top) and scaled quail (bottom) in the Rolling Plains of Texas, 1978–2000, based on TPWD roadside counts and BBS data. The Rolling Plains region is referred to as the Rolling Red Plains by the BBS and includes data from Oklahoma and Texas.

Across the state, bobwhite abundance in Texas declined an average of 5.6 percent annually from 1980 to 2002, but there was a smaller decline of 3.5 percent in the Rolling Plains. Roadside count data from TPWD generally support the BBS trends. Scaled quail abundance statewide was basically stable (1.4 percent increase annually) during the same time period. However, scaled quail declined 9.2 percent annually in the Rolling Plains from 1980 to 2000 according to BBS. Scaled quail abundance in this region declined rapidly after 1988 for unknown reasons (Rollins 2000).

Although the data are not standardized by hunter effort, harvest data from TPWD seem to support the declining trends from the roadside count and the BBS data. Annual bobwhite harvest for the Rolling Plains from 1981 to 2001 ranged from a high of 688,167 birds in 1982 to a low of 87,570 in 1996 (table 7.2). Scaled quail harvests during the same period ranged from a high of 110,287 in 1982 to a low of only 5,557 birds in 1995.

The Texas Quail Index (TQI) was initiated in 2002 as a long-term demonstration effort to monitor quail abundance in about 40 counties. Data are collected on spring call counts, forb diversity, simulated nest success, predator abundance, roadside covey counts, fall covey call counts, and a habitat score. Sample TQI data from several sites in the Rolling Plains are summarized in table 7.3. More information on the TQI is available online at the TeamQuail Web site.

Table 7.2.
Bobwhite and Scaled Quail Harvest on the Rolling Plains of Texas, 1981–2001

Year	Bobwhites			Scaled quail		
	Hunters	Harvest	Birds/hunter	Hunters	Harvest	Birds/hunter
1981	29,964	333,529	11.1	10,627	50,095	5.4
1982	44,937	688,167	15.3	20,484	110,287	5.4
1986	38,897	418,700	10.8	16,376	60,895	3.7
1987	43,492	528,643	12.2	18,399	65,510	2.3
1988	36,098	285,782	7.9	13,353	41,671	3.1
1989	33,865	234,814	6.9	12,642	34,051	2.7
1990	28,531	203,145	7.1	9,840	25,856	2.6
1991	30,636	249,233	8.1	8,332	18,054	2.2
1992	40,829	534,295	13.1	9,456	21,649	2.3
1993	50,007	543,511	10.9	11,167	35,656	3.2
1994	30,478	199,540	6.6	7,846	9,320	1.2
1995	25,178	114,293	4.6	5,840	5,557	1.0
1996	20,613	87,570	4.3	4,010	12,875	3.2
1997	27,439	253,987	9.3	5,946	20,183	3.4
1998	28,450	200,715	7.0	4,005	15,910	4.0
1999	23,618	199,529	8.4	4,598	13,808	3.0
2000	26,010	218,518	8.4	3,497	7,499	2.1
2001	19,257	109,585	5.7	4,488	6,369	1.4
Mean	32,128	300,198	8.8	9,495	30,847	2.9

Source: Texas Parks and Wildlife Department data.

Table 7.3.
Population Parameters Relating to Bobwhite Abundance from Selected Counties in the Rolling Plains of Texas, 2002

Index	Unit	County						
		Collingsworth	Coke	Childress	Fisher	Kent	Shackelford	Stonewall
Spring call count	Cocks heard/stop	10.2	4.6	8.1	10.2	8.7	3.3	5.7
Fall covey call count	Coveys heard/stop	—	5.7	9.4	6.2	17.2	—	13.4
Roadside count	Quail observed/mile	18.3	1.0	2.5	11.0	4.5	13.1	9.1
Flushing rate	Coveys flushed/hour	—	3.6	1.0	5.2	—	4.0	2.3
Age ratio	% subadults	—	82	—	80	—	91	62
Nest success	% surviving	47	36	75	75	50	64	81
Nest-site density	No. clumps/acre	249	216	137	172	237	273	516
Predator index	No. visits/100 SSN	5	30	9	14	2	—	23
Habitat score	1 = poor; 10 = perfect	5.9	5.6	7.0	6.7	7.1	7.3	6.4

Note: Parameters from the Texas Quail Index demonstration. These data were compiled from participating landowners and do not reflect abundance for the county as a whole. Sampling protocols described at http://teamquail.tamu.edu.

Natural History

The purpose of this section is to describe the natural history of the Rolling Plains in the context of quail ecology and management. I will describe how aspects of the Rolling Plains landscape provide food, habitat, and other life requisites for quails.

Diet

Quail diets in the Rolling Plains are well documented only for the hunting season (November–February). Typically, 90 percent or more of the diet during fall and winter consists of seeds of forbs, grasses, and woody plants (e.g., mesquite, chittam); greens and insects complete the diet (figure 7.4). Greens tend to be more common during late winter and early spring, and presumably insect consumption mirrors their availability and is greatest during summer and fall (Jackson 1969). Bobwhite and scaled quail in this area have essentially the same diets where the two species occur sympatrically (Rollins 1981).

Staples in the diets are summarized in table 7.1 and include seeds of forbs (e.g., western ragweed [*Ambrosia cumanensis*], buffalobur [*Solanum rostratum*]), woody plants (e.g., mesquite, chittam), and a few grasses (e.g., johnsongrass [*Sorghum halepense*]). The annual importance of any particular class or species of plants can vary considerably. Although western ragweed is likely the single most important seed for bobwhites in northwestern Texas, its composition of the fall-winter diet ranged from only 1 percent in 1963 to 50 percent in 1964 (Jackson 1969). During such busts of annual and perennial forbs, seeds of woody plants become especially important. Seeds of common broomweed (*Xanthocephalum dracunculoides*) are important items during "broomweed years," years in which short-term droughts have been broken by above-average rainfall during fall and winter (Rollins 1981; Linex 1999).

Grasshoppers (Orthoptera) are the primary insects consumed, with beetles (Coleoptera), bugs (Hemiptera), leafhoppers (Homoptera), and ants (Hymenoptera) the less common items in the diet. Desert termites (Isoptera), whose mud tubes often characterize the landscape during droughts, have been documented in quails from the Permian Basin (P. Dickerson, Texas Parks and Wildlife Department, pers. comm.) and Rio Grande Plains (Lehmann 1984; Campbell-Kissock, Blankenship, and Stewart 1985).

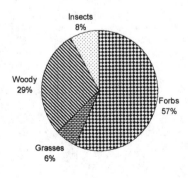

Figure 7.4.
Seeds of forbs, grasses, and woody plants compose the bulk of the fall-winter diets of bobwhites in the Rolling Plains. Insects are taken as they are available. These graphs represent crop contents of quail taken from the Matador and Gene Howe wildlife management areas during the 1958–59 season (Jackson 1969).

An analysis of the crop contents from the day's hunting bag is a good way to introduce land managers to quail diets. Interested managers can assemble their own seed reference collection (Rollins 1991). Photographs of important seeds in quail diets are available in Jackson (1969) and online at the TeamQuail Web site.

Cover Requirements

Bobwhites need a landscape that has low brush interspersed with open grass and forb communities. Cover needs, which constitute usable space for quails (Guthery 1997), must address their physical and behavioral limitations. Scaled quail in this region typically prefer more open landscapes with shallower soils or shorter-grass communities (Schemnitz 1964; Rollins 1980, 2000). Cover management should address nesting, brooding, loafing, and feeding habitats.

Nesting Cover

Adequate nesting cover is a key consideration for quail managers in the Rolling Plains (figure 7.5). In my opinion, suitable nesting cover *across the landscape* is perhaps the single most limiting factor for bobwhites across West Texas. Short-term droughts, overgrazing, and desert termites often interact to reduce suitable nesting cover, thus reducing nesting success. Bunchgrasses, such as little bluestem, are the preferred nesting substrate for bobwhites (Hernández 1999; Townsend et al. 2001). Peoples et al. (1996) found 98 percent of bobwhite nests located on the Packsaddle WMA in little bluestem. Larger threeawns and clumps of tobosa (*Hilaria mutica*) become more common nesting sites in western portions of the Rolling Plains.

My students have used simulated nests to study hatch rates relative to various management practices. Simulated nest survival tends to be greater than 50 percent when the number of suitable bunchgrass clumps exceeds about 640/hectare (260/acre) (Slater et al. 2001). The manager's goal should be to enhance nesting cover across the landscape, not just

Figure 7.5.
Ideal nesting cover should provide a minimum of 250 suitable bunchgrass plants per acre. Little bluestem (pictured here) is a preferred nesting site wherever it is available.
Photo by Dale Rollins

in small islands of nesting habitat (e.g., 1 hectare, or about 2.5 acres). Lower stocking rates and timely deferments from grazing can be used to improve the availability of good nesting cover.

Prickly pear clumps were identified as important nesting sites in Irion, Coke, and Shackelford counties (Hernández 1999; Carter, Rollins, and Scott 2002). Nests situated in prickly pear had greater hatch rates relative to nests situated in bunchgrasses when bunchgrass cover was limited (Slater et al. 2001; table 7.4). Nests may be situated occasionally at the base of small shrubs such as sand sagebrush (Jackson 1969), but quails typically do not nest under shrubs. Other nesting sites include sacahuista (*Nolina texanum*) and yucca (*Yucca glauca*) (Carter 1995). Increasing the number of potential nesting sites on the landscape generally increases nesting success. Slater et al. proposed a density of about 640 bunchgrass plants/hectare (260/acre) as a minimum threshold.

Loafing Cover
Adequate loafing coverts are key to the location of bobwhites and scaled quail across the landscape (figure 7.6). A good covert should be dense above to minimize exposure to raptors, yet open at ground level to permit visibility of mammalian predators. A useful covert should ideally be 1–3 meters tall (3–10 feet) and at least 1.5 meters in diameter (about 5 feet). Plants that provide adequate coverts include lotebush, sandplum, sumacs, some mesquites, elbowbush (*Forestieria pubescens*), catclaw mimosa, chittam, and fourwing saltbush (*Atriplex canescens*). Taller forms of prickly pear and cholla (*O. imbricata*) also provide coverts along the western edge of the Rolling Plains.

Escape Cover
Escape cover is a habitat component that permits quails to elude their enemies. It may consist of low brush (e.g., catclaw mimosa), dense brush (e.g., mesquite), prickly pear, bunchgrasses, or combinations of any of these.

Figure 7.6.
Loafing coverts, or "quail houses," are key components of quail habitat in the Rolling Plains. A desirable loafing covert should be about the size of a pickup truck, provide dense foliage above, offer good visibility at quail height, and be spaced on the landscape about the distance of a softball throw.
Photo by Dale Rollins

Thermal Cover

Quail seek landscape features that minimize thermal stress (Forrester et al. 1998). Coverts that provide protection from hypothermia (i.e., cold-weather coverts) commonly used by quails in the Rolling Plains include sandplum, lotebush, and skunkbush. Generally, shelters that provide protection against hyperthermia (i.e., hot-weather coverts) are taller and denser than cool-weather coverts (Johnson and Guthery 1988); sandplum, skunkbush, and chittam thickets are examples of hot-weather coverts in the Rolling Plains.

Roosting Cover

Both bobwhite and scaled quail coveys roost in open areas with relatively short grass (e.g., old fields or rangelands). Less is known about roosting habitat during breeding season, but pairs were often found roosting in association with catclaw mimosa as screening cover in Fisher County (J. L. Brooks, Texas Agricultural Experiment Station, pers. comm.).

Brooding Cover

Brooding cover for quail chicks should address nutritional needs, such as insect availability, and physical constraints of chicks, such as their small size and low mobility. Ideal brood cover consists of areas with good forb diversity, ample bare ground, and moderate canopies about 0.3–1.0 meters (1–3 feet) above ground level. Old fields and ecotones between different land-use types usually provide such conditions. Particularly good plants attractive to insects and that meet these structural characteristics in the Rolling Plains include pigweed (*Amaranthus* spp.), kochia (*Kochia scoparia*), Russian thistle (*Salsola iberica*), alfalfa (*Medicago sativa*), and even cotton (*Gossypium hirsutum*). Disking or other soil disturbance can be used to promote such areas.

Water

Quail require water, but they do not necessarily require access to free-standing water (Guthery 2000:44). Quail will use free water when it is available, but providing supplemental water has not proved to be an effective technique for increasing quail populations in South Texas (Guthery and Koerth 1992). Another aspect of water that may prove more beneficial than providing drinking water per se is water harvesting. Water harvesting is basically capturing and retaining precipitation runoff that would otherwise be lost from the site. A bulldozer or motor grader can be used to build spreader dams that divert runoff into small collection pits. The additional runoff makes these sites mini-wetlands that often produce more or different plants than the adjacent uplands do (figure 7.7). Such moist-soil areas in Pecos County produced about 25 times more vegetation and 5 times more arthropods than the adjacent uplands (R. J. Buntyn, Angelo State University, unpublished data). However, the value of these areas to quails remains unproved. No research to date has demonstrated that this management practice results in more quails or increases quail survival.

Habitat Management: Usable Space

Guthery's (1997) concept of usable space underpins quail habitat management. Quail managers seeking to increase quail abundance should

Figure 7.7.
The use of spreader dams to harvest runoff can be used to create moist-soil sites that promote desirable plants for quail. The response by western ragweed is impressive on this site in Fisher County.
Photo by Dale Rollins

try to maximize the percentage of the landscape that is habitable to quails. Under this maxim, managers should seek to increase the quantity, not the quality, of quail habitat.

Jackson (1962) characterized bobwhite population variations in the Rolling Plains as an interaction among drought, livestock grazing practices, plant succession, and periodic episodes of above-average precipitation. His explanation of the situation may be described as a five-step process:

1. A drought of several years, coupled with livestock overgrazing, depletes much of the habitat and hence most of the bobwhite population.
2. A year of average rainfall promotes expanses of annual forbs (e.g., doveweed, buffalobur) useful to bobwhites. The nutritional situation is good, and the predator population has probably lagged during the dry years. Bobwhites undergo a lateral increase and occupy sites across the landscape.
3. A second year of average or above-average rainfall breaks the drought. The landscape is now covered with a dense canopy of common broomweed, which provides excellent winter ground cover yet is open at quail level for easy travel. The quail increase is a rapid vertical increase.
4. A year of normal rainfall follows with good moisture carryover from the previous year. The bobwhite population explodes and occupies all available habitat.
5. Several dry years set in. The bobwhite population crashes if food or cover fails before spring. Conditions revert to phase one.

Jackson used bobwhite population irruptions in 1942 and 1958 as the basis of his observations. His data were based largely on hunting preserve records of quail harvested. It is not possible to compare bobwhite abundance indices available today, such as BBS data (Sauer, Hines, and Fallon 2002), for the purpose of comparing the relative abundance levels observed by Jackson (1962). Breeding Bird Survey data suggest that

Figure 7.8.
"Broomweed years" are generally correlated with good quail production. The broomweed canopy helps insulate quail from their enemies, and quail also gorge themselves on the tiny seeds during the winter.
Photo by Dale Rollins

the largest bobwhite irruption in the Rolling Red Plains (generally synonymous with Jackson's "Lower Rolling Plains") from the period 1966–96 occurred in 1967. Although irruptions have occurred several times since then, none have approached 1967 levels, at least with respect to the BBS data.

The most visible herald of a banner quail year in the Rolling Plains is a broomweed year (figure 7.8). Even though the seeds of broomweed can be a major diet item during such years, I suspect that broomweed's major contribution to quail production is increasing the quantity of habitat, making virtually all the landscape usable space (Guthery 1997).

The 1987 irruption, which conforms well to Jackson's model, is the one that most hunters of my generation use as a benchmark. Dry conditions prevailed during 1983–84, and range conditions were deplorable. Accentuating the dilemma for quails was the bitter-cold winter of 1983–84. I estimate that bobwhites composed less than 20 percent of the quail population in Harmon County, Oklahoma, during the 1984–85 hunting season. Scaled quail made up the remainder of the quail population. Precipitation in the fall of 1985 resulted in a good broomweed stand in 1986, at which time the lateral increase occurred. More rain in 1986 resulted in a bumper broomweed year in 1987. The anticipated vertical increase occurred, resulting in a banner quail year. Interestingly, a year later—during winter of 1988—scaled quail virtually disappeared from this area (Rollins 2000).

A dense canopy of broomweed probably provides a measure of predator protection for bobwhites that is unavailable during other phases of Jackson's model. Several studies (Roseberry and Klimstra 1984; Giuliano and Lutz 1993) suggested that the best predictor of bobwhite abundance is the previous year's abundance. Broomweed probably helps increase overwinter survival, thereby increasing density of birds available for the breeding season.

Factors Affecting Habitat

Several factors impact the quantity and quality of habitat for quails in the Rolling Plains, including weather, brush management, grazing management, and desert termites (Rollins 2002). Of these, only brush and grazing management are under the direct control of the land manager. Weather accounts for about half of the variability seen in South Texas bobwhite populations (Hanselka and Guthery 1991), and the impacts are likely similar in the Rolling Plains, especially for areas receiving less than about 60 centimeters (25 inches) of precipitation annually.

In the preface of his classic *Game Management,* Leopold (1933) argued that "game populations can be restored by the creative use of the same tools which have heretofore destroyed it—axe, plow, cow, fire, and gun." Four of those tools deal directly with habitat management. In the Rolling Plains, the ax takes the form of brush management, the plow represents farming practices and related USDA farm programs, the cow represents livestock grazing management, and fire represents prescribed burning. A more thorough discussion of each of these tools follows.

Brush Management

Brush diversity and growth form are important components of quail habitat in the Rolling Plains. An area should have three or more species of brush (e.g., mesquite, lotebush, hackberry) with a suitable loafing covert at least every 30 meters (100 feet). Important quail coverts in the Rolling Plains are made of lotebush, sandplum, chittam, sumacs (littleleaf and skunkbush), elbowbush, shinoak, wolfberry, catclaw mimosa, and some mesquites, especially the ones that look like large mushrooms. One should be able to throw a softball in the air from one covert to the next.

Brush control has been a common practice in the Rolling Plains, with mesquite, juniper, and prickly pear being the species most commonly targeted for control. Although large-scale brush control is detrimental to quails (Jackson 1969), more judicious approaches can be of benefit (Guthery 1986; Guthery and Rollins 1997). The concept of brush sculpting promotes the planned, selective control of brush to enhance wildlife habitat (Rollins, Ueckert, and Brown 1997). As Guthery (1999a) noted, there is a certain amount of slack in habitat prescriptions for quails. Areas with taller grasses need less brush to be habitable for bobwhites than areas lacking taller grasses. Moreover, the quantity and dispersion of woody cover can change without affecting quail abundance, at least to some degree.

Brush sculpting can be used to enhance habitability and huntability of the landscape for quails. Excessively dense stands of mesquite or juniper are not very attractive to quails or quail hunters. Reducing brush canopies to perhaps 15 to 20 percent canopy cover (on grazed rangelands) and to 5 to 10 percent (on ungrazed or lightly grazed rangelands) will maintain or improve habitability while enhancing hunter access. Clearing may be accomplished in strips or in a motte pattern (which may be aesthetically more pleasing). Regardless of the pattern chosen, a quail should never be forced to be farther than about 45 meters (50 yards) from brush cover.

The brush manager has basically two options: chemical (e.g., herbicides) or mechanical (e.g., bulldozing). Generally, mechanical means are preferable because they can be more selective and increase forb production caused by soil disturbance. However, mechanical means are typically two to four times more expensive than herbicides.

Most mechanical brush control in the Rolling Plains historically

Figure 7.9.
Although bulldozers have traditionally been the implement of choice for mechanical brush control, excavators such as this one have become more popular in recent years. Any method that permits a degree of selectivity can be used to sculpt brush-infested rangelands for quail habitat.
Photo by Dale Rollins

has been done via bulldozers to grub, root-plow, or chain brush, mostly mesquite. Increasingly, the use of excavators has become popular (figure 7.9). Any mechanical treatment that affords some degree of selectivity—that is, the ability to leave a hackberry next to a juniper tree—may be used effectively to sculpt quail habitat. Rollins (1997a) described the various levels of brush sculpting that can be applied to benefit wildlife habitat. A general plan would address the following points: (1) a suitable loafing covert should be left at least every 30 meters (100 feet); (2) older mesquites with other species growing in them should be spared; (3) some larger clumps of brush, perhaps an acre in size, should be spared about every 350 meters (400 yards); and (4) clearing instructions should be communicated directly to the dozer operator using flagging tape to mark specific instructions until it is evident that the operator understands the clearing plan.

A common shortcoming of many brush management operations is the failure to consider wildlife needs a priori. One should not wait until the dozer is running or the airplane is overhead to factor in cover needs for quails. Remember the carpenter's advice: "Measure twice and saw once." It is critical that intentions are communicated clearly—and often—to the brush contractor, or you may be unpleasantly surprised.

Some landowners try to counter overzealous brush control by leaving brush piles, which they assume adequately meet a quail's cover needs. I do not advocate brush piles as a substitute for poor planning. Brush piles offer more habitat for some enemies of quails, such as skunks (*Mephitis mephitis* and *Spilogale* spp.) and raccoons (*Procyon lotor*), than they do for quails (Doty 2003). A landowner in Coleman County once told me he had spent most of the winter burning brush piles, per my recommendation. He estimated that he flushed raccoons from about 30 percent of the burned piles. The piles with the most raccoons were the ones near his farm ponds.

That said, brush piles can and do provide loafing cover for quails in the absence of other coverts. If you are making brush piles, build a frame out of pipe or fence posts and set them atop concrete blocks so that the resulting brush will be suspended about 25 centimeters (about 10 inches) off the ground (Webb and Guthery 1982).

If larger mesquites have been top-killed either mechanically or with herbicides, the site will eventually, after about 10 years, be dominated by multistemmed resprouts. One method for improving the structure of such regrowth for quails is by half-cutting (Jackson 1969; Rollins 1997b). Half-cutting involves scoring the tops of smooth-stemmed mesquite branches (usually those less than 5 centimeters, or 2 inches, in diameter) with a limb saw. Saw no farther than is necessary to break the limb while applying downward pressure. Select trees that have 5–10 limbs so that the resulting tree looks like an umbrella. The best time of the year to half-cut mesquites is during April and May, when the limbs are most flexible. Half-cut 5–15 mesquites over an area the size of a basketball court, then move about 225 meters (250 yards), and repeat the process.

Another option is to make tepee shelters using wooden fence posts or cut mesquites. Take the stump ends of cut trees, and prop the cut end up into a live tree. Place four or five such cut limbs/trees until you form a tepee.

Chemical control with herbicides is a popular means of treating mesquite and shinoak but is not generally an option for controlling junipers. Herbicides are usually less expensive to apply than mechanical means and have been especially popular on mesquite-dominated rangelands. Broadcast herbicide applications are generally less desirable than mechanical brush control methods because they are less selective. Applications of herbicide by individual plant treatment (IPT), however, can provide a level of selectivity similar to that achieved by mechanical methods. By choosing the appropriate herbicide and application rate, a land manager can use the herbicide as an effective tool for sculpting rangelands. Care should be taken when the spray mixture includes herbicides such as picloram that result in more broad-spectrum control of woody plants. Including picloram in a mesquite spraying mixture will kill desirable shrubs such as netleaf hackberry. Although a variety of herbicides have been applied aerially for mesquite control (Scifres 1980), the current recommendation is a 1:1 mixture of triclopyr (Remedy®; mention of trade name is for information of reader only and does not constitute an endorsement) and clopyralid (Reclaim®) (McGinty et al. 2000). The Brush Busters program (McGinty and Ueckert 1995) promotes IPT spraying for controlling mesquite regrowth that is shorter than 2 meters (about 7 feet) and at densities less than 1,000 trees/hectare (about 400 trees/acre). Benefits of IPT versus broadcast applications of herbicides for quail managers include (1) the degree of selectivity it provides, such as kill a particular mesquite but leave the adjacent hackberry unharmed; and (2) lower occurrence of forb shock (suppression of forbs) from the herbicide treatment.

Sand shinnery oak or shinoak dominates some sandy soils in the western half of the Rolling Plains. Whereas sparse stands of shinoak offer good quail habitat, vast, dense stands usually do not. Controlling shinoak is best accomplished by applying the pelleted herbicide tebuthiuron (Spike® 20P) at rates ranging from 0.3 to 1.2 kilograms/hectare (0.25 to 1.0 pound/acre). Recommended rates usually provide at least 80 percent control. Innovative ways to apply tebuthiuron pellets within the context of brush sculpting involve the use of variable-rate patterning (Koerth 1996) or backpack blowers (figure 7.10). The variable-rate

Figure 7.10.
Pelleted herbicides (e.g., Spike ® 20P for shinoak control) can be applied on smaller acreages via a backpack-mounted blower. When an all-terrain vehicle, such as shown here, is used to make the application, a digital speedometer is needed to accurately gauge the speed of the vehicle (thus application rate).
Photo by Dale Rollins

patterning approach applies half-rates of pellets in alternating strips. Flight lines flown in the first direction (north to south) are then re-flown at a right angle to the previous strips (east to west). The resulting pattern makes a checkerboard arrangement of totally killed (usually 25 percent of resulting landscape), partially killed (50 percent), and untreated (25 percent). The backpack blower can be used on foot or in conjunction with an all-terrain vehicle (ATV) to treat intermittent or irregularly shaped strips through shinoak areas.

PRICKLY PEAR

Although not a woody plant per se, prickly pear cacti are common components of quail habitat in the Rolling Plains. Prickly pear provides a source of seed during fall and winter and can be an important source of nesting cover (Slater et al. 2001; Carter, Rollins, and Scott 2002; Hernández et al. 2003).

Ranchers often seek to control prickly pear by using herbicides (i.e., picloram [Tordon®]), prescribed burning, or a tandem application of picloram following a fire. The latter treatment usually provides greater than 95 percent control (Ueckert et al. 1988). Quail management concerns regarding prickly pear control focus on two points: forb shock in the acute sense and possible impacts on nesting habitat by the removal of prickly pear (Hernández et al. 2003), assuming no response from bunchgrass.

Lehmann (1984) reported only 1 of 189 bobwhite nests situated in prickly pear in South Texas. By contrast, Carter (1995) reported that prickly pear was the most common nesting site of bobwhite (12 of 21 nests) and scaled quail (8 of 12 nests) in Irion County. Slater et al. (2001) tested whether nests situated in prickly pear were more successful than those situated in grass microhabitats. They used artificial nests (three chicken eggs) to simulate nest survival at eight sites in west-central Texas (table 7.4). Simulated nests situated in prickly pear had higher survival than nests located in bunchgrass. Once a transect offered more than about 700 suitable bunchgrasses/hectare (280/acre), there was no difference in nest survival between grass nests and artificial nests made of cactus. That threshold suggests that if sufficient grass nests are present on the landscape, the searching efficiency of nest predators can be diluted.

Hernández (1999) monitored bobwhite nesting ecology on four sites in Shackelford County during 1997–98. Of the 81 bobwhite nests located, 47 were found in bunchgrasses, 24 in cactus, and 10 in shrubs.

Table 7.4.
Mean Survival Time of Simulated Nests in Grass or Prickly Pear Microhabitats at 8 Sites in West-Central Texas, 1995–96

County	1995		1996		Density of potential nesting sites (plants/acre)	
	Grass	Prickly pear	Grass	Prickly pear	Grass	Prickly pear
Coleman	0.28	2.08	1.22	2.61	278	173
Crockett	2.08	2.94	0.06	0.33	218	256
Shackelford	2.97	3.06	3.53	3.39	545	117
Tom Green	0.03	1.06	0.53	1.83	137	202
Cottle	—	—	2.69	3.11	200	183
Fisher	—	—	2.78	2.83	419	134
Reagan	—	—	1.44	2.36	261	75
Sterling	—	—	2.00	2.47	304	129

Source: Slater et al. (2001).
Note: Survival time given in weeks.

Given the relative densities of bunchgrasses and cactus, Hernández concluded that bobwhites were selecting for prickly pear as a nesting substrate. Quail nesting in cactus averaged 53 percent higher survival than those nesting in bunchgrass.

Prickly pear can become too thick, if not for habitability by quails, then certainly for huntability by people. Results from Hernández et al. (2003) suggest that good grazing management, such as maintaining adequate bunchgrass cover, can mitigate any potentially negative impacts on nesting habitat from controlling prickly pear. One means of strip-spraying prickly pear involves a boomless nozzle attached to an ATV, a method that is area-specific for applying picloram. Additional studies are needed to better define thresholds of prickly pear density as it relates to quail habitat in different sites, especially during drought periods.

Farming Practices

The plow can be discussed in three contexts relative to quails: impacts of prevailing agriculture and government farm subsidy programs on quail habitat; food plots; and soil disturbance, such as disking.

THE AGRICULTURAL LANDSCAPE

The interspersion of dryland agriculture, especially for milo, wheat, and livestock production on rangeland, is one reason the Rolling Plains provides excellent quail habitat. Prior to the advent of the Conservation Reserve Program (CRP) in 1986, much of the cropland in the Rolling Plains was planted in wheat, milo, and various forage sorghums. Provided woody cover is adjacent, fallow wheat fields during summer can provide excellent brooding habitat, and milo fields provide abundant feed during winter. Such farming practices interspersed with rangeland and woody cover resulted in excellent quail habitat (Jackson 1969).

Approximately 1.2 million hectares (3 million acres) of Rolling Plains cropland were converted to permanent grass plantings in the CRP. The primary grass species used included native mixtures (e.g., sideoats grama, little bluestem), Old World bluestems (*Bothriochloa* spp.), weeping lovegrass (*Eragrostis curvula*), and bermudagrass (*Cynodon dactylon*). Monocultures of the last three species are generally unproductive for quails, although Old World bluestems and weeping lovegrass may provide some nesting cover.

Grass plantings provide good quail habitat initially for one or two years. They are usually dominated by pioneer plants (weeds, e.g., Russian thistle). But as the grasses become established, the sites become less attractive to quails. The absence of brush on such areas precludes widespread use by quails. Brush, typically mesquite, invades such sites, but it takes about 15 years before the site will consistently hold quail.

Lutz et al. (1994) provided recommendations for improving CRP acreages for wildlife, including quails. Generally, these include complementing the existing grass stand—a native mixture of grasses preferred over exotics—with woody plantings such as plums; field borders of annuals, which are food strips; and prescribed burning.

FOOD PLOTS

Planting various annual food plots for quails is a popular practice, although it has not been proved as a management technique that increases populations. Turner (1999) listed various species and planting recommendations for the Rolling Plains. My experiences with food plots in the Rolling Plains suggest two things: when you need them, such as during dry years, you cannot grow them; and when you can grow them, such as during wet years, you probably do not need them. Food plots will be more dependable in the eastern half of the Rolling Plains—on areas receiving more than 50 centimeters (about 20 inches) of annual precipitation—and on sandy soils, which have better moisture-holding and release capabilities than clay soils. Candidate species include various sorghums (primarily milo and sorghum alum), millets (either browntop or German), and cowpeas. The use of cool-season food plots (such as hairy vetch) as a means of promoting insect abundance the following spring warrants investigation. If seeding with perennials is being considered, recommendations include Illinois bundleflower (*Desmanthus illinoensis*), plains bristlegrass, and even johnsongrass.

DISKING

Soil disturbance at any time of the year promotes the subsequent growth of forbs. Disking in winter (January–February) is recommended to promote important food-producing forbs and grasses in the Rolling Plains. Disking a sandy-loam range site in Dickens County increased the frequency of occurrence of desirable quail food plants (Webb and Guthery 1983; table 7.5). Western ragweed was 6–20 times more abundant on disked sites up to six years later, whereas pigweed was 25 times more common on disked strips. Larger-seeded grasses, such as Hall's panicum (*Panicum hallii*) were 5 times more common on disked strips than on undisked areas.

Grazing Management

The most pervasive habitat problem in the Rolling Plains is overgrazing, which changes the composition, species diversity, and structure—most important, fewer tall bunchgrasses—of the vegetation. The novice quail manager sees such sites as awash with good food-producing plants, such as western ragweed and doveweed, but food is rarely the limiting factor for bobwhites in Texas (Guthery 2000:68).

Quail managers often promote grazing to manipulate plant succession (Guthery 1986:36). The need for heavier stocking to provide adequate bare ground is rarely a problem west of the 99th meridian. Good grazing management that promotes higher successional prairie species, such as bunchgrasses, is recommended for quail range in most of the Rolling Plains.

Table 7.5.
Frequency of Occurrence of Important Seed-Producing Plants after Spring Disking, Dickens and King Counties, Texas

	1978		1979		1980	
Species	Disked	Not disked	Disked	Not disked	Disked	Not disked
Forbs						
Annual sunflower	0.0	0.0	21.3	0.0	14.7	0.0
Common broomweed	0.0	0.7	12.7	89.3	1.3	9.3
Pigweed	16.0	0.7	13.3	0.0	18.0	0.0
Western ragweed	18.0	15.3	30.0	5.3	40.0	2.0
Grass						
Hall's panicum	57.3	12.7	38.0	7.3	11.3	6.0

Source: Adapted from Webb and Guthery (1983).
Note: Disking was done in March 1978 and 1979. Data from 1978 and 1979 are from counts conducted in July and August; 1980 data are from May.

Although the value of a quail hunting lease can equal or surpass the value of a grazing lease in the Rolling Plains and South Texas Plains (D. Rollins, unpublished data), cattle are still king on most quail range in West Texas. Much of the quail range suffers from high stocking rates and continuous grazing. Unfortunately, federal farm subsidy programs, such as drought disaster feed programs that allow high stocking rates to be maintained during drought, sometimes exacerbate the multitude of problems caused by heavy grazing. However, attitudes are changing, especially as more ranches are purchased with the goal of increasing quail populations. The importance of quail hunting as a factor driving real estate values in West and South Texas is an interesting new development. From 1990 to 2000, 19 percent of Texas Quail Unlimited members had purchased property for the primary purpose of hunting quails (D. Rollins, unpublished data). If such trends continue, and I believe they will only escalate over the next 10 years, there will be growing interest in the idea of prescribed grazing—grazing for the purpose of attaining specific quail habitat management goals—as opposed to traditional use of cattle for generating income.

Grazing is a double-edged sword as a tool for managing rangelands for quails. Grazing can be used to retard plant succession, thus promoting the lower successional species, such as doveweed and western ragweed. But overgrazing degrades quail habitat when too much grass is removed. Even though quails can cohabit with cows on the same range successfully, populations of both cannot be maximized simultaneously (figure 7.11). There will always be trade-offs, and the aspiring quail manager should anticipate and understand the pressure points.

Knowledge of plant succession is important to appreciate how a practice such as grazing affects quail habitat. Succession is the orderly, predictable process of change in plant communities. Rangelands are often classified according to range-condition class (Dyksterhuis 1949), that is, how similar the current plant community on the site is relative to what it was like in pristine condition. Excellent-condition range has most of the plant species present that would be expected in pristine conditions on that particular range site. At the other end of the spectrum, poor-condition range has less than 25 percent of the original plant commu-

Figure 7.11.
Grazing can be a double-edged sword for quail managers in the Rolling Plains. As quails continue to increase in their importance, more emphasis will be placed on grazing plans (e.g., lighter stocking rates) aimed at enhancing quail habitat.
Photo by Dale Rollins

nity. Fair condition connotes 25–50 percent of the climax plant community, and good suggests 50–75 percent. Range-condition classes do not necessarily conform to quail habitat condition (Rollins, Guthery, and Richardson 1993). For example, a site in fair range condition may provide excellent quail habitat, especially in the relatively mesic eastern portions of the Rolling Plains. But in the arid west, sites in good or excellent range condition likely provide better quail habitat. Higher stocking rates and lower successional stages are more optimal for quails in mesic climates, whereas lower stocking rates and higher seral stages are preferred in more arid regions or less productive sites (Spears et al. 1993). A lack of bare ground is often cited as a management concern in some areas (Guthery 2000:175), but such is rarely the case on West Texas rangelands.

A desirable grazing regime for quails must be, above all else, flexible. Weather has a tremendous impact on the amount of forage available for livestock grazing and the resulting condition—either good or bad—of quail habitat. One approach to mitigate potential negative impacts of grazing is to stock conservatively with cow-calf pairs (at perhaps 50 percent of grazing capacity) and then complement herd numbers with stocker animals, such as steers, when conditions allow. Such a flexible stocking plan is the best approach for drought-proofing rangeland and minimizing undesirable impacts on quails. Seasonal stocking plans should provide rest during the growing season (generally May–October), especially where bunchgrasses are limited.

Increasingly, ranches in the Rolling Plains are being purchased and managed primarily for quails. This trend heralds a shift from the historical livestock-grazing paradigm of land use. Having cows and quails simultaneously and having cows as a tool to manage quail habitat are not the same thing. There are no optimal grazing systems, or schemes, for quail habitat other than the incorporation of flexible stocking rates. The most critical factor relative to grazing is not the grazing system but the stocking rate. To optimize quail habitat, I recommend a light stocking rate—perhaps 30–50 percent of the stocking rate recommended by the Natural Resources Conservation Service (NRCS)—either in a continuous or slow rotational grazing scheme, such as a Merrill four-pasture, three-herd system.

A limited amount of spot or patch grazing is beneficial and helps promote spatial and floral heterogeneity across the landscape. Eastern portions of the Rolling Plains can accommodate heavier stocking rates. On ranches owned specifically for quail hunting, undergrazing should be considered. I define undergrazing as "the conscious decision to leave more grass standing than suggested by historical grazing paradigms." Undergrazing might be considered as grass sculpting: the use of planned, selective grazing as a tool to enhance quail habitat.

Quail managers should have various benchmarks in mind as they assess the role of grazing. If nesting cover is limited because of drought, overstocking, or desert termites, then complete rest from grazing may be needed for at least two years.

Fire
Fire can be used as the primary method of brush control in some plant communities (e.g., *Juniperus* spp.) or used as a secondary method to

provide maintenance control in mesquite-grassland communities. The plant response to burning varies with the intensity of the fire involved, the season of burning, and the postburn grazing management. Generally, cooler fires produce a more mosaic result, which is desirable for species such as bobwhites, whereas hotter fires may be more appropriate for reclamation of dense brush. Fall-winter burns usually promote more cool-season grasses and forbs, whereas winter-spring burns promote more warm-season grasses. In recent years, Texas wintergrass (*Stipa leucotricha*) seems to have become more prevalent over the southern half of the Rolling Plains. Although graziers laud this cool-season perennial grass, I consider it to have low value for quails.

The impacts of burning on quail habitat in Texas are unclear (Guthery 2000:70). Burning generally promotes good brood habitat by increasing desirable forbs (especially legumes) and increasing insect abundance/availability. Late-winter burning improves bobwhite habitat in southern pine forests (Stoddard 1931; Speake 1967; Rosene 1969). But because the western range of bobwhites is more xeric, for example, 50 centimeters (about 20 inches) of annual precipitation in West Texas versus more than 125 centimeters (about 50 inches) in Florida, the impacts of fire on bobwhite habitat may be less quail-friendly. As with grazing, burning may be less important to a quail manager in the Rolling Plains than in more mesic areas. Its applications for quail management will be greatest east of the 100th meridian.

There is some concern that prescribed burning may increase the vulnerability of bobwhites to predators, especially raptors, via reduction of escape cover (Mueller and Atkinson 1985). The abundance of northern harriers (*Circus cyaneus*) that spend the winter in the Rolling Plains makes cover considerations for quails a priority, as harriers are likely the most important raptor preying on quails in this area (Jackson 1947). Lotebush, a preferred covert for quails in the Rolling Plains, is top-killed by fire and takes 10 years or longer postburn to provide adequate cover (Renwald, Wright, and Flinders 1978). Likewise, the reduction of perennial bunchgrasses and prickly pear may reduce nesting success (Slater et al. 2001). Carter, Rollins, and Scott (2002) concluded that prescribed burning had no effect on short-term survival rates (0–6 months postburn) of bobwhites in Irion and Coke counties under the conditions of their study (i.e., cool, patchy burns less than 160 hectares, or about 400 acres, in size).

An innovative approach to managing livestock grazing to achieve desirable patches of vegetation for quails involves the use of patch burning (Fuhlendorf and Engle 2001). Burning small patches on the larger landscape concentrates grazing pressure. Such localized spot grazing promotes greater floral and structural diversity, which should benefit a quail's need for feeding and brooding habitat interspersed with nesting and escape cover.

Other Considerations: Predation

Rollins and Carroll (2001) provided an overview of the impacts of predation on bobwhite and scaled quail. Predation is the most common source of mortality for quails at all stages in their life cycle. The average nesting success for bobwhites across their range in the United States is about 28 percent (Rollins and Carroll 2001). Recent changes in land

Table 7.6.
Predators of Bobwhite and Scaled Quail (including eggs) on the Rolling Plains of Texas

Class and species	Life stage of quail		
	Egg	Chick	Adult
Insects			
Red-imported fire ant (*Solonopsis victa*)	X	X	
Reptiles			
Bullsnake (*Pituophis melanoleucus*)	X	?	
Coachwhip (*Masticophis* spp.)	X	?	
Ratsnake (*Elaphe* spp.)	?	X	X
Western diamondback (*Crotalus atrox*)		X	X
Birds			
Cooper's hawk (*Accipiter cooperii*)			X
Great-horned owl (*Bubo virginianus*)			X
Greater roadrunner (*Geococcyx californianus*)	?	?	
Northern harrier (*Circus cyaneus*)			X
Red-tailed hawk (*Buteo jamaicensus*)			X
Sharp-shinned hawk (*A. striatus*)			X
Wild turkey (*Meleagris gallopavo*)	X	?	
Mammals			
Armadillo (*Dasypus novemcinctus*)	X		
Badger (*Taxidea taxus*)	X	?	?
Bobcat (*Lynx rufus*)	X	X	X
Cotton rat (*Sigmodon hispidus*)	X		
Coyote (*Canis latrans*)	X	X	X
Feral cat		X	X
Feral hog	X		
Fox (*Vulpes vulpes, Urocyon cinereoargenteus*)	X	X	X
Ground squirrel (*Spermophilus* spp.)	?	?	
Opossum (*Didelphis virginiana*)	X	X	X
Raccoon (*Procyon lotor*)	X	X	X
Skunk (primarily *Mephitis mephitis*)	X		
White-tailed deer (*Odocoileus virginianus*)	?		
Woodrat (*Neotoma* spp.)	X		

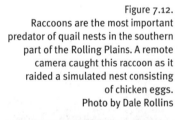

Figure 7.12.
Raccoons are the most important predator of quail nests in the southern part of the Rolling Plains. A remote camera caught this raccoon as it raided a simulated nest consisting of chicken eggs.
Photo by Dale Rollins

use that have fragmented what were once large, continuous tracts of bobwhite habitat may have made quails more vulnerable to predation (Hurst, Burger, and Leopold 1996; Rollins 1999a). Additional studies are needed to assess the role of predation and predation management in light of these landscape-level changes.

The list of predators of quails or their nests in the Rolling Plains is long (table 7.6). Mortality during summer months tends to be primarily by mammals, whereas during the winter most mortality is caused by raptors (Hernández 1999; Carter, Rollins, and Scott 2002). Mammalian predator communities tend to be rather simple: for example, mostly coyotes (*Canis latrans*) and striped skunks in the northern parts of the Rolling Plains, but a more diverse mesomammal predator community in the southern portion (south of Interstate 20).

Common nest predators in the Rolling Plains include raccoons, skunks, and coyotes. I consider raccoons to be the most significant nest predator for quails in the southern portions (figure 7.12). Snakes are considered to be major predators of quail eggs in the southeastern United States, but Hernández, Rollins, and Cantu (1997) never photographed snakes depredating simulated nests near San Angelo. Feral hogs are an increasingly important nest predator as their populations continue to increase across West Texas (Tolleson et al. 1995).

Comparing earlier studies (Stoddard 1931; Jackson 1952) to more contemporary studies (Frost 1999; Lyons 2002) suggests that changes have also occurred within populations and communities of various predators that are often implicated in the decline of quail populations. Raccoons have apparently increased sharply during the past 30 years over much of this region (Jackson 1952; Frost 1999; Rollins and Carroll

2001; Lyons 2002). The increasing popularity of feeding deer over much of Texas may be one factor responsible for the increase in raccoon abundance (Cooper and Ginnett 2000).

Supplemental Feeding

The use of feeders has been, and continues to be, a popular, yet neutral management practice (figure 7.13). Several studies (Peoples 1992; Doerr and Silvy 2002; DeMaso, Townsend, et al. 2002) suggested that feeding was a neutral practice under most conditions. However, Townsend et al. (1999) reported higher survival of bobwhites from a fed area in western Oklahoma during two out of four winters that were colder than average or had greater snowfall. It is perhaps noteworthy that the studies done at Packsaddle WMA (DeMaso, Townsend, et al. 2002) were on a site characterized by sandy soil; sandy soils are the least likely soils to have a shortage of good quail food plants. Feeders do help concentrate quails for hunting.

Figure 7.13.
Quail feeders are popular but unproven methods for increasing quail survival during winter months. The "Currie Quail Feeder," being visited here by scaled quails, is an inexpensive, rugged feeder design.
Photo by Dale Rollins

DeMaso, Townsend, et al. (2002) listed four assumptions that must be met in order for a supplemental feed program to be successful: (1) the native food supply, such as the availability of insects, is limiting quail numbers; (2) no other habitat parameters, such as nesting cover or brood-rearing cover, restricts the population from increasing when supplemental food is provided; (3) quails will utilize supplemental feed; and (4) quails will be more fit in terms of higher survival, more productive, or more adept at escaping predators when the food supply is improved.

A major problem with quail feeders is use by nontarget species (Guthery 1986), which may account for more than 70 percent of feed disappearance (Guthery 2000:66). Henson (2006) used motion-sensing cameras to monitor species surveillance at free-choice quail feeders at six sites across the Rolling Plains. Her data confirmed that quail use at most sites was less than 15 percent of the total visitations recorded. Feed disappearance tended to be greatest during the spring season, when wintering songbirds were most common. Raccoons were the most frequent mammalian visitor at feeders and often fed most of the night at a feeder. Harvester ants (*Polygomyrmex* spp.) are major nontarget species at quail feeders during April–October. I have seen red ants (the common harvester ant in West Texas) attracted to quail feeders from as far away as 27 meters (about 75 feet). A colony of harvester ants can eat as much milo in a year as a covey of quail can (Guthery 1986:50). Feral hogs can be especially problematic, as they not only consume the feed but tear up feeders.

Concern is often expressed that the presence of feeders can actually increase mortality by increasing predation, focusing hunters, or spreading disease (Townsend et al. 1999; Guthery 2000:64). However, researchers have not documented these concerns. Townsend et al. reported that predation by raptors was slightly higher on an area with feeders. However, Henson (2006) reported no incidences of predation on quails (a few incidents on mourning doves [*Zenaida macroura*] were observed) during surveillance of quail feeders at several sites in West Texas.

A variety of feeding systems have been tried (Guthery 1986). Most employ some type of fixed feeder, usually a steel drum with some kind of dispensing mechanism. Guthery has reported that the best feeders have long life expectancy, require no fencing, minimize use by nontarget species, and have adjustable openings to control the amount of feed disbursement. One feeder that I recommend is a homemade design I call the "Currie Quail Feeder" in honor of J. Currie of Garden City (figure 7.13). This rugged, inexpensive feeder consists of several holes (0.77 centimeter, or 9/32 inch, for feeding milo; 0.55 centimeter, or 7/32 inch, for feeding wheat) drilled about an inch off the bottom of the barrel. The barrel is then placed on a wheel rim for a support, leaving the feeder holes about quail's-eye height. Steel T-posts can be used to secure the feeder in the presence of livestock.

J. E. Huston and I explored an innovative way to feed quails, but it has not been thoroughly tested. Our goal was to produce a range cube for livestock (cottonseed cake) that contained whole milo: 135 kilograms (about 300 pounds) of whole milo per ton of cottonseed cake. Most of the milo passes intact through the cow and is deposited in the dung. Quails learn readily that the dung pats offer a source of feed and quickly dissect the pats. We proposed that this method of supplemental feeding (what we coined the "Patty Melt Quail Feeder") might be a compromise between grazier and hunter. The dispersion of dung pats across the landscape avoids one potential liability of feeding, that is, predisposing quails to hawks at a fixed feeder. The system has yet to be field-tested.

In summary, if you want to feed, and can afford to feed, then feed. At worst, feeding appears to be a neutral practice.

Hippocratic Management

Changes in quail habitat may be very apparent, such as pasture conversion to tame grasses, or more cryptic, such as chronic overgrazing. When discussing cryptic habitat loss, I often cite the Hippocratic oath as an axiom for quail managers: First do no harm. Hippocratic management includes those practices that would at first glance appear benign to quails but may ultimately be liabilities. Examples include (1) the proliferation of deer feeders in Texas, resulting in the concentration of egg-eating mesomammals (Cooper and Ginnett 2000; Rollins and Carroll 2001); (2) the proliferation of farm ponds that may fragment prairie landscapes and enhance their habitability by raccoons (Rollins 1999a); (3) government-subsidized livestock feeding programs during droughts that postpone, or preclude, destocking procedures and, ultimately, range recovery; (4) range management practices (e.g., grazing methods) that strive for plant community homogeneity (Fuhlendorf and Engle 2001); and perhaps (5) intensive coyote control efforts that may release mesopredators that are more efficient predators of quails (Rollins 2002).

Epilogue

The next 10 years promise to be especially exciting, and anxious, times for quail managers in the southern Great Plains (Rollins 2002). If bobwhite abundance continues to decline in more eastern ranges, the demand for wild bobwhite hunting will undoubtedly sustain, and likely increase, the appetite for those interested in improving quail habitat.

Because of lower land prices and a history of sustained quail success, the Rolling Plains will be a focal point for this interest.

Slowly but surely ranchers in this region are acknowledging that the quail tail is wagging the livestock dog as the primary motivation for rangeland ownership in the Rolling Plains. I am excited about the current hunger for information and technical assistance among both traditional ranchers and absentee landowners who purchase properties for recreational use.

I am cautiously optimistic that an early diagnosis of the quail decline in the Rolling Plains will permit and promote appropriate therapeutic management. Certainly, we can glean much from successes and failures on the research, outreach, and political fronts from our colleagues in the southeastern United States. Efforts will require the coordination and support of state game agencies, universities, landowners, conservation organizations, and an increasingly apathetic public. The rapidly growing population in Texas tempers my optimism, however. As such, the challenge in Texas will be the same as in points farther east: how to keep bobwhites on an increasingly fragmented landscape.

8 Bobwhites on the Cross Timbers and Prairies

Stephen J. DeMaso and James Dillard

Originally the prairie grew beneath the oaks as an understory. Grazing has since reduced the grasses and allowed an undergrowth of shrubs.
The tall grasses are still present and grow luxuriantly in some woodlands
as well as in the prairie openings. The area is of geological interest since
the existence of the cross timbers is largely traceable to "beaches" left by
the retreat of the sea in Cretaceous times. The beaches were alternatively
sandy and clayey and these today are characterized by savanna or forest
and grassland, respectively. The combination of grassland and woodland,
with its many miles of grassland-timber border, and the added influence
of streams and rivers crossing the vegetation bands, provides a remarkable
variety of habitats for plant species and animal life hardly excelled anywhere in the mid-continent prairie.

Costello (1969)

142

The Cross Timbers and Prairies (CTP) were named by early Texas settlers who found belts of oak forests crossing strips of prairie grassland
(Bolen 1998). The vegetation of the CTP is similar to that of the Post
Oak Savannah. The post oaks (*Quercus stellata*) and blackjack oaks
(*Q. marilandica*) of the CTP are shorter than those found in the Post
Oak Savannah ecoregion. The Grand Prairie (GP), historically an ex-
panse of tall grasses broken by an occasional mesquite or cedar, lies
between the eastern and western portions of the CTP. Diggs et al. (1999)
provide detailed descriptions of the CTP in the north-central Texas region. The characteristics of the CTP in central Oklahoma and north-
central Texas are similar (Duck and Fletcher 1943; Gould 1975). Quail
research in the CTP has been characterized by diverse studies lacking
theme. The objectives of this chapter are to provide an overview of quail
population trends and habitat-relationships in the CTP ecological region and summarize the various quail research conducted in the CTP.

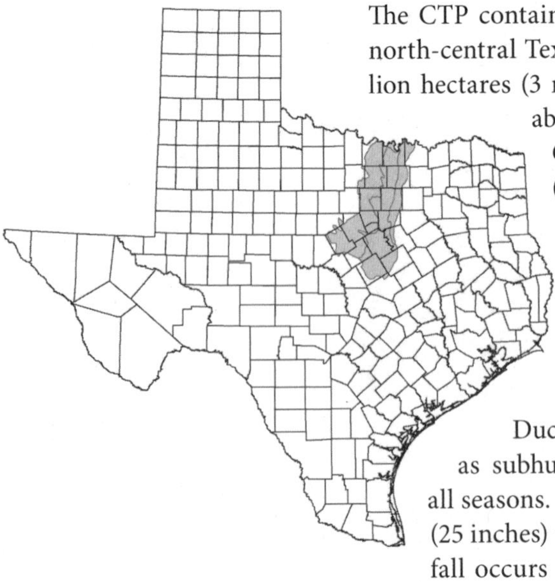

Figure 8.1.
The Cross Timbers and Prairies
ecoregion of Texas.
Courtesy Caesar Kleberg Wildlife
Research Institute (CKWRI)
GIS Laboratory

Location and Area

The CTP contains roughly 6.9 million hectares (17 million acres) in
north-central Texas (figure 8.1). The area is made up of about 1.2 million hectares (3 million acres) in the western Cross Timbers (WCT),
about 404,687 hectares (1 million acres) in the eastern
Cross Timbers (ECT), and about 2.4 million hectares
(6.5 million acres) in the GP. The remaining acreage is
called the north-central prairies (NCP). Most of the
region is rolling to hilly and deeply dissected with
creeks and rivers that promote rapid surface drainage (Gould 1975b).

Climate

Duck and Fletcher (1943) characterize the CTP climate
as subhumid and mesothermal, with adequate moisture for
all seasons. Average annual rainfall ranges from 63.5 centimeters
(25 inches) to 101.6 centimeters (40 inches). The majority of rainfall occurs during April, May, and June (Gould 1975b). Annual

snow accumulation ranges from 5.1 centimeters (2 inches) to 10.2 centimeters (4 inches) (Dyksterhuis 1946, 1948).

Soils

The soils in the ECT and WCT are acidic or slightly acidic sandy or sandy loam. The GP has dark-colored calcareous clay soils over limestone. Soils in the NCP are brown, neutral to slightly acid sandy or clay loams; however, some areas are rocky (Gould 1975b).

Vegetation Characteristics

Vernon Bailey, author of the 1905 *Biological Survey of Texas,* recognized the importance of the CTP as a faunal transition area (Schmidly 2002:365). Duck and Fletcher (1943:19–22) describe the "Post Oak Blackjack–Game Type" in Oklahoma. Their description of vegetation characteristics of the CTP is similar to the one by Gould (1975b). Dyksterhuis (1946, 1948) provides a historical review of previous documentation of vegetation characteristics in the region. Major species mentioned in these accounts are similar to those identified by Gould.

Presently, even with a wide variation in soil and range sites, the climax understory vegetation is fairly uniform. Predominant grasses are little bluestem (*Schizachyrium scoparium*), big bluestem (*Andropogon gerargi*), indiangrass (*Sorghastrum nutans*), switchgrass (*Panicum virgatum*), Canada wild rye (*Elymus canadensis*), sideoats grama (*Bouteloua curtipendula*), hairy grama (*B. hirsuta*), tall dropseed (*Sporobolus asper*), and Texas wintergrass (*Stipa leucotricha*) (Gould 1975b). The ECT and WCT vary from open savanna to closed-canopy post oak and blackjack oak forests.

Bobwhite Population Trends

Northern bobwhite populations have declined significantly in the CTP (DeMaso, Peterson, et al. 2002). Two different surveys, the Texas Parks and Wildlife Department (TPWD) August quail roadside survey and the U.S. Fish and Wildlife Service Breeding Bird Survey (BBS), conducted in early spring, show similar declines (figures 8.2 and 8.3).

Small-game harvest mail surveys conducted by the TPWD from

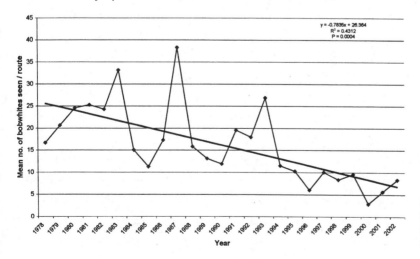

Northern Bobwhite Texas Parks and Wildlife Department Quail Survey Population Trend in the Cross Timbers and Prairies of Texas

$$y = -0.7835x + 26.384$$
$$R^2 = 0.4312$$
$$P = 0.0004$$

Figure 8.2.
Northern bobwhite population trend in the Cross Timbers and Prairies, TPWD quail survey, 1978–2002.

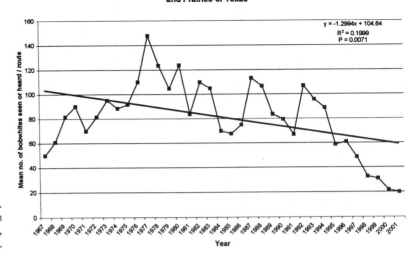

Figure 8.3.
Northern bobwhite population trend in
the Cross Timbers and Prairies, BBS,
1967–2001.

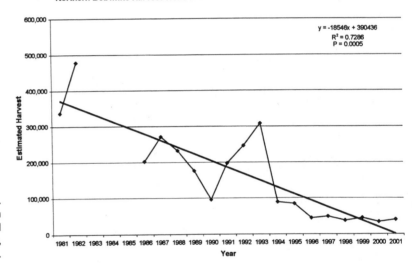

Figure 8.4.
Estimated hunter harvest of northern
bobwhites in the Cross Timbers and
Prairies, TPWD small-game survey,
1981–2001.

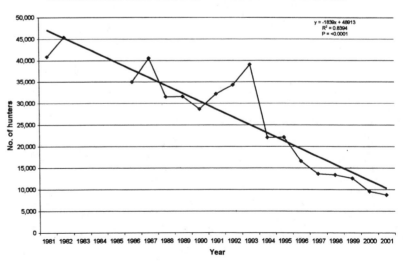

Figure 8.5.
Estimated number of northern bobwhite hunters in the Cross Timbers
and Prairies, TPWD small-game survey,
1981–2001.

1981 to 2001 show a significant decline in the estimated number of bobwhites harvested and the estimated number of bobwhite hunters (figures 8.4 and 8.5).

Changing Land-Use Impacts on Bobwhite Populations

Farm tenancy averaged 65–70 percent in the CTP portion of Oklahoma during the early 1940s (Duck and Fletcher 1943). Average farm size was about 32 hectares (79 acres). The primary crop was cotton; however, grain sorghums, berries, peanuts, and orchards were important in certain areas of the CTP in Oklahoma. Duck and Fletcher (1943) reported that about 75 percent of the CTP in Oklahoma was woodland.

Grazing

By 1883, most ranchers and farmers on the CTP had fenced their properties with barbed wire; and by 1889, portions of the CTP had been plowed for cotton production (Dyksterhuis 1946). The CTP was subjected to its first severe overstocking in the late 1880s. Grazing occurred largely on natural vegetation; however, some permanent tame pastures (bermudagrass) had been established before the middle of the twentieth century (Dyksterhuis 1948). Grazing by domestic livestock was the primary cause of CTP vegetation modification.

Fire

Early settlers near Jacksboro, Texas, recall no undergrowth of shrubs, but mid- and tall grasses, which commonly burned during dry periods (Dyksterhuis 1948). Dyksterhuis also reported that 44 percent of the trees in 269 sample plots had not been burned for one to five years. Elwell, Daniel, and Fenton (1941) reported average annual soil and water losses as a result of burning in the CTP of Oklahoma.

Cultivation and Crops

During 1945, 17.8 percent of the WCT was in cultivation (Dyksterhuis 1948). Peanuts, grain sorghums, small grains, corn, and cotton were the principal crops.

Present Land-Use Practices

Dyksterhuis (1948) reported that the subdivision of large ranches on the CTP began about 1890 and continued for 20–40 years, depending on the location. Erosion caused the abandonment of many fields and farms. Consolidation of small-crop farms into livestock ranches occurred after only two to four decades of cultivation. Today, land use in the CTP is variable, with agriculture and cattle ranching the two largest land uses (Gould 1975b).

The elimination of fire and overgrazing by livestock transformed much of the historic prairie areas into scattered brushlands that are now dominated by mesquite, juniper, and other native woody species. In many areas, native grasses have been replaced by introduced species, such as coastal bermudagrass, to provide forage and permit higher stocking rates for livestock. Considerable acreage throughout the region that once supported populations of bobwhites no longer provides habitat.

As property size decreases and land use changes, habitat for bobwhites is often directly impacted in a negative manner. Many of the basic components of good bobwhite habitat become fragmented, depleted, or otherwise altered. Large tracts of continuous habitat that are needed to sustain populations of bobwhites have become scarce in the CTP ecoregion.

Natural and human-caused influences have and always will have dramatic effects on populations of bobwhites in the CTP. Annual bobwhite reproduction is most influenced by rainfall and temperature patterns. The CTP is known for periodic drought, record-breaking high temperatures during the summer months, and occasional extremely cold winters. The intensive application of proven land management practices known to improve habitat for bobwhites may ultimately fail if extreme climatic conditions occur and limit reproductive success or survival. In addition, these extremes have a broader effect on growth of vegetation that provides food and cover for bobwhites. Bobwhites have to compete in the CTP for a place at the landscape table with other wildlife and other land uses.

Future Land-Use Practices and Bobwhite Management Opportunities

The human population in Texas is projected to increase 100.7 percent from 2000 to 2050 (figure 8.6). In 2000, the CTP had a human density of about 1 person/2.4 hectares (5.9 acres). By 2050, the projected human density will be about 1 person/1.2 hectares (2.9 acres). Where will these additional people live? What will they eat? Human population factors alone present huge management challenges with respect to sustaining wild quail populations on the CTP.

As human population increases, fragmentation of the landscape increases, property size declines, and fewer and fewer areas of sufficient size are available to support viable bobwhite populations. Guthery, Peterson, and George (2000) suggested that bobwhite populations need a minimum of 800 bobwhites at the lowest point in their population cycle if they are to persist for 100 years. Assuming a bobwhite density of 1 bird/4 hectares (about 10 acres), an assumption that is quite generous for most of the CTP, we need at least 3,240 hectares (8,000 acres) of bob-

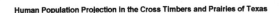

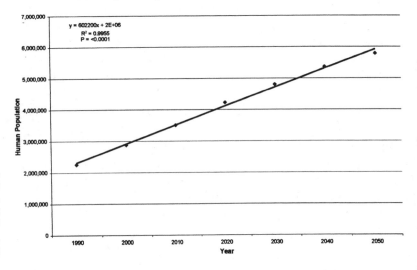

Human Population Projection in the Cross Timbers and Prairies of Texas

$y = 602200x + 2E+06$
$R^2 = 0.9955$
$P = <0.0001$

Figure 8.6.
Projected human population growth in the Cross Timbers and Prairies, 1990–2050 (http://www.twbd.state.tx.us/data/popwaterdemand/main.asp).
Courtesy GIS Lab at CKWRI–TAMUK

white habitat to sustain just one viable, long-term bobwhite population in the CTP ecoregion.

There are several ways to develop large areas to support viable quail populations in the CTP. Three examples come to mind. First, the Lyndon B. Johnson National Grassland near Decatur, Texas, was once an area that supported good bobwhite numbers. With some prescribed burning and better grazing management, this area could again support viable bobwhite populations. Second, Fort Hood, the U.S. Army post near Killeen, Texas, provides a large area that, with some habitat improvements, could restore bobwhite populations. Last, landowners of any size property can join together to form wildlife cooperatives (see chapter 21 on forming quail management cooperatives). By working together, having common goals, and modifying their current land-use practices, landowners can supplement their agricultural income by marketing the wildlife on their properties for both consumptive and nonconsumptive uses (see chapter 18 on quail economics).

The following list describes the most important land-use practices in the CTP that will affect bobwhites in the future:

1. Land and habitat fragmentation: Bobwhites need large areas of usable habitat for long-term viability. Proactive planning to preserve blocks of good remaining bobwhite habitat will help protect bobwhite populations. Because weather conditions are variable, conservative cattle stocking rates will help ensure suitable nesting and brood-rearing cover during normal and drought years.
2. Increased use of fire: Fire helps keep the canopy open so that sunlight can reach the ground. Periodic fire improves nesting and brood-rearing cover, especially in forested and brushy areas.
3. Increased use of native grasses: Many improved grasses form dense mats of sod and lack suitable structure required for good bobwhite nesting and brood-rearing cover. The exotic species range in the amount of usable space they provide for quails, from bermudagrass, about 0 percent, to buffelgrass and weeping lovegrass, which actually can be a quail savior in drought years in South Texas and provide nesting cover in the Texas Panhandle.

There are no known bobwhite management case histories in the CTP.

What Do We Know about Bobwhites in the CTP?

In central Oklahoma, total nitrogen content of four preferred bobwhite seeds was composed of 28–43 percent nonamino nitrogen of limited nutritional value (Boren et al. 1995). Boren et al. suggest that assays of crude protein may overestimate the true protein content of food for wildlife. Amino acid content of seeds in lieu of crude protein may better describe the nutritional ecology of bobwhites.

Calling Behavior

Hansen and Guthery (2001) noted that bobwhite calling activity and count precision were maximal during a one-hour period beginning 10–20 minutes after sunrise. Calling activity varied seasonally between years, violating an assumption required to determine annual trends in population abundance. Calling activity, as perceived by a human observer, declined as air temperature, wind speed, and light intensity increased. Calls increased as humidity increased.

Diet

Boren et al. (1996) reported that four-week-old, captive-raised northern bobwhite body mass was reduced on 8 and 15 percent crude protein diets. They reported that total concentrations of sulfur-containing amino acids, ratios of branched chained to nonbranched chain amino acids, essential amino acid to nonessential amino acids, and glycine to (leucine + valene) in blood serum were useful for discriminating among diet groups.

Dabbert, Lochmiller, Waldroup, and Teeter (1996) fed captive-reared bobwhite hens diets with varying amounts of methionine. Mean egg weight, percentage of egg production, total cumulative egg production, yolk weight, yolk volume, and percentage of fertility and percentage of hatch of fertile eggs did not differ among diets.

Disturbance during Field Trials

Wiseman (1977) evaluated the effect of field trials on bobwhite coveys in the CTP of Oklahoma. He reported that disturbed coveys neither temporarily nor permanently abandon their previous home ranges. Dogs found only 20 percent of the birds available on hunt courses, and the gallery was responsible for a large percentage of disturbance to coveys.

Food Habits

Baumgartner (1946) stressed the effect of land-use changes on bobwhite foods contained in crops of birds collected during fall and winter in north-central Oklahoma. Lee (1948) provided a list of the fall and winter foods used by bobwhites in the CTP of Oklahoma. Baumgartner et al. (1952) reported that 99 percent of total bobwhite food was vegetable matter (seeds); 51 percent, seeds of annual plants; 27 percent, seeds of perennial plants; and 21 percent, seeds of genera containing both annuals and perennials. He also noted that overgrazing, cultivated crops, and by-products of cultivation were important land uses related to bobwhite food production. Morris (1957) reported that many high-ranking bobwhite foods in the CTP are considered pests by landowners.

Habitat Management

Results of a five-year study of bobwhite management near Stillwater, Oklahoma, suggested that (1) overgrazing reduces fall populations; (2) fall and early-winter fires destroy covey ranges for that season; (3) pole and board shelters do not provide suitable escape cover; and (4) planting ornamental trees, shade trees, and shrubs provides food and cover for bobwhites during winter (Baumgartner 1945).

On habitat management, Morris (1957:99) stated, "Very little habitat management for bobwhite will probably be done by anyone except the private landowner. Thus, the management practiced must offer him an economic return either directly or indirectly."

Derdeyn (1975) reported that burning, disking, and fertilizing all increased the number of food-producing plants but failed to produce more seeds available to bobwhites. Burning and burning-disking treatments reduced ground-litter accumulation. Early-spring burning followed by fertilization showed the best potential for improving bobwhite habitat in the tallgrass prairie in Oklahoma.

Engle, Stritzke, and McCollum (1991) reported that standing crop of grasses and forbs increased following herbicide treatments in the CTP of Oklahoma. Grass production was greater with tebuthiuron, whereas production of forbs and browse was greater with triclopyr. Tebuthiuron and triclopyr both reduced the canopy of blackjack oak and post oak (Stritzke, Engle, and McCollum 1991). Crown reduction and tree kill of these hardwood species were generally better with tebuthiuron. Neither herbicide was effective on eastern red cedar (*Juniperus virginianus*). Areas treated with tebuthiuron resulted in a better fine-fuel release, allowing fire to reduce woody plants.

Schulz et al. (1992a) found that more birds and more bird species were found on herbicide-treated sites in the CTP of Oklahoma than on control sites. Herbicide type (tebuthiuron and triclopyr) had no effect on bird-species abundance. Herbicide-treated sites had the highest bird-species richness, but untreated areas were important for interior woodland bird species.

Boren et al. (1993) reported that brush management by herbicide, herbicide plus fire, and mechanical removal had minimal long-term effects on bobwhite body condition. However, seasonal differences in weight of gizzards, gizzard fat, liver, and lipid reserves (body and gizzard fat) were observed.

Habitat Use

DeArment (1950) described timbered ravines, hedges, thickets, forbs, and ungrazed tall grass as the most important habitats for bobwhites. Cultivating, grazing, clearing ravines of protective and productive vegetation, cutting out hedges and thickets, removing weed patches, and burning affected and often impaired bobwhite habitat.

Wiseman and Lewis (1981) estimated bobwhite home range to be 4.4 ± 0.6 hectares (10.9 ± 1.5 acres) in the northeastern portion of the CTP in Oklahoma. Bobwhites preferred tall and short shrub habitats, used woodland in proportion to its availability, and used large-seeded forb and grassland habitats less than would occur if use were random.

Guthery, Green, et al. (2001) reported that calling rates of male bobwhites in Oklahoma declined with increasing quantity of mature woodland and increased with increasing quantity of brushy prairie or early-successional woodland. Bobwhites responded more strongly to the composition than to the configuration of land-cover classes on areas. The highest populations were observed in the absence of cropland agriculture.

Hunting

Baumgartner (1944a) found similar spring densities between hunted and unhunted areas in the CTP of Oklahoma. He suggested that bobwhites could tolerate a harvest rate between 20 and 55 percent. This could be true only if fall densities were higher in the hunted area (Guthery 2002). Baumgartner admitted that the hunted area had a "more favorable distribution of food and cover" than the unhunted area. Strictly interpreted, the results show that spring populations on hunted areas with good habitat are about the same as on unhunted areas with poor habitat (Guthery 2002).

Gore, Holt, and Barron (1971) suggested that the opening date of quail hunting season in north-central Texas should coincide with the average date when 90 percent of juvenile bobwhites weigh 150 grams (5.3 ounces). The average date that bobwhites achieved this weight during the five-year study was November 25.

Nesting Habitat

Reid, Grue, and Silvy (1978) reported that bobwhites selected shrublands and deciduous savanna as nesting habitat in the CTP. Mesquite habitats did not appear to be important for bobwhites in the CTP of Texas.

Pen-Raised Bobwhites

Results of a study on releasing birds to supplement wild populations in the CTP of Oklahoma indicate that heavy restocking with game-farm birds appears to be costly and a futile method to increase bobwhite populations for hunting or to increase spring breeding populations (Baumgartner 1944b).

Maple and Silvy (1988) reported that recovery rate of pen-reared bobwhites varied depending on when birds were released for hunting purposes. The largest recovery occurred on birds released during the last two months of hunting. The cost per bird was lowest for birds released just prior to hunting.

Population Status

DeMaso, Peterson, et al. (2002) compared bobwhite population trends based on the TPWD August quail roadside survey and the BBS. The surveys showed similar population trends in the CTP of Texas.

Weather Effects

Dabbert, Lochmiller, and Teeter (1996) reported that thermal stress did not affect serum asparate aminotransferase or albumin concentrations of captive-reared male bobwhites. Lactate dehydrogenase and uric acid in serum of cold-stressed birds were greater than concentrations in thermoneutral or heat-stressed birds. Serum total protein was greater in cold-stressed birds than in heat-stressed birds.

Dabbert, Lochmiller, and Teeter (1997) found that thermal stressors did not influence spleen mass or cell-mediated and humoral immunity. Disease resistance of bobwhites to *Pasturella multocida* was not influenced by heat stress but increased following cold stress.

Bridges et al. (2001) reported that neither the 12-month Modified Palmer Drought Severity Index (MPDI) nor 12-month raw precipitation was correlated to bobwhite abundance in the CTP of Texas. November, December, January, and February MPDIs were most correlated with bobwhite abundance in the CTP.

Toxicology

Dabbert, Sheffield, and Lochmiller (1996) reported no difference in percentage of egg viability, percentage of egg hatchability, apparent chick malformations, and immunocompetence of chicks exposed to different levels of diazinon.

Problems Facing Bobwhites

Habitat conditions and weather are the factors that have the greatest influence on bobwhite populations. Weather cannot be managed, but habitat can. The biggest factor facing bobwhites in the CTP of Texas is isolation that results from habitat fragmentation. Once a bobwhite population becomes separated from other bobwhite populations, the probability of extinction increases because a population is increased only through reproduction and immigration into the population.

Land-use practices are working against bobwhites in the CTP. As the CTP landscape becomes more fragmented, bobwhite populations become separated by larger distances, thus decreasing opportunities for dispersal. Lack of fire and overgrazing by livestock reduce nesting cover and brood-rearing cover, decreasing reproduction. The result is bobwhite populations that cannot produce enough young birds to be self-sustaining.

Research Needs

Bobwhite research in the CTP of Texas needs to focus on the following, in no particular order.

1. Geographic information systems (GIS) need to be utilized to determine where suitable bobwhite habitat exists. This information can be used to protect existing habitat from destruction and link bobwhite populations that are isolated (figure 8.7).
2. For quail management in the CTP to be effective, we need a better understanding of bobwhite movements and dispersal in landscapes with varying degrees of fragmentation.
3. We need a better understanding of how metapopulation theory and dynamics apply to bobwhites. Much of what is known about bob-

Figure 8.7.
Examples of good bobwhite habitat in the Cross Timbers and Prairies.
Photos by Jim Dillard

white population ecology comes from areas with large amounts of suitable bobwhite habitat.

4. Knowledge of the economic worth of bobwhites in the CTP of Texas is a critical aspect of quail management that has not been investigated. For example: How much will a quail hunter in Dallas pay for a productive CTP lease three hours from home, taking into account the added time and expense required for traveling to South Texas to hunt bobwhites?

5. We need a better understanding of landowner attitudes in the CTP of Texas. Land managers should use bobwhite-friendly management practices. What would it take to get them to manage for bobwhites?

6. It would be a great step forward to develop a TPWD Wildlife Management Area located in the CTP. Such an area should be large enough to conduct research on bobwhites and other wildlife species. The results of research conducted on the area could provide landowners with knowledge to help sustain and increase populations of bobwhites and improve habitat management practices throughout the region. Research and demonstration of proper land management practices beneficial to bobwhites could be tested and applied under different land uses.

Bobwhite Management on Private and Public Lands

Bobwhite management can be frustrating because results from management efforts are often not immediate. Weather conditions can negatively influence management practices. Land management practices on one tract of land can influence the bobwhite population on neighboring property. A land manager can do everything perfectly, but if the land being managed is in the wrong spatial (i.e., too small an area) scale or temporal (too little time since management was initiated) scale relationship to everything else that affects the property, populations are not likely to respond.

One practice to ensure that there is enough property to manage a bobwhite population is the formation of wildlife cooperatives (see chapter 21). Cooperatives involve owners of small tracts of land agreeing to manage their properties in a similar manner to achieve a common goal. The cooperative system has worked well for managing deer on small properties in East Texas.

Many owners of small tracts of rural land do not need the agricultural income from their property. Many have purchased their land for recreational purposes. This provides an opportunity to improve lands for bobwhites. If these landowners have specific goals and plans, they can often improve wildlife habitat on their properties. See chapter 22 on technical information for quail managers.

Many agencies offer programs to financially assist landowners in managing wildlife habitat on their properties. The TPWD has a Landowner Incentive Program (LIP) that assists landowners managing for threatened and rare species and rare and declining habitats. Bobwhite habitat requirements are similar to those of many rare wildlife species in the CTP, so what is good management for one often benefits many other species (figure 8.8). For more information about the LIP, contact LIP Coordinator, Texas Parks and Wildlife Department, 4200 Smith School Road, Austin, TX 78744-3291; (512) 581-0657.

Assistance is also available from TPWD under the Private Lands and Habitat Program and the staff of regional technical guidance biologists, private lands biologists, district wildlife biologists, and district wildlife technicians that help landowners develop written wildlife and habitat management plans for bobwhites and other wildlife species.

The U.S. Fish and Wildlife Service Partners Program assists landowners with wildlife habitat management. For more information, contact Partners Program, U.S. Fish and Wildlife Service, 711 Stadium Drive, Suite 252, Arlington, TX 76011; (817) 277-1100.

The TPWD Pastures for Upland Game Birds Program focuses on increasing native vegetation and plant diversity in coastal bermudagrass pastures (figure 8.9). For information, contact Pastures for Upland Game Birds Program, Private Lands and Public Hunting Program, Texas Parks and Wildlife Department, 4200 Smith School Road, Austin, TX 78744; 1-800-792-1112 (menu #5).

The Natural Resources Conservation Service (NRCS) implements

Figure 8.8.
Timber that is periodically burned has an open canopy and more suitable nesting and brood-rearing habitat for bobwhites.
Photos by Jim Dillard

Figure 8.9.
Coastal bermudagrass field. Note the lack of suitable nesting structure, brood-rearing structure, and bare ground.
Photos by Jim Dillard

Figure 8.10.
A closed canopy of tree limbs allows
little sunlight to reach the ground,
leaving little nesting cover and
brood-rearing habitat.
Photos by Steve DeMaso

Figure 8.11.
Overgrazed native rangeland leaves
little to no nesting cover or brood-
rearing habitat for bobwhites.
Photos by Jim Dillard

the federal Farm Bill at the local level. Wildlife is a coequal with soil and water in many Farm Bill programs. Farm Bill programs such as the Conservation Reserve Program (CRP), Environmental Quality Incentives Program (EQIP), Wildlife Habitat Incentives Program (WHIP), and many others can be used to better manage rangeland, natural resources on that land, and bobwhites (figures 8.10 and 8.11). Contact your local TPWD technical guidance biologist and your local county district conservationist for assistance with Farm Bill programs and wildlife.

9 Bobwhites in the East Texas Piney Woods

R. Montague Whiting Jr.

> A forest of longleaf pine . . . which once occupied an area of about
> 5,000 square miles . . . is an extension of the same forest in Louisiana.
> This forest . . . is now heavily cut-over or replaced with twentieth-century
> plantings of introduced trees, especially the quick growing slash pine.
> Oberholser (1974)

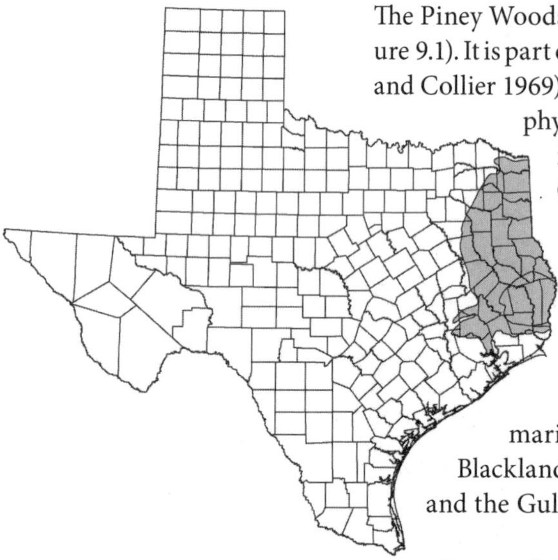

Figure 9.1.
The Piney Woods ecoregion
of East Texas.
Courtesy Caesar Kleberg Wildlife
Research Institute (CKWRI)
GIS Laboratory

The Piney Woods ecological region is on the eastern edge of Texas (figure 9.1). It is part of the West Gulf Coastal Plain (Fenneman 1938; Walker and Collier 1969), which includes much of western Louisiana. Based on physiography, the West Gulf Coastal Plain is separated into the Upper Gulf Coastal Plain and the Lower Gulf Coastal Plain; approximately half of the Piney Woods is in each. Dice (1943) and Blair (1950) included the Piney Woods region in the Austroriparian Province. The region encompasses 16 counties entirely, more than 50 percent of 11 counties, and somewhat less than 50 percent of 10 counties. It adjoins Louisiana to the east and is bordered on the north and west primarily by the Post Oak Savannah region. A finger of the Blackland Prairies intersects the Piney Woods in the southwest, and the Gulf Prairies and Marshes are to the south (Gould 1962).

Extent of the Piney Woods

According to Gould (1962), the region contains approximately 6,073,000 hectares (15 million acres) in 37 counties. However, the Texas Forest Service classified the Piney Woods as occupying 4,575,000 hectares (11.3 million acres) in 43 counties (Anonymous 1970). Murphy (1976) listed about 5,870,000 hectares (14.5 million acres) in the region, and McWilliams and Lord (1988:5) stated that "the total land base of the East Texas Piney Woods is 21.6 million acres," thus 8,740,000 hectares; Rosson (2000) used the same numbers. No doubt the latter estimates include eastern portions of the Post Oak Savannah region. Approximately 4,777,000 hectares (11.8 million acres) are classified as timberland suitable for production of timber products (Ramos 1997). In 1986, commercial forests and croplands made up approximately 55 percent and 15 percent, respectively, of the 5,870,000 hectares. The remainder was in rangelands and residential areas. Both timber and agricultural (including range) lands were lost to urban and industrial uses between 1975 and 1986. However, about 296,000 hectares (731,000 acres), almost all agricultural lands, were converted to forests; thus, the net loss to forest land was only 0.8 percent (McWilliams and Lord 1988). Between 1986 and 1992, there was an increase in forest lands of 82,000 hectares (202,700 acres), most of it from agricultural lands (Rosson 2000).

Approximately 93 percent of the land is in private ownership. Of the total, forest industry owns about 32 percent, private individuals own 61 percent, and 7 percent is in public ownership. The U.S. Forest Service manages most public land. That agency has responsibility for about 259,000 hectares (640,000 acres) in the Piney Woods. Other federal agencies manage about 36,000 hectares (90,000 acres), excluding reservoirs; state and county governments manage slightly less than 28,000 hectares (70,000 acres) (McWilliams and Lord 1988).

Climate

The Piney Woods region extends approximately 370 kilometers (230 miles) from north to south and is approximately 200 kilometers (125 miles) wide at its widest point. Elevation above sea level ranges 60–150 meters (200–500 feet) (Gould 1962). As a result, the region is subject to a wide range of climatic conditions. Generally, average annual precipitation and average annual temperature increase from northwest to southeast. Average annual precipitation ranges 100–148 centimeters (40–56 inches). Average normal annual temperature ranges 30°C–32°C (64°F–68°F). Length of the growing season averages 230–245 days throughout most of the Piney Woods (Orton 1969).

Soils

Soils on the Upper Gulf Coastal Plain of the Piney Woods are mostly on rolling topography and generally have fine sand to fine sandy-loam surfaces; subsoils are clay loams and sandy clays. Surface soils are light in color, relatively low in organic matter, slightly acidic, and low in natural fertility. Subsoils are often red due to high ferric acid content. Alluvial soils are derived from surrounding uplands and are therefore slightly acidic. Soils on the Lower Gulf Coastal Plain are on near-level topography, sometimes called flatwoods. These soils generally have poor internal drainage; thus, subsoils lack bright colors. Textures of the surface soils range from fine sands to silt loams; the soils are acid with low fertility. Subsoils are generally heavy, gray clays. Due to slow internal drainage, flatwood soils often remain saturated throughout late fall, winter, and early spring (Carter 1931).

Vegetation and Land Use

Plant geographers have subdivided the Piney Woods into two or three subregions. Most have agreed that prior to the 1880s the longleaf pine (*Pinus palustris*)–bluestem (*Andropogon* spp.) community dominated the southeast-central portion of the region. Some authors described a belt of loblolly pine (*P. taeda*) in the southwest and a large area of shortleaf pine (*P. echinata*) in the northwest portions of the region (Bray 1904; McWilliams and Lord 1988). Other writers have grouped the loblolly and shortleaf pines and named the area simply pine-hardwood (Smeins and Slack 1982). Vegetative structure of the Piney Woods probably was relatively stable for thousands of years before the arrival of Europeans (Walker 1991). Based on descriptions of early explorers and settlers, uplands in the Piney Woods were dominated by open stands of pines; hardwoods were dominant along streams and river bottoms.

The importance of fire in creating and maintaining the vegetative structure of the Piney Woods cannot be overstated. The pines, the prairies, and the lack of hardwoods were the result of regular fires. Pines, especially longleaf, are very tolerant of, even dependent on, fire; most hardwoods are not. Although lightning started some fires, most probably were started by American Indians. The use of fire by American Indians was widespread and long term. In the 1540s, Cabeza de Vaca noted that American Indians regularly burned the forests of the Gulf Coastal Plain, including those in Texas (Fehrenbach 1968; Hodge and Lewis 1984). Traveling less than 120 kilometers (72 miles) in and around the Piney Woods in the 1680s, René-Robert Cavelier, Sieur de La Salle, recorded seven major fires set by American Indians; one such fire was in what is now the Davy Crockett National Forest (Foster 1998). In the 1720s, Le Page du Pratz commented on clouds of smoke during the fall (du Pratz 1774). Indians told early settlers that the woods were burned in spring and fall to kill ticks, fleas, and snakes and to capture and drive mammals. Early settlers and then stock raisers followed the same tradition until the 1950s (Reid 1953; Sitton 1995).

Prior to the arrival of Europeans, the Caddo Indians had a complex culture with well-defined social strata. They lived in more or less permanent towns and villages, growing corn, beans, and other vegetables (Cowdry 1983). Lacking fertilizer, Indians probably practiced a modified slash-and-burn agriculture; towns and villages abutting fertile river-bottom soils were the most enduring. These practices affected the pattern of forest types and ages of timber stands first noted by European explorers (Walker 1991).

Early European settlers used similar agricultural practices. Permanent communities were established adjacent to streams and rivers. Newcomers, especially those in the lower socioeconomic strata, were scattered throughout the Piney Woods, where they practiced subsistence agriculture on less fertile soils. However, that pattern began to change about 1880 when the vast pineries caught the eyes of entrepreneurs who had exhausted the forests of the Lake States (figure 9.2).

Forest Lands

What has been called the "bonanza era" of logging in East Texas began in the early 1880s (Maxwell and Baker 1983); some have called it the cut-out-and-get-out era or the boom era. Regardless, steam-powered sawmills, steam-powered locomotives, and cheap labor made harvesting the virgin forest economical. By 1907, there were 600 sawmills, at least 100 of which could be classified as large, in East Texas. By 1932, virtually all the virgin stands had been harvested, and most of the large lumber companies had moved west or shut down. What remained of the Piney Woods were abandoned cutover areas (figure 9.3), understocked second-growth stands, and thousands of miles of railroad beds (figure 9.4). The vegetation structure of the Piney Woods had been drastically altered.

The tradition of burning the woods continued, however, primarily to improve grazing for free-ranging livestock (Goodrum 1949; Lay 1952). The frequent, relatively hot fires prevented even the fire-tolerant pines from regenerating. As a result, foresters with the Texas Forest Service began promoting fire prevention and exclusion in 1916. In 1936, the federal government established four national forests in the Piney Woods, mostly on cutover lands abandoned by forest industries. Shortly thereafter, the Civilian Conservation Corps (CCC) began replanting these lands; thus, federal foresters were also promoting fire exclusion (McWilliams and Lord 1988). Over time, the success of these efforts also altered the vegetation structure of the Piney Woods.

After World War II, forest industry was again a shaping force in the

Figure 9.2.
Harvesting a stand of virgin old-growth longleaf pines in eastern Texas. From the Thomas Family Enterprises Collection, Stephen F. Austin State University

Figure 9.3.
An area that was regularly burned and probably grazed after the virgin pine stands had been harvested. From the Sawdust Empire Collection, Stephen F. Austin State University

Figure 9.4.
Map of eastern Texas showing railroads used to haul logs when the virgin forests were harvested. From the Sawdust Empire Collection, Stephen F. Austin State University

Piney Woods; a few forward-thinking companies had survived from the boom era, and others had moved into East Texas. Companies hired professional land managers, primarily foresters, and began to practice intensive forest management. Research throughout the South, including East Texas, demonstrated that industrial forests managed by using uneven-aged regeneration systems showed declining inventories (Walker 1991). By the early 1970s, most companies had converted to even-aged management of pine forests.

Even-aged management dictates that either seed trees be retained in harvested areas or the areas be clear-cut and planted. With longleaf and shortleaf pines, seed-tree regeneration is not dependable; thus, most companies elected to plant loblolly pine seedlings. Regardless, either regeneration system requires site preparation, that is, the removal of unmerchantable stems and logging debris.

Site-preparation techniques in the late 1950s and early 1960s were fairly simple. Chaining, cabling, or similar techniques uprooted unmerchantable stems. Debris may or may not have been burned. By the early 1970s, techniques had intensified such that unmerchantable vegetation was sheared and, along with logging debris, was raked into long piles called windrows. Windrows may or may not have been burned. The shearing and raking set plant succession back to the pioneer stage and created habitat for a wide array of early-successional birds (Whiting 1978). However, it was expensive, and sheared woody plants sprouted with renewed vigor and competed with the planted pine.

Throughout the late twentieth century, management of industrial and nonindustrial commercial forests continued to intensify. Rotation lengths for the planted pines shortened as site-preparation techniques reduced woody and herbaceous competition. Current intensive site-preparation techniques may include roller-chopping unmerchantable vegetation, spraying with herbicides to control both herbaceous and woody vegetation, burning the site, and then subsoiling and bedding as the seedlings are planted. After the first growing season, pine seedlings and goatweed (*Croton* spp.) will compose the vast majority of the vegetation on the site. Pines will have attained crown closure by year 3 or 4, and the landowner could have a first thinning by year 10 or 12; rotation lengths will range between 18 and 25 years.

At the opposite extreme are landowners who own small, nonindustrial forested tracts on which little or no management is practiced. Although such tracts are found throughout the Piney Woods, most are concentrated on the southern and western fringes and in the northern half of the region (McWilliams and Lord 1988). Often, merchantable timber on such tracts is harvested, and the landowner depends on nature to reforest the site. The resulting stand may be pure pine, pine-hardwood, hardwood-pine, or pure hardwood. In recent years, such practices, coupled with the abandonment of pastures and farmlands, have led to an increase in upland stands dominated by an oak-hickory type (*Quercus* spp.–*Carya* spp.) (McWilliams and Lord 1988; Rosson 2000).

U.S. Forest Service Lands

Currently, management of U.S. Forest Service lands is in limbo. Prior to about 1975, such lands were managed on a multiple-use, sustained-yield basis. Forests in each of the four national forests in Texas were made up of a multitude of even-aged stands; thus, each forest was un-even-aged. These stands, which ranged from 1 to greater than 100 years old, provided habitat for virtually every animal species that occurred in the Piney Woods. There were also numerous cattle-grazing allotments on Forest Service lands. Cattle grazing reduced the grass cover to the benefit of herbaceous annuals. Also, cattle movements created trails through thickets that allowed access by various wildlife species (Reid and Goodrum 1959).

Since 1977, the Forest Service has been under one or more federal court injunctions that have severely restricted management of national forest lands. For four years, the Angelina and Sabine national forests were under contradictory decrees by two federal judges: one (1988) required prescribed burning; the other (1999) prohibited that activity. Both injunctions were lifted in July 2003. Regardless, various decrees have virtually eliminated regeneration harvests and restricted burning and thinning. As a result, there is a lack of early-successional habitats in the national forests in Texas. Most such habitats are in the Sabine National Forest in an area devastated by a major windstorm in February 1998. The Forest Service received permission to site-prepare and regenerate approximately 4,000 hectares (10,000 acres) in the storm area.

Bobwhite (*Colinus virginianus*) habitat may be a by-product of southern pine forest management for red-cockaded woodpeckers (*Picoides borealis*), hereafter RCW, a federally listed endangered species. Thus, discussion of RCW management has direct bearing on bobwhite populations in the Piney Woods ecological region.

Court decrees also dictated how the Forest Service manages RCWs on national forests. This woodpecker has very specific habitat requirements, including open pine stands with little or no hardwood midstory and a ground cover of lush herbaceous grasses and forbs. The birds excavate cavities in living pines; cavity trees typically range from 40 to 60 centimeters (16 to 24 inches) in diameter at breast height (dbh). Usually, a RCW family group will excavate cavities in several trees in close proximity to one another (Conner, Rudolph, and Walters 2001). Such an aggregate of trees was referred to in the past as a colony but is currently called a cluster.

In 2002, there were approximately 280 clusters in the Texas national forests. Regulations require that the cluster areas be intensively managed for the woodpecker. Each cluster is a minimum of 4 hectares (10 acres) in size. In the cluster area, basal area of midstory stems should be no more than 1 meter^2/hectare (5 feet^2/acre); overstory basal area should be between 9 and 16 meters^2/hectare (40 and 70 feet^2/acre). Each cluster area must be burned, mowed, or treated with herbicide at least once every five years and preferably at shorter intervals to control the midstory.

Surrounding the cluster is a foraging habitat area and a habitat management area (HMA). In the 50-hectare (120-acre) foraging habitat, the midstory should be sparse or lacking, and basal area should be 9–16 meters^2/hectare. The HMA contains at least 2,500 hectares (10,000 acres) and generally encompasses numerous clusters. The current Forest Management Plan calls for the upland pine stands within the HMA to be managed in open, parklike conditions with grassy understories. Basal area should range 14–18 meters^2/hectare (60–80 feet^2/acre), with a minimum of 8 meters (25 feet) between trees. The HMA is to be burned at least once every five years, but preferably every second or third year, and then appropriate regeneration methods can be used. Plans are for the Forest Service to manage approximately 121,000 hectares (300,000 acres) as RCW habitat in the Piney Woods.

Agricultural Lands

The boom era of logging did not impact agricultural lands as drastically as it did forest lands. Perhaps the greatest impact was the expansion of the railroad system. Prior to 1875, railroads skirted the edges of the Piney Woods (Maxwell and Baker 1983). As a result, farmers and landowners had to haul cash crops, primarily cotton, beef, and pork, by wagon or steamboat to markets north and south of the Piney Woods. The first railroad between Shreveport and Houston was the Houston, East and West Texas Railroad, completed in 1886. The line passed through Nacogdoches and then through "Tenaha, Timpson, Bobo, and Blair."

At that time, the Piney Woods was a patchwork of small communities. The economy was based on agriculture, but mostly it was subsistence farming. Although most small farms were within a one-day wagon ride of a community, some were scattered throughout the Piney Woods. Regardless, the major cash crop was cotton. Most other crops were for personal use; these included peas, beans, corn, and other fresh vegetables. Corn was perhaps the most extensive crop. Not only was it used for human consumption but it was necessary for feeding livestock throughout the winter. Although beef cattle and hogs were allowed to roam free, milk cows, draft animals, and chickens had to be fed (Maxwell and Baker 1983).

All farm labor was by hand or draft animals. As a result, weed control was minimal. Once the crop plants established dominance, weed control was discontinued, even in cotton fields. Also, as cattle ranged free, it was necessary to build rail fences around crops. Fence lines, neither tilled nor burned, acted as reservoirs for weed seeds.

Although the logging activities improved transportation facilities, little changed in the agricultural community until well after World War I. Bailey (1905:18) described the Piney Woods as "a rich though only half-developed agricultural region." In 1924, the proportions of croplands in East Texas counties ranged from 40 percent in the central portion of the region to less than 3 percent in the southeastern portion (Carter 1931). Economically, cotton continued to be the most important crop; acreage planted in East Texas doubled between 1900 and 1930 (May 1981).

The arrival of the tractor in the 1920s was a first step toward drastically changing the agricultural landscape of East Texas (May 1981). Factors involving World War II accelerated the changes. Tenant farmers left the Piney Woods to enlist in the armed forces or go to work in the shipyards on the coast. After the war, most young people did not return to the farms; thus, tenant farming waned. Transportation systems, especially for the automobile, improved greatly. As a result, farmers no longer needed to plant gardens for themselves nor cornfields for their livestock. Likewise, counties passed stock laws that prohibited free-ranging livestock. Also, the use of mechanical farm implements greatly increased. Mechanization coupled with the loss of tenant farmers required larger fields and fewer fences. Finally, farmers rapidly adopted the use of synthetic pesticides for controlling weeds and insect pests. Among these pesticides was DDT (dichloro-diphenyl-trichloroethane), which was widely used on cotton to control boll weevils (*Anthonomus grandis*). As DDT lost its effectiveness, farmers turned to other chlorinated hydrocarbon chemicals for insecticides (Trefethen 1975). These chemicals not only killed the insects necessary for bobwhite chicks but also the birds themselves (D. W. Lay, Texas Parks and Wildlife Department [TPWD], retired, pers. comm.).

Although cotton remained the most economically important crop after the war, its importance declined as the East Texas cattle industry grew. Research involving pasture grasses and legumes in the 1960s led to a lengthened grazing season and increased weight gains for cattle. Between 1968 and 1970, the area in winter pasture increased 300 percent (May 1981). By the mid-1970s, cotton had practically disappeared from the East Texas landscape, and beef cattle had replaced it in importance. The growth of the cattle industry led to the conversion of row crops to pastures and hay fields.

Poultry research in the 1950s led to expansion of the broiler industry into East Texas by the early 1960s (May 1981). For about 20 years thereafter, the industry was dependent on producers with relatively small poultry houses. Such producers were scattered throughout the central and northern portions of the Piney Woods. Income from the broiler industry further depressed row-crop production. By the late 1970s, commercial row crops were no longer an important part of East Texas agriculture (J. L. Young, Agriculture Department, Stephen F. Austin State University, pers. comm.).

Currently, the primary agricultural crops in the Piney Woods are beef cattle and poultry. Most cattle are grazed on improved pastures of bahiagrass (*Paspalum notatum*), bermudagrass (*Cynodon* spp.), and/or tall fescue (*Festuca arundinacea*); hay fields are usually bermudagrass. Many producers use herbicides to control undesirable plant species and fertilizers to maximize production of desirable species. Producers that do not have improved pastures often severely overgraze native pastures and provide supplemental feed in the form of hay, cottonseed meal, or chicken litter.

In the poultry industry, the economy of scale has eliminated the many scattered small producers. These have been replaced by producers with as many as 10 houses, each capable of growing 20,000 broilers in a seven-week period. This development has forced small producers to seek other cash crops. Some are growing blackberries, blueberries, Christmas trees, and watermelons on a limited scale. However, the lack of a broadscale, profitable agricultural crop has forced many to convert their lands to tree farms. Although some grain crops are grown on the northern and southern fringes of the Piney Woods, most feed for the many chickens is produced outside the region.

Northern Bobwhite Population Trends

Although there are no data about bobwhite populations prior to the late 1960s, inferences can be made based on knowledge of habitat conditions, hunter-success stories, and early agency reports. When the Europeans arrived in the Piney Woods, bobwhite populations were probably relatively high (Reid and Goodrum 1959). The primitive agriculture practiced by Indians and their sedentary nature probably created scattered, weedy fields in which bobwhites thrived. Likewise, the regular burning of the forest benefited the species. Both bobwhites and their eggs were probably part of Indian diets.

Little changed as European settlers replaced the Indians. Although the settlers had better tools than the Indians did, agricultural practices still produced weedy fields, and the tradition of burning the forest continued. The settlers possessed guns that could be used to hunt bobwhites, and they probably trapped birds using lattice-type traps with figure-four triggers. However, the harvest probably had little or no impact on bobwhite populations. An early reference to bobwhite hunting comes from the diary of Adolphus Sterne, who lived in Nacogdoches. On Sunday, December 10, 1843, he wrote, "Cloudy at noon went hunting to Kill time, but did Kill nothing else except four little partridges" (McDonald 1969:84), which were obviously bobwhites. Earlier in that year he noted that "millions of Pidgeons [*sic*] flew over Town today. Shot only one. . . . Spent the afternoon in shooting grouse" (48). No doubt these were passenger pigeons (*Ectopistes migratorius*) and greater prairie-chickens (*Tympanuchus cupido*).

Bobwhite populations in the Piney Woods likely remained relatively high throughout the eighteenth century and the first half of the nineteenth century. Populations probably peaked between World War I and World War II (Reid and Goodrum 1959). By World War I, much of the virgin timber had been harvested, the cutover areas were burned on a regular basis, and cattle ranged free. Agricultural practices were still relatively primitive, and farmers continued to grow crops for home use. These conditions created vast areas of early-successional habitats that were ideal for bobwhites. Also, most people disposed of all "varmints" on sight, whether they flew, walked, or slithered. These predator-control efforts were to protect free-ranging chickens, not bobwhites, however.

The sport hunting of bobwhites evolved during the same time period. Guns and ammunition improved, as did transportation systems. Prior to the arrival of the railroad, hunters were restricted to the distance that they could walk or ride a horse or buggy. Railroads effectively doubled the distance because hunters could ride into the countryside and hunt on the way back home. By 1920, the automobile, sporting firearms, and ammunition were available and affordable (Trefethen 1975). Between then and World War II, the Piney Woods was known as the quail hunting capital of Texas (Reid and Goodrum 1959; Baker 1999).

Although bobwhites were plentiful during that period, there were real or perceived depressed local populations. The first game law in Texas, in 1860, "prohibited the hunting of quail (or partridge) for two years" (Doughty 1983:158). The Game, Fish and Oyster Commission of Texas was purchasing bobwhites for distribution to private landowners by 1916. At least 200,000 quail were purchased from Mexico between then and 1926; per-bird costs ranged $0.74–$1.00 (Hubby 1926; Tucker 1939). The practice continued through 1940 (Baker 1999), with 20,000 birds distributed that year (Tucker 1941). Bobwhites were also purchased from other states and private breeders for up to $2.50 each (Hubby 1926); some birds were trapped and relocated within Texas. Examination of quail distribution lists in the 1927–37 commission reports indicates that landowners in most Piney Woods counties received birds from Mexico and/or other southern states.

Although there was concern about declines in bobwhite numbers throughout much of Texas, the Piney Woods seemed to have been the exception (Tucker 1940). There were indications that bobwhite numbers increased during World War II (Dodgen 1945). During the late 1940s, a biologist with the Texas Game, Fish and Oyster Commission gathered more than 10,000 bobwhite wings from hunters in southeastern Texas during a seven-year period. The wings were used to evaluate age ratios (Lay 1952; D. W. Lay, TPWD, retired, unpublished data).

However, changing agricultural and land-use patterns in the Piney Woods after World War II led to the decline in bobwhite populations (Goodrum 1949). Into the early 1960s, the decline probably was almost imperceptible. Hunters continued to bag good numbers of bobwhites. One party of three hunters bagged 150 birds during a three-day hunt in Angelina County in the mid-1950s. An engineer for the U.S. Soil Conservation Service lived six blocks north of the Stephen F. Austin State University campus. He regularly walked from his house and killed a limit of birds after work in the early 1960s. He and a friend hunted every weekend and usually bagged limits (G. Adams, U.S. Soil Conservation Service, retired, pers. comm.). Likewise, a Texas Game and Fish Commission biologist collected 600 wings from a small group of Hardin County hunters in 1960 (C. D. Stutzenbaker, TPWD, retired, pers. comm.).

In 1967, the first Breeding Bird Survey (BBS), which is coordinated by the U.S. Fish and Wildlife Service, was conducted in the Piney Woods. Each spring, numerous volunteers record birds at 50 points along 39.2-kilometer (24.5-mile) routes. Each survey starts 30 minutes before local sunrise, and the observer spends 3 minutes at each point, recording all birds seen or heard.

Data for 1967 were available from only two routes in the Piney Woods, and 29 bobwhites were recorded. In 1970, 242 bobwhites were recorded along nine routes. However, by 2001, only 4 birds were recorded along six routes (figure 9.5); TPWD roadside surveys show a similar trend (figure 9.6). That survey, initiated in 1978, was discontinued in 1987 because of low numbers of bobwhites recorded. Finally, TPWD hunter surveys demonstrate the declines in numbers of hunters and in bobwhites harvested in the Piney Woods (figure 9.7). In 1981, 14,076 hunters bagged 73,456 bobwhites. In 2001, 953 hunters bagged 9,492 birds; no doubt some of these were pen-reared birds.

Bobwhites bagged by American woodcock (*Scolopax minor*) hunters

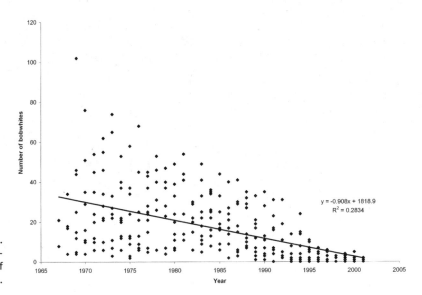

Figure 9.5.
Numbers of northern bobwhites recorded by BBS in the Piney Woods of East Texas, 1967–2001.

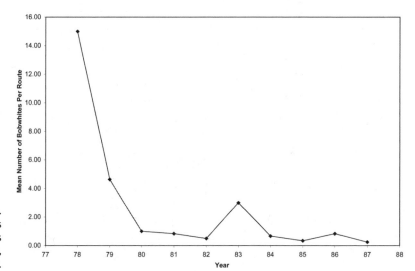

Figure 9.6.
Numbers of northern bobwhites recorded on TPWD roadside surveys in the Piney Woods of East Texas, 1978–87.

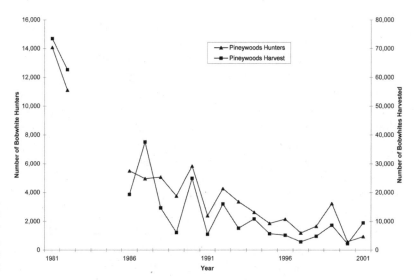

Figure 9.7.
Numbers of northern bobwhite hunters and bobwhites harvested in the Piney Woods of East Texas, 1981–2001. Data courtesy Texas Parks and Wildlife Department

mirror these declines. In the 1979–80, 1984–85, 1989–90, 1994–95, and 1999–2000 hunting seasons, 48, 30, 2, 5, and 1 bobwhites, respectively, were bagged. In 2000, the last grazing lease in the Texas national forests was discontinued. In three woodcock hunting seasons since then, no bobwhites have been found in a longleaf pine regeneration area that had previously supported two coveys. In fact, no bobwhites were observed or bagged during the 2000–2001 or 2001–2002 woodcock hunting seasons. However, during the 2002–2003 season, three coveys were observed and five birds bagged on site-prepared portions of the windstorm area in the Sabine National Forest (R. M. Whiting Jr., unpublished data). The inevitable conclusion is that wild northern bobwhites are disappearing from the Piney Woods landscape.

The Temple-Inland Boggy Slough Project

Temple-Inland Forest Products Corporation was one of the few large companies to remain in the Piney Woods after the timber boom faded. Founded in 1907, Temple-Inland prided itself on being a good steward of the land. In the late 1980s, the company committed to a project to manage approximately 610 hectares (1,500 acres) for northern bobwhites on land used by the South Boggy Slough Hunting and Fishing Club. The project area was in Trinity County, which is in the south-central portion of the Piney Woods region. It was approximately 24 kilometers (15 miles) west of Lufkin and 37 kilometers (23 miles) southwest of Nacogdoches. The objectives of the project were twofold: to rehabilitate and manage a bobwhite population on the area and to scientifically examine the effects of habitat modification and bobwhite relocation on the population recovery.

Habitat Modifications

Prior to habitat modifications, the project area was typical of second-growth forests managed for timber in the Piney Woods. The even-age overstory was primarily pure pine with mixed pine-hardwood types along drainages. Basal areas ranged 21–28 meters^2/hectare (90–120 feet^2/acre). Due to overhead competition and sporadic prescribed fire, the midstory was mostly open with scattered oaks, hickories, and sweetgum (*Liquidambar styraciflua*). The understory was dominated by grasses and scattered clumps of low-growing woody species, primarily American beautyberry (*Callicarpa americana*) and yaupon (*Ilex vomitoria*).

Habitat modifications began in 1988. Harvesting reduced basal area of overstory trees to 9–14 meters^2/hectare (40–60 feet^2/acre). Excepting escape-cover blocks and food plots, the entire area was burned in February 1989 (figure 9.8). Prior to the prescribed burn, 150 escape-cover blocks were established throughout the project area. Islands of natural vegetation, primarily yaupon, were protected. Where such vegetation was lacking, strips of thunburg lespedeza and autumn olive were planted. Excluding two 10-hectare (25-acre), five-year-old pine plantations, escape cover totaled 122 hectares (300 acres).

Food plots, both temporary and permanent, were established throughout the area. Temporary plots were small openings of less than 0.1 hectare (0.25 acre); roadsides, fire lines, and pipeline rights-of-way were planted seasonally. The 69 permanent food plots ranged 0.11–

Figure 9.8.
A loblolly pine stand managed for northern bobwhites. It was thinned and prescribed-burned in the winter prior to being photographed.
Photo by Don Dietz

Figure 9.9.
A northern bobwhite food plot with planted escape on its border.
Photo by Don Dietz

2.10 hectares (0.25–5.00 acres) in size and were located such that each was visible from at least one other.

Generally, the plots were divided into fourths. Current-year, warm-season species made up one-fourth; and current-year, first-year fallow, and second-year fallow fall-winter crops composed the remaining three-fourths. Most permanent food plots were bordered by natural or planted escape cover (figure 9.9). Food plots were disked and fertilized before they were seeded. Warm-season species planted included brown-top, Japanese, and pearltop millets (*Panicum* spp.), Egyptian wheat (*Sorghum* sp.), American jointvetch (*Aeschynomene americana*), kobe lespedeza (*Lespedeza striata*), partridge pea (*Cassia fasciculata*), cowpea (*Vigna* sp.), and Florida beggarweed (*Desmodium* sp.). Fall-winter portions of the plots contained winter wheat (*Triticum* sp.), ryegrass (*Secale* sp.), vetch (*Vicia* sp.), kobe lespedeza, partridge pea, and crimson and red clover (*Trifolium* spp.). Permanent food plots were protected from prescribed fires.

Habitat Maintenance
Beginning in 1991, approximately half of the area, including escape cover composed of natural vegetation, was burned late each winter. However,

permanent food plots and planted escape cover plots were protected from prescribed fire. In the mid-1990s, weather conditions considered acceptable for burning were restricted due to scorch to residual pines; these restrictions plus a series of wet winters severely reduced the effectiveness of the burns. Thus, hardwoods, especially sweetgum and yaupon, sprouted with renewed vigor. Therefore, the entire area, excluding food plots and escape cover, was treated with broadscale herbicides to control hardwoods in the spring of 2000. Since then, approximately one-third of the area has been burned each year; thus, the entire area is burned on a three-year cycle. Herbicides are still used on problem spots.

A major habitat management problem on Boggy Slough has been control of hardwoods and turfgrasses, especially bermudagrass and bahiagrass, both exotics, and southern crabgrass (*Digitaria ciliaris*), a native (D. R. Dietz, Temple-Inland Forest Products Corporation, pers. comm.). Winter burns do not adequately control these species, and summer burns may lead to unacceptable scorch. Grazing the area with domesticated livestock has been discussed but probably will not happen.

Bobwhite Population Rehabilitation

In the fall of 1988, a drive count of the project area did not flush any bobwhites. However, one covey was known to be on the area, and another was on its periphery. In January 1990, 13 bobwhites were captured on the project area and 31 were captured on North Boggy Slough Hunting Club in Houston County, 20–26 kilometers (12–15 miles) north of South Boggy. The resident birds were sexed, aged, banded, radio-tagged, and released at the point of capture. The North Boggy birds were likewise processed and released at predetermined points on the project area; both subpopulations were of the *mexicanus* subspecies. Additionally, 50 bobwhites of the *texanus* subspecies were captured on the King Ranch in Kenedy County and transported to South Boggy, where they were processed and released.

A drive count in February 1991 indicated approximately 200 bobwhites on the project area. Trapping was initiated immediately thereafter, and 71 birds (9 adults and 62 juveniles) were captured; 50 were radio-tagged and released at the point of capture. Also, 50 bobwhites from North Boggy and 50 from Kenedy County were radio-tagged and released on the project area; monitoring of these birds and 7 birds with active radios from the 1990 release continued throughout the year.

In February 1992, a drive count suggested approximately 225 bobwhites on the project area and about that many in the woods adjacent to the area; three coveys containing radio-tagged birds moved off the area in front of the drivers. That winter, 67 resident birds (14 adults and 53 juveniles) were captured in the two days; 55 were radio-tagged and released, as were 55 from North Boggy and 55 from Kenedy County. Monitoring of all radio-tagged birds (including 8 carryovers from 1991) continued until the start of white-tailed deer (*Odocoileus virginianus*) season in November 1992. At that time, the data-collection portion of the project was completed; results of the associated studies are in the research section of this chapter.

Population Trends

In June 1990, biologists with Temple-Inland initiated a roadside whistle-count survey on the project area. Since then, whistling bobwhites

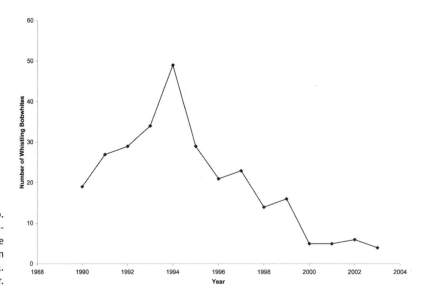

Figure 9.10.
Numbers of whistling bobwhites recorded along a 9.75-km route on the South Boggy Slough Hunting Club in Angelina County, Texas, 1990–2003.
Courtesy R. Montague Whiting Jr.

have been counted at 10 stops along a 9.75-kilometer (3.9-mile) transect around the periphery of the project area. Three surveys took place during mid-June of each year. Each survey day, the biologist was at the first stop by sunrise and recorded the number of different males heard during a three-minute period. This procedure was repeated at the second and then at the remaining stops. The data showed an increase in the numbers of whistling bobwhites until 1993 (figure 9.10). Thereafter, the numbers declined through 1999, probably reflecting a decline in habitat quality. The very low number in 2000 is an artifact of the herbicide treatment, which killed much of the understory and ground-cover vegetation. Thereafter, as herbaceous vegetation recovered, numbers increased for two years but then decreased in 2003. The low number in 2003 was probably an artifact of poor weather conditions and noise associated with a logging operation adjacent to the project area (D. R. Dietz, pers. comm.).

Bobwhite Research in the Piney Woods

Although the Boggy Slough project was perhaps the most intensive northern bobwhite research study in the Piney Woods, it was certainly not the first. As early as 1932, Valgene Lehmann, an instructor at the University of Texas, was investigating the impact of nine-banded armadillos (*Dasypus novemcinctus*) on bobwhite nests. The study was supervised by the U.S. Bureau of Biological Survey. He reported that armadillos destroyed 18 of 100 dummy nests. Hogs (*Sus scrofa*), foxes (family Canidae), skunks (family Mustelidae), crows (*Corvus* spp.), Virginia opossums (*Didelphis marsupialis*), snakes (suborder Serpentes), and rats (family Cricetidae) each destroyed 5 or more nests (Tucker 1934). It is unclear where the research took place, but the absence of raccoons (*Procyon lotor*) suggests it was not the Piney Woods. However, Baker (1999) indicated that there were several such studies, some of which examined feeding habits of the armadillo; all exonerated the species. He did not indicate where the studies were performed, but as armadillos appeared in eastern Texas about the same time that a decline in bobwhite numbers became noticeable (Lay 1952), some may have taken place in the Piney Woods.

In 1935, the Cooperative Wildlife Service Unit was formed under the direction of W. P. Taylor; the field biologists were Henry Hahn, Daniel W. Lay, and Valgene Lehmann (Tucker 1937). One of the first projects supported by the unit was the study of quail food plants in southeastern Texas by S. R. Warner, head of the Department of Biology, Sam Houston State Teachers College (Tucker 1937). Warner (1940) described the seeding and fruiting habits and food value to bobwhites of more than 90 herbaceous species or species groups and more than 40 woody species or species groups. He also noted the soils on which these plants performed best and the effects of grazing on them.

By 1938, biologists with the Texas Game, Fish and Oyster Commission had begun questioning the practicality of importing bobwhites from Mexico. In 1939, Game Division Chief Phil Goodrum assigned biologists Rollin Baker and Paul Jones the task of evaluating the program. These biologists banded 4,000 of the 20,000 Mexican bobwhites imported in 1940. Only 30 of the banded birds were reported by hunters; these birds had moved an average of 10.1 kilometers (6.3 miles) from their release sites; one bird moved 40.2 kilometers (25 miles). The biologists found that most release sites, including several in the Piney Woods, had abundant native bobwhites. As a result, despite much hue and cry, the practice was discontinued in 1941 (Tucker 1941; Baker 1999).

Studies by Dan Lay

By 1936, Lay was studying the wildlife resources of Walker County, which is in the pine-hardwood type on the southwestern edge of the Piney Woods. The emphasis was on bobwhites. Using CCC "boys" to make drive counts, Lay estimated 40,000 quail in the county. Roaming cats and dogs were considered a problem, as was tenantry (Tucker 1937). Tenantry was likely considered a problem because tenant farmers used box traps with figure-four triggers to capture "partridges." This practice continued into the 1950s, much to the chagrin of bird hunters. Also, Lay believed that blue jays (*Cyanocitta cristata*) were an important link between bobwhites and oaks in that jays knocked acorns from oaks and also dropped acorn chips to the ground where they were available to bobwhites (Lay and Siegler 1937; Tucker 1937).

In 1937, President Roosevelt approved the Pittman-Robertson Federal Aid to Wildlife Restoration Act. Texas' first Pittman-Robertson project, approved in 1938, was a long-range research, management, and demonstration program under the general supervision of Phil D. Goodrum. A part of that project was to continue studies of bobwhites and other species in Walker County. An early result of that project allayed concerns about skewed sex ratios resulting from hybridization by introduced Mexican and resident bobwhites (Tucker 1938).

Lay's (1940) bulletin on bobwhite populations also resulted from that project. It was perhaps the first Texas publication addressing bobwhite populations. He recorded more bobwhites in 5- to 9-year-old cutover stands than elsewhere. Areas on which the virgin timber had been cut 10–14 years earlier ranked second, and 1- to 4-year-old cutovers ranked third. The reason that bobwhite numbers were not highest in 1- to 4-year-old cutovers was that the best food plants had not had time to develop following removal of the overstory and subsequent fires (Tucker 1937; Lay 1940). Lay noted that bush clover (that is, common or kobe lespedeza [*Lespedeza striata*]) and doveweed (*Croton capitatus*) made up 57.8 percent of the diet of 56 bobwhites taken in late winter. Although he recorded the highest numbers of bobwhites in the 5-to 9-year-old cutovers, he wrote that the plant species present were more important than the age of the cutover. In the bulletin, he expressed reservations about burning cutover areas but supported it in longleaf pine forests. He found that cutover lands had more bobwhites than blackland farms did, but fewer than farms on sandy land. He recommended controlling brush by cutting, plowing, or burning. Grazing should be excluded on newly plowed, burned, or planted tracts and well regulated in other situations. Finally, he saw no benefits from restocking and suggested limited predator control (Lay 1940).

As a result of the Walker County work, Lay and Taylor (1943) developed a successional gradient of plants and animals (primarily game species). That gradient started with virgin pine stands and traced relative abundances through 45 years after harvest. Bobwhites and gray foxes (*Urocyon cinereoargenteus*) were the only animal species found completely across the spectrum. Jackrabbits (*Lepus californicus*) were recorded "almost as soon as the forest is cut" (Lay and Taylor 1943:448).

Lay continued to work on problems concerning bobwhites into the 1960s. However, at some point prior to 1946, he moved his research to Newton County, which is in the longleaf pine belt of the Piney Woods. There he initiated a five-year study to determine the effects of normal land use on bobwhite numbers and to evaluate trial plantings of bobwhite food and cover. Most of the material in this section is based on Lay (1952) unless otherwise noted.

The study area was composed of scattered, naturally seeded longleaf pines, slash pine (*Pinus elliottii*) plantations, a few small fields of row crops, and unimproved native grass pastures. At the time the study was initiated in 1946, the primary landowner began developing pastures and planting slash pines. These were among the major land-use conversions taking place in the Piney Woods at the time of the study.

During the study, bobwhite numbers increased from one bird per 17.4 hectares (43 acres) to one bird per 2.4 hectares (6 acres). Lay attributed the increase to the change in agricultural use during the period. Prior to the study, most of the study area was cutover pine stump land. During the study, much of the land was converted to improved pastures planted in kobe lespedeza for hay. Most of the fields were in small blocks or strips that allowed bobwhites to make maximum use of seeds produced by the lespedeza. Disturbance associated with the conversion was also an important factor benefiting the bobwhites. The removal of stumps and construction of roads and fire lanes through thick grass roughs produced seed-bearing annuals important to the species. However, bobwhite numbers declined as the hay fields increased in size and in proportion to fire lanes and roads.

The highest numbers of bobwhites were recorded where grazing was moderate. Lay wrote that not grazing at all and overgrazing both produced poor bobwhite habitat in unimproved native grasslands of the longleaf pine type. He recommended the use of fire in ungrazed habitats, pointing out that climax perennial grasses were not killed by most fires; thus, burns improve bobwhite habitat for about a year. Very hot fires do kill such grasses and may result in stands of partridge pea (*Cassia fasciculata*), crotonopsis (*Crotonopsis linearis*), and croton.

Lay noted that in a study in the Angelina National Forest, CCC workers had recorded one covey per 24.7 hectares (61 acres) in a fenced, newly planted slash pine plantation and one covey per 25.9 hectares (64 acres) outside the fence. Both areas had been burned the previous year. After three years of fire exclusion, the enrollees recorded one covey per 90.2 hectares (223 acres) and one covey per 70.8 hectares (175 acres) inside and outside the fence, respectively. Lay concluded that grazing outside the fence partially compensated for the lack of fire therein.

Using data from throughout the Piney Woods, Lay found that 1,325 of 1,513 bobwhites hatched before mid-August; 87 others hatched in late August, as did 91 in September and 10 in October. Percentage of young of the year in the population ranged from 68 in 1951–52 (D. W. Lay, unpublished data) to 82 in 1949–50. Sex ratios of the immature birds were about 50:50, whereas those of mature birds were skewed toward males. Lay attributed this to female mortality during the spring.

The effectiveness of food and cover plantings for bobwhites was also examined. Lay noted that many seed-producing species were unsatisfactory because they have to be cultivated, fenced against livestock, and replanted every year. Also, they were expensive, and their seeds deteriorated rapidly in winter. However, he wrote that bicolor lespedeza (*Lespedeza bicolor*) was the most promising plant for producing bobwhite food. Trial plantings began in 1945. By 1951, cooperators had planted the species in all Piney Woods counties and numerous counties in other regions (Lay 1952:37–39). He recommended 1,000 seedlings per unit with four or five rows of seedlings and 4.5–7.4 meters (15–25 feet) between rows; seedlings should be 0.6 meter (2 feet) apart.

Cover was not lacking on the study area. However, in planting trials, Lay had poor success with several native species. He wrote that multiflora rose (*Rosa multiflora*) was a first-rate bobwhite cover; it did not spread from runners or seeds as did some native roses (Lay 1952:46). When heavily fertilized in spring and fall, the species made excellent cover in three years and could be used as fencerows. At the time of the report, there were trial plantings of the species in counties throughout all but western Texas.

The research led to the publication of the *Quail Management Handbook for East Texas* (Lay 1954). Many of Lay's recommendations were based on the work done in Newton and Walker counties. He recommended against predator control. He also stated that restocking was unnecessary. Bobwhites move constantly, and if acceptable habitat is unoccupied, birds will move into it. He opposed the use of artificial feeders.

Lay (1954) continued to recommend planting kobe and bicolor lespedeza for food plots and multiflora rose for cover. He also recommended planting, or at least disking, rights-of-way and fire lanes. He emphasized the benefits of fire and moderate grazing to bobwhites. Finally, he listed and provided photographs of plants that produce winter foods for bobwhites in eastern Texas. The bulletin was very well received; it was revised and updated several times. In the last revision, Lay (1965) strongly recommended against planting multiflora rose for cover because it may spread and become a pest, especially on fertile soils.

In a cooperative study, Rosene and Lay (1963) investigated the disappearance and visibility of bobwhite remains. They placed bobwhite carcasses in areas known to have wild birds in Alabama and Newton

County, Texas, then tracked the fate of the carcasses for four days. They estimated visibility of bobwhite remains by throwing carcasses of female bobwhites over their shoulders, then measuring the distances at which the carcasses could be seen with the sun at the observer's back.

By the fourth day, 46.7 percent and 13.3 percent of carcasses had disappeared in Alabama and Texas, respectively. The dead birds disappeared at a rate of 3.5 percent per day in Texas and 14.0 percent in Alabama. Average visibility of dead bobwhites was 3.1 meters (10.5 feet). Rosene and Lay (1963) concluded that failure to find dead bobwhites does not necessarily mean there are no dead birds, and that finding even a small number of dead birds is reason to suspect heavy mortality.

Studies by Phil Goodrum and Vincent Reid

In 1947, Goodrum and Reid, biologists with the U.S. Fish and Wildlife Service, initiated a long-term study of bobwhites. Their primary study area was in the longleaf pine–bluestem region of west-central Louisiana. However, some data were collected in the same habitat type in Sabine and Newton counties, Texas, and on Elgin Air Force Base in western Florida. The 11-year study had a multitude of objectives that can be summarized as a study of the ecology of bobwhites in the longleaf pine ecosystem. The results were presented in a final report (Reid and Goodrum 1959) and several publications (Goodrum and Reid 1954; Reid 1953; Reid and Goodrum 1960; Reid and Goodrum 1979).

Reid (1953) reported that desirable bobwhite food plants were more abundant the first year after a winter burn than the fourth year. During the four years, numbers of stems of four of the five most abundant legume species declined drastically, as did the two abundant members of the spurge (*Euphorbia* spp.) family. Overall, stems of bobwhite food plants declined by 50 percent in four years. Reid also applied combinations of plowing, annual burning, and fertilizer to a heavy stand of broomsedge (*Andropogon virginicus*) that had not been burned for eight years. After three years, grass ground cover remained very dense on the unburned plots. On the annually burned plots, such cover was reduced to less than 50 percent, and common lespedeza, partridge pea, and tick-clover (*Desmodium* spp.) plants were abundant.

Although the Louisiana study plots were on open range, cattle grazing was light. Several species of bobwhite food plants showed light to moderate use by the cattle. However, Reid (1953) wrote that the grazing was beneficial in that light to moderate grazing complements use of prescribed fire.

Reid and Goodrum (1960) surveyed bobwhite numbers for seven years using dogs and whistle counts. The whistle counts were unsatisfactory, so they used hours-per-covey-find as an index to the bobwhite population. Additionally, using 6,654 bobwhite wings obtained from cooperating hunters, they determined adult:subadult ratios and hatching dates of some subadults. They used these data to trace population trends and reproduction success during the study.

Population trends across years were similar on hunted and nonhunted areas. Likewise, when the nonhunted area was opened to hunting after 14 years, the adult:subadult ratio was similar to that of the continuously hunted area. There was also a significant negative regression of hours-per-covey-find to the proportion of young birds in the population. However, there was no trend in percentages of young birds bagged by month of the hunting season. When a large proportion of the young birds pipped after July 31, there was a high fall population; a small proportion after that date resulted in a low fall population (Reid and Goodrum 1960).

Climatic factors during the summer affected annual bobwhite production and thus population indices. There was a negative linear function between hours-per-covey-find and highest average maximum monthly temperature. When proportions of young birds in the bag were compared to hours-per-covey-find, a significant negative relationship was observed. Reid and Goodrum (1960) found that annual production was greatest when average maximum monthly temperature did not exceed 33°C (91°F); production was lowest when that value exceeded 36°C (97°F).

Precipitation during April through October also affected annual production of bobwhites (Reid and Goodrum 1960). Production was greatest when rainfall during the breeding period exceeded 76 centimeters (30 inches); it was lowest when rainfall was less than 69 centimeters (27 inches). The authors concluded that cool, moist summers resulted in the highest proportions of young birds.

Reid and Goodrum (1979) also examined feeding habits of bobwhites. During the 11-year study, they collected 7,147 crops of hunter-killed birds; 6,902 of these came from the vicinity of the western Louisiana and eastern Texas study areas. Contents of the crops were dried and sorted by taxa, and volume of each taxa was measured. The authors used aggregated volume and frequency of occurrence to evaluate food habits.

Woody and herbaceous plant seeds and fruits comprised more than 90 percent of the foods consumed; green, leafy vegetation and animal material made up the remainder. Seeds and fruits of woody plants constituted more than 45 percent of the volume consumed during 9 of the 11 years. In 1955, longleaf pine had a good seed year, and its seed comprised 72 percent of the volume of bobwhite foods in November but only 2 percent in February. The authors believed that by late winter, most longleaf seeds had germinated or been consumed. The birds consumed significant quantities of red bay (*Persea borbonia*) drupes and white and red oak acorns. Bobwhites also ate small quantities of seed from numerous other tree species (Reid and Goodrum 1979).

Seeds from leguminous species, especially lespedeza and partridge pea, also were important foods for the bobwhites. However, volume of legume seeds in crops declined in the latter years of the study. The authors hypothesized that improved fire suppression reduced the abundance of legumes. When consumption of pine seeds decreased as winter progressed, consumption of legume seeds tended to increase. Conversely, when legume seed consumption decreased across winter, croton seed consumption increased. With some exceptions, seeds of grasses, spurges, sedges (*Carex* spp.), and other herbaceous plants comprised less than 20 percent of the crop volumes each year. However, seeds of several of these taxa did have relatively high frequency-of-occurrence values. The authors pointed out that in their forested study area, seeds and fruits of woody species were salient winter food items, whereas studies in agricultural settings showed seeds of herbaceous plants to be most important.

Finally, Reid and Goodrum (1979) listed 10 management activities that could either positively or negatively influence abundance and availability of bobwhite foods in longleaf pine forests. These could be grouped as timber harvesting and site preparation, prescribed burning and wildfire prevention, and grazing activities. They stated that optimum bobwhite habitat in forested areas is dependent on maintaining and enhancing diverse, abundant food-producing woody plants, and they emphasized the value of fire for accomplishing such goals.

Studies at Boggy Slough

Research on the Boggy Slough study area addressed several objectives. The primary objective was to compare survival, reproduction, movement patterns, and habitat preferences of resident, East Texas–relocated, and South Texas–relocated bobwhites. Other objectives addressed food-plot use by juvenile bobwhites and food habits and preferences of adults.

Survival

During a three-year study, 155 bobwhites translocated from South Texas, 136 bobwhites from East Texas, and 139 resident bobwhites on the Boggy Slough area were radio-marked. Survival among the three groups did not differ (Liu et al. 2000).

Nesting Losses

Seventy percent of all nests were initiated between May 1 and July 17. Of the known-fate bobwhites alive on May 1, 40 percent, 38 percent, and 68 percent of resident, North Boggy, and South Texas birds, respectively, were lost to predators by mid-July (Liu et al. 2000). Of all known-fate bobwhites, avian predators took 58 percent, 14 percent died of unknown causes, and mammalian predators and capture processes each caused 9 percent of the mortality. Three birds (1 percent), were radio-located inside snakes; the remaining 9 percent were alive at the end of the study.

Reproduction

Nesting efficiency of the three groups of bobwhites was evaluated using number of hens alive at the beginning of the nesting season, number of nests recorded, and number of hens for which no nests were recorded (Parsons, Whiting, Liu, et al. 2000). The 39 resident, 33 North Boggy, and 33 South Texas hens alive on May 1 produced 22, 13, and 6 nests and 9, 4, and 0 fledged broods, respectively.

Nine males assumed incubation duties; all were resident or North Boggy birds. Also, 10 fledged broods with radio-tagged males but from unknown nests were recorded. Although 2 such broods were with South Texas adults, evidence suggested that 1 brood was lost shortly after fledging and that the other may have been adopted by the South Texas birds. Parsons, Whiting, Liu, et al. (2000) concluded that the South Texas hens contributed little to the population recovery.

In an earlier study, Nedbal et al. (1997) reached the same conclusions. In February 1991, blood samples were collected from 40 North Boggy and 46 South Texas bobwhites before they were released in the study area. Likewise, samples were collected from 45 resident birds in both 1991 and 1992; 88 percent of these were subadults. Genetic material from these birds was analyzed, and restriction-site variation of mitochondrial DNA was used to evaluate differences in genetic variation among the resident, North Boggy, and South Texas bobwhites. Both tests indicated that there were no differences in heterogeneity of the mitochondrial DNA of North Boggy bobwhites and of resident birds hatched the second or third year after restocking was initiated. Conversely, both groups were genetically distinct from the South Texas birds.

Habitat Preferences

Habitat relationships of the three groups of bobwhites were examined at the macro- and microlevels in 1991 and 1992 (Liu et al. 1996). Macrohabitat components included forest type and food plots and their areas of influence (i.e., within a radius of 40 meters, or 133 feet). All three groups of bobwhites were associated with food plots and preferred stands of pure pines greater than 30 years old. Likewise, all groups avoided 6- to 15- year-old pine stands and hardwood or mixed pine-hardwood stands greater than 30 years old. Use of other forest types varied among groups. The authors pointed out that these results indicated that food plots seemed to attract and concentrate bobwhites in forested ecosystems. They also noted that the forest stands selected by the bobwhites provided the most open ground conditions on the study area.

Microhabitat components included characteristics of overstory and ground-cover vegetation and several variables associated with edge. Data to evaluate microhabitat were recorded at bobwhite-centered and random points. There were higher proportions of bare ground (11.4 vs. 2.1 percent) and dead grass (9.7 vs. 3.6 percent) and lower proportions of living grass (32.2 vs. 48.2 percent) at bobwhite-centered points than at random points each year. Ground cover at bobwhite points was taller than at random points in 1991 (98.3 vs. 72.7 centimeters, or 38.7 vs. 28.6 inches) but shorter in 1992 (28.5 vs. 37.4 centimeters, or 11.2 vs. 14.7 inches) (Liu et al. 1996). The authors hypothesized that the habitat on the study area was so heterogeneous that the birds did not respond to the edge components.

Home Range and Movements

Liu et al. (2002) examined home-range sizes and movement patterns of the three groups of bobwhites on South Boggy. The South Boggy residents had larger home ranges during March (10.5 vs. 5.5 and 6.1 hectares, or 25.9 vs. 13.5 and 15.0 acres) and the nesting season (61.9 vs. 46.9 and 42.6 hectares, or 152.9 vs. 115.8 and 105.2 acres) than did North Boggy or South Texas bobwhites, respectively. South Boggy birds moved longer distances (182 vs. 123 and 134 meters, or 166 vs. 112 and 122 yards) between consecutive days in March than did North Boggy or South Texas bobwhites. The difference was not significant in April, however.

Use of Food Plots

Nine hens that hatched clutches moved their chicks an average of 217 meters (712 feet) from the nest site to a food plot in an average of 2.1 days. Two unmarked hens with radio-tagged males and chicks about 7 days old were also recorded in food plots. One male that hatched a clutch was not recorded in a food plot for 36 days (Parsons, Whiting, Liu, and Dietz 2000).

Sixty-five percent of the 774 radio locations were associated with food plots. Quail-level foliage density was lower (44.5 vs. 64.0 contacts/50 pins) and insect biomass higher (0.302 vs. 0.105 gram, or 0.01 vs. 0.003 ounce) in food plots than in native vegetation. Parsons, Whiting, Liu, and Dietz (2000) stated that their results emphasized the value of warm-season food plots to juvenile bobwhites. They recommended that food plots be located within 200 meters (660 feet) of nesting cover and that plots be associated with escape cover.

Foods

In 1994 and 1995, Dietz (1999) examined food habits and preferences of bobwhites collected on South Boggy, North Boggy, and private and U.S. Forest Service lands. He classified the three areas as intensively, extensively, and unmanaged, respectively, for bobwhites.

In 1994, seeds of pines were the most important food item. Seeds of that genus, partridge pea, and Hercules-club (*Zanthoxylum clava-herculis*) and leaflets of clover (family Leguminosae) made up approximately 92 percent of digestive tracts of birds collected on South Boggy and North Boggy; partridge pea and clover were planted in food plots on each area. Pine, American beautyberry, and flowering dogwood (*Cornus florida*) seeds composed approximately 96 percent of crop contents of the two birds from Forest Service lands.

Proportions of pine seeds in the crops declined drastically in 1995. Seeds of partridge pea, butterfly pea (*Centrosema virginianum*), bush clover, waxmyrtle (*Myrica cerifera*), browntop millet (*Panicum fasciculatum*), and wildbean (*Strophastyles* spp.) each made greater than 10 percent of the diet of at least one group of birds. However, clover leaflets, which made up 21–26 percent of the diet, were the most consistently consumed food item by the three groups of birds. In 1995, the bobwhites consumed food items from at least twice as many taxa as in 1994. This may have been due to the reduced availability of pine seeds in the latter year.

In 1994, when pine seeds were readily available, they were in the top-ranked group of food items for South Boggy and North Boggy bobwhites. Seeds of hairy vetch (*Vicia villosa*), Hercules-club, hawthorn (*Crataegus* spp.), oaks, and browntop millet also were in the top-ranked group. In 1995, pine seeds were in the middle- or lower-ranked groups. The top-ranked group contained seeds of several legume and rush (*Juncus* spp.) species and waxmyrtle. Greenery, primarily clover, was in the top-ranked group of foods for bobwhites from unmanaged areas only. Dietz's (1999) results support Lay's (1952) conclusions that when pine seeds are scarce in forested areas, bobwhites increase use of legume seeds.

Other Studies

Although importation of bobwhites from Mexico was discontinued after 1940, distribution of pen-reared birds either continued or was reinitiated. In 1956, the Texas Game, Fish and Oyster Commission began operation of a bobwhite hatchery in Tyler. Bobwhites were raised at the facility for distribution to landowners. In 1958, R. B. Davis initiated a study to compare survival of pen-reared and wild bobwhites. He established study areas in Bowie County on the U.S. Army Red River Arsenal and on the Gibbs Ranch in Walker County (Davis 1970). Bowie County is on the northern tip of the Piney Woods, and the Gibbs Ranch is the same area that Dan Lay had used earlier.

Pen-reared bobwhites were released in early fall 1959, 1960, and 1961, and in spring 1961. Surveys were made of birds present on the study areas before and after each release. Dogs were used during the surveys to increase the wildness of the hatchery birds. When the hunting season opened, hunters were encouraged to kill as many birds as possible (Davis 1970).

Prior to the study, the estimated bobwhite population on the Red River Arsenal was about 1,900 birds, thus 1 per 1.2 hectares (3.0 acres). The estimated population on the Gibbs Ranch was 150 bobwhites, or 1 per 5.0 hectares (12.7 acres). Estimated numbers of wild birds on the Arsenal declined to 750 during the study period; on the Gibbs Ranch, the wild-bird population increased to 250 in fall 1960 but then decreased to 100 in the last year. The numbers of pen-reared bobwhites released on the Arsenal was increased from 1,000 in 1959 to 2,855 in 1961; likewise, numbers released on the Gibbs Ranch increased from 400 to 1,250 (Davis 1970).

Davis (1970) calculated the ratio of the number of wild or pen-reared bobwhites killed to the number available (i.e., estimated or released) at the start of the hunting season. He used these ratios as an index of survival. On the Arsenal, wild birds had three to six times better survival than pen-reared birds. On the Gibbs Ranch, only 9 wild birds were bagged in 1959, whereas 60 hatchery birds were bagged. This would suggest that pen-reared birds survived better than wild birds. However, the study area was severely overgrazed that year, and the wild birds had disappeared by hunting season. In the following two years, survival ratios of wild birds to hatchery birds on the Gibbs Ranch were 6:1 and 21:1. Overall, return of pen-reared bobwhites to the hunter was 15 percent and 6 percent on the Arsenal and the Gibbs Ranch, respectively.

Davis (1970) pointed out that although bobwhite habitat was better on the Arsenal than on Gibbs Ranch, habitat on both areas was better than that on which hatchery bobwhites were released in the early phases of the program. He predicted that most releases of pen-reared birds would yield less than 5 percent return to the hunter, and he closed by noting that the financial costs of such operations are high.

Between the completion of Davis's (1970) project in 1962 and the initiation of the Boggy Slough project in 1988, only one research project addressed bobwhites in the Piney Woods. Reid (1977) correlated habitat characteristics along TPWD bobwhite whistle-count transects with numbers of whistling males recorded in the ecological regions of Texas. Road shoulder width and seven structural features associated with edge and habitat interspersion were positively correlated with whistle counts. Likewise, nine vegetation features were positively correlated and four negatively correlated with the counts. The authors noted that many of the features positively correlated with whistle counts were associated with openings in the forest.

Laing (2003) attempted to create bobwhite habitat by converting vegetation in an abandoned bermudagrass pasture to native grasses and forbs. He used various combinations of disking, burning, and applying herbicides to eliminate vegetation on the study area. He then planted four species each of native grasses and legumes. After one growing season, the planted species composed no more than 8 percent of the vegetation cover, regardless of treatment. For various reasons, the treatments did not satisfactorily control numerous undesirable species, including bermudagrass, johnsongrass (*Sorghum halpense*), southern crabgrass, and blackberry (*Rubus* spp.). Some desirable native species, especially croton and ragweed (*Ambrosia* spp.), were present, however. Laing believed that herbicide application and burning in the fall prior to the study reduced the effectiveness of the herbicides that he applied. He suggested that multiple disking or a two-stage herbicide treatment might control the undesirable vegetation.

Research Needs

The northern bobwhite is a species that thrives in early-successional, even pioneer, habitats in East Texas. This habitat-use pattern is quite different from that of advanced-successional vegetation in the more xeric parts of their geographic range. In the Piney Woods of East Texas, precipitation far exceeds evapotranspiration; thus, maintaining vegetation in an early-successional stage is difficult and ongoing. Prescribed burning, livestock grazing, disking, and applying herbicides are tools that can be used to do so. However, the details of how to use these individually and in various combinations need clarification.

Prescribed fires have been used extensively for timber management in the Piney Woods; such fires definitely benefit bobwhites. However, the timing, frequency, and intensity of prescribed fires that are most beneficial to bobwhites and other resources are unknown. In particular, there is a need for information on the use of growing-season burns to control turfgrasses and hardwoods, especially in pine-hardwood types. Likewise, although Lay (1952) supported the use of fire in the longleaf pine type, there are no data on the specifics of its use for bobwhite management in the West Gulf Coastal Plain. However, there is a large body of literature regarding prescribed fire and livestock forage yields from the longleaf pine type in western Louisiana (e.g., Halls et al. 1964; Grelen 1978a).

Although livestock grazing in the forest has fallen into disfavor in recent years, it might become an important tool for managing bobwhites if the use of fire is restricted. Researchers working in western Louisiana have published numerous studies addressing forest grazing (e.g., DuVall and Linnartz 1967; Grelen 1978b), but none addressed the impact on bobwhites. The timing and intensity of grazing on bobwhite food plants and the effectiveness of grazing for controlling undesirable grasses need investigating. Likewise, information regarding the interactions of grazing and burning is also needed. Work by DuVall (1962) in western Louisiana that addressed grazing and burning but not bobwhites might be a starting point.

Although disking obviously retards plant succession, there are no data from the Piney Woods that address how timing impacts production of insects for bobwhite chicks or plants that produce food for adults. Likewise, the impacts of disking following prescribed fire or disking combined with fertilization have not been investigated.

There is virtually no information on how herbicides can be used to benefit bobwhites in the Piney Woods. However, it is obvious that broad-scale use of herbicides to control herbaceous and woody vegetation in young pine plantations is detrimental to bobwhite populations. During 2002–2003, two mourning dove (*Zenaida macroura*) hunters spent portions of 11 days in one-year-old pine plantations and did not see or hear a bobwhite. Although there was abundant croton, there was no nesting or brooding cover. Methods to incorporate nesting and brooding cover into intensively managed pine plantations are definitely the most pressing research need in the Piney Woods.

Other areas that need investigating involve competition and predation. Throughout the Southeast, as white-tailed deer numbers have increased, bobwhite numbers have decreased. Although this relationship is primarily a result of habitat changes, the impact of deer foraging on bobwhite food plants, especially in marginal bobwhite habitat, is unknown. Even though there is evidence that red imported fire ants (*Solenopsis invicta*) normally do not depredate bobwhite nests (Parsons, Whiting, Liu, et al. 2000) or healthy chicks (Johnson 1961), their competitive interactions with bobwhite chicks is speculative at best (Parsons, Whiting, Liu, and Dietz 2000). Competition with and predation by numerous other species, including hogs and wild turkeys (*Meleagris gallopavo*), would be fruitful research areas. Finally, the potential of commercial poultry operations exposing bobwhites to diseases, especially if the litter is spread on pine plantations, might warrant investigation.

Bobwhite Management in the Piney Woods

The key to managing bobwhites in the Piney Woods is fire. If fire is used judiciously, the species can be maintained throughout a pine rotation, regardless of its length. On tracts with sawtimber-size trees (i.e., minimum dbh of 30 centimeters, or 12 inches), the Boggy Slough model is appropriate. However, depending on soil fertility and management history, it may be necessary to graze and/or aggressively control hardwoods using hot fires or herbicides.

Landowners whose primary emphasis is timber production can maintain bobwhites by incorporating some relatively inexpensive practices into their management regime. When harvesting the residual stand, the clear-cut or seed-tree regeneration method should be used. Regardless, most logging debris needs to be removed. For bobwhites, shearing and windrowing are probably the best ways to accomplish this. Windrows may be burned, but some portions should be maintained for escape cover. Some areas where windrows are burned should be used for food plots.

If the residual timber is clear-cut and the tract planted, the rows of seedlings should be 3.0–3.6 meters (10–12 feet) apart. If it is necessary to use herbicides to control competing vegetation, the widely spaced rows will allow the landowner to band-spray over the pines while maintaining some residual vegetation between rows. Likewise, the spacing will allow disking between rows. Alternatively, distances between rows could be staggered with several rows closer together and then a pair wide enough to disk between. Until the planted pines are large enough to withstand fire, it will be necessary to disk; frequency of disking will depend on soil fertility. As soon as it is safe to do so, the stand should be burned, and burning should continue at regular intervals. Burning intervals will depend on soil fertility but should not exceed three years. Generally, food plots and escape cover should be protected. Finally, the stand should be thinned early and often. Maintaining basal-area value of the residual pines below that of the site index will result in an open canopy, which is necessary for bobwhites (Stransky 1971). Using similar techniques in a 1,400-hectare (3,500-acre), 15-year-old pine plantation, a southern Nacogdoches County landowner increase his bobwhite population from virtually zero to 1 bird/16 hectares (40 acres) in five years (D. S. Parsons, TPWD, pers. comm.).

If the seed-tree regeneration method is used, the seedlings should be precommercially thinned as early in the life of the stand as possible. This can be done using a tractor-operated mower or shredder to cut strips in the regeneration (i.e., corridor thinning). On some occasions, the precommercial thinning can be accomplished while removing the seed trees. Regardless, some corridors should be disked until the use of prescribed fire is feasible. Thereafter, the stand should be burned and thinned in a manner similar to that of a planted plantation.

The Future

On private lands in the East Texas Piney Woods, the future does not look bright for the northern bobwhite. Except for individuals specifically managing for the species, landowners trying to incorporate bobwhites into their management face numerous problems. The most important of these is liability associated with prescribed fire. Landowners can acquire liability insurance for burning on their own land. However, although Texas has a program to certify individuals to prescribe-burn properties other than their own, it is not functional because no insurance is available to such individuals. Texas needs a program similar to those of other southeastern states whereby, if a certified individual has an approved burning plan and adheres to the plan, that person is exempt from liability.

Currently, a weakening market for pulpwood reduces the incentive for private landowners to thin young stands. However, if this trend continues, it may benefit bobwhites by dictating that landowners plant seedlings farther apart. Also, as the forest industry no longer uses shearing and windrowing for site preparation, contractors to do such work are scarce.

The best hope for bobwhites in the Piney Woods is U.S. Forest Service lands. If the Forest Service is allowed to manage 121,000 hectares (300,000 acres) for the RCW, there again may be huntable numbers of bobwhites in the Piney Woods. Brennan (1991a) noted that forest stands managed for RCW can support up to 17 times more bobwhites than stands not managed for the woodpeckers. Likewise, RCW management benefits a multitude of other species, including Bachman's sparrows (*Aimophila aestivalis*), Henslow's sparrows (*Ammodramus henslowii*), and Louisiana pine snakes (*Pituophis melanoleucus ruthveni*), all of which are listed by one or more states as threatened or endangered.

Management for the RCW will entail harvesting timber, including regeneration harvests. Unfortunately, some portions of the American public view any regeneration area, especially one that is clear-cut, as a blight on the landscape rather than a first step in a successional gradient that will include numerous unique communities. Likewise, many people oppose prescribed burning, which is necessary for management of RCWs and critical for Bachman's and Henslow's sparrows and pine snakes. Most likely, management of the national forests will continue to be challenged in courts, and the Forest Service will remain in what has been called bureaucratic gridlock. Legislation that provides for timely public oversight while allowing the resource managers to perform their duties is sorely needed. However, perhaps the greatest need for the Forest Service and the entire natural resource management community is a strong information and education program.

10 Bobwhites on the Blackland Prairies

Markus J. Peterson

> This [blackland] prairie has been largely converted to farmland, although a few relicts remain in wildlife habitat and on ranches.
> Sims and Risser (2000)

184 The Blackland Prairies physiographic region of Texas (figure 10.1) is not currently thought of as prime quail country, although northern bobwhites (*Colinus virginianus*) certainly occur there. Rich blackland soils, however, once supported substantial numbers of bobwhites (Texas Game, Fish and Oyster Commission [TGFOC] 1945:46–60). In many ways, this ecological area serves as a useful microcosm for understanding bobwhite trends across Texas; abundance probably increased after European-American settlement, then decreased to levels where hunting could not be supported over much of the region. Both changes resulted from human activities. Lessons learned from the Blackland experience have direct relevance to today's bobwhite strongholds, such as the Rolling Plains and South Texas Plains (Gould 1962). Thus, the purpose of this chapter is to briefly (1) describe the Blackland Prairies, (2) present historical trends in bobwhite abundance in this region—including their causes and possible futures, (3) explore relevant ecological relationships, (4) evaluate attempts to enhance bobwhite abundance in this region, (5) outline gaps in our knowledge about bobwhites in this ecoregion, and (6) summarize this material and outline management implications.

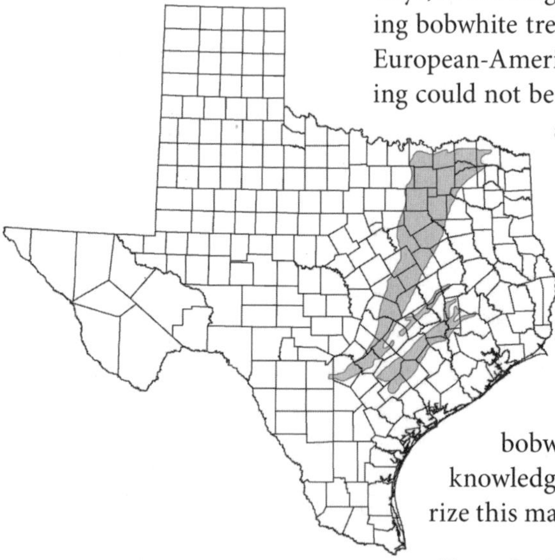

Figure 10.1.
The Blackland Prairie ecoregion of Texas.
Courtesy Caesar Kleberg Wildlife Research Institute (CKWRI) GIS Laboratory

Description of the Blackland Prairies

The Blackland Prairies consists of about 5.1 million hectares (12.6 million acres)—including the San Antonio and Fayette prairies—and represents the southern extreme of the true prairie that once extended from Canada to Texas (Gould 1962:10; Hatch, Gandhi, and Brown 1990:7,12–13). Topography is nearly level to gently rolling and is well dissected with rapid surface drainage. Elevation varies from 76 to 213 meters (250 to 700 feet) above mean sea level. Because this region intermingles with the Post Oak Savannah in the south, some of the past bobwhite research conducted in this area (e.g., Parmalee 1952a) occurred on Blackland Prairies and Post Oak Savannah sites, although he referred to the entire study area as Post Oak Savannah. Average annual precipitation in the Blackland Prairies varies from 76 centimeters (30 inches) in the west to about 114 centimeters (45 inches) in the east (Carr 1969; Hatch, Gandhi, and Brown 1990:6–8). Precipitation is seasonally bimodal, with primary and secondary peaks in May and September, respectively. There are 230–280 frost-free days annually.

Uplands in the Blackland Prairies are characterized by dark, calcareous, shrink-swell clayey soils, changing gradually with depth to light

marls or chalks (Hatch, Gandhi, and Brown 1990:12). Bottomland soils generally are reddish brown to dark gray, slightly acid to calcareous, loamy to clayey and alluvial. These soils are quite fertile, but many have lost productivity through erosion and continuous cropping.

Hatch, Gandhi, and Brown (1990:12) maintained that "this once-luxuriant tallgrass prairie" previously was dominated by little bluestem (*Schizachyrium scoparium*), big bluestem (*Andropogon gerardii*), yellow indiangrass (*Sorghastrum nutans*), tall dropseed (*Sporobolus asper*), and Silveus dropseed (*S. silveanus*) (figure 10.2). Grasses, such as sideoats grama (*Bouteloua curtipendula*), hairy grama (*B. hirsuta*), Mead's sedge (*Carex meadii*), Texas wintergrass (*Stipa leucotricha*), and buffalograss (*Buchloe dactyloides*), increased with grazing pressure. Common forbs include asters (*Aster* spp.), prairie bluet (*Hedyotis nigricans*), prairie-clovers (*Petalostemon* spp.), and late coneflower (*Rudbeckia serotina*). Common legumes include snoutbeans (*Rhynchosia* spp.) and vetches (*Vicia* spp.). Oaks (*Quercus* spp.), elms (*Ulmus* spp.), cottonwoods (*Populus* spp.), and native hickories and pecans (*Carya* spp.) probably always were widespread along drainages. Mesquites (*Prosopis glandulosa*), huisache (*Acacia smallii*), oaks, and elms are common invaders on abandoned croplands and poor-condition rangelands.

Approximately 98 percent of the Blackland Prairies was cultivated to produce cotton, sorghum, corn, wheat, and forage crops during the late nineteenth and early twentieth centuries (Hatch, Gandhi, and Brown 1990:12–13). After the drought of the 1950s, only about 50 percent of this physiographic region was used as cropland, with pasture and forage crops making up the difference. By 2001, 24 and 19 percent, respectively, of the total and nonurban area of the Blackland Prairies was used for crop production (Wilkins et al. 2003). Conversely, urban-suburban sprawl took up 23 percent of the Blackland Prairies, whereas 21 percent of the remaining rural lands were in tame pasture, primarily coastal bermudagrass (*Cynodon dactylon*). Other pasturelands still made up approximately 52 percent of nonurban landscapes in this region (40 percent of total) (Wilkins et al. 2003). From 1991 through 2001, more than 1.5 percent of rural land in the Blackland Prairies was lost to urban expansion, primarily in the Dallas–Fort Worth metropolitan area and along the I-35 corridor. Only about 2 percent of the native Blackland Prairies remains undisturbed (Hatch, Gandhi, and Brown 1990:12–13); these scattered, remnant patches are primarily used for grazing or hay production.

Figure 10.2.
A remnant Blackland Prairie in southeastern Brazos County dominated by little bluestem (left); and a Blackland site in western Washington County restored to native vegetation (right). Note green sprangletop (*Leptochloa dubia*), indiangrass, and Maximilian sunflower on near side of fence. Photos by Matthew Wagner and Brian Hays, respectively

Historical Trends in Bobwhite Abundance

Before the 1960s, little reliable data existed regarding northern bobwhite abundance in the Blackland Prairies. During 1945, biologists working for the TGFOC (1945) speculated that bobwhites probably were quite numerous near streams where suitable woody cover was present, but more rare elsewhere in this region prior to European-American settlement (pp. 46–47). Early agriculture probably benefited bobwhites in the Blackland Prairies by opening climax grasslands through livestock grazing, producing weedy field borders that provided food and cover, and introducing woody vegetation. For these reasons, 1875–1910 might represent the period of peak bobwhite abundance in this region. During Word War I, however, high agricultural prices led to almost complete removal of brush along creeks and fencerows so that every potential area could be planted to crops (p. 48). Not surprisingly, quail declines began in earnest in the 1920s. By 1945, TGFOC biologists considered bobwhite abundance in the Blackland Prairies to be among the lowest in the state (p. 51). They maintained that although "the Blackland Belt is basically satisfactory quail range, . . . agriculture has removed virtually all of the quality woody and grassy cover, as well as much of the native weeds that produce seeds for food" (p. 51).

By today's standards, bobwhites were still numerous and quail hunting excellent during the mid-twentieth century in much of the Blackland Prairies. For example, Parmalee (1953c) documented a mean harvest of 6.9 and 5.4 bobwhites per hunter per day in the field during the 1950–51 and 1951–52 hunting seasons, respectively, in Brazos, Robertson, Madison, and Grimes counties. Although these quail undoubtedly were taken on both Blackland and Post Oak sites, these harvest rates eclipse those seen since the early 1980s in the both the Rolling and the South Texas Plains (respectively, 1.7–4.1 and 1.8–3.4 bobwhites per hunter per day in the 1981–82 through 1982–83 and 1986–87 through 2001–2002 hunting seasons) (Texas Parks and Wildlife Department [TPWD], unpublished data). Clearly, bobwhite abundance in the Blackland Prairies has declined substantially since the 1950s.

More recently, reliable long-term data on avian abundance have become available. Statistical evaluation of data collected by the North American Breeding Bird Survey (BBS) (Sauer, Hines, and Fallon 2002) demonstrates that northern bobwhite abundance has declined dramatically in the Blackland Prairies since the mid-1970s (figure 10.3). Similarly, the number of bobwhites harvested, as well as the number of individuals hunting quail in the Blackland Prairies, has decreased since the early 1980s (figure 10.4). Unfortunately, TPWD discontinued its quail production survey for this physiographic region in 1988. During the 10 years it was conducted, however, it documented trends similar to those of the BBS. Further, because the TPWD quail production and harvest surveys are highly correlated (Peterson and Perez 2000), it is likely that if the production survey had been conducted during the last 15 years, it would have documented a trend much like that of the harvest survey. At any rate, there is no doubt that northern bobwhite abundance has declined markedly since at least the mid-1970s in the Blackland Prairies of Texas; this decline is similar to trends documented for bobwhites across most of the southeastern United States during this

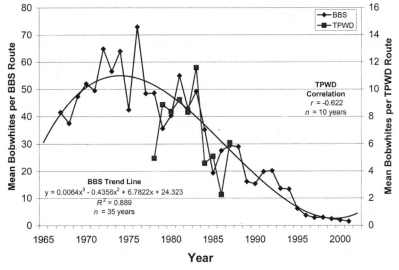

Figure 10.3.
Mean number of northern bobwhites observed per North American BBS and TPWD quail production survey route in the Blackland Prairies of Texas (Sauer, Hines, and Fallon 2002; TPWD unpublished data).

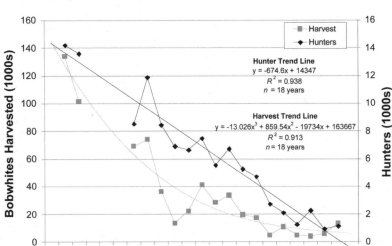

Figure 10.4.
Estimated numbers of northern bobwhites harvested and number of individuals hunting bobwhites in the Blackland Prairies of Texas (TPWD unpublished data).

period (Peterson, Wu, and Rho 2002). Moreover, declining bobwhite abundance in this region probably began much earlier, perhaps in the 1920s (TGFOC 1945:48).

Reasons for the Decline

Although it is clear that northern bobwhite abundance in the Blackland Prairies has decreased markedly, reasons for this decline are less obvious. After all, a large proportion of the Blackland Prairies has been in crop- or pastureland since the early 1900s, so cropland and pasture, per se, cannot be the entire problem. People interested in managing lands where bobwhite production is a priority must understand why this decline occurred if they hope to devise strategies that will reverse this trend.

The short answer to this question is that in recent decades insufficient habitat space has been available in the Blackland Prairies that can be used by bobwhites to fulfill all life requisites throughout the year (Guthery 1997). Instead, this space has been taken up by types of land cover that are essentially incompatible with bobwhite persistence. As detailed previously, these uses include vast urban areas, tame pastures, and cleanly farmed croplands. As of 2001, approximately 60 percent of the Blackland Prairies was used in ways essentially incompatible with bobwhite production (Wilkins et al. 2003). Urban-suburban landscapes are probably the worst possible land use for bobwhites; not only do they support no quail but there is no reasonable possibility of their being reconverted to bobwhite habitat. Although coastal bermudagrass pastures and large, cleanly farmed croplands are little better than urban sprawl as far as bobwhites are concerned, there is at least the possibility that agricultural areas could be reconverted to native vegetation and managed to benefit quail (see later discussion of case histories in the management section).

Approximately 40 percent of the Blackland Prairies consists of abandoned croplands now used as pastures (Wilkins et al. 2003). These pasturelands have potential as bobwhite habitat, and some still support huntable populations. Unfortunately, management of these landscapes during recent decades has not always benefited quail. Many pastures, particularly during periods of drought, have been stocked with cattle and grazed in ways that are incompatible with bobwhites. Further, these areas often have been invaded by mesquites, huisache, oaks, elms, and other woody vegetation. Although a certain amount of woody vegetation benefits bobwhites, lack of fire in these systems results in substantial areas becoming too thickly covered with woody vegetation to support bobwhite populations. As with other Texas physiographic regions, overly thick brushlands and periodic overgrazing could be remedied through management.

The Future

Prognosticating the future is always fraught with difficulty. There is no reason to think, however, that bobwhite numbers in the Blackland Prairies will suddenly rebound to levels observed in the 1950s. In fact, there is every reason to assume they will not. All of the social and environmental attributes that caused quail numbers in this region to decline are still in place. There is also no reason to think that the massive conversion of rural lands to urban landscapes observed during recent decades will not continue unabated. Similarly, there is no sign that farmers will suddenly decide to again employ the cropping practices used during the first half of the twentieth century or that all tame pastures will be converted to native vegetation and managed to benefit grassland birds such as the northern bobwhite. In fact, Wilkins et al. (2003) found that proliferation of smaller tracts of land in the Blackland Prairies was strongly tied to amounts of tame pasture. Apparently, many urban dwellers who purchase mini-ranches enjoy the golf-course-like vistas provided by coastal bermudagrass. This trend toward ownership-cum-landscape fragmentation in the Blackland Prairies seems almost certain to continue. Finally, there is no reason to assume that the land managers will suddenly reduce stocking rates to levels that benefit bobwhites, particularly during droughts, or begin managing woody vegetation at spatial scales relevant to bobwhite populations.

Does this mean nothing can be done for bobwhites in the Blacklands? Certainly not, but the broadscale changes required will be difficult to achieve. It is likely that in southern latitudes at least, the quantity of habitat necessary to support viable bobwhite populations that can withstand sustained human harvest is much greater than previously thought. Using viability analyses, Guthery et al. (2000) found that under a criterion of quasi extinction at ≤14 bobwhites (one covey), an autumn population of 700 bobwhites would be required to ensure a ≥95 percent probability of persistence for 100 years in southern latitudes. They assumed that droughts and extreme heat occurred during some summers and that approximately 30 percent of the population was harvested during the winter hunting season annually (e.g., approximately 210 bobwhites harvested from a population of 700). Thus, if 100 percent of the landscape under consideration could support bobwhites throughout the year (Guthery 1997), and 1–2 hectares (2.5–4.9 acres) were needed per individual, then approximately 700–1,400 hectares (1,730–3,500 acres) of habitat would be needed to support such a population. By way of illustration, if managers wished to restore numbers of bobwhites harvested in the Blackland Prairies to the levels enjoyed in the early 1980s, as compared to those of 1997–2001, then 590,046–1,180,093 *additional* hectares (1,457,984–2,915,970 acres) of bobwhite habitat that could be used throughout the year—in blocks of at least 700–1,400 hectares— would be required in the Blackland Prairies of Texas. This is the approximate area of *all* cropland, *all* tame pastureland, or about *half* of all other rangelands in this physiographic region (Wilkins et al. 2003). A change of this magnitude will never occur through application of the failed, localized bobwhite management practices of yesteryear (e.g., brush tepees, half-cutting mesquites, field borders). Instead, if there is to be a bright future for bobwhites in the Blackland Prairies of Texas, regional (multicounty) cooperatives among land managers will be needed to produce the requisite 0.6–1.2 million new hectares (1.5–3.0 million acres) of usable space; this undoubtedly will require conversion of vast areas of tame pasture, overgrazed native pastures, overly thick brushland, croplands, or other types of land cover to bobwhite habitat. Additionally, the conversion of rural lands to urban landscapes must also be slowed dramatically. These changes will have significant economic and social costs. I will leave it to the reader to decide whether these scenarios, or some suitable combination, are likely to come to fruition.

Ecological Relationships

Even in the absence of human exploitation, nonhuman predation, infectious agents, resource limitation, inclement weather, or other vagaries of the natural environment, approximately 44 percent of adult bobwhites die annually as a result of senescence (Guthery 2002:49–51). When other sources of mortality, with the exception of harvest, are factored in, one would expect approximately 75 percent of adult bobwhites to die annually. Bobwhites are not a long-lived species. Thus, factors controlling annual production, such as the number of females that go into reproductive condition, length of time females stay reproductively active, nesting success, and brood and chick survival, are key to northern bobwhite population dynamics (Guthery, Koerth, and Smith 1988; Guthery and Kuvlesky 1998; Peterson 2001; Guthery 2002:69–94).

Little modern research has addressed these ecological relationships in the Blackland Prairies of Texas, although studies conducted between the mid-1930s and 1950s explored some of these issues. These projects, combined with modern research conducted elsewhere, provide useful insights into northern bobwhite ecology in the Blackland Prairies. Because basic bobwhite life history, ecology, and management are detailed in chapter 4, I do not repeat this information here. Rather, I present what is known for the Blackland Prairies, point out features that might differentiate the Blacklands from other bobwhite habitats in Texas and elsewhere, and attempt to interpret these data within the context of the Blackland Prairies.

Habitat Use

The objective of this section is to summarize and synthesize what is known about bobwhite habitat use in the Blackland Prairies ecological region.

Nesting and Brood Rearing

Parmalee (1955) found that 46 of 61 (75.4 percent) nests in 13 Blackland and Post Oak counties during 1950 and 1951 occurred in grasslands and pastures (including associated roadsides and fencerows). Of the remaining nests, 11 (18.0 percent) were found beside buildings, in fallow fields, in oak woods bordering roadsides, or in brush thickets. Only 4 (6.6 percent) were located in cultivated fields. Considering the proportion of these counties under cultivation and the likelihood of locating nests in fields as opposed to other locations, it appears that cultivated areas probably did not contribute significantly to bobwhite production even in the 1950s. Unfortunately, Parmalee did not record nesting success by habitat characteristics, although 34 of 59 (57.6 percent) nests evaluated during May–July 1951 were successful.

Reid (1977) found that during the breeding season bobwhite whistle counts along 10 randomly placed 24-kilometer (15-mile) transects in the Blackland Prairies were negatively correlated with plowed land and mesquite-shrub savanna. Whistle counts were positively correlated with shrub and mixed savanna, but these areas composed less than 1 percent of the land area intersecting the whistle-count transects. They speculated that because approximately 38 percent of land intersecting the whistle-count transects was cleanly cultivated, with almost no fencerows, and 39 percent was tame pasture, inadequate nesting cover was available over much of the Blackland Prairies.

No reliable data are available regarding exactly where bobwhites rear their broods in the Blackland Prairies. Typically, however, bobwhite brood rearing and nesting occur in the same general areas (see chapter 4 for details).

Covey Habitat

Lehmann (1937b) documented three coveys inhabiting broomweed (*Amphiachyris dracunculoides*) and brushland on a 32.4-hectare (80-acre) Blackland cattle pasture southeast of Brenham. The land manager mowed the entire pasture and cleared the brush, extirpating the quail. Parmalee (1952a:102–106) evaluated covey ranges for two Blackland study areas in southwestern Robertson County and found that occupied areas were characterized by scattered woody vegetation, with birds using forest edges, brushy draws, and fencerows. Based on banding returns and other observations, Parmalee reported that bobwhites on these areas exhibited a "higher-than-usual degree of mobility" as compared to that typically reported in the literature of the day, and that these "data tend to indicate the 'flexibility' exhibited by quail coveys in this region" (p. 106). This flexibility, or "slack," regarding habitat use by bobwhites was more formally explored by Guthery (1999a) and is discussed in chapter 16. Reid et al. (1978) found that clean farming practices and tame pasture resulted in little suitable cover for bobwhites in the Blackland Prairies, with shrub and mixed savanna being the only habitat types positively correlated with whistle counts.

Diet

Lehmann (TGFOC 1945:55) evaluated crop contents from 905 bobwhites collected during the winter of 1934–35 in unrecorded areas of the Blackland Prairies and Post Oak Savannah. He found that woolly croton (*Croton capitatus*), acorns (*Quercus* spp.), Texas signalgrass (*Brachiaria texana*), johnsongrass, and one-seed croton (*C. monanthogynus*) made up 13.1, 9.5, 9.1, 4.4, and 4.0 percent of the diet, respectively.

Parmalee (1953a) conducted the first formal study of adult bobwhite diet in the southern Blackland Prairies and Post Oak Savannah regions of Texas. One aspect of the study evaluated crop (*n* = 32) contents by month between February 1 and November 30, 1951. Although several food items were eaten, acorns and croton (*Croton* spp.) made up at least 80 percent of the diet by volume during February and March. By April, unidentified green vegetation made up 37 percent of the diet and, along with acorns and croton, accounted for 90 percent of crop contents by volume. Panicum (*Panicum* spp.) and animal matter dominated the diet in May (87 percent by volume). Grasshoppers (Acrididae, Tettigoniidae), stinkbugs (Pentatomide), leafhoppers (Cicadellidae), and cucumber beetles (Chrysomelidae) composed most of the animal matter, but snails also were taken. During the summer months (June–August), animal matter, panicum, croton, and corn made up approximately 95 percent of the diet by volume. During fall (September–November), croton and evening primrose (*Oenothera* sp.) dominated the diet (85 percent by volume).

It is important to realize that due to differential food availability, bobwhite diets in this same area probably would have differed had data been collected during other years. For example, Parmalee (1953a) also evaluated 185 and 361 crops collected by hunters from 11 and 13 Blackland and Post Oak counties between December 1, 1950, and January 16, 1951, and between December 1, 1951, and January 16, 1952, respectively. During the 1950–51 hunting season, acorns, croton, elm, lespedeza (*Lespedeza* spp.), cowpeas, ragweed (*Ambrosia* spp.), johnsongrass, corn, panicum, and sorghum made up 39.7, 15.1, 8.3, 8.3, 5.1, 4.8, 2.6, 2.5, 2.1, and 1.1 percent, respectively, of the diet by volume. At least 39 additional species composed the remaining 9.4 percent. Conversely, during the 1951–52 hunting season, croton, Texas signalgrass, snow-on-the-prairie (*Euphorbia bicolor*), johnsongrass, corn, sunflower (*Helianthus* spp.), and ragweed composed 72.2, 6.8, 3.5, 3.5, 2.5, 2.2, and 2.1 percent of the diet, respectively, with at least 44 other species accounting for the remaining 7.2 percent.

Few data are available on adult bobwhite diets elsewhere in the

Blackland Prairies. Springs (1952:20) noted the plants that bobwhites appeared to be eating during various times of year and spot-checked crops from hunter-killed birds on his 3,561-hectare (8,800-acre) study area in the transition zone between the Blackland Prairies, Post Oak Savannah, and South Texas Plains (hereafter, Pandora Study Area) in Gonzales and Wilson counties. He maintained that croton, sunflowers, partridge peas (*Chamaecrista* spp.), ragweed, panicum, dropseeds, paspalums (*Paspalum* spp.), acorns, Hercules-club (*Zanthoxylum clava-herculis*), wild grapes (*Vitis* spp.), johnsongrass, sesbania (*Sesbania* spp.), corn, peanuts, and insects were the principal foods used at various times of year. Gore, Holt, and Barron (1971) evaluated an unrecorded number of bobwhite crops collected during the winter of 1962 in Wise County. They identified 47 different food items, with none greater than 10 percent by volume. The most common items were corn, acorns, sunflowers, johnsongrass, and browntop signalgrass (*B. fasciculata*).

No data are available regarding the diet of bobwhite chicks in the Blackland Prairies, although insects are undoubtedly important. See chapter 4 and accounts from better-studied physiographic regions, such as the South Texas and Rolling Plains, for more details regarding chick diet.

Mortality Factors

When one considers the ubiquity of recommendations to plant food plots, strip-disk, or otherwise provide bobwhites food in the Blackland Prairies and neighboring physiographic regions (e.g., Lehmann 1937a:34–38, 1939; Baker 1940:13–15; Chenault 1940; Coleman 1941; TGFOC 1945:54–55), one might reasonably assume that starvation or other nutritional deficiencies are the primary mortality factors in this region. Careful review of the literature, however, reveals no unambiguous examples of food limiting juvenile or adult bobwhite abundance in Texas or elsewhere (Guthery 1997, 2002:148–49). Management strategies intended to produce more food for adult bobwhites, however, might still be beneficial regardless of whether food limits the population, if more habitable space-time is developed during attempts to produce more food (Guthery 1997; also see chapter 9). The situation with newly hatched chicks is less clear. The diet of chicks typically consists of greater than 80 percent arthropods during the first two weeks of life (Handley 1931; Eubanks and Dimmick 1974), apparently in order to provide sufficient protein for rapid growth. In the Blackland Prairies and elsewhere in Texas, the proportion of chicks that die of starvation or other nutritional deficiencies before they are able to obtain required nutrition from vegetation (6–8 weeks of age) is unknown, but might be substantial during some years.

Little is known regarding predators of northern bobwhites in the Blackland Prairies. Feral house cats (Parmalee 1953b) and great horned owls (*Bubo virginianus*) (Parmalee 1954), at least, are known to take bobwhites in this region. Of 47 nests located by Springs (1952:24–38) during 1947 and 1950 in the Pandora Study Area, 13 (27.7 percent) were successful; 11 (23.4 percent) were abandoned; and 15 (31.9 percent) were depredated by snakes and mammalian predators, including striped skunks (*Mephitis mephitis*), spotted skunks (*Spilogale putorius*), and opossums (*Didelphis virginianus*). Of the remaining 8 nests, 1 was trampled by a horse and another by a cow, 2 were destroyed by humans, and the remaining 4 were taken by predators thought to be snakes. Because of the apparent importance of snake predation, Springs (1952:30–36) paid a bounty for snakes during the 1948 and 1949 nesting seasons. He evaluated the stomach contents of 88 snakes of seven species. Evidence of bobwhite predation was found for only two species. Of 35 Texas ratsnakes (*Elaphe obsoleta linheimeri*) evaluated, 12 (34.3 percent) had empty stomachs. Of the remaining 23, 16 (69.6 percent) contained bobwhite eggs, eggshells, or young. Only 1 of 34 (2.9 percent) stomachs of the western coachwhip (*Masticophis flagellum testaceus*) contained bobwhite eggs. Other snakes evaluated included the eastern hognose snake (*Heterodon platyrhinos*), Texas glossy snake (*Arizona elegans arenicola*), bullsnake (*Pituophis melanoleucus sayi*), copperhead (*Agkistrodon contortrix*), and western diamondback rattlesnake (*Crotalus atrox*). It is likely that bobwhite predation in the Blackland Prairies is similar to that known to occur in better-studied regions of the state that border this area. See chapters discussing neighboring physiographic regions for details.

Bobwhite parasites were surveyed in the Blackland Prairies and Post Oak Savannah during the 1950s (Parmalee 1952b; Parmalee and Price 1953). See chapter 6 for details. Although infectious agents undoubtedly infect and sometimes kill bobwhites in the Blacklands, it is unclear whether these parasites limit bobwhite populations or otherwise influence population dynamics in this region or elsewhere in the state.

Population Dynamics

Biologists have long recognized that bobwhite abundance varies considerably among years in the Blackland Prairies and neighboring physiographic regions (Springs 1952:21–26; Parmalee 1955), as well as elsewhere in Texas (Peterson 2001:fig. 1). Lehmann (1946a, 1953) and Jackson (1947) argued that weather, primarily precipitation, accounted for these variations in the South Texas Plains and Rolling Plains, respectively. These reports probably led Springs (1952:38–39) and Parmalee (1955) to assume that precipitation might be critically important to bobwhite production in the Blackland Prairies and Post Oak Savannah as well. Using visual comparison of weather data, juvenile-adult ratios, and hatching dates, Parmalee suggested that average to heavy winter and early-spring precipitation led to high bobwhite production in the Blackland and Post Oak counties he studied. It is important to remember, however, that fluctuations in abundance among years typically are much greater in semiarid regions of Texas than in more mesic locales, such as the Gulf Prairies and Marshes and Blackland Prairies (Bridges 1999:4–33; Peterson 2001).

During the 1970s, researchers began to explore these hypothesized relationships statistically. For example, Kiel (1976) found that the amount of precipitation during the reproductive season was correlated with the ratio of juveniles per adult in the South Texas hunting bag, and Rice et al. (1993) documented that Thornthwaite's (1948) index of precipitation effectiveness (12-month) was correlated with bobwhite abundance in the semiarid South Texas and the Rolling Plains, but not in the wetter Gulf Prairies and Marshes. Similarly, Bridges et al. (2001) found that Palmer drought indices (Palmer 1965; Alley 1984; http://www

.ncdc.noaa.gov) could account for bobwhite production in the South Texas Plains, Rolling Plains, Edwards Plateau, and Cross Timbers and Prairies but not in the Gulf Prairies and Marshes. Because both the Thornthwaite and Palmer indices combine precipitation, temperature, and other data to compute a single value representing precipitation effectiveness, the individual importance of precipitation and temperature to bobwhite production could be obscured. Lusk et al. (2002) addressed this issue by explicitly representing both precipitation and temperature variables in a neural network model designed to predict bobwhite abundance for six Texas ecological regions. Like Bridges et al. (2001), they found that fall precipitation could account for the number of bobwhites observed during August roadsides counts. Guthery et al. (2002), using a similar analytic approach, found that the number of juveniles per adult in South Texas hunter bags increased asymptotically with fall, spring, and summer precipitation and were insensitive to maximum daily July temperature up to 36°C (97°F), when they began to decline rapidly. Conversely, Lusk et al. found that numbers of bobwhites observed during August roadsides counts increased with increasing July temperatures. For details regarding how weather influences bobwhite abundance in Texas, see chapter 4.

Quantitative explorations of how weather might influence bobwhite production in the Blackland Prairies have yet to be completed. However, because regional aridity is inversely correlated with how well the Modified Palmer Drought Severity Index predicts bobwhite production (Bridges et al. 2001), we can reasonably estimate how weather might influence variations in bobwhite abundance among years in the Blackland Prairies. Based on the regional aridity index developed by Bridges et al., one would expect bobwhite production in the southern Blackland Prairies to be strongly tied to weather conditions, whereas precipitation and temperature probably would be less influential in the northern Blacklands. The mechanisms accounting for exactly how weather influences differences in bobwhite abundance among years remain unclear in the Blacklands and elsewhere in Texas. See chapter 24 for an outline and evaluation of proposed hypotheses. At any rate, it is likely that the influence of precipitation, temperature, and soil moisture on vegetation, and possibly bobwhites themselves, as mediated by an array of land-use practices such as livestock grazing, ultimately accounts for the variation in bobwhite abundance among years, at least in the more arid portions of the Blackland Prairies.

Management

Initial habitat management recommendations for bobwhites in the Blackland Prairies of Texas were based primarily on research conducted in the southeastern United States (e.g., Stoddard 1931), as well as the perceptions of the biologist making the recommendations. For example, Lehmann (1937a:27–28) recommended dividing prairie into blocks of 20–121 hectares (50–300 acres) by strip-disking; disking around clumps of woody vegetation; burning ≤60 percent of an area per year using spot burning; grazing moderately; joining with neighbors to regulate hunting; and eliminating sheep, goats, stray dogs and cats, domestic turkeys, and other barnyard fowl from quail ranges. Based on demonstration areas in the Gulf Prairies and Marshes, Lehmann (1939) added recommendations to build pole and brush shelters, fence areas near brush, and plant and fence food plots. Baker (1940:13–15) provided the following recommendation for the northern Blackland Prairies: limit harvest to one-third of the total population, refrain from clearing brush, eliminate grazing in woodlots and cultivated fields, leave unharvested strips of grain and legumes in fields adjacent to cover, reserve grassy areas free from grazing and burning as roosting and nesting areas, delay mowing to avoid nest destruction, leave fields uncultivated until spring to provide food and cover, plant brush, provide food plots, and kill all house cats. The TGFOC (1945:51–55) provided similar management advice. None of these recommendations were explicitly tied to manipulative field experiments and therefore remain unsubstantiated.

Grounded in the assumption that food limited bobwhite abundance in the southern Blackland Prairies and Post Oak Savannah, Chenault (1940)—working in Brazos County—evaluated the phenology of 91 plant species known to be used by bobwhites for food and/or cover somewhere within their range. Coleman (1941), also working in Brazos County, used 26 food plots to evaluate the relative merits of 17 of these plant species. Although all plots were accessible to bobwhites, Coleman recorded quail in only a single plot. For this reason, the influence of food plots on bobwhite populations, if any, could not be evaluated. Therefore, these studies provided no evidence that food plots benefited bobwhites in the Blackland Prairies or Post Oak Savannah. Parmalee (1952a: 79–88) used one treatment and one control area in the Blacklands of Robertson County to evaluate supplemental feeding (October 1949–51). During this short-term study, he was unable to detect differences in population trends. There is no clear evidence that food typically limits bobwhite populations in Texas or elsewhere, and although supplemental feeding may concentrate bobwhites around feeders, it does not necessarily increase density (Guthery 1997, 2002:148–49; Doerr and Silvy 2002). Despite these facts, some wildlife biologists still recommend planting food plots or providing supplemental food.

Case Studies

Springs (1952), working on the Pandora Study Area in the transition zone between the Blackland Prairies, Post Oak Savannah, and South Texas Plains during 1946–51, completed the only evaluation of habitat management practices designed to benefit northern bobwhites that occurred across an area large enough to be relevant at the population level in the Blacklands. Springs (1952:7–9) initially evaluated Lehmann's (1937a: 34–35, 1939) notion that food was limiting during late winter and early spring as well as his recommendations to build pole and brush shelters and fence areas to prevent livestock grazing. Springs found "that a shortage of food did not exist" during any season on the Pandora Study Area, "even during extreme drought" (p. 7). Therefore, he did not recommend attempting to enhance food plants or provide supplemental food. Springs maintained that although fenced areas seemed to localize coveys, they "probably had little effect on the overall [bobwhite] population" (p. 9). He also determined that native brush piles deteriorated so rapidly "that such brush piles seldom benefit quail after two or three years" (p. 9). Interestingly, despite the fact that Springs found no support for food shortages or benefits of brush shelters or fenced areas, food plots, supplemental feeding, brush shelters, and fenced areas continue to be recommended by some wildlife biologists working in this region.

Springs (1952:9–13) also conducted experimental half-cutting of native woody vegetation and plantings to provide cover on the Pandora Study Area. Mesquites, huisache, and Hercules-club ($n = 674$) were half-cut and pruned in order to provide living brush piles. Mesquites and huisache responded favorably to these techniques as long as the limbs were not too large or brittle. Hercules-club did not respond well to half-cutting and was better left in its natural state. Although huisache responded well, Springs maintained that time and effort were better spent on mesquites, because huisache was difficult to work with due to dense foliage and thorns (p. 11). Half-cut shrubs were used by bobwhites throughout the year, including singles, pairs, and broods during the reproductive season.

Springs (1952:13–19) evaluated experimental plantings of both native and exotic herbaceous and woody vegetation of 21 species. Of these, only Japanese rose (*Rosa multiflora*) and silverleaf sunflower (*Helianthus argophyllus*) showed any promise. Bicolor lespedeza (*L. bicolor*) was a spectacular failure. Of 12,150 seedlings transplanted during the winter of 1948, less than 1 percent survived. Because only 25.8 percent of approximately 5,000 Japanese rose cuttings survived more than two years, and silverleaf sunflower already grew in profusion along roadsides and cultivated fields, Springs questioned the value of these plantings as well (p. 18). Clearly, "planting something" is not necessarily the solution to every problem with bobwhite populations.

Probably the greatest contribution of Springs's (1952) study was that it illustrated how landowners, quail hunters, and wildlife biologists could be brought together to cooperatively manage an area sufficiently large to be relevant to a bobwhite population. The Pandora Study Area comprised 3,561 hectares (8,800 acres) under of the control of 33 individuals, with a mean ownership size of only 108 hectares (267 acres). Many of these landowners were "only passively interested" (p. 1) in bobwhite management. Springs, a Texas Game and Fish Commission biologist, was able to directly involve the San Antonio Bird Dog and Quail Club in this cooperative effort. Because managing habitat tracts the size of the Pandora Study Area is key to the future of bobwhites in the Blackland Prairies, those interested in developing or maintaining huntable populations of bobwhites in this region should explore how Springs was able to coordinate this effort.

Recently, there has been renewed interest in cooperative wildlife habitat management in the southern Blackland Prairies and Post Oak Savannah. Although the wildlife cooperatives in Fayette, Lee, and Washington counties primarily emphasize white-tailed deer (*Odocoileus virginianus*) management, some land managers also want to improve habitat for bobwhites. As discussed earlier, replacing tame pastures (e.g., coastal bermudagrass) with native vegetation is probably the most likely way sufficient space can be provided to support bobwhite populations through time in this region. Currently, research is under way on a Blackland site in Grimes County and two Post Oak sites in Falls County to determine how best to replace bermudagrass with native vegetation (Wagner et al. 2003; figure 10.5). Preliminary results

09/24/2003

suggest that coastal bermudagrass is considerably more difficult to kill with Glyphomax Plus on Blackland than on looser Post Oak soils but that satisfactory kills probably can be obtained with higher application rates. Using a Truax no-till drill, a native seed mix (seven species) was planted in previously sprayed areas during both spring and fall 2002. Sideoats grama dominated the Blackland site, whereas switchgrass (*Panicum virgatum*), yellow indiangrass, and Maximilian sunflower (*H. maximiliani*) dominated on the other two sites. Switchgrass, yellow indiangrass, and Maximilian sunflower also were established on the Blackland site but were less dominant. Further monitoring is necessary to determine how successful these conversions to native plants will be after intensive management is discontinued.

Texas Cooperative Extension personnel, in cooperation with TPWD's Pastures for Upland Game Birds Program and the Natural Resources Conservation Service Environmental Quality Incentives Program (EQIP), now have two demonstration areas on Blackland sites in Washington County (Wagner et al. 2003). One site was dominated by coastal bermudagrass and the other by King Ranch bluestem (*Bothriochloa ischaemum*). They used techniques developed during the research studies discussed previously and offer field days so land managers can observe what was accomplished. Since 2001, TPWD has offered the incentives of technical assistance and cost sharing to land managers willing to convert bermudagrass or bahiagrass (*Paspalum notatum*) pastures to native grasslands. To date, only modest conversions have occurred, but at least the potential to provide sufficient quantities of additional space usable by bobwhites throughout the year now exists in the Blackland Prairies.

Figure 10.5.
A pasture in western Washington County dominated by King Ranch bluestem (top left); sprayed with Glyphomax® Plus at 4 quarts/acre (top right); plowed, then broadcast-seeded with a native seed mix containing little bluestem, indiangrass, sideoats grama, switchgrass, green sprangletop, Maximilian sunflower, Engelmann daisy (*Engelmannia pinnatifida*), and Illinois bundleflower (*Desmanthus illinoensis*) (lower left); and restored to native vegetation (lower right) (note indiangrass, sideoats grama, green sprangletop, Maximilian sunflower, and Engelmann daisy).
Photos by Brian Hays

Knowledge Gaps and Research Needs

Because almost no research has addressed northern bobwhites in the Blackland Prairies since the 1950s, one could argue that nearly every topic is a gap in our knowledge. Realistically, there is no need to reevaluate all important issues discussed in chapter 4 and elsewhere in this book for the Blacklands. Guthery (1999a) found that there are a large number of habitat configurations that can lead to fully usable space through time for bobwhites. Thus, there is no need to study every pasture within the range of the northern bobwhite in order to know how to design management strategies that will benefit populations in a given area. Actually, we know quite a lot about the habitat requirements of bobwhites, and we typically know how to manage landscapes to provide these features. The difficulty is determining how to effectively implement this knowledge.

There is a pressing need to fill three fundamental gaps in our knowledge upon which bobwhite management either will rise or fall in the Blackland Prairies:

1. We must perfect effective prescriptions for converting coastal bermudagrass and other tame pastures into space usable through time by bobwhites.
2. We must determine how to convince sufficient numbers of land managers that it is in their best interest to provide landscapes suitable for bobwhites. At a minimum, this will require three fundamental changes in how land managers perceive their world. First, land managers must convert large acreages of tame pasture to bobwhite habitat. Next, livestock grazing must be viewed as a tool for bobwhite management. As discussed in chapters 4 and 24, if land managers wish to have robust bobwhite populations, particularly during hot, dry years, they must have the ability to greatly reduce and even eliminate livestock grazing. Finally, land managers must work cooperatively with their neighbors to provide minimum blocks of quail habitat of about 700–1,400 hectares (1,800–3,500 acres). Hundreds of such blocks will be needed.
3. We must find ways to make these changes economically and socially feasible. Although some exurban landowners can pay for these changes, many traditional owners of rural lands cannot. Thus, research addressing how best to provide economic incentives, including removing disincentives; technical assistance; cost sharing; purchase of development rights; and public-private partnerships is needed (Peterson et al. 2000; Wilkins et al. 2003). Stated another way, we should determine whether proposed incentives are likely to be effective prior to implementing these socially expensive programs.

Somewhat ironically, one class of badly needed incentives for conservation on private lands is abatement of the governmentally induced disincentives already in place (Peterson et al. 2000). For example, property and inheritance taxes can lead rural landowners to sell their landholdings to developers, thus causing ownership and, eventually, habitat fragmentation. Similarly, in order to qualify for certain types of conservation funding, such as the Conservation Reserve Program (CRP) administered by the Natural Resources Conservation Service, landowners must ensure that weeds do not occur in CRP fields (Capel et al. 1993). Weeds benefit bobwhites and many other wild species. Landowners are also allowed—and sometimes forced—to plant vegetation that is detrimental to quail. Similarly, the Farm Services Administration often has allowed emergency haying on CRP fields and sometimes has required mowing (Allen, Cade, and Vandever 2001). Mowing and haying reduce cover, annual weeds, and bare ground, at least in the short term (Burger et al. 1990; Burger, Burger, and Faaborg 1994; Allen, Cade, and Vandever 2001). If conducted during the nesting season, these activities can cause nest destruction as well as hen and brood mortality (Allen 1994). Finally, Texas Cooperative Extension still actively promotes tame pasture grasses as alternatives to cropland or native vegetation. Wilkins et al. (2003:12) found that "from 1992 to 2001 the most notable land use trend was the conversion of native rangelands and croplands to nonnative 'improved pastures.' Thus, significant amounts of important wildlife habitat were lost, especially in the central and eastern portions of the state."

Nongovernmental disincentives also exist. For example, the economic value of rural land near metropolitan areas can reach levels at which few landowners can afford not to sell such properties to developers. In some parts of the United States, zoning and property tax relief have been used to limit this trend.

Beyond removing conservation disincentives, what can be done to promote the broadscale bobwhite management so desperately needed? Public-private partnerships could be formed to share costs of conversion of cropland or tame pastures to bobwhite habitat at relevant spatial scales. For example, various provisions of the current Farm Bill offer sources of funding for broadscale alterations of the landscape that could benefit bobwhites. It should be noted, however, that although CRP and other Farm Bill programs have long been touted as possible solutions to the problem of declining bobwhite abundance (Howell and Isaacs 1988; Dimmick, Gudlin, and McKenzie 2002), there is little evidence to date that these programs have benefited this species over broad spatial scales (Brennan 1991a; Roseberry and David 1994; Ryan, Burger, and Kurzejeski 1998). Because land prices are higher in the Blackland Prairies than in any other Texas physiographic region (Wilkins et al. 2003), another approach would be for willing landowners to sell the development rights, in the form of a conservation easement, of their farm or ranch to governmentally approved land trusts. The landowner could still retain all other rights of ownership, including the ability to sell or bequeath the property to others, yet enjoy lower tax rates as well as the funds generated by the sale. This approach has been used for at least 25 years in other states and has slowed the conversion and fragmentation of rural lands (Peterson et al. 2000; Wilkins et al. 2003).

Wildlife and rangeland ecologists are well equipped to determine how best to convert tame pastures to bobwhite habitat and already know how to manage native vegetation to benefit quail. By and large, however, they are not well prepared to address societal issues—these typically have been perceived as the purview of the social sciences and humanities. Moreover, because those with expertise in economics and other social sciences usually know little about quail ecology and management, cross-disciplinary teams of researchers will be required to determine how best to fill these knowledge gaps.

Summary and Implications

Prior to European-American settlement, the rich soils of the Blackland Prairies of Texas probably supported substantial numbers of northern bobwhites near streams where suitable woody cover was present. Early agriculture may have benefited bobwhites by opening climax grasslands and producing cover that provided usable habitat space. During World War I, high agricultural prices led to almost complete removal of brush along creeks and fencerows, and declining bobwhite abundance was noted in this physiographic region as early as the 1920s. By the 1940s, TGFOC biologists considered bobwhite densities in the Blackland Prairies to be among the lowest in the state. In the early 1950s, however, the typical number of bobwhites taken per hunter per day in the southern portion of this region was still much higher than now seen in the Rolling and South Texas Plains. Systematic surveys of bobwhite abundance and harvest began in the late 1960s and 1980s, respectively. Bobwhite numbers have declined since at least the mid-1970s in the Blackland Prairies, and both bobwhite hunters and harvest have declined since the early 1980s.

Cropland and pastureland have been dominant land uses in the Blackland Prairies since the early 1900s, so cropland and pastures per se cannot be blamed entirely for declining bobwhite abundance in this region. Rather, in recent decades insufficient space has been available in the Blackland Prairies that can be used by bobwhites to fulfill all life requisites throughout the year. This space has instead been taken up by types of land cover that are essentially incompatible with bobwhite persistence, such as vast urban areas, coastal bermudagrass pastures, and cleanly farmed croplands. Moreover, many abandoned croplands have become too thickly covered with woody vegetation to support bobwhites; and pastures, particularly during droughts, have often been stocked at rates that excluded this species.

Although little research has addressed bobwhite ecology in the Blackland Prairies since the 1950s, information from other areas is relevant to bobwhite management in this region. We know what excellent bobwhite habitat in the Blackland Prairies looks like, and in most cases, we know how to develop it. The major obstacle is this: If northern bobwhites are to again thrive in the Blackland Prairies of Texas, vast amounts of new quail habitat are required, that is, 0.6–1.2 million hectares (1.5–3.0 million acres). Accomplishing this goal will require fundamental changes in how humans use these landscapes. Conversion of range- and farmland to urban expanses must either cease or be greatly curtailed. Tame pastures must be converted to quail habitat. Livestock grazing on wild pastures must be controlled to benefit quail. Fire must again be allowed in pasturelands and woody vegetation managed to benefit bobwhites. If sufficient quantities of usable habitat space through time are to become available to support robust bobwhite populations, these changes must occur at unprecedented spatial scales—minimum blocks of 700–1,400 hectares (1,800–3,500 acres). Traditional, localized, or fine-scaled quail management practices have failed. No amount of half-cutting of mesquites or distribution of brush piles will provide the requisite millions of acres of new bobwhite habitat in sufficiently large blocks. Instead, management at a regional rather than at a pasture scale is needed.

How can this be accomplished? Although a few individual ranches and farms in the Blackland Prairies are large enough to provide sufficient habitat to support a bobwhite population, most are not. Therefore, regional wildlife management cooperatives will be needed to secure requisite large blocks of habitat. Similarly, although some exurban landowners have the financial means and inclination to pay for required landscape changes, many traditional landowners who rely at least in part on agricultural income cannot afford to make required changes even if they wanted to. Incentives will be needed if sufficient space to support bobwhite populations through time is to be developed in the Blackland Prairies. These might include abatement of governmentally induced disincentives to bobwhite conservation, technical support, sharing costs of habitat management, coordination of landowner cooperatives, purchase of development rights, and public-private partnerships. Cross-disciplinary teams of researchers and managers will be required to put together incentives programs that will allow northern bobwhites to again thrive in the Blackland Prairies of Texas.

11 Quails on the Trans-Pecos

Louis A. Harveson

After a long climb through artemesias, fouquieria, yuccas and other thorny plants of thorn-infested country, we arrived late in the afternoon at the summit of the hill towards which our burros have all day been headed. As the burros were stopped to gain a breathing spell, I looked around me at the extensive view. It was a goodly sight, for on three sides of me the peaks and mountains of two thousand miles of territory were visible.

To the south could be seen a crevice in the gigantic wall of limestone, out of which crept the Rio Grande, trembling as if it had been doing penance in its tortuous long and dark course through the Grande Canyon. To the east the circled tips of the Chisos (Ghost) Mountains glistened in the western sun like the pearly points of a coronet.

O. W. Williams (quoted in Myers 1965)

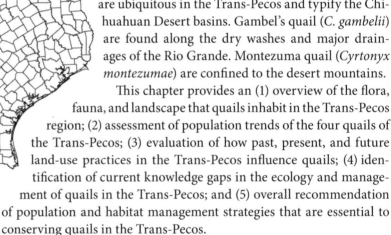

Figure 11.1.
The Trans-Pecos ecoregion of Texas.
Courtesy Caesar Kleberg Wildlife
Research Institute (CKWRI)
GIS Laboratory

The four quail species known to Texas can all be found in the Trans-Pecos, making it the most quail-diverse ecoregion in the state (figure 11.1). The western limit of northern bobwhites (*Colinus virginianus*) is found along the eastern boundary of the ecoregion, where they are restricted to the Pecos River watershed and its tributaries. Scaled quail (*Callipepla squamata*) are ubiquitous in the Trans-Pecos and typify the Chihuahuan Desert basins. Gambel's quail (*C. gambelii*) are found along the dry washes and major drainages of the Rio Grande. Montezuma quail (*Cyrtonyx montezumae*) are confined to the desert mountains.

This chapter provides an (1) overview of the flora, fauna, and landscape that quails inhabit in the Trans-Pecos region; (2) assessment of population trends of the four quails of the Trans-Pecos; (3) evaluation of how past, present, and future land-use practices in the Trans-Pecos influence quails; (4) identification of current knowledge gaps in the ecology and management of quails in the Trans-Pecos; and (5) overall recommendation of population and habitat management strategies that are essential to conserving quails in the Trans-Pecos.

Trans-Pecos Mountains and Basins

The Trans-Pecos is an area of contrast and diversity. Located in the Chihuahuan Desert Biotic Province, the region is about 7.3 million hectares (18 million acres) and is bordered to the east by the Pecos River, to the west and south by the Rio Grande, and to the north by New Mexico (Hatch, Gandhi, and Brown 1990). Desert islands are scattered throughout the Trans-Pecos with elevations ranging between 762 and 2,667 meters (2,500 and 8,750 feet). Mountain ranges that occur in the Trans-Pecos include the Barilla, Baylor, Beach, Christmas, Chinati, Chisos, Davis, Del Norte, Eagle, Franklin, Glass, Guadalupe, Santiago, Sierra Diablo, Sierra Vieja, Van Horn, and Wiley. Mountain ranges receive more precipitation (30–46 centimeters, or 12–18 inches), primarily in the form of monsoonal rains, than the lowlands and basins (20–30 centimeters, or 8–12 inches). Soils in the region vary, with deep sands along desert washes; gravel mulch in desert lowlands; and shallow, rocky soils on slopes and mountains.

The Trans-Pecos is diverse in flora and fauna. More than 2,188 plant species have been recorded in the region (Texas Parks and Wildlife Department [TPWD] 2002). Plant life of the region has been described by Warnock (1970, 1974, 1977) and Powell (1998, 2000). Creosote bush (*Larrea tridentata*) and tarbush (*Flourensia cernua*) are the prevalent shrubs and dominate more than 80 percent of the plant communities in the region (Hatch, Gandhi, and Brown 1990). Other common plants in the lowlands include catclaw acacia (*Acacia greggii*), whitethorn (*A. constricta*), sotol (*Dasylirion* spp.), lechuguilla (*Agave lechuguilla*), dropseeds (*Sporobolus* spp.), gramas (*Bouteloua* spp.), and threeawns (*Aristida* spp.). Juniper (*Juniperus* spp.) savanna, pinyon (*Pinus edulis*)-juniper-oak (*Quercus* spp.) woodlands, and ponderosa pine (*Pinus ponderosa*) forest lands become prevalent with increased elevation and precipitation.

The Trans-Pecos region has more than 500 species of birds (Bryan 2002), more than 100 species of reptiles and amphibians (Dixon 2002), and more than 75 species of mammals (Schmidly and Martin 1997).

Distribution and Trends of Trans-Pecos Quails

This section provides an overview of the geographic distributions and population trends of the four species of quails that inhabit the Trans-Pecos ecological region.

Northern Bobwhites

Oberholser (1974) described the western limit of northern bobwhite distribution in the Trans-Pecos as being limited to Terrell and Pecos counties and the immediate uplands along the Pecos River valley (figure 11.2). Bobwhites have been reported in areas on the Trans-Pecos other than the western limit of their contiguous distribution. Oberholser reported that bobwhites were rare in the Davis Mountains (Jeff Da-

Figure 11.2.
Northern bobwhites are commonly found in the oak woodlands and mesquite savannas in the Pecos River watershed of the Trans-Pecos.
Photo by Louis A. Harveson

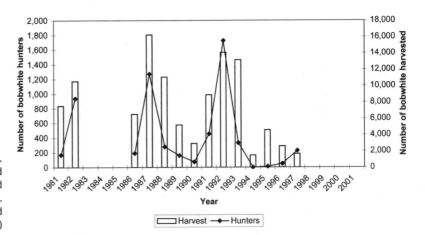

Figure 11.3.
Number of bobwhite hunters and
number of bobwhites harvested
in the Trans-Pecos, 1981–2001.
Data from Texas Parks and
Wildlife Department (TPWD)

vis County) and introduced in El Paso County. Bobwhites were also introduced in Culberson County (Johnsgard 1975). Bobwhites were frequently seen in the Glass Mountains (Brewster and Pecos counties) and persisted for more than 10 years (B. J. Warnock, Sul Ross State University, pers. comm.). They have also been documented calling during spring 2000 at Elephant Mountain Wildlife Management Area, Brewster County (unpublished data) and were observed later that summer (S. P. Lerich, TPWD, pers. comm.). The status of the introduction attempts in Culberson and El Paso counties and the origin and persistence of the scattered observations of bobwhites in Brewster and Jeff Davis counties are unknown.

Reid, Grue, and Silvy (1979) did not document bobwhites along nine 32-kilometer (20-mile) transects in the Trans-Pecos. TPWD, which subsequently adopted the transects established by Reid, Grue, and Silvy, has not recorded bobwhites in its annual quail surveys in the Trans-Pecos. An evaluation of Breeding Bird Survey (BBS) data suggests that northern bobwhites appear to have a stronghold in Terrell and Pecos counties adjacent to the Pecos River. The only trend data available for northern bobwhites in the Trans-Pecos are from hunter surveys conducted by TPWD (figure 11.3; see DeMaso et al. [2002] for descriptions of hunter-survey and roadside counts by TPWD). Hunter and harvest data are thought to be indicators of quail abundance (DeMaso et al. 2002). The number of hunters that pursued bobwhites and the number of bobwhites harvested in the Trans-Pecos during 1981–2001 ranged from 165 to 1,806 and 0 to 15,539, respectively. Two obvious peaks occurred in 1987 and 1992, but no trend is apparent from the data.

Scaled Quail

Aside from their presence on upper elevations of large mountain ranges, scaled quail are found throughout the Trans-Pecos (Wallmo 1957; Oberholser 1974; figure 11.4). Scaled quail populations, hunter effort, and harvest in the Trans-Pecos have been monitored by TPWD. The number of quail seen per route (figure 11.5), the number of hunters that hunted scaled quail, and the number of scaled quail harvested (figure 11.6) indicate that scaled quail populations exhibited large annual fluctuations.

Overall, they have remained stable or have slightly declined. Wallmo (1957) was the first to document the effects of drought on scaled quail

Figure 11.4.
Scaled quail are strongly associated
with the mesquite shrublands that are
found throughout the Trans-Pecos.
Photo by Louis A. Harveson

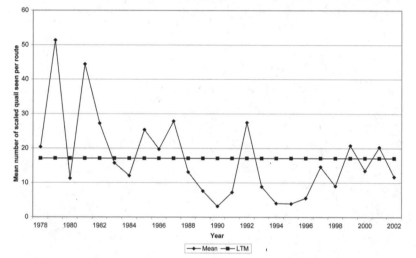

Figure 11.5.
Number of scaled quail observed
(mean number of quail per route) and
long-term mean (LTM) during survey
routes in the Trans-Pecos, 1978–2002.
Data from TPWD

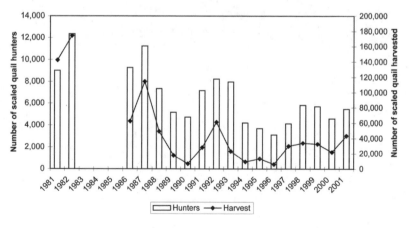

Figure 11.6.
Number of scaled quail hunters and
number of scaled quail harvested
in the Trans-Pecos, 1981–2001.
Data from TPWD

populations in the Trans-Pecos. In his study, scaled quail numbers
decreased by 12 percent during a year of below-average precipitation.
Recently, Bridges et al. (2001) demonstrated that annual fluctuations
in scaled quail abundance were correlated with precipitation-based
weather indices in the Trans-Pecos.

Gambel's Quail

In Texas, Gambel's quail are found only in the Trans-Pecos region and are primarily restricted to the Rio Grande corridor from the northwestern extent of El Paso County to the Big Bend in southern Brewster County and major drainages in El Paso, Culberson, Hudspeth, and Presidio counties (figure 11.7). The distribution of Gambel's quail has not deviated with time. Oberholser (1974) considered Gambel's quail fairly common in this region and documented them as far as Alpine, Brewster County; Limpia Creek, Jeff Davis County; and along the Rio Grande in Terrell County. Gambel's quail have been detected along BBS routes in El Paso County but have not been detected in any other routes in the Trans-Pecos. According to BBS data, Gambel's quail have increased in recent years (figure 11.8); however, Sauer et al. (2003) cautioned against using BBS data at this spatial scale. Volunteers with the Christmas Bird Count (CBC) have also accounted for Gambel's quail in their surveys, and data suggest a declining trend in abundance (figure 11.9). Gambel's quail populations or hunter-harvest data have not been surveyed by

Figure 11.7.
Gambel's quail are limited in their distribution to the Rio Grande corridor and desert washes characterized by catclaw, mesquite, and desert willow in the Trans-Pecos.
Photo by Louis A. Harveson

Figure 11.8.
Number of Gambel's quail seen or heard in Texas, 1967–2001.
Data from the Breeding Bird Survey (BBS)

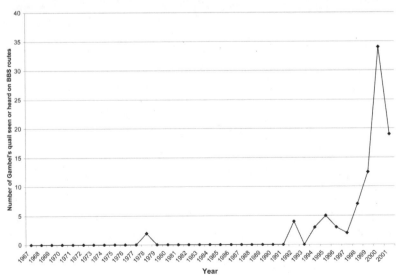

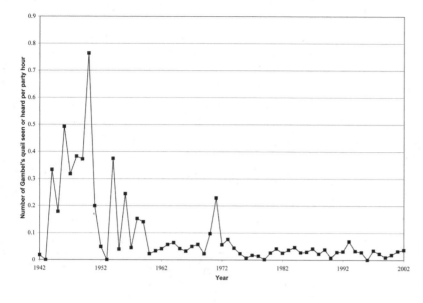

Figure 11.9.
Number of Gambel's quail observed
per party hour in Texas, 1942–2002.
Data from the Christmas Bird
Count (CBC)

TPWD; thus, no substantiating data on the current trend of this quail
are available.

Montezuma Quail

Presently, Montezuma quail are virtually restricted to desert grassland
and woodland communities of the mountains of the Trans-Pecos region,
although populations persist in the Edwards Plateau (figure 11.10). Historically, Montezuma quail had a wider distribution, and populations
have been extirpated from several isolated mountain ranges (Oberholser 1974; see chapter 3). Montezuma quail are difficult to survey (Brown
1976; Hernández 2002a, 2002b) and have not been monitored by TPWD
on an annual basis. Data collected by the BBS and CBC on Montezuma
quail are too spotty to determine a general trend in populations (figures
11.11 and 11.12); however, their numbers have likely decreased with loss
of habitat.

Figure 11.10.
Montezuma quail primarily occur in
the pine-oak woodlands and desert
savannas of the major mountain
ranges in the Trans-Pecos.
Photo by Louis A. Harveson

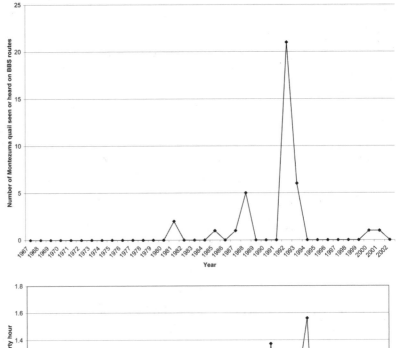

Figure 11.11.
Number of Montezuma quail seen
or heard in Texas, 1967–2002.
Data from the BBS

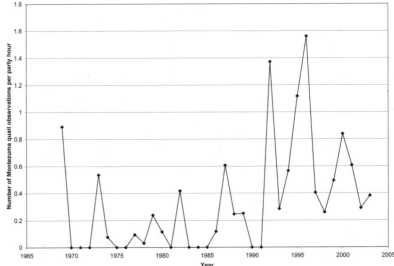

Figure 11.12.
Number of Montezuma quail observed
per party hour in Texas, 1967–2003.
Data from the CBC

Factors Influencing Trends of Trans-Pecos Quails

Many of the factors (e.g., habitat fragmentation and loss) influencing quails in other parts of Texas have had little influence in the Trans-Pecos ecoregion. In fact, the Trans-Pecos was considered the most conserved ecoregion in the state, with 8 percent of the region in conservation lands (state, federal, or nongovernmental organization) (TPWD 2002). Wallmo and Uzzell (1958) reported that ranches in the Trans-Pecos in the 1950s averaged greater than 10,125 hectares (25,000 acres), and more than 90 percent of the region was used for farming and ranching purposes. In 2000, ranches in the Trans-Pecos averaged between 2,025 and 8,100 hectares (5,000 and 20,000 acres) (Wilkins et al. 2000), and 76 percent of the region was in farm- or ranchland (Wilkins et al. 2003). However, the interaction of drought, overgrazing, and fire has changed the landscape of the Trans-Pecos over the past 150 years.

Prior to European settlement, the Trans-Pecos consisted of productive grasslands, savannas, and woodlands. Currently, most rangelands are shrublands, have low grass production, and are highly erodible. Warnock and Loomis (2002) provide a historical overview of how rangelands in West Texas have transformed from prolific grasslands to unproductive shrublands. Large, natural fires maintained the grasslands (Wrinkle 2002), prevented encroachment of shrubs, and provided enough grass to support as much as 65 animal-units/section in wet years (an animal-unit is one cow and her calf). Since the turn of the twentieth century, droughts were frequent (2–4 years/decade), and the catastrophic drought of the 1950s severely affected the rangelands of the Trans-Pecos (Nelle 2002). The once-widespread fires of the past soon came to an end as drought and overgrazing eliminated fine fuels (i.e., grasses) (Cottle 1931).

Northern Bobwhites

Although not well documented, the distribution of northern bobwhites has likely contracted with heavy stocking rates along the western edge of its distribution. Bobwhites are a grassland/woodland species but require a grass component during various stages of their life (e.g., nesting). Based on the seral-stage model proposed by Spears et al. (1993), bobwhite numbers should decrease in the Trans-Pecos with increased grazing and decreased ground cover. Rollins (2000) noted a range expansion of bobwhites into the Chihuahuan Desert during wet years. Thus, as precipitation and site productivity decrease, the abundance of bobwhites decreases.

Scaled Quail

It is likely that land-use changes and the resulting desertification of rangelands in the Trans-Pecos have positively affected scaled quail. In New Mexico, scaled quail avoided climax vegetation (*Bouteloua* grasslands) and preferred sites in lower ecological condition (*Prosopis* shrublands) in the Chihuahuan Desert (Smith, Holechek, and Cardenas 1996; Saiwana et al. 1998). Reid, Grue, and Silvy (1993) also found more scaled quail in mesquite shrublands than in other habitats surveyed in the Trans-Pecos. Although shrublands are important to scaled quail, grass is essential for nesting habitat. In Pecos County, under conservative stocking rates, scaled quail nested almost exclusively in tobosa grass (*Pleuraphis mutica*) (B. Buntyn, Angelo State University, unpublished data). However, scaled quail nested in shrubs when grass was limited (Lerich 2002). Saiwana et al. (1998) concluded that scaled quail managers should strive for a mixture of late- and mid-seral plant communities that provide shrubs for food and cover and adequate grasses for food and nesting.

Gambel's Quail

Gambel's quail are more adapted to the arid environments of West Texas than other Texas quails and are thus less susceptible to the desertification process previously described. However, the availability and structure of Gambel's quail habitat in Texas have changed significantly in the last 150 years. First, water availability and flow of the Rio Grande have decreased. Although Gambel's quail do not need free water to survive and reproduce (Hungerford 1960b), the reduced amount of water has affected other components of their habitat (e.g., food and cover). Specifically, native plants such as desert willow (*Chilopsis linearis*), catclaw acacia (*Acacia greggii*), and cottonwood (*Populus* spp.) have been replaced by salt cedar (*Tamarix ramosissima*). Gambel's quail habitat has also been lost to agricultural practices along the Rio Grande and to the expanding urbanization of El Paso. The human population in El Paso has grown from 16,000 in 1900 to more than 600,000 in 2000 (Texas State Data Center 2001) and is expected to continue to grow by 15 percent annually. The impacts of these habitat alterations to Gambel's quail populations have not been studied.

Montezuma Quail

Because of their dependence on adequate grass cover, Montezuma quail populations have decreased in distribution and abundance. The range of Montezuma quail was once contiguous throughout the mixed prairies, desert grasslands, and mountain savanna zones of the Trans-Pecos, as well as the oak woodlands of the Edwards Plateau. As herbaceous cover was reduced, habitat for Montezuma quail was lost and their distribution reduced to isolated mountain ranges that retained adequate grasses (see chapter 3).

Current and Future Trends

Land ownership is changing in Texas (Wilkins et al. 2000). Historical cattle ranches are being sold because of financial constraints, and buyers are purchasing ranches primarily for recreational activities (i.e., wildlife). This shift in ownership is now and has been occurring across the state, including the Trans-Pecos. Although the size of ranches in the Trans-Pecos has decreased, the rate of fragmentation is lower than in other regions to the east (Wilkins et al. 2000). Cattle and sheep numbers have declined in the past 30 years and are predicted to continue to decrease (figure 11.13). Nelle (2002) hypothesized that as ranches in the Trans-Pecos shift from livestock production to wildlife enterprises, rangelands will recover more rapidly than with traditional ranching (e.g., livestock-based enterprises). However, this prediction needs to be evaluated with long-term monitoring and research. The new land-owners are considered to be more wildlife-friendly, with a renewed interest in restoring natural habitats (Warnock and Loomis 2002).

With shifting demographics of landowners and land-use trends,

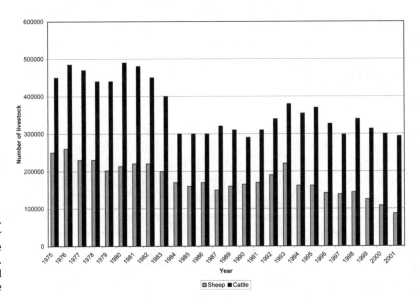

Figure 11.13.
Livestock production (number of sheep and cattle) in the Trans-Pecos, 1975–2001. Data from USDA, National Agricultural Statistics Service

quails in the Trans-Pecos may receive more attention in the future. For example, as bobwhites in the southeastern United States continue to decline (Brennan 1991a), more emphasis will be placed on the ecology, conservation, and management (e.g., hunting) of western quails. Burger, Miller, and Southwick (1999) chronicled the economics of bobwhite hunting and the impact that the decline in bobwhite numbers will have in the southeastern United States. However, as hunting opportunities begin to decrease in the southeast, hunting markets elsewhere (e.g., western quails) may increase.

Northern Bobwhites

The distribution and abundance of northern bobwhites in the Trans-Pecos will never reach the levels of those in South Texas or the Rolling Plains. The frequency of droughts and the low productivity of rangelands in the Trans-Pecos prohibit high densities. However, several factors are in favor of bobwhites. First, the changes in land ownership and attitudes that are presently occurring will help accelerate bobwhite habitat restoration. Specifically, habitat quality will increase with reduced stocking rates and increased participation in landowner incentive programs (Wetland Habitat Incentives Program [WHIP], Riparian Buffer Program of the Conservation Reserve Program [CRP], and Environmental Quality Incentives Program [EQIP]) in the Trans-Pecos. If riparian woodlands and adjacent shrublands become better suited to bobwhites, it might be possible for them to slowly recolonize habitats in the Trans-Pecos.

Scaled Quail

Nesting habitat may be a limiting factor for scaled quail in heavily grazed lands of the Chihuahuan Desert (Evans 1997; Joseph et al. 2003). As rangelands support more grass following destocking of livestock associated with market values or land-use changes, scaled quail populations will benefit from higher nest success and recruitment.

Gambel's Quail

Although Gambel's quail habitat will continue to disappear as El Paso grows, much of their distribution will benefit from human-made changes. Gambel's quail will benefit from riparian habitat improvements associated with the WHIP, CRP, and EQIP programs, as well as international efforts to restore native habitat, water flow, and water quality to the Rio Grande.

Montezuma Quail

Montezuma quail are especially vulnerable to local extirpation. The future of Montezuma quail in the Trans-Pecos will lie in the hands of private landowners and resource agencies that manage lands where the quail currently occur (e.g., desert mountains). If habitats are able to support adequate herbaceous cover, Montezuma quail populations will persist and may expand. However, many of the mountain ranges where Montezuma quail occur may be too isolated for natural recolonization. In those cases, reintroduction efforts should be established, evaluated, and executed in historic ranges. Effective management of Montezuma quail will be necessary as their hunting status (e.g., open or closed season) is reevaluated and if they are to continue to be a flagship species for ecotourism in the Davis Mountains (see chapter 3).

Management Case Histories

Documented management case histories are relatively rare for quails in the Trans-Pecos. Nevertheless, there are several such documented management efforts in the literature and unpublished reports, which are summarized here.

Northern Bobwhites

Quail hunters harvest between 0 and 15,000 bobwhites annually from the Trans-Pecos region. This accounts for less than 1 percent of the statewide take. No studies have documented any aspect of bobwhite status, ecology, or management in the Trans-Pecos.

Scaled Quail

Harveson, Harveson, and Richardson (2002) highlighted several ranches and their management efforts for scaled quail in the Trans-Pecos. Landowners successful in managing scaled quail had conservative stocking rates that allowed for adequate nesting cover, conservative hunting seasons (self-imposed bag limits, shortened seasons, or no hunting during years of low abundance), abundant watering sites, and predator management programs. Although these aforementioned management efforts are confounding, a limited amount of data are available on the management of scaled quail in the Trans-Pecos.

Habitat

Few studies have been conducted to evaluate scaled quail habitat in the Trans-Pecos. Howard (1981) and Reid, Grue, and Silvy (1993) noted that scaled quail were strongly associated with mesquite shrublands. Recommended stocking rates vary with site productivity. Rollins (2000) recommended more conservative grazing practices (1 animal-unit/30 hectares, or 75 acres) in drier areas and moderate grazing (1 animal-unit/15 hectares, or 37 acres) in more productive sites. Little is known regarding scaled quail responses to herbicidal and mechanical treatments of brush; however, Rollins notes that chemical treatments typically result in forb shock and may decrease scaled quail foods.

Scaled quail use a variety of nesting structures and substrates but prefer bunchgrasses (Rollins 2000). B. Buntyn (Angelo State University, unpublished data) documented 39 of 42 and the majority of 31 scaled quail nests in bunchgrasses in Pecos County in 1999 and 2000, respectively. In a drier area, Lerich (2002) located 5 scaled quail nests in bunchgrasses and 6 in shrubs. Rollins recommended 1–3 loafing sites/hectare (about 0.5–1.0 per acre) for scaled quail in the Rolling Plains and Trans-Pecos regions.

Water

One of the benefits of the cattle industry on all wildlife populations in the Trans-Pecos is the increased availability of water (e.g., cattle troughs, stock tanks). Although Wallmo and Uzzell (1958) contested that scaled quail abundance was independent of water sources, Evans (1997) suggested that water availability affects their distribution and density. Regardless of the effect water has on scaled quail, maintenance of watering sites should be practiced. Both Evans (1997) and Lerich (2002) documented that scaled quail can drown in water troughs lacking appropriate access. Managers should provide better access (ramps, floating platforms, perches) to water sites, as well as allow vegetation to grow around the sites for better escape cover.

Diet

Scaled quail diets are diverse and dependent upon food availability. Diets in Brewster County were predominantly grass seeds and shrub fruit and mast (Wallmo 1957). In Pecos County, scaled quail diets changed with season and availability (Howard 1981). In that study, scaled quail diets consisted of grass and forb seeds in winter; invertebrates and shrub, grass, and forb seeds in spring; invertebrates and shrub fruit and mast in summer; and green material and forb seeds in fall.

Hunting

Wallmo and Uzzell (1958) claimed that scaled quail were the most difficult game bird to hunt in the state. They noted that scaled quail hunters in the Trans-Pecos increased from about 1,400 to 1,900 in the 1950s; TPWD data indicated an increase from about 3,000 to 8,000 in the 1990s. Currently, scaled quail hunters harvest between 6,000 and 174,000 birds in the Trans-Pecos region, accounting for 5–22 percent of the statewide scaled quail harvest (TPWD data). Wallmo and Uzzell (1958) and Peterson and Perez (2000) speculated that scaled quail hunting was self-regulating. Further, resource managers have done a poor job of communicating with hunters and landowners to help facilitate use of the scaled quail resource in Texas (Wallmo and Uzzell 1958). Little is known about the economics of scaled quail hunting in the Trans-Pecos, but one ranch in the 1990s leased scaled quail hunting privileges for $2.50/hectare ($1/acre) (L. A. Harveson, unpublished data).

Gambel's Quail

No studies have documented the status, ecology, or management of Gambel's quail in the Trans-Pecos outside that in chapter 2 in this book. Further, TPWD has not monitored Gambel's quail populations or hunter-harvest characteristics despite the status of the quail as a game bird with a hunting season. Tarrant (2002), using information from Arizona, identified five management strategies that would benefit Gambel's quail in Texas: (1) enhance forb production with deferred rotational grazing, (2) protect riparian areas with fencing, (3) maximize water infiltration with various water catchments and diversions, (4) disk parallel to contours in late winter to enhance forb production, and (5) distribute water sources and allow water to overflow during dry periods. The effects of these management strategies on Gambel's quail in Texas are unknown and need to be tested through research.

Montezuma Quail

Aside from the three reintroduction efforts of Montezuma quail to historic ranges (see chapter 3), Montezuma quail have not been managed in Texas. Other than an exploratory investigation on their distribution (Sorola 1986), Montezuma quail are not surveyed annually by TPWD.

213

Quails on the Trans-Pecos

The lack of knowledge on population levels in Texas was the primary reason TPWD withdrew a petition to open a hunting season on Montezuma quail. Despite the lack of knowledge, overgrazing appears to be the primary cause of the distribution reduction that Montezuma quail have experienced in Texas (Hernández, Harveson, and Brewer 2002a). Hernández (2004) documented a Montezuma quail population crash following a reduction in ground cover resulting from a freeze in October.

Future Research Needs

Little is known about northern bobwhites, scaled quail, Gambel's quail, and Montezuma quail in this region. The Trans-Pecos offers many opportunities to investigate the status, distribution, life history, ecology, and management of regional quails. The following is a brief profile of knowledge gaps that exist in our understanding of these quails in the Trans-Pecos.

Northern Bobwhites

Northern bobwhites reach their western limit in the Trans-Pecos, and their distribution shrinks and expands with variation in precipitation. This unique environment would lend itself to a comprehensive investigation in landscape ecology (e.g., corridor use, dispersal and colonizing strategies, minimum habitat area, minimum viable population).

If cattle grazing continues to decrease in the Trans-Pecos, landowners and managers along the Pecos River watershed will need information to maximize habitat space to sustain bobwhites once they colonize new habitats (Guthery 1997). Information on habitat (e.g., grazing, brush, nesting requirements) and population (e.g., hunting impacts, dynamics) management will be essential to maintain populations of bobwhites in the eastern portion of the Trans-Pecos. Additionally, efforts should be made to initiate a monitoring program of bobwhite abundance (e.g., expansion of TPWD quail lines) along the Pecos River watershed. A great deal of the recent research on bobwhites in South Texas (see chapter 16) may be applicable to the Trans-Pecos.

Scaled Quail

Compared to the information available on the other three species of quails in the Trans-Pecos, much is known on the ecology and management of scaled quail. Several descriptive studies have chronicled the general ecology of scaled quail in the region (table 11.1), yet no experimental studies have been conducted regarding their management. Priorities should be given to studies investigating the habitat preferences, movements, and effects of various habitat management practices (chemical, mechanical, grazing) on their distribution and abundance. Because scaled quail are the primary quail resource of the region, more information is needed to help landowners both manage and market them. Scaled quail in the Trans-Pecos are an underutilized resource; Wallmo and Uzzell (1958) speculated that 99 percent of scaled quail in the Trans-Pecos "have never seen a hunter." Basic research focusing on population dynamics should also be a priority; long-term data sets on scaled quail dynamics based on radiotelemetry are nonexistent. The Trans-Pecos also allows for investigations on interactions of sympatric

Table 11.1.
Characteristics of Scaled Quail Populations on the Trans-Pecos, Texas

Characteristic	Estimate	County	Source
Sex ratio (M:F)[a]	1.07–1.33:1	Eastern Brewster	Wallmo (1957)
	1.12:1	Eastern Pecos	Howard (1981)
	0.78–1.25:1	Central Brewster	L. A. Harveson (Sul Ross State University, unpublished data)
Age ratio (J:A)[b]	0.32–3.93:1	Eastern Brewster	Wallmo (1957)
	0.33–5.29:1	Central Pecos	B. Buntyn (Angelo State University, unpublished report)
	0.25–1.14:1	Central Brewster	L. A. Harveson (Sul Ross State University, unpublished data)
Annual survival rate	0.30	Central Brewster	Lerich (2002)
Density (bird/hectare)	3.3–6.7	Central Brewster	L. A. Harveson (Sul Ross State University, unpublished data)
Nest success	62%–84%	Central Pecos	B. Buntyn (Angelo State University, unpublished report)
	45%	Central Brewster	Lerich (2002)

[a] M = male; F = female.
[b] J = juvenile; A = adult.

species of quails (scaled quail and Montezuma quail, scaled quail and Gambel's quail, and scaled quail and northern bobwhites).

Gambel's Quail

Investigations on Gambel's quail are sorely needed. The first tier of priorities for research on Gambel's quail should include determining their current distribution and status (relative abundance), establishing and validating a monitoring program that can be implemented by TPWD, and evaluating hunter effort and success, as well as determining ways to further the economic benefit (e.g., marketing) of managing Gambel's quail in the Trans-Pecos. The second tier should be the investigation of the basic life history of Gambel's quail in Texas: determining seasonal food habits, evaluating habitat use and preferences, assessing population demographics (sex and age ratios, densities, dynamics, movements and ranges, survival rates, mortality factors), and investigating their breeding and nesting ecology. The third tier should focus on applied research: determining appropriate grazing systems, assessing the effects of salt cedar on their ecology, evaluating brush management programs, and enhancing upland sites to maximize use by Gambel's quail.

Montezuma Quail

Little is known about Montezuma quail in Texas and throughout its distribution in the United States and Mexico. A general assessment of the distribution and status of Montezuma quail is the first step to managing this species. Once distribution is established, efforts should be made to establish survey routes for Montezuma quail in various mountain ranges. A better understanding of the ecology of Montezuma quail is needed; only one study using radiotelemetry has been conducted on this secretive bird. Radiotelemetry will provide managers insight into the habits of Montezuma quail, including their demographics, movements and ranges, survival rates, mortality factors, and breeding strategies. Studies implementing new technologies in conservation genetics will be especially useful to determine dispersal strategies, understand the effects of habitat fragmentation, estimate effective population sizes of mountain-specific populations, and evaluate the success of previous reintroduction efforts. After the life history of Montezuma quail in the Trans-Pecos is revealed, researchers should focus on reintroducing them to historic ranges. A reintroduction protocol should be drafted, implemented, and evaluated (with radiotelemetry). Once baseline information is gathered on Montezuma quail, harvest scenarios should be modeled, habitat management strategies (e.g., prescribed fires) should be evaluated in the field, and the economic impact of Montezuma quail tourism in the Davis Mountains should be assessed.

Summary

Over the past century, the quails of the Trans-Pecos region have been affected by different environmental, social, and ecological factors. Northern bobwhites and scaled quail populations have demonstrated high annual fluctuations but have remained relatively constant; Gambel's quail populations have remained stable; and Montezuma quail populations have decreased in distribution and abundance. Drought, overgrazing, and lack of fire, which were the primary factors that converted most of the Trans-Pecos from a grassland savanna to a shrubland, have had a significant effect on the distribution and abundance of the quails in the region. Recent changes in land ownership and uses show promise for the conservation and management of quails in the Trans-Pecos. As stocking rates decrease across the region, more habitats will be made available for quails, resulting in wider distribution and higher abundance. Despite this optimistic forecast, very little information is available relative to the conservation and management of quails in the Trans-Pecos ecoregion of Texas. Researchers and managers need data relative to the life history and ecology of the quails of the Trans-Pecos before they can be properly managed.

Quails on the Edwards Plateau

12

John T. Baccus and Jack C. Eitniear

> Serious problems confront wildlife in many parts of the Edwards Plateau.
> These problems are interwoven with the problems of the stockman.
> Texas Game, Fish and Oyster Commission (1945)

Three species of quails inhabit the Edwards Plateau ecological region of Texas. The northern bobwhite (*Colinus virginianus*), the best-known and most widely distributed species, occurs in virtually all counties east of the Pecos River. Two species—scaled quail (*Callipepla squamata*) and Montezuma quail (*Cyrtonyx montezumae*)—occupy the arid western part of the region. Although diminishing in recent years, populations of the northern bobwhites are still the most abundant of the three quail species. Since the 1940s, populations of scaled quail have decreased on the Edwards Plateau (Oberholser 1974). The Montezuma quail, which was evidently never abundant on the Edwards Plateau, presently inhabits only a few ranches and a state park northeast of Del Rio (Sorola 1986). During recent years, however, Montezuma quail populations have increased (S. Sorola, Texas Parks and Wildlife Department [TPWD], pers. comm.; Lockwood 2001).

The purpose of this chapter is to summarize what has happened to quail populations on the Edwards Plateau since European settlement of this region. We describe the landscape components of the Edwards Plateau, summarize changing land-use trends, and cast these changes in the context of how they have influenced the distribution and abundance of quails in this region.

Characteristics of the Edwards Plateau

The Edwards Plateau consists of all or part of 42 counties. This ecological region covers 12,000 square kilometers (31,000 square miles; figure 12.1). The central and western parts have broad, nearly level uplands that are moderately dissected by gently sloping streams. In the south, several river systems dissect the surface, creating a rough and well-drained landscape, typified by the Balcones Canyonlands or Hill Country, adjacent to the Balcones Escarpment. The Central Mineral, or Llano, Uplift, formed by granitic soils, occurs in the northeastern part of the plateau. The Blackland Prairies and South Texas Plains border on the east and south; the Cross Timbers and Prairies, Rolling Plains, and High Plains border on the north; and the Trans-Pecos ecological regions abut the western boundary.

The overall topography slopes gently eastward and ranges in elevation from 305 meters (1,000 feet) to more than 900 meters (3,000 feet) above sea level.

Climate

Climatic factors of the plateau influence quail populations and distributions. With an average annual temperature of about 21°C (70°F),

217

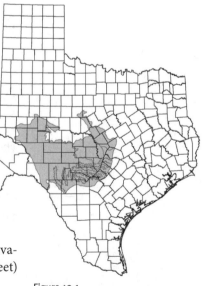

Figure 12.1.
The Edwards Plateau ecoregion of Texas.
Courtesy Caesar Kleberg Wildlife Research Institute (CKWRI) GIS Laboratory

monthly average temperatures vary from around 11°C (52°F) in January to 30°C (86°F) in August. The western, higher elevations have the lowest temperatures, and higher temperatures occur in the eastern areas with lower elevation. July afternoon highs often range to 42°C (108°F), and January nighttime lows often decrease to −10°C (14°F). The lowest nighttime temperature ever recorded on the plateau was −23°C (−4°F). The average last spring frost usually occurs in late March; and the earliest frost in autumn, in mid-November.

Precipitation varies on an east-west gradient from 84 centimeters (33 inches) at Austin to 38 centimeters (15 inches) in the west (Hatch, Gandhi, and Brown 1990). Seasonal rainfall patterns peak in May–June and September.

Vegetation

The original (circa 1800) vegetation of the Edwards Plateau consisted primarily of grassland or, more commonly, a type of open savanna, with shrubs and low trees along rocky slopes and drainages (Correll and Johnston 1970; Stanford 1976; Weniger 1988; Hatch, Gandhi, and Brown 1990). Prior to settlement by the first Europeans in the mid-1800s, grazing by bison (*Bison bison*) and pronghorn antelope (*Antilocapra americana*), combined with frequent natural and human-caused fires, maintained the Edwards Plateau vegetation in a condition that was about half grassland and half forest (Schmidly 2002) or a grassland savanna (Weniger 1988). The land supported a rich diversity of forbs and grasses. Early Texas explorers described the region as "a waving sea of grass, often stirrup-high on a horse or high as a cow's back" (Bentley 1898:7). Before European settlement, recurrent fires suppressed woody plants and maintained the open, grassy nature of the landscape on relatively level ground but not on steeper slopes and canyon walls (Weniger 1988).

Some of the common grasses first identified on upland sites (Bailey 1905) included little bluestem (*Schizachyrium scoparium*), big bluestem (*Andropogon gerardii*), indiangrass (*Sorghastrum nutans*), sideoats grama (*Bouteloua curtipendula*), Canada wildrye (*Elymus canadensis*), Texas wintergrass (*Stipa leucotricha*), and buffalograss (*Buchloe dactyloides*). Riparian area grasses included switchgrass (*Panicum virgatum*), eastern gamagrass (*Tripsacum dactyloides*), Virginia wildrye (*E. virginicus*), dropseeds (*Sporobolus* spp.), and the smaller bluestems. The drier western section grew shorter grasses such as tobosa grass (*Hilaria mutica*), common curlymesquite (*H. belangeri*), and threeawns (*Aristida* spp.). Trees and shrubs on the plateau include many oaks, such as live (*Quercus fusiformis*), Spanish (*Q. buckleyi*), bur (*Q. macrocarpa*), shin (*Q. havardii*), blackjack (*Q. marilandica*), and post (*Q. stellata*); hackberries (*Celtis* spp.); elms (*Ulmus* spp.); mesquite (*Prosopis glandulosa*); junipers (*Juniperus* spp.), catclaws (*Acacia* spp.); yuccas (*Yucca* spp.); bumelia (*Bumelia lanuginosa*); cenizia (*Leucophyllum* spp.); mountain laurel (*Sophora secundiflora*); and sumacs (*Rhus* spp.). The cooler, moist bottomlands and canyons contained a mixture of eastern and western plants. Pecan (*Carya illinoiensis*), ash (*Fraxinus* spp.), baldcypress (*Taxodium distichum*), walnut (*Juglans* spp.), mulberry (*Morus* spp.), maple (*Acer grandidentatum*), willows (*Salix* spp.), sycamore (*Platanus occidentalis*), and cottonwood (*Populus deltoides*) occupied less xeric environments (Bray 1901, 1904; Buechner 1944; Gould 1975b; Riskind and

Diamond 1988). In scattered sites across the region, less common plants, such as Texas madrone (*Arbutus xalapensis*), black hickory (*Carya texana*), and even pinyon pine (*Pinus edulis*), occurred on many southwestern hilltops (Palmer 1920).

Landscape and Vegetation Changes

The plateau had already undergone extensive landscape and habitat change by the time Vernon Bailey and his agents arrived in the region (Goetze 1998). When Bailey and Oberholser surveyed the plateau, most of the area had already been overgrazed by cattle, goats, and sheep, and most of the grasses had been depleted and replaced by less desirable woody shrubs (Schmidly 2002). Bailey (1905) described an area about 19 kilometers (12 miles) west of Kerrville as covered with scrubby timber, which became dense and of considerable size in canyons and gulches but was scattered and dwarfed on mesas. In June 1900, Oberholser depicted the landscape at Rocksprings as having a cover of live oak brush as the prominent vegetation across the entire face of the country, with the exception of frequent, though not often extensive, open grassy areas (Schmidly 2002). Oberholser noted occasional patches of mesquite, but documented that it did not grow among the live oak thickets. Some *Juniperus* occurred in the area (Schmidly 2002). Although grasslands of the plateau may have been mostly devoid of Ashe juniper (*Juniperus ashei*), also known as cedar, in pre-European settlement times, an increase in density of this species occurred, creating cedar thickets in former grasslands (Bray 1905; Foster 1917; Beuchner 1944; Smeins 1980). Historically, woodlands and primarily Ashe juniper thickets have occupied overgrazed areas along rivers and streams, areas of shallow soils, hillsides, and steep canyons with infrequent fires (Sellards, Adkins, and Plummer 1932).

The prominent and widespread brush invaders—junipers, live oak, mesquite, shin oak, and cacti—distinguished an ecosystem-wide change in the composition and structure of the plant community. In much of the Edwards Plateau, Ashe juniper and redberry juniper (*J. pinchotii*) became the dominant plants, causing a once-diverse and healthy landscape to become a "cedar break" with diminished plant diversity (figure 12.2). In the western plateau, mesquite began to take over the plant community. In addition, poor-quality forb and grass species domi-

Figure 12.2.
Unsuitable habitat for quails in a decadent Ashe juniper stand in Kerr County.
Photo by John T. Baccus

nated the plant community. As the more palatable grasses and forbs decreased or disappeared, many ranchers on the plateau switched from primarily cattle to sheep and Angora goat operations, often grazing all three types of livestock to better use the dominant shrubby vegetation (Buechner 1944).

European settlement brought fences, cows, sheep, goats, and control of fire. Livestock continuously grazed in fenced pastures, disrupting the natural movement patterns of native grazing animals that allowed plants to rest and recover from grazing. By 1900, continuous overgrazing and suppression of fire had caused a change in the composition and structure of plant communities from grassland to brushland. Sheep, goats, cattle, and an increasing deer herd readily browsed the increasingly abundant woody brush species. Through the selective eating habits of these animals for the climax plant species of the relic grassland, less desirable plants became dominant in the community. By 1930, shrubs and trees had invaded the uplands. By the 1940s, populations of good-quality, climax herbaceous plants could not be readily found on most ranges, and most rangelands had deteriorated into a landscape dominated by short grasses, rocks, shrubs, cacti, and trees (Weniger 1988).

What brought about this change in the rangeland? In part, the cultural philosophy of Europeans and implementation of an agricultural system of livestock grazing incompatible with sustaining wildlife habitat caused changes in plant communities. The philosophy of conquering nature and maximizing the production of land for human use prevailed. The Europeans developed grazing systems under a more mesic-climate philosophy that was not reflective of the arid environments of the plateau. The application of the wrong philosophy and grazing systems led to the transformation of the rangeland vegetation from a region that once supported from 300 to 500 cattle/section (260 hectares, or 640 acres) in the 1860s (Buechner 1944) into a deteriorated range with a recommended stocking rate for livestock of no more than 50 animal-units/section (an animal-unit is a cow and her calf). Combined with the effects of climatic instability, the landscape changes on the Edwards Plateau reached their present condition in the last quarter of the 1900s.

Presently, a scrub forest plant association dominated by a dense growth of shrubs and small trees 3–8 meters (9–25 feet) tall dominates the plateau. This vegetation consists mostly of oaks, Ashe juniper, and stunted live oak. It occupies not only the rocky slopes and the more dissected southern and eastern canyonlands but also many of the undulating uplands, especially in the eastern and southern halves of the plateau. Mesquite occurs throughout the plateau. With live oak, it dominates the woody vegetation in the western region. Some savanna-type vegetation still occurs. Tall prairie grasses still exist on level or nearly level rocky outcrops and protected areas that have good soil moisture. Unfortunately, such relic sites are widely distributed, sporadic, and uncommon.

Shallow soils and more xeric, exposed sites support midsize grasses. Areas with extensive, continuous grazing have a predominance of short grasses about 15 centimeters (6 inches) in height. At the northwestern margin of the plateau, the vegetation grades into the mesquite–tobosa grass community of the Rolling Plains, also a short-grass savanna with mesquite dotting the short tobosa grass, forming vast, almost monospecific stands on flatlands.

nated the plant community. As the more palatable grasses and forbs decreased or disappeared, many ranchers on the plateau switched from primarily cattle to sheep and Angora goat operations, often grazing all three types of livestock to better use the dominant shrubby vegetation (Buechner 1944).

Quail Population Trends

Information on the distribution and size of quail populations on the Edwards Plateau remained vague until near the end of the nineteenth century. The inventory of wildlife and assessment of its practical value became the job of the U.S. Biological Survey in the U.S. Department of Agriculture (Sterling 1989). C. Hart Merriam, director of the U.S. Biological Survey, picked a series of states, including Texas, for intensive biological survey and inventory. Over about a 20-year period (1889–1905), a team of 12 scientists and field agents led by Vernon Bailey conducted field surveys and prepared written reports that described the state's physiography, plants, birds, and mammals observed or captured at 178 different sites in all ecological regions of the state.

Ornithologist Harry C. Oberholser prepared the bird report from this biological survey. It contained the first comprehensive discussion of the distribution and habitats of quails in Texas. In this chapter, we used his information on quails as a historical baseline for a discussion of quail species of the Edwards Plateau.

During the early to mid-1990s, articles in magazines discussed habitat and populations of quails in different areas of the state. Texas Parks and Wildlife Department conducted studies of quails and published progress reports. However, no structured plan existed for collecting consistent information on quail population trends for the state. During 1976, TPWD implemented a roadside quail survey to track quail production trends at a regional spatial scale. A series of randomly assigned, 32-kilometer (20-mile) routes covered the state, with most counties having one route. On the Edwards Plateau, biologists established routes to record occurrences of northern bobwhites in Bandera, Blanco, Concho, Crockett, Edwards, Gillespie, Irion, Kendall, Kerr, Kimble, Kinney, Llano, Mason, Reagan, Real, San Saba, Schleicher, Sutton, Taylor, Uvalde, and Val Verde counties. Biologists established routes to record occurrences of scaled quail in Concho, Crockett, Irion, Kinney, Reagan, San Saba, Sutton, and Val Verde counties but did not include routes for Montezuma quail. Biologists traveled each route once annually during the first two weeks of August and recorded by 1.6-kilometer (1-mile) increments the number of singles, pairs, coveys, relative age of broods, and number of quail within coveys for each quail species. Because of legislatively mandated budget cuts and lack of bird sightings on some routes, TPWD discontinued northern bobwhite routes in Bandera, Blanco, Crockett, Edwards, Gillespie, Kendall, Kerr, Llano, Real, and Uvalde counties in 1988. We based our discussion of population trends for northern bobwhites on 16 routes with 25 years of continuous data.

Northern Bobwhites

Oberholser (1974) listed records for the northern bobwhite quail in almost all of the counties of the Edwards Plateau. During the past 30 years, quail numbers have declined and the species has become uncommon to rare in some localities of the plateau. This decline is consistent with the overall decline in quail numbers throughout most of the bobwhite's geographic range (Brennan 1991a; Church, Sauer, and Droege 1993; Brady, Flather, and Church 1998).

Because of the decline of the northern bobwhite on the plateau, Partners in Flight listed the species as a priority bird with respect to populations and habitats in the juniper-mesquite savanna and brushland associations. As a priority bird, the northern bobwhite has management priority equal to that of the golden-cheeked warbler (*Dendroica chrysoparia*) and black-capped vireo (*Vireo atricapillus*), two endangered species. In contrast, Lockwood (2001) suggested a stable population of northern bobwhites exists on the plateau.

The long-term population trend for northern bobwhites on the plateau, using TPWD survey data, shows an erratic, bimodal curve with a consistent decline since 1994 (figure 12.3). A five-year moving average applied to the data depicts a decline in the mid- to late 1980s with a brief recovery from 1990 to 1994. Since 1995, a steady decline in the population trend has resulted in an all-time low. At the beginning of the survey in 1978, 27 survey lines provided data on the population trend. Many of these lines for counties in the southern and central plateau had few or no counts from 1984 to 1987, and 11 lines were discontinued in 1988. From 1988 to 2002, the population trend was based on 16 lines. For these 16 lines from 1978 to 2002, the average number of quail seen per line varied from 0.92 to 27.96. To assess the source of the variation through time, we subsumed the data into lines associated with the periphery and core of the quail's distribution on the Edwards Plateau. Survey lines from counties in the central and southern plateau composed the core area. The peripheral lines occurred in Concho, San Saba, and Taylor counties along the northern boundary of the plateau. A contrast of the mean number of quail seen per line in core and peripheral areas showed fewer quail were recorded on core lines than peripheral lines. The core lines averaged 6.6 quail per line, and the peripheral lines averaged 16.6 quail per line. This suggests that the declining trend for northern bobwhites on the plateau has resulted from data showing fewer birds on core lines, as opposed to those on the periphery. The low standard error of the mean for core lines indicates little difference in number of birds seen year to year. The peripheral lines showed higher numbers of quail, but the number seen from year to year was more variable. This would suggest that some of the year-to-year variation in the population trend for the plateau stems from fluctuations in peripheral quail populations.

Even with a population decline in recent years, the northern bob-

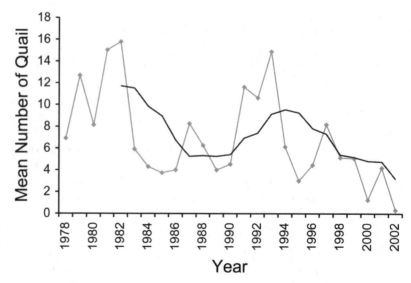

Figure 12.3.
Population trend for northern bobwhite quail based on Texas Parks and Wildlife Department quail survey lines in the Edwards Plateau, 1978–2002. A 5-year moving average is shown.

white remains a common and permanent resident in open shrublands and woodlands over the entire Edwards Plateau. However, in the arid western regions of the live oak–mesquite savannas, the distribution tends toward river drainages and mesic habitats (Lockwood 2001).

Overall habitat loss has played a major role in the decline. The habitat of a covey must be confined and nonfragmented within a relatively small area. Good northern bobwhite habitat must have an interspersion of cover types with an even mixture of bunchgrasses and forbs and open ground underneath. Throughout the Edwards Plateau, suitable habitat for the northern bobwhite is severely fragmented or nonexistent in many areas. To restore quail habitat, two obvious changes in land use and management must receive immediate attention: control of overgrazing caused by extreme livestock stocking rates (figure 12.4) and removal of excessive stands of noxious, invasive plant species. Restoration of pastures dominated by bunchgrasses has to be a major objective in land management. This type of habitat produced the richness of quail on the historical vegetation of the plateau. Overstocking of the range with livestock—and the ensuing overgrazing and exacerbation by drought—led to the change from the bunchgrass rangeland of the 1800s to the brush-dominated rangeland of today (Buechner 1944). Based on current stocking rates on most ranches on the plateau, the adequate density and height of bunchgrasses needed for suitable quail habitat cannot be established. Goats graze many pastures until a monoculture of the unpalatable horehound (*Marrubium vulgare*) dominates the plant community. There is no economic or ecological logic to such management; it is not cost effective nor does it exhibit good land stewardship. Such landowners need to receive educational materials from the county agent. Under such stocking rates, livestock will eat any recovering grasses. For recovery of quail populations, livestock stocking rates must be reduced on the Edwards Plateau.

Areas with dense cedar thickets preclude viable populations of northern bobwhites (figure 12.2). Under such conditions, the lack of ground cover, nesting cover, and food limits use by birds. The opening of such areas can be accomplished by brush management and prescribed burning. Prescribed burning remains the most effective and least expensive habitat management practice to control invasive brush species (White

Figure 12.4.
Unsuitable habitat for quails caused by overgrazing the rangeland.
Photo by John T. Baccus

Figure 12.5.
Northern bobwhite habitat on the Kerr
Wildlife Management Area, Texas.
Photo by John T. Baccus

and Hanselka 1989). However, the effect of burning grasslands remains
unclear (Carter, Rollins, and Scott 2002). Prescribed burning may increase mortality of northern bobwhites from predation in grasslands
with a complete removal of escape cover (Mueller and Atkinson 1985;
Guthery 2000). On the plateau, sporadic fine-fuel distribution generally
results in a mosaic of burned and unburned patches. Northern bobwhites seem to prefer unburned patches of perennial bunchgrasses for
nesting sites (Rosene 1969; Dimmick 1971). Such patchy burns provide
suitable habitat for quail (Guthery 1986) because the unburned areas
provide habitat refuges and protection from predators while burned
vegetation regrows. During periods of average or above-average precipitation, burning pastures on a three- to five-year burning rotation
sustains growth of important seed-producing forbs and grasses, sup-
presses invasive woody vegetation, and removes excessive plant litter,
allowing quail travel lanes and easier access to forage.

Throughout the Edwards Plateau, the native grassland community
has been altered and fragmented to the point that it is extremely difficult to find sufficient contiguous habitat to sustain viable populations
of wild quail. The reduction or elimination of once-dominant native
bunchgrasses (i.e., little bluestem, big bluestem, and indiangrass) has
severely limited successful quail reproduction. The declining population trend for the plateau indicates that one or more factors inhibit successful production by northern bobwhites. Overgrazing and the shift
from native pastures to improved grass pastures (i.e., coastal bermudagrass) have contributed to the loss of nesting habitat.

Larger areas of nesting cover can potentially improve reproduction,
if provided in conjunction with areas of weedy forbs and shrub cover.
Simply put, without good nesting habitat, females can not successfully
raise their young. Increasing the population for northern bobwhites
depends on reproductive success. Quail have a short life span (Rosene
1969); therefore, it is important that every female in the population have
access to nesting cover. Without sustained reproductive success, the viability and stability of a population decline over time. With depressed
populations generally throughout the plateau, nesting cover functions
as the single most important cover type controlling population size for
northern bobwhites.

Adequate nesting cover consists of a moderately dense, even mixture of native bunchgrasses and forbs with mostly bare ground around grass clumps. Lehmann (1984) found that northern bobwhites typically nested in perennial bunchgrasses with leaves that fold over to create overhead canopies. In the western plateau, northern bobwhites selected three microhabitats for nesting: grass, brush-grass, and cacti associations (Carter, Rollins, and Scott 2002). However, Carter, Rollins, and Scott did not identify optimal prickly pear and bunchgrass densities for increasing nest survival.

Nesting cover isolated in only small areas may be one possible explanation for decreased nesting success because these small, isolated patches give predators, especially raptors, an advantage (Mueller and Atkinson 1985). If nesting cover is spread over a large enough area, predators will have more difficulty locating nests and reproductive success will increase.

Kerr Wildlife Management Area

Personnel on the Kerr Wildlife Management Area near Hunt in Kerr County have used a general philosophy of holistic land management and incorporated prescribed burning, rotational grazing, proper stocking rate for livestock, control of Ashe juniper, and reduction of the white-tailed deer (*Odocoileus virginianus*) herd in white-tailed deer management. The removal of stands of Ashe juniper on the area occurred in the 1960s. During the late 1970s and early 1980s, rotational grazing of livestock was combined with prescribed burning. While working in pastures on the area at that time, Baccus saw no northern bobwhites. Personnel on the area considered the bird to be rare (Bill Armstrong, TPWD, pers. comm.). Intensive range management continued into the 1990s and proved successful in the restoration of a northern bobwhite population on the area. In a helicopter survey for white-tailed deer in January 2003, personnel documented 12 large coveys of northern bobwhites (Gene Fuch, TPWD, pers. comm.). Habitat management for white-tailed deer resulted in reestablishment of suitable habitat for northern bobwhites (figure 12.5). The Kerr Area model of range management demonstrates the benefits of holistic range management for white-tailed deer and all other wildlife species (figure 12.6). Some ranchers

Figure 12.6.
A contrast between two management systems. The foreground represents holistic management, and the background portrays continuous grazing with high stocking rates of livestock. Photo by John T. Baccus

on the plateau have implemented these practices on their land, but to have a landscape level of quail population restoration, more ranchers need to become involved in this strategy of range management.

Scaled Quail

The scaled quail has been listed as a declining permanent resident in open grasslands and mesquite and juniper savannas on the western plateau (Hamilton 1962; Lockwood 2001). Scaled quail reach the easternmost limit of their geographic distribution on the plateau (Johnsgard 1973, 1988). The historical distribution of the species extended as far east as Mason, Llano, Gillespie (sight breeding record), Kerr (breeding record), Bandera (fall specimen record), Travis (fall sight record), and Bexar (sight breeding and winter specimen records) counties (Oberholser 1974; Lockwood 2001). Near the boundary of distribution, a species may have viable populations but be uncommon to rare with smaller population size than in the core distribution. Recently, the distribution of scaled quail on the plateau has regressed westward to Crockett, Irion, Reagan, and Val Verde counties, but birds may still be present locally in western Menard, Kimble, and Edwards counties and uncommon in Schleicher and Sutton counties (Lockwood 2001).

Through time, scaled quail have become increasingly scarce in all but the most arid parts of the plateau (Lockwood 2001). To understand this reduction in populations and distribution, we examined data for eight survey lines on the population trend for scaled quail from 1978 to 2002 (figure 12.7). The mean number of quail seen per line varied from 0.16 to 16.24. To assess the source of the variation through time, we subsumed the data into lines associated with the eastern and western areas of the quail's distribution. Survey lines from Concho, Kinney, San Saba, and Sutton counties formed the eastern subset. The western lines occurred in Crockett, Irion, Reagan, and Val Verde counties. A comparison of the mean number of quail seen per line in eastern and western areas showed fewer quail were recorded on eastern lines (average 1.2 birds per line) than western lines (average 11.5 birds per line), suggesting that the declining trend for scaled quail on the plateau is moving downward because there are fewer birds on the eastern survey lines. The low standard error of the mean indicates little difference in number

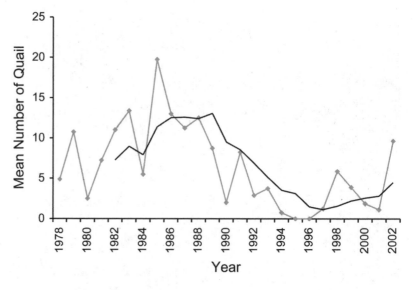

Figure 12.7.
Population trend for scaled quail based Texas Parks and Wildlife Department quail survey lines in the Edwards Plateau, 1978–2002. A 5-year moving average is shown.

of birds seen year to year. The western lines showed greater numbers of quail with more year-to-year variability in number of birds. This would suggest that some of the year-to-year variation in the population trend stems from fluctuations in western populations.

Scaled quail often experience extreme fluctuations in population size, with low numbers following dry years and high numbers following years with above-average rainfall. Their numbers also may diminish because of overgrazing by livestock and the loss of desirable groundcover plants (Leopold, Gutiérrez, and Bronson 1981). Declines in the distribution and populations of scaled quail in the western plateau may have resulted from increasing dominance of a juniper monoculture for the plant community and loss of nesting habitat. The historical pattern of land use caused a loss of bunchgrasses and vertical structure in the grassland community. Thus, cover became a limiting factor over much of the range of scaled quail on the plateau because lack of cover diminishes the suitability of habitat. Leopold (1959) reported that scaled quail thrived in Mexico in a habitat containing a combination of annual weeds, some shrubby or spiny ground cover, and available surface water.

Montezuma Quail

On the Edwards Plateau, the Montezuma quail was almost consumed by that great hazard of all earthly creatures: extinction (Oberholser 1974). In Mexico, the Montezuma quail is listed as endangered (Stromberg 2000; Tapia et al. 2002). Certainly, the loss of habitat and decline in populations during the last century indicate the precarious state of this bird on the plateau. Oberholser showed a historical eastern boundary extending from Mason County (summer and winter sight records) southward to Bexar County (breeding sight record and winter specimen record) and listed unconfirmed reports of birds in Llano and Burnet counties. As late as 1901, the species had begun to fade on the Edwards Plateau portion of its geographic range but still had a toehold in Nolan, Tom Green, Concho, Crockett, Schleicher, Menard, Mason, Llano, Burnet, Val Verde, Sutton, Kimble, Edwards, Real, Kerr, Bandera, Kinney, Uvalde, and Bexar counties (Oberholser 1974). Sorola (1986) reported that older ranchers thought Montezuma quail were common in some of these counties prior to a major decline caused by drought in the 1930s. By 1940, overgrazing of rangeland diminished the distribution of Montezuma quail into two small pockets—an area where Val Verde, Edwards, and Kinney counties join and near Concan in extreme northern Uvalde County, where Oberholser saw a healthy pair in 1938 (Texas Game, Fish and Oyster Commission 1945; Oberholser 1974). Oberholser suggested that by the 1960s, Montezuma quail populations of the plateau consisted of a small remnant on a private ranch in western Edwards County. By 1970, Oberholser had no firm information on the existence of the Edwards County population and suggested extirpation as a probability. However, probably unknown to Oberholser, Thomas (1959) saw 12 coveys of Montezuma quail on white-tailed deer lines in Edwards County.

Because of sparse populations, secretive behavior, and infrequent sightings of Montezuma quail, hunters and wildlife managers showed little interest in these quail on the Edwards Plateau. Other than the work of Oberholser (1974), TPWD has provided some information on the species (Texas Game, Fish and Oyster Commission 1945; Uzzell, Moore, and Wallmo 1953; Thomas 1959), but managers lacked the basic natural history and demographic information necessary for management of the species on the Edwards Plateau. Therefore, from 1983 to 1986, TPWD personnel studied and assessed the historical and current distribution, described habitat requirements, and developed guidelines necessary to manage remnant populations and stock populations within the former range of the species on the plateau (Sorola 1986).

Sorola (1986) verified that Montezuma quail had not been extirpated in the wild and still occurred in five counties, primarily on private ranches. An estimated 126 coveys occurred on about 131,580 hectares (325,000 acres), or 1,050 hectares (2,600 acres) per covey on 47 ranches. Edwards County had the largest population and widest distribution, where an estimated 93 coveys occurred on 35 ranches with areas near 93,120 hectares (230,000 acres). Sorola estimated that 19 coveys inhabited about 13,360 hectares (33,000 acres) on 4 ranches in Uvalde County. In Val Verde County, he found 10 coveys occupying about 14,575 hectares (36,000 acres) on 5 ranches. Three ranches in Kinney and Real counties (2 and 1, respectively) on about 10,930 hectares (27,000 acres) had 4 coveys (3 and 1, respectively). Sorola considered his estimate of the number of coveys to be conservative based on the unfamiliarity of many ranchers with this quail. Other than the covey counts observed by Sorola, no population estimates exist for Montezuma quail on the Edwards Plateau.

Current Status: Populations and Habitat

Today, Montezuma quail exist on the Edwards Plateau as a rare and local resident in open habitats with abundant tall grasses (Lockwood 2001). Sorola (TPWD, pers. comm.) considered the demise of the mohair industry and removal of most Angora goats from rangelands of the plateau as the primary reason for the improvement of rangelands (i.e., higher growth and greater cover of grasses), leading to increases in populations of Montezuma quail on ranches surveyed in the 1980s. Since the purchase of Kickapoo Cavern State Park by the state in 1986, the populations of Montezuma quail have shown a steady increase as the plant community in the park recovered from prior abusive land use (Lockwood 2001).

Montezuma quail are sensitive to changes in the quality of grasslands and savannas they inhabit (Lockwood 2001). On the Edwards Plateau, Montezuma quail usually inhabit environments in a live oak–juniper–pinyon pine association with annual rainfall of 61 centimeters (24 inches), a moderate stocking of livestock of about 10 hectares/animal-unit (25 acres/animal-unit), and elevations of 395–950 meters (1,500–2,400 feet) above sea level (Sorola 1986; figure 12.8). Pastures with quail had about a 25 percent canopy composed of live oak, juniper, and pinyon pine with an understory of Mexican persimmon (*Diospyros texana*), agarita (*Mahonia trifoliolata*), and mountain laurel (*Sophora secundiflora*). Sorola found that *Cyrtonyx montezumae* did not prefer areas with dense Ashe juniper but used areas with mountain laurel and concluded that dense stands of Ashe juniper could be a limiting factor of suitable habitat. The predominant grasses included threeawn, Texas wintergrass, sideoats grama, and common curlymesquite.

Figure 12.8.
Montezuma quail habitat at Kickapoo
Cavern State Park.
Photo by John T. Baccus

In pastures with quail, Wright's threeawn (*Aristida purpurea*), a bunchgrass, was the most common grass; however, the dominance of this grass in the community, which apparently provided sufficient cover for quail, may have resulted from historical grazing excesses by livestock (Sorola 1986). Albers and Gehlbach (1990) characterized the quail's feeding habitat as Madrean oak woodlands on dry slopes with tall grasses and terrain that is not rocky. They found feeding sites associated with patches of tall grasses on overgrazed pastures with patchy grass cover. In recent studies at Kickapoo Cavern State Park, Lockwood (2001) reported that removal of 40 to 50 percent of tall-grass cover caused extirpation of *C. montezumae*.

Quail Conservation on the Edwards Plateau

The Montezuma quail is intolerant of heavy grazing, particularly of grazing by sheep and goats. It is almost gone from the Edwards Plateau, which is its most eastern distribution in the state. The welfare of scaled quail is contingent on the presence of a diversified flora of grassland, arid-adapted shrubs, and cacti. Changes in land use, that is, the replacement of native food-bearing forbs and grasses with non-food-bearing exotic grasses, have severely reduced both the quantity and quality of quail habitat for all three species, especially the northern bobwhite. Although a rapidly expanding human population along the eastern and southern boundaries leaves fewer acres for practical quail restoration, large areas in the central and western plateau provide ample space for restoration of the three quail species.

An acute threat to quails on the Edwards Plateau in recent years has been the development of land for residential and light-industrial purposes, especially in the Hill Country near the largest cities. Large ranches located at commutable distances from cities have been sold for subdivision. Land in these areas is in jeopardy of becoming fragmented; thus, more quail habitat could be lost. Diffuse urbanization, the result of literally thousands of independent decisions to buy small parcels and settle in the suburban and rural locales, appears mostly immune from governmental regulation, especially if an endangered species does not occur on the tract of land.

However, outside the metropolitan-influenced areas, a change has taken place with respect to the ownership of land (Baccus 2002). A dynamic flux of land ownership developed during the last 30 years shows an increasing number of properties owned by nonresidents. For example, in Kimble County, the majority of current landowners do not reside in the county. These landowners use their land for hunting, wildlife viewing, and weekend retreats, not primarily for the traditional livestock production. These individuals have an entirely different philosophy of land use than the residents do, whose families in many cases have ranched for several generations. Many of these nonresident owners are appalled by the overgrazed landscape and have interest in good land stewardship. We believe this changing trend in land ownership provides an opportunity to educate and recruit these landowners into the cause of landscape management for quails. By applying habitat management practices, landowners can take pride in restoring and maintaining quality quail habitat on their property.

Despite the renewed management interest on the part of TPWD and selected individual quail enthusiasts, there has been a general lack of interest in quails on the plateau (Don Wilson, TPWD, pers. comm.). Because of poor huntable quail numbers on the plateau, hunters have been drawn to the Rolling Plains and South Texas Plains, which have greater bird populations. The meager hunting probably explains the deficiency of interest in quails by wildlife biologists on the plateau. A paucity of basic information on natural history and demography exists for the three species of quails inhabiting the plateau. The TPWD quail survey lines provide the only consistent and substantial data set on quail population trends for the region, but these data are limited by the few lines per county and lack of survey replication.

Land use at the broadest scale has been the most important factor impacting quail populations. In particular, grazing practices that reduce the amount of cover and eventually change the percent composition of bunchgrasses in the plant community could be the single most important factor causing declines in many quail populations. To combat the factors that jeopardize quail habitat, we must resolve to restore health to the grassland communities that support these popular game birds and all other grassland species. Unlike the situation for several species, it is not too late to restore populations of quails on the Edwards Plateau.

The three species of quails on the Edwards Plateau evolved and flourished in a grassland-savanna ecosystem. The successful restoration of viable quail populations on the plateau requires a united effort and commitment by a large contingency of private landowners to implement ecosystem management in land-use decisions and carry out these practices in perpetuity. One does not have to travel far on the highways of the plateau and look at the range conditions to see a broken system of land stewardship. We need ranchers to realize that their use of the land can deter or promote the recovery of quails. Most important, successful results from habitat improvement strongly depend on the number of landowners willing to change their current farming or ranching practices to suit the habitat needs of quails. The poor range conditions of today have resulted from 150 years of mismanagement. Habitat restoration cannot be expected to occur overnight. It took about 25 years on the Kerr Wildlife Management Area. However, with commitment, knowledge, hard work, and patience, positive results are possible.

As quail habitat and numbers have declined, the economic value of quails, particularly northern bobwhites and scaled quail, has increased. The fees that people pay for quail hunting rights on private lands have risen dramatically in price. Landowners need to recognize that good habitat management leading to the recovery of quail populations has economic benefits. For example, very limited quail hunting occurs on the plateau, and viable quail populations would provide landowners with another source of revenue. With the current depression in live-stock prices, ranchers have incentives to implement wildlife-friendly land-use practices. However, cultural attitudes conflict with needs of quails. The ranching culture emphasizes the use of land for human benefits, even to the extent of razing the land. Which is more economically viable: a goat herd destroying the range vegetation so that a rancher has to use supplemental feed for the herd to survive, or a multifaceted hunting and wildlife watching program with limited capital investment and good land stewardship? As a result of economics, an increasing number of ranchers now incorporate the needs of wildlife into their land-use management. When most do, the future of quails will be assured.

We need an outside-in and inside-out ecosystem management approach to restore and sustain viable quail populations throughout the Edwards Plateau. Initial efforts should concentrate on counties with the lowest human density. Destructive land uses of the past resulted in large tracts of land with habitats unsuited for quails. Populations of northern bobwhites and scaled quail in the Rolling Plains and South Texas Plains could serve as sources for recovering quail populations in the boundary counties of the plateau. This is the outside-in approach.

In the central plateau, landowners can form cooperatives for quail management. Tracts of land of 5,000–8,000 hectares (12,000–20,000 acres) under common management for the restoration of bunchgrass habitat can be dedicated, depending on the size of the cooperative. The application of management practices, such as those used at the Kerr Wildlife Management Area, to lands in cooperatives would form a nuclear population of quail for dispersal into adjoining lands. This is the inside-out approach. The attempts to improve land management on a small tract can produce positive results, and we applaud any landowner working to improve quail habitat on any size tract of land, but for substantial increase of quail populations on the plateau, management must be conducted on a far greater scale.

Generally, in matters of threatened species the state and/or federal government selects tracts of land for their relatively undisturbed state in establishing biological reserves for species. Although this concept is not new to policy makers and those with financial resources, at the present time only a minuscule area of the Edwards Plateau ecological region has been set aside as public land. It should be noted that in contrast to the vast amounts of public lands in other western states, Texas has virtually no federal and limited state lands on the plateau. State and municipal parks total only a few square miles in contrast to the huge size of the region. The only national park is devoted mainly to historical interpretation in San Antonio. We believe that no pristine sites presently survive on the plateau; however, tracts of several hundred to several thousand acres still exist with potential for restoration.

Finally, hunter revenues and research will not save quails on the Edwards Plateau. A cultural change concerning how private landowners view land use and wildlife will determine the fate of quails on the plateau. What incentives do landowners have to change land-use practices? Several programs of TPWD, such as the Landowner Incentive Program, assist private landowners in protecting and managing rare species by providing financial incentives that encourage landowners to help conserve rare species. The program is flexible and open to all private landowners who have a desire to voluntarily manage rare species on their land. Another incentive is the agriculture property tax conversion for wildlife management. This program passed by the legislature provides for equal tax conversion of land use from primarily livestock grazing to wildlife management. The problem with implementing this conversion in land use has been the reluctance of county tax assessors to accept wildlife management as a viable use of land. The attorney general of the state needs to insist that the tax assessors abide by the law and allow tax exemption for wildlife management. With this tax conversion, landowners have no incentive to continue livestock grazing to receive a tax exemption.

Landowner education should clearly be a part of the mix. Education about incentives and the economic benefits of a holistic approach to land management and quail-friendly management that involves the views of landowners, wildlife biologists, Partners in Flight, agricultural extension, hunters, professional ornithologists, and interested citizens should be promoted. Clearly, using white-tailed deer management on the Edwards Plateau as a strategy for restoring quail habitat, such as on the Kerr Area, needs marketing. Education should not be limited, however, to landowners. Information promoting ecosystem management, good land stewardship, and quail habitat should be distributed to public schools. After all, the reason for our campaign to restore quail habitat and populations on the plateau is to give future generations opportunities to see quails in the wild.

232
Quail Populations in the
Ecoregions of Texas

Quails on the High Plains 13

C. Brad Dabbert, Duane R. Lucia, and Robert B. Mitchell

> Agriculture, especially cotton production,
> has drastically changed the bird life of Texas.
> Oberholser (1974)

Wild quails are one of the most popular objects of pursuit for bird-watchers and hunters in Texas. In many areas of the state, their economic value rivals that of traditional agricultural enterprises such as 233 livestock. Unfortunately, this importance is not realized in the Southern High Plains of Texas. Land-use practices in this region of intensive agricultural activity leave relatively few areas of suitable habitat available for quails. Though Farm Bill programs have influenced millions of acres in the High Plains, this influence has not resulted in increases in quail populations in the region. Description and analysis of the current state of knowledge concerning quails and their management in the Southern High Plains of Texas should help direct the efforts of parties interested in the maintenance and restoration of quail populations. Thus, the purpose of this chapter is to (1) discuss the present and future state of quail populations and their relationship to land use in the Southern High Plains of Texas, (2) review the quail research literature concerning the region, and (3) describe future research needs.

Description of the High Plains

The ecoregion of the Southern High Plains of Texas is classified as the Southwest Plateau—Plains Dry Steppe and Shrub Province within the Tropical and Subtropical Division of the Dry Ecosystem Domain (Bailey 1998). The Texas High Plains are on the southern end of the North American Great Plains and occupy about 8 million hectares (20 million acres) (Scifres 1980; figure 13.1). The Texas High Plains are bordered by Oklahoma on the north, New Mexico on the west, the Trans-Pecos and Edwards Plateau on the south, and the Rolling Plains on the east. The Canadian River breaks, an extension of the Rolling Plains, bisects the northwestern portion of the region. The Caprock Escarpment provides a clear delineation of the eastern border.

The region is a flat to slightly rolling high plateau with numerous playa lakes (Scifres 1980). Elevation above sea level typically decreases from north to south. Elevation at English Field in Amarillo is 1,095 meters (3,591 feet); at Lubbock International Airport, 1,006 meters (3,257 feet); and at Midland International Airport, 875 meters (2,866 feet) above sea level. The lack of natural landmarks forced early explorers to drive stakes or pile rocks for navigation points, earning the region the nickname Llano Estacado, or Staked Plains (Morris 1997). The region has a long history of human habitation. Lubbock Lake, a National Historic Landmark, represents the span of North American culture from the Clovis period (ca. 11,000 years B.P.) to the present.

The climate of the Southern High Plains is semiarid. Long-term (90-year) average annual precipitation at Lubbock is 48 centimeters (18.9 inches), with about 81 percent of the precipitation occurring

Figure 13.1.
The High Plains ecoregion of Texas.
Courtesy Caesar Kleberg Wildlife Research Institute (CKWRI) GIS Laboratory

from April through October (National Oceanic and Atmospheric Administration [NOAA] 2003b). However, from May to October, potential evapotranspiration is about twice the annual precipitation (Bailey 1998). Since 1911, annual precipitation at Lubbock has been highly variable and ranged from 22 centimeters (8.7 inches) in 1917 to 103 centimeters (40.5 inches) in 1941 (NOAA 2003b). Average decadal precipitation has ranged from 40 centimeters (15.7 inches) in the 1950s to 52.5 centimeters (20.7 inches) during the decade of the 1910s.

The decade of the 1910s indicates the variable nature of precipitation in the region. This decade had the driest year on record yet had the highest average annual precipitation of any other decade. During 1914, 1915, and 1919, Lubbock received more than 78 centimeters (31 inches) of precipitation per year. However, the total precipitation received during 1916, 1917, and 1918 totaled only 91 centimeters (35.9 inches).

Vegetation Characteristics

The historic vegetation of the Texas High Plains was short-grass plains (Gould 1975a). Dominant grasses included blue grama (*Bouteloua gracilis*), buffalograss (*Buchloe dactyloides*), purple threeawn (*Aristida purpurea*), sideoats grama (*Bouteloua curtipendula*), and little bluestem (*Schizachyrium scoparium*). Dominant forbs included blueweed (*Helianthus ciliaris*), prairie coneflower (*Ratibida columnifera*), cutleaf germander (*Teucrium laciniatum*), lambsquarter (*Chenopodium album*), and scarlet globemallow (*Sphaeralcea coccinea*). Dominant woody plants were honey mesquite (*Prosopis glandulosa*), shinoak (*Quercus havardii*), and sand sagebrush (*Artemisia filifolia*).

Intensive agricultural activity throughout much of the historic range has reduced and fragmented the native vegetation. The remaining perennial native vegetation is predominantly degraded native rangeland and monocultures of exotics such as weeping lovegrass (*Eragrostis curvula*) and Old World bluestems (*Bothriochloa* spp.). Historically, the canopy cover of trees and shrubs was low (likely less than 5 percent) and was maintained by fire, thereby preventing seedling establishment on productive sites.

Quail Species on the High Plains

Two species of quails, northern bobwhites (*Colinus virginianus*) and scaled quail (*Callipepla squamata*), occur on the Texas High Plains. Their historical distribution and abundance are unclear, but both species have been reported from all counties within the region and during all seasons of the year (Seyffert 2001). McCauley (1877), who explored a significant portion of the Texas High Plains, including Palo Duro Canyon, never heard or saw either quail species. By as late as the 1930s, northern bobwhites and scaled quail were being reported as fairly common in Palo Duro Canyon and the woody areas surrounding the canyon (Seyffert 2001). It is likely that populations of both quail species increased on the High Plains as the canopy cover of trees and shrubs increased because of fire suppression and increased grazing pressure by cattle.

Various authors have discussed range boundaries of these species on the High Plains, indicating dominance of scaled quail in the west, dominance of northern bobwhites in the east, and an area of sympatry somewhere in the center, of which the size and shape are governed by precipitation (Hawkins 1945; Rollins 2000; Seyffert 2001). It appears that annual precipitation patterns may have governed the historic distribution of these species on the Texas High Plains.

Long-Term Population Assessment and Trends

Evidently, northern bobwhite populations have been slowly increasing on the High Plains during the last few decades. Breeding Bird Survey (BBS) data indicate an average annual rate of increase of 2.11 percent from 1966 to 2000 (Sauer, Hines, and Fallon 2002). Data from Texas Parks and Wildlife Department (TPWD) roadside counts display the irruptive pattern typical of northern bobwhite populations (figure 13.2). In contrast, scaled quail populations appear to be declining in the High Plains ecoregion. BBS data indicate an average annual rate of decline of −1.10 percent from 1966 to 2000. Data from TPWD roadside counts also display the irruptive pattern typical of scaled quail populations (figure 13.3). Calling route data between 1978 and 2002 appear to agree

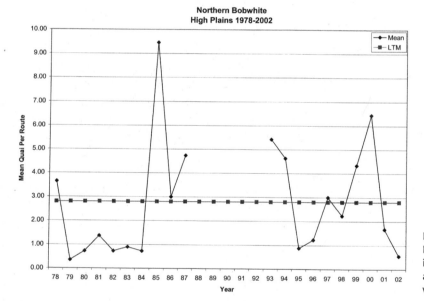

Figure 13.2.
Northern bobwhite population trends in the High Plains. Based on U.S. Fish and Wildlife Service Breeding Bird Survey data (LTM = long-term mean).

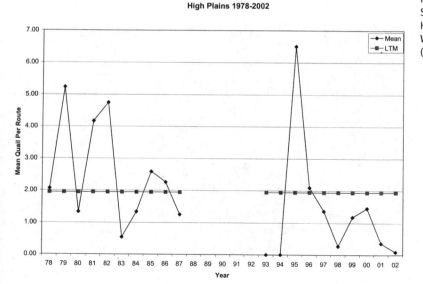

Figure 13.3.
Scaled quail population trends in the High Plains. Based on Texas Parks and Wildlife Department roadside counts (LTM = long-term mean).

with BBS data for scaled quail in the High Plains. Though there is extreme variability among years, population fluctuations appear to be drifting below the long-term mean toward local extinctions.

Lusk, Guthery, and DeMaso (2002) recently examined relationships between weather and land-use variables and abundance of northern bobwhites in several regions of Texas, including the High Plains. Their modeling suggested average conditions of land use and weather in the High Plains were less suitable than in most other regions in Texas for northern bobwhite populations. Simulations pointed to suboptimal winter and fall precipitation as the limiting weather factors. Livestock density and cropland were land-use variables that impacted northern bobwhite abundance in all regions examined. Abundance became severely limited as average cropland of a county approached 50 percent. Livestock density greater than 0.15 head/hectare (0.6 head/acre) also caused decreases in abundance of northern bobwhites. Unfortunately, these negative factors generally describe the condition of much of the land in the High Plains of Texas. Such factors are one of the main reasons that this region has one of the lowest average quail abundances of any physiographic region in Texas.

Land Use

Currently, land use in the High Plains of Texas is dominated by intensive agricultural activity. Cropland constituted roughly 42 percent of the land use by 1997. Some counties in the High Plains have few acres not occupied by cropland. For example, in Hockley and Terry counties, only 13 percent of the land area remains in rangeland (National Resources Conservation Service [NRCS] 1997). The greatest portion of cropland in the Texas High Plains is planted in cotton. Cotton production became common by early 1920 when hybrid cotton varieties were developed for the semiarid environment and farmers learned to tap the Ogallala Aquifer to irrigate their crops (Sharp 1992). Irrigation wells are estimated to have increased from 14,000 wells in 1950 to 65,000 in 1970. Unfortunately, the cropping system used for cotton provides generally unusable habitat for quails for at least six months of the year, when ex-

Figure 13.4.
The cropping system used for cotton provides generally unusable habitat for quails for at least six months of the year, when exposed soil is the only available feature of the landscape.
Photo by C. Brad Dabbert

Figure 13.5.
Quails can often survive in small coveys in abandoned homesites, often the only usable habitat in large portions of the High Plains.
Photo by C. Brad Dabbert

posed soil is the only available feature of the landscape (figure 13.4). Frequently, tillage occurs right up to the roads. Quails can often survive in small coveys in abandoned homesites, which may be, unfortunately, the only usable habitat in the area (figure 13.5).

Abandonment of cotton acreage can result in quick response of native forbs, some of which provide sufficient structural cover to provide usable space for quails. Infrequently, a mixture of forbs, grasses, and shrubs is left untilled in the corners of irrigated fields of cotton where center-pivot irrigators do not reach. These corners can provide usable habitat space for quails, but most corners are planted as dryland cotton, hayed, or sprayed because of weed concerns (figure 13.6). Cotton is by no means the only bane of quails on the High Plains of Texas. It is easy to envision, however, how conversion of cotton acreage to native warm-season grass pastures with sufficient forb diversity and woody cover could increase quail populations throughout the region.

Conservation Reserve Program (CRP) fields are a common site adjacent to cropland. The CRP was established under the 1985 Farm Bill to

Figure 13.6.
Most "corners" on the edge of irrigated areas are planted as dryland cotton, hayed, or sprayed because of weed concerns. If left to grow into native forbs and grasses, these areas can provide modest amounts of usable habitat for quails.
Photo by C. Brad Dabbert

Figure 13.7.
Conservation Reserve Program (CRP) fields planted in native warm-season grass are generally devoid of woody cover with the exception of an occasional invading woody species such as elm, mesquite, lotebush, or willow baccharis.
Photo by C. Brad Dabbert

remove highly erodible land from crop production. The CRP revegetated more than 1.3 million hectares (3.2 million acres) in the High Plains of Texas. Weeping lovegrass, an introduced, warm-season, perennial bunchgrass, was seeded extensively because of ease of establishment and production potential on sandy soils (Gamble 1970). Consequently, more than 0.4 million hectares (1.0 million acres) of weeping lovegrass were seeded in the High Plains of Texas during the CRP. Monocultures of weeping lovegrass CRP appear to be unsuitable for quails because of their lack of available food sources, often overly dense habit, and lack of woody cover. Weeping lovegrass CRP that was never well established or has been invaded by native forb species can provide food for quails. A few quail inhabit weeping lovegrass CRP when woody cover is available, such as near abandoned homesites.

Lack of woody cover is prevalent in weeping lovegrass CRP. Native warm-season grass CRP also is generally devoid of woody cover, with the exception of an occasional invading woody species such as elm (*Ulmus crassifolia*), mesquite (*Prosopis* spp.), lotebush (*Ziziphus obtusifolia*), or willow baccharis (*Baccharis salicina*) (figure 13.7). Although CRP has been a success at preventing soil erosion, it has not resulted in widespread increases in quail populations across the High Plains of Texas.

Rangeland provides the most usable habitat for quails on the High Plains of Texas. Reid, Grue, and Silvy (1979) reported that almost all positive correlations between both northern bobwhite and scaled quail abundance were with some type of rangeland. Today, both species can probably do well in their respective ranges, if rangelands are managed with some type of rotational grazing system and stocking rates monitored and adjusted as precipitation dictates (figure 13.8). This is frequently not the case. Rangeland that would be considered generally suitable habitat has been excessively grazed over much of the Texas High Plains to the point that it is no longer usable habitat (figure 13.9). Definitive research on relationships between quail populations and cattle grazing needs to be conducted on the High Plains.

Figure 13.8.
When High Plains rangelands are managed with some type of rotational grazing system and stocking rates monitored and adjusted as precipitation dictates, residual grass and shrub cover can provide habitat for scaled quail and northern bobwhites.
Photo by C. Brad Dabbert

Figure 13.9.
Rangeland in the High Plains that would be considered generally suitable habitat (behind the fence) has been excessively grazed over much of the Texas High Plains to the point that it is no longer usable habitat (in front of the fence).
Photo by C. Brad Dabbert

How Will Future Land-Use Practices Influence Quail Management on the High Plains?

Paisley (1968) chronicled the land-use change from cotton production in 1860 to northern bobwhite hunting plantations in Leon County, Florida. He suggested that the Mexican boll weevil, which arrived in Leon County in 1916, and a lack of diversification on farms led to bankruptcy of many large farms, their abandonment, and subsequent repurchase by parties interested in hunting quail. Today, Leon County and the adjacent Thomas and Grady counties in Georgia contain more than 150,000 hectares (300,000 acres) of excellent quail habitat. A landscape once dominated by cotton plantations has had a major impact on quail research and management in the United States since the 1920s (Stoddard 1931; Brennan 1991a).

We certainly do not want the agricultural demise that occurred in Leon County, Florida, to occur on the Texas High Plains. However, we do take hope in the fact that an area once dominated by intensive cotton production eventually became home to significant quail populations. Because of obvious climatic differences, the Texas High Plains will likely never support the same density and stability of quail populations that occur in Florida. Future trends in land use will undoubtedly determine the future of quail populations in the Texas High Plains.

We do not envision many major changes in land use in the High Plains of Texas that will have a significant, positive impact on quail habitat. Most producers involved in cotton production are heavily invested in equipment, time, and money. Economic pressures and good business practices encourage them to optimize production from every possible area. However, a major concern for agriculture in the Texas High Plains is the long-term availability of irrigation water. Just how long the Ogallala Aquifer can be pumped or if it will ever run dry is a matter of current debate. But barring serious limitations on irrigation water or more substantial subsidies that discourage production, it is unlikely that cotton acreage in the High Plains will significantly decline, at least in the foreseeable future.

Grazing Management

Like cotton production, overgrazing can render the landscape useless to quails. Rollins (2002) argued that overgrazing is the most important problem limiting quail populations in the eastern Rolling Plains. He described relationships among federal programs, drought, and continuous grazing activities that lead to severe range degradation.

The High Plains of Texas is caught in much the same situation as the Rolling Plains. Low livestock prices and drought can make it difficult for landowners to generate profit from rangeland. Cow-calf operators are reluctant to reduce herd sizes during a low point in the market, and stocker operations are eager to accept more animals. Concurrently, drought conditions limit grass production and rangeland carrying capacity. Consequently, many producers feed hay and supplement on rangeland, causing localized rangeland degradation (figure 13.10). Although this degradation is not desirable, these locations may provide quail habitat after a drought by growing large quantities of early-

Figure 13.10.
Many livestock producers feed hay and other cattle food supplements on High Plains rangelands, causing localized rangeland degradation and allowing no opportunity for quail production.
Photo by C. Brad Dabbert

successional vegetation (Jackson 1962). Nevertheless, landscape-scale rangeland abuse in the name of quail habitat improvement is unacceptable. Such an approach renders the landscape unusable by quails for an extended time period and opens it to other environmental problems such as erosion and poor water infiltration when precipitation returns. Instead, land managers should seek to maintain stocking rates that maintain quality nesting cover across the landscape through periods of drought and abundant rainfall.

Conservation Reserve Program

In contrast to the problem with rangeland, CRP has supplied nesting cover but is largely deficient in woody cover and food. Changes in CRP regulations could benefit quail management. For example, allowing desirable woody plants (shrubs) to be planted or to increase naturally would improve habitat diversity and structure and provide escape cover and loafing coverts (figure 13.11). Additionally, increasing the percentage of wildlife food plots allowed on CRP acreage would probably further improve quail habitat if the plantings were conducted on a sufficient scale. Requiring more of these features in future CRP contracts and providing programs to encourage their incorporation into existing contracts could greatly increase the benefit of CRP to quails on the High Plains of Texas. The recent emergence of the Conservation Practice 33, or "bobwhite buffers" program, may have a positive influence on High Plains quails.

Changing Demographics

Changes in landowner demographics could impact High Plains quail habitat in the future. The demographic of landowners is changing as current landowners age and traditional agriculture becomes less profitable. The primary income source for these new landowners is not agricultural income; therefore, income from the property is not required to maintain ownership. The new landowners are acquiring farmland and rangeland for recreational activities as a first priority and traditional land uses as a secondary priority. Farmland is being converted to

Figure 13.11.
Shrubs are significant habitat features for successful quail nesting sites.
Photo by Greg Pleasant

native perennial species, and rangeland is being managed specifically for wildlife habitat. With proper plant species selection and good grazing management, these areas can provide excellent quail habitat. The Farm Bill that is offered through the Department of Agriculture can be of major assistance in habitat modifications for quails. Conservation Reserve Program, Riparian Buffer Program, Environmental Quality Incentives Program, Wildlife Habitat Incentives Program, and other programs that are being offered in the Farm Bill through NRCS are usually done with matching funds. Depending on the program, this assistance could be up to a 75 percent cost share from the NRCS.

A positive impact of the change in land ownership is the increased landscape heterogeneity. These new landowners usually do not want to consider landscape-scale brush management projects that could decrease loafing and escape cover. They often manage the brush density to provide ample brush in strategic locations throughout their property. Many of these new landowners see wildlife and quail management as a priority and agriculture as a hobby or as a tool for wildlife management.

An example can be found in shinoak-dominated rangeland. The primary objective of traditional treatments was to reduce shinoak density in an entire grazing unit to maximize grass production for increased livestock grazing. The primary objective for many landowners today is to reduce shinoak density in strips or in a checkerboard pattern to increase grasses in the treated strips but maintain the shinoak in the nontreated areas.

Fragmentation

The fragmentation of large tracts of rangeland that used to support healthy quail populations may become the primary negative impact of this changing pattern in land ownership. Typically, large tracts are being split up into smaller ranches or ranchettes. Prior to fragmentation, relatively large pastures would be grazed inefficiently and thus provide nesting cover in areas away from watering sites. It remains to be seen whether the benefits of better management will offset the disadvantages of fragmentation.

Quail Research from the Texas High Plains

After we examined the literature concerning northern bobwhites and scaled quail, it became apparent that relatively few studies have been conducted in the Texas High Plains, especially compared to other physiographic regions in Texas, such as the South Texas Plains (chapter 16). Information from the High Plains of New Mexico concerning scaled quail (Campbell et al. 1973) and the Rolling Plains of Texas concerning both species (chapter 7) brackets our area of interest.

Foods

Davis, Barkley, and Haussamen (1975) studied scaled quail food habits on the High Plains of New Mexico only 15 kilometers (9 miles) from the western border of Texas. They reported that seeds of mesquite and croton, as well as insects, were consumed throughout the year. Snakeweed (*Gutierrezia sarothrae*), crown-beard (*Verbesina encelioides*), and cycloloma (*Cycloloma atriplicifolium*) were important winter foods.

Ault (1981) reported the food habits of a small sample of scaled quail inhabiting the Texas High Plains. Important seeds included bladderpod, fragrant sumac (*Rhus aromatica*), gromwell, honey mesquite, sorghum, crotons, Russian thistle (*Salsola kali*), western ragweed (*Ambrosia psilostachya*), and sand sagebrush (*Artemisia filifolia*). Animal matter, principally grasshoppers and beetles, were eaten throughout the year.

Burd (1989) studied food habits of scaled quail on the High Plains near the New Mexico border. He stratified sampling to prereproductive (January–April) and reproductive (April–June) periods. Birds ate primarily seeds (79.6 percent dry volume) during the prereproductive period, with the remainder of the diet being split almost equally between insects and green vegetation. Percentages of these diet components shifted to 23.8 percent vegetation, 36.9 percent insects, and 39.3 percent seeds during the reproductive season. Grasshoppers were the dominant insect food throughout the study.

Important seeds included those of Russian thistle, barnyardgrass (*Echinochloa crusgalli*), belvedere summercypress (*Kochia scoparia*), and western ragweed. Important sources of green vegetation included pinnate tansymustard (*Descurainia pinnata*), western ragweed, prairie pepperweed, Gordon bladderpod (*Lesquerella gordonii*), broom snakeweed (*Xanthocephalum sarothrae*), and nuttall milkvetch (*Astragalus nuttalianus*). Though sand shinnery oak (*Quercus havardii*) and sand sagebrush were major woody plants on the study areas, no seeds from these plants were detected during the two years of the study. Seeds from honey mesquite, fragrant sumac, and broom snakeweed, the other dominant species of woody vegetation on the study sites, were consumed during the two-year study. We were not able to find any publications with data on the diets of northern bobwhites in the High Plains of Texas.

Rainfall and Populations

Campbell (1968) detected a positive relationship between hunter success for scaled quail in eastern New Mexico and spring-summer rainfall. Giuliano and Lutz (1993) examined relationships between northern bobwhite and scaled quail abundance (using Christmas Bird Count data) and seasonal rainfall between 1966 and 1991 in study sites from both the High Plains and the Rolling Plains. Rainfall patterns were not correlated with abundance changes of either species from year to year. Scaled quail abundance was negatively correlated with fall and winter rainfall, but no differences among regions were detected. Giuliano and Lutz suggested that differences between their study and Campbell's were likely due to differences in the timing and amount of rainfall between their study areas. The study sites used by Giuliano and Lutz were located on the eastern edge of scaled quail range in Texas and received a mean October–March rainfall of almost 23 centimeters (9 inches). In contrast, the study area of Campbell received less than 10 centimeters (4 inches) of rainfall during the same time period.

Giuliano and Lutz (1993) suggested that fall-winter precipitation in the arid area was likely important for habitat maintenance but might limit usable habitat in the more mesic edge of their range. They were puzzled, however, to find that rainfall was not more strongly and positively correlated with northern bobwhite abundance in their study areas, which represented the more arid edge of the western range for northern bobwhites. As previously mentioned, Lusk et al. (2002) analyzed the relationship between mean weather conditions and bobwhite populations on the High Plains of Texas. Their simulations pointed to suboptimal winter and fall rainfall as possible limiting weather factors.

Habitat Management

We know of no published studies of specific habitat management techniques and concurrently monitored quail response occurring on study sites in the Texas High Plains. Some information on the potential response of quails to different management actions can be gleaned from studies where grass management was the primary objective. For example, Heirman and Wright (1973) found that March burning decreases forb composition of rangeland on the Texas High Plains. Specifically, western ragweed and annual broomweed were greatly reduced. Robertson and Box (1969) provided planting date and depth prescriptions for interseeding sideoats grama into rangeland in the High Plains.

Several studies have been conducted on sites that closely border or bisect the High Plains of Texas. We mention a few of these studies because of their applicability to the High Plains. Renwald, Wright, and Flinders (1978), working in the Rolling Plains near the border of the High Plains, reported that lotebushes about 3.9 cubic meters (5 cubic yards) in size were important as loafing cover and were used at a density as low as approximately 3.9 lotebushes/hectare (2/acre) following prescribed fire. Mature mesquites were also used but at a much lower rate. Annual broomweed was used when lotebush and mesquite were defoliated. Lotebush should be protected in quantity to preserve quail habitat when burning is considered.

Stormer (1984) described roost sites used by scaled quail in the Canadian River section of the High Plains. Scaled quail roosts on consecutive nights were from 0 to almost 400 meters (about 430 yards) apart. Favored vegetation included yucca (*Yucca angustifolia*), walkingstick cholla (*Opuntia imbricata*), true mountain mahogany (*Cercocarpus montanus*), and fragrant sumac. In general, roost sites contained no overhead canopy, and vegetation height was less than 0.5 meter (about 1 foot).

Stormer (1981) also described loafing coverts of scaled quail in the same area. Cholla was the dominant species used by scaled quail, but fragrant sumac and mesquite-cholla associations were also used. These shrubs protected significant amounts of lateral herbaceous cover encircling the shrub with a bare area in the center. Stormer indicated that scaled quail would use artificial cover sources made of limbs, poles, or other structures and provides details for building the structures.

Prescribed fire and grazing can be important tools for managing quail habitat, and the combined impact of these tools may provide additional benefit. Burning patches within larger management units attracts large herbivores and creates islands of diversity that function similarly to food plots. Vermeire et al. (2004) burned 4-hectare (1.6-acre) patches within large pastures in western Oklahoma. They reported that cattle were strongly attracted to burned sites and reduced grass standing crop by 78 percent within burned areas but only 19 percent outside burned patches. Forbs increased by 60 percent on patches that were burned and grazed. These increases in forbs not only provide increased seed production but likely promote invertebrate diversity for the high-protein diet necessary for brood rearing. This management strategy can be effectively utilized in the Texas High Plains.

Growth and Development

Smith and Cain (1984) determined that scaled quail from the High Plains attained 50 percent of their mean, 177-gram (6.2-ounce) body weight by 6 weeks and 90 percent of this weight by 13 weeks. They also provided data concerning wing and bone growth and methods to age juvenile scaled quail ±1 week.

Population Dynamics

Campbell and Harris (1965) detected dispersal distances of scaled quail from 16 to 40 kilometers (10 to 25 miles) during the summer and fall. Birds traveled from Lea County, New Mexico, to Andrews County, Texas, in the High Plains. They were unclear of the cause or frequency of these movements but believed habitat conditions of the site they left were suitable. Burd (1989) used the date of the first calling scaled quail male as an indicator of the beginning of reproductive season; April 20 was the average date from 1980 through 1982. The average date when hatch was 50 percent complete was June 21. Burd estimated this date by capturing juvenile quail in walk-in traps and back-dating their age from feather-molting patterns. Pleasant (2003) monitored nest success and chick survival of scaled quail in Cochran County, Texas. Nest success was 44 percent and 64 percent during 1999 and 2000, respectively (figure 13.12). Forty-six percent of hens had chicks present with them 21 days after hatch during 2000, but only 10 percent had chicks present with them 21 days after hatch during 1999. Predation appeared to be the primary cause of hen mortality and unsuccessful nests. It is unclear why there was so much variation in chick survival between years. Pleasant, Dabbert, and Mitchell (2003) used scaled quail as a model to

Figure 13.12.
Scaled quail nest success was 44 percent and 64 percent in 1999 and 2000, respectively.
Photo by Greg Pleasant

examine the moisture-facilitated nest depredation hypothesis. Rainfall, however, was not related to the rate of nest predation in the semiarid environment of the Texas High Plains.

Research Needs

Though there are few published studies concerning quail management in the Southern High Plains of Texas, we are not suggesting that quails cannot be effectively managed in this region. We can still use descriptions of quail habitat requirements and management techniques for similar regions such as the Rolling Plains (chapter 7) and apply them to areas in the High Plains. Grazing management, burning, disking, and brush management can all be used to manage quail habitat in this region. Future research endeavors should start to refine use of these management tools for this region. Several areas of investigation will be most beneficial at this time. Increasing the woody cover and forb components of CRP in the Texas High Plains could create major increases in quail habitat. Methods need to be developed for optimal planting or transplanting of shrub species and for interseeding forbs. Further, methods should be developed to optimally convert monocultures of exotic grasses to native warm-season grass and forb communities.

For example, in Lynn County, Texas, we converted more than 200 hectares (500 acres) of weeping lovegrass on a CRP site to a mix of native grasses and legumes. In early October, two quarts of Roundup were applied per acre to reduce weeping lovegrass density. Mortality was evaluated in early spring, and the treatment was deemed successful. In May, a mixture containing sideoats grama, blue grama, little bluestem, switchgrass, green sprangletop, and Illinois bundleflower was sod-seeded at 4.4 kilograms/hectare (4 pounds/acre) into the weeping lovegrass stubble. Although drought has negatively impacted the stand, plant species diversity is high, and weeping lovegrass has been reduced by more than 90 percent. Illinois bundleflower is established in the field and has increased the available food supply (figure 13.13).

As we have previously mentioned, lack of woody cover is the other major negative factor concerning CRP besides food supply. Establishing and growing woody plants in CRP require one to five years before any quail habitat improvement is realized. We initiated a study in Lynn County, Texas, to evaluate the usefulness of artificial structures to provide adequate cover for bobwhite quail in weeping lovegrass CRP. Our goal was to develop an artificial cover structure that could be used while woody plants were establishing. Artificial cover structures consisted of a cone-shaped structure about a meter (a yard) tall and wide, covered in 5- × 10-centimeter (2- × 4-inch) wire with juniper boughs covering the wire (figure 13.14). Feed and water were provided inside the cones. We installed 24 of these structures on a 65-hectare (160-acre) area.

Figure 13.13.
Establishment of Illinois bundleflower might increase the available food supply for quail in old-field habitats in the High Plains.
Photo by C. Brad Dabbert

Figure 13.14.
Where woody cover is lacking, cone-shaped brush piles might provide this element of structure for quail.
Photo by C. Brad Dabbert

We trapped and transplanted 94 northern bobwhites into weeping lovegrass CRP containing artificial cover structures between February and April during 2002 and 2003 (Abbott 2003). Quail were radio-marked to allow us to monitor their survival, habitat use, and nesting success. We recorded extremely high nest success of 70 percent in 2002 and 71 percent in 2003. Northern bobwhites were often seen using artificial brush structures, and this use appeared to peak during summer when high ambient temperatures may have forced them to seek shade. Weeping lovegrass CRP at the composition available in our study area appears to be suitable nesting cover for northern bobwhites.

In addition to refining prescriptions for habitat management, understanding quail demographics on the High Plains of Texas is an important future research area. We have discussed the lack of demographic data concerning northern bobwhites in this region, and Rollins (2000) lamented the paucity of modern demographic data for scaled quail throughout its range. Certainly, knowledge of the relationships among quail survival, nest success, population growth rate, and habitat improvements (i.e., woody plantings, interseeding, and grazing reform) are key to stewardship management for quails on the High Plains of Texas. Additional understanding of habitat overlap between northern bobwhites and scaled quail is also an important facet of stopping the decline of scaled quail in this ecoregion.

Finally, economic analyses may play an important role in defining future land-use changes, especially for rangelands. The bottom line for producers is that they must make a profit to stay in business. Producers will likely have to be convinced that income losses caused by changes in land use that are beneficial to quails can be recouped via other avenues, such as hunting leases, wildlife photography and viewing tours, and/or western experience and historical tours (Blodgett 2002).

It is easy to be pessimistic about the major challenges facing quails on the Texas High Plains. Alternatively, the solution is not wholly unknown, and the reality is that there are millions of acres that could be improved for quail habitat. We hope the future will bring creative economic and habitat management solutions that will be beneficial to quail and producers on the Texas High Plains.

14 Bobwhites on the Post Oak Savannah

Nova J. Silvy

> [The] restriction of naturally occurring fires and continual overgrazing have converted much of the Post Oak Savannah from true savannah to complex, heavy thickets of woody plants.
>
> Scifres (1980)

Today, the Post Oak Savannah of Texas supports few huntable populations of northern bobwhites (*Colinus virginianus*). In this ecoregion, small and relatively isolated populations of quail currently exist in fragmented patches of habitat.

There are few published studies of northern bobwhites in the Post Oak Savannah, and little recent work has been done. Some of the classic natural history studies of quail in this region were conducted in places where it intergrades into the Blackland Prairies (chapter 10).

This chapter describes the ecological aspects of the Post Oak Savannah in the context of bobwhite management. It presents population trends and provides a general overview of aspects of bobwhite life history that are germane to this region. The chapter also discusses limiting factors and management options and outlines research needs that pertain to bobwhite ecology and management. It summarizes the land-use and management changes that will need to occur if northern bobwhite populations will ever increase within the Post Oak Savannah region of Texas.

Post Oak Savannah

The Post Oak Savannah comprises about 3.4 million hectares (8.4 million acres). This ecoregion is situated in east-central Texas, extending southward from the Texas-Oklahoma border for a distance of about 563 kilometers (350 miles) and varying in width from 80 to 121 kilometers (50 to 75 miles) (Parmalee 1953a; figure 14.1). Topography is mostly level to gently rolling, with some steep slopes and hilly areas (Gould 1975b). Many areas are considerably eroded, largely by formation of gullies. Kirvin (Norfolk group) and Lufkin (Susquehanna group) are the two major soil types; they are mostly loose, light-colored, sandy-loam topsoil with a subsoil of clay and sandy clay (Parmalee 1953a). Elevation ranges from 91 to 242 meters (250 to 650 feet) (Gould, Hoffman, and Rechenthin 1960). The average annual temperature is 19.3°C (66°F), average annual rainfall is 98.3 centimeters (approximately 40 inches) (Grue 1977), and average length of the growing season is about 250 days (Parmalee 1953a).

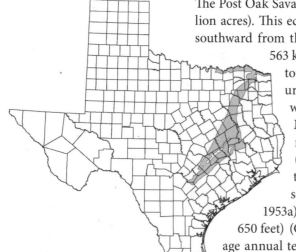

Figure 14.1.
The Post Oak Savannah ecoregion of Texas.
Courtesy Caesar Kleberg Wildlife Research Institute (CKWRI) GIS Laboratory

Climax vegetation is basically a post oak (*Quercus stellata*) savanna (Gould, Hoffman, and Rechenthin 1960). Most of the Post Oak Savannah is in native or improved pasture, although small farms are common. Almost 75 percent of the area is in pastureland grazed primarily by

cattle. Due to intensive grazing practices, much of the area has degener-
ated to dense stands of oak with an understory of yaupon (*Ilex vomitoria*). Post oak and blackjack oak (*Q. marilandica*) are the two dominant
species in the upland areas. Several other woody species are often found
growing in association with them: hackberry (*Celtis occidentalis*), eastern red cedar (*Juniperus virginiana*), mesquite (*Prosopis glandulosa*),
and cedar elm (*Ulmus crassifolia*). The understory is dominated by yaupon, winged elm (*U. alata*), poison oak (*Rhus toxicidendron*), American beautyberry (*Callicarpa americana*), and trumpet creeper (*Campsis
radicans*). Wild plum (*Prunus mexicana*), honey locust (*Gleditsia triac-
anthos*), hawthorn (*Crataegus spathulata* and *C. marshalli*), prickly ash
(*Xanthoxylum clava-herculis*), sumac (*R. copallian*), Osage orange (*Tox-
ylon pomiferum*), and cedar (*J. lucayana*) also are commonly found sin-
gly in open areas, along streams, and in thickets. Bottomlands consist
of hardwoods, predominantly oaks (water oak [*Q. nigra*] and overcup
oak [*Q. lyrata*]), with pecans (*Carya* spp.) and black hickory (*Hicoria
buckleyi*) in some areas.

The dominant grasses include little bluestem (*Schizachyrium scoparium*), indiangrass (*Sorghastrum nutans*), switchgrass (*Panicum
virgatum*), purpletop (*Tridens flavus*), silver bluestem (*Bothriochloa
saccharoides*), grama grasses (*B. curtipendula* and *B. hirsute*), Texas
wintergrass (*Stipa leucotricha*), panicgrass (*Panicum halli, P. obtusum,
P. lindheimeri,* and *P. texanum*), bullgrass (*Paspalum longipilum* and
P. pubescens), buffalograss (*Buchloe dactyloides*), spike uniola (*Uniola
laxa*), and longleaf uniola (*U. sessiliflora*) (Parmalee 1953a; Gould, Hoffman, and Rechenthin 1960).

Most of the large tracts of Post Oak Savannah were cleared in the early
1900s. By the early 1950s, much of the cleared areas had been reclaimed
by brush and woody species. Today, very little original savanna vegetation remains; most has been plowed and converted to tame pasture for
cattle grazing (Gould 1975b). Tame pastures are commonly planted in
common and coastal bermudagrass (*Cynodon dactylon*), crimson clover (*Trifolium incarnatum*), and white clover (*T. repens*). Fallow fields
consist of common and coastal bermudagrass, threeawn grass (*Aristida
purpurescens, A. olingantha,* and *A. intermedia*), johnsongrass (*Sorghum
halepense*), ryegrass (*Lolium perenne*), goatweed (*Croton lindheimeri,
C. lindheimeranus, C. mananthogymus,* and *C. texensis*), broomweed
(*Gutierezia texana*), western ragweed (*Ambrosia psilostachya*), southern
dewberry (*Rubus trivialis*), showy partridge pea (*Chamaecisita fascicu-
late*), and other forbs. Grain sorghum, cotton, corn, forage crops, tame
pasture, and pecans are important crops within the bottomlands (Godfrey, Carter, and McKee 1967).

Dominant vegetation types within the Post Oak Savannah intersecting nine random quail call-count transects in 1976 were tame pasture
and unmanaged fields (34.8 percent), woodlands (25.1 percent), parklands (18.1 percent), and savanna (10.0 percent), with the latter three
primarily post and blackjack oak (Grue 1977). Grue observed that
cropland composed 4.1 percent; forests, 3.4 percent; and urban areas,
0.8 percent of area along transects. Mesquite in the form of shrubs and
trees occupied about 7.7 percent of vegetation types along transects.
Vegetation type interspersion and diversity were high (exceeded only

by those of Piney Woods and Cross Timbers and Prairies ecological regions) compared to those within the other ecological regions of Texas (Gould 1975b).

Quail Distribution and Abundance

Oberholser (1974) indicated that northern bobwhites were found in every county within the Post Oak Savannah region of Texas. In 1976, Reid (1977) noted an average northern bobwhite whistle count of 30 whistles/transect on nine 24-kilometer (15-mile) call-count transects within the Post Oak Savannah. This average whistle count ranked fourth highest among 10 ecological regions in Texas, being exceeded only by those of the Cross Timbers and Prairies (average = 46), Gulf Prairies and Marshes (average = 43), and Rolling Plains (average = 38) regions.

From 1978 to 1987, Texas Parks and Wildlife Department (TPWD) evaluated quail abundance within the Post Oak Savannah. A series of 32.2-kilometer (20-mile) census routes, randomly selected, were run annually during the first two weeks of August. Northern bobwhites were observed along each route either one hour before sunset or at sunrise. Quail routes were designed to evaluate trends in quail populations at an ecological-region scale. Initially, these routes were to be run each year; however, due to budget cuts, routes within the Post Oak Savannah were discontinued in 1987 (M. J. Peterson, pers. comm.). During the 10 years for which the routes were run, mean numbers of northern bobwhites/route (Bridges 1999) ranged from 4.3 in 1987 to 11.1 in 1983. Bridges noted that the population trend appeared stable for this 10-year period (figure 14.2). During this period, the Post Oak Savannah ranked fifth highest in mean number of quail seen per route (being exceeded by the South Texas Plains, Rolling Plains, Cross Timbers and Prairies, and Gulf Prairies and Marshes).

The Present

Unfortunately, there are no current data available for quail abundance within the Post Oak Savannah. Once TPWD stopped the trend surveys, little information was available on quail numbers or distribution within the region. However, TPWD has conducted hunter surveys in the region to obtained estimates of the number of hunters and the number of quail harvested. Data for both the number of hunters and the number of quail harvested have declined from 1981 to 2001 (figure 14.3).

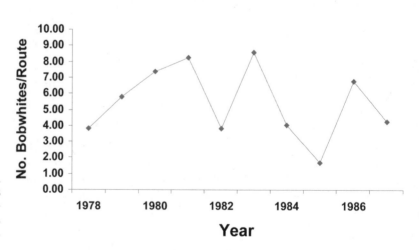

Figure 14.2.
Mean number of northern bobwhites per Texas Parks and Wildlife Department route in the Post Oak Savannah, 1978–87.

The Future

Data from TPWD hunter-survey trends indicate that the quail harvest will be basically nonexistent by the year 2005 within the Post Oak Savannah (figure 14.3). Brennan (1991a) had a similar projection for the southeastern United States, based on Christmas Bird Count (CBC) data, indicating that the CBC index for bobwhite numbers would effectively be 0 by the year 2005. Undoubtedly, bobwhites will continue to exist for some time within the Post Oak Savannah if they are given priority by landowners. However, unless habitat loss is abated and additional habitat is created, they will ultimately become extinct within this region of Texas.

Ecological Relationships: Life History

Much of the information in this section is summarized from Parmalee (1952a, 1954) unless otherwise noted.

Covey Breakup

The first "bob-white" calls in the Post Oak Savannah are typically heard between March 1 and April 30. Calls reach a maximum, both in number and in intensity, in May. Covey dispersal and pairing occurred the second and third weeks in April 1950 and 1951, respectively. As temperature increased, coveys broke up into groups of four and five birds and moved to roadsides, to open pastures, and along fencerows. By May 1, pairing was completed.

Nesting

In the Post Oak Savannah, the majority of quail used pasture or grassland for nesting, although brush and woodland edges were also used to a limited extent. Of 61 quail nests located in 1950 and 1951, 44 were in open pastures, fields, or meadows; 2 were beside buildings; 5 were in fencerows; 5 were in cultivated fields; 3 were in oak woods; and 2 were in brush.

From a nesting survey, Parmalee (1955) tracked 59 northern bobwhite nests during the 1951 nesting season. Of these, 54 were of known fate and 34 (62.9 percent) were successful. Parmalee also noted that hatching success for 1950 had been even higher. Of the 20 unsuccessful nests, 9 were abandoned or destroyed by human interference (losses primarily to mowing), and 5 were destroyed by predators. The average

251

Bobwhites on the Post Oak Savannah

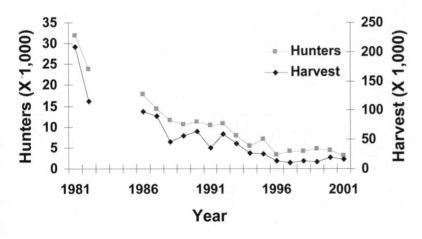

Figure 14.3.
Number of hunters and the number of quail harvested within the Post Oak Savannah, 1981–2002
(TPWD, unpublished data).

number of eggs/nest was 12.9, and the average number of eggs hatching/nest was 11.9. The largest number of eggs hatching from one nest was 23, and the smallest, 3.

Based on wing samples from hunter-harvested quail, 86.3, 90.0, and 98.9 percent of young hatched prior to August 15 in 1949, 1950, and 1951, respectively. Production appeared to be correlated with rainfall. Parmalee (1952a) noted that late broods (July and August) in 1951 averaged only 8.9 birds (n = 12). One hen observed on August 18 had 4 chicks from 3 to 5 days old. Laying also occurred late during 1951, for on October 29, 1951, a fresh quail egg was taken from beneath a rosebush on his main study area. In addition, during the first week of December 1951, three fresh eggs were picked up and a fourth fresh egg was collected during the first week of January 1952 by a landowner. Parmalee considered late nests to be a result of a second or third nesting attempt after the first nest had been destroyed. He also noted that juvenile hens normally nested later in the season than did adults based on development of ovaries.

Brood Survival

No direct data on brood survival are available for northern bobwhites within the Post Oak Savannah. The best data available are from young/adult age ratios obtained from hunter kills. Wings from hunters obtained in 1949 indicated that bobwhites had an average reproductive year, with a 50:50 adult sex ratio and 5.0 young/adult. In 1950, there were 9.7 young/adult. This is one of the highest juvenile/adult ratios ever recorded for bobwhites. In 1951, there were only 2.4 young/adult, classified by Parmalee as a relatively poor hatch.

Habitat Use

Reid (1977) and Reid, Grue, and Silvy (1978) noted that within the Post Oak Savannah, grain crops (corn and sorghum), hay, and mesquite habitats were probably the most important vegetation types used by bobwhites. They also noted that snags served as whistle posts and cropland may have been utilized as feeding areas.

Cover used by northern bobwhites has been classified into three categories: brush thickets, grassland, and edge of woodlands. Reid, Grue, and Silvy (1978) found that stretchberry (*Smilax bona-nox*) was one of the most satisfactory native plants providing protective cover for bobwhites in the Post Oak Savannah. It was common throughout the area, grew rapidly, and formed thick tangles. Occasionally, it combined with other brush types and became too thick for quail (figure 14.4). Wild grape (*Vitis candicans*) also supplied good quail cover.

Another important plant for quail cover in the Post Oak Savannah is Macartney rose (*Rosa bracteata*). It was introduced and planted to serve as fencerows or to control erosion. However, if left unattended, it forms large thickets and spreads into neighboring areas within a short time. This plant was condemned by many ranchers and farmers because of its ability to take over a field or pasture.

The edge of woodlands provided both food and cover during certain periods of the year but was used by bobwhites only if adjacent to grasslands (Parmalee 1952a). Cover of this type often constituted a sizable

Figure 14.4.
Invading woody plants are gradually
replacing the pasture and form-
ing cover too thick for quail. Brazos
County, Texas, October 2003.
Photo by Nova Silvy

portion of a covey's range, especially during fall and winter. Bobwhites
used it for protection, and in years of high mast production, as an area
in which to feed.

During the nesting season and during summer, bobwhites were dependent upon the grass cover for their life requisites (Parmalee 1952a).
Grasslands provided cover and an abundant food supply. In addition,
areas surrounding water tanks, stock barns, holding pens for livestock,
and old farmsteads were often trampled or heavily overgrazed. Such locations provided winter food as well as some cover in summer.

Diet

Chenault (1940) observed four seasonal waves of potential food plants
for northern bobwhites in Brazos County, Texas, within the Post Oak
Savannah ecoregion. He noted that plants furnish food to quail in the
form of seeds and green vegetation and also serve as cover. He placed
plants into four major groups according to the season in which they
flowered. During winter, bobwhites utilized Virginia rockcress (*Arabis
virginia*), common chickweed (*Stellaria media*), mouse-ear chickweed
(*Cerastium viscosum*), chervil (*Chaerophyllum dasycarpum*), annual
bluegrass (*Poa annua*), panicgrass (*Panicum hellrei*), and dichondra
(*Dichondra carolinensis*) as green food. In early spring, they also used
fruits of dewberry (*Rubus trivialis*) and honeysuckle (*Lonicera semper-
virens*), both of which produced flowers in winter. Chenault frequently
observed 35–50 bobwhites feeding upon dewberries during June.

Chenault (1940) noted that even though the plants flowering in
spring were most numerous, they were not of most importance as food
sources for quail. Summer-flowering plants were by far the most important for the entire year: showy partridge pea, goatweed (*Croton* spp.),
and knotweed (*Polygonum acre*).

During the breeding season, bobwhites utilized primarily animal
matter (31 percent), grass seeds (29 percent), and forb seeds (22 percent).
During the nonbreeding season, bobwhites utilized primarily forb seeds

(64 percent), mast (20 percent, mainly acorns), and grass seeds (10 percent). Goatweed was the most utilized forb during both seasons of the year, and oak acorns were the primary mast utilized (Parmalee 1953a). Parmalee (1952a) considered goatweed to be the most important food item for quail in the Post Oak Savannah. Acorns were utilized greatly during winter; however, production varied considerably between years, and few acorns were available in some years. Parmalee (1952a) observed 120 goatweed seeds/929 square centimeters (120 square feet) in 1950 and 115 seeds/929 square centimeters in 1951. He estimated that a bobwhite, during two daily feedings, would eat about 136 goatweed seeds.

Parmalee (1952a) observed northern bobwhites drinking from a spring-fed creek on several occasions. When disturbed, they would either flush or run to trees that grew to the edge of the water. He noted that quail hunters and landowners had observed bobwhites congregating in the vicinity of available surface water in periods of drought. He also noted a covey of 10 bobwhites that frequented a stock tank on one of his study areas. At low water levels, quail had to cover 4.6–6.1 meters (15–20 feet) of exposed ground to obtain water.

Mortality Factors

Numerous factors contribute to quail mortality. This section summarizes those factors known to be responsible for quail mortality in the Post Oak Savannah ecological region. See chapter 6 for a discussion of parasites and diseases of quails.

Nutrition

Coleman (1941) suggested that winter food was limiting, and Chenault (1940) observed that there were fewer plant species available for bobwhites during winter months. With reduced winter food, quail numbers could be limited due to competition with other vertebrates. However, Parmalee (1952a) observed that songbirds did not consume quantities or species of food that were important in the diet of northern bobwhites. However, he noted that rodents may remove large quantities of seeds that form important components of the bobwhite's diet. Therefore, rodents may be in direct competition with bobwhites for food within the Post Oak Savannah. This is a difficult hypothesis to test. Along with the food-limitation hypothesis, it remains unproven.

Weather Events

Bridges (1999) found that only May precipitation was correlated with northern bobwhite abundance within the Post Oak Savannah.

Predation

Parmalee (1952a) considered snakes to have taken quail eggs from nests where eggs disappeared completely. In contrast, however, recent work (Hernández, Rollins, and Cantu 1997) has shown that such an assumption may be wrong; of 10 snakes collected, none had quail eggs in the stomach. Parmalee also collected 14 nine-banded armadillos (*Desypus novencinctus*) and found no quail eggs. Nevertheless, the majority of ranchers and farmers destroyed them because they considered armadillos predators of quail eggs.

Parmalee (1952a) noted that during summer 1951, a large percentage of young bobwhites were lost, probably from predation. However, he obtained no evidence concerning which species of predators were possibly preying upon the young quail. He did not consider the road-runner (*Geococcyx californianus*) to be a significant predator of quail chicks—as was commonly believed—because few roadrunners were found within the Post Oak Savannah.

Predation by red imported fire ants (*Solenopsis invicta*) has been suggested by many hunters as the reason for the decline of northern bobwhites in the Post Oak Savannah. Coon and Fleet (1970) noted that fire ants were first found in Brazos County, Texas, in 1970. During this same year, Mirex (a chlorinated-hydrocarbon pesticide) was aerially broadcast from low-flying aircraft across much of the Post Oak Savannah in an effort to control the advancing fire ants. Mirex was later banned for use as a pesticide by the Environmental Protection Agency because of its carcinogenic properties, bioaccumulation, and effects on wildlife and animal reproduction. Both Mirex and fire ants may have had negative effects on the northern bobwhite population of the Post Oak Savannah.

Pedersen (1994) and Pedersen, Grant, and Longnecker (1996) examined the response of pen-raised northern bobwhite chicks to the presence of red imported fire ants during a nine-week field experiment in Brazos County. During the first six days posthatching, chicks were observed responding directly to fire ants by altering daily activity budgets. Time spent avoiding fire ants affected the time chicks spent moving, sleeping, and feeding. Pederson, Grant, and Longnecker suggested that fire ant–related mortality probably occurred during the first few days posthatching. They also noted that for species with extended nesting seasons, such as the bobwhite, nesting success might be higher for earlier or later nests (fire ants were less active earlier and later in the nesting season due to cold and dry weather, respectively). Wilson and Silvy (1988) recorded nest abandonment by a northern bobwhite hen and subsequently fire ants swarming into broken eggs.

Wood (1952), working in Brazos County, Texas, analyzed stomachs of 43 raccoons (*Procyon lotor*), 22 opossums (*Didelphia virginians*), 18 striped skunks (*Mephitis mephitis*), 9 ringtails (*Bassariscus astutus*), and 12 gray foxes (*Urocyon cinereoargenteus*) but observed no bobwhite remains. Parmalee (1952a) observed that an opossum had killed two bobwhites in a trap he had left unattended with the top door opened. Apparently, the two quail and then the opossum entered the trap during the 30 minutes he was away banding other quail taken earlier from the trap.

Of 24 hawks (five species) and 17 owls (three species) Parmalee (1952a) collected, no quail remains were found. However, he observed what appeared to be a raptor kill of a bobwhite at a stock tank, and he had been informed by hunters of a hawk killing a male bobwhite. From the hunters' description, he speculated it was either a red-tailed (*Buteo jemaicensis*) or a red-shouldered (*B. lineatus*) hawk. In addition, he found the remains of one bobwhite in a thicket, possibly killed by a raptor, and another bobwhite in a roadside ditch, possibly killed by a house cat. Of 44 pellets he collected from under a nest containing three young great horned owls (*Bubo virginianus*), 1 contained a leg band of a juvenile female bobwhite.

Hunting

Parmalee (1953b) speculated that hunting during his study in the Post Oak Savannah did not lower the breeding stock below the normal carrying capacity of the land. Parmalee (1952a, 1953b), however, did propose that reduction of the bag limit in years of low quail populations might prevent overshooting in local areas. He further recommended that the quail hunting season start earlier in the year (e.g., October 15–November 30 instead of December 1–January 16, inclusive, as were the season dates in 1950 and 1951). By starting and closing the season earlier, hunters would be able to take the fall surplus before they were lost from natural causes, and the seed stock would not suffer too great a loss in local areas during years of low populations. This was apparently qualitative support for the doomed-surplus hypothesis (see chapter 24). Parmalee (1953b) also noted that 20.8 percent of the quail shot down by hunters were never recovered and should be taken into account when figuring loss due to hunting.

Population Dynamics

In spite of the low survival of nests, chicks, and adults, northern bobwhites continue to maintain small, isolated populations in the Post Oak Savannah. To sustain their populations, northern bobwhites breed at one year of age, have large clutch sizes and high egg hatchability, are persistent renesters, and can produce more than one brood per year. These factors tend to compensate for low nest success and brood and adult survival.

Variation in Production

In the Post Oak Savannah, population densities of northern bobwhites vary between years (Bridges 1999). Yearly densities ultimately are influenced by variations in precipitation. Bridges et al. (2001) found that May precipitation was correlated with mean numbers of northern bobwhites observed in the Post Oak Savannah.

Mechanisms Accounting for Variation in Production

Northern bobwhites have declined throughout the Post Oak Savannah (Bridges 1999; Bridges et al. 2001). Although weather ultimately controls much of the variation in northern bobwhite annual abundance in Texas (Bridges et al. 2001), the proximate processes governing this variation are unknown. Disease, predation, brush encroachment, overgrazing, land fragmentation, and possible other unknown factors have been proposed (Parmalee 1952a). Parmalee found, however, that northern bobwhites are able to disperse through movements that would allow recolonization of adjacent areas. He observed one banded bird (later shot) to have moved 1 kilometer (0.6 mile) from where it was trapped.

Any of the factors discussed in the previous section on mortality factors probably could singularly or in combination be responsible for variations in northern bobwhite numbers in the Post Oak Savannah. Land use and land-use practices, such as livestock grazing (Parmalee 1952a), in addition to influence of weather, ultimately account for changes in population densities of northern bobwhites. Regardless of the cause, the variation in the percentage of hens that successfully produce young has the greatest effect on populations in this region.

Wilkins et al. (2003) noted that from 1992 to 2001, the most notable land-use trend within the Post Oak Savannah was the conversion of croplands (−13.7 percent) to nonnative improved pastures (3.1 percent). Conversion of croplands to improved pastures and the reduction of available habitat for northern bobwhites are considered to have the greatest effect on populations.

I reanalyzed vegetation types along the nine 32-kilometer (20-mile) quail whistle-count transects originally analyzed by Reid (1977) and found that pastures and old fields along the transects had decreased from 34.6 percent to 3.1 percent from 1976 to 2002. Further, during the same time period, parkland vegetation types had increased from 18.2 percent to 50.6 percent; tree savannas, from 10.0 percent to 35.2 percent; forest vegetation types, from 3.8 percent to 21.5 percent; and urban areas, from 0.7 percent to 6.6 percent. During this 26-year period, pastures and fields (preferred habitat for nesting quail) had decreased more than 1,100 percent, and closed-canopied habitats (unused by quail) had increased more than 700 percent. Also, there was a more than 900 percent increase in urban areas during the same period, causing increased fragmentation of quail habitat.

It is clear that livestock grazing influences northern bobwhite populations in the Post Oak Savannah. There must be enough cover left during all periods of the year, even during times of drought, if bobwhites are to exist and prosper in this region (Parmalee 1952a). The nesting observed along roadsides by Parmalee indicated that bobwhites were apparently leaving overgrazed pastures and looking for nesting cover along roadsides. Conservatively or moderately grazed native pastures contained areas with a mix of grazing intensities ranging from ungrazed to heavily grazed areas, which are important quail habitat requisites.

During drought years, fewer quail nested and grazing reduced available nesting habitat, leading to higher predation on nests, young, and adults (Parmalee 1952a). Also, the nesting season was shorter due to the hot, dry weather. However, many of the interactions between the various proximate causes that affect annual northern bobwhite abundance in the Post Oak Savannah are largely unknown at this time.

Management

Coleman (1941) used 17 plant species to evaluate 26 food plots within Brazos County. Quail used only 1 of these plots. Parmalee (1952a) noted that food plots usually failed because of low plant quality, poor choice of sites, incorrect site preparation and lack of cultivation the first year, insufficient fertilizer, destruction by livestock, wrong patterns, seasonal drought, and wildlife damage.

Parmalee (1952a) also evaluated supplemental feeding and did not find a relationship between providing food and increasing quail abundance. Doerr (1988), Doerr and Silvy (1987, 2002), and Silvy (1993, 1999) noted that although supplemental feeding concentrated bobwhites for hunters, it did not increase spring densities of quail.

Grazing pressure was the primary factor affecting the vegetation composition of pastures. Pastures under careful management often contained a high percentage of grasses used by bobwhites for nesting and cover, and those that are overgrazed produce abundant annual weeds used by quail for food. Parmalee (1952a) also considered roadsides to be important for quail nesting and travel. Timing of mowing on rights-of-way was critical.

Knowledge Gaps and Research Needs

Within the Post Oak Savannah ecological region of Texas there has been only one study (Parmalee 1952a) conducted on northern bobwhites. This was done over a half century ago, before the advent of radiotelemetry. Therefore, relatively little is known about northern bobwhite populations and habitat relationships within this region. The curtailing of quail censuses within the Post Oak Savannah in 1987 by TPWD exacerbated the situation. Of greatest need is to restart the TPWD quail census routes within the region. Without knowledge of what the population is doing, how can the population be managed?

Reversing the trend of native pastures and old fields succeeding to brush, woodlands, and forests or being converted to improved pastures (figure 14.5) would greatly help bobwhite populations within the Post Oak Savannah. Some initial work on restoration of native plants in bermudagrass pastures (figure 14.6) has been started by Wagner et al. (2003) and Hays et al. (2004). However, a comparative study of the long-term economics of native versus improved pastures is desperately needed. As wildlife managers, we promote (without economic data) na-

258

Quail Populations in the Ecoregions of Texas

Figure 14.5. Contrasting fencerows: with woody vegetation suitable for quail habitat (left) and with little cover for quail (right). Brazos County, Texas, October 2003. Photo by Nova Silvy

Figure 14.6. Open bermudagrass pastures offer little cover for quail. Brazos County, Texas, October 2003. Photo by Nova Silvy

tive pastures over improved pastures for wildlife. However, to convince landowners, we must show that there is a greater long-term economic return from native pastures (including leases for quail hunting) than from improved pastures, if there is one. Only with convincing economic data can we succeed in changing the land-use practice of converting native to improved pastures, a practice that is harmful to quail populations.

Eliminating closed-canopy woody habitats will require that efficient and economic methods be developed. Because of overgrazing and the lack of a fuel load to carry prescribed fires, and the liability associated with fire management, many pastures and old fields have changed to woody-dominated landscapes. Public attitudes about fires must be changed and liabilities to landowners must be minimized if such management is to succeed.

The urbanization of the Post Oak Savannah has and will continue to create problems for quail management. Urbanization causes fragmentation of the landscape and isolation of individual quail populations, reducing their population size until they are unsustainable. Today, we do not know the minimal land area needed to support a viable population of quail within the Post Oak Savannah, nor do we know the minimal number of quail needed to support a viable population. Because of the potential genetic inbreeding problem associated with small, isolated populations, it may not be feasible to support a single population in isolation from adjoining populations. Therefore, northern bobwhite management within the Post Oak Savannah must be accomplished in unison throughout the region if quail are to be sustained within the region.

Summary

The potential for northern bobwhite populations to return to their former glory days within the Post Oak Savannah region of Texas is probably unrealistic. With the current economic situations of the state and nation, there is little hope for economic incentives that will produce additional quail habitat within the Post Oak Savannah.

With the human population of Texas increasing at a phenomenal rate, urbanization will continue to fragment existing quail habitat. Rural lands near urban areas will be taken out of production prior to being subdivided for sale, leading to brush encroachment and thereby decreasing quail habitat. In Texas, the areas along and east of Interstate 35 and along and west of Interstate 45 (which includes much of the Post Oak Savannah) are being urbanized at an unprecedented rate. During the same period, northern bobwhite habitat and numbers are being lost at an unprecedented rate. A look into the future only sees these trends continuing.

15 Bobwhites on the Gulf Coast Prairies

Robert M. Perez

> Because little of the coastal prairie vegetation remains undisturbed,
> it is difficult to determine the nature of the original vegetation.
> Sims and Risser (2000)

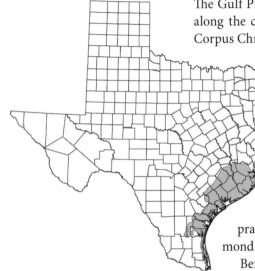

Figure 15.1.
The Gulf Prairies and Marshes
ecoregion of Texas.
Courtesy Caesar Kleberg Wildlife
Research Institute (CKWRI)
GIS Laboratory

The Gulf Prairies and Marshes physiographic region of Texas extends along the coast from the Louisiana border in Orange County to the Corpus Christi Bay in Nueces County and continues south as a narrow band less than 16 kilometers (10 miles) to the southern tip of the state (figure 15.1; Gould 1962). The prairies have never been a popular destination for quail hunters, but they once supported respectable densities of northern bobwhites (*Colinus virginianus*). Today, bobwhites persist at low densities because of tremendous reductions in available habitat since the mid-eighteenth century. Remaining areas of native prairie and semi-prairie are vital to bobwhites and many other declining grassland birds, including the endangered Attwater's prairie-chicken (*Tympanuchus cupido attwateri*) (Smeins, Diamond, and Hanselka 1991:288; Knopf 1994).

Before European settlement, the Gulf Prairies probably did not produce large numbers of bobwhites. Early accounts make no reference to quails, but they do mention species associated with mid- and tallgrass prairie, such as prairie-chickens, buffalo (*Bison bison*), and antelope (*Antilocapra americana*). Post-European settlement activities enhanced bobwhite populations, but eventually fire suppression, intense grazing pressure, woody encroachment, mechanized farming, industrial development, and introduced grasses greatly reduced native grassland habitat in the region (Texas Game, Fish and Oyster Commission [TGFOC] 1945:47; Smeins, Diamond, and Hanselka 1991:287). Smeins, Diamond, and Hanselka estimated that less than 1 percent of the original prairie remains in pristine condition (p. 270). Changes in the quantity of quail habitat in the Gulf Prairies are similar to those that have occurred throughout the bobwhite range. An understanding of these land-use changes is critical to bobwhite conservation efforts.

This chapter will address the description of the Gulf Prairies and Marshes ecoregion, historical accounts, bobwhite population status, reasons for the bobwhite decline, human impacts and trends, summary of regional research, knowledge gaps and research needs, habitat management, and the future.

The Gulf Prairies and Marshes Ecoregion

The Gulf Prairies and Marshes ecoregion covers approximately 5.3 million hectares (about 13.1 million acres) in Texas. The marshes are small subregions comprising about 125,000 hectares (about 300,000 acres), but they are especially important to many species of waterfowl and Neotropical migrant birds (Schmidly 2002:391). The prairies are nearly level plains dissected by rivers and streams (Gould 1962) and are generally thought of as a continuum of the north-south range of tall-grass communities in Texas (Diamond and Smeins 1984). The inland boundary of this area ranges from 15 to 150 kilometers (approximately 10 to 90 miles) from the coast, and elevations vary from sea level to 76 meters (250 feet), characterized by slow surface drainage (Smeins, Diamond, and Hanselka 1991).

Average annual precipitation in the Gulf Prairies ranges from 64 to 140 centimeters (25 to 55 inches). Temperature averages 20°C–21.1°C (68°F–70°F), and the growing season lasts 280–320 days. Other climatic influences include occasional tropical storms and hurricanes (Smeins, Diamond, and Hanselka 1991).

Prairie soils are dark, neutral to slightly acidic clay loams and clays in the northeastern parts. Farther south in the Coastal Bend, the soils are less acidic. A narrow band of light acidic sands and darker loamy to clayey soils stretches along the coast; farther inland is another narrow belt of lighter acidic, fine, sandy-loam soils. Soils of the river bottomlands and broad deltaic plains are reddish brown to dark gray, slightly acidic to calcareous, loamy to clayey alluvial (Gould 1962; Smeins, Diamond, and Hanselka 1991).

The original vegetation types of the Gulf Prairies were tallgrass prairie and post oak savanna (Gould 1962). The lower third of the region also contained occasional shrublands consisting of mesquite (*Prosopis glandulosa*), huisache (*Acacia smallii*), blackbrush (*A. rigidula*), lime prickly ash (*Zanthoxylum fagara*), and Texas persimmon (*Diospyros texana*) (Johnston 1963). However, native trees and shrubs, including mesquite, oaks (*Quercus* spp.), acacia (*Acacia* spp.), and exotic species such as Macartney rose (*Rosa bracteata*) and Chinese tallow (*Sapium sebiferum*) have greatly increased in abundance throughout the prairies. Prickly pear (*Opuntia* sp.) are common throughout the area. Characteristic oak species are live oak (*Q. virginiana*) and post oak (*Q. stellata*) (Johnston 1963; Smeins, Diamond, and Hanselka 1991).

Climax grasses include gulf cordgrass (*Spartina spartinae*), big bluestem (*Andropogon gerardii* var. *gerardii*), seacoast bluestem (*A. scoparium* var. *littoralis*), little bluestem (*Schizachyrium scoparium*), indiangrass (*Sorghastrum nutans*), eastern gamagrass (*Tripsacum dactyloides*), gulf muhly (*Muhlenbergia capillaris*), tanglehead (*Heteropogon contortus*), and several species of panicgrasses (*Panicum* spp.). Common increasers and invaders are yankeeweed (*Eupatorium compositifolium*), broomsedge bluestem (*A. virginicus*), smutgrass (*Sporobolus indicus*), western ragweed (*Ambrosia psilostachya*), tumblegrass (*Schedonnardus paniculatus*), threeawns (*Aristida* sp.), and many annual forbs and grasses (Gould 1962; Diamond and Fulbright 1990).

Historical Accounts

Late seventeenth- and early eighteenth-century explorers described the central portion of the Gulf Prairies as wide, flat, treeless plains dissected by wooded streams and rivers (Inglis 1964; Bartlett 1995). Explorer accounts during the early to mid-nineteenth century mention belts of timber (hackberry [*Celtis* spp.], post oak, blackjack oak [*Q. marilandica*]), and thinly timbered mottes of post oak in the central to upper portion of the region (figure 15.2; Inglis 1964; Lehmann 1965). These belts of timber were likely associated with the soil types previously described, river bottoms, and coastal cheniers (ancient beachfront ridges).

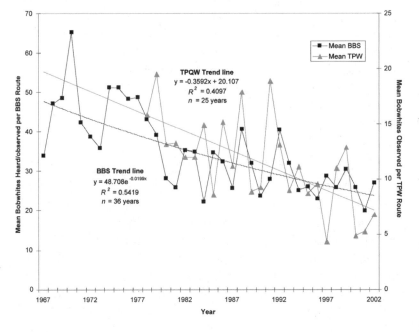

Figure. 15.2.
Stand of relict prairie in Goliad
County, Texas, December 2003.
Courtesy Wade Harrell,
The Nature Conservancy

The lower portion of the Gulf Prairies was referred to as "brush prairie," with mottes of mesquite and live oak interspersed throughout with occasional fields of dense, low, thorny chaparral (Johnston 1963; Inglis 1964; Schmidly 2002:318). It is difficult to determine vegetation shifts through qualitative information, but it is clear that woody plants have increased throughout the ecoregion (Smeins, Diamond, and Hanselka 1991).

Status of Bobwhite Populations

The North American Breeding Bird Survey (BBS) documents a long-term decline in breeding numbers at a rate of 3.2 percent per year from 1966 to 2002 and 3.7 percent per year from 1980 to 2002 (Sauer, Hines, and Fallon 2002). Texas Parks and Wildlife Department (TPWD) production surveys also indicate a decline within the region at a rate of 2.3 percent per year from 1978 to 2002 (figure 15.3). TPWD annual quail production survey methodology and sampling framework are de-

Figure. 15.3.
Mean number of northern bobwhites observed per North American Breeding Bird Survey (BBS) and Texas Parks and Wildlife Department (TPWD) quail production survey route in the Gulf Prairies and Marshes (Sauer, Hines, and Fallon 2002; TPWD, unpublished data).

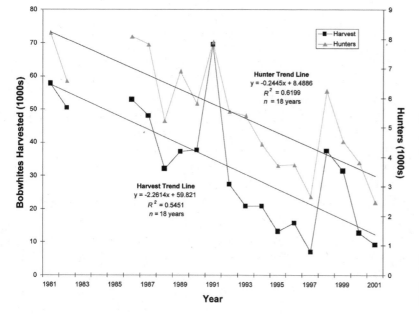

Figure 15.4.
Trends in bobwhite harvest in the Gulf
Prairies and Marshes. Data from Texas
Parks and Wildlife Department

signed to provide information at the ecoregion level and are more reflective of actual declines than the BBS at this scale (DeMaso, Peterson,
et al. 2002). Additionally, TPWD harvest surveys, although an indirect
measure of population status and trend, are highly correlated with the
annual quail production surveys and provide further evidence of decline (figure 15.4; Peterson and Perez 2000).

Prior to the initiation of the BBS in 1966, there was very little information regarding bobwhite abundance in the Gulf Prairies. However, somewhere between 1875 and 1910, bobwhite numbers most likely
reached their peak. Farms and ranches broke up vast areas that had
once been mid- to tallgrass prairie. As a result, woody cover and forbs
increased, and the density of bunchgrasses was reduced. Landowners
inadvertently managed the prairies with farming and soil disturbance
that enhanced usable habitat space for bobwhites (TGFOC 1945:47;
Guthery 2000:131).

Reasons for the Decline

After World War I, agricultural commodity prices rose to such a level
that most farmers removed riparian and fence-line brush to maximize
crop production. Such actions effectively eliminated quail habitat. Additionally, rice farms almost completely covered the best-drained portions of the Gulf Prairies. Because rice depletes soil nutrients, optimum
production requires that fields rest for two to three years. During rest
periods, fields become very weedy and provide quail foods, but there is
not sufficient time for native grasses to recover (Lehmann 1941; TGFOC
1945:48; Jurries 1979). During the 1920s, many game species, including white-tailed deer (*Odocoileus virginianus*), prairie-chickens, pronghorn (*Antilocapra americana*), wood ducks (*Aix sponsa*), wild turkeys
(*Meleagris gallopavo*), and bobwhites became noticeably less abundant
across Texas. Consequently, the Texas Game, Fish and Oyster Commission closed seasons and reduced bag limits for various species, including a reduction in the bag limit for quail and dove from 25 to 15 birds
per day (TGFOC 1945:48; Doughty 1983:178).

Despite dramatic landscape-level changes, bobwhites remained relatively abundant within the Gulf Prairies. In 1939, a quail census of various habitat types in Colorado County averaged 1 bird/10.5 hectares (26 acres) over 16,000 hectares (39,500 acres), ranging from 1 bird/2 hectares (5 acres) in huisache-grassland to 1 bird/98 hectares (243 acres) in rice country (Lehmann 1984:142). From 1937 to 1941, quail counts in Victoria, Matagorda, Jackson, Lavaca, and Calhoun counties recorded densities of 1 bird/0.36 hectare (0.88 acre) to 1 bird/2 hectares (5 acres) in good habitat (Lehmann 1984:141). Densities of 1 bird/1.6–2 hectares (4–5 acres) were common along the Gulf Prairie–Post Oak Savannah ecotone in the early 1940s (TGFOC 1945:49).

After World War II, industrialization, especially petrochemicals, began in earnest along the coast from Orange to Houston. Food demands led to heavier grazing pressure and the cultivation of marginal areas (TGFOC 1945:48; Schmidly 2002:390–91). Mowing became an increasingly popular method to maintain pastureland for cattle, producing pure stands of shorter grasses; however, mowing pastures reduces quail foods and severely compromises the quality of ground cover (Lehmann 1941; TGFOC 1945:54). By 1950, bobwhites were declining in 25 of 39 states surveyed, including Texas. Declines were attributed to widespread changes in land use, including clean farming and increased livestock (Goodrum 1949). In the transitional zone between the Gulf Prairies and the Post Oak Savannah, coastal bermudagrass and other so-called improved grasses became widespread and popular for haying and livestock operations in the early 1960s. Along with these changes, the rice industry continued to grow (Royce Jurries, TPWD, pers. comm.). An assessment of land use in 1979 determined that 71 percent of the Gulf Prairies had been converted to rice, other crops, and improved pastures or was lost to invasive woody species. Rice cultivation alone accounted for 568,000 hectares (1.4 million acres) in 17 Gulf Prairie counties (Jurries 1979). By 1974, Macartney rose was considered a severe range management problem on more than 198,000 hectares (490,000 acres) of the central and upper Gulf Prairies, and running live oak began to degrade rangelands in the lower Gulf Prairies (Bovey et al. 1969; Scifres 1975). Woody encroachment has led to many areas becoming so thick that grasses are shaded out, rendering them largely unsuitable for bobwhites. During the 1970s, hunter opportunity was still good to excellent in many areas of the region, including Goliad, Refugio, and Victoria counties. It was common to find 20–30 coveys a day with good dogs, and 12–15 coveys a day closer to the coast in Brazoria, Jackson, and Matagorda counties (Royce Jurries and David Reid, TPWD, pers. comm.). Huntable populations currently persist on tracts of rangeland greater than 400 hectares (1,000 acres) where proper range management practices are being implemented. In summary, post–World War II human-induced habitat changes have gradually altered the Gulf Prairies to a degree that very little usable space for bobwhites remains.

Human Impacts and Trends

Of all the physiographic areas in Texas, the Gulf Prairies and Marshes is second only to the Blackland Prairies in human population. Based on the 2000 census, the Gulf Prairies region is home to approximately 9.9 million people (25 percent of the state total), and the Blackland Prairies region includes 11.9 million people (30 percent of the total).

Together they account for more than half of the population of Texas but represent only 17 percent of the land base (Wilkins et al. 2003). Increased urban and suburban development is likely as the human population continues to grow.

Land Use

In 2001, agricultural lands made up 59.8 percent of the total land use in the Gulf Prairies. Native rangelands accounted for about half of the agricultural lands (33 percent), whereas improved pasture (6.8 percent), dryland crop (13 percent), and irrigated cropland (7 percent) made up the remainder (Wilkins et al. 2003). From 1992 to 2001, there was an overall loss of cropland, including a 12 percent loss of irrigated cropland, that is related to changes in federal farm subsidy requirements. Over the same time period native rangelands increased by 5.6 percent and improved pasture by 15 percent. Considering that modern farming practices are not quail-friendly and improved pastures are viewed as ecological deserts for most wildlife, including quail, only a third of the Gulf Prairies currently offers potential good bobwhite habitat in the form of native rangeland. Not all rangelands are created equal, and habitat space varies greatly by property and year. As a result, bobwhites remain locally abundant on large islands of suitable habitat. The recent increase of native rangelands is beneficial to quail only if such lands are managed for both cattle and quail through proper grazing management.

Land Fragmentation

Land fragmentation can be defined as the division of rural lands into smaller parcels that remain in rural use (Wilkins et al. 2000). Fragmentation within the Gulf Prairies and throughout Texas poses a serious threat to wildlife habitat, especially quail habitat. In general, as landholdings become smaller than 200 hectares (500 acres), total acreage of improved pasture and forest land increases and native rangeland is lost (Wilkins et al. 2003). Fragmentation rates are increasing over much of the central and upper Gulf Prairies. From 1987 to 1997, the number of rural landowners in Brazoria, Chambers, Liberty, and Walker counties increased by 10–25 percent; and in Orange, Jefferson, Galveston, Matagorda, Wharton, and Fort Bend counties, by 3–10 percent (Wilkins et al. 2000).

Bobwhites and other upland game birds are more vulnerable to harvest, predation, and ultimately, local extinction in fragmented landscapes (Roseberry and Klimstra 1984:147–48; Burger, Burger, and Faaborg 1994; Jimenez and Conover 2001; Rollins 1999a). Guthery et al. (2000) modeled the viability of bobwhite populations subject to weather catastrophes and harvest. For southern climes subject to summer catastrophe (e.g., drought or hurricane) and a predicted 30 percent harvest, the probability of a bobwhite population remaining viable for 100 years required a fall population of 700 birds. In other words, fragments of habitat must be large enough to support 700 bobwhites. Based on reported quail densities for good habitat in the Gulf Prairies, a minimum of 1,400–2,800 hectares (3,500–7,000 acres) would be necessary to maintain a viable bobwhite population. If model probabilities are representative of actual processes, very few lands in the Gulf Prairies meet the criteria necessary for sustaining populations of wild bobwhites. Thus, bobwhites are probably in danger of being extirpated from this ecoregion of Texas.

What We Know About Bobwhites on the Gulf Prairies

This section provides an overview of what we know about bobwhite habitat use, movements, mortality, and other factors that influence their ecology and management in the Gulf Prairies ecological region.

Habitat Use

Reid, Grue, and Silvy (1978) correlated whistle-count data with habitat types and found that bobwhite calling activity was correlated with edge in the Gulf Prairies. Specifically, whistle counts were greatest along borders between dissimilar crops, intersecting fences, dirt roads, buildings, parallel windbreaks, and power lines. These edge associations offered nesting, travel, and escape cover and access to food. These findings are similar to those regarding breeding habitat used by bobwhites in other agricultural landscapes, such as in Illinois and Iowa (Hanson and Miller 1961; Crim and Seitz 1972).

Spears et al. (1993) measured bobwhite density in relation to vegetative seral stage (low, mid, and high) and site productivity (potential annual herbaceous biomass production) in the western South Texas Plains (low), central South Texas Plains (medium), and Gulf Prairies (high). Of the three sites, low seral stage (i.e., early-successional habitat) supported the greatest densities of bobwhites in the most productive site, whereas high seral stage favored bobwhite density in the medium productive site (see chapter 16). In areas of moderate to abundant precipitation, bobwhites thrive on the early-successional vegetation stages associated with disturbance (Ellis, Edwards, and Thomas 1969; Rosene 1969:122; Roseberry and Klimstra 1984:32; Guthery 2000:192). This seems to be the case for bobwhites in the Gulf Prairies, where remnants of habitat exist. However, in semiarid environments such as the South Texas Plains, later stages of vegetation succession appear to provide appropriate habitat structure for bobwhites (Guthery 2002:150–51).

Movements

There is very little information regarding the seasonal movements and home-range size of bobwhites on the Gulf Prairies, with the exception of a banding study completed in Colorado County. From 1938 to 1940, 249 bobwhites were banded, of which 4 were recovered in the same winter territories the following year. Sixteen moved 0.48–17 kilometers (0.3–10.5 miles) away from the capture site, with an average distance of 1.9 kilometers (1.2 miles) (Lehmann 1984:117). These results are consistent with seasonal movements and annual home-range estimates reported in contiguous habitat, which ranges 4–32 hectares (10–80 acres) (Lehmann 1946b; Murphy and Baskett 1952; Rosene 1969:89). However, home-range sizes may be larger in the Gulf Prairies today, given that the distance to adequate food and cover becomes greater in fragmented landscapes (Puckett et al. 2000; Oakley et al. 2002).

Mortality

A comparison of winter mortality on hunted versus unhunted areas from 1938 to 1941 in Colorado County recorded an average total winter loss of 51 percent on hunted areas and 31 percent on protected areas. Preharvest, unhunted bobwhite populations were higher (1 bird/3.2 hectares, or 8 acres) than in hunted areas (1 bird/7.7 hectares, or 19 acres); date of harvest was not recorded (Lehmann 1984:218). These results suggest that hunting mortality was additive in this case and lend credence to other studies that indicate late-season harvest or harvest in years of low production may be additive to annual mortality (Pollock, Moore, et al. 1989; Johnson and Braun 1999; Guthery et al. 2000; see chapter 24).

Fire Ants

By 1957, the red imported fire ant (*Solenopsis invicta;* hereafter RIFA) had taken hold in the upper Gulf Prairies (Vinson and Sorenson 1986). Before this exotic ant ever reached Texas from its point of introduction in Alabama, managers and biologists were concerned with the potential negative impacts of fire ants on bobwhites (Stoddard 1931:193–94; Travis 1938). The majority of the Gulf Prairies is currently infested with single and multiple queen forms of RIFA. In Texas, more than 50 percent of all fire ant colonies are multiple queen that can reach densities up to greater than 1,900 mounds/hectare (about 800 mounds/acre) (Porter et al. 1991). Researchers have differing interpretations of the realized impacts of RIFA based on the evidence to date (Brennan 1991a, 1993; Allen, Lutz, and Demarais 1993, 1995; Allen et al. 2000). These differences of opinion may be related to the greater impact of high-density, multiple-queen colonies.

Allen, Lutz, and Demarais (1995) used two methods to evaluate the impacts of RIFA on bobwhites. First, bobwhite-abundance trends (Christmas Bird Count data for 1966–92) for 15 Texas counties, including 3 counties in the Gulf Prairies, were compared before and after fire ant infestation. Using correlation analysis, no significant trend in abundance existed prior to infestation, whereas postinfestation abundance declined and was negatively correlated with years of infestation. As a control, 16 uninfested Texas counties were examined for the same time period and showed no trend. These results suggest that bobwhite populations are stable in uninfested areas and decreasing in areas of RIFA infestation. However, there are inherent biases in Christmas Bird Count data, including a lack of precision, variability in volunteer observer experience and sample size, and appropriateness at fine scales. Furthermore, another limitation of this study was that the authors did not factor out land-use changes and expanding urbanization as potentially confounding variables.

The second method involved reducing RIFA densities on five of ten 202-hectare (500-acre) study sites in the Gulf Prairies. Bobwhite abundance was monitored via line transects and whistle counts for two years. Bobwhite autumn density was higher on treatment areas than on control sites in the second year and may have been the result of more effective fire ant control. However, some of the control sites in this study had excellent initial bobwhite densities, which potentially confounded their results.

Allen, Lutz, and Demarais (1995) and Allen et al. (2000) suggested that RIFA may be another factor depressing bobwhite populations in the region, although not directly. Indirect effects examined to date include reduction of available insects, reduced weight gain and survival of chicks, and altered foraging and activity patterns (Porter and Savignano 1990; Giuliano et al. 1996; Pederson et al. 1996; Mueller et. al 1999).

Allen, Lutz, and Demarais (1995) noted that a precipitation-habitat model (Rice et al. 1993) performed poorly in predicting bobwhite abundance in the Gulf Prairies, implying that other factors such as RIFA may be influencing populations. Although weather can account for up to 90 percent of the annual variation in quail populations in semiarid climes (Bridges et al. 2001), Brennan et al. (1997) and Reid and Goodrum (1960) found that weather variables could account for only about 25 percent of the variation in production and abundance in southeastern humid climes. This suggests that weather is not a good predictor of abundance across the humid portions of the bobwhite range, including the Gulf Prairies (see chapter 4). An intensive nesting study using infrared video cameras showed that direct losses of bobwhite nests to RIFA may be as high as 10 percent (Staller 2001). Mueller et al. (1999) compared hatching success and chick survival for bobwhites between nesting areas treated for RIFA suppression and untreated areas in the Gulf Prairies. Fire ants were reduced by 70 percent in 1997 and by 99 percent in 1998. There was no difference in hatching success between treatment and control sites. However, the proportion of chicks surviving to 21 days was greater on treated sites. Treated nest sites had 60 percent survival of 21-day-old chicks, and untreated areas, 22 percent. These results, along with field observations of stung chicks, suggest that the indirect effects of fire ant stings, shortly after chicks hatch, can lead to death and may degrade the suitability of habitat for bobwhites in the Gulf Prairies (Pederson, Grant, and Longnecker 1996; Giuliano et al. 1996; Mueller et al. 1999).

Prescribed burning, fallow disking, and mowing are common disturbance-based habitat management practices used to set back vegetative succession to create food and desirable cover types for bobwhites (Lehmann 1984; Guthery 1986). There is some evidence that the spread of RIFA may be facilitated by disturbance along power line rights-of-way and highways (Tschinkel 1988; Stiles and Jones 1998). Forbes et al. (2002) evaluated the effects of prescribed burning and disking in the Gulf Prairies and found no differences in RIFA mound density between treatments and controls in Refugio County. However, fire ant colonies were predominantly single-queen and occurred at densities near recorded maximums at the beginning of the study. Williamson et al. (2002) conducted a similar study in central Mississippi and found that prescribed burning, disking, and mowing increased RIFA mound density (presumably, multiple-queen colonies) compared to that in control areas.

The possibility that RIFA have negative impacts on bobwhite quail populations certainly exists and may be more relative to ant density than to actual presence or absence of the ants. Current research suggests that RIFA can indirectly decrease bobwhite chick survival, and this may be a limiting factor in heavily infested areas. Because fire ant management is expensive and impractical at large scales, resource managers' time and efforts may be better spent improving nesting cover and the amount of usable space available for bobwhites (Mueller et al. 1999; Brennan 1993).

Supplemental Feeding

Quail managers have long used supplemental feed in attempts to bolster native bobwhite populations (Hawkins 1937). Several well-designed research projects have examined the effects of supplemental feeding on bobwhites since 1954 (Guthery 1997). For a more complete discussion on supplemental feeding, see chapter 16.

In the Gulf Prairies, Kane (1988) examined the effects of supplemental feeding on bobwhite density in Victoria County. Twelve feeders were distributed on a 162-hectare (400-acre) treatment site (1 feeder/ 14 hectares, or 34 acres) and filled with grain sorghum (milo) every 2–3 weeks. No differences could be detected in bobwhite abundance between treatment and control sites. Doerr and Silvy (2002) completed a similar study with three paired sites in the South Texas Plains and one paired site in the Gulf Prairies (San Patricio County). They found no differences in bobwhite densities between areas with supplemental feed and those without in the Gulf Prairies, where natural food production was not considered limiting and habitat structure was determined to be inappropriate (Doerr and Silvy 1987).

Weather

The Gulf Prairies region is subject to occasional tropical storms or hurricanes. These destructive storms can decimate local bird populations (Welty and Baptista 1988:393). For example, Hurricane Beulah hit the Texas coast in September 1967 and flooded thousands of acres in Refugio County. During a helicopter survey after the hurricane, quail were observed bunched up on dry ridges and perched in trees and on buildings scattered across flat, flooded prairie. Observers estimated quail losses as high as 95 percent (Lehmann 1984:111). Hurricane Bret hit the South Texas coast in 1999 during an ongoing bobwhite telemetry study in Brooks County. Researchers documented a 14 percent loss of adults and a 47 percent loss of broods. Remaining broods were reduced from an average size of 11 chicks before the storm to an average size of 4 after the hurricane (Hernández, Vasquez, et al. 2002). The resilience of birds to recover after such events depends on species breeding potential (Welty and Baptista 1988:393). Bobwhites have the ability to quickly recover via a high reproductive potential and the immigration of new birds into the population (Roseberry and Klimstra 1984). However, isolated bobwhite populations within the Gulf Prairies are at risk of extirpation from such weather events if there are no sources of ingress. Further discussion of the effects of weather on bobwhites can be found in chapter 4.

Knowledge Gaps and Research Needs

The lack of knowledge in regard to bobwhites in the Gulf Prairies is similar to that in other Texas ecoregions, including the Post Oak Savannah and Blackland Prairies. See chapter 10 for the discussion relating to the Blackland Prairies. In addition to the enumerated fundamental knowledge gaps in chapter 10, there is a need to develop better native prairie restoration techniques in the Gulf Prairies, especially in previously cropped lands where the seed bank in the soil is greatly depleted. Currently available ecotypes of native seeds are often obtained from sources thousands of miles from Texas. These seeds often have reduced vigor, forage production, seed set, and longevity when planted in Texas (Riskind and Davis 1975). The conservation of remaining fragments of native prairie is critical for many reasons, one of which is their value as a seed source for locally adapted ecotypes in restoration efforts. The South Texas Natives project of the Caesar Kleberg Wildlife Research Institute has developed a successful methodology for the collection and cultivation of native seeds in 33 South Texas counties (http://www .southtexasnatives.org). This project could serve as a model for the development of similar programs in other ecoregions.

Management

Habitat management techniques have been evaluated for many years across much of the bobwhite's range (Stoddard 1931; Rosene 1969; Lehmann 1984; Guthery 1986). Many of the habitat recommendations, such as prescribed burning, fallow disking, brush management, proper grazing, half-cutting, and cover plantings, have become standard. Other recommendations may have limited benefit to quail but continue to be made (e.g., predator control, food plots, supplemental feeding). Historical recommendations made by the TGFOC (1945:46–60) for bobwhite management in the Gulf Prairies are still valid today. Such practices include (1) allowing heavier grazing in the spring and lighter in the winter to benefit quail and livestock—if rainfall is adequate, (2) discontinuing mowing practices that destroy nests and reduce quail food and quality of ground cover, (3) leaving well-drained ridges and hills unmowed and unburned for nesting cover, and (4) planting trees and shrubs for cover and improved drainage. Lehmann (1939) recommended using tepee and brush shelters, fencing areas near brush (riparian zones), and planting fenced food plots in the region. Today, concepts regarding usable space support the idea that only practices that increase the amount of space that can be used by bobwhites will increase abundance (see chapter 24). With the exception of fenced food plots, these historical recommendations all potentially result in more usable space.

Prescribed Fire

Fire suppression is likely the primary reason for the dramatic landscape-level vegetation changes on the Gulf Prairies (Smeins, Diamond, and Hanselka 1991:276). Frost (1998) estimated that as much as 90 percent of the prairie was burned every 4–6 years and was likely more frequent (1–3 years) when influenced by early Native Americans. Fire frequency in the prairies kept native woody species restricted to riparian zones and other areas inaccessible to fire. Range managers in the Gulf Prairies can use prescribed fire as a tool to suppress woody species and encourage grasses and forbs. However, proper grazing management is also required for the success of any prescribed burning program (White and Hanselka 1989). If cattle consume the grasses that provide the fine fuels required to carry a fire, it will be impossible to implement a prescribed burn.

Grazing Management

The most important factor influencing remaining bobwhite populations in the Gulf Prairies today is grazing management. Heavy grazing pressure results in a loss of grass species needed for screening, roosting,

and nesting cover. In many instances, the first grazing recommendation made by natural resource professionals is deferment. Range recovery can take anywhere from two to seven years depending on degree
of abuse (Homerstad and Brown 2001). Once the range has recovered,
grazing becomes another tool along with prescribed fire and mowing
that can be used to create a density, structure, and composition of vegetation favorable to bobwhites.

Generally speaking, during periods of average to above-average
rainfall, employment of moderate grazing regimes will favor the key
habitat components and structure needed for grassland bird production, including bobwhite quail. Integrated grazing and brush management plans developed in consultation with a qualified range specialist
that take into account soil types, range-site capability, brush species and
stature, and long-term rainfall regime in the immediate vicinity will
prove to be the most important land management tools for quail and
other prairie wildlife in the region (Gene Miller, TPWD, pers. comm.).

Vegetation Management

Improved pastures do not meet the habitat requirements for many species of grassland birds; where possible, the conversion of these areas
to native prairie will benefit wildlife. However, conversion can be difficult and expensive and will likely not occur on a large scale without
incentive-based programs such as Pastures for Upland Birds (TPWD)
and the Environmental Quality Incentives Program (Natural Resource
Conservation Service) (see chapter 10).

Vegetation management objectives on native rangelands should include the development of pastures containing residual bunchgrasses at
least 20 centimeters (8 inches) tall and 30 centimeters (12 inches) in diameter at a density greater than 620 clumps/hectare (about 250 clumps/
acre), or 1 clump every 15–20 steps. There should be evenly distributed
brush canopy coverage (15–30 percent) that is closed above and that is
open below, up to 30 centimeters (12 inches) (Oklahoma Department of
Wildlife Conservation 1992; Homerstad and Brown 2001). If met, these
objectives will provide optimum nesting, roosting, escape, and screening cover.

Brush or woody vegetation management objectives should target
either reducing or increasing the woody component to create evenly
distributed mottes of thick cover approximately 15 meters (50 feet) in
diameter. Keep in mind that it is easier to remove brush than to add it.
Huisache, mesquite, and running live oak are native species that can
dominate rangelands. Grubbing, bulldozing, and chaining can control mature huisache and mesquite. Several herbicides, including Rem-
edy® and diesel, are also effective. Running live oak can be controlled
by roller-chopping (aeration) followed by summer burns or with aerially sprayed herbicides containing picloram followed by deferment and
then fire. Invasive, nonnative species such as Chinese tallow and Macartney rose can be reduced via prescribed burning and herbicides.
Grazon P+D applied at 9.3 liters/hectare (1 gallon/acre) seems to work
well on Chinese tallow when applied in late August or early September.
Seedlings quickly emerge after treatment and may be controlled by fire
(Hanselka 2002). Both undisturbed and disturbed stands of Macartney
rose can be controlled by spot-spraying with a variety of herbicides and
maintained with fire (Homerstad and Brown 2001).

The Future

Current human population and fragmentation trends are likely to continue. In the process, increasing acreages of native range will be lost, further degrading quail habitat in the Gulf Prairies. As local bobwhite populations lose the benefit of ingress, they may be subject to decreased genetic fitness by a potential loss in heterozygosity and may become vulnerable to catastrophic events that may lead to extirpation (Vucetich and Waite 1999; Guthery et al. 2000). However, it is possible to halt declines and even increase bobwhite populations in the Gulf Prairies.

In the central and lower portions of the Gulf Prairies, fragmentation rates have not been as dramatic. Consequently, large landholdings greater than 400 hectares (1,000 acres) still support viable populations of bobwhites (Wilkins et al. 2003). Conservation opportunities exist for interested landowners in the form of wildlife cooperatives (see chapter 22). Landowner interest usually stems from recreational use and/or the economic value of leasing out to quail hunters. It is critical that state and federal natural resource agencies provide well-known habitat management information for bobwhites in the form of technical assistance. Agency personnel must be of one voice. Additionally, multiagency partnerships must be developed to assist landowners financially through existing and new incentive-based programs.

All forms of assistance should stress the importance of proper grazing management, which can be defined as "the degree and time of use of current year's growth which, if continued, will either maintain or improve the range condition consistent with conservation of other natural resources" (Anderson 1969:362). To maximize the benefit to bobwhites, grazing duration and intensity should target a stubble height and density of bunchgrasses favorable to quail. If grazing is not an option, other management techniques can achieve the same structure (e.g., late-summer mowing, prescribed fire, aerating, and fallow disking). In a broader sense, clearly defined focus areas that build off existing bobwhite populations are necessary to meet regional restoration goals defined in national (Northern Bobwhite Conservation Initiative) and state (Texas Quail Conservation Initiative) conservation plans.

The upper portion of the Gulf Prairies and metropolitan areas throughout the region require a different conservation strategy. Nothing short of a paradigm shift in societal values is needed to conserve prairie habitats for bobwhites and other grassland birds in these areas. In general, Western culture places a high aesthetic value on manicured landscapes, whereas forbs produced by necessary disturbance in grassland ecosystems are perceived as unattractive. In too many cases, people who purchase land for recreational purposes lack either the desire to protect native habitat or the information necessary to conserve and manage their property for wildlife. In any case, natural resource managers and professionals must rise to the challenge of reaching these "new" Texas landowners to counteract the tendency of smaller acreages to be converted to coastal bermudagrass or other habitat-deficient cover types. If bobwhite conservation is to become a reality in the Gulf Prairies, an adaptive strategy is necessary to inform and educate this fast-growing segment of landowners to the benefits of native habitats and their ecological importance.

Bobwhites on the South Texas Plains 16

Fidel Hernández, Robert M. Perez, and Fred S. Guthery

> In an inherently unstable environment, it is
> inevitable that quail populations are unstable.
> Lehmann (1984)

Quail management, despite an extensive foundation of knowledge, generally is perceived more as an art than a science. Northern bobwhites (*Colinus virginianus*) have been studied since the beginning of the twentieth century (Scott 1985). Their life history, ecology, and habitat requirements are well known (Stoddard 1931; Rosene 1969; Lehmann 1984; Roseberry and Klimstra 1984), and years of research have been devoted to their management (Hernández, Guthery, and Kuvlesky 2002). Yet managers often associate quail management with uncertainty and guesswork. The truth is that we have the knowledge to manage bobwhites properly.

In addressing quail management, we begin with an overview of bobwhite population trends in South Texas to provide a biological and social context under which management currently is operating. We then discuss two unifying concepts, usable space (Guthery 1997) and slack (Guthery 1999a), that serve as a theoretical basis for habitat management. Relative to management practices, we have categorized management into two categories: habitat management and cultural practices. We do not focus on the specifics of management but emphasize limitations regarding certain practices. We give added emphasis to incorrect information (based on current knowledge) contained within the book *Beef, Brush, and Bobwhites* (Guthery 1986). We are not doing so to criticize the book (many of the recommendations remain useful); however, because of its popularity with landowners, we have an opportunity to make corrections and to highlight advances in knowledge since its publication. We conclude with a brief philosophical perspective on bobwhite management.

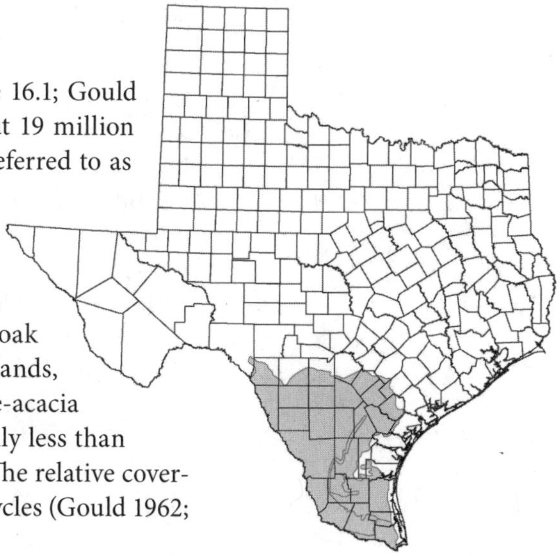

Ecoregion Description

The South Texas Plains physiographic region (figure 16.1; Gould 1962) covers approximately 9 million hectares (about 19 million acres) in southern Texas. This region is commonly referred to as the brush country and is part of the Tamaulipan Biotic Province that extends into northern Mexico. Chaparral, or thorn-brush vegetation, and fairly recent agricultural fields dominate this semiarid region. The region also includes fairly extensive grasslands, oak forests, and some tall riparian forests. In the brushlands, much of the area was originally covered by mesquite-acacia savanna, and areas of semi-open thorn scrub generally less than 3 meters tall (10 feet), alternating with grassy areas. The relative coverage of grassy areas may have varied during wet-dry cycles (Gould 1962; Inglis 1964).

Figure 16.1.
South Texas Plains ecoregion of Texas.
Courtesy Caesar Kleberg Wildlife
Research Institute (CKWRI) GIS
Laboratory

Average annual rainfall decreases from 76 centimeters (30 inches) at the Gulf Coast around Corpus Christi to 50 centimeters (20 inches) at the western edge of the region in Laredo. Soil types are very diverse and include fine sands, sandy loams, clays, caliche, and other rocky soils with areas of alkaline, saline, and gypseous soils (Johnston 1963; McLendon 1991). Today, much of the acreage in the South Texas Plains is used for livestock, commercial hunting, and recreational wildlife operations. Although bobwhite abundance can be highly variable in this region, quail hunting is of major economic importance to local communities (Guthery 1986; Doerr and Silvy 1987).

Historical Accounts

Prior to European settlement, bobwhites were probably locally abundant along riparian corridors and areas of chaparral and less abundant in the pure grassland portions of the South Texas Plains (Texas Game, Fish and Oyster Commission [TGFOC] 1945:46–47). From 1675 to 1722, early Spanish explorers described much of the area as "flat country" devoid of trees. They saw large numbers of quails, turkeys, and rabbits associated with chaparral and live oaks in present-day Atascosa, Zavala, and Webb counties (Inglis 1964:90–91). Based on explorer accounts, much of the flat country was presumably grassland and grassland savanna. Beginning in the mid- to late 1800s, the suppression of fire along with intense livestock grazing led to the encroachment of brush (Inglis 1964:3; Lehmann 1969; Archer and Smeins 1991). Although brush was certainly present when Bailey (1905) was conducting biological surveys in the region during the 1880s, it had just begun to spread from fire-protected areas along hillsides, riparian corridors, and other areas of topographical relief into the uplands (Inglis 1964; Schmidly 2002). Post-European settlement, ranching, and farming activities greatly increased the amount of quail habitat. At some point between 1875 and 1910, bobwhites likely reached maximum abundance (TGFOC 1945:46–47), although remarkable densities have been observed in modern times (e.g., 1987, 1992). By the 1930s, most of the South Texas Plains was in livestock production, and dramatic changes in the density and distribution of mesquite were apparent. Mesquite progressed from open groves of large trees in low areas and along streams to vast acreages of mesquite-dominated brush (Schmidly 2002:385). By 1963, grassland areas had contracted considerably in South Texas (Johnston 1963). Although bobwhites have been shown to prefer mid- to late-seral stages of vegetation succession in the South Texas Plains, continued brush encroachment resulting in canopy coverage greater than 50 percent greatly diminishes the amount of usable space for quail (Spears et al. 1993). Other factors influencing Texas landscapes include land conversion, invasive and/or exotic plants, and more recently, land fragmentation (Schmidly 2002). Although many habitat changes have transpired, vegetation succession is reversible. The knowledge and management tools necessary to enhance South Texas habitats for bobwhites are well known.

Population Trends

The North American Breeding Bird Survey (BBS) documents a long-term decline in South Texas bobwhite breeding numbers at a rate of

2.1 percent per year from 1966 to 2002 (Sauer, Hines, and Fallon 2002). However, there are inherent biases in BBS data, including a lack of precision at fine scales and variability in observer experience and sample size. The Texas Parks and Wildlife Department (TPWD) annual quail production surveys (1978–2002) indicate no trend, although populations fluctuate from year to year (figure 16.2). TPWD annual quail production survey methodology and sampling framework are designed to provide information at the ecoregion level and are more reflective of actual trends than BBS at this scale (DeMaso, Townsend, et al. 2002). Additionally, TPWD harvest surveys, although an indirect measure, are highly correlated with the annual quail production surveys and provide further evidence of stability (figure 16.3; Peterson and Perez 2000).

For any given population, annual fluctuation is more pronounced at the edges of its range than in the interior (Brown and Gibson 1983:49–81). These fluctuations are even more apparent with more r-selected species (animals whose populations are typically characterized by having a high potential rate [r] of population increase), such as bobwhites. Even within the center of the bobwhite's range, we see annual fluctuation. However, it is the amplitude of this fluctuation that is much more pronounced along the western edge of the distribution, where rainfall patterns can be erratic (Rosene 1969; Roseberry and Klimstra 1984; Guthery 2000:121; Peterson and Perez 2000).

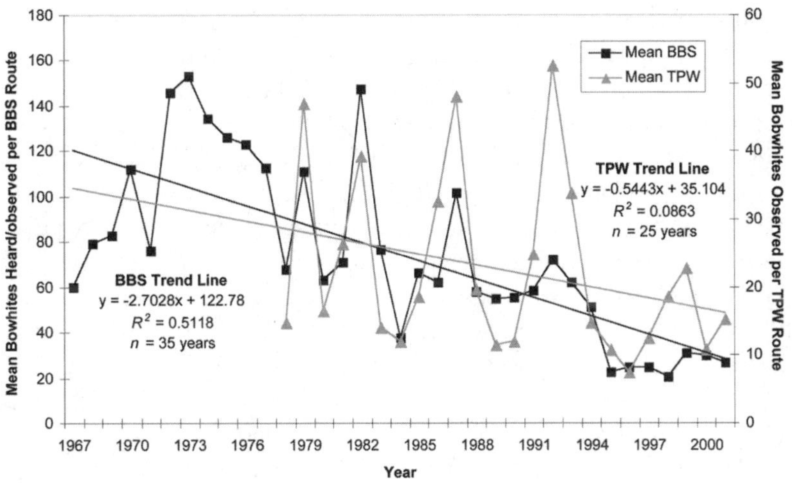

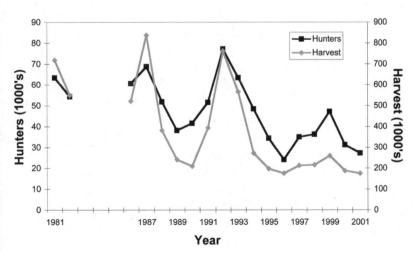

Figure 16.2.
Mean number of northern bobwhites observed per North American Breeding Bird Survey (BBS) and Texas Parks and Wildlife Department (TPWD) quail production survey route in the South Texas Plains
(Sauer, Hines, and Fallon 2002; TPWD, unpublished data).

Figure 16.3.
Estimated numbers of northern bobwhites harvested and number of individuals hunting bobwhites in the South Texas Plains
(TPWD, unpublished data).

Weather dictates the growth of plants and the foods they produce and thereby has a major effect on bird populations (Welty and Baptista 1988). The growth stage of shrubs and grasses and the amount of food available throughout any given year affect the population dynamics of ground-nesting birds such as bobwhites (McMillan 1964; Roseberry and Klimstra 1984:128; Giuliano et al. 1996). However, we still lack evidence that lack of food limits populations. Lehmann (1946a) and Kiel (1976) noted an increase in bobwhite abundance during wet years in the South Texas Plains.

Abundance, breeding success, and harvest have been correlated with weather variables for bobwhites, and these relationships are more apparent in semiarid environments than in mesic climes (Rice et al. 1993; Bridges et al. 2001; Guthery, Land, and Hall 2001; Perez, Gallagher, and Frisbie 2002).

Lusk, Guthery, and DeMaso (2002) developed a neural model to examine the influence of weather and land use on bobwhite population dynamics. Statewide simulations indicated that bobwhites decreased with increasing June temperature and livestock density. Bobwhites increased with July and August temperature (potentially due to survey bias), fall rainfall, and cultivation up to 20 percent of county area. The neural model accounted for 65 percent ($n = 72$) of the variation in training data and 61 percent ($n = 17$) of the variation in cross-validation data. These findings begin to shed light on factors affecting quail populations rangewide.

Trends in the abundance of bobwhites in the South Texas Plains seem to show cyclic behavior. Cyclicity in North American grouse (Tetraonidae) has long been recognized; northern bobwhites were early on considered noncyclic, and the dynamic behavior of southwestern quails has not been studied (Leopold 1933:58). Cycles occur when there is a consistent period (elapsed time) between population peaks or population lows. If the period between highs and lows is not consistent, animal populations are said to fluctuate rather than cycle.

We used harmonic analysis to assess cyclic behavior in South Texas bobwhites based on roadside counts conducted by the TPWD. Harmonic analysis involves describing population behavior through time as a sum of cosine terms. Generally, one first detrends a time series to analyze the data for cycles, because a trend over the period of interest would appear as a cycle in harmonic analysis.

The analysis suggested that bobwhite dynamics in South Texas could be described as a sum of 6.3- and 5.0-year cycles, resulting in a cycle with a period of about 6 years (figure 16.4). Cyclic behavior explained about 52 percent of the annual variation in abundance. Thogmartin, Roseberry, and Woolf (2002) examined 73 long-term time series for evidence of cyclicity in bobwhite abundance. Cyclic populations were found in the northern and western portion of the bobwhite's range, where weather events (e.g., drought, extreme cold temperatures) had a regular negative influence on populations. Whether cycles truly exist for bobwhite populations in South Texas will have to be determined with more data.

Figure 16.4.
Apparent cyclicity (6-year) in the dynamics of South Texas bobwhites based on harmonic analysis of counts conducted by the Texas Parks and Wildlife Department. The period of record was 1978 (year = 1) through 2002.

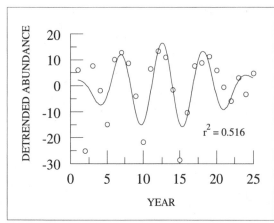

Theoretical Basis for Habitat Management

The formalization of two management concepts provides a theoretical basis for bobwhite management: the concepts of usable space (Guthery 1997) and slack in bobwhite habitat (Guthery 1999a). The notion of providing usable habitat for wildlife is an old management paradigm. Early researchers alluded to the concept (Stoddard 1931:374; Leopold 1933:52). For example, Lehmann (1984:189) believed that virtually every square foot of habitat should provide continuous use for bobwhites. However, in contrast to earlier researchers, Guthery (1997) formalized the concept and viewed it as the fundamental principle in the theory of habitat management for bobwhites.

Usable space can be viewed as habitat that is compatible with the physical, behavioral, and physiological adaptations of bobwhites (Guthery 1997:294). The management implication is that bobwhite populations are maximized when bobwhites are able to use any part of an area during any time of the year. Usable space provides a meaningful measure for evaluation of any habitat or management treatment (figure 16.5). Further, it serves as the basis for patterns applied in habitat management.

Guthery (1999a) introduced the concept of slack in habitat. "Slack" is a term used to describe the concept that different arrangements of habitat patches (herbaceous cover, woody cover) may result in equally valuable habitat for bobwhites. Slack partly arises because the adaptations of bobwhites allow them to use habitat over a broad range of values for specific features. For examples, bobwhites select for habitat containing 20–60 percent woody cover (Kopp et al. 1998). An ideal landscape for bobwhites therefore may exhibit high relative variability resulting in woody cover.

The concept of slack in bobwhite habitat has important management implications (Guthery 1999a). First, ideal bobwhite habitat is not a singular instance but rather a composite of different habitat arrangements, each of which maximizes bobwhite abundance (Guthery and Rollins 1997:71). Second, in theory, situations could arise in which habitat management (managing brush, creating edge, enhancing diversity) could have a null effect on bobwhite populations. This sce-

Figure 16.5.
Example of an area with a high degree of usable space for northern bobwhites in Brooks County, Texas.
Photo by Robert Perez

nario can arise when management results in a habitat configuration of equal value to the habitat existing prior to management. Therefore, the goal of management should be to identify and recognize the conditions when management may be applied with reasonable expectations of a positive response (Guthery 1999a). It is within this context that we discuss habitat management for bobwhites; for further discussion, see chapter 24.

Habitat Management Practices

Habitat management for bobwhites in the South Texas Plains involves manipulation of brush by a variety of means (mechanical, chemical, and fire). It also involves manipulation of herbaceous cover by grazing and/or disking. The goal of this section is to provide an overview of how these techniques are used to manage quail habitat on the South Texas Plains.

Brush Management

South Texas rangeland has been converted from open grasslands and savannas to shrublands during the past 100–200 years (Scifres 1980:3–22). As a result, much of the ecoregion has been managed for brush via mechanical, chemical, and fire treatments. When considering brush management for bobwhites, it is important to realize that rangeland can have either too little, the appropriate amount, or too much brush. Put differently, brush cover on rangeland can either provide usable space (appropriate amount of brush) or unusable space (too little or too much brush). The goal of managers then is to recognize the bounds of brush cover for bobwhites and implement appropriate brush management practices to provide the appropriate cover.

In selecting a brush management practice for bobwhites, it is important to recognize that there is no single best practice for managing bobwhite habitat. Different management practices can achieve similar results. Identifying the appropriate brush management practice for a given situation requires quantifying the amount of brush cover present on the rangeland relative to bobwhite requirements. For example, in areas with high brush canopy cover (e.g., dense stands of regrowth brush), practices such as root-plowing or reclamation fires can be used to create usable space for bobwhites (figure 16.6). However, in areas exhibiting the appropriate amount of brush cover, root-plowing or reclamation fires would not be advisable because they probably would result in the loss of usable space (i.e., result in too little brush). Rather, in these situations, other practices such as roller-chopping or maintenance fires could be applied as needed to help maintain usable space. Further, brush management can be conducted using either a species or holistic approach. A species approach is one in which bobwhites are the sole interest of management, disregarding other wildlife species.

We define a holistic approach as one in which bobwhites are the primary interest but some consideration is given to the habitat needs of other wildlife species. We chose to discuss bobwhite management from a holistic perspective because multiple-species management is the predominant management approach in South Texas.

Figure 16.6.
A common brush management practice in South Texas is clearing strips of brush to increase the amount of usable space for bobwhites. Photo taken in McMullen County by Macy Ledbetter

Mechanical Methods

Mechanical methods of brush management may be categorized into three general classes based on the resulting degree of soil disturbance: high, moderate, and low. A mechanical method resulting in relatively high soil disturbance is root-plowing. Root-plowing results in high mortality of woody plants and often causes long-term reduction in species diversity (Fulbright and Beasom 1987). In a study by Mutz et al. (1978), mesquite (*Prosopis glandulosa*) and huisache (*Acacia smalli*) composed about 95 percent of the woody plants on root-plowed rangeland and 25 percent on nontreated rangeland. Root-plowing also generally destroys a high percentage of perennial grasses in the near term and disturbs the soil to a degree that reseeding may be necessary to reestablish herbaceous vegetation (Vallentine 1989:88–124). Because perennial grasses represent important nesting cover for bobwhites, we generally would not recommend root-plowing as a mechanical method for bobwhite habitat management. However, root-plowing might be the only feasible method of habitat management in mature, dense stands of brush.

Mechanical methods resulting in moderate soil disturbance include roller-chopping, aerating, and disking. These methods reduce the height of brush but do not result in high brush mortality as root-plowing does. The growth form of resprouting brush species is also affected, changing from single- to multiple-stem shrubs. Further, the density of mesquite and other woody legumes may increase following roller-chopping (Fulbright and Beasom 1987). Despite the low mortality in brush, these methods probably are more appropriate mechanical methods for management of bobwhite habitat when the goal is to maintain usable space (figure 16.7). Bozzo et al. (1992) reported that forb and grass canopy cover increased following treatment. All these methods (root-plowing, roller-chopping, aerating, and disking) may also increase rainfall infiltration, especially when applied on compacted soils.

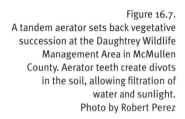

Figure 16.7.
A tandem aerator sets back vegetative
succession at the Daughtrey Wildlife
Management Area in McMullen
County. Aerator teeth create divots
in the soil, allowing filtration of
water and sunlight.
Photo by Robert Perez

Mechanical methods of brush management resulting in the least amount of soil disturbance include shredding and chaining. Shredding reduces height of woody plants but alone does not control sprouting species; and chaining generally uproots mature, single-stem woody plants but not small plants or plants with limber stems (Vallentine 1989:89–124). Double-chaining often is recommended for maximum uprooting of trees. Chaining therefore does result in some soil disturbance and represents an appropriate practice to manage bobwhite habitat, especially in areas containing mature brush. Shredding may result in a relatively level plant height (Wiedemann 1997), thereby reducing structural (vertical) diversity. A relatively uniform plant height might be of no concern to bobwhites if shredding results in a plant height that falls within the bounds of acceptable habitat structure.

When planning brush management for bobwhites by using mechanical methods, it is essential to remember that brush represents an important component of bobwhite habitat. Bobwhites use shrubs such as granjeno (*Celtis pallida*), brasil (*Condalia obovata*), and lotebush (*Ziziphus obtusifolia*) as coverts for resting during the midday inactive period and for thermal protection (Johnson and Guthery 1988). Woody cover is important escape cover and reduces vulnerability to predation (Kopp et al. 1998). Bobwhites also use the mast of woody plants for food.

Recent research has disclosed discrepancies regarding the amount of woody cover appropriate for bobwhites. These discrepancies might be an artifact of the scale at which brush is viewed. Early researchers generally considered brush cover at the pasture scale, whereas more recent research use a point scale (i.e., brush surrounding points of bobwhite use, such as flush sites). For example, Jackson (1969:32) recommended retaining brush on as little as 1–3 percent of the land if bobwhites were desired. Guthery (1986:18–19) stated that 5–15 percent woody cover was sufficient for bobwhites, a percentage similar to Lehmann's (1984:248) recommendation of less than 20 percent. However, more recently, Kopp et al. (1998) documented that bobwhites avoided habitat points with less than 20 percent woody cover (within 4 meters, or about 13 feet, of the point). They reported that bobwhites preferred flushing points with 25–90 percent woody cover and landing points with 15–65 percent woody cover. Other studies using habitat points also support Kopp et al.'s finding. Johnson and Guthery (1988) reported that bobwhite midday coverts were located in areas with greater amounts of woody cover (30 percent; within 30 meters, or about 100 feet, of coverts) than what was available at the landscape (13 percent). On these same study areas, Johnson, Guthery, and Kane (1990) documented that whistling posts used by calling males were located in areas with greater amount of woody cover (20 percent; also within 30 meters) than available at the landscape.

The optimal amount of brush required by bobwhites is broad and variable (i.e., has slack) and probably is a function of amount and height of herbaceous cover (Guthery 1986). To some extent, the cover functions provided by woody plants are interchangeable with tall, robust herbaceous cover. Therefore, the amount of brush required on a landscape is inversely related to the amount of tall herbaceous cover, a point acknowledged by previous researchers (Leopold 1933:130; Errington and Hamerstrom 1936:386; Lehmann 1984:248; Guthery 1986:20).

Brush management should be conducted in a manner such that the remaining brush cover falls within the range of percentage of cover used by bobwhites. We recommend about 15–25 percent brush cover at the pasture scale. Untreated areas should be in the form of brush mottes instead of individual trees because bobwhites prefer areas (30 meters, or 100 feet, from point of use) with greater brush coverage than that of the surrounding landscape (Johnson and Guthery 1988; Johnson, Guthery, and Kane 1990). Tall, mature brush should also be preserved. Bobwhites use loafing coverts averaging 2.8–4.5 meters (9–15 feet) in height during the summer (Johnson and Guthery 1988). Further, bobwhite males prefer to display from perch sites 1.5–2.5 meters (5–8 feet) aboveground that have overhead protection (Johnson, Guthery, and Kane 1990). The habitat component of interspersion of woody cover needs to be arranged such that no point is more than 50 meters (about 150 feet) away from escape cover. Our recommendation is more conservative than that of previous researchers, who recommended 100–200 meters (about 300–600 feet) (Stoddard 1931:181; Lehmann and Ward 1941:135). Because most bobwhite flights typically are less than 75 meters (250 feet; average = 47 meters, or 154 feet), a maximum distance of 100 meters (about 300 feet) from cover to cover should be compatible with typical flight behavior of bobwhites (Kassinis and Guthery 1996).

Chemical Methods
Chemical methods generally have limited applicability in management of bobwhite habitat. Mechanical and pyric methods of brush management represent better alternatives.

Application of herbicides may have detrimental effects on bobwhite habitat. Herbicides often reduce the abundance of forbs (important seed-producing plants for bobwhites) for at least one growing season after application (Scifres and Mutz 1978). Consequently, abundance of phytophagous (plant-eating) insects also may be negatively affected because they depend on herbaceous plants for food. However, the effect of herbicides on broad-leaved plants can vary depending on factors such as type of herbicide, rate of application, soil disturbance, and rainfall. For example, picloram (4-amino-3,5,6-trichloropicolinic acid) controls a broad spectrum of plants and can damage forb production (Scifres 1980:165–70). Conversely, many forb species are tolerant to tebuthiuron (N-[5-(1,1-dimethylethyl)-1,3,4-thiadiazol-2-yl]-N,N′-dimethylurea), given low application rates.

Guthery et al. (1987) evaluated the effects of 14 herbicide treatments of autumn-disturbed soil on canopy coverage of forbs in Kleberg County. Twelve of the 14 treatments reduced plant diversity compared to diversity in untreated areas. Total forb canopy cover was reduced in 4 of the 12 treatments, but croton (*Croton* spp.) and sunflower (*Helianthus annuus*) responded favorably to certain herbicides. They speculated that the positive response of these two plants resulted from herbicides suppressing cool-season forbs during fall-winter, thus preserving soil moisture and reducing competition for the warm-season plants. Because their study was conducted during a year with abnormally high precipitation (60 centimeters, or 24 inches, from October to May; 28 centimeters, or 11 inches, above average), their results need to be interpreted with caution and may not apply during typical arid conditions of South Texas rangelands.

A potential benefit resulting from chemical treatments is that herbaceous production will increase dramatically following herbicide application (Koerth 1996). Production of warm-season grasses varies inversely with shrub canopy coverage (Wilson and Tupper 1982). Nesting cover for bobwhites therefore may be limiting in rangeland with high shrub canopy coverage. Doerr and Guthery (1983) improved habitat for lesser prairie-chickens (*Tympanuchus pallidicinctus*) in Cochran County by controlling sand shinnery oak (*Quercus harvardii*) with variable rates of tebuthiuron. They reported increased canopy cover of grasses, forb diversity, and seed production of grasses where tebuthiuron was applied at rates of 0.2 and 0.4 kilogram/hectare (0.17 and 0.35 pound/acre).

Herbicide type, rate, method of application, and pattern of application should be considered when using herbicides to manage bobwhite habitat. As mentioned previously, herbicide type and rate will affect the response of vegetation to treatment. Becoming knowledgeable about plant susceptibility and response to herbicides will improve the probability that management objectives will be met. Method of application (i.e., broadcast or individual plant treatment) will determine the selectivity and resolution at which the treatment may be applied. Individual plant treatment may be useful in bobwhite habitat management as a follow-up maintenance treatment on areas previously cleared via other methods.

Various patterns of herbicide application have been used to manage wildlife habitat, such as blocks, strips, or variable-rate patterning (Beasom and Scifres 1977; Scifres and Koerth 1986). Blocks involve treating a more-or-less-square tract of contiguous rangeland, whereas strip patterning involves an arrangement of treated and untreated strips. Variable-rate application, in its simplest form, involves applying herbicide at half the normal dose in treated and nontreated strips in two directions (Scifres and Koerth 1986). The second set of strips is applied in a direction perpendicular to the first, resulting in a checkerboard application. Recommending a pattern of herbicide application is difficult because, in theory, there are infinite ways to pattern brush management that would yield fully usable space. Thus, it is more important to recognize bounds (e.g., when blocks are too large or strips too wide) than to identify a particular pattern.

The size of the square block at which 100 percent spraying exceeds habitat suitability will vary as a function of the species life history and habitat requirements, being directly related to mobility. Beasom and Scifres (1977) documented that in Willacy County, the density of white-tailed deer (*Odocoileus virginianus*), feral hogs (*Sus scrofa*), javelinas (*Pecari tajacu*), and wild turkeys (*Meleagris gallopavo*) was lower on a 1,620-hectare (4,000-acre) block sprayed (2,4,5-T + picloram; 1:1; 1.1 kilograms/hectare, or 0.98 pound/acre) than on an untreated site. For bobwhites, assuming a square shape and uniform treatment effect (e.g., complete defoliation of brush), we speculate that treating blocks larger than about 2 hectares (5 acres) probably will result in a loss of usable space because of quail's low mobility (less than 400 meters, or 440 yards) and small home-range size (10–30 hectares, or 25–50 acres). We base this recommendation on the fact that most bobwhite flights are ≤75 meters (82 yards) (Kassinis and Guthery 1996), and therefore bobwhites should have access to brush cover within this range. If 75 meters is used as the maximum radius from a point to be treated, then the resulting circular treated area would be 1.7 hectares (4.2 acres; 2.25 hectares for a block 150 meters square, or 5.5 acres for a block 500 feet square). Thus, the estimate of blocks 2 hectares (5 acres) square as the threshold of suitability for bobwhites appears reasonable. If an average home range for bobwhites is 10 hectares (about 25 acres), this treated block would represent about 20 percent of the covey's home range.

The width of a treated strip at which the strip becomes too wide (i.e., portion of the strip that is unusable) for bobwhites can also be estimated based on typical bobwhite flight. Using 50 meters (about 150 feet) as the mean distance of bobwhite flight to cover and assuming uniform treatment effect, then it can be reasoned that treated strips should not exceed a width of 100 meters (about 300 feet). It should be noted that a strip is merely an elongated block (a rectangle rather than a square). Thus, the shape of the treated plot plays a more significant role than the area of the plot. For example, treating 1,000 hectares (2,500 acres) in a square shape (a block) could be detrimental to bobwhites. However, it is conceivable that treating 1,000 hectares in a rectangular shape (a strip, with a relatively small width but very long length) could increase usable space, especially if bounded on at least one side by brush. Perhaps a general rule is that treatment should be conducted so that about 15–25 percent brush cover remains at the pasture scale.

Prescribed Fire
The use of prescribed fire in managing bobwhite habitat is limited and generally overrated in Texas rangelands (Guthery and Rollins 1997). The popularity of prescribed fire as a management tool arose from the early work of Stoddard (1931) conducted in the southeastern United States. This area receives more than 100 centimeters (40 inches) of annual rainfall, resulting in rapid succession of woody cover and accumulation of vegetation litter and herbaceous cover if areas are not burned periodically. Frequent application of prescribed fire (every 1–5 years in mesic

sites) is considered essential for maintaining bobwhite populations with about 50–75 percent of the understory burned (Stoddard 1931:401–14; Brennan 1999). In semiarid land sites, this interval can be much longer, but fire coverage should still be about 50–75 percent, depending on vegetation. In subtropical areas, prescribed fire maintains bobwhite habitat by removing accumulated litter, increasing percentage of bare ground and therefore seed availability, increasing insect abundance, and stimulating forb growth (Hurst 1972; Lewis and Harshbarger 1986).

The South Texas Plains ecoregion is a semiarid environment receiving less than 50–60 centimeters (20–25 inches) of annual rainfall. The low annual rainfall and grazing pressure limit the accumulation of sufficient ground cover to conduct prescribed burns (Guthery and Rollins 1997). Food supplies may not increase following prescribed fire in semiarid environments (Koerth, Mutz, and Segers 1986), unlike in subtropical areas (Hurst 1972; Lewis and Harshbarger 1986). Koerth, Mutz, and Segers reported no difference in total biomass of seeds (grass and forbs) or invertebrate density between burned and nonburned areas in southern Texas (Jim Hogg County). Annual precipitation during their two-year study was 61.9 and 39.1 centimeters (25 and 15 inches)— a long-term county average of 52.8 centimeters (20 inches)—compared to 121.9 centimeters (48 inches) in the southeast (Lewis and Harshbarger 1986).

Prescribed fire may be useful in semiarid regions in certain scenarios, such as for opening dense Gulf cordgrass (*Spartina spartinae*) stands or as a follow-up maintenance treatment in areas previously treated with other methods (figure 16.8). Scale, intensity, and frequency of the prescribed fire should be considered when managing bobwhite habitat. Prescribed fires should be conducted on small areas of less than 100 hectares (250 acres) to benefit bobwhite populations (Wilson and Crawford 1979; Carter, Rollins, and Scott 2002).

Managing bobwhite habitat with prescribed fire can be achieved with maintenance fires or reclamation fires, depending on the amount of brush existing on the rangeland. Maintenance fires are low-intensity fires intended to suppress encroachment of woody plants, whereas rec-

Figure 16.8.
Prescribed burning activities at the Daughtrey Wildlife Management Area in McMullen County. Regular maintenance fires in the eastern South Texas Plains remove ground litter and rank grasses, temporarily increase the amount of bare ground, and can slow brush encroachment and invigorate native warm-season grasses.
Photo by Macy Ledbetter

lamation fires are high-intensity fires intended to destroy woody plants (Scifres 1980:226). Maintenance fires result in a mosaic pattern of burned to nonburned patches, the latter being used as refuge and nesting cover by bobwhites (Mueller, Atkinson, and DeVos 1988; Carter, Rollins, and Scott 2002). Reclamation fires can be used to create bobwhite habitat in areas with dense, mature brush. However, reclamation fires may top-kill loafing coverts such as lotebush, which once burned, may take up to 6–7 years before they become useful to bobwhites (Renwald, Wright, and Flinders 1978). These important habitat areas should be protected from fire via fire guards.

Prescribed fire cannot be applied as frequently to the same area in semiarid rangelands as in subtropical areas. In Texas, fire frequency prior to settlement is estimated to be 4–6 years for the eastern South Texas Plains and 7–12 years for the western portion (Frost 1998). Scott (1985) estimated Interstate Highway 35 as the approximate boundary between the two regions. We recommend that prescribed fire be conducted as needed to maintain usable space for bobwhites.

Livestock Grazing

Livestock grazing occurs over much of the bobwhite range in Texas and impacts habitat composition, structure, and usability. Livestock grazing traditionally has been viewed as being detrimental to bobwhites in both subtropical and semiarid areas. Stoddard (1931:351) believed that maximum quail production was seldom attained in the southeastern United States on grazed areas. Lehmann (1937a:21) stated that Texas rangeland generally was severely overgrazed, and consequently, bobwhite abundance could be increased if grazing pressure was reduced.

During the 1980s, research was conducted on the impacts of grazing on bobwhite habitat. However, this research did not produce a general consensus on the topic but muddled the issue by yielding inconsistent results. For example, Campbell-Kissock, Blankenship, and White (1984) documented that grazing systems (short-duration and rotational 3-herd, 4-pasture) provided better nesting cover for bobwhites than continuous grazing. Conversely, Bareiss, Schulz, and Guthery (1986) reported no difference in density and dispersion of suitable nesting sites between short-duration and continuous grazing. Guthery (1996b) noted that literature on the use of grazing in management of upland game-bird habitat was a potpourri of unsupported conjecture, mixed research results, and conflicting recommendations. Grazing technology in management of bobwhite habitat therefore lacked a theoretical basis. Guthery (1997) presented a theoretical approach to resolve these inconsistencies and provide the foundation for grazing recommendations:

1. Bobwhites are adapted to certain habitat structures (e.g., height, density, and biomass of herbaceous and woody cover), not composition.
2. Structure and composition of herbaceous cover are confounded with each other.
3. Vegetation structure varies with climate, weather, and soils.
4. Bobwhite abundance is positively correlated with usable space.

Grazing for bobwhites, therefore, should maximize usable space through time by optimizing habitat structure (Guthery 1996b). Because the optimum seral stage for bobwhites on southern rangeland varies inversely with site productivity (Spears et al. 1993), optimum grazing can range from no grazing to heavy grazing (Guthery 1996b). For example, in subtropical areas with abundant precipitation and high site productivity, late-seral stages would contain greater biomass, and heavy use of forage by livestock would therefore improve bobwhite habitat (i.e., use grazing to result in lower seral stage). In semiarid regions, sites with low productivity would contain relatively less biomass; therefore, little or no grazing would be recommended to result in higher seral stages. The key issue is the quantity of herbaceous ground cover available to quail.

Grazing management to improve bobwhite habitat generally involves three considerations: stocking rate, type of grazer, and type of grazing system. Stocking rate has more influence on vegetation, livestock, and wildlife than any other factor (Holechek, Pieper, and Herbel 1998:191). The proper stocking rate for bobwhites will depend on site productivity. In semiarid areas, a stocking rate of 12–17 hectares/animal-unit (30–40 acres/animal-unit, where an animal-unit is one cow and her calf) is compatible with bobwhite management under most conditions, although lighter stocking rates or no cattle at all might be better for bobwhites. However, stocking rate is not a static number and will vary through time depending on factors such as amount of precipitation. No grazing may be advisable at certain times, such as during drought, or in particular areas, such as deteriorated, overgrazed landscapes (figure 16.9).

Type of grazer (i.e., stocker vs. cow-calf) can be an important consideration given that stocking rate should be adjusted to habitat conditions. Cow-calf operations offer the least flexibility in stocking-rate adjustments. Stocking rates may not be readily adjusted during certain times, such as calving season, because disturbance may affect parturition and separate calves from cows. Stockers provide the greatest flexibility to adjust stocking rate. Stockers are animals not directly involved in production (e.g., steers). Both types of operations are compatible with bobwhite management if proper stocking rate is maintained and readily adjusted to changing conditions.

Figure 16.9.
An overgrazed pasture in
McMullen County.
Photo by Alan Cain

The type of grazing system that is most favorable for bobwhites might be a moot point given that proper stocking rate is used relative to maintaining usable space for bobwhites. Although grazing systems were designed primarily to distribute livestock uniformly across the landscape and for uniform use of forage (Hart 1978), grazing systems will not impact bobwhite habitat if grazing results in habitat structure within the bounds acceptable to bobwhites. Alternative grazing approaches have been proposed to promote landscape heterogeneity by shifting grazing focal points (areas where grazing is concentrated) through time to produce a dynamic habitat mosaic (Fuhlendorf and Engle 2001). Using practices such as patch burns and feed blocks can create grazing focal points. Regardless of the grazing system used, the key consideration is whether grazing results in usable space for bobwhites.

Exact knowledge does not exist concerning the initial time when stocking rates should be reduced or livestock removed to maintain usable space. We can identify the extremes of the grazing continuum (overgrazed and undergrazed habitat) but have little theoretical basis for decision making for the in-between area. Several correlates of usable space (e.g., stubble height and bunchgrass density) may provide helpful guidelines. Holechek et al. (1982) stated that grazing should not be evaluated by the amount of forage removed (traditional perspective), but by the remaining stubble height. Applied to bobwhite management, optimum mean stubble height for bobwhites may be a function of their morphology (e.g., bobwhite height) (Guthery 1996b) or habitat preferences. For example, bobwhites generally nest in perennial, warm-season bunchgrasses of at least 25 centimeters (10 inches) in height and 45 centimeters (18 inches) in diameter (Lehmann 1984:81). Thus, the optimum stubble height for bobwhites could be 25 centimeters, and grazing should be discontinued when stubble height of grasses declines below this level. This does not necessarily imply that a homogeneous habitat of one height should be pursued but does set a boundary for the minimum height.

Another potential correlate of usable space relative to grazing might be bunchgrass density (i.e., potential nesting clumps/hectare). Unfortunately, there are no empirical data to provide a basis for recommendation. Lehmann (1976) and Guthery (1986) arbitrarily recommended that about 625–3,125 nesting clumps/hectare (300–770 clumps/acre) were adequate for bobwhite nesting cover. We expect under slack that a range of acceptable nest-site densities exists, but research is warranted to provide an empirical recommendation.

Early biologists understood that grazing is compatible with bobwhite management. Lehmann (1937a) recognized that grazing was not necessarily harmful and, under certain circumstances, could be beneficial to bobwhite habitat, depending on the type of grazing animal and carrying capacity of the range. However, the critical realization is that grazing affects usable space, and this in turn determines its impact— positive, negative, or neutral—on bobwhite populations.

Disking

The value of disking has been challenged by recent habitat management philosophy (Guthery 1997), a notable challenge given that disking of rangeland traditionally has been considered a valuable management practice to improve bobwhite habitat (Stoddard 1931:365–66; Rosene 1969:315–23; Lehmann 1984:270–71; Guthery 1986:71–75). However, the efficacy of disking as a bobwhite management practice ultimately is determined by the bobwhite response to it, which is dependent on the impact that disking has on usable space (Guthery 1997). The pertinent question, therefore, is how does disking affect usable space?

The impacts of disking on habitat basically are changes in food resources and changes in habitat structure. Increases in food resources often associated with disking do not impact usable space because research indicates that food generally is not limiting in the field (Guthery 1997:299). For example, Peoples et al. (1994) documented that cumulative seed production (June–February) averaged over two years was greater on disked areas (37.8 kilograms/hectare, or 33.7 pounds/acre) compared to control plots (16.9 kilograms/hectare, or 15.1 pounds/acre). However, Guthery (1999b) determined that the nondisked rangeland in the study by Peoples et al. provided ample energy for a dense population (2.5 bobwhites/hectare, or 1 bird/acre) and that disking would not be expected to increase bobwhite density. Therefore, from the perspective of increased food supplies, disking might be a meaningless practice, except maybe as an indicator of land stewardship and its subsequent effect on lease pricing.

Disking also results in a change of habitat structure, such as increasing bare ground, forb canopy cover, screening cover, and so on. From this perspective, disking may increase bobwhite density if it increases structurally suitable habitat (usable space) (figure 16.10). Guthery (1997) provided evidence (e.g., Ellis, Edwards, and Thomas 1969) that management practices such as prescribed fire increased bobwhite abundance because favorable habitat was created. Disking and prescribed fire have similar impacts on habitat; therefore, disking could conceivably increase usable space. The impact of disking on usable space will depend on what the initial habitat deficiencies of the study area were and how the vegetation changes created by disking addressed these deficiencies.

Empirical data demonstrating the impacts of disking on usable space or bobwhite density do not exist. Limited evidence is provided

Figure 16.10.
Fallow disking over a pipeline right-of-way at the Daughtrey Wildlife Management Area, McMullen County. This activity promotes the growth of seed-producing plants and can potentially increase the amount of usable space available for bobwhites.
Photo by Robert Perez

in a study conducted by Webb and Guthery (1983) in the Rolling Plains of Texas (Dickens County). Relative to an indication of usable space, they documented that March disking resulted in a percentage of bare ground (51.9 percent) that was more favorable for bobwhites (greater than 40–60 percent) than that of nondisked areas (21.4 percent). Webb and Guthery (1982) also documented an increase in bobwhite abundance in response to habitat management (i.e., grazing exclosures, brush piles, and disking). However, we cannot isolate the effects of disking on bobwhite abundance because the various treatments confounded the results.

The value of disking for managing bobwhite habitat is therefore debatable, especially in semiarid areas that are grazed. Like prescribed fire, disking may be more applicable in mesic subtropical areas, where vegetation and litter buildup occurs rapidly, than in semiarid rangelands. Given the previous admonition, we present the following arbitrary recommendations (Guthery 1986:71–75):

1. Disk areas where grass covers more than 85 percent of the soil surface and is ≥75 centimeters (30 inches).
3. Disk within 50–75 meters (about 150–200 feet) of woody cover, given some perceived benefit from disking.
3. Disk sandy soils or sandy loams (more effective than on loam or clay soils).
4. Disk between first freeze in fall and last freeze in spring when the goal is to decrease grass cover.

We emphasize that the usable-space theory (Guthery 1997) predicts that disking may be a neutral practice in management of bobwhite habitat in grazed, semiarid rangeland.

Cultural Management

This section addresses aspects of cultural management for bobwhites on the South Texas Plains. We use the term "cultural management" to describe aspects of quail management that are based on the assumption that they are intrinsically good for bobwhites, despite the lack of scientific evidence to support it.

Supplemental Feeding

Since the early 1930s, quail managers have used supplemental feed with the goal of improving bobwhite survival and reproduction and increasing the probability of locating wild coveys (Hawkins 1937; Rosene 1969:335; Doerr and Silvy 1987). By its very definition, *supplement* is "something added" and is certainly not a replacement for natural foods. Rosene (1969:324), Lehmann (1984:272–76), and Guthery (1986:48) hypothesized that there was no biological reason for continuous (year-round) feeding and recommended the practice only when bobwhites were stressed by harsh winters or drought, which limited their food. Signs of stress include daylight feeding; short, silent flight; reduced fear of humans; and weight loss (Lehmann 1984). Food plots are another form of supplement but are not discussed here because of their limited use in South Texas. Food plots within this physiographic region are regarded as unnecessary when rainfall is above average and as impractical in drought.

The potential benefits of supplemental feeding must be weighed against the possible detriments, which may include the concentration of predators, facilitation of avian disease and parasite transmission, possible poisoning by aflatoxins, and potential overharvest of birds (Lehmann 1984; Guthery 1986).

The concentration of predators, and thus a presumable increase in depredation, is often cited as a reason not to feed. However, there is little evidence it occurs. Using radiotelemetry, DeMaso et al. (1998) and Townsend et al. (1999) could find no increase in annual bobwhite mortality near feeders. But DeMaso et al. did report differences in cause-specific mortality. Specifically, the proportion of mammalian depredation was higher on fed versus unfed areas. In South Texas, Doerr and Silvy (2002) found no differences in mammal-scent station visits or observed avian predators between fed and unfed sites. Furthermore, Sisson, Stribling, and Speake (2000) hypothesized that feeding may enhance survival by reducing covey home-range size and movements, thereby decreasing the amount of time bobwhites are exposed to predators.

There is very little information available regarding disease transmission at quail feeders, although feeder transmissions of protozoan diseases have been recorded in mourning doves and wild turkeys (Guthery 2000:64). Cause-specific mortality studies have not attributed any bobwhite deaths to disease (DeMaso et al. 1998; Townsend et al. 1999).

The differential maturation of corn in drought years leads to the production of molds in the harvest. Improperly stored corn or birdseed mix containing corn can also begin to produce molds. Some of these molds produce poisonous compounds called aflatoxins, which can kill domestic poultry, quails, and turkeys. Available lab research on game species indicates a range of maladies, including liver damage, depressed immune system, lowered reproductive ability, and death. The effects of directly ingesting aflatoxins on the immune system of wild-caught quails have been examined at 100, 500, 1,000, and 2,000 parts-per-billion (ppb) treatment levels. Preliminary results of white blood cell proliferations indicate that bobwhites were only about half as responsive to the introduced antigen in all treatments (Deana Moore, unpublished data). In other words, immune systems of wild bobwhites are dramatically suppressed at aflatoxin levels as low as 100 ppb, a level that is commonly found in corn marketed as game feed (Henke et al. 2001). Some researchers argue that birds may discriminate against individual kernels of corn with high levels of aflatoxin. Perez, Henke, and Fedynich (2001) evaluated the ability of white-winged doves (*Zenaida asiatica*), northern bobwhites, and green jays (*Cyanocorax yncas*) to select against contaminated feed and found that green jays could detect and avoid toxins, whereas white-winged doves and bobwhites could not. Despite the potential dangers, there have been no reported aflatoxin-related reductions in wild quail populations, so poisoning may pose only a minor threat (Guthery 2000:64–66). However, managers should take care to minimize the potential short- and long-term effects of aflatoxins by following guidelines outlined in Guthery (1986:54–56) and Thompson and Henke (2000), including purchasing only corn that has been labeled safe for wildlife (less than 20 ppb).

As previously mentioned, one of the reasons managers feed is to concentrate birds for harvest. A potential consequence of this practice is overharvest. If surrounding habitats are not conducive to ingress, long-term declines may become apparent in local populations. Sisson, Stribling, and Speake (2000) reported that coveys seen per-hour hunted were higher on broadcast-fed sites than unfed sites. DeMaso et al. (1998) also reported an increase in harvest on fed areas but only when food was considered limiting. In South Texas, Doerr and Silvy (2002) flushed birds more frequently near feeders than at random sites, except on sites where populations were low. Conversely, Townsend et al. (1999) found no differences in harvest between fed and unfed sites. The evidence to date suggests that harvest management strategies that involve feeding may need to adjust harvest rates accordingly.

Another factor to be considered is the economics of a supplemental feeding operation. Depending on the feeder type, much more than half of the feed may be consumed by a variety of nontarget animals, including harvester ants, rabbits, rodents, raccoons, feral hogs, deer, livestock, mourning doves, and nongame birds (Hawkins 1937; Doerr and Silvy 1987; Kane 1988). Also, the costs associated with year-round feeding can be quite high. For more information regarding the economics of feeding in South Texas, see Guthery (1986) and Doerr and Silvy (1987).

Stationary and roadside feeding are the two delivery systems for supplement. Stationary feeders come in a variety of shapes and sizes and most often are homemade. For more information on feeder types, see Guthery (1986:49–52).

Roadside feeding is usually accomplished by attaching an electric broadcast spreader to a vehicle. Both delivery systems are regularly used in wildlife operations in the South Texas Plains (Doerr and Silvy 1987). There are also two categories of feed, whole and partial ration. Whole ration provides all of the nutrients and minerals necessary for survival, whereas partial ration does not meet the nutritional requirements of bobwhites (Nestler, Bailey, and McClure 1942; Guthery 1986:53; Doerr and Silvy 1987). Whole rations certainly offer greater benefit but are more expensive and harder to deliver than partial rations (Guthery 1986:48–59; Doerr and Silvy 1987). The most commonly used feeds for quails in South Texas are grain sorghum (milo) and corn, both of which meet the nutritional needs of nonbreeding adult bobwhites. However, neither provides sufficient protein, calcium, or phosphorus for laying hens (Guthery 1986:53, 2000:67).

Guthery (1986:57, 2000:60–64) describes supplemental feeding as a viable management tool only where annual rainfall is less than 75 centimeters (about 30 inches) but later regarded the practice overall as unnecessary and a failure as a management tool. In Alabama and western Oklahoma, studies examining bobwhite population response to fed versus unfed sites concluded that supplemental feeding programs were ineffective (Keeler 1959; DeMaso, Peterson, et al. 2002). Conversely, in southern Florida and South Texas, researchers found that bobwhite survival increased when food was considered limiting (Frye 1954; Doerr and Silvy 2002). Townsend et al. (1999) demonstrated that feeding enhanced survival in the first two of three years and decreased survival in the third year. The only evaluation we found of broadcast feeding in the literature showed that fed areas had higher survival than unfed areas in one year and no difference the next (Sisson, Stribling, and Speake 2000). Based on the research to date, the potential benefits of supplemental feeding remain unclear. It is important to note that none of the aforementioned studies measured an increase in reproduction. In other words, no birds were added to the fall population as a result of feeding.

Perhaps supplemental feeding is of more importance in South Texas, where frequent periods of drought may limit natural food supplies. The only comprehensive feeding study to be completed in South Texas concluded that survival could be increased only when food was limiting and that feeding was ineffective when the basic habitat requirements of bobwhites were not met (Doerr 1988). In certain years, Doerr found that the native food supply was limited from January through March in deep sands. Koerth and Guthery (1987) reported bobwhite body condition to be low in late summer. It remains to be seen if a properly applied full ration can increase productivity, as stated in Guthery (1986:48). Managers would likely see more benefit to bobwhites if their time, energy, and resources are focused on habitat management rather than feeding.

Supplemental Water

The bobwhite's need for surface water has been a subject of debate for many years. Stoddard (1931:503) believed that bobwhites in the southeastern United States did not need surface water for drinking purposes but rather obtained sufficient moisture from preformed water (water contained in food) and dew. However, in semiarid regions, the perception differed, as bobwhites had been observed drinking surface water, especially during drought. Lehmann (1984:87) reportedly observed 468 bobwhites drinking water from an earthen reservoir in two hours during a drought, but we are skeptical of his biological interpretation of this observation—that this illustrated that bobwhites require surface water. Prasad and Guthery (1986) observed no quail visits (157 hours of observation) to earthen reservoirs at a mesic site (54 centimeters, or 21 inches, of precipitation) but observed 27 quail visits (166 hours of observation) at a more xeric site (22 centimeters, or about 9 inches, of precipitation). These general observations resulted in the belief that bobwhites needed surface water in arid environments and that water deprivation may explain their reproductive failure during drought.

Laboratory research appeared to support the water-deprivation hypothesis. Koerth and Guthery (1991) documented that female bobwhites on restricted water intake had lower masses of reproductive organs than hens receiving water ad libitum. They concluded that their data were consistent with the hypothesis.

Guthery and Koerth (1992) subsequently field-tested the water-deprivation hypothesis by documenting the availability of preformed water in forbs during drought and evaluating whether water supplementation would prevent reproductive failure. They documented that daily water demand of bobwhites was minuscule relative to the amount of preformed water available during both wet and drought years. Further, percentage of summer gain did not differ between the control (average = 34 percent) and watered site (average = 53 percent) during drought years. Guthery and Koerth concluded that water supplementation would not be a productive practice to reverse drought-induced reproductive failure and rejected the hypothesis.

Research indicates that bobwhites do not require surface water

(Guthery and Koerth 1992; Guthery 1999b). Bobwhites may obtain water from three sources: metabolic water (produced by metabolism of foods), preformed water, and free water (e.g., dew). If the equations and example provided in Guthery (1999b) are used, a 160-gram (5-ounce) bobwhite requires about 23 milliliters (0.78 ounce) of water per day. Metabolic water would provide about 4 milliliters (0.13 ounce), implying that exogenous water sources (preformed and free water) would have to account for the remaining 19 milliliters (0.64 ounce). The bobwhite summer diet would provide about 18 milliliters (0.60 ounce) of preformed water (Wood, Guthery, and Koerth 1986). Therefore, it is possible for bobwhites to meet their water requirement without free water. The total water from metabolic water (4 milliliters, or 0.13 ounce) and preformed water (18 milliliters, or 0.60 ounce) approximates the estimated water requirement (22 vs. 23 milliliters, or 0.74 vs. 0.77 ounce, respectively).

Based on current knowledge, we concur with Guthery (1999b) that bobwhites are adapted to habitats that lack free water. In fact, it appears that bobwhites can be relatively abundant during drought conditions and in areas removed from surface water, given usable space. Armory R. Starr wrote, "In September, 1884, I went on a bear-hunt . . . in the southwestern portion of Texas. It was during a severe drought. Water was to be found only on the Nueces River and a few of its tributaries, and while the cattle had eaten all the grass within several miles of the stream . . . , in other places we found it quite abundant, because the cattle would not go so far from water to graze upon it, and yet in those places I saw more bobwhites than I ever saw before or since" (quoted in Stoddard 1931:500–501).

Surface water is not necessary, assuming that preformed water is present in sufficient quantities to meet bobwhite requirements, an assumption supported by Guthery and Koerth (1992). Therefore, Guthery's (1986:103–108) recommendation of establishing waterers in areas receiving less than 75 centimeters (30 inches) at a density of 1 waterer/120 hectares (about 300 acres) appears to be wrong (Guthery 2002).

Predator Control

Predator control often is resorted to as a management practice given the relatively high levels of predation sustained by bobwhites. Based on band recovery, annual survival rates have been documented to range from 9.7 percent to 24.1 percent (Pollock, Moore, et al. 1989). Guthery (1997:292) estimated that annual survival for stable populations was 30 percent in low latitudes (warm climates) and 20 percent in high latitudes (cold climates).

Individual nests also have a relatively low probability of hatching (i.e., nest success). Nest success estimates range from 17 percent in Georgia (Simpson 1976) to 45 percent in Florida (DeVos and Mueller 1993). Depredation often is cited as the primary cause of nest failures. In Illinois, Klimstra and Roseberry (1975) reported that of 863 nests, only 34 percent were successful. Depredation accounted for 55 percent of nest failures. In southern Texas, Lehmann (1984:91) documented that 45 percent of 532 nests were successful, with predators accounting for 84 percent of nest failures.

The low annual survival and nest success have led to the speculation that predation may be a limiting factor of bobwhite populations (Hurst, Burger, and Leopold 1996; Rollins and Carroll 2001). However, research does not provide convincing evidence to support this speculation. Beasom (1974) conducted predator control on approximately 2,347 hectares (5,000 acres) in Kleberg County during 1971–72. In the two years of the study, he reported moderate gains in bobwhite abundance in the experimental pasture (98.7 percent and 213.8 percent, respectively) compared to the untreated pasture (39.2 percent and 154.6 percent, respectively). Beasom concluded that predator removal seemed to enhance, to a limited extent, the reproductive success of bobwhites.

Guthery and Beasom (1977) also conducted predator control on approximately 1,550 hectares (3,800 acres) in Zavala County, Texas, during 1975–76. They evaluated the response of scaled quail (*Callipepla squamata*) and bobwhites to the treatment. Preexperiment populations were higher on untreated pastures for scaled quail (0.89/kilometer, or 1.4/mile) and bobwhites (6.07/kilometer, or 9.7/mile) than on the predator removal area (0.51/kilometer, or 0.8/mile; and 3.32/kilometer, or 5.3/mile, respectively). This trend continued for the duration of the project, even after predator removal. Guthery and Beasom concluded that predator suppression at their level had little discernible effect on density trends of bobwhites or scaled quail.

These two studies were not replicated; therefore, their results are limited to their sites. However, to our knowledge, they represent the only published studies conducted on bobwhite response to predator control and thus provide an underlying basis for assessment.

We do not believe that predator control is necessary to sustain bobwhite populations under most circumstances. It may be economically unfeasible or logistically impractical to control predators at a level required to elicit a positive bobwhite response. Because neither mortality nor recruitment depends solely on predation, it cannot account completely for a given population density (Newton 1993). Further, given that sufficient suitable habitat exists, weather is a primary influence on the population dynamics of bobwhites. We acknowledge that certain situations might exist where predator control may be effective or necessary (e.g., fragmented habitat). Therefore, the role of management is to scientifically determine the conditions under which these circumstances exist and to apply predator management according to scientific prescriptions (Guthery 1995:107). It is important to note that although predator control has proven effective for increasing production of various other game birds, such as wild turkeys and waterfowl (Wadsworth and McCabe 1996), the life-history variables of bobwhites differ from those of other species; hence, contradictory findings on the value of predator control are consistent with biological expectations.

Harvest Pressure

Animal populations are complex systems, and parameters that affect changes in any given population are interrelated. Harvest is one of many variables influencing bobwhite populations. Other variables include reproduction, emigration, immigration, predation, weather, habitat changes, and fragmentation (Roseberry and Klimstra 1984; DeMaso 1999). The degree to which harvest affects bobwhite populations depends on scale. At a statewide scale harvest may have little or no effect on populations, but at finer scales (e.g., ranch or pasture) intense harvest can result in long-term population declines (see chapter 24). Additionally, harvest, predation, weather, and other parameters can cause local extinction where there is no source of ingress (i.e., fragmented landscapes). A definitive set of decision rules regarding late-season harvest are not clear. In theory, late-season harvest can be more additive, or more compensatory, depending on the strength of density dependence in relation to survival and harvest rate.

In South Texas, 30 percent annual survival can be expected in non-hunted populations (Guthery 2000:116). Considering this high level of annual turnover and limited evidence that late-season harvest is more additive than compensatory (Roseberry and Klimstra 1984), managers must exercise sound harvest management strategies to avoid declines in local populations (see chapter 24).

The overall goal of harvest management should be to maintain the number of quail during the reproductive season that are capable of producing as many as or more offspring than total losses during the preceding year (Guthery 1996a; Peterson 1999). In order to reach this goal, the manager must have some idea of the preharvest population. Recording morning covey-call counts, a form of avian point counts, is a good way to do this (Guthery 1986; DeMaso et al. 1992). Healthy bobwhite populations can sustain about a 30 percent harvest of the fall population (Guthery et al. 2000). Harvest rates should be adjusted up or down to match production surveys and adult:juvenile ratios, although ratios may be positively biased (Shupe, Guthery, and Bingham 1990). In South Texas, age ratios of less than 2:1 are considered poor, whereas ratios above 3.5:1 are considered to reflect a good year (Howard 1994). Good record keeping is essential to sound harvest management and can illuminate potential problems. For example, poor age ratios in particular pastures may indicate habitat deficiency (DeMaso 1999; Peterson 1999). Additionally, certain methods of harvest are commonly used to minimize detrimental effects to quail populations, including limiting gun hours, limiting birds taken per covey, and resting management units from cattle grazing (Howard 1996).

Summary

Certain advancements in knowledge have occurred since the publication of *Beef, Brush, and Bobwhites* (Guthery 1986). Following, we highlight the primary fallacies or limitations contained therein, based on current knowledge.

1. Practices aimed at increasing food, such as feeders, food plots, and disking, may not increase bobwhite density because food generally is not limiting for bobwhites. Usable-space theory does not incorporate food. Because disking impacts habitat structure and therefore potentially usable space, disking may increase bobwhite density.
2. Water supplementation is unnecessary. Research indicates that bobwhites are capable of meeting their water requirement without exogenous sources, such as surface water. The notion that incubating adult quail dip their bellies in water to foster humidity at the nest (Lehmann 1953) appears to be a myth. Birds regulate humidity at nests by "choosing" the "correct" nesting season and location, ma-

terial, and construction and simply by being part of the system (Ar and Sidis 2002).

3. The early recommendation of 5–10 percent brush cover may be too low for bobwhites. Based on recent research, about 15–25 percent brush cover appears adequate for bobwhites.

4. The recommended number of nesting sites, 625–3,125/hectare (300–770/acre), is an arbitrary number, though probably reasonable. Research is warranted to provide an empirical recommendation.

We emphasize that the foundation of bobwhite management appears to rest upon the concept of usable space. The decision-making process of management therefore centers on which practice(s) will maximize usable space for bobwhites, assuming a sole interest in bobwhites. Land stewards must realize that even in areas saturated with usable space, bobwhite populations still can exhibit considerable annual variability due the influence of weather (Lehmann 1953; Kiel 1976; Guthery, Koerth, and Smith 1988; Lusk et al. 2002). Weather can account for about 30 percent of the variability observed for bobwhite populations in semiarid environments (Rice et al. 1993). Because weather cannot be controlled or accurately predicted, management should initiate corrective habitat measures before habitat deterioration has occurred to maintain maximum usable space through time.

A nagging question still remains relative to bobwhite management: Why does bobwhite management appear to be a backwater science, given an extensive knowledge base (Hernández, Guthery, and Kuvlesky 2002)? Philosophically, it is worthwhile to entertain a potential explanation for the existence of this perception.

The answer to the question may lie in human nature. It is human nature to desire simple solutions to complex problems and expect immediate, predictable results. We seek and anticipate simple cause-and-effect relationships from complex, multivariate systems. We pursue complete control in a dynamic, stochastic environment. However, we fail to realize that management operates under the time scale of natural processes, not hunting seasons.

We judge management success in terms of hunting success, not the wildlife demographic capacity of the land. As a result, management results often fall short of our expectations, giving the impression that management has failed, but more detrimentally, that management involved guesswork. In the process, the science that once built management is forgotten, and with each new disappointment, management begins to evolve and become perceived more as an art, resulting in lingering disappointment, frustration, and confusion with management. If we are to become effective managers, we need to realize that the technology of management exists and adjust our expectations accordingly.

Section III
Culture, Heritage,
and Future of
Texas Quails

Quail Regulations and the Rule-Making Process in Texas

17

Jerry L. Cooke

> Many sportsmen still habitually place the blame for game shortage on
> "vermin" or "politics" or even "too many restrictive laws." Many non-
> shooting protectionists with equal regularity, place the blame on "too
> many sportsmen." Such verdicts are hardly entitled to be diagnoses.
> They represent . . . the age-old insistence of the human mind to fix on
> some visible scapegoat the responsibility for invisible phenomena which
> they cannot or do not wish to understand.
> Leopold (1933)

Although bird hunters have always been interested in quails, there has been a developing concern about quails among birders and other conservationists. Why the growing interest in quails among nonhunters? Populations of northern bobwhites, by far the species of quail most popular among Texas bird hunters, are disappearing from portions of their historic range at an alarming rate. For example, the southeastern United States, a region that was historically considered the major quail hunting area in North America, has lost more than 90 percent of its wild bobwhites.

Birders have noticed that many other ground-nesting birds are disappearing from their annual surveys as well (e.g., the Audubon Christmas Bird Count and the U.S. Fish and Wildlife Service Breeding Bird Survey). Many populations of ground-nesting and grassland birds are apparently headed, like quails, to oblivion. As a result of these mutual concerns, birders have joined quail hunters in an effort to identify the problem and repair it.

However, what many Texans, and most birders, do not realize is that this problem is not new. Neither the quail nor grassland bird decline—which has been progressing across the United States for more than 50 years—nor the desire to do something about it has been ignored. Unfortunately, many people think that the solution to the quail decline should involve changing hunting regulations rather than understanding what is happening on a landscape scale from a management perspective.

The purpose of this chapter is to provide a brief history of how the people of Texas have tried to increase quail populations by using regulations. It will describe how the rule-making process works and show how it has been used in the context of developing and enforcing hunting regulations as they pertain to quails in Texas.

Why Do We Need Rules?

At the heart of wildlife regulations and, therefore, all actions related to making laws and rules, is the fact that regulations are nothing more than a formally accepted solution to problems. Such laws and rules are made in the context of how those problems are understood by the public and their representatives.

In the case of quails, the public's understanding of factors that influence quail populations is deficient. If we had a complete understanding of such factors, we would not be writing about restoring quails in this book. We would be loading up to go quail hunting.

If you think that I do not believe the solution to quail management problems will be found through regulation, you are correct. Rule making is complicated and, at times, confounding. Unfortunately, meticulous procedures that ensure an exacting legal process do not ensure that the process is aimed in the right direction. An old cowboy saying is, "If you don't know where you are going, any road will get you there," or "There's no right way to do the wrong thing." With quails, many roads have been tried. Only a few have taken quail enthusiasts to the right destination.

Sick quail populations reflect sick landscapes and not the impact of unruly, overzealous, or unscrupulous hunters and poachers. Some quail populations have declined and disappeared where no hunting was conducted. Despite this fact, many have tried to repair quail populations with regulations. All such attempts have failed.

A statement that has not yet been offered in testimony before wildlife commissioners or legislators is a hunter or landowner saying, "Please regulate me, I'm completely out of control!" On the other hand, the statement "Please regulate my neighbors. They will not do what I want them to do on their land!" is a common one. Although proposals are never stated in these exact words, requests from the public come almost exclusively from this perspective. Apparently, many landowners and hunters are not willing to make personal sacrifices unless they are assured that everyone else will make such sacrifices. For example, human nature and the tragedy of the commons points to a view such as "Why should I pass up a hunt if someone else is just going to come along and take the wildlife that my personal discipline has provided?"

In reality, I do not think that self-interest, in most of its forms, is a bad perspective, because it is an honest, evolutionary one. Self-interest is, after all, the perspective that has led to the development of cooperative wildlife management associations (see chapter 21).

The real problem, in my opinion, with thinking that a problem will be solved by a rule change from the legislature or Texas Parks and Wildlife Commission (TPWC) is the fact that you can spend a dollar only once. If you spend it promoting a cause or fighting what you consider to be a bad cause, you cannot spend it restoring habitats or coalescing existing habitats into a landscape that again can support a quail population. You also will be embracing the notion that the solution to the problem lies with the actions of someone else or, more accurately, anybody else.

Sources of Regulations

In Texas there are four sources of regulations that affect quail hunting: (1) statutes adopted by the Texas legislature, (2) regulations adopted by the TPWC, (3) hunting-camp rules adopted by landowners, and (4) hunting-camp rules adopted by quail hunters themselves. In this chapter, I will cover the first two sources of regulations.

The Legislative Process
The Texas legislature meets for 140 days in odd-numbered years. During this 140-day period, anything can happen and frequently does. I think

there is a typographic error in the Texas Constitution. In my view, the framers of the Texas Constitution really intended the legislature to meet for 2 days every 140 years, but it is too late to change that now.

To change the laws and statutes of Texas, a member of the Texas House of Representatives or the Texas Senate has to file a bill. One of the greatest gifts the framers of the Texas Constitution provided the people of Texas is the requirement that any changes to Texas statutes included in a bill must be germane to the title of the bill. In other words, you cannot hide an action in a bill that is supposed to be acting on something completely different. Of course, this means that the title of an action needs to be read very carefully (e.g., with and without punctuation, upside down, and backward).

Before a representative or senator files a bill, it must be reviewed by the parliamentarian in the Office of Legislative Council (LC) (figure 17.1). The LC reviews the language in the bill that will change a statute and then reviews whether each section in the bill is germane to the title. For simplicity's sake, I will assume that our hypothetical bill has been filed in the Texas House, though in reality it can be filed in either the House or the Senate, or in both houses simultaneously (i.e., companion bills) with separate authors. Once the bill is filed, the Speaker of the House reviews it and decides which standing committee in the House will hold hearings on it. When a bill has been assigned to a committee, the author has to convince the chairman of the committee to allow it to have a hearing. With several thousand bills filed during a normal session—there were more than 4,000 bills files in the 2003 legislative session—not many bills will ever see the light of day after they have been filed.

When a hearing is held, the author puts the bill before the committee by explaining what it does and what the intent of the action is. The public is allowed to provide comments on the bill, such as identifying strengths, weaknesses, or unintended results, and the committee either then passes the bill to the House floor, amends the bill, offers a substitute for the bill, or kills the bill. If the bill is passed to the House floor with the committee's recommendation for passage, the bill must survive three readings on three separate days—when it can be amended from the floor by any member with approval of the author or with the approval of a majority of members present—before the House members are allowed to vote on it for passage. If the bill passes, it is then sent to the Senate, where the entire process is repeated.

Sometimes bills passed by the House and the Senate are not the same because each version was amended differently. When this happens, the bill is sent to a conference committee appointed by the Speaker of the House and the lieutenant governor, who chose the committee chairs who held hearings on the bill. Also present at the conference committee are the author(s) of the bill(s) and, generally, any members who have an interest in the bill and request appointment. The bill that leaves the conference committee may not resemble the original bill, but it often does. Whether it is identical to or completely different from the original bill, it will have to be reapproved by the House and the Senate before it can be sent to the governor. The governor can veto it, sign it into law, or allow it to become law of its own accord. A bill becomes law 10 days after the governor receives it, if the governor takes no action on it. If

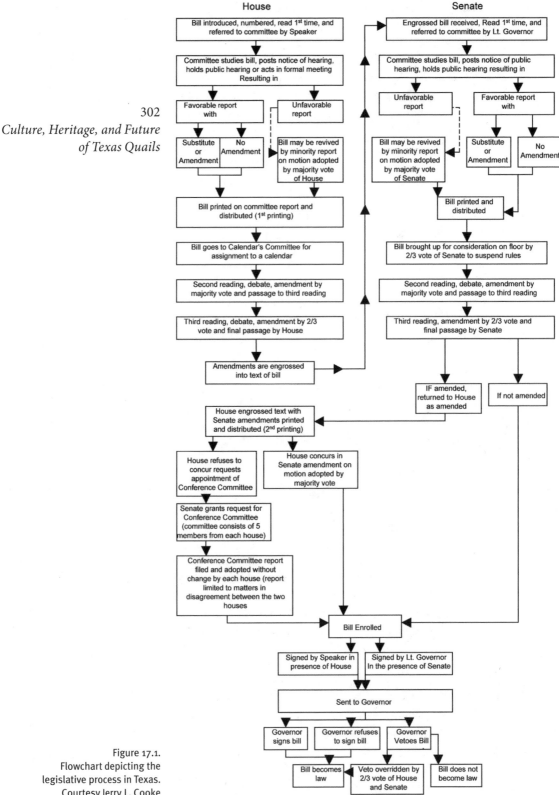

Figure 17.1.
Flowchart depicting the
legislative process in Texas.
Courtesy Jerry L. Cooke

the governor vetoes the bill, it can still be made law if two-thirds of the members of the House and Senate vote to override the veto. Of course, overcoming a veto requires time. Toward the end of the session, this becomes a very important factor. Clearly, the governor's veto becomes more effective as the session progresses.

The Rule-Making Process

Legislation is the people speaking their will. Such speech is the State's policy concerning wildlife. You do not have to like it. However, you have to do it. It has to be done exactly as the legislature said it should be done. For example, some statutes use the word *shall,* as in "The department shall issue the licenses authorized by this chapter," meaning that when all the conditions of the statute are met, the department issues the license, no more discussion. Some statutes use the word *may,* as in "The department may issue a license for a private bird hunting area under this subchapter." When the word *may* is used, there usually is a provision somewhere in the statute such as "The commission may adopt regulations necessary to administer this subchapter." This is called "regulatory authority" and is the reason why TPWC can act on some issues (such as seasons and bag limits) and not others (such as exotic introductions and high fences).

Many legislative acts contain provisions directing the TPWC to make rules that implement the legislated policies. These statutes will be worded as "may issue a permit" or "the commission shall adopt regulations." Sometimes the wording results because legislators do not want to make the final decision on an issue—sometimes this increases their chances of reelection. In general, regulatory authority is conveyed in this way because TPWC has access to the Texas Parks and Wildlife Department (TPWD) professional staff. Such a system allows more time to think through problems. The TPWC meets more often than the legislature and therefore can be more sensitive to changing conditions related to wildlife and resource management issues. Basically, the legislature tells TPWC where the boundaries of an issue are, and TPWC sets what it believes to be the best rule within those boundaries to address the issue.

Some issues become so fluid through time that it becomes necessary to return to the legislature to change the boundaries. Sometimes this is initiated by TPWC and at other times, by the regulated community (e.g., landowners, hunters, shrimpers).

Basically, the legislature has said that TPWC rules should provide reasonable and equitable access to the wildlife resources that are owned by all Texans; TPWC rules should always prevent depletion or waste of the wildlife resources of this state; and the hunting seasons on all game animals and game birds in Texas are closed by the legislature unless data collected by TPWD suggest that a hunt can safely be conducted on a species and this suggestion becomes a finding of fact by TPWC.

Virtually every other TPWC rule related to hunting seasons is to carry out what hunters and landowners prefer or what hunters and landowners can tolerate, or to administer a permitting program created by the legislature.

Rule Making, a Complicated Process

Rule making is complicated for a reason. If it were too easy to make rules, you would get a lot of rules! Rule making begins with the identification and definition of an issue. As discussed previously, sometimes this is initiated by TPWD staff in response to changing population and or harvest estimates or to improve the enforceability of existing rules. Sometimes rule making is initiated by the public because they do not like the hunting season that they have; they have heard about a season somewhere else that sounds appealing; they want to make their neighbor adopt the management practices that they have adopted on their own land or hunting lease; or they think that they are being taken advantage of by neighboring landowners or hunters and want it stopped. Public-initiated requests for rule changes are much more common than agency requests for rule changes based on wildlife population changes or enforcement needs.

Once the issue is identified and defined, an experienced biologist or game warden will scope the issue. Scoping an issue means having formal or informal meetings with everybody who is going to be impacted by the new rule. If this is not possible, then a representative sample of those who will be impacted is used. At these meetings, the biologist or game warden will (1) clarify the issue for the attendees, (2) help the public decide what the system should look like within a defined future, (3) help the public decide the most appropriate approach to bringing the issue to closure (i.e., either making a rule to fix a problem or simply accepting that there will be a problem and take no action), and (4) assure that everybody understands how long a rule should be in effect if it is adopted.

Generally, this conversation also includes how you are going to measure the changes brought on by the rule along with when and how you will know that the rule is no longer needed. If you have survived this process, which at times will seem impossible, you now have a proposal that can be brought before TPWC.

The first formal presentation of a proposal to TPWC is to explain the need for the rule, how the rule will work, and generally, the language that the rule will contain. The ideal proposal is one that brings solutions to TPWC rather than one that dumps a problem, or an only partially solved problem, on the commission. The purpose of the initial presentation is to seek permission from the commission to publish the proposal in the *Texas Register* for public comment. Permission is requested, because there are times when TPWC does not want to move forward on a proposal and they need an opportunity to end the process. Basically, if a majority of TPWC does not think that there is a problem, there is not a problem regardless of what the data suggest or the staff may think. Sometimes the TPWC will recognize that there is a problem but will postpone a proposal because they want staff to spend more time improving the proposal by talking to individuals or groups that may have been missed during the scoping process. Or perhaps they just think that the proposal will get a better review by the public at another time.

The TPWC cannot adopt a rule unless the public is provided at least 30 days to comment on the proposal (i.e., following publication in the *Texas Register*) and the public is also provided at least one public hearing during which questions can be asked about the proposal and comments formally accepted. Normally, TPWD will have several meetings across the state, particularly in areas most affected by a proposal, to facilitate the public's opportunities to comment. But it is important to note that TPWD accepts and includes all comments whether they are received by phone, public hearing, public meeting, letter, or e-mail.

After the comment period, the proposal is again brought before TPWC to explain one more time the need, as before; to provide an accurate summary of public comments that have been received; and to point out any changes to the proposal that staff may recommend in response to those comments. The TPWC can adopt the proposal as is, adopt it with changes, postpone action, or reject the proposal.

Published proposals can be amended by TPWC only so long as the amendment does not expand the rule to include people who were not included in the original proposal, does not expand the rule to include areas of Texas not included in the original proposal, and does not make the rule more restrictive than the original proposal.

Before those kinds of amendments can be made, the proposal with these changes must be published for another 30-day comment period before it can be adopted. The proposal becomes a regulation when it receives a majority vote from TPWC and 20 days have lapsed following filing the adoption with the Texas secretary of state.

Not only is the process for making a new rule complicated but the same process must be followed for changing an existing rule or simply clarifying a rule when the intent is not clear from the language. For example, the clarity of language is confounding when the person(s) who created the rule or carried it through the process is not around anymore. Sometimes conditions change such that nobody knows how the rule should apply under new circumstances. At any rate, this is the torturous process that prescribes how, when, and where you may hunt in Texas.

Quails and Hunting Regulations in Texas

The first game law ever adopted by the Texas legislature occurred in 1861. The purpose of this law was to close the bobwhite quail season on Galveston Island for two years to allow the quail population to recover. In 1861, Galveston was the only real seaport in Texas and the first real Texas city. It was the first geographic portion of Texas fragmented by urban sprawl. This law to protect and recover quail did not work. The quail population did not recover on Galveston Island because quail habitat was eliminated, not because the quail season was open. However, wildlife regulation was launched with that legislative action. Such wildlife regulation has increased, rather than decreased, through time.

Texans do not just value independence—they demand it. Although a modern Texan would barely consider the hunting and fishing regulations adopted by the legislature and the Texas Fish Commission (which was created in 1879) as real limitations, in 1883, 130 counties declared themselves exempt from all game laws. This action was followed in 1885 by the legislature's abolishing the Texas Fish Commission because regulations were considered "too tight."

With the exception of the brief quail-season closure in Galveston County, there was a no-closed season throughout Texas. People could hunt whenever they wanted, and there was no bag limit. People could take as many quails in a day as they chose. During 1903, the Texas legislature established a quail bag limit of 25 birds "at any one time." This was cut back to 15 birds per day in 1915, but still no season had been established.

Starting about 1925, county-by-county quail seasons began to appear in Texas statutes. The one consistent aspect of these seasons and bag limits was their inconsistency. Because each legislative action was a local issue—such actions did not impact anyone outside a single county—the season and bag limit each were adopted to be pretty much whatever the folks in the county wanted. Some actually provided regulatory authority to the Texas Game, Fish and Oyster Commission (TGFOC) (which was established in 1907 by the legislature, with the directive that it needed to sell enough licenses to support itself) so long as the season did not open before a certain date nor close later than a different date and the bag limit was no larger than some prescribed number with only so many daily bag limits making up a possession limit.

Some county exceptions within the statutes were as extraordinary as prohibiting discharging a firearm within 200 yards of a church; prohibiting hunting on Sunday; or allowing quail hunting only on Mondays, Wednesdays, and Fridays during the open season. As you can imagine, each of these regulations had virtually no impact on the wild quail populations.

As an example of how some things never change, consider the following anecdote. During 1926, the director of education, publicity, and research for the TGFOC was quoted in department news releases as saying that the people of Texas are natural conservationists. He then was quoted to have said that what was really needed in Texas were 10 game-propagation farms and public shooting grounds; and further, he urged the public to exercise their natural conservationist perspective to exterminate all crows, roadrunners, hawks, snakes, and other predators that affected quails. This was the perspective that guided both the legislature and the agency in regulating hunting and guiding wildlife management activities.

Informing the Public

Texas Game and Fish Magazine was first published in 1942, and the first quail article appeared in the magazine in 1945. There were three articles published that year. The bobwhite appeared on the first magazine cover in 1946. Between 1945 and 1959, the magazine published nearly half (44 articles, or 46 percent) of all the quail articles ever to appear in its pages. This was the first time the public had been exposed to quail biology and the best management perspective the profession had to offer. For example, the first article published on quails was titled "Why Texas Doesn't Pen-Raise Quail" (February 1945). The result of this and other articles in the magazine was the construction of the Tyler Quail Hatchery in 1956. Thanks to the operation of this facility, quail stocking with pen-reared birds continued as a TGFOC function until 1965, when the hatchery was switched from quail to pheasant production.

Contemporary Quail Regulations

The first quail-season statute that began to resemble current quail-season characteristics was adopted in 1959, when the season ran from December 1 through January 16 and the bag limit was 12 birds per day. However, the quail hunting seasons adopted by the TGFOC continued to vary across the state, but with bag limits that were fairly similar to one another. Very few changes occurred in quail statutes or regulations throughout the 1970s.

The most complex quail regulations ever promulgated by TPWC

started in 1979, whereby daily bag limits varied across the state—and overlaid the variable county opening and closing dates that already existed—depending on the results of the August quail population surveys conducted by TPWD. This meant that not only did the bag limit vary from county to county but each of these limits changed each year. This continued until 1984, when the TPWC adopted one quail season and bag limit for the whole state and with minor adjustments in these state-wide regulations. This framework remains in place today.

There is a reason that I wrote this brief history of Texas quail regulations: The next time you hear someone describing what they think is "the perfect season or bag limit" for quail management, be assured that whatever it is, it has already been tried somewhere in Texas for at least some period of time. You can also be assured that whatever it is, it did not work the first time. However, on the positive side, although it did not help, neither did it hurt the populations.

The lesson to be learned here is that it really comes down to how you want to expend your energy and political capital. Should you seek a quick fix through regulations that basically do not work, or should you attempt to repair a landscape so that quails can live in it again?

The Politics of Quail Regulations

As mentioned previously, most proposed changes to wildlife regulations or statutes that come from the public are aimed at forcing others to conform to a personal belief that is, sometimes for obvious reasons, not popular. Being effective, which I define as "actually succeeding in changing a regulation or statute," is problematic at best. Efforts are often confounded because the initiators of a rule change often ignore proven successful approaches in the name of expediency, political clout, or just plain inexperience. In this final section, I will describe two legislative efforts to influence quail management in Texas that failed and explain why they failed.

Forcing a Season

During 1983, there were still 13 of 254 counties in Texas that were not under the regulatory authority of TPWC and 72 counties that were only partially under its authority. Also, there were 30 counties in which TPWC rules were subject to county commissioners courts. The Wildlife Conservation Act of 1983 was adopted during the Sixty-eighth Texas Legislature. This act placed all wildlife resources in every county under full TPWC authority. After that date, seasons, bag limits, means, and methods were determined by TPWC. Although actions were often questioned during public comment, no real challenge to that authority was initiated.

During the Seventy-fourth Texas Legislature (1995), bills were introduced to suspend seasons and bag limits set by TPWC for quails for several counties. Not unlike the 1861 season closure on Galveston Island that was intended to allow quail numbers to recover, the actions were introduced to reduce the quail season from the Saturday nearest October 28 through the last Sunday in February (approximately 125 days) to December 1 through January 31 (approximately 62 days). The proposal also was designed to reduce the daily quail bag limit from

15 birds (maximum of 45 birds in possession) to 12 birds (maximum of 36 birds in possession). The position of TPWD was that the average quail hunter hunted less than six days in a season and took less than one-third of a daily bag limit during that season. The main effect these bills would have—from the TPWD point of view—was limited hunting opportunity. For example, hunters hunt a limited number of days because of other commitments. Therefore, providing a narrower window for fitting in a hunting trip could exclude some that would otherwise have hunted because they would not be free to do so when the season was open. Research also suggests that very few quail hunters hunt after late-winter quail mortality has occurred and, therefore, hunting quails during the current open season has no detectable biological effect on populations.

These bills were introduced on behalf of Cottle (S.B. 1246), Hardeman (S.B. 1247), Wilbarger (S.B. 1522), and Foard (S.B. 1523) counties. Following the bill filings, TPWD staff met with the bill author. During the meeting, the purpose and procedures of the regulatory process (i.e., rule making) of TPWC were explained. Basically, during the regulatory process, the public has more than ample opportunity to comment on proposed changes—as opposed to the very limited opportunity the public has to comment on legislative actions—and if the author or the constituent-sponsors of the bills wanted to see what the public thought about such a proposal, it needed to be part of the regulatory process, not as a local and uncontested action of the legislature. The author agreed, and the bills were never called to hearing.

As promised to the legislator, during the next regulatory cycle (January 1996), the seasons and bag limits that had been included in the bills noted earlier were proposed for the four counties. As expected, during each public hearing and throughout the public comment period, the proposals were widely criticized by landowners and hunters alike. The hunters and landowners who were going to be affected by these proposed changes apparently had no problem realizing that these proposals had nothing to do with quail biology or population dynamics and that someone was trying to force their hunting and wildlife management opinions on everybody else.

It did not require sophisticated statistical analysis of the comments to see that the public did not like the proposal. The seasons and bag limits in those counties remained unchanged because only those few constituents who had proposed the change to their legislator thought that the proposal was a good idea. The best thing to come out of this exercise was that everybody learned something from the process. We all have the scars to prove it.

For Lack of a Little Money

There are generally two recognized approaches to bringing about a change in behavior: using a carrot or using a stick. In Texas politics, it is common to use both. It is also common to fool someone into believing that the carrot is a stick. Another trick is to paint a stick to look like a carrot. The introduction of H.B. 1390 in the Seventy-fourth Texas Legislature (1995) is an example of this kind of subtlety. It is also a good example of how doing something is not always better than doing nothing.

During the late 1980s and early 1990s, there was a perception among some that TPWD was not paying quails the attention that the species deserved. Put another way, TPWD was not paying the species the attention that was desired by some. After all, there was only one quail season statewide, only one bag limit, and only a couple of wildlife management areas where there was good quail hunting; and the most current research from TPWD was almost 20 years old, based on a couple of 4-year studies on the Matador and Chaparral wildlife management areas in the early 1970s. Perhaps the most unforgivable thing was the fact that TPWD biologists kept saying things such as the following:

- "Quails are an r-selected species characterized by their high potential reproductive rate [which they are] and so promoting nesting success directly affects population size" [which is still true].
- "If there is no soil moisture, nesting success will usually be poor" [which is still true].
- "If you don't have quails, it is because you don't have the habitat to support them" [which is still true].
- "Coastal bermudagrass is not quail habitat" [which is still true].
- "You don't have quails because it didn't rain." [The TPWD biologists are good, but we are not good enough to fix this problem.]

The comeback was generally something such as, "But my habitat hasn't changed, and my quail have still gone away." Although it is hard to refute that kind of statement without studying the habitats involved, it is interesting to note that during the period that "my habitat hasn't changed," white-winged doves shifted their range and began nesting 500 miles north of what had been their northern-most historic range in Texas, but that is a story for another discussion.

Despite, or because of, the misconceptions about the status of quail work in Texas, a bill was introduced to address perceived deficiencies by securing funding through the creation of a quail stamp. This stamp would be required, in addition to a valid hunting license, for any hunter wanting to hunt quails in Texas. The major provisions of the bill included boiler-plate language from other stamp statutes with some significant differences unique to the quail stamp:

1. A "special quail stamp fund" would be set up for depositing funds from the sale of this stamp. Note: No other TPWD stamp has such a special fund except the nongame or endangered species conservation stamp.
2. Money in this account could be used only for "research, management, and protection of quail" and "acquisition, lease, and development of quail habitat." Note: Every other TPWD stamp that provides for acquisition of habitat applies to species that have been shown biologically to have a critical habitat that limits and/or endangers the species.
3. Money in this account would be exempt from appropriation requirements. Note: No other TPWD stamp has such an exemption.
4. Money in this account would be exempt from the state comptroller's authority to sweep appropriated funds into general revenue if they are not used during the budget year. Note: No other TPWD stamp has such a specific exemption.

5. The TPWC shall appoint an advisory committee that would recommend how best to spend the money. Note: No other TPWD stamp has such an advisory committee required by statute.
6. The TPWD would provide an annual itemized report to the advisory committee on how much money was available from stamp sales and what had been spent from those funds. Note: TPWD does not report to its advisory committees in this way.
7. Members of the advisory committee could draw travel expenses from the fund. Note: No other advisory committee has access to state funds for its own use.

Some of the problems of the bill are highlighted by the amendments added to the bill from the House floor during the second reading: (1) there would be no travel expenses for the advisory committee members, (2) no land would be leased or acquired for quail management, (3) funds could be used only for developing quail habitat on publicly owned land or on private land if the landowner gives permission and allows the public hunting access to the land, (4) everyone under 17 would be exempt from the stamp requirement, and (5) the stamp would be required only of hunters who came from outside the county within which they were hunting. In other words, landowners and their local friends did not need to buy a stamp.

Despite the floor amendments—which usually relieve legislative member concerns—the bill failed to pass the third reading and thus died without being heard by the Senate. Representatives saw the bill as a request for money when there was no plan for using the money and no clear explanation for why this money was needed. Actually, that was how quail hunters, landowners, and many TPWD biologists also saw this situation.

Regardless of who might be expected to pay fees, the legislature sees licenses and permit fees for what they are: taxes. The lesson learned here is that when you ask the legislature to tax its citizens, you need a good reason for the money and you need the people who are going to be taxed up there with you supporting your request.

The failure of this bill has had a continuing impact on all quail-related actions that have been brought before the legislature since the Seventy-fourth Session. That is, everything is now viewed as just another way to get around having been told no to the quail stamp. The quail-stamp failure means that new quail initiatives start out with several strikes against them. Also, by and large, all failed initiatives since the quail-stamp failure have suffered from the same deficiencies: no clear definition or explanation of a need, no clear or demonstrable path for filling the need, and no demonstration that the job cannot be done unless there is new money.

If you want to be successful in a legislative initiative—regardless of the issue—do your homework, prove that there is a concern or need that somebody other than the initiator shares, have a plan to address the concern or need that you can prove will work, know how much it will cost, show an available and untapped funding source—with support from those providing the funds—and then go for it. If you fail to complete any of those steps, the results will be problematic. A final cowboy adage is appropriate here: "The only place success comes before work is in the dictionary."

This just in May 30, 2005:

The Seventy-ninth Texas Legislature has just gone home, and one of the actions taken during the session was the adoption of H.B. 2940, a bill relating to stamps for migratory and upland game-bird hunting and providing a penalty. The adoption process of this bill is a perfect example of the principles presented at the end of this chapter.

1. Give a clear definition or explanation of a need: H.B. 2940 was justified during its public committee hearings by showing that bobwhite quail have been and are in decline in the southeastern United States, including parts of Texas. Concurrently, mourning dove surveys have shown a significant enough decline in bird numbers that serious investigation is warranted (i.e., is the population in decline or is the survey technique failing?). Also, two of the major Rio Grande turkey regions of Texas, which have been used to establish free-ranging, wild populations in at least six other states, have declined alarmingly.
2. Give a clear or demonstrable path for filling the need: Pilot studies using geographic information systems (GIS) and landscape ecology techniques have suggested that important scales within the habitat components used by each of these species have changed significantly in the past 20–30 years. Investigating the agricultural practices that brought on that change and modification or replacement of these practices show promise for each species—at least promising enough to warrant new effort.
3. Demonstrate that the job cannot be done unless there is new money: Budgets are stretched and priorities were strained to conduct the pilot studies. Expanding the studies or using the results to conduct management experiments cannot be accomplished as funded.
4. Prove that there is a concern or need that somebody other than the initiator shares: Witnesses that spoke in favor of H.B. 2940 were from the Texas Audubon Society; Texas Wildlife Association (a large private landowner organization); Quail Unlimited; Dove Sportsman Society; Ducks Unlimited, Inc.; Texas State Chapter of National Wild Turkey Federation; and the National Wild Turkey Federation. It also helped that these same organizations represent the people who would ultimately fund any initiatives that might result from the legislation.
5. Show an available and untapped funding source: Before H.B. 2940 was adopted, Texas hunters paid for hunting white-winged doves, turkeys, and waterfowl by purchasing special stamps in addition to their licenses. The only problem with these funds was that they could be used only for any work aimed at white-wing doves, turkeys, or waterfowl. As mentioned above, white-winged doves have spontaneously expanded the northern extent of their range in Texas by more than 500 miles in less than 30 years (i.e., doesn't look like they need much more help). Texas has stocked eastern wild turkeys in just about every place you can put them (this program was the primary justification for adopting the turkey stamp initially). Texas

can always spend money on waterfowl, but how much is enough? Re-prioritizing the use of funds already being taken from Texas hunters seemed appropriate. H.B. 2940 did away with each of these species-specific stamps and in their place created a stamp for "upland game birds" and one for "migratory game birds." This meant that TPWD gave up the white-winged dove stamp outright (i.e., reducing taxes) and was given the authority to use the new stamp fees where they would do the most good (i.e., new quail research, etc.).

That's called being effective.

Economic Aspects of Texas Quails

18

J. Richard Conner

Quail have moved along the spectrum towards European style hunting
and management, once abundant and available to every man, now rarer
and harder to obtain.
Mahoney (2002)

In past decades throughout most of the southern United States, all a
person needed to hunt quail was a shotgun, a dog, and access to habitat.
Moreover, due to the proliferation of small farmsteads and the subsistence nature of the agricultural enterprises, habitat was plentiful and
access quite freely granted by the farm operators.

During the first several decades of the twentieth century, quail hunting grew in popularity. Not only was it relatively easy to gain access
to quails in numbers adequate for hunting but also quail hunting was
unique in the southern United States in that it offered the opportunity to hunt with pointing dogs. Over time, the sport helped foster the
growth of kennels specializing in the various breeds of pointing dogs,
as well as the development and marketing of shotguns developed especially for quail hunting.

From an economic perspective, the proliferation of quail habitat and,
therefore, quail populations was an "externality" of the southern agricultural production industry (see chapter 1). An externality is an unintended, or accidental, impact on individuals or entities other than the
business responsible for creating the effect. Externalities may be either
positive, as in the case of quail habitat being created by the early-day
cultural practices of small-farm agricultural production, or negative, as
in the water pollution resulting from nutrient- and/or pesticide-laden
runoff from some crop-producing areas.

Over the past several decades small-farm, crop-oriented agricultural
production has largely disappeared in the South. Land use and land
cover have largely changed to improved pasture (coastal bermudagrass
[*Cyndon dactylon*], bahiagrass [*Paspalum notatum*], and fescue [*Festuca* spp.]), pine plantations, large-scale commercial farms, or urban-
suburban development. These land use–land cover changes have also
resulted in loss of habitat for quails.

As quail numbers declined throughout most of this area, quail hunters begin focusing on the southern Great Plains region as the last remaining area with habitat to support quail numbers sufficient for hunting. Unlike the southern United States, the southern Great Plains was
characterized by a drier climate with large-scale livestock ranching as
the dominant land use. Nonetheless, it could be argued that quail habitat was maintained as an externality of livestock grazing practices and
land management practices designed primarily to enhance forage production for livestock (e.g., brush control).

Another difference between the regions was that hunter access to
quail habitat in the Great Plains region was different from that in the
South. In the latter region, access to private agricultural lands could often be obtained by word-of-mouth permission from the farmer-owner.

Some public lands also were accessible for quail hunting. In Texas, quail hunting access was limited because landholdings tended to be much larger and located in sparsely populated areas. The more rigid adherence to, and enforcement of, trespass laws in the Great Plains, and especially Texas, also limited access.

By the last quarter of the twentieth century, the lore and legacy of quail hunting, which had developed over the first three-quarters of the century, had fostered a relatively large and enthusiastic following. In addition, as personal incomes had generally increased rapidly over the last half of the twentieth century, quail hunters were able and willing to spend ever-increasing sums in pursuit of their sport. These quail hunting enthusiasts formed the basis of the consumer or demand side of the current quail hunting economic equation.

This basis of demand for quail hunting was, and is, enhanced by the development and proliferation of the corporate client-employee entertainment package. The corporate objective is to provide entertainment opportunities for clients and/or employees, and quail hunting is but one of many outdoor recreation activities that the corporation is willing to pay for. Along with the growth in importance of the corporate entertainment consumer is the demand for consistency in the quality of the hunting experience and for associated amenities, such as high-quality food, lodging, and comfortable access to the hunting site (see chapter 20).

The Supply Side of Quail Hunting Economics

The supply side of the quail hunting economic equation is complex. There are several categories of goods and services that are associated with supplying the various types of quail hunting experiences sought by quail hunting consumers. Although there are probably many different ways of categorizing the various goods and services associated with supplying quail hunting opportunities, I like to think of them first in terms of the old-fashioned basics: land and quail habitat, shotguns, and dogs. Modern-day developments require the addition of two additional categories: services and amenities and, in some cases, pen-raised and released quails.

Land and Quail Habitat

All rural land can be put to a variety of potential uses in support of the goals and objectives of landowners. However, all rural land cannot support all of these potential uses with equal efficiency. From one location to another, land differs with respect to soils, topography, climate, current land cover (vegetation), and proximity to both natural and human-made support resources (e.g., ports, roads, markets, etc.). Because of these natural and location differences, each parcel or tract of rural land will be relatively more efficient in some land uses and relatively less efficient in others. In addition, as the associated human population undergoes cultural and institutional changes, the relative efficiency for any given tract or parcel of land can change between or among potential uses.

As mentioned in the previous section, quail habitat was historically supplied as an externality, or unintended by-product, of other land uses, namely, crop or livestock production. In recent decades, however, agri-

Box 18.1.

My Perspective

I was asked to write this chapter to try to promote a clearer understanding of the current and future impact that quails, or actually quail hunting, have and will have on the economy of Texas. I come to this task from three perspectives. First, and the obvious reason the editor asked for my contribution, I am a economist with interest and experience in analyzing the economic and managerial aspects of privately owned rangeland, livestock, and wildlife enterprises and the government policies and programs that, either intentionally or unintentionally, impinge on them. Over the past 20-plus years, most of my professional research and consulting work has been fostered by a desire to help private rangeland owners explore alternative ways to use their land to achieve their financial and/or lifestyle-related goals and objectives. Increasingly, this has required exploring alternative ways to exploit the potential of the rangeland as wildlife habitat, as well as or instead of a source of forage for livestock.

My second perspective is that of a lifelong quail hunter. I grew up on a small ranch in Central Texas (Coryell and Lampasas counties) and first hunted quail as a teenager with family and friends by simply walking up coveys. Although this was not as efficient as hunting with a bird dog, it was sufficiently productive to keep us entertained on fall and winter afternoons. By the time I was 16 or 17, I never missed an opportunity to go hunting with my uncle behind his dogs. After a couple of years of real bird hunting, I was hooked! Since then, as I progressed through young adulthood and middle age, I enhanced my enjoyment of quail hunting through purchasing better shotguns, hunting vests, and so on and by buying and training bird dogs. I then began joining with groups of friends and family to acquire access to more quail hunting opportunities through hunting leases. As I approach my golden years, I still own a couple of bird dogs and do not miss many quail hunting opportunities.

My final quail hunting economics perspective is that of private rangeland owner. My family and I still own the Central Texas ranch. During the past 10–12 years, our quail numbers have declined by 70–80 percent despite our conservative livestock stocking rates and generally improving range condition. Like many other landowners in Texas and across the southeastern United States, we are anxious to learn more about how to manage our land and related resources to encourage improvement in our quail population.

cultural production practices have changed drastically, and quail habitat is now much less likely to be a by-product of agricultural enterprises, especially crop production. This reduction in habitat, particularly in the southeastern states; the increased income of consumers, including hunters; the initiation and enforcement of strong antitrespass laws; and the development and growth of corporate entertainment expenditures combined to make the leasing of hunting rights a profitable enterprise for many Texas landowners with habitat to support wild game, especially quails and white-tailed deer (*Odocoileus virginianus*).

The key issue from the landowner perspective is the potential of a specific tract of land to provide habitat to support sufficient quantity and quality of wildlife to attract paying lease hunters, with habitat maintenance costs low enough to make the enterprise sufficiently efficient to compete with other potential land uses. It should also be noted that "sufficiently efficient" depends on each individual landowner's goals, preferences, and income level.

The differences in the potential of each tract of land to provide habitat and differences in landowner goals, preferences, and so on have resulted in the availability of a wide array of quail hunter habitat-access opportunities across Texas. These different types of hunting leases vary from those in which quail hunting is only an incidental, secondary benefit for the lessee to other types of leases in which quails are the primary and/or only game hunted.

Hunting Leases with Quails as the Secondary Game Species

The most common hunting lease in Texas is designed primarily to provide the lessee with access to land to hunt white-tailed deer. In many cases, these leases also have provisions that allow the lessee to hunt other species, such as quails, doves, and turkeys. This type of lease, which includes quails as the secondary game species available to the lessee, is quite common in areas where habitat and/or climatic conditions are such that quail populations are either relatively low or relatively inaccessible, thus making them relatively less attractive to hunters. Although the lessee's primary interest may be deer hunting, the addition of the opportunity to hunt other species, such as quails, is often attractive to hunters because it offers opportunity to access the land at times other than deer season and provides an opportunity to involve a wider array of friends and/or family in their outdoor life. Obviously, this type of lease usually involves one set of lessees obtaining access to a specified tract of land year-round, or at least for the duration of the hunting seasons for the specified game species. As will be discussed later, this type of lease can involve a variety of different amenities and services provided by the landowner and/or the landowner's agent, from almost none (most commonly) to near-resort accommodations.

Hunting Leases with Quails as the Coprimary Game Species

In areas where the habitat provided by a tract of land supports both quails and white-tailed deer in sufficient quantity and quality to be attractive to lease hunters with primary interest in each species, leases can be developed to accommodate the two groups of lessees. Two types of lease provisions are commonly used to provide for the two types of hunting interest. The first involves only one lease contract with the landowner, in which case the lessees include two groups each with a specific interest in hunting either deer or quails. In this type of arrangement the lessees have access year-round, or the season's duration, and decide among themselves how to allocate the times during which each type of hunting may be conducted on the different parts of the tract and what percentage of the lease cost is to be borne by each of the two groups.

A second type of lease involves the landowner leasing to two separate groups of lessees: one interested in deer and the other interested in quail hunting. In this case, the quail hunters usually have to forgo the early part of the hunting season because it coincides with deer hunting season. A variation on this theme involves the deer hunter group as the only lessees with the landowner, but then subleasing to a group of quail hunters who would be given exclusive access to the property after the deer hunting was concluded.

Hunting Leases with Quails as the Primary Game Species
In areas where the habitat provided by a tract of land supports quails in sufficient quantity to be attractive to lease hunters with primary interest in quails, landowners may prefer, for a number of reasons, to lease their land primarily, or exclusively, to quail hunters. The landowner may make this choice even if the land supports other game species in sufficient quantity and quality to attract lease hunters, because the lease to quail hunters may be more profitable or fit better with other resource management objectives. As was mentioned in conjunction with leases designed primarily for deer hunting, the lease focusing on quail hunting can involve a variety of different amenities and services provided by the landowner and/or the landowner's agents. These different services and amenities will be discussed later.

Resource Management and Quail Habitat
With the development and growth of the demand for lease hunting, landowners have, in most cases, experienced a change in the relative efficiency of land use from livestock production to lease hunting. Fortunately, this switch in relative efficiency required landowners to make only minor changes in their resource management practices in order for their livestock production enterprise to provide support to the lease-hunting endeavor. The increased economic attractiveness of lease hunting did, however, have a significant impact on vegetation manipulation practices. Primarily, the roles of woody shrubs and forbs were recognized as important in providing wildlife habitat. This recognition resulted in reduced emphasis on the traditional livestock-oriented goal of striving to maximize forage (grass) production. Although shrubs and forbs are important elements in quail habitat, maintaining shrubs in the proper growth form and maintaining both forbs and shrubs in the proper distribution with grasses across the landscape usually require specific management practices, such as roller-chopping, disking, and/ or prescribed burning.

Implementing these vegetation manipulation practices will cost from a few to many dollars per acre. Not all land would be subjected to such practices, and the practices would likely be applied to any given acre at three- to seven-year intervals; however, the use of the practices represents a real cost associated with maintaining or enhancing wildlife habitat. Other quail habitat maintenance and enhancement practices that land managers may use include water development, controlled or prescribed burning, grazing by livestock, and periodic supplemental feeding. Differences in soils, topography, climate, and landowner goals and preferences assure that none of these practices will be cost effective for maintaining and enhancing quail habitat on every tract of Texas rangeland. Also, for the same reasons, it is highly unlikely that they

Box 18.2.

Quail Habitat—Vegetation Manipulation Costs

Maintenance or enhancement of habitat for quail can entail a variety of vegetation manipulation practices. Costs associated with use of these practices vary widely from one location to the next and are impacted by a number of factors, including soil type; terrain; current land cover, especially density and growth form of trees and/or shrubs; and for mechanical practices, type and size of equipment used. The following list shows sample costs.

Practice	Typical cost ($/acre)
Prescribed fire	4–9
Roller-chopping	20–40
Disking (heavy)/seeding	50–100
Disking (light)/seeding	30–60
Chaining	18–36
Crawler-tractor operations (dozing, raking, stacking, etc.)	60–90 ($/hour)

would all be cost effective on any one tract. Obviously, these differences in the cost-effectiveness of quail habitat maintenance and enhancement practices have an impact on whether quails are the primary or secondary game species featured in the development of a lease-hunting enterprise for any given tract of land.

It should also be noted that despite use of the "best management practices" for maintenance or enhancement of quail habitat, quail populations normally fluctuate widely from year to year in response to droughts and floods, which are beyond the control of resource management. Thus, landowners, managers, and hunters must be willing and able to deal with the fact that despite the effort and expense of maintaining the habitat and obtaining the lease, there will be a great deal of year-to-year variation in the quality of hunting offered on any given tract of land.

Shotguns and Other Quail Hunting Equipment

Although a shotgun may be a basic requirement for quail hunting, current-day quail hunters commonly invest in a much larger set of supplies and equipment. First, the shotgun used will likely be one suited especially for quail hunting. Such guns are double-barreled or automatic, short, lightweight, and 20-gauge or smaller, with a cylinder and/or improved cylinder choke(s). Excluding equipment related to dog handling, the array of equipment and special clothing used by quail hunters commonly includes a hunting vest or shell and game-bag belt, hunting pants with a double-thick front-leg panel usually made of thorn-resistant nylon, and either snake-proof boots or snake-guard leggings for the lower legs. Additional equipment commonly includes bright orange vests and/or hats, shooting gloves, noise-dampening earplugs, and knives and/or scissors designed especially for dressing quail.

The demands of hunters for shotguns, ammunition, clothing, and

Figure 18.1.
Quail hunting equipment includes specialized protective clothing, trained pointing dogs, shotguns, and customized or modified vehicles for traveling in the field.
Photo by J. Richard Conner

other accessories have grown tremendously over the last two to three decades (figure 18.1). The extent and significance of this demand have helped foster the development and growth of sports equipment supermarkets, not just in Texas but across the nation.

Bird Dogs

One of the distinguishing aspects of quail hunting is the use of pointing dogs to locate and fix the birds prior to their being flushed for wing shooting (figure 18.2). Essentially all quails are hunted with the aid of pointing dogs, but probably more than half of the quail hunters in any given season do not own a bird dog. Thus, providing dogs is a service business essential to quail hunting.

The business of supplying pointing dogs for quail hunting starts with the dog-breeding kennels. Breeding kennels range from the very large, multiple-breed, high-volume commercial businesses to the individual dog owner–hunter who may raise only one or fewer litters per year and may or may not own the male used as sire. Kennels, and most indi-

Figure 18.2.
A bird dog pointing a covey of quail in brushy cover. Considerable training and expense are required to breed, raise, and train these working dogs.
Photo by Neta S. Conner

Box 18.3.

Bird-Dog Costs

Bird dogs are like cattle in that their purchase price can vary widely. Pointing-breed weaned puppies from reputable kennels or breeders usually sell in the $250–$550 range, depending on breed, reputation of the breeder or kennel, and the reputation and characteristics of the parent bloodlines. Prices for dogs of the same parentage or kennel, but with training and of hunting age, will commonly sell for two to five times the price of a weaned puppy. Dogs with exceptional credentials and/or proven hunting excellence in performance may fetch much higher prices.

vidual breeders, typically sell most of the dogs as weaned pups, leaving the training to the owner or the services of a professional trainer. Some kennels and breeders also do training and sell significant numbers of their dogs as trained young adults. It should also be noted that pointing dogs are used in hunting species other than quails (e.g., grouse, snipes, and woodcocks).

Bird-dog breeding and/or training is practiced as both a vocation and avocation. For those who enjoy dog training and handling more than bird hunting, there is a viable market for their talent and expertise through the provision of dog-training services for those more interested in the actual hunting sport. There are also opportunities to show the product of their breeding and training expertise in competitions such as dog shows and field trials. Thus, all pointing-breed dogs do not end up as pointers for hunters. Significant numbers are simply family pets, and others are used as breeding stock and show or field-trial entrants.

The use of dogs necessitates a variety of dog-support equipment and services. Regardless of whether a dog is owned by a kennel, a trainer, or an individual, it requires food, water, health care, and shelter. Thus, businesses that supply these goods and services flourish. Pet food companies and veterinarians are perhaps the largest such businesses, but suppliers of feeding, watering, and shelter/containment equipment and facilities are important industries partially supported by quail hunters. If the dogs are trained and used as hunters, then additional equipment is required (e.g., radio-controlled training collars, location beepers, whistles, dog boots, and kennel trailers or other portable dog boxes).

Services and Quail Hunting Amenities

Quail hunting today incorporates a large array of services and amenities that were not present in the early days of the sport. I briefly explore them in four categories: resource management, hunt booking and outfitting, lodging and associated services, and guiding and dog-handler services.

Resource Management
Wildlife biologists have a long history of consulting with landowners regarding the status of their wildlife habitat and populations. This type of service can be as simple as involving the consulting biologist in periodic

visits to a tract of land. The landowner is then provided with a report of changes or trends in habitat and wildlife populations and prescriptions for management practices (e.g., habitat manipulation or harvest quotas) that might enhance opportunities to attain landowner goals. A more encompassing arrangement involves the resource management company making the site visits, providing the trend assessment, and taking responsibility for implementing the prescribed management practices. In some cases, the resource management function is integrated into an outfitting or hunting operations company. In such cases, the resource management service company may enter into a lease agreement with the landowner under which specific resource management functions are made the responsibility of the lessee. An alternative arrangement involves the integrated resource management or operating company acting as an agent for the landowner. The company collects management and operating fees from the landowner or takes a commission from the hunting activity revenues generated.

Hunt Booking and Outfitting

The primary purpose of this segment of the quail hunting service industry is to connect the individual or groups of hunters with a specific habitat location and time for their hunt. In its simplest form a booking agent or company simply develops agreements with landowners, or hunting operation managers or outfitters, to advertise the availability of their hunting opportunities. They either refer hunter inquiries to the landowner/manager or actually contract directly with the hunter(s), acting as agent for the landowner/manager. The booking agent incurs expenses associated with advertising the hunting opportunities, usually via the Internet and perhaps through ads in hunting magazines or large metropolitan newspapers. The booking agency collects revenue through a booking or referral fee paid by the landowner/manager or a commission of a percentage of the fees collected from the hunter(s). In most cases, after a hunting event is booked, the booking agency simply provides the hunters with directions to the hunting site where they are to meet the landowner/manager, who conducts the hunt and coordinates other services such as lodging, guides, and so on. It should also be noted that booking agencies provide access to a variety of hunting and fishing opportunities in addition to quail hunting. Typically, deer, dove, and hog hunting opportunities are bigger sources of booking agency business than quail hunting.

"Outfitting" is a term used to describe the role of an agent or company providing a multitude of services that facilitate a complete and enjoyable experience for the hunter. For quail hunting in Texas, the outfitter (an individual or a company) usually obtains hunting rights to land via a lease or contract with the landowner. Customers are secured through advertising the hunting opportunities on the Internet and/or in other media or through the services of a booking agent. The outfitter may then arrange, if necessary, for transportation for the hunters from an airport to the hunting site. The outfitter is responsible for managing the hunt, including such services as providing a guide and dog handler and transportation to the actual hunting location(s); providing, or making arrangements for, food and lodging; and providing for other entertainment/amenities while the hunters are not actually in the field.

As mentioned in the section on resource management, in some cases the outfitter's relationship with the landowner will also make the outfitter responsible for specified resource management functions. As with the booking agencies, most outfitters offer a variety of hunting opportunities, many of which are available on the same properties that support quail hunting.

Lodging and Associated Services

Hunting lodges differ from other lease-hunting operations in several ways. In fact, they are operated more as resort hotels in that they aim to provide an array of entertainment and relaxation opportunities and offer a high level of high-quality service and comfortable facilities. Most lodges cater to short-term "packaged" hunting opportunities, the price of which reflects not only the quality of the hunt but also the quality of service and amenities. Typically, a landowner or a company that has a long-term lease with the landowner operates hunting lodges. The lodge-operating company may either lease or own the buildings and other facilities. In some cases, outfitters may also act as lodge operators.

A typical quail hunt package offered by a lodge is for a three-day hunt, including lodging of two nights in an air-conditioned room with private bath and six meals (often gourmet quality). A guide and dog handler with dogs and a kennel-platform truck escort the hunts. The guide/handler is either an employee of the lodge trained to operate the dogs and equipment or a contractor who brings his or her own dogs and equipment. The guide/handler usually also processes birds shot by the hunters. Typically, the hunters are in the field for three to four hours in the morning, return to the lodge for lunch and a rest, and hunt for another three hours in the afternoon. Lodges usually have a full bar, pool tables, big-screen TV, sauna and/or swimming pool, and courses for skeet/sporting clay shooting available for use by the hunters when they are not in the field.

Hunting lodges generally offer a variety of packages that include a range of hunting opportunities (e.g., doves, turkeys, deer, and wild hogs). Offering a diversity of hunting and other nature-based activity packages allows the lodge to be used by more guests over more months of the year, thus keeping its occupancy rate as high as possible. Nonetheless, lodges incur high overhead and operating costs. Overhead costs are high due to the large investments required to build, equip, and maintain the lodge and associated facilities and equipment. Operating costs are high due to the number of people required (e.g., a chef; other kitchen, dining room, and housekeeping assistants; groundskeepers; guides/dog handlers; and marketing, public relations, and management personnel and/or services). Other operating costs typically include utilities; veterinary services; pen-raised birds and bird feed; dogs and dog feed; and fuel, maintenance, and repairs for vehicles and equipment.

The high-cost, high-quality entertainment packages offered by lodges are primarily targeted to corporations entertaining clients. In fact, the growth in demand from this segment is largely the reason that hunting lodges have proliferated in Texas over the past two decades. For this same reason, lodges face serious slumps in demand for their services during economic downturns. Due to the periodic slumps in de-

Box 18.4.

Packaged Hunt Prices

Packaged quail hunts offered by lodges in South Texas generally range $700–$1,700 per hunter-day. These prices usually include food and lodging, plus dogs, guide, bird processing, and transportation while hunting. In addition, the price may also include ammunition, open bar, sauna, swimming, skeet and/or sporting clays, and transportation to and from a local airport.

mand, plus their relatively high overhead and operating costs, hunting lodges are financially vulnerable and thus suffer relatively high closure and ownership turnover rates.

Guiding and Dog-Handler Services

Quail hunting requires the use of pointing dogs. In the early days, the quail hunter most often owned a couple of bird dogs that may also have doubled as family pets. Keeping two or more bird dogs, however, is expensive and time-consuming, especially for present-day, highly mobile urban residents. Over the past couple of decades, many quail hunting lessees, outfitters, and lodge operators have increasingly found that engaging the services of a hunting guide/dog handler is more efficient than owning and handling their own dogs.

Persons operating a guide and dog-handler service normally provide the dogs and a truck that doubles as a hunter transport and observation platform and a portable dog kennel. The trucks are typically one ton, with four doors and a custom cargo bed that serves as a portable kennel and observation platform for hunters to use while in the field (figure 18.3). A typical day of hunting begins with the

Figure 18.3.
Customized truck used for quail hunting. These trucks, of which there are scores of design variants, are used for travel and observation during the hunt and as portable kennels to transport dogs, water, and other hunting equipment. Courtesy Michael Rader

Box 18.5.

Hunting Guides and Dog Handlers

Hunting guides and dog handlers typically work on contract with a lodge, outfitter, or hunter lessees. Typical prices are $450–$600 per day, for which the guide/dog handler furnishes the dogs, transportation while on the hunt, and bird processing/packaging. In addition to the per-day price, hunters commonly pay tips. Besides the costs of owning, training, and maintaining the necessary dogs, guides/dog handlers must own, maintain, and provide fuel for the kennel/hunter transport truck they use. Trucks typically cost $30,000–$40,000, and the kennel/hunter transport bed is an additional $10,000–$15,000. These trucks usually last several years and are typically expected to provide service for 150,000–225,000 miles.

guide picking up the hunting party of two to four persons shortly after breakfast. The guide transports the hunters and dogs to the assigned hunting tract for the morning hunt. Once on site, the guide/dog handler will put down one to two pointing dogs, which will scout the area around the truck as it proceeds slowly across the landscape. When the dogs locate and point a covey, the guide stops the truck, fetches a retriever dog from the truck kennel, and accompanies two of the hunters to the location of the point. After the birds are flushed, hunters shoot, downed birds are retrieved, and the procedure is repeated. The handler will normally rotate the pointers about every 20–40 minutes so that the dogs remain fresh. The morning hunt will typically last three to four hours and require eight pointers. The guide then returns the hunters to the lodge or other point of departure for lunch and rest. In the afternoon the process will be repeated with the hunt ending about sundown. The guide is usually responsible for processing the birds and presenting them to the hunters in freezer-ready packages shortly after the hunt concludes.

To be able to offer this kind of service, the guide/dog handler must maintain a kennel with approximately 10–12 pointing dogs for each truck that is operated. Typically, only 8 pointers are on the truck at any given time, but reserves are required in case of injury. Many guide/dog handlers also breed and train some or all of the dogs they use. In such cases, the number of dogs being maintained at any one time will likely be even larger because some of the dogs will not be sufficiently mature and trained to use in the field with paying customers.

Pen-Raised, Released Quails

Hatchery-produced quails and other game birds have long been a primary source for shooting preserves, restaurants, and bird-dog trainers. As the popularity of hunting lodges and their packaged hunts grew over the past two decades, the demand for quail hunts began to exceed the capacity of even well-managed land resources to provide populations that could support the number of hunts being demanded over the entire season. This was especially true when quail populations were experiencing a periodic bust, or down year. Although traditional quail hunters would be likely to understand year-to-year fluctuations of quail populations and be willing to adjust their hunting pressure accordingly, corporate entertainment customers wanted a consistently good experience for their guests every time they went out. To accommodate this increased demand for consistently good hunting experiences, the hunting lodges and outfitters began supplementing their wild birds with pen-raised, released birds (see chapter 19).

Hatcheries that cater to the demand for quails that will provide a reasonable substitute for wild birds produce and market what is commonly referred to as "flight-conditioned" birds. To produce flight-conditioned quails, the hatchery first hatches eggs and then grows out the chicks in much the same manner as a chicken hatchery. Flight-conditioned quail production, however, differs from chicken production in the growing phase in two important ways. First, after the quail chicks are hatched and throughout their growth to maturity and ultimate release into the wild, care is taken to keep them isolated as much

Box 18.6.

Pen-Raised, Released Quails

Hatcheries typically get between $2.70 and $3.50 per bird for flight-conditioned, pen-raised quails. The price varies with the time of year when the order is placed, the delivery date, and other factors. Hunting lodges that market large numbers of packaged quail hunts typically supplement their available wild birds with several thousand pen-raised birds each year.

as possible from seeing and hearing humans and their pets. This is to ensure that they maintain a natural fear of humans in their immediate vicinity so that they will flush and fly away as a wild bird does when humans get too close. The second difference is that as they reach the stage of development and growth where flight is possible, the quail chicks are enclosed in large, screened-in flyway pens and periodically frightened into flight so that they get sufficient exercise to develop their flight capability. Nevertheless, flight-conditioned, pen-raised quails still suffer swift and devastating mortality to all sorts of predators.

Generally, pen-raised birds are released in the designated hunting area about one hour prior to the hunters going to the field. The number released at one time usually is equal to the number that the hunters are expected to shoot the same day, because their survival rate in the wild is very poor. Because they are artificially hatched and pen reared, they have little or no foraging or predator-avoidance instincts.

The purchase of flight-conditioned quails represents a significant expense to the hunting lodges and outfitters that use them. In addition to the expense of purchasing the birds, they must provide facilities for holding, feeding, and watering the birds on the property prior to their release and labor to care for and take the birds to the designated release sites.

Summary

Clearly, quail hunting is an economically important sport and industry in Texas. With the advent and growth of lease hunting, many landowners were able to maintain the economic viability of their ranches by making lease hunting and the habitat management that supports it a primary focus, equal to or exceeding traditional livestock production. To the extent that quail hunting supports the lease-hunting enterprise, it shares in the support of large numbers of rural Texans maintaining their land ownership and livelihoods.

The service aspects of the quail hunting industry have experienced phenomenal growth, especially over the last two decades. For the most part, this rapid growth in demand for services has been fueled by the increased popularity of corporate entertainment. The continued urbanization and increases in income of the Texas population—including quail hunters—have also contributed to the trend. The growth of services associated with quail hunting has provided new employment opportunities in both the rural quail hunting areas and urban settings. It

Box 18.7.

Problems with Estimating Exact Economic Impact of Quails

It should be obvious by now that the economic impact of quail hunting in Texas is indeed very large. However, it is probably also clear that the exact impact of quail hunting alone on the economy of the state, a region, or a county is almost impossible to quantify. In almost every aspect of the demand and supply side of the quail hunting market, the available data for revenue and expenditures are aggregated over several types of hunting, other sports, and/ or large geographic areas. For example, information on expenditures for hunting licenses is not sufficiently detailed to determine whether the licensee hunts quails or not. Similarly, expenditures on other items such as guns, ammunition, and transportation are not reported in sufficient detail to ascertain the proportion spent on quail hunting versus dove hunting or other activities.

Given the data-aggregation problem when dealing with secondary data, about the only approach to estimating quail hunter expenditures is to interview quail hunters and ask them to estimate the amount that they spend in a specific time period on goods and services related to quail hunting. In addition to being expensive to conduct, such studies often fall short of producing accurate estimates of total economic impact for a specific area per time period. Typical shortcomings in such studies arise because of the difficulty in obtaining a sample of survey respondents that is truly representative of the entire population of quail hunters using the specified area and time frame. For example, such studies often omit, or underrepresent, hunters who use a hunting lease developed primarily for deer but that supports limited quail habitat that may be exploited on a limited basis after the deer hunting season has ended. Another difficulty in obtaining information on the economic impact for a specific region is in segregating the geographic location of the hunter expenditures. For example, other than paying the cost of the lease itself, hunters typically spend a relatively small proportion of their hunting-related expenditures in the county where the lease is located. That is, costs associated with dogs, veterinary fees, dog and hunter food, sporting equipment and ammunition, and a large portion of transportation are, in large part, incurred in the geographic area of the hunter's home, not in the vicinity of the lease.

should be noted, however, that like employment in most service industries, especially those associated with the provision of entertainment, the employment is seasonal, often less than full-time even in the peak of demand, and quite susceptible to significant reductions in demand when the general economy experiences a downturn.

Managing and Releasing
Pen-Raised Bobwhites

19

Fidel Hernández and Robert M. Perez

> Despite the wretched history of bobwhite releases,
> interest in artificial stocking remains high.
> Guthery (2000)

The release of pen-raised northern bobwhites (*Colinus virginianus*) has 327
been a controversial aspect of quail management for more than six decades. Initial discussions about using pen-raised quail in wildlife management focused on the effectiveness of the practice to augment or restore depleted wild populations of bobwhites (Clark 1942; Buechner
1950). When research indicated that stocking of pen-raised bobwhites
to increase wild bobwhite populations was ineffective (Baumgartner
1944b; Pough 1948; Roseberry, Ellsworth, and Klimstra 1987; DeVos
and Speake 1995), releasing pen-raised bobwhites continued to be used
but for a different purpose, namely, to supplement commercial hunting
opportunities. Thus, discussions have now started to focus on the potential negative impacts that releases of pen-raised quail could have on
wild populations, such as disease and parasite transmission and changes
in habitat use, social structure, genetic fitness, and survival rates of wild
bobwhites (Brennan 1991a).

We will not address the ethical decision of whether or not pen-raised
bobwhites should be released. Rather, our objectives are to summarize
the existing knowledge concerning pen-raised bobwhites and synthesize this information in the broader context of northern bobwhite
conservation.

History of Releasing Pen-Raised Bobwhites

The practice of releasing pen-raised bobwhites initially was used as a
public relations tool instead of a game-restoration practice based upon
reliable information (Clark 1942; figures 19.1, 19.2, 19.3). Releasing pen-

Figure 19.1.
Pen-raised bobwhites begin their lives
after hatching in an incubator.
Photo by Mario Gonzalez,
courtesy TPWD

Figure 19.2.
Many pen-raised quail operations
use automated systems to provide
food and water to the birds.
Photo by Mario Gonzalez,
courtesy TPWD

Figure 19.3.
A flight pen ready for occupancy by
pen-raised bobwhites. Although flight
pens provide opportunities for quail
movement and exercise, losses to
avian predators are still swift and
high even a short time after the
birds are released in the wild.
Photo by Mario Gonzalez,
courtesy TPWD

raised bobwhites was used as a means of demonstrating to the public that the bobwhite decline was being addressed (Backs 1982). The pressure to restock wild populations via such releases apparently arose from hunters, who argued that annual restocking by pen-raised bobwhites was warranted due to excessive hunting pressure in certain areas, as well as in naturally unproductive land (Pough 1948). Thus, game commissions advocated these releases in order to maintain good relations between game administrators and the public (Bennett 1945). Einarsen (1945:254) stated, "Many annual game programs involving the annual stocking of artificially-reared birds have been carried on to please sportsmen. While this procedure usually results in the waste of most of the game birds involved, it has merit from the game department point of view of satisfying public opinion." However, the merit of such a justification soon would succumb to the high costs and low success of restocking programs.

The release of pen-raised bobwhites resulted in the expenditure of large sums of money from resource agency budgets. A survey of 35 states indicated that releasing pen-raised game composed an average (*n* = 19 states) of about 39 percent ($726,500) of the states' total game-restoration budget. Thirty-two states expended a total of $1,270,745 for the propagation or purchase of pen-raised game (Clark 1942). In our current economic climate, this sum translates into tens of millions of dollars. Nestler and Nelson (1942) reported that state game departments raised or purchased about 362,000 bobwhites in 1940. The cost of each pen-raised bobwhite was $0.77 at time of liberation (Hart and Mitchell 1941). Although this represented an expenditure of about $278,740, the low annual survival of these bobwhites increased the cost when reported in terms of harvested bobwhites. At an average annual rate of band recovery of 1.26 percent (Hanson 1947), the cost of a pen-raised bobwhite would increase from $0.70 upon release to $55.56/harvested bobwhite (Buechner 1950). Further, harvest of pen-raised bobwhites represented only a fraction (less than 1 percent) of the total bobwhite harvest (Barnes 1947). Thus, although it was probably economical to raise a bobwhite, it was not financially practical for state game departments to maintain restocking programs (Buechner 1950). Further concerns arose regarding the utility and effectiveness of restocking programs.

Pough (1948) presented economic, biological, and psychological arguments against restocking. In addition to the economic concerns aforementioned, he warned about potential genetic pollution of wild bobwhites, threat of disease transmission, and impacts on predation rates. An important concern was the public perception that restocking was the solution to the bobwhite decline and that as long as a restocking program was maintained, there was no need or incentive to attempt any other solution.

Buechner (1950) conducted a survey of 17 states, showing that about 82 percent of the states were in agreement that restocking via pen-raised bobwhites was an ineffective means of increasing wild bobwhite populations or adding to the annual harvest of bobwhites. The Wildlife Society concurred that no permanent increase in game resources could be achieved by artificial propagation and that funds, often diverted from useful programs, were better spent in habitat improvement (Anonymous 1948). Steen (1948) attacked the justification of restocking as a public relations tool, arguing that critical time and resources were lost by applying the wrong remedy to the decline; habitat improvement was the solution for the future. Clark (1942:181) also supported this philosophy by stating, "Restocking of depleted areas is commonly considered to be justified in the name of game restoration. For purposes of discussion, I submit the theory that such restocking may be classed as game restoration only when the causes of depletion have been corrected, or are being corrected, and when such restocking does not tend to defeat efforts to correct the causes of depletion."

Survival and Movements

Pen-raised bobwhites generally experience low survival rates across the United States (Buechner 1950), but the mechanisms responsible for this low survival are poorly understood. One hypothesis is that pen-raised quail chicks do not learn predator-avoidance behavior from adult quail (figure 19.4). Although survival over the winter, based on censuses and trapping, has been reported as high as 45 percent in Oklahoma (Baumgartner 1944b) and 58 percent in Florida (Frye 1942), most studies have reported much lower survival estimates for pen-raised

Figure 19.4.
Wild quail chicks may learn predator-
avoidance behavior from adult birds.
Pen-raised quail chicks lack this, and
apparently many other, elements of
inherited wildness.
Photo by Glenn Mills, courtesy TPWD

bobwhites. In Oklahoma, 83,000 bobwhites were released from 1940 to 1942, with only 1.1 percent recovered over the three-year period (Anonymous 1942). Gerstell (1938) reported only 0.61 percent band returns from 12,420 bobwhites released in Pennsylvania. In South Carolina, Webb and Nelson (1972) released 1,915 pen-raised bobwhites prior to the hunting season, and another 1,134 during the hunting season in 1969. They reported that of the total 3,049 quail released, only 35.0 percent were harvested during that season, of which 56.6 percent were recovered during the first two weeks following liberation.

Radiotelemetry studies also support the low survival rates reported using band returns. DeVos and Speake (1995) reported that pen-raised bobwhites experienced low survival (0.18 percent) 22 weeks postrelease, pooling data gathered over two years in Alabama. Oakley et al. (2002) also reported low survival of pen-raised bobwhites for areas in Maryland with and without buffer strips (0.11 and 0.00 percent, respectively). In Texas, Perez, Wilson, and Gruen (2002) reported that pen-raised bobwhites reached 50 percent mortality 9 days after liberation and 100 percent mortality by 12 weeks postrelease.

Two basic reasons have been proposed to explain why pen-raised bobwhites do not survive for an extended period of time: rearing technique and genetic deficiencies. An early evaluation of pen-raising techniques showed that most efforts concentrated on increasing the efficiency of the raising process (Anonymous 1945b). Thus, most breeders attempted to decrease cost, time, and labor, thereby maximizing profit but possibly decreasing bobwhite survivability after liberation (Anonymous 1945a). A resulting perception was that long-term breeding of captive bobwhites led to loss of vigor and reduced viability. Some biologists speculated that differences in performance between pen-raised and wild bobwhites were due to genetic differences (Nestler and Studholme 1945) and that infusing genes from wild bobwhites would improve survival (i.e., F_1 offspring [wild $\times$ pen-raised cross]). However, research did not support this speculation. In Illinois, Roseberry, Ellsworth, and Klimstra (1987) reported similar band-recovery rates 90 days postrelease between pen-raised (0.08 percent) and F_1 bobwhites (0.10 percent). Perez, Wilson, and Gruen (2002) also reported that survival to

12 weeks postrelease was similar between pen-raised (0.00 percent) and F_1 bobwhites (0.05 percent) in Texas.

Recently, manufacturers of commercially produced release systems (e.g., Anchor Covey Release System® [ACRS], manufactured by Quality Wildlife Services, Inc., Waynesboro, Georgia) claim that survival of pen-raised bobwhites is improved by using their product. However, little data exist to support this claim. Fies, Fischer, and Steffen (2000) compared survival of pen-raised, F_1, and relocated wild bobwhites using ACRS and a habitat-release method.

The ARCS consists of a metal frame camouflaged with a cordura nylon cover and contains a feeder, water, and callback bobwhite. The habitat-release method involved releasing bobwhites at sites with woody cover adjacent to planted food plots. Fie, Fischer, and Steffen (2000) reported no difference in mean days of survival between the ARCS and habitat-release methods for either pen-raised (2.3 vs. 3.0 days, respectively) or F_1 bobwhites (3.2 vs. 6.1 days, respectively). However, relocated wild bobwhites experienced higher mean days of survival with ARCS (50.3 days) than with the habitat-release method (26.3 days). The researchers could not explain the higher survival for relocated bobwhites, in particular because they found no evidence (e.g., droppings, feathers, reduced amounts of feed) that relocated bobwhites used ARCS. They concluded that ARCS did not enhance survival of pen-raised or F_1 bobwhites.

Pen-raised bobwhites generally do not exhibit long-distance movements (Gerstell 1938; Webb and Nelson 1972). Brill (1941) reported that they ($n = 252$) moved an average 3.6 kilometers (2.2 miles). Baumgartner (1944b) reported average movements of 280 meters (306 yards) for pen-raised bobwhites within the first six weeks of liberation. Roseberry, Ellsworth, and Klimstra (1987) reported that 75 percent of F_1 bobwhites ($n = 83$) and 64 percent of pen-raised bobwhites ($n = 86$) were captured within 250 meters (273 yards) of their release site. Average movements from release site to capture site was 124 and 157 meters (135 and 172 yards), respectively. During their second year of study, released birds were even more sedentary. More than 60 percent of F_1 ($n = 83$) captures were within 50 meters (54.5 yards) of the release site compared to 50 percent for pen-raised bobwhites ($n = 83$). Longer movements have been reported for pen-raised bobwhites. Clark (1942) reported that at least 1 individual of 1,064 released bobwhites moved 12.8 kilometers (7.9 miles). Bennitt (1946) also reported that of 366 released bobwhites, 2 of 3 bands reported were farther away than 11.3 kilometers (7.0 miles).

Flight Behavior of Pen-Raised Bobwhites

Several studies have attempted to describe the behavior of pen-raised bobwhites upon liberation (Frye 1942; Dollar 1969; Roseberry, Ellsworth, and Klimstra 1987; Perez, Wilson, and Gruen 2002). One of the most obvious differences between the two groups is flight. Frye qualitatively described the flight of pen-raised bobwhites as lacking the speed, power, dexterity, and endurance observed in wild bobwhites. He further observed that released bobwhites frequently made sudden swerves during flight in the wild, as if expecting to encounter the wire mesh of their earlier flight pens (figure 19.3). Perez, Wilson, and Gruen provided empirical data regarding differences in flight behavior of pen-raised and wild bobwhites. They reported that mean flight speeds were greater for wild and wild-transplant bobwhites (45.2 and 46.5 kilometers/hour, or 27.1 and 27.9 miles/hour, respectively) than for pen-raised and F_1 bobwhites (29.9 and 31.4 kilometers/hour, or 17.9 and 18.8 miles/hour, respectively). Further, the mean distances flown were greater for wild and wild-transplant bobwhites (60.3 and 70.4 meters, or 65.7 and 76.7 yards, respectively) than for pen-raised and F_1 bobwhites (27.8 and 31.8 meters, or 30.3 and 34.6 yards, respectively). There were no differences in flight speed or distance flown between wild and wild-transplant bobwhites or pen-raised and F_1 bobwhites.

Perez, Wilson, and Gruen (2002) also noted that direction of departure after release differed between their categories of released bobwhites. Wild-resident, wild-transplant, and F_1 bobwhites were nonrandomly distributed in direction of departure, whereas pen-raised bobwhites were randomly distributed. They measured vector length (R), which is a measure of concentration of departure direction and ranges from 0 (data are too dispersed to describe a mean direction) to 1.0 (data are all concentrated in the same direction). Resident bobwhites had the greatest vector length (R = 0.741) when compared to wild-transplant (R = 0.534), F_1 (R = 0.360), and pen-raised bobwhites (R = 0.374).

Intermixing between Pen-Raised and Wild Bobwhites
Roseberry, Ellsworth, and Klimstra (1987) documented the degree of intermixing between pen-raised, F_1, wild-transplant, and wild bobwhites during 1984–86. Generally, wild transplants showed the least fidelity to released mates, whereas F_1 bobwhites were the least associative with wild residents. DeVos and Speake (1995) reported that in Alabama, only 4 of 15 wild coveys were not mixed with pen-raised bobwhites. They noted that pen-raised and wild coveys were either established during the first month or were not established at all. Perez, Wilson, and Gruen (2002) found that 15 F_1 ($n = 50$) and 1 pen-raised bobwhite ($n = 50$) integrated into wild coveys. This recent research contrasts with the early belief that wild bobwhites did not allow pen-raised bobwhites to join their coveys (Mueller 1984; Landers and Mueller 1986).

There is considerable interest in the integration of pen-raised bobwhites with wild bobwhites and how this association with wild bobwhites affects their survival, flight, and behavior. Subjective observations have been reported, but no empirical data have been published. Frye (1942) noted that pen-raised bobwhites appeared to adopt some of the instincts of wild bobwhites, although not to the degree observed in wild bobwhites. He further observed that flight endurance appeared to improve over time as the pen-raised bobwhites were exposed to the elements of predation, weather, and other environmental conditions. He speculated that this adaptive response was a result of their association with wild bobwhites. DeVos and Speake (1995) noted that pen-raised bobwhites surviving past one month seemed to fly farther and stronger than birds immediately after release. By one to two months, most pen-raised bobwhites mimicked wild behavior and were difficult to distinguish from wild bobwhites. In contrast, Roseberry, Ellsworth, and Klimstra (1987) made qualitative observations that pen-raised bobwhites were relatively tame upon release and even 5–10 weeks postrelease were often reluctant to fly when approached. Although they became less tame and their flight capabilities improved noticeably, they could still be readily distinguished from wild bobwhites based on behavior. Perez, Wilson, and Gruen (2002) noted, but provided no empirical data, that pen-raised bobwhites that became integrated into wild coveys seemed to survive longer than those in groups containing no wild birds.

Genetics of Pen-Raised Bobwhites

To our knowledge, only one published article exists concerning the genetic differences between pen-raised and wild bobwhites. Ellsworth, Roseberry, and Klimstra (1988) compared the genetic composition of wild, pen-raised, F_1 (wild × pen-raised), and F_2 (F_1 × F_1) bobwhites. Wild bobwhites exhibited 21.1 percent polymorphism compared to 10.5 percent, 15.8 percent, and 10.5 percent for pen-raised, F_1, and F_2 bobwhites, respectively. Thus, crossing wild bobwhites with pen-raised bobwhites produced F_1 offspring with a genetic constitution more similar to that of wild bobwhites, whereas crossing F_1 bobwhites produced F_2 offspring that were almost as genetically distant from wild bobwhites as were pen-raised bobwhites. The mean number of alleles/ polymorphic locus was similar between wild bobwhites (2.3) and pen-raised bobwhites (2.5), as was mean heterozygosity (0.050 and 0.048, respectively). Although variability that was present at certain loci in wild bobwhites was fixed in pen-raised bobwhites, wild bobwhites were not consistently more variable across all loci.

Genetic deficiencies in pen-raised bobwhites have been proposed to cause their observed low survival (Backs 1982). However, Ellsworth, Roseberry, and Klimstra (1988) reported that genetic variability in pen-raised bobwhites was not markedly deficient. Although heterozygosity of pen-raised bobwhites was slightly lower than that of wild bobwhites, it was considerably higher than levels observed in wild bobwhites (0.027) in New Mexico (Gutiérrez, Zink, and Yang 1983). Further, the inbreeding coefficients of pen-raised bobwhites were not supportive of high inbreeding levels (Ellsworth, Roseberry, and Klimstra 1988). Therefore, they hypothesized that early environmental conditions may be a more crucial factor determining survivability of pen-raised bobwhites than genetically programmed instincts dealing with behavior. They expressed caution that additional differences between the two groups could exist because many proteins were not detectable with the methods they employed.

Nedbal et al. (1997) revealed geographic subdivision between South Texas bobwhites (*C. v. texanus*) and East Texas bobwhites (*C. v. mexicanus*). They used restriction-site variation of mitochondrial DNA to reveal geographic subdivision between the species. They suggested that wild bobwhites might consist of several genetically distinct stocks throughout their range. However, the true extent of genetic differences between pen-raised and wild bobwhites remains largely unknown.

Effects of Pen-Raised Bobwhites on Wild Populations

Although augmenting wild bobwhites with pen-raised bobwhites is considered ineffective with respect to elevating and stabilizing their populations, the practice remains in use, but not at the state agency level or for restocking purposes. Commercial enterprises now release pen-raised bobwhites for recreational purposes, such as hunting and dog field trials. Many hunting enterprises supplement hunting opportunities of wild bobwhites with releases of pen-raised quail, especially when hunting opportunities of wild bobwhites diminish because of drought or other factors. As a result, concern exists regarding the potential negative impacts that these releases may have on wild populations, such as disease transmission (Brennan 1991a).

Some biologists believe that there is little concern regarding impacts on wild bobwhite populations because pen-raised bobwhites often experience low survival. The main idea behind this belief is that the released birds die so quickly that they have little or no opportunity to impact wild bobwhites. Others counter, arguing that although pen-raised bobwhite survival may be low, wildlife enterprises release more than 2,000 pen-raised bobwhites throughout the hunting season, and their continued presence for a prolonged period of time may be impacting wild populations. To our knowledge, no published study has investigated the realized impacts of pen-raised bobwhites on wild populations. Realized impacts may be reduced survival due to disease or parasite transmission and increased predator abundance, as well as habitat displacement.

DeVos and Speake (1995) compared survival between wild bobwhites on control sites and release sites. Survival on control sites (0.41 percent) to 22 weeks was similar to that on release sites (0.36 percent). Regarding habitat displacement, Bennitt (1946) reported that unstocked areas carried a higher population of wild bobwhites and the population on the stocked area was progressively smaller each year in relation to the unstocked area. In Texas, Davis (1970) also reported a decrease in the population of wild bobwhites associated with pen-raised bobwhite releases. Although these declines might indicate that pen-raised bobwhites affect home ranges of wild bobwhites, DeVos and Speake (1995) speculated that introduced bobwhites did not appear to displace wild bobwhites from established covey ranges, because wild bobwhites were found less than 50 meters (55 yards) from pen-raised coveys shortly after release.

Management Considerations for Releasing Pen-Raised Bobwhites

Pen-raised bobwhites provide an unlimited source of birds for harvest. They are especially useful as supplements to wild bobwhites in commercial hunting operations in Texas. However, it is important to make the distinction between shooting-preserve management techniques and population management techniques. Doing well in one arena does not necessarily reflect positive achievement in the other. Well-established techniques for shooting-preserve management are essentially aimed at getting the highest return rate of released birds and a quality hunting experience (Kozicky and Madson 1966; Kozicky 1987). As with any commercial enterprise, the highest possible return on an investment is desirable.

Maple and Silvy (1988) estimated the cost of a pen-reared bird in hand 14 days postrelease to be about $18.65 (20.9 percent return) as compared to $6.50 (55.4 percent return) for birds released just prior to the hunt. These results are similar to Buechner's (1950) findings of $0.68–$3.00

($3.04–$13.42, when adjusted for inflation to 1985). Preseason releases (one to two months prior to the hunting season) are even more expensive considering that harvest rates for banded birds range from 10 to 30 percent (DeVos and Speake 1995). Managers pass these costs on to the hunter; therefore, as long as there is a demand, pen-raised released birds likely will continue to be released for recreational purposes.

Although released game birds are often intended to offset heavy hunting pressure, the release and subsequent harvest of large numbers of pen-reared birds can be detrimental to wild game-bird populations if the manager's attention is diverted from habitat management (Robertson and Rosenburg 1988). Additionally, there is some evidence from partridge shooting preserves in Italy to suggest that the harvest of resident birds may be increased to a level that could lead to the loss of the wild population (Potts 1986). Another potential detriment to using pen-raised birds is a postrelease increase in predator abundance. This occurrence has been mentioned only incidentally, with no supporting data. Some researchers question whether an influx of predators in response to released birds increases depredation rates of resident wild bobwhites (Pough 1948; DeVos and Speake 1995; Perez 1996).

Summary

The failure of pen-reared birds to survive and reproduce in the wild is well documented; as such, they are not a viable option for restoring wild quail populations. Some interrelated causes of failure examined to date include inability to escape depredation, sedentary behavior, and slower flight speed compared to that of wild bobwhites. However, there are knowledge gaps in regard to the interaction and possible negative influence released birds have on wild bobwhite populations. Areas requiring attention and further research include increased harvest of wild birds (in fragmented and intact landscapes), disease and parasite transmission, increased predator abundance, habitat displacement, and integration of pen-reared birds into wild coveys.

Pen-reared bobwhites have long been used in attempts to bolster wild populations and as quarry in shooting preserves. More recently, they have been used as supplements to commercial hunting operations in response to reduced availability of wild birds as a result of annual variation and long-term population declines. In Texas alone the mean number of licenses sold for commercial game-bird breeders (more than 1,000 birds) and hobby breeders (less than 1,000 birds) from 1983 to 2001 is 89 (minimum 59; maximum 116) and 858 (minimum 527; maximum 1,152), respectively. Shooting-preserve licenses sold from 1989 to 2001 average 357 per year (minimum 320; maximum 384). Thus, pen-reared bobwhites remain a commercially viable enterprise in Texas that will most likely persist and expand in the future.

20 Operating a South Texas Quail Hunting Camp

Ronnie Howard

> Unless the habitat is maintained, there will be
> little wildlife left to hunt or to see.
> Leopold (1978)

The San Tomas Hunting Camp was established on the Encino Division of King Ranch during the summer of 1979. It was formed as a corporate hunting facility for Blocker Energy Corporation in Houston, Texas. John Blocker was a farsighted man with close ties to the Wildlife Science Department at Texas A&M University. He made the decision to build a world-class facility to entertain corporate and family guests in the heart of South Texas quail country. He also made a decision to hire a professional biologist to run the operation, rather than the standard hunting guide–dog trainer that was normally chosen for such a position. During 1979, I knew of only two individuals (Bill Kiel with King Ranch and myself) who were privately employed in the field of wildlife management in South Texas.

In the beginning, San Tomas consisted of 4,000 hectares (10,000 acres) of prime quail habitat. The hunting success during our first year dictated that we expand the operation to 9,700 hectares (24,000 acres) to accommodate the number of hunters we wanted to entertain. The lease was further increased to 14,500 hectares (36,000 acres) in 1986 and has remained at 13,770 hectares (34,000 acres) since 1988.

John Blocker set a precedent for hunting camps throughout South Texas. He provided the resources needed to manage the camp and to develop professional guidelines required to run an intensive wild quail hunting operation that also sustained native northern bobwhites (*Colinus virginianus*). My responsibilities were to run the operation from an entertainment standpoint but also to develop the habitat and hunting management plans that would allow us to offer quality hunts in a sustainable manner.

In 1982, Blocker added partners at the hunting camp, one of whom purchased the camp in 1983. This partner brought in Freeport McMoRan (FMI) as a partner in 1983, and together they purchased the camp in 1985. It has operated as a corporate hunting facility continuously from 1979 until today. James Moffett, chairman of the board of FMI, and Richard Adkerson, CEO of FMI, have supported and expanded this operation with the same professional attitude that Blocker used to establish it. Our hunts have always emphasized a quality experience for a few guests (normal groups are six to eight guests) rather than entertain a maximum number of people at a time. San Tomas now employs four full-time people, three student interns (to gain practical field experience for their associates degree in commercial wildlife management from Southeastern Illinois College), and four seasonal employees. In addition, the camp is host to two to three graduate students from the Caesar Kleberg Wildlife Management Institute who have been conducting quail-related research at San Tomas since 1998.

During the 26 years that San Tomas has been in operation, we have learned many lessons about the camp, hunting, and habitat management strategies that are required to sustain wild quail and quality hunting under a private land lease agreement. The purpose of this chapter is to share the history and experience of these lessons.

Personnel and Facilities

The hunting-camp staff can make or break a hunting lease. San Tomas has existed for more than 26 years under three different companies. When one company hit hard times and had to give up the camp, there was always someone from another company who had experienced San Tomas as a guest and wanted to step in and have his or her company represented as an owner of the camp. Through the years, one common link has held the camp together. We run a very personable, very relaxed camp. Guests are treated with respect, but they are also treated as friends. I have always encouraged camp staff to interact with guests. Over the years, we have developed a friendship bond with every host that comes to the camp and brings guests. After 26 years many of these guests are as familiar with our operation as the hosts who bring them.

Camp employees wear shirts with name tags so that guests get to know them quickly and personally, and the staff is encouraged to learn the names of each guest. Everyone that comes to the camp has one of two first names: Mr. or Mrs. Many of the camp employees are younger men and women, and I insist that they use proper manners when referring to the guests.

The goal of any well-run hunting camp is to allow the guests to enjoy hunting and develop a personal relationship with their host. Since 1979, I have always tried to show our guests that we enjoyed entertaining them and that we were willing to go an extra mile to make their hunt whatever they wanted it to be—within the limits of the law. Imparting this attitude to your employees is one of the most important things a hunting-camp manager can do.

We never mix two hosts with different groups of people at the camp at the same time. When a host arrives with 10 guests or 2, they have the entire camp and pasture at their disposal. There are three full-time guides (myself included), three student interns, two seasonal guides, one full-time chef, and two seasonal employees that guide guests or work on keeping up the facilities. With this number of employees, I have the ability to run three quail trucks and two big-game trucks, clean and repair the lodge, prepare the meals, and still send someone to town for the inevitable emergency purchase. Having the correct number of staff members who have the right attitude about entertainment is paramount to a well-run operation. Trying to operate a quality operation without enough employees to provide personalized service will result in restricting the flexibility your guests have in their hunting choices. Allowing hosts to guide hunts and play a role in running the camp is a disaster in the making. Nearly everyone I know who does this runs into problems with equipment, gets lost, has poor hunts, or never eats on time. It defeats the purpose of trying to provide the guests a quality experience. Camp management inevitably ends up apologizing for the numerous errors that occurred.

I have a large pool of replacement guides from the student intern program. Guides and camp employees come from all over Texas and other states. These people are very dedicated to San Tomas and work hard for the four months of hunting season. They have the freedom to be involved in all aspects of the camp. Employees are allowed to harvest does, selected management bucks, feral hogs (*Sus scrofa*), and nilgai (*Boselaphus tragocamelus*) with my approval. I encourage them to get out in the pasture and learn their way around. The chef, maid, and lodge maintenance man know their way around the pastures almost as well as the guides do. This costs extra gasoline but makes these employees 100 percent more valuable in the event of an emergency or when unexpected circumstances occur. These same employees are knowledgeable about our game management program and impart a sense of total team effort to the guests.

Facilities at hunting camps in South Texas vary from lavish Spanish-style haciendas to rebuilt ranch houses to the log cabin design we use at San Tomas. Normally, a camp consists of a central lodge where meals and entertainment of guests are conducted (figure 20.1), one or more guesthouses, employee quarters, dog kennels, laundry room, storage facilities for food and other necessary camp supplies, game-cleaning facilities (figure 20.2), walk-in cooler, and equipment shed. A commercial-grade kitchen is essential for meal preparation (figure 20.3).

The size of the camp facilities depends on the number of people that are entertained at the camp at one time. We have found that one bedroom for two guests allows the hunters to get to know each other better and creates an atmosphere of camaraderie. We have a smaller guesthouse with two bedrooms for couples and world-class snorers.

Quail hunting trucks are customized crew cab trucks capable of carrying five guests, a driver, dog handler, and up to 10 dogs. Normally, two to three guests at a time hunt from a vehicle. Each truck is self-contained, carrying shotgun shells, cold drinks, dog water, and gun scabbards. I maintain five quail trucks but use only three at a time. This allows us to have a full-time backup vehicle in the event one of the primary trucks needs repair. The fifth quail truck serves as another

Figure 20.1.
The hunting lodge is the center of social activities at San Tomas.
Photo by Michael Rader

Figure 20.2.
Keeping the game-cleaning area clean
and organized is essential to good
hunting-camp management.
Photo by Michael Rader

Figure 20.3.
A commercial-grade kitchen is essential for producing meals for camp
guests, guides, and other staff.
Photo by Michael Rader

backup when one truck is in town for major repairs. We customize the
dog boxes and other truck accessories at the camp to carry the number
of dogs and amount of equipment needed for a day hunt.

Dog kennels are necessary if dogs are kept at the camp all year. Our
kennels consist of about 35 runs and a puppy pen. Each run has two
dogs (a male and a female to prevent fighting) and ample space for the
dog to run around. The kennels have a tin roof to provide shade during
hot weather and a suspended barrel for the dogs to get in when we wash
the kennels. In cold weather, we block the wind using tarps, add hay to
the barrels, and increase the dogs' feed to compensate for heat loss. Kennels have a concrete floor and are washed twice daily. All dogs are fed
once a day, and their eating habits are monitored. A dog that does not
eat well is considered sick and evaluated by a veterinarian.

Game cleaning areas must be kept sanitary and covered from the
weather. Our game-processing facility consists of a skinning rack with

scales for weighing big game and three large sinks for cleaning birds. This is the area where we record all the data (age, weight, crop contents) collected from the harvested quail. Game birds are cleaned, packaged, and sent home with guests.

Although we cannot control the weather to create a good quail hatch each year, it is fundamental that we control the quality and efficiency of the camp and the hunt. Having a tire blow out in the pasture is inevitable—being prepared to fix it rapidly and get right back to the hunt is something we can control. The guests judge the camp and my staff by our ability to react to and control situations such as this.

The motto we live by at San Tomas is "Don't be penny wise and pound foolish." Although we do not endeavor to re-create the lush environment of a vacation retreat, we do spend money to keep up the basic needs of an efficient camp. Most camps follow this motto regarding their equipment, but some operations try to save money with a bare-bones staff. The result is that the camp employees are so overworked that they cannot provide the attention to detail that is essential to a quality operation.

Safety

The primary responsibility a manager carries at any hunting facility is to maintain a safe environment for guests and guides. Safety rules are discussed in letters to all the hosts before the season begins. All guests receive a list of basic safety rules at San Tomas when they receive their letter of invitation to the camp.

When the guests arrive at the camp, they are assigned quarters and then sent to the lodge to get their hunting license and have a safety talk that covers everything from safety at the skeet range to safety in the field. Rule number one is "Do not mix guns with alcohol." No alcohol is allowed in the field or on the skeet range.

Rule number two is "When you drive away from this camp, my guides are the boss." Guides are empowered with keeping hunts in accordance with camp safety rules. I have always emphasized to the guides that even though they must be courteous to guests, they must also control the hunt. This is best handled by a quick review of safety once they get to the field. Guides do not need to go over each rule in the pasture. Merely asking the guests if they have been informed reminds them that the rules will be applied now that the hunt is ready to start. Anytime they find it necessary to reiterate safety rules to guests, they do so by emphasizing that these are the rules I have instructed them to follow. If there is an exception to the rule, it must come from me. In 26 years of running the camp, I have never had a guest question these safety rules. The heads of the companies that hunt at San Tomas realize that all the fun and good times we have had would be for naught if we were to have a serious accident. My guides and I speak with their authority.

Preseason Preparation

Each year, *before* the season begins, I send a letter to our guests that discusses the status of our quail population and any necessity to emphasize conservative harvest measures. I have found it is too late—and very disappointing—to inform guests of a poor bird crop once they arrive at the camp. If the host informs the guests of a poor situation ahead of time, they will generally be happy to comply with any measures necessary to follow the game management program. An ill-informed host—or a nonhunting host—that has not been to the camp in several years may encourage people to hunt quail on a year when we should take only the most avid quail hunters to the pasture. Rather than correct the hosts at the camp in front of guests, it is always better to have them receive a letter explaining the situation ahead of time. This way, the host and the camp management all preach the same lesson—be conservative in your harvest this year. Most of my hosts will call the week before their hunt to get a more current update of the game situation.

Establishing rapport with hosts and guests is paramount to any good game management or camp management plan. The purpose of any hunting camp is to provide the guests with a good time, regardless of the quality of the game population. The quality of the camp, the professionalism of the staff, the upkeep of the facilities, and the effort expended by the guides reflect the attitude of the companies that are part of San Tomas Hunting Camp. The more you can educate hosts and hunters about the game management plan, the more willing they will be to follow the management program. Our guests regularly watch us clean their game, take harvest information concerning quail and deer, and ask questions about why we hunt a particular way. All of my guides and camp personnel are briefed about commonly asked questions and are encouraged to get to know the guests as friends. Since the camp is primarily about allowing the company hosts to establish a relationship with their guests, guides and camp personnel have to learn when they should participate in conversations with the guests and when they should leave the socializing to the hosts.

Hunting Intensity

Bobwhite quail populations in South Texas are extremely variable due to the sporadic nature of rainfall in this region. To accommodate the 30 three-day hunts (from 200 to 240 guests a season) we have annually (November–February), we found that we needed to maintain at least 13,700 hectares (34,000 acres) to handle our hunting pressure. During the last 20 years, we have averaged about 220 outings (one outing = one quail truck with two to three guests shooting for at least three hours) a year. The quail hunting intensity has varied annually from a maximum of 340 outings during the 1984–85 season to a scant 76 outings during the 1998–99 season. Harvest has averaged about 3,150 birds (4.0 hectares/bird, or about 10 acres/bird) over the 20-year period with a range of 7,712 (1983–84) to 471 birds (1998–99).

Hunting intensity varies according to the annual quail population. Total harvest is a reflection of, and is regulated by, factors such as (1) the amount and timing of nesting-season rainfall and our observation of the success of the hatch; (2) our preseason perception of the quail population as determined by general observation while driving the pastures in the fall, and by conditioning and training our bird dogs in September and October; (3) our level of success during November and December; (4) the condition of the habitat in our pastures going into the winter months; (5) a working knowledge of past harvests under similar rainfall, pasture, and population situations; and (6) an early evaluation of the juvenile-to-adult (J:A) ratio, which is a fundamental indicator of the previous breeding season productivity.

In every case, the total quail harvest does not reflect an absolute number of birds that could be harvested. Rather, it represents a number we feel we can safely harvest without jeopardizing the breeding population of birds for the next spring. Outings can be conducted in very brushy areas where hunting success is extremely low or in areas where we know there are plenty of birds and can expect a high harvest. Annually, we entertain a certain percentage of hunters (maybe 40 percent) that come to San Tomas for one reason—to hunt wild quail. The other hunters either enjoy quail and big game or are new hunters that have not yet picked a favorite quarry. Once these hunters are recognized, they are the ones that help swing harvest to a high level or a low one. Essentially the same number of hunters will come to the camp every year, so we control harvest by encouraging big-game harvest; running fewer trucks (two trucks with three hunters each, rather than three trucks with two hunters each); providing alternative hunts using released bobwhites, chukar (*Alectoris chukar*), or pheasants (*Phasianus* sp.) one of the four times the hunters go to the field; and by shortening one afternoon hunt to 1.5 hours by conducting a flighted mallard shoot during the early part of the evening.

Thirty hunts provide 120 sessions (mornings and evening sessions) to shoot birds. Using these methods of harvest control, we can often reduce shooting pressure by two trucks each hunt by encouraging big-game harvest (60 outings annually) or by one to two trucks each hunt by consolidating six hunters on two trucks (30–60 outings annually). And we can reduce the pasture time after duck shooting to one outing rather than two (30 outings annually). Reducing the shooting pressure by 90 to 150 outings annually conserves quail for the breeding season and allows serious quail hunters to continue hunting quail without harming the population.

Keeping Hunting Records

When I began managing San Tomas in 1979, I had just completed six years in the Range and Wildlife Departments at Texas A&M University. One of the foremost lessons preached to us was to keep records on everything we did. Having never seen a corporate quail camp and having little to no precedent before me, I established a set of records based on the most obvious parameters of a quail population: numbers harvested by pasture, age, and sex and types of foods in the crops of birds.

That database was slowly expanded as experience taught me which other factors should be monitored. We soon realized that each "hunt" was not equal. Sometimes we went out for three to four hours, sometimes for only one to two hours. On some days we ran one truck and on other days, three. Therefore, we developed the concept of a quail "outing" as a measure of our effort to harvest birds. Our standard of shooting pressure is now measured by the "outing," which is one truck running for at least three full hours with two or more guests.

Early-season evaluation of the J:A ratio can show you how good your hatch was during the previous summer. Examination of approximately the first 300 birds harvested will usually reveal an accurate picture of the hatch. An average J:A ratio at San Tomas will be around 2–2.5:1. A J:A ratio of 4:1 or more suggests a banner season for reproduction. However, an evaluation of the pasture and its ability to hold the birds through the season must be taken into account to determine if a heavier than normal harvest can be applied. The highest J : A ratio we have seen was 5.1 : 1 in 1983.

Since 1984, we have kept the following records on our quail harvest:

1. Date and pasture hunted
2. Number of hours on an outing
3. Number of hunters on an outing
4. Number of coveys found on an outing
5. Number of quail harvested on an outing
6. The primary and secondary foods in the crop of each quail harvested
7. Age of each bird (juvenile or adult)
8. Sex of each bird
9. Weight of each bird
10. Wing molt patterns on the first 200 juveniles harvested each season

The data in numbers 6–9 are recorded on the first 100 birds per week if it is a productive quail season. Pasture management records have been generally kept on disking, burning, and half-cutting and creation of artificial escape cover.

Research

San Tomas opened its doors to wildlife research projects conducted by the Caesar Kleberg Wildlife Research Institute in 1999. Our camp has provided housing, vehicles, fuel, meals for researchers, tractor time, and personnel assistance to research projects dealing with habitat manipulation, nesting, and radiotelemetry of bobwhites, as well as avian predator projects and wild turkey research.

Assisting with research projects such as these allows us to gain first-hand knowledge of our wildlife populations. Such information is much more valuable than the insights we would gain from otherwise general observations. Information from research is used to determine what we are doing right or wrong in the pastures. It also helps us understand current or potential shortcomings in our management program.

Factors Influencing Quail Populations and Harvest

Volumes have been written about the factors—both environmental and human-caused—that affect quail populations, factors that have been adequately covered in other sections of this book. Populations will rise and fall annually, even on the best-managed quail lands. Mother Nature and her timing and generosity of rainfall will annually determine the density of a quail population. This, unfortunately, is beyond the reasonable control of humans. However, we can control many other factors that determine the volatility of our quail populations and, most important, how low they go. The factors that we can control are (1) plant succession, (2) foods, (3) grazing management, (4) access to the pasture, and (5) harvest. Although some of these factors are interdependent, how we deal with each one at San Tomas will be addressed separately.

Plant Succession

The most basic principles of quail management center around the ability of the manager to control plant succession and to recognize the optimum succession level of the plant community for quail. San Tomas is blessed with sandy soils that promote water infiltration and allow annual seed-producing plants (both forbs and grasses) to thrive (figure 20.4). Therefore, even a moderate to high range condition will still produce a large number of annual forbs. In loam and clay soils, moderate to high range condition often is composed only of grasses that do little to feed a quail. Forb seeds are the basic foods for quail and also provide the primary ingredient necessary for a thriving insect population. The most beneficial annual plants at San Tomas from a seed-producing standpoint are crotons (*Croton* spp.), sunflower (*Helianthus* spp.), partridge pea (*Cassia* spp.), cow-pen daisy (*Verbesina encelioides*), and ragweed (*Ambrosia* spp.) (figure 20.5). A host of others provide seeds for quail, but year in and year out, these are the most important five. Important annual seed-producing grasses include thin-seed paspalum (*Paspalum setaceum*) and signalgrass (*Brachiaria decumbens*). Although grasses

Figure 20.4.
Croton and sunflowers, two important food-producing forbs for quails, are maintained by soil disturbance from disking or hoof action of cattle.
Photo by Michael Rader

Figure 20.5.
A lush stand of western ragweed provides insects for bobwhite broods during summer and seeds during winter.
Photo by Michael Rader

contribute diversity to quail diets, they make up only a small percentage of the overall biomass consumed by quail. Management for annual grasses is essentially the same as management for forbs.

As range condition declines, a greater percentage of the plant community is composed of annual plants, many of which are attractive to insects. This can be an optimal condition for bobwhites as long as the pastures are managed to contain some areas with adequate grass and woody cover to provide nesting and escape cover for the birds during each month of the year. At no point during the year should grasses be grazed shorter than about half their annual growth.

Higher plant succession provides more perennial grasses that afford the best nesting and escape cover for quail. Predominant perennial grasses are little bluestem (*Schizachyrium scoparium*), tall dropseed (*Sporabolus cryptandrus*), brownseed paspalum (*P. plicatulum*), switchgrass (*Panicum virgatum*), bristlegrasses (*Setaria* spp.), yellow indiangrass (*Sorghastrum nutans*), and sacahuista (*Nolina texana*). Perennial grasses are much more drought hardy than annual grasses and will often be the only cover left standing when the inevitable drought hits the area. Droughts and below-average rainfall are the norm for this area. Therefore, in order to keep the pastures from becoming barren during drought, it is essential that every pasture contain a good mix of perennial grasses. A grazing management plan that does not leave adequate standing perennial grass for nesting cover after missing rainfall in two consecutive growing seasons is not sufficiently flexible for providing sustainable quail habitat and populations.

The other extremely important role played by perennial grasses is as holding cover for quail. Trucks, dogs, and hunters have ardently pursued bobwhites at San Tomas for more than 20 years. The quail quickly learn to run from these dangers until they find a grassy area with good cover in which they feel secure. If they do not encounter or have access to heavy grass cover (generally perennial grasses), they will either run away from the hunters and dogs or flush wild before the hunters get close enough to get a shot. Having good grass cover that encourages birds to hold tight and then flush all at once offers the experience that makes quail hunting the great sport it is.

We control herbaceous plant succession by disking in the winter and early spring and by burning in late February and early March. Disked strips provide strips of primary plant succession (mostly crotons, sunflowers, and cow-pen daisies) that yield abundant food and bugging areas for chicks. As long as there is abundant perennial grass cover over most of the pasture, disked strips can occupy 10 percent or more of the area. These strips should be strategically placed to provide food in every part of the pasture. Keeping the strips narrow (3–7 meters, or 10–20 feet, wide) allows the birds to feed here but always be steps away from the protective cover of perennial grasses.

Differences in soil types and the depth of the sand will also influence plant succession. Dense sands with clay layers just below the surface provide more nutrition for the plant community, and grazing animals will seek these areas first. High–clay pan areas usually support a lower level of plant succession than deeper sands. Looking at plant communities within the same pasture that are rich in perennial grasses versus communities supporting a large percentage of annuals will show the manager where these differences in soil type occur. We concentrate disking in the deeper soils to promote greater food production and make these areas more attractive to quail. Livestock tend to graze these high–clay pan areas first, so it is sometimes necessary to allow these areas to be grazed short before the cattle have sufficiently thinned the perennial grasses. The key to grazing a diverse soil pasture is to graze hard enough to promote forb growth everywhere and still allow these high–clay pan areas to recover sufficiently for quail to be secure in them during the winter.

I suggest disking different strips in consecutive years to increase diversity of the forb community. Second-year disk strips tend to provide a better cover of annual grasses, partridge pea, and ragweed. Strips that have been disked in the current year tend to provide more croton, sunflower, and cow-pen daisy.

Disking enough pasture to impact the food source on a large pasture 1,200–2,000 hectares (3,000–5,000 acres) in area can be excessively costly during years when large grass accumulations occur. In this case, burning can rid the area of grass buildup and allow annual plants to germinate. Cool-season burns (January–early March) tend to encourage forb production without hurting perennial grasses. Given conservative grazing practices, perennial grasses should be sufficiently recovered by the next winter to provide winter cover (holding cover) for bobwhites. We normally burn 20–30 percent of a pasture annually (as rainfall and grazing management allow). Burns are generally 135–180 meters (150–200 yards) wide with 270–360 meters (300–400 yards) between burns. A covey whose home range centered on the burn need only move 68–90 meters (75–100 yards) to be out of the burn. When possible, we will burn another 135–180 meters (150–200 yards) off the old fire lanes the next year. Although rainfall and grazing seldom allow a strict burning schedule, the entire pasture would be burned about every four to five years under this plan. Eventually we will have a mosaic of plant succession that includes heavy grass next to the current winter burn, which is adjacent to a two- and three-year-old burned area. Two- and three-year-old burns often provide optimum nesting and winter habitat for birds, whereas current-year burns will provide better feeding and bugging areas for chicks.

Foods

Although foods are generally not considered a factor that limits quail production in the sandy areas of South Texas, we keep track of what quail eat during the hunting season because it tends to enhance the hunting program. Quail foods have been studied at San Tomas for more than 26 years during the winter (November–February) and during two summers. We attempt to record the contents (primary and secondary food) of at least 100 birds a week during the hunting season. Forb seeds, as a whole, compose 60–70 percent of a quail's winter diet annually. During 18 of 20 seasons the most common quail food was croton. Although we have at least six species of croton and their seeds are distinguishable, I lump all six species into the general category of croton. Crotons normally provide 40–60 percent of all quail-food observations made during the season. During November and December they are often found in 90 percent of the crops observed. During 1989 and again in 1998, other plants provided more food than croton. During 1989, we

had such a devastating drought in the summer and fall that a very limited amount of forb seeds was produced. Green leaf material from forbs
and corn and milo (provided by us) composed the bulk of feed for that
winter. During 1998, following a devastating drought all summer and
most of the fall (this left most of our pastures in a state of bare ground
during the fall), October rains brought a flush of erect dayflower (*Com-
melina erecta*) (normally little more than 2–5 percent of the food material). That year dayflower far exceeded croton in importance.

Forb seeds in general order of importance for quail are croton, partridge pea, sunflower, cow-pen daisy, ragweed, erect dayflower, and a
host of others, including milk pea (*Galactia* spp.), dollarweed (*Hydro-
cotyle* spp.), ground cherry (*Physalis* spp.), Mexican clover (*Euptoitea*
spp.), *Sesbania* spp., *Neptunia* spp., little-leaf sensitive briar (*Mimosa*
spp.), scarlet pea (*Indigofera miniata*), southern corydalis (*Corydalis mi-
crantha*), trailing wildbean (*Strophostyles helvula*), bluebonnet (*Lupinus
texensis*), and morning glory (*Ipomoea* spp). Quail to some degree will
use virtually any seed-producing plant. Partridge pea and sesbania may
be abundant in the early season but are seldom used in quantity until
other seeds start to disappear from the diet (January and February).

Grass seeds normally make up about 3–5 percent of the total food
supply for quail. Bristlegrasses and brown-seed paspalum are the only
perennial grasses that make any real contribution to feeding quail. The
most important grasses for quail food are thin-seed paspalum, *Sarita
dicanthelium*, signalgrass, and to a lesser extent, round-seed panicum
(*Panicum laeve*).

Insects and green leaf material (from fresh, growing green weeds)
are equally as important as forb seeds in that they provide the bulk of
insect production. Insects are essential for chick survival for about the
first month of their life. Winter diets show that insects can make up
10–20 percent of the overall diet. Cold weather, especially a freeze, can
reduce the proportion of insects in quail diets to nearly zero during
January and February. Green leaf material from cool-season forbs is a
staple diet of quail during most years (starting sometime in January)
and can make up 20–40 percent of their diet during January and February. I have heard many people raise the question of green weeds being
a starvation diet for late-season quail. My observation is that quail will
switch to this food source in late winter, regardless of the availability of
seed. This may be explained by a need for increased protein in their diet
as they prepare for the upcoming nesting season.

As long as we observe a variety (at least four to six species of different plant seeds) of quail foods in the crops during November and December, we are not terribly concerned that food will become limiting.
Studying the difference in food selection and variety of seed in crops
confirms the success or failure of management within a pasture. For
instance, a burned area within a pasture may produce an abundance
of croton, thin-seed paspalum, and legumes such as dollarweed and
trailing wildbean late in the season (January and February) where these
plants have disappeared in other pastures early in the year.

Grazing Management

A basic of any quail habitat management plan is the provision of perennial grasses through the winter and into the springtime for nesting
sites. Although quail seem to prefer the previous year's growth from

perennial grasses (at San Tomas the most popular seem to be bluestems, paspalums, dropseeds, and sacahuista), they often attempt nesting in whatever cover is available (grassburr [*Cenchrus* spp.], threeawn (*Aristida purpurea*), and annual cool-season forbs) as long as it will initially cover the nest. During years when cover was sparse, but climatic conditions were good, we saw birds use all kinds of cover for nesting. Cactus (*Opuntia* spp.) was used several years when it was essentially the only cover offered. Other years, we saw great movements of birds (1.6 kilometers, or 1 mile or more) to take advantage of sacahuista for nesting. Several times, nests from different birds were placed under the same sacahuista clump, suggesting a definite lack of good nesting locations. Following winters when pastures were heavily grazed, birds often nested under forbs such as Indian blanket (*Gaillardia pulchella*) and stinging nettle (*Urtica* spp). At the onset of egg laying, nests were well concealed. Before incubation was completed, plants would die and fall, leaving the nest visible from yards away.

Grazing management and practices such as burning must be planned to leave adequate nesting cover through the winter. Birds left unharvested in February are often entering the most stressful period of the year. Late-winter hawk migrations take a huge toll on birds as they feed in pastures that are stripped of their herbaceous cover. This predation can remove a huge number of the birds that our conservative hunting management practices left as a breeding population and further reduce your quail numbers to a skeleton population by nesting season.

Although I have heard arguments both ways, I prefer a mid-level to high range condition to a low range condition. Low range condition consists of a higher percentage of annual forbs and grasses that tend to produce more food for quail. High range condition guarantees that the pasture contains a larger percentage of deep-rooted, drought-tolerant grasses that provide year-round nesting and escape cover for birds. The sandy soils that exist at San Tomas nearly always ensure that some seed-producing annual plants are present. Having a solid stand of perennial grass with few forbs and a great deal of litter for birds to move through is seldom as detrimental to quail as having an overgrazed overexposed area. The primary difference is that there are management practices such as disking and burning that will add food to a heavy grass area. During times of drought, the perennial grasses will still provide adequate nesting cover and escape cover for birds to survive. An overgrazed, barren area will lose what little cover it has after a few months of drought. Deferment does not help once this situation has occurred. The only solution for this situation after deferment from grazing is rainfall, then time.

A pasture that is kept in low range condition may be very good quail habitat during an exceptional rainfall year because of the abundance of feed. However, given a short, three- to four-month drought, the plants in these pastures can die, fall over, and leave quail with no nesting cover, no escape cover, and no food. When rains finally do occur, the result can be a pasture that is either covered in grassburr or solid sunflower (depending on the timing of the rain). Pastures covered in grassburr or sunflower are almost impossible to hunt, even when you boot the dogs, until very late in the season (when the burrs fall and soften and the sunflower stalks start falling).

Grassburr seeds can be fatal to a hunting dog if they are ingested or stuck in the dog's sinus (where they can cause infection). Both grassburr seeds and rough sunflower stalks can easily damage a dog's eyes. Pastures in poor range condition generally provide poor grass cover for at least part of the year, leading to inadequate nesting cover or exposure to predators.

Grazing management, whether continuous or rotational, should be geared toward reducing ground cover to its lowest point in February to encourage germination of annual plants but should never allow the pasture to lose adequate ground cover for nesting and protection. Pastures should be either grazed very lightly or deferred following the winter, until spring rains occur. If rains do not occur in March and April, the pastures should be deferred from even light grazing pressure.

Harvest

Of all the tough quail management lessons I have learned at San Tomas, the hardest has been figuring out how to control the harvest. As previously stated, harvest is not always a barometer of how many birds can be shot in a 30-hunt season. Using various methods of harvest control, we can entertain the same number of people each year and yet voluntarily decrease harvest by as much as 50 percent. Over the years, we have learned how to appeal to the hunters to get them to take a conservative approach to harvest in years when the quail population is average or below average.

Human nature and pride dictate that my guides want the hunters to have their best quail hunt each time they go into the field. I have found that guides have a tendency to want to return repeatedly to the areas where they have previously had success until the area is either shot out or the birds become so wild that you cannot have a quality shoot. I have found it necessary to predetermine where in the pasture a group hunts and assign my guides to that area. Each truck is given a pasture map that delineates the area where they are to stay during that hunt. The driver and guide attempt to stay in those boundaries while thoroughly covering as small an area as possible—and without encountering the same coveys twice.

By controlling where and how often an area gets hunted, that is, by regulating the access to the pastures, I can stop hunting a certain area while there are still an adequate number of birds to repopulate the area the next nesting season. Areas with the highest potential for quality hunts are strongly protected from overshooting. This protection seems to be more important to establishing a huntable population when the ensuing year has poor to average reproduction—such as a short window of production the next summer—than when there is a good rainfall year with excellent production—such as optimum nesting conditions all spring and summer.

Breeding Population

From 1980 to 1986, we banded wild bobwhites in the spring and fall and monitored the hunting recovery rate of the banded birds. Using this information, we got an idea of what percentage of the population we were harvesting from each pasture. Harvest percentages ranged from 5 to 55 percent over the study. Normal harvests from 20 to 30 percent seemed to have no effect on the population the following year. When we returned 40 to 55 percent of the bands during hunting season, we saw a marked decline in the number of birds in these pastures the next year (in addition to normal year-to-year fluctuations). With this information, we learned to stop shooting birds in a pasture when we consistently were seeing coveys of less than 8–10 birds (generally occurring during mid- to late February).

Leaving plenty of birds at the end of the season and leaving them adequate cover to survive until the spring rains begin are probably the two key factors in taking the bottom out of low quail populations during dry years. Harvest control at the end of the season is accomplished by designating which areas the hunting trucks are sent to and keeping good records on the number of coveys seen and number of birds harvested. These records are worthless for decision making unless they are tallied as the season progresses. When harvest data start showing a decline in coveys found and birds harvested, shooting pressure can be shifted to other areas of the pasture, preserving the population that is left for breeding.

I also drive quail trucks during hunts as often as possible throughout the season, allowing me to assess the situation firsthand. When I cannot drive, I try to discuss each hunt with both the driver and dog handlers. Hunters make poor interviewees for this type of information. They are often reluctant to admit that they saw 12 coveys in a morning and shot only three birds. Also, hunters that have never hunted South Texas may feel that they have had a great hunt when they saw 6 coveys in a morning, because this would be a great hunt in many parts of the country that no longer have huntable populations of quail. Hunters nearly always underestimate the number of coveys seen on a hunt. Either they were slow getting off the truck and did not see a covey flush, or they were on the wrong side of the bush when the covey flushed. Hunters tend to count only the coveys flushed in front of them while they were holding their shotgun.

Normally, by February we are skipping areas in our hunting rotation that we feel are approaching a minimum number of birds to be left as a breeding population. In poor bird years, we often restrict late-season hunting to the more brushy areas where hunting success is lower.

Predator Management

Predation is probably the number-one cause of death for a bobwhite quail. At the same time, predators are probably one of the last things a quail manager in South Texas needs to try to manage. It is very simplistic to imagine that if there were no predators, all bobwhites would live to a ripe old age and be around for several seasons to be hunted. My feelings are that even the most intensive predator management program will not eliminate enough mammalian predators to truly influence the number of birds available for hunting in the fall. If you hired someone full-time to trap predators, the cost of salary, benefits, gasoline, vehicle, and equipment would probably be $45,000–$55,000 a year. In our case, the person would be tasked with eliminating predators over a 145-square-kilometer (56-square-mile) area. Research has shown that as soon as you stop removing predators, the predators reoccupy that area within the year. To see any real long-term benefit, predation control would have to continue indefinitely. The birds saved by removing these mammalian predators would still be subject to avian predators (of which nothing can legally be done), reptilian predators (quail are low on the food chain, so just about everything out there eats them), and the remaining mammalian predators that move in to take advantage of the increased food supply. I do not believe anyone will ever be able to remove all of the mammalian predators. Even under a best-effort circumstance, not all of these birds would be available for harvest in the fall.

Because bobwhite quail and predators evolved together over the centuries, it makes sense that quail have been programmed to compensate for predation loss by their ability to have large and multiple hatches. From my observation, the only thing that really depresses a quail population is to adversely affect the habitat by removing the herbaceous and woody cover that feeds and protects them and hides their nesting efforts. If the same amount of money were applied to pasture deferment, ensuring that overgrazing did not occur or that brush control and plant succession were manipulated in the quail's favor, I think the benefits seen would be 10-fold compared to those of predator management.

Bird Dogs

Just as camp personnel can make or break a hunting camp, so can the bird dogs. I will not discuss the merits of having your own full-time dog trainer versus hiring a handler by the day to bring dogs to the camp and conduct your hunts. Both situations have merit in expense and in expertise. Day handlers may be cheaper because the dogs are not cared for at the expense of the camp on a year-round basis. However, a full-time trainer generally has a better working knowledge of the terrain and the guests. I am aware of camps that successfully handle their dogs both ways. At San Tomas, we have a full-time dog trainer that is responsible for purchasing, feeding, training, and hunting of our dogs, as well as tending to their health. We have two seasonal dog handlers who have worked at the camp for 5 and 15 years, respectively. Both of these men are responsible for conditioning and training the dogs that our trainer assigns them. They assist in the training of these dogs as well as several new dogs each year during the five months they are at the camp. Each handler has 20 dogs in his string. Normally, 2–4 of those are "started" dogs (young dogs with basic training in the kennel that still need work in the field) that need work before they are considered a "finished" dog that can hunt in front of our guests. My dog trainer conditions dogs year-round by letting them run in the cool, early-morning hours. We normally raise 3–4 dogs a year and will purchase 10–12 started dogs a year. We lose about 6–10 dogs a year (out of 60 finished dogs) to death or retirement.

Starting in September, the trainer will take dogs to the field during the cool part of the morning and work them on wild birds. My seasonal handlers usually arrive the first week of October and work dogs early and late in the day to get them in shape and ready for hunting season. We start hunting around November 10, giving the handlers a little more than a month to get their dogs ready. Younger dogs will be worked all season on afternoons and days off until they are ready to put on the truck and hunt in front of guests.

Dogs must be "snake broken" and learn to ignore other animals such as hogs, javelinas, and deer while on a hunt. The handler must develop a rapport with his dogs and be able to call them back to the truck when he is ready. Some of the worst quail hunts ever attempted in San Tomas occurred when the dogs ran off from the truck and we spent half the morning looking for them or hunting with one dog.

It takes a very tough dog with a lot of heart to hunt through the thorns, heat, and cactus of South Texas. We have found that English pointers handle the terrain and heat better than most other breeds. There are exceptional individuals of other breeds that can perform as well as pointers, but as a breed, they seem to be the best suited for this area.

Dog handlers must maintain control of their dogs throughout the hunt as well as advise the hunters on how to approach the covey. The handler and the truck driver are responsible for marking and retrieving the downed birds and leading dogs and hunters to the singles. Most drivers and handlers have a Labrador retriever to assist them with finding downed birds and are also responsible for enforcing safety rules and bird limits.

We always run two dogs at a time (a male and a female) and try to pair the dogs so that we have one dog that likes to run "big" and one that stays closer to the truck. Dogs are taught to watch the truck and hunt in front of it no matter which way it turns. The truck drivers are responsible for dictating where the hunts go. They must learn where the most likely areas are to find quail and learn the pace they must move to get the dogs downwind of these areas. The most common mistake a driver makes is to rush the dog past good quail cover or to turn the dog (by changing the direction of the truck) before it gets downwind of the cover. Dog handlers have to keep the dogs in sight of the truck, water the dogs, and learn to read the dogs' ability to continue hunting or to rest them and hunt with new dogs.

Some people run one dog at a time, with the consideration that a fresh dog will find more quail. In my opinion, you should carry twice as many dogs on the truck and find more birds by having two noses searching rather than one.

South Texas bird dogs are notorious for *not* being steady to wing and shot, this is, they run after the hunter shoots at a quail rather than stay on point. As a good friend of mine—who is a dog trainer—once said, "I wouldn't own a bird dog that I had to run back to and tap on the head to get him to hunt." South Texas bobwhites have learned to consider bird dogs, hunters, and trucks as predators. Whereas quail that have never been hunted or have been lightly hunted will hold tight in front of a dog, San Tomas bobwhites have learned to move away from the dogs when they are pointed. Dogs are trained to hold until the hunters arrive and then move forward on command and relocate a moving covey. When cover is sparse, this can be 40–90 meters (50–100 yards) or more. Once the covey rises and the shots are fired, the dog can be released by command to find the downed birds.

Regardless of how good dogs are, they will not perform perfectly every time they go out. Some people blame variable dog performance on weed odors, others on heat and humidity, and others on barometric pressure. I have seen dogs have great days and terrible days under what appeared to be similar conditions. About all a handler can do is keep the dogs in shape, carry cold water on the truck to keep the dogs from overheating, and hope for the best.

Habitat Management

Much of our habitat management program is covered in other areas of this chapter. Here, I will concentrate on the bigger picture of habitat management. The two most influential management tools at San Tomas are grazing management and brush management. Most other management tools are just "tweaking" a specific situation that occurs within the pasture.

Grazing Management

The stocking rates, grazing system, timing, and duration of grazing have never been under our control, even though poor grazing management for quail can negate about anything else positive that is done for quail. On the other hand, proper grazing management can be the easiest, most economical, most effective, and the most widely influential management practice that can be applied for quail. For years, we had no control over the grazing management practices of the ranch. More recently (since July 2002), we have begun to compensate the cattle managers for revenue lost from grazing by reducing stocking rates and completely deferring pastures. This has been highly effective in keeping pastures in the condition we need them for optimal quail production and range improvement. Pastures that have carried sufficient cover and food for two consecutive nesting seasons have allowed quail populations to rebound dramatically. We also have been extremely fortunate because rainfall patterns have been exceptional since this program began. Pastures have responded by increasing the perennial grasses that will help carry us through our next inevitable dry period. Compensation for grazing has increased our costs considerably, but it allows us to attain the hunting quality necessary to justify the other expenses of the camp.

Brush Management

In South Texas, one of the most important and expensive needs for quail management is the ability to control brush to keep access to all parts of the quail pasture. About half of the current San Tomas lease was root-plowed in 1969, with strips of brush approximately 27 meters (30 yards) wide left every kilometer (about one-half mile). This resulted in a coverage of about 3.4 percent brush and 96.6 percent open rangeland. The other half of the lease was chained two ways at about the same time. Only live oak areas (perhaps 1,000 hectares, or 2500 acres, or about 7 percent of the lease) were unaffected by these brush-control methods.

When I arrived in 1979, root-plowed areas were still very open except along the remaining tree lines. Very little woody loafing cover existed between these tree lines. For several years we concentrated on half-cutting mesquites and building brush shelters in areas that lacked loafing cover for birds. Chained pastures had a great deal of regrowth, and it was difficult, if not impossible, to drive a quail truck through about 60 percent of these pastures.

During the 1980s and 1990s, brush invasion occurred in both of these areas at a rapid rate. Dry years in the mid- to late 1990s and heavy grazing pressure allowed mesquite to germinate throughout the root-plowed areas to the point that formerly open areas would soon become inaccessible. To some degree, brush invasion in these root-plowed areas increased the usable space for bobwhites. Our management goal was to keep these areas from getting so dense in brush that they were no longer accessible by truck. By the early 1990s, chained pastures had so much brush in them that they were 80–90 percent inaccessible for hunting. In 1991, we were paying to lease 13,770 hectares (34,000 acres) but could effectively access only 66 percent of it (approximately 9,100 hectares, or about 22,500 acres). This situation was causing us to pay for a huge area in which we could not effectively hunt quail. It also put extra pressure on the areas that we could access. Following the chaining of strips through about 2,400 hectares (6,000 acres) in 1992, we went from harvesting 200–300 birds in these areas before chaining to harvesting more than 900 birds from the same areas.

Chemical Brush Control

Since 1980, we have used two methods of chemical brush control (aerial spraying and individual plant treatment [IPT] administered from all-terrain vehicles) (figure 20.6) and two methods of mechanical brush control (two-way chaining and grubbing with a dozer) to improve inaccessible areas for quail hunting.

Aerial spraying of brush was conducted in 1980 and again during 1986 in selected areas that had been chained in 1969. Some areas responded well, with a significant root kill (90 percent), whereas other areas responded poorly (20–30 percent root kill). Forbs were devastated in these sprayed areas, and quail hunting in these areas did not return to normal for at least two seasons. Having witnessed this response to aerial spraying, in 1986 we developed our current method of IPT from all-terrain vehicles mounted with a 58-liter (15-gallon) tank of either Remedy or Velpar. We have experimented with various chemical concentrations and eventually developed mixtures that work very well for us.

IPT is primarily used in previously root-plowed pastures (figure 20.6). We basal-spray newly germinating mesquite. Care is taken to avoid granjeno and other woody species important to deer as browse

Figure 20.6.
Results of individual plant treatment (IPT) with herbicide. Note dead mesquite in the foreground. This type of brush management keeps the brush motte in the background from becoming excessively large.
Photo by Michael Rader

Figure 20.7.
An ideal mix of grasses, ragweed, and brush that provides essential elements of quail habitat. It takes cooperation and collaboration among lessees and lessors to provide and maintain habitat as part of the overall quail hunting-camp operation.
Photo by Michael Rader

and as quail loafing cover. From 1986 through 2002, we struggled to cover all the areas where brush invasion was becoming a problem, but we were rapidly losing the battle. We have used IPT in certain heavily grazed pastures as many as three times since 1986. It costs about $44–$74/hectare ($18–$30/acre) per treatment to maintain the pastures in an open state. Other pastures that have had better grass cover since 1986 have cost around $12–$25/hectare ($5–$10/acre) and are still in need of more work to maintain them in the open state we would like.

With the advent of grazing control, we are getting ahead of the problem of excess mesquite germination. Leaving more vegetation on the ground year-round will slow down mesquite invasion and hopefully allow us, within the next few years, to address new problem areas that have cropped up on the lease. Once we have thinned brush on problem areas, we should be able to keep up with new mesquite germination with a normal maintenance program (figure 20.7). We have found IPT to be especially effective where we can burn a hot fire through the area. This top-kills the mesquites and then allows us to spray the regrowth as it sprouts from the base of the tree.

The beauty of IPT is that we have never seen it hurt our quail populations after we applied it to an area. Even though the chemicals will suppress forbs in the immediate sprayed area, there are still plenty of forbs only a short distance away from the sprayed spots. It is much more selective and compatible with wildlife management than a pasturewide application of chemical from an airplane.

Chaining
During 1992 and 1993, we chained strips 72–90 meters (80–100 yards) wide two ways through about 4,800 hectares (12,000 acres) of large mesquite regrowth, leaving 72–135 meters (80–50 yards) of brush between strips. In 2002, we grubbed mesquite through some of the strips that were chained in 1992. This was effort to thin problem areas too thick to control with chemicals. Again in 2003, we chained strips through approximately 1,600 hectares (4,000 acres) of large mesquite regrowth and

grubbed another 400 hectares (1,000 acres) of strips previously chained in 1993. The 2003 effort was designed to treat 65 percent of the pasture and leave 35 percent untreated.

Chaining is an economical method of opening the pasture for increased forage production. This is beneficial for both wildlife and livestock. Given good soil moisture conditions (which we had in 1992 and 2003), I estimate that we killed 30–40 percent of the brush in the chained strips. We have since followed the 1992 chaining with IPT to further reduce the brush in these strips to about 20 percent woody cover. This has been an ongoing process—about every three years we cover a strip by spraying all newly germinating mesquite and thinning mesquite regrowth. I estimate we have spent an additional $29–$37/hectare ($12–$15/acre) chemically maintaining these strips chained in 1992. The drawback of chaining is that the debris from fallen trees restricts your ability to thoroughly cover the area by driving. If we can get sufficient deferment from grazing pressure for two years following chaining, we can carry a hot fire through the area to eliminate much of this debris, making the area somewhat more accessible to a truck over time.

Grubbing

Grubbing with a dozer is expensive. It has been selectively used to thin chained strips that were not feasible to re-cover with herbicides because of the density of regrowth. Soil disturbance from chaining and grubbing creates a flush of annual forbs that can create abundant food for quail. These same measures tend to reduce grass cover in the area, making grazing deferment necessary to ensure nesting cover for quail. It is highly important to use a dozer operator that has some "quail sense" when grubbing. A poor operator can tear up the landscape by gouging holes in the ground that will restrict the ability to drive over the land for years to come. Mechanical brush control is best accomplished during late winter and early spring, before birds begin to nest. This also gives a pasture eight to nine months to build grass before the hunting season begins.

Harvest Management

When I first came to South Texas to manage San Tomas, the rule of quail management was, "You can't stockpile quail! You might as well shoot them when you have them!" State quail biologists pointed to booms and busts in the population and observed that hunting pressure—and statewide harvest—had no influence on next year's population. Certain public wildlife management areas boasted that they had quail harvest rates of 2.5 birds/hectare (1 bird/acre) in boom years. These rates far exceeded the quail harvests at San Tomas. Fortunately for these management areas, their hunters go away or never show up in years of poor quail production. After the first few weekends of the season, the word gets out that there are few quail and the hunters stop coming. This is not the case at a corporate camp, where 30 hunts are scheduled during the summer and hunters must be entertained every year to justify the expense of the camp. San Tomas was one of the first corporate camps in this area to apply four-month-long shooting pressure of six to seven days a week to a piece of property year in and year out. For the first few years this "shoot them while you have them" philosophy worked. Then we began to realize that we were having some rather exceptional reproduction years. Over time, we found that when we applied heavy shooting pressure on pastures that had marginal winter habitat because of droughts and heavy grazing, our shooting pressure had a profound effect on next year's population. By 1986, we added 4,000 hectares (10,000 acres) to the lease in order to sustain normal shooting pressure without hurting the birds. Although we have seen quail populations rise and fall since 1979, we have never seen them as high as they were in 1979, 1981, and 1983. The next boom cycle we saw was in 1992 and 1993. Bird numbers were high, but never quite as good as they were during the early boom years at San Tomas. Grazing management became more of an issue in the late 1980s and late 1990s as continuous grazing started to eliminate perennial grasses that had always dominated our pastures. Each year we would harvest quail conservatively, leave plenty of birds in a pasture for breeding, then watch their numbers dwindle to a skeleton population as excessive grazing pressure destroyed their habitat through the winter and into the nesting season. At this time, we realized that harvest control was completely necessary, but it was not the root cause of our problem. It was just the part of quail management that, unlike the grazing, we could control.

During 1984 and 1985, we had below-average rainfall and production (the J : A ratio was 1.7 : 1) from an extremely large breeding population. That year our hosts decided that the answer to fewer birds was to run four or five quail trucks rather than two or three. The previous year (1983) had yielded one of the highest quail harvests over a large area that I had ever heard of (4 birds/7.4 hectares, or 1 bird/3 acres), and we still left plenty of birds for breeding. Following the 1983 harvest, the hosts felt the bird population could not be hurt through shooting pressure and proceeded to shoot certain pastures almost to oblivion. During that year, I witnessed the results of overshooting coupled with overgrazing. Overall populations have never again been as high as pre-1984 levels, even in the boom years of 1992 and 1993. The harvest control measures we instituted fell under two categories: rules and management tools.

Hunting Rules

During 1986, we instituted the following rules to conserve quail and keep harvest under control.

1. Stop hunting from any truck when 10 birds/hunter are harvested on an outing—regardless of the number of birds the hunters shot during the morning or if they were not going to shoot that afternoon.
2. Wait at least two weeks before returning to an area to shoot.
3. Shoot a maximum of 3 birds/covey, and then find a new covey.
4. Hunt according to areas designated on the map by a hunt coordinator.
5. Eliminate any betting on which truck gets the most birds.
6. Eliminate the individual tip to guides, and encourage a year-end bonus or group tip.

These rules allow guests to continue their pursuit of quail without damaging the individual covey or total number of birds on a given area. Shooting 10 birds/person on an outing is plenty of shooting for a morning or afternoon, does not overshoot your better areas, and satisfies the shooter's feeling of success at having shot a limit of birds.

Resting each area for two weeks and recording on a map where the hunt took place accomplish two goals. First, the birds are allowed to regroup and settle down between hunts, keeping them from getting so wild that they flush ahead of the dogs or scatter to the winds when flushed. Second, I learn where the quail are concentrated and can plan my hunts to cover smaller and smaller areas more thoroughly as the season progresses. This also allows me to increase success as the hunt progresses, ultimately showing the die-hard quail hunters the best hunt on their last outing. The last outing is the one that they remember the most and can make or break their image of a successful hunt.

Mapping a hunt allows me to determine which areas are being used and which areas (and coveys) are not. Our goal is to accomplish each hunt in as small an area as possible. Making a thorough hunt over a 100-hectare (250-acre) area rather than wandering aimlessly across 200 hectares (500 acres) creates twice as many hunting areas in the rotation. Guides are encouraged to systematically hunt an area by moving back and forth across the area, hunting across the wind rather than straight into it. By doing this, we cover the area more closely, encounter a higher percentage of coveys, and never have to turn and hunt downwind. To accomplish this, a driver and dog handler must have a complete knowledge of the terrain and a sense of where they are in the pasture to keep from covering the same coveys twice on the same hunt. In open terrain, we never hunt a specific route, choosing not to have specific hunting roads. We are often forced to hunt the roads we have created in brushier pastures that have limited access.

Human nature dictates that every good hunting guide wants each hunt to be the very best. By assigning dog handlers an area to hunt rather than leaving it up to them, they are relieved of responsibility for finding a good area. The dog handler will go where assigned and will make the best of the circumstances. Because we do not allow individual tips, the guide does not have the incentive to return to better areas and overshoot them. Paying guides a good wage (rather than their depending on tips to make ends meet) makes them more responsive to a long-term management program.

Management Tools

Over the years, management experience at San Tomas has led me to implement the following hunting management tools.

1. Hunt three persons per vehicle rather than two in poor to average bird years.
2. Hunt both poor areas and productive areas with each group of guests. Start weak and finish strong.
3. Encourage big-game hunting (hogs, javelinas [*Tayassu tajacu*], management bucks, does, and nilgai) by enough people on each outing so that no more than two trucks are needed to hunt quail.
4. Encourage dual hunts. Get staunch quail hunting guests to go out early with the turkey, hog, or deer hunters, and then bring them in midmorning for a late quail hunt (9:30 to 11:30).
5. Establish alternative entertainment in the afternoons that will shorten the evening hunt (flighted mallards).
6. Hunt heavier brush more often than open areas in very poor years.
7. Implement one outing of shooting released game (out of four outings per hunt).

8. Eliminate an area from your hunting rotation when you start finding a majority of the coveys with eight or fewer birds.
9. Save brushier pastures for January–February hunts.
10. Inform guests through preseason letters about rule changes, the need for conservative harvest, and situations that have caused problems with previous hunts.
11. Use supplemental feed to concentrate quail and create a better hunt in marginal or difficult-to-hunt pastures.

We have learned that the hunters' last impression of the hunt—the final morning hunt—can be the most important to their opinion of success. When guests arrive, they are given the opportunity to hunt quail, big game, or both. Dyed-in-the-wool quail hunters will quail hunt all four outings regardless of how many birds are available. Hunters new to the sport often follow the majority, generally meaning that they quail hunt. These new hunters are seldom successful at quail hunting because wild quail are an extremely difficult target upon which to start a hunting career. When these hunters find out just how difficult it is to shoot wild birds, they often decide they should try big game. By providing your weakest hunting area first, you often get two or three newcomers to drop out of quail hunting and reduce your shooting pressure by a full truck following the first outing.

Before each hunt, we review which areas have had their two weeks' rest and decide which 12 areas we will hunt with that group (assuming 12 are necessary). Having kept meticulous records throughout the season to determine where the best areas for quail hunting are, we send the first afternoon groups to what we feel will be the weakest area to hunt. The areas are better the next morning and even better the next evening. We save the best areas we have for the last morning. Hunters that find 6, 8, 10, and 12 coveys on their four outings have a better experience each time they go out and culminate their hunt by seeing plenty of birds. In contrast, the hunters who find 12 coveys the first afternoon expect to find 12 or more coveys each time they go out. This can lead to disappointment the last morning if they find only 10. By any standard, 10 coveys in a half day of hunting should be considered a good hunt.

At San Tomas, we never allow the harvest of big game from a quail truck. Dog handlers spend countless hours training their dogs to leave other game animals alone. Shooting big game from the quail truck teaches the bird dogs that these animals are to be hunted as well. Feral hogs, does, management bucks, javelinas, wild turkeys (*Meleagris gallopavo*), nilgai, and predator hunting can keep hunters entertained and off the quail trucks. Although many people consider feral hogs and nilgai a nuisance, I consider them one of the best management tools I have to reduce pressure on the wild quail population. If we have eight guests, we only need to get two at a time to hunt big game to cut back to two trucks per outing. If we have three or four new guests that want to hunt big game, we often stagger them so we never have more than six quail hunters and run two trucks at a time.

Released Game Birds

In our 26 years of quail hunting, we have gone through three hunting seasons (1989, 1990, and 1998) in which our quail population was so low that we felt we had to reduce shooting pressure even further. In 1990 and 1998, we implemented a released-bird program (primarily bobwhite quail, with some pheasant and chukar) in selected areas of the pasture. One evening per group, we required any bird hunter that hunted that evening to hunt released birds. This action normally replaced about 60–80 outings a season of wild quail hunting. The beauty of this operation was that not only did we relieve pressure from the wild population but we gave guests an opportunity to harvest 30–50 (we normally released 50 birds per area the evening of the hunt) birds per truck in one afternoon, in a season in which the entire group might harvest 40–60 wild birds on 6–8 wild bird outings.

Released birds were always taken to the same three areas of approximately 80 hectares (200 acres) each. About midseason, we started to find a covey or two of birds left over from the previous hunts, allowing guests to find and shoot into sometimes 60–70 birds rather than just the 50 that were released that evening. Telemetry work at San Tomas has shown that the majority of released birds that are not harvested that same day are dead within a week, most in a matter of days. Avian or mammalian predation was the cause of death in almost every case.

Releases of 5 birds were done under natural cover in 10 places along each course immediately before the hunt began. Dogs run ahead of the trucks, just as they do on wild coveys. Five-bird coveys work well, as dog handlers are usually able to keep up with where the 2 or 3 singles landed that were not shot on the rise. Working ten 5-bird coveys takes more time (occupying a full afternoon of hunting) and is more efficient in harvest than working five 10-bird coveys. Guests were aware that they were shooting released birds and gladly followed our program. They knew we were trying to save wild birds for next year. By minimizing the areas where we released birds, we minimized any chance for spreading disease into our wild quail population. In every instance where we released birds, the area of release carried as many coveys the next year as the surrounding areas did. This practice alone can reduce shooting pressure on wild quail by 25 percent, or the same as canceling seven or eight hunts.

Other Alternatives to Shooting Wild Quail

In addition to released-bobwhite hunts, we created other means of entertainment with a quail walk and a flighted mallard shoot. Early on, we found that guests will shoot skeet only long enough to warm up before the hunt. Forcing them to stay and shoot at a skeet machine only gives them the impression that you do not want them to have a good time hunting. Hunting is what a quail camp is about. The "quail walk" is a walking skeet course where 1, 2, or a covey of 4–6 clay birds is thrown at 17 different locations. The shooter is not aware of when the birds will be thrown and simply walks the path with gun at ready as if approaching a dog on point. Shots are scored for hits and misses, bringing out the competitive nature in the shooter. This is the time when we allow guests to bet on their scores—normally a one-dollar bet plus bragging rights. We walk the quail walk the second afternoon of the hunt starting about two o'clock and ending around three o'clock. An added benefit of the quail walk is that it occupies the hunters from lunchtime until the hunt. They have no idle time to sit around the camp and drink alcohol before the afternoon hunt. Immediately following the quail walk, we shoot flighted mallards at a pond about 30 minutes from camp. This shoot, which takes about an hour from start to finish, allows a completely different kind of shooting for the guests and is red-hot action from start to finish. Pen-raised ducks are purchased for this shoot from Arkansas and are held in our flight pens until time to shoot them. We have a feed pen on the pond where any birds that were not harvested can be recaptured the next day and used again on a later hunt. Normally, about 200 ducks are released during a 45-minute period, with each guest shooting from four to six boxes of shells. Ducks are shot over water, flying to decoys, and are retrieved by an arsenal of 5–7 very excited Labrador retrievers. By the time we finish our duck shoot and guests head to the pasture, they have time for a short 1.5-hour quail hunt (about half the time of a normal outing). The quail walk and mallard shoot have become an integral part of our program at San Tomas. They are part of virtually every hunt we have in both good and bad seasons.

During the winter dove season, we can go straight from the duck shoot to dove ponds to finish the evening. This completely eliminates an afternoon of hunting quail but still keeps the guests shooting nonstop all evening long.

Supplemental Feeding

We use supplemental feed as a tool to increase the success of our hunts in brushier pastures where our trucks cannot cover the entire area. When hunting designated roads through restrictive (brushy) pastures without feed, dogs have to be kept close to the truck, and many coveys will never be pointed during the year. Those coveys that live along the roads get too wild to hunt and quickly learn to flush into the brush to avoid hunters and dogs. Using supplemental feed on these roads (we try to feed them at least twice the week before we hunt them) will bring more and new coveys to the area, allowing dog handlers to find enough coveys to conduct a satisfactory hunt. It allows us to have a good hunt in areas that would yield a marginal hunt otherwise. It is most important to make use of the entire lease and all your coveys, rather than just those that are easy to get to.

Summary

Managing a South Texas quail camp, and providing a quality hunting experience for guests during both boom and bust years, is a challenging and rewarding task. In addition to the logistics of running the camp facility, the success or failure of the operation hinges on the leaseholder working with the landowner to identify and implement practical management actions that allow usable habitat space to be maintained for quail during all months of the year (figure 20.7). Taking this approach to habitat management may help dampen the wild fluctuations that quail populations experience in the variable South Texas environment. It definitely helps maximize the opportunities for guests to have quality hunting experiences.

One of the most important aspects of quail management that a leaseholder can influence is harvest management. Our experience at San Tomas has shown us that judicious management of hunting pressure is absolutely essential for assuring that an adequate breeding population will be conserved for the next year. There are numerous strategies that a camp manager can use to reduce hunting pressure on quail populations. These strategies involve both the provision of alternative activities and distribution of hunting activities across all parts of the lease in relation to what is known about where quail are (and are not) most abundant. However, without competent and effective habitat management, harvest management will most likely be a moot point because there will be few quail to hunt or to see (Leopold 1978).

If a quail hunting lease and quail hunting camp are managed correctly, a great deal of quail habitat—and habitat for dozens of other species of wildlife—can be conserved. This is absolutely essential for sustaining the tradition of hunting wild coveys of quail on the Texas landscape.

Strategies for Forming a Quail Management Cooperative

21

Stephen J. DeMaso, William P. Kuvlesky Jr.,
and Jason B. Hardin

> A long pull, and a strong pull, and a pull all together.
> Charles Dickens

Quails need space! The more space—or habitat—the better. So how do 363
landowners who own 20, 32, 41, or 81 hectares (50, 80, 100, or 200 acres)
manage for wildlife species that need lots of space? They have to work
cooperatively with neighbors and other partners in the community who
have similar interests in wildlife. The objectives of this chapter are to introduce the concept of wildlife management associations and cooperatives, show how quail management cooperatives can be used to assemble
enough acreage to realistically manage quail populations, and provide
information about how to create a quail management cooperative.

Information for this chapter has been taken or modified from the
Texas Parks and Wildlife Department (TPWD) Web site: http://www
.tpwd.state.tx.us/conserve/pdf/72wildlife_co-op.pdf. For more details
on forming wildlife management cooperatives, see this Web site.

History of Wildlife Management
Associations and Cooperatives

Wildlife management associations and cooperatives are groups formed
by landowners to improve wildlife habitats and associated wildlife populations. The idea of wildlife management associations and/or cooperatives has been around since the early 1930s (MacNamara 1936; Hill
1940; Leopold 1940).

In Texas, the first wildlife cooperatives are thought to have evolved
during the 1950s in the Hill Country for management of white-tailed
deer (*Odocoileus virginianus*) (G. Homerstad, TPWD, Victoria, pers.
comm.). The first-known wildlife management association in Texas,
the Peach Creek Wildlife Management Cooperative, was organized in
1973. The cooperative was developed in response to landowners' desire
to improve the quality of white-tailed deer. This cooperative forged a
new type of relationship among Texas landowners—a process in which
groups of landowners work together with wildlife biologists to learn
about wildlife and make improvements to wildlife habitat and populations on the cooperative acreage.

Wildlife cooperatives—or similar entities—have been defined and
amended by the Texas legislature since 1975 (1975 Parks and Wildlife
Code, Title 5, Subtitle A, Chapter 43, Subchapter D, § 43.041). The Texas
legislature defined *wildlife associations* in 1993 (1993 Parks and Wildlife
Code, Title 5, Subtitle E, Chapter 81, Subchapter D, § 81.301). The mean-
ings have remained similar, but the semantics have changed through
the years. Roughly, a cooperative is more than two landowners managing wildlife within a county. An association is more than two contiguous landowners managing wildlife within a county. Also, in some areas
of the state there are social issues with deep cultural and political roots

that influence the type of group that is formed and the ultimate success of that group.

Why Quail Associations and/or Cooperatives Are Essential

Land ownership fragmentation is defined as the division of rural lands into smaller parcels that remain in rural land uses. Ownership fragmentation is a result of the combined influence of weakened agricultural economies and increased demands from large, urban populations. Impacts of land ownership fragmentation include loss of open space; localized loss of farm, ranch, and forest production; higher demand for public services in rural areas; and reduced space for wildlife and their habitats (Wilkins et al. 2000).

In Texas, about 80 percent of farms and ranches are less than 200 hectares (500 acres) in size, most of these occurring in the eastern part of the state. About 81 percent of Texas rural land is owned by 23 percent of the rural landowners (Wilkins et al. 2000).

Harvest is problematic for bobwhite (*Colinus virginianus*) populations that struggle to exist in fragmented landscapes (Roseberry and Klimstra 1984:147–48). Bobwhite populations on small patches of permanent cover appear extremely vulnerable to extinction, whether harvested or not (Guthery 2002:145).

It is easy to see that the largest threats to quails are the smaller and smaller areas of habitat and usable space. As quail populations become more isolated from each other, the probability of extinction increases. The use of wildlife associations and/or cooperatives can increase the acreage suitable for quails, keep populations from becoming isolated, and thereby reduce the risk of localized extinctions.

How big does a quail association or cooperative need to be? The bigger the better! Research has shown that for bobwhite populations to thrive for long periods of time there need to be at least 800 birds at the lowest point in the population's annual cycle (Guthery et al. 2000). The size of an area needed to support about 800 bobwhites will vary depending on the density of bobwhites (number of birds per unit area), the position of the association or cooperative in relation to the surrounding landscape, and the land-use practices on those surrounding properties. The general rule of thumb is that 1,200–2,000 hectares (3,000–5,000 acres) of habitat would usually be needed to support a bobwhite population over the long term.

Benefits of Quail Associations and/or Cooperatives

Managing wildlife on small acreages presents a special challenge. Success in managing habitat for healthy wildlife populations depends on the actions and attitudes of neighboring landowners. This is especially true for bobwhites in many areas of Texas.

In addition to receiving technical assistance in wildlife management from a wildlife biologist, each association and cooperative member receives a gate sign from TPWD, showing that he or she is a member of the landowner group. There is a "Posted" notice at the bottom of each sign, and many co-ops design and pay for their own signs.

Increased surveillance for law enforcement purposes is an option some associations and cooperatives choose. As in a neighborhood crime-watch program, landowners help each other by watching for trespassers and/or poachers. Association and cooperative members may post "No trespassing" signs on association or cooperative lands and may ask their hunters to produce permission cards. Some groups may enable their members to file trespass charges on behalf of agreeable, absentee landowners (if authorized in writing) and may participate in patrolling under the supervision of a TPWD game warden during times of suspected or known abuse. In some areas of the state where trespassing, poaching, and night hunting repeatedly occur, landowners have successfully curtailed these activities and feel that they have regained control of their property.

Legitimate hunters are usually agreeable and often actively assist the association or cooperative in law enforcement and data collection. In areas where wildlife populations are low, some folks by nature are often too kind to say no to the overhunting of their property by friends or relatives. These landowners have found that agreements benefit their wildlife populations and take them off the hook by giving them a sound method of control through the wildlife association or cooperative plan. Special hunting-lease licenses are available to members of wildlife management associations and cooperatives. Examples of newsletters, announcements, and other materials produced by other wildlife management associations and cooperatives are available from TPWD by writing to Private Lands and Public Hunting Program, 4200 Smith School Road, Austin, TX 78744, or calling 1–800–792–1112 (menu #5).

Often, as cooperative wildlife plans begin to work, co-op members and their families turn into wildlife activists—pursuing, watching, and appreciating the animals they are managing. Landowners earnestly begin to address habitat issues and improve conditions for many species of wildlife, not just the ones they hunt. Through its Lone Star Land Steward Awards Program, TPWD recognizes the best examples of habitat management each year. The first statewide winner of this prestigious award was the North Central Fayette County Wildlife Management Association in 1995. This resulted in a new award category specifically for wildlife management associations and cooperatives.

In summary, these are among the potential benefits to landowners in wildlife management associations or cooperatives:

1. Personal knowledge gained through educational programs and materials
2. Better stewardship of land (habitat)
3. Knowing the neighbors better, meeting new people, and sharing common interests
4. Improved quality and quantity of wildlife
5. Decreased poaching and trespass

The major reasons for failure of wildlife management associations or cooperatives include the following:

1. Inadequate wildlife population information
2. Inadequate wildlife harvest information
3. Lack of consensus among members about goals and objectives
4. Lack of enthusiasm, interest, or participation due to skepticism
5. Lack of attention to habitat

How to Form a Quail Association or Cooperative

Wildlife biologists provide information that is useful for the development of landowner groups. They provide information and assistance in wildlife habitat and population management. Also, biologists at TPWD are available to help landowners schedule meetings to discuss possibilities for associations and cooperatives. The service is free through TPWD's Private Lands and Public Hunting Program. A biologist's time is in high demand, so call early to schedule meeting times. For information about how to contact a TPWD biologist, see figures 21.1 and 21.2.

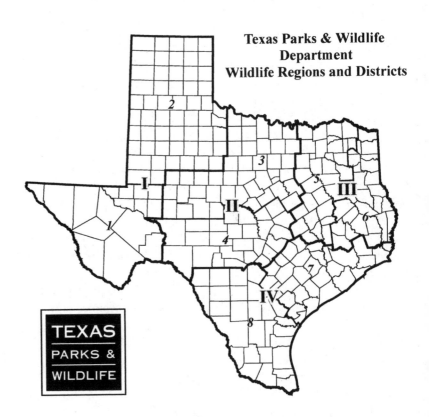

Region I Director
3407-B Chadbourne
San Angelo, TX 76904
(325) 651-4748

District 1 Leader
109 S. Cockrell St.
Alpine, TX 79830
(432) 837-2051

District 2 Leader
P.O. Box 659
Canyon, TX 79015
(806) 655-3782

Region II Director
301 Main St., Suite D
Brownwood, TX 76801
(325) 641-9234

District 3 Leader
301 Main Street, Suite D
Brownwood, TX 76801
(325) 643-5977

District 4 Leader
309 Sidney Baker South
Kerrville, TX 78028
(830) 896-2500

Region III Director
11942 FM 848
Tyler, TX 75707
(903) 566-1626

District 5 Leader
11942 FM 848
Tyler, TX 75707
(903) 566-1626

District 6 Leader
1342 South Wheeler
Jasper, TX 75951
(409) 384-6894

Region IV Director
715 S. Hwy 35
Rockport, TX 78382
(361) 790-0306

District 7 Leader
111 E. Travis, Suite 200
LaGrange, TX 78945
(979) 968-6591

District 8 Leader
1607 2nd Street
Pleasanton, TX 78064
(830) 569-8700

Figure 21.1.
Telephone numbers and addresses for Texas Parks and Wildlife Department regional and district wildlife offices that can help you contact your local biologist to assist in forming a quail association or cooperative.

**Landowner Request for Technical Assistance
In Enhancement of Habitat and Management of
Wildlife Populations**

1. I hereby request technical assistance of wildlife biologists of the Texas Parks and Wildlife Department, Wildlife Division, in my efforts to enhance habitat and manage wildlife populations on lands under my control.

2. The lands in question comprise approximately _____ acres in
    _____ County(ies) and are known collectively as the
    _____ Ranch.

3. Permission is granted to Wildlife Biologists and Wildlife Technicians of the Texas Parks and Wildlife Department, Wildlife Division, to enter upon these lands and conduct, at a mutually agreeable time, wildlife and habitat inventories which may include the use of ground vehicles, aircraft, or nighttime spotlight counts to gather data necessary for the development of management recommendations.

THIS NOTICE IS REQUIRED BY LAW

> HB 2012 by the Texas Legislature adds section 12.0251 to TPW Code and requires that information collected in response to a landowner request for technical guidance on private land relating to the specific location, species identification or quantity of any animal or plant life is confidential and may not be disclosed. The Department may release game census, harvest, habitat or program information if the information is summarized in a manner that prevents the identification of an individual or specific parcel of land and the landowner.

4. I understand that management recommendations will address needs of all wildlife species, but will emphasize the management of certain species or aspects which I have identified from my goals and objectives as follows:

    _____

    _____

5. I understand that recommendations will be provided to me in the form of oral and/or written guidelines which are confidential by law and are non-binding and voluntary on my part.

Signed: _____

              Landowner   Date

Period of Agreement: Beginning date: _____   Termination date: _____

Title V Compliance: The Texas Parks and Wildlife Department provides this service to land managers without discrimination in respect to race, color, national origin, age or handicap.

PWD – 153-7100-12/95
Dispersal of this publication conforms with Texas State Documents Depository Law, and it is available at Texas State Publications Clearinghouse and Texas Depository Libraries.

Figure 21.2.
Form for landowners to request technical assistance for enhancing wildlife habitat and populations on their property. This form is required by state law.

The biologist will also need information about contacts on the property, past and present land uses, past and present management regimes, past harvest data, and wildlife population data. Figure 21.3 provides an example data sheet containing the kinds of information required by a biologist.

The county Tax Appraisal District can often provide useful information. Tax offices can provide maps showing land ownership and lists of mailing addresses so that invitations can be sent to landowners to attend a meeting to form an association or cooperative. Maps can be valuable in setting up survey routes to measure population status. New associations and cooperatives often invite the game warden and local county agent to meetings as additional sources of assistance.

Involving the Neighbors

Invite the neighbors to a meeting to discuss mutual interests in wildlife. Associations and cooperatives are good ways to meet new neighbors and reestablish relationships with longtime neighbors and friends.

**Private Lands Enhancement Program
LANDOWNER DATA SHEET**

DATE _____

NAME OF TRACT OR RANCH _____

LANDOWNER _____ PHONE: Office_____

Home _____

ADDRESS _____

_____

RESIDENT FOREMAN _____ PHONE: Office_____

Home _____

ADDRESS _____

_____

COUNTY AND LOCATION _____

_____

ACREAGE _____

VEGETAION TYPE(S) _____

LAND USE HISTORY _____

TYPE OPERATION _____ Recreation _____ Livestock _____ Farming

PRINCIPAL CROPS AND/OR CLASS OF LIVESTOCK (Grazing system, stocking rates)

_____

PRINCIPAL WILDLIFE SPECIES _____

_____

LANDOWNER INTENT _____

_____

INDIVIDUAL REQUESTING TECHNICAL ASSISTANCE _____

PWD-152-7100-12/94
**Dispersal of this publication conforms with Texas State Documents Depository Law, and it is available at Texas State
Publications Clearinghouse and Texas Depository Libraries.**

Figure 21.3.
Example of data that will be needed
by a wildlife biologist when visiting
your property to develop a wildlife
management plan or assist in forming an association or cooperative.

Meetings should be scheduled to maximize attendance and conve-
nience. Weekend and church-night dates should be avoided to reduce
scheduling conflicts. Residents, absentee landowners, and land managers should be invited and given ample notice to arrange their schedules.
Absentee landowners are often very interested in wildlife and many
times are key participants in an association or cooperative. Wildlife
management programs often take two hours, allowing for questions,
answers, and discussion about forming an association or cooperative.
Coffee and cake or barbecues with neighbors are generally very successful at drawing folks together.

The formation of an association or cooperative typically involves the
development of a landowner agreement that is not legally binding. The
biologist can provide examples of agreements (figure 21.4). Landowners
enter into an agreement with the expressed intent to comply in good
faith with the program to manage for wildlife. In addition, participat-

Landowner's Cooperative Agreement

1. _____   _____

   Landowner's name   Date

_____   _____

   Address   Telephone number

_____   _____

   City   State   Zip code

2. I am the owner or authorized agent of tract or tracts of land located on county/state road

_____ containing _____ acres,

_____ containing _____ acres,

_____ containing _____ acres.

3. I agree to cooperate with the goals and bylaws of the Barton Creek Game Management Co-op.

4. This agreement does not give any unauthorized person the right to trespass on above listed property.

5. I am in no way obligated to the Texas Agricultural Extension Service, the Texas Parks and Wildlife Department, or the Barton Creek Game Management Co-op. I may or may not agree with the management practices recommended. The only thing I have agreed to is to recognize the need for wildlife management in order to improve the wildlife on my property.

6. This agreement is valid for the life of the co-op unless revoked in writing.

7. Annual membership dues are $5.00 which will be used for postage, advertisement, and educational programs.

_____

Signature of Landowner/Agent

Figure 21.4.
Example of a landowner's cooperative agreement.

ing landowners often agree to comply with recommendations from a management plan developed with the assistance of a TPWD wildlife biologist. Landowners also agree to put forth a good-faith effort to get their hunters to comply with these recommendations. Implementation of the wildlife management plan should have an effective starting date and a term of three to five years. All parties should agree to participate in uniform data collection and methods of documenting wildlife observations. Every property does not have to be involved for the association or cooperative to be successful. Many of the good associations and cooperatives have "holes" where some landowners do not participate for one reason or another, but excellent progress is occurring.

The following steps are usually involved in forming a wildlife association or cooperative:

1. Planting the seed: Use the power of suggestion. Get someone to start talking to the neighbors, and the word will spread.
2. Cultivation: Make it clear that landowners, hunters, and interested public are welcome. Host the initial meeting of landowners to provide information, education, and organization.

3. Birth of the organization: Select leaders and form a steering committee (or vice versa, depending on participation).
4. The law: Generate a statement of purpose and bylaws of the association, establishing goals and objectives.
5. First session: Approve bylaws, elect officers, and establish member records (collection of dues) and agenda. Plan annual meeting, fundraisers, and other meetings.

The Lease Cooperative

Another perspective on cooperatives that few people consider when they think of quail or deer cooperatives might be termed the *lease cooperative*, which is simply the working relationship that exists between a landowner, a lessee such as a corporation, and the wildlife manager of the lease. Good communication between these three parties is absolutely essential to effective wildlife and hunting-camp management on a lease.

Communication begins with negotiating the lease agreement. Clearly, the landowner and lessee are involved in the negotiating process, but if at all possible, the wildlife/hunting-camp manager should also be involved because professional expertise in managing quails and hunters can be very helpful in ensuring that the landowner and lessee are fully aware of what will be required to implement and sustain a successful quail hunting operation. Expectations and responsibilities for each party should be clearly stated in the lease agreement. For example, the landowner should state in writing what the rules and expectations are concerning liability; damage to property; and client, guest, and hunting-camp employee behavior. Similarly, the lessee and wildlife/hunting-camp managers should state what their requirements will be to provide quality quail hunting to camp guests. The landowner should be made aware of brush and grazing management requirements that will be necessary to produce healthy quail populations.

Agreement on livestock grazing management is very important relative to quail management, because excessive grazing pressure can have detrimental impacts on quail habitat. The landowners should state what their livestock needs are, and the wildlife managers should offer their professional judgment on how this will impact quail populations. Livestock stocking rates, herd rotation, and a drought management plan should be clearly identified and agreed upon by the landowner, lessee, and wildlife/hunting-camp manager before a lease agreement is signed.

After the lease is signed, everyone should keep clear lines of communication open. If a problem occurs, everyone involved in the lease agreement should be immediately notified and then work together to resolve the problem. Maintaining any successful personal or professional relationship is built upon a foundation of trust and integrity. Maintaining a cooperative relationship between the landowner, lessee, and wildlife/hunting-camp manager requires the same commitment to honesty and integrity.

Audubon Texas Quail Initiative

Audubon Texas began its Texas Quail and Grassland Birds Initiative in September 2003. The goals of the initiative follow those of the Texas

Quail Council, which are to stabilize the decline of quails and other grassland birds and return quails and other grassland birds to densities similar to the early 1980 densities on available suitable habitat.

Audubon's Quail Initiative differs little from the priorities identified by the Texas Quail Council. Audubon's approach is to form and maintain quail co-ops in all areas of Texas, but specifically on areas of Texas where landowner tracts are about 202 hectares (500 acres) (figure 21.5).

Audubon conceptually uses the five steps mentioned previously for forming quail co-ops, practices that have been successful. It is important that at least one co-op meeting be held each year with biologists (Audubon, Cooperative Extension, TPWD, etc.) involved to identify the status of the co-op, new members, future goals and objectives, the success of the habitat management practices, and the quail/grassland bird population status. The importance of bylaws largely depends on the members of the co-op.

Audubon Texas makes an effort to involve as many professional wildlife biologists, land managers, and landowners as possible in the formation and implementation of management goals of the co-op. Audubon Texas feels that this cross-pollination of ideas will help slow declining bird populations and return quails and other grassland birds to their former densities.

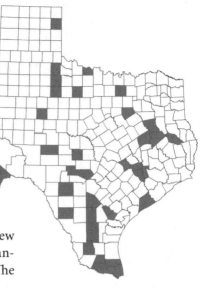

Figure 21.5.
Counties with Audubon quail cooperatives and/or demonstration areas.
Courtesy Jason Hardin

Texas Organization of Wildlife Management Associations

The Texas Organization of Wildlife Management Associations (TOWMA) was founded in 1996 to serve as a parent organization for a large number of wildlife management associations and cooperatives in south-central Texas. The TOWMA became a statewide organization in 1998. The purpose of TOWMA is to promote coordination between members of wildlife cooperatives by providing a forum for exchange of ideas and information. This forum helps maintain interest among existing cooperatives and provides support for establishment of new associations. The organization currently represents more than 60 wildlife management associations in 33 counties of Texas. The 3,000-plus landowners in these cooperatives control more than 600,000 hectares (1.5 million acres) of the Texas landscape. For more information about TOWMA, visit its Web site at http://www.towma.org/.

22 Sources of Information and Technical Assistance for Quail Managers

Dale Rollins

> Farming looks mighty easy when your plow is a pencil
> and you're a thousand miles from the cornfield.
> Dwight D. Eisenhower

372 The recent quail population declines in Texas have stimulated interest in quail management among landowners, hunters, and other stakeholders. Brennan (1991a) recognized the importance of education in helping stem the decline of bobwhites (*Colinus virginianus*). Historically, such interests have focused on management practices such as what to plant in food plots (Ramsey and Shult 1984) and the basic habitat requirements of bobwhites (Gore and Wilson 1987). Fortunately, landowners are becoming interested in looking beyond simply planting food plots for quail management. They want to know how to apply landscape-scale conservation practices that will benefit quails along with other species of wildlife.

Prior to 1970, quail management literature applicable to Texas was quite common (Lay 1954; Jackson 1969). The next 30 years saw few efforts toward enhancing the libraries of quail managers. Two key books, *The Bobwhite in the Rio Grande Plain of Texas* (Lehmann 1984) and *Beef, Brush, and Bobwhites* (Guthery 1986), are important compilations for quail managers in South Texas. Texas' other quail species, such as scaled quail (*Callipepla squamata*), garnered little attention until the last few years (Rollins 2000). Recently, national and statewide quail symposia (Cearley 1999; De Maso, Peterson, et al. 2002; DeMaso, Kuvlesky, et al. 2002), short courses (Cohen 1993, 1996), quail appreciation days (Rollins 2002), and related tours have become popular. The Internet clearinghouse for quail-related information from Texas is http://teamquail.tamu.edu.

This chapter lists and describes various types of technical assistance that are available—and mostly free—to quail managers in Texas. Sufficient information and expertise exist so that lack of advice about what people can do to enhance quail populations and habitat should not be a limiting factor.

Technical Advice

Technical advice on quail management is available from a variety of sources within Texas (table 22.1). Some provide on-site assistance, whereas others provide pamphlets or other publications. The more common sources of information for quail managers in Texas fall into five categories: agencies, universities, foundations, nongovernmental conservation organizations, and private industry (including consultants). Finally, local landowners who are successful quail managers should not be overlooked as sources of information and advice.

State agencies that provide technical assistance to quail managers include Texas Parks and Wildlife Department (TPWD) and Texas Cooperative Extension (hereafter Extension). Other state agencies that have

Table 22.1.
Sources for Technical Assistance on Quail Management in Texas

Entity	Technical assistance	Information	Cost share	Web site
Agencies: State				
Texas Parks and Wildlife Department 512-389-4800	X	X	X	www.tpwd.state.tx.us
Texas Cooperative Extension 979-845-7800	X	X		http://texasextension.tamu.edu
Texas Agricultural Experiment Station 979-862-4384		X		http://agresearch.tamu.edu
Texas Forest Service 979-458-6650	X	X		http://txforestservice.tamu.edu
Texas State Soil and Water Conservation Board 800-792-3485			X	http://www.tsswcb.state.tx.us
Texas Wildlife Damage Management Service 210-472-5451	X	X		http://wls.tamu.edu/
Agencies: Federal				
Farm Service Agency 979-680-5150		X		http://www.fsa.usda.gov/tx
Natural Resources Conservation Service 254-742-9800	X	X	X	www.tx.nrcs.usda.gov
U.S. Fish and Wildlife Service 817-277-1100	X	X	X	http://arlingtontexas.fws.gov/pfw.htm
Universities				
Angelo State University 325-942-2211		X		http://www.angelo.edu
Texas State University 512-245-2111		X		http://www.txstate.edu/
Stephen F. Austin State University 936-468-2011		X		http://www.sfasu.edu
Sul Ross State University 432-837-8011		X		http://www.sulross.edu
Tarleton State University 888-214-4636		X		http://www.tarleton.edu
Texas A&M University 979-845-5777	X[a]	X		http://wfscnet.tamu.edu
Texas A&M University–Kingsville 361-593-2111		X		http://www.tamuk.edu
Texas Tech University 806-742-2011		X		http://www.ttu.edu
Foundations and institutes				
Caesar Kleberg Wildlife Research Institute 361-595-3922		X		http://ckwri.tamuk.edu
National Fish and Wildlife Foundation 202-857-0166			X	www.nfwf.org
Noble Foundation 580-223-5810	X[b]	X		www.noble.org
Welder Wildlife Foundation 361-364-2643		X		http://hometown.aol.com/welderwf/welderweb.html
Conservation organizations				
Quail Unlimited 620-443-5834		X		www.qu.org
Society for Range Management (Texas Section) 979-845-5579		X		www.tssrm.org
Texas Audubon Society 512-306-0225		X		http://www.audubon.org/chapter/tx/tx
Texas Wildlife Association 210-826-2904		X		www.texas-wildlife.org
The Wildlife Society (Texas Chapter) 979-845-7471		X		www.tctws.org
Private industry				
Texas Flightbird Association 979-845-4319		X		www.texasflightbirdassn.org
Quail Forever 651-209-4980	X	X		www.quailforever.com

[a] Through Texas Cooperative Extension.
[b] Certain areas of north-central Texas.

relevance to quail managers include Texas Agricultural Experiment Station, Texas Forest Service, Texas Department of Agriculture, and Texas Wildlife Services. Federal agencies within the U.S. Department of Agriculture include the Natural Resources Conservation Service (NRCS) and Farm Services Agency (FSA), as well as local Soil and Water Conservation Districts. The U.S. Fish and Wildlife Service (USFWS) within the U.S. Department of the Interior administers some cost-share programs that may be helpful for quail habitat management. University departments within Texas that are often identified with quail management and research efforts are housed in the graduate wildlife research programs at Texas A&M University, Texas A&M University–Kingsville, and Texas Tech University. Other Texas universities involved with quail management and research include Angelo State University, Texas State University, Stephen F. Austin State University, Sul Ross State University, and Tarleton State University.

Foundations and institutes that address quail needs in Texas include the Caesar Kleberg Wildlife Research Institute at Texas A&M University–Kingsville, the Welder Wildlife Foundation at Sinton, and the Noble Foundation in Ardmore, Oklahoma, which serves parts of North Texas. Outside Texas, Tall Timbers Research Station (www.ttrs .org) and Ames Plantation (www.amesplantation.org) have information useful to quail managers, especially those managers interested in sustaining and elevating quail numbers in the Piney Woods of East Texas. The National Fish and Wildlife Foundation (not to be confused with the U.S. Fish and Wildlife Service) has grant funds available for cooperative quail habitat management efforts.

Nongovernmental conservation organizations that address quail conservation include Quail Unlimited, Bobwhite Brigade, Texas Wildlife Association, Audubon Texas, Texas Chapter of The Wildlife Society, and the Texas Section of Society for Range Management.

Private industry of interest to quail managers may include brush-control contractors, seed dealers, game-bird breeders, hunting outfitters, and other allied industries.

Types of Assistance

The information available to quail managers has been coordinated mostly by state agencies (such as TPWD), federal agencies (such as NRCS), and land-grant universities with cooperative extension programs.

On-Site Consultation

In a perfect world, any landowner seeking technical assistance on quail management could arrange a personal visit by a trained quail biologist to design and oversee implementation of a suitable management plan. Certainly such assistance is available, but staffing and budget constraints limit these opportunities. Such arrangements are likely to become even more restrictive in the future. The TPWD private-lands biologists can make site visits and prepare management plans (see table 22.1 for contact information for various agencies). Similarly, wildlife specialists with Texas Cooperative Extension, the outreach component of Texas A&M University, are located around the state and work through the network of local county Extension agents. The NRCS regional biologists and district conservationists can provide information on various

Farm Bill programs and other land management strategies. The Noble Foundation has a staff of wildlife biologists who provide free consultation to landowners within a 160-kilometer (100-mile) radius of Ardmore, Oklahoma.

Given the growing economic importance of quails, there are surprisingly few private consultants who specialize in quail management. A private consultant works on a fee basis to provide on-site assistance in a turnkey fashion. As a number of ranches trade hands and move from traditional livestock operations to quail management, there is a growing need for more private consultants. When considering a private consultant, seek references and credentials to ensure that he or she knows the business. Currently, there is no registry or directory of private consultants in Texas.

Technology Transfer

Technology transfer is a flow of knowledge from some source—such as university scientists—to the practitioner and results in a positive change or a solution to a problem. For the most part, the technology of quail management is not rocket science, nor does it change quickly. Quail management is rooted in the basics of land stewardship and conservation—including soil, water, and human resources. Unfortunately, far too much of the Texas landscape is uninhabitable from a quail perspective. Technology transfer for quail information in Texas involves several agencies, but mostly Extension, TPWD, and NRCS. Other quail-related entities, such as Caesar Kleberg Wildlife Research Institute and Quail Unlimited, are usually involved as cosponsors of Extension activities.

Extension Education

Beginning in 1914, the Extension partnership between the USDA, land-grant universities (Texas A&M University in Texas), and county governments formed the backbone of outreach education for agriculture and natural resources. County Extension agents, who are present in nearly every county of Texas, work locally with interested cooperators to identify educational needs and implement educational programs. There are presently five Extension wildlife specialists from various regions of the state. They typically deliver the educational programming in conjunction with other resource specialists. Recent Extension education programs that focused on quails are summarized in table 22.2.

The goal of an Extension education effort is different from that of a consultant and is characterized by the adage "Give a man a fish and you

Table 22.2.
Some Educational Programs and Products on Quail Management Offered by
Texas Cooperative Extension, 1990–2002

Name	Type of program	Description
Quail Appreciation Days	Workshop	1-day workshops on quail biology and management for landowners
Texas Quail Index	Demonstration	Series of counts to estimate quail abundance and trends
Preserving Texas' Quail Heritage into the Twenty-first Century	Symposium	3-day symposium to assemble current art and science of quail management in Texas into the twenty-first century
Key seed-producing plants for quail	Color poster	Important plants for quails
Aging and sexing northern bobwhites	Fact sheet	How to determine age and gender of bobwhites by examining plumage

Figure 22.1.
Extension events focused at quail conservation include "Quail Appreciation Days" (top left), demonstrations (top right), regional symposia (bottom left), and the Bobwhite Brigade Wildlife Leadership Camps (bottom right). Photos by Dale Rollins

have fed him for a day. Teach a man to fish and you have fed him for a lifetime." Accordingly, the strategy of Extension education corresponds to the Chinese proverb "Tell me and I forget; show me and I remember; involve·me, and I understand."

Grassroots educational efforts generally focus on county-level meetings complemented with demonstrations, tours, and field days with the objective of having land managers involved in the process. The educational approach will likely involve passive learning (such as the distribution of fact sheets [e.g., Ramsey and Shult 1984], news articles, or symposia, but hands-on teaching through demonstrations is the preferred method. Hands-on learning activities for quail managers include collection of harvest records (such as wing surveys) (Koerth, Kuvlesky, and Payne 1991); collection of plants and seeds (Rollins 1991); and habitat management (such as brush management).

Extension events focused at quail conservation include a series of one-day workshops called "Quail Appreciation Days," demonstration efforts such as the "Texas Quail Index," regional symposia in North and South Texas, and the Bobwhite Brigade Wildlife Leadership Camps (Rollins et al. 2000; figure 22.1). For more information about these events, see http://teamquail.tamu.edu.

Printed Information
Various publications of interest to quail managers include books, leaflets, newsletters, and symposia proceedings (table 22.3). Some of the older, out-of-print regional bulletins such as those by Jackson (1969) and Lay (1954) are collectors' items. Perhaps the easiest way to get a

Table 22.3.
Selected References for Quail Managers in Texas

Type	Title	Source	Availability
Books			
	Beef, brush, and bobwhites	Guthery (1986)	Out of print
	Bobwhites of the Rio Grande Plain	Lehmann (1984)	Out of print
	On bobwhites	Guthery (2000)	Available
	The technology of bobwhite management	Guthery (2002)	Available
	Texas quail	Meinzer and Sasser (1997)	Available
	The bobwhite quail	Stoddard (1931)	Out of print
	The bobwhite quail	Rosene (1969)	Available
	Population ecology of the bobwhite	Roseberry and Klimstra (1984)	Available
	Seed identification manual	Martin and Barclay (1961)	Out of print
Bulletins			
	A handbook for bobwhite quail management in the West Texas Rolling Plains	Jackson (1969)	Available (pdf)[a]
	Quail management handbook for East Texas	Lay (1954)	Available (pdf)
	A guide for aging scaled quail	Cain and Beasom (1983)	Available (pdf)
	Habitat appraisal guide for bobwhite quail	Bidwell et al. (1991)	Available (pdf)
Fact sheets			
	Sexing and aging the northern bobwhite	Koerth, Kuvlesky, and Payne (1991)	Available (pdf)
	Bobwhite quail management in South Texas	Hanselka and Guthery (1991)	Available (pdf)
	Northern bobwhite (Colinus virginianus)	Brennan (1999)	Available
	Scaled quail (Callipepla squamata)	Schemnitz (1994)	Available
	Bobwhite facts and fantasies	Gore and Wilson (1987)	Available (pdf)
Posters			
	Upland game birds of Texas	Rollins and Hysmith (1997)	Available
	Key seed-producing plants for quail	Rollins (1999b)	Available
	Woody plants for wildlife of the Rolling Plains	Rollins and Cadenhead (1995)	Available
Symposia proceedings			
	Proceedings of the 5th National Quail Symposium	DeMaso, Peterson, et al.(2002); DeMaso, Townsend, et al. (2002)	Available
	Preserving Texas' quail heritage into the 21st century	Cearley (1999)	Available
	Proceedings of the Texas quail short course (Vols. 1 and 2)	Cohen (1993, 1996)	Available (pdf)

[a] Portable document format; publication is available on the Internet (see http://teamquail.tamu.edu).

copy of these classic bulletins is to photocopy an original if you can find a colleague who owns one. Most are available electronically at the TeamQuail Web site.

Books

Books of particular value to quail managers in Texas include those covering quail biology and management (Guthery 1986, 2000), quail hunting (Meinzer and Sasser 1997), plant identification (Taylor, Rutledge, and Herrera 1997), seed identification (Martin and Barclay 1961; Rosene and Freeman 1988; Davis 1993), and related habitat management practices (Scifres 1980; Wright and Bailey 1982). Several of these are out of print but can be purchased through a used-book seller. Two bobwhite classics that apply to East Texas Piney Woods habitats include those by Stoddard (1931) and Rosene (1969). Other books on quails, albeit more technical, include those by Roseberry and Klimstra (1984) and Guthery (2002).

Periodicals

Several magazines (such as *Farmer-Stockman, Progressive Farmer,* and *Livestock Weekly*) have occasional articles on quail management. *Quail Unlimited Magazine, Quail Forever,* and *The Covey Rise* are the only periodicals dedicated to quail hunting and management. Similarly, various newsletters from organizations such as Noble Foundation and Caesar Kleberg Wildlife Research Institute address quail-related matters.

Symposia Proceedings

Printed proceedings from various regional, state, or national quail symposia are available. Some (DeMaso, Peterson, et al. 2002; DeMaso, Kuvlesky, et al. 2002) are quite technical, whereas others (Cearley 1999) are more oriented toward landowners and managers. Extension has conducted various wildlife symposia since 1993, including such quail-related topics as brush sculpting and grazing management. The proceedings of these symposia are available in printed or electronic form (see http://tcebookstore.org for availability).

Online Sources

The Internet has made a variety of quail-related information readily available. Quail-related Web sites are listed in table 22.4. Only a few will be mentioned in detail here. The TeamQuail Web site is a good portal to find information pertaining to quail management in Texas. The Noble Foundation's Web site has an excellent online plant identification gallery. Several universities have Web sites that feature various quail management publications (for example, http://wildlife.tamu.edu).

Cost-Share Assistance

Various federal and state-funded programs may provide cost-share assistance or incentives for landowners to implement habitat management practices (table 22.5). As of 2003, some of these included federally administered programs offered by the FSA and the USFWS.

Various USDA Farm Bill programs that can be used to enhance quail habitat include the Environmental Quality Incentives Program (EQIP), Wildlife Habitat Incentives Program (WHIP), and the Conservation Reserve Program (CRP). The USFWS Partners for Wildlife and

Table 22.4.
Selected Web Sites Offering Information Pertinent to Quail Management in Texas

Name	Web site	Comments
Albany Area Quail Management Project	www.quailmanagement.com	News and publications from south-eastern U.S. quail efforts
Bobwhite Brigade	www.texasbrigades.org	Youth leadership camps focusing on quail conservation
Breeding Bird Survey	http://www.mbrpwrc.usgs.gov/bbs/bbs.html	Allows estimation of quail trends for various regions and time periods
Caesar Kleberg Wildlife Research Institute	http://ckwri.tamuk.edu	Newsletter and publications from South Texas
Noble Foundation	www.noble.org	Newsletters and plant gallery
Quail Unlimited	www.qu.org	Links to various events and information
Southeastern Quail Study Group	http://seqsg.qu.org/seqsg/index.cfm	Source for Northern Bobwhite Quail Initiative
Tall Timbers Research Station	http://ttrs.org	Source for national quail symposia proceedings; research findings
TeamQuail	http://teamquail.tamu.edu	Good starting point; links to other quail sites
TEXNAT	http://texnat.tamu.edu	Range and wildlife management information; source of numerous symposia proceedings
WILDLIFE	http://wildlife.tamu.edu	Online publications through Texas A&M University
Texas Parks and Wildlife Department	www.tpwd.state.tx.us	Population trends for quails in various ecoregions

Table 22.5.
Types of Cost-Share Assistance for Quail Habitat Management

Program	Contact	Website
Conservation Reserve Program	USDA Farm Service Agency	www.fsa.usda.gov
Environmental Quality Incentives Program	USDA Natural Resources Conservation Service	www.tx.nrcs.usda.gov
Wildlife Habitat Improvement Program	USDA Natural Resources Conservation Service	www.tx.nrcs.usda.gov
Landowner Incentive Program	Texas Parks and Wildlife Department	www.tpwd.state.tx.us
Partners for Wildlife	U.S. Fish and Wildlife Service	http://arlingtontexas.fws.gov/pfw.htm

state-funded programs administered by TPWD (the Landowner Incentive Program) may be aimed at species other than quails, but such cost-shared projects can usually be made to work for quails. The Texas State Soil and Water Conservation Board has provided funding for brush control—which can benefit quail habitat—for water-related conservation efforts in parts of West Texas. Eligibility rules for cost-sharing programs change frequently and may have regional or county restrictions.

Other Useful Tools

Resources such as remote imagery and other tools such as cameras, seed and plant collections, and access to native plant materials can be very useful to a quail manager.

Remote Imagery

Aerial photographs and geo-referenced satellite imagery are useful when planning quail habitat management efforts such as brush management or prescribed burning. The advent of geographic information systems (GIS) has been a boon to land planning. Many local NRCS offices have GIS capabilities for using color infrared imagery to help plan brush sculpting or other land management practices. Several universities have GIS labs that can—usually for a fee—produce maps and various imagery useful to quail managers. The Texas Natural Resource Information System offers color infrared imagery for many locations across Texas at a reasonable fee. Local NRCS offices and Soil and Water Conservation Districts also have aerial photographs (black and white) for helping landowners construct a conservation plan.

Cameras

A good-quality 35-millimeter or digital camera is an asset for quail managers. Photographers can assemble a photographic plant collection for their property and also use photography to monitor vegetation change over time (McGinty and White 1998). Recently, motion-sensing cameras (35-millimeter, digital, or video) have become popular. They can be used for monitoring quail feeders or waterers. A listing of various models is available at the TEXNAT Web site (http://texnat.tamu.edu). More expensive versions of such cameras are used by researchers to monitor predator activity at quail nests (see Web sites for Tall Timbers Research Station and Ames Plantation).

Seed Collections

A seed collection tailored to one's local area is an invaluable tool for studying quail diets. Online photographs of some common seeds from

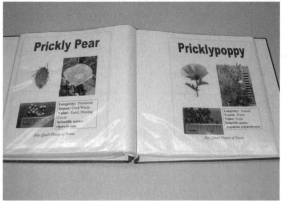

Figure 22.2.
Seed and plant collections are valuable references that can be tailored to a specific region.
Photo by Dale Rollins

quail crops can be found at the Bobwhite Brigades' Web site (www.texasbrigades.org). A handy seed reference can be made by identifying seeds from quail crops taken from your property, segregating them to species, and then cataloging the seeds in cellophane coin holders (Rollins 1991). The individual seed specimens can be placed in plastic sleeves (used for storing 2- × 2-inch color slides) for storage in a three-ring binder.

Plant Collections

Similar to the seed collection, a collection of key plants for quails, specific to one's region, is a valuable reference (figure 22.2). Plant specimens can be pressed and mounted, or the photographs can simply be printed and assembled for the collection. Color posters featuring key seed-producing and woody plants for quails in Texas (Rollins 1999b; Rollins and Cadenhead 1995) can be found at http://tcebookstore.org.

Plant Materials

Shrubs for improving woody cover on quail range can be obtained from the Texas Forest Service as bare-root seedlings. Local Soil and Water Conservation Districts usually serve as ordering points for such materials. Other sources for plant materials of interest to quail managers include the Plant Material Centers (located at Knox City) of the NRCS and South Texas Natives plant initiative of the Caesar Kleberg Wildlife Research Institute.

Summary

Texas landowners interested in enhancing their quail management skills can access a variety of information sources. Various state and federal agencies have published bulletins, fact sheets, and related information, many of which are available on the Internet. Educational programs on quail management are offered at the county, regional, and state levels. Some agencies, such as the NRCS, offer cost-share assistance or incentives to landowners interested in implementing habitat management practices. Conservation organizations, such as Quail Unlimited, and commodity groups, such as the Texas Wildlife Association, provide outlets for quail-related information. Despite its place in the importance in the future of quail conservation, Texas has few private consultants who specialize in quail management. Landowners interested in quail management are encouraged to locate, organize, and support local wildlife management associations or co-ops that can result in management at larger scales than is possible on individual properties.

Effects of Quail Management on Other Wildlife

23

William P. Kuvlesky Jr.

> The apparent link between red-cockaded woodpecker and bobwhite
> habitat management in mature pine forests can, and should, be used
> to demonstrate the value of adaptive, integrated habitat management
> for terrestrial vertebrates.
> Brennan (1991a)

A lucrative recreational hunting economy has emerged in South Texas and is emerging elsewhere, such as in the Rolling Plains. Typically, ranchers in South Texas can expect, on average, to net $5.00–7.50/hectare/year (about $2.00–3.00/acre/year) from cattle operations. Currently, hunting leases range $20–$62/hectare/year (about $8–$25/acre/year) (Rhyne 1998). Hunters who lease both hunting and grazing rights often end up, on average, paying ranchers more than $37/hectare/year ($15/acre/year). Hunters sometimes lease an entire ranch, or at least a large pasture consisting of several thousand acres. Clearly, the gross profits generated from wildlife production frequently exceed those of livestock production on many South Texas ranches. This new economic force continues to grow and has the potential to dramatically impact how rangelands are used and managed throughout Texas.

Quail Hunting

Texas ranchers clearly have a financial incentive to actively manage vegetation in a manner that provides habitat conditions conducive to quail production. However, although quails may be the driving force behind habitat management programs on millions of acres of private land in Texas, quail habitat management has a profound impact on many non-target wildlife species that represent an additional potential source of revenue.

For example, wildlife watchers spent more than $1 billion in Texas during 2001 compared to the approximately $2 billion spent by hunters (U.S. Fish and Wildlife Service 2002). Also, like Texas quail hunters, the majority of nonconsumptive wildlife enthusiasts are from demographic categories that generally have substantial discretionary funds, which they are willing to devote to their favorite outdoor activities. It is therefore important to understand how quail habitat management impacts other valuable species of wildlife.

Wildlife watchers have become a significant economic force in Texas. The money they spend in pursuit of their activities has a tremendous real and potential impact on rural economies. Ranchers should understand that because of the growing popularity of nature tourism, they have an opportunity to market the nongame wildlife resources on their lands to individuals who have no interest in hunting. Today more than ever, nongame wildlife can be a valuable commodity to ranchers who want to diversify their wildlife programs beyond hunting.

Consequently, the purpose of this chapter is to review how quail management in Texas impacts other native wildlife species. Because most active quail management programs currently occur on private ranches, much of this chapter will focus on management practices applied to rangelands. However, active quail management also occurs in East Texas, where timber management is an important land use. The final section of the chapter will be devoted to how quail management in forest ecosystems impacts other wildlife.

Quail Management on Texas Rangelands

Most quail populations in Texas inhabit rangeland vegetation communities. Consequently, quail management in most parts of Texas involves aspects of grazing (figures 23.1 and 23.2) and/or brush management. Numerous factors influence and determine how rangelands are managed for quails. Land-use history and the financial resources available to a landowner have a substantial impact on management decisions. Nevertheless, maintaining an appropriate configuration of woody and herbaceous cover on a sufficiently large area is generally the basic requirement needed to maintain a self-sustaining quail population. Numerous management practices can be implemented to meet the habitat

Figure 23.1.
On rangeland habitats, the cattle-grazing regimes have a huge impact on populations of quails and other grassland birds.
Photo by William P. Kuvlesky

Figure 23.2.
Two views of quail and grassland bird habitat. The right side of the fence represents good grazing stewardship and good habitat for quails and grassland birds. The left side of the fence represents overgrazing and lack of grass cover essential for quails and grassland birds.
Photo by Dale Rollins

requirements of quail populations on rangelands. The following section will summarize the potential impacts of some of the most common quail habitat management practices on other species of wildlife.

Prescribed Burning

Although prescribed burning has been used for decades to improve bobwhite habitat in the southeastern United States and has become a cultural tradition in that part of the world, no such tradition has yet developed in Texas. In contrast, livestock grazing has been a cultural tradition in Texas for more than 150 years. Destroying forage with fire is anathema to many livestock producers. However, because quail production has become so lucrative in recent years, more landowners are reducing cattle stocking rates and implementing prescribed burning as means of managing herbaceous vegetation.

Numerous quail biologists have extolled the virtues of prescribed burning relative to quail production (Stoddard 1931; Rosene 1969; Lehmann 1984; Guthery 1986; Brennan, Cooper, et al. 1995; Brennan et al. 1998). It is clear that fire can be used to improve quail habitat if it is prescribed under the right circumstances and conditions. However, few prescribed burning studies have been devoted to the impacts of fires on rangeland wildlife in Texas, especially with regard to nongame species. Nevertheless, Scifres and Hamilton (1993) believed that prescribed burning applied with the intention of improving livestock production will generally benefit wildlife populations because the majority of prescribed burns are patchy and result in a mosaic of different habitat types that support a diversity of wildlife species.

Nongame Birds

Prescribed fire does not appear to negatively affect rangeland nongame bird communities in Texas. Species-specific responses to prescribed fires vary depending on the habitat requirements of each species. For example, winter prescribed fires affect postfire abundance of species that prefer dense herbaceous vegetation, such as Brewer's sparrows (*Spizella gramnieus*), Le Conte's sparrows (*Ammodramus leconteii*), grasshopper sparrows (*A. savannarum*), sedge wrens (*Cistothorus platensis*), and wrens (*Troglodytidae*) (table 23.1). In contrast, bird species that prefer shorter, less dense herbaceous habitats, such as some sparrow species in the family Emberizinae and brown-headed cowbird (*Molothrus ater*), are often more abundant on burned areas one year postfire.

As in Texas, prescribed burning research conducted elsewhere on southwestern rangelands indicates that fire generally has little long-term negative impacts on bird communities. For instance, Bock and Bock (1992) noted that the abundance and diversity of the bird community changed in response to prescribed fire for at least two years postfire. Fall bird populations increased on burned areas compared to those on unburned control sites in response to greater availability of seeds. Species of breeding birds that preferred open habitats with reduced litter also preferred the burned sites, whereas species that required tall, thick grass cover and those that needed shrubs were less abundant on burned sites. Nevertheless, Bock and Bock concluded that the bird community's response to the summer wildfire was largely ephemeral because the

Table 23.1.
Response(s) of Selected Rangeland Wildlife Species to Range Management Practices Utilized to Improve Quail Habitat in Texas

Source	State or region	Management practice	Species affected and response,[a] (+), (−), (n)
Adams (1978)	Texas	Grazing	White-tailed deer (−)
Beasom and Scifres (1977)	Texas	Herbicides	Feral hog (n), javelina (−), nilgai (n), white-tailed deer (−)
Best (1972)	California	Herbicides	Brewer' sparrow (−), vesper sparrow (n)
Black and Frischknecht (1971)	Intermountain West	Grazing	Harvest mouse (−)
Bozzo, Beasom, and Fulbright (1992)	Texas	Root-plowing	White-tailed deer (+)
Bozzo, Beasom, and Fulbright (1992)	Texas	Roller-chopping	White-tailed deer (+)
Bryant, Kothman, and Merrill (1979)	Texas	Grazing	White-tailed deer (−)
Buttery and Shields (1975)	Intermountain West	Grazing	Nongame birds (−)
Castrale (1982)	Intermountain West	Prescribed burning, chaining, and plowing	Brewer's sparrow (−), horned lark (+), sage thrasher (−), vesper sparrow (n), western meadowlark (n)
Clary and Holmgren (1981)		Grazing	Pronghorn (n)
Cohen (1986)	Texas	Grazing	White-tailed deer (−)
Crouch (1982)	Colorado	Grazing	Cottontail (−)
Drawe (1991)	Texas	Grazing	White-tailed deer (−)
Ellis (1970)		Grazing	Pronghorn (−)
Fagerstone and Ramey (1996)	North America	Grazing	Pocket mouse (−), jackrabbit (+)
Feldhamer (1979)	Oregon	Grazing	Cotton rat (−), harvest mouse (−), deer mouse (+), white-footed mouse (+)
Fitzgerald and Tanner (1992)	Florida	Roller-chopping	Shrub-dependent birds (−), grassland birds (+)
Ford (1977)	Indiana	Grazing	Harvest mouse (−)
Fulbright and Guthery (1996)	Texas	Root-plowing	White-tailed deer (−)
Germano, Hungerford, and Martin (1983)	Arizona	Chaining	Bird community (−), antelope jackrabbit (−), black-tailed jackrabbit (−), cottontail (−)
Gruver and Guthery (1986)	Texas	Herbicides	Bird community (n)
Guthery, Anderson, and Lehmann (1979)	Texas	Grazing	Cotton rat (−)
Hanley and Page (1982)	Intermountain West	Grazing	Pocket mouse (−)
Hawbecker (1975)	California	Grazing	Ground squirrel (−)
Jones, Armstrong, and Choate (1985)	Great Plains	Grazing	Black-tailed jackrabbit (−)
Kaufman, Finck, and Kaufman (1990)	Kansas	Prescribed burning	Deer mouse (+), grasshopper mouse (+), ground squirrel (+), harvest mouse (−), heteromyids (+), microtines (−), wood rat (−), zapodids (+)
Koerth (1996)	Texas	Herbicides	White-tailed deer (n)
Lochmiller et al. (1991)	Oklahoma	Prescribed burning, herbicides	Cottontail (+)
McNay and O'Gara (1981)	Intermountain West	Grazing	Pronghorn (−)
Meeker (1981)	Nevada	Grazing	Pronghorn (n)
Merrill, Teer, and Wallmo (1957)	Texas	Grazing	White-tailed deer (−)
Mix, Kuvlesky, and Drawe (2003)	Texas	Prescribed burning	Brown-headed cowbird (+)
Moulton (1978)	Colorado	Grazing	Deer mouse (+)
Nolte and Fulbright (1997)	Texas	Herbicides	Bird community (n)
O'Meara et al. (1981)	Colorado	Chaining	Bird community (−), rodent community (+)
Overmire (1963)	Oklahoma	Grazing	Dickcissel (−), Bell's vireo (−)
Powell (1968)	Texas	Root-plowing	Rodent community (+)
Pyrah and Jorgenson (1974)	Intermountain West	Herbicides	Brewer's sparrow (−)
Reynolds and Krausman (1998)	Texas	Prescribed burning	Grasshopper sparrow (−), LeConte's sparrow (−), sedge wren (−)
Rollins et al. (1988)	Texas	Chaining	Bird community (+), cottontail (−), white-tailed deer (+)
Ruthven, Hellgren, and Beasom (1994)	Texas	Root-plowing	White-tailed deer (+)
Saab et al. (1995)	Western United States and Great Plains	Grazing	Bell's vireo (−), cactus wren (−), Cassin's sparrow (−), common ground dove (+), curve-billed thrasher (−), grasshopper sparrow (−), groove-billed ani (+), horned lark (−), lark sparrow (−), long-billed curlew (−), northern cardinal (+), savanna sparrow (+), Sprague's pipit (−), verdin (−), vesper sparrow (+), western meadowlark (−)
Schulz et al. (1992a)	Oklahoma	Herbicides	Bird community (+)
Senzota (1986)	Texas	Prescribed burning, herbicides	Cotton rat (+), cottontail (+)
Smith (1940)	Oklahoma	Grazing	Nongame birds (−)
Stamp and Ohmart (1978)	Arizona	Grazing	Kangaroo rat (+), hispid cotton rat (−)
Stangl et al. (1992)	Texas	Grazing	Kangaroo rat (+)
Steenburgh and Warren (1977)	Arizona	Grazing	Wood rat (−)
Tanner, Inglis, and Blankenship (1978)	Texas	Herbicides	White-tailed deer (n)
Taylor, Vorhies, and Lister (1935)	Arizona	Grazing	Jackrabbit (−)
Taylor (1989)	Texas	Herbicides	White-tailed deer (n)

(*continued*)

Table 23.1.
(*continued*)

Source	State or region	Management practice	Species affected and response,[a] (+), (−), (n)
Teer (1996)	Texas	Grazing	White-tailed deer (−)
Tewes (1982)	Texas	Prescribed burning	Cotton rat (+), rice rat (−)
Tewes and Schmidly (1987)	Texas	Mechanical operations	Ocelot (−)
Van't Hul, Lutz, and Mathews (1997)	Texas	Prescribed burning	Wren (−), sparrow (+)
Vega and Rappole (1994)	Texas	Roller-chopping and disking	White-eyed vireo (−), olive sparrow (−), common ground dove (+), lark sparrow (+)
Yoakum, O'Gara, and Howard (1996)	Intermountain West	Grazing	Pronghorn (−)

[a] + = positive population response, − = negative population response, n = neutral.

observed fire-related changes in bird abundance did not persist after the vegetation began to recover from the fire.

Brawn, Robinson, and Thompson (2001) also noted that grassland bird responses to fire were species specific based on natural-history requirements of individual species. Like Bock and Bock (1992), Brawn, Robinson, and Thompson observed that birds that preferred short grasses and bare ground were more abundant a year or two postfire and that they become less abundant as the vegetation recovered. These species are gradually replaced by species that become more abundant as herbaceous cover becomes taller and thicker. Eventually, species that prefer shrubs gradually replace mid- to tall grassland species as woody vegetation begins to invade an area several years after a fire.

Small Mammals

Like nongame bird populations, small-mammal populations display variable responses to prescribed burning depending on species-specific habitat requirements. Scifres and Hamilton (1993) reported that fire might affect small mammals directly by impacting food and cover or indirectly by stimulating inter- and intraspecific interactions. Moreover, Riggs, Bunting, and Daniels (1996) stated that rodent species richness is not impacted by fire, although the relative abundance of certain species can be affected. For instance, species that require relatively dense vegetation and litter, such as microtines, harvest mice (*Reithrodontomys* sp.), cotton rats (*Sigmodon hispidus*), rice rats (*Oryzomys palustris*), and wood rats (*Neotoma floridana*), typically display negative responses to fire. Table 23.1 provides a summary of responses of selected wildlife species to range management practices that benefit quails and can be consulted in relation to the following discussion. Conversely, species that prefer open habitats, such as heteromyid and zapodid rodents, deer mice (*Peromyscus* sp.), grasshopper mice (*Onychomys* sp.), cotton rats (*S. hispidus*), and ground squirrels (*Spermophilius* sp.), respond in a positive manner to fire.

Lagomorphs also appear to respond in a species-specific manner to fire. Cottontails (*Sylvilagus floridanus*) prefer lower successional habitats that are typical of disturbed areas, and because fire represents a significant disturbance, it often has a positive impact on cottontail populations. Indeed, Lochmiller et al. (1991) reported that cottontail densities increased in response to prescribed burning in Oklahoma because fires created or maintained forest-prairie ecotones.

In the absence of dramatic habitat alteration, small-mammal populations are characteristically resilient in response to manipulation of plant communities. The duration of fire impacts on small-mammal populations is influenced by the timing and intensity of prescribed burns, though most impacts are brief due to the rapid recovery of vegetation communities and the high reproductive potential of most small-mammal species (Riggs, Bunting, and Daniels 1996).

Large Mammals

White-tailed deer (*Odocoileus virginianus*) are the most popular big-game mammal in Texas. Consequently, most large-mammal habitat management research, including that devoted to prescribed burning, has focused on white-tailed deer. Scifres and Hamilton (1993) provide an excellent review of the impacts of prescribed fire on white-tailed deer in South Texas. They stated that white-tailed deer generally benefit from application of prescribed burns to habitats they occupy because most prescribed fires ignited in South Texas do not result in uniform burns. Patches of burned and unburned habitats prevail on most burn units and thus provide deer with the diversity of plant successional stages that they prefer (Bailey 1984). Moreover, because white-tailed deer are grazers and prefer forbs over any other food class (Drawe 1968; Walsh 1985) and because prescribed fires, particularly late-winter fires, promote forb growth, prescribed burning that benefits and maintains quail habitat can also provide deer with a preferred source of food. Browse, however, is also an important source of food, especially during drought and in drier areas of Texas (Arnold and Drawe 1979). Consequently, prescribed fires ignited at any time of the year on shrublands provide deer with nutritious woody regrowth that is more accessible than mature brush for variable lengths of time, depending on the species composition and diversity of the brush community (Scifres and Hamilton 1993).

In addition to food, white-tailed deer habitat must have sufficient screening cover to support a quality deer population. However, unlike other brush management practices that are poorly planned and either remove too much woody cover or remove woody cover in favored deer habitats such as draws or creeks, fires generally leave adequate woody cover to meet the requirements of white-tailed deer on Texas rangelands. Moreover, because South Texas fires are usually patchy due to a lack of fine fuel (in thick stands of brush, for example) and they leave standing woody material and stimulate brush regrowth, sufficient screening cover for deer typically remains on most burned pastures (Scifres and Hamilton 1993). Therefore, application of prescribed fire to improve quail habitat also usually benefits white-tailed deer populations.

Other common big-game mammals that inhabit Texas rangelands managed for quails include javelinas (*Dicotyles tajacu*), pronghorns (*Antiolocapra americana*), feral hogs (*Sus scrofa*), and a variety of exotic mammals, such as nilgai (*Boselaphus tragocamelus*). However, little information exists about how prescribed burning impacts these species. Nevertheless, we do know something about the life history of each of the mammals, so we can speculate about how prescribed burning impacts each of them.

Javelinas, for example, typically have a strong preference for brush, which provides important cover and, to a lesser extent, food. Therefore, prescribed fire that results in extensive top-kill of brush can be expected to reduce the utility of habitats for javelinas for several years posttreatment. Conversely, pronghorns prefer grasslands. Thus, prescribed fire could improve pronghorn habitat conditions if a significant amount of brush is removed from a landscape by fire.

Nilgai and feral hogs have more flexible habitat requirements than javelinas or pronghorns. Like white-tailed deer, nilgai consume forbs and woody species; however, they can also eat grass, which deer rarely consume. This makes nilgai more efficient competitors than deer. Although plant materials constitute the bulk of feral hog diets, they typically consume a wider variety of plants than other large wild mammals inhabiting rangelands. Feral hogs are omnivorous—they consume animal matter on an opportunistic basis. Consequently, food availability rarely limits feral hog populations. Both nilgai and feral hogs require some woody cover but probably do not require screening cover to the extent that white-tailed deer and javelinas do. Therefore, because nilgai and feral hogs are flexible in their diets, prescribed fires probably do not negatively impact their populations. More likely, nilgai and feral hog populations, as do white-tailed deer populations, benefit from the impacts of prescribed burning on rangeland vegetation communities.

Predators

A variety of predators also inhabit Texas rangelands; however, in the absence of fires that uniformly consume significant amounts of standing vegetation on several thousand acres—such burns are extremely rare events in Texas—fires probably do not negatively affect most mammalian predator species. Coyotes (*Canis latrans*), bobcats (*Lynx rufus*), mountain lions (*Felis concolor*), gray foxes (*Urocyon cinerageneus*), badgers (*Taxidea taxus*), and skunks (*Mephitis mephitis*) are all capable of escaping conflagrations. Although they may avoid burned areas because of lack of cover and a temporary reduction in prey abundance, most predator populations undoubtedly benefit from application of prescribed fire, because usually within a year of a fire, prey populations have either recovered or increased beyond preburn levels.

Mechanical Habitat Management

Although it is more expensive and time intensive than prescribed burning, mechanically manipulating rangeland vegetation communities to improve quail habitat is popular among Texas landowners because it is possible to dramatically alter the structure and composition of plant communities on specific areas in specific patterns in a reasonably short period of time. Soil aerating and roller-chopping are used on many ranches in South Texas to improve quail habitat—brush can be removed in specific locations and in specific patterns. Significant ground disturbance occurs, stimulating the growth of important quail foods provided by forbs. Similar to soil-aerating and roller-chopping, range disking can be applied with great specificity to small acreages. Forb production increases as a result of the significant soil disturbance that occurs after such an operation.

Clearly, most other wildlife species that inhabit rangelands mechanically improved for quails are also impacted by the treatment operations. However, certain species and classes of wildlife are more dramatically impacted than others.

Nongame Birds

Several studies have indicated that mechanical habitat management has a negative impact on bird communities occupying rangelands, though other studies have noted that bird communities respond favorably to such operations. It appears that mechanical habitat management can be detrimental to shrub-obligate species but benefit grassland species (O'Meara et al. 1981; Germano, Hungerford, and Martin 1983; Fitzgerald and Tanner 1992). For example, populations of olive sparrow (*Arremonops rufivirgatus*), sage thrasher (*Oreoscoptes montanus*), and white-eyed vireo (*Vireo griseus*) decline in habitats manipulated mechanically, whereas those of common ground-dove (*Columbina passerina*), horned lark (*Eremophila alpestris*), lark sparrow (*Chondestes grammacus*), vesper sparrow (*Pooecetes gramineus*), and western meadowlark (*Sturnella neglecta*) increase or are unaffected.

Fulbright and Guthery (1996) concluded that species adapted to woody communities decline in response to mechanical habitat treatments, whereas species adapted to herbaceous habitats increase. They believed that the size and configuration of treated areas were important relative to how bird communities would respond to mechanical habitat management. The results of a study they conducted in a complex mesquite–mixed-brush community in South Texas indicated that bird species richness and diversity were not impacted when undisturbed strips of brush 140 meters (154 yards) wide were preserved every 200 meters (220 yards) within a pasture that was subjected to range disking. Similarly, O'Meara et al. (1981) believed that the adverse effects of chaining on bird communities could be mitigated by reducing the widths of cleared areas and increasing survival of shrubs and young trees, as well as retaining tree cavities in treated areas. Castrale (1982) also demonstrated that applying mechanical treatments in 100-meter (110-yard) strips could maximize avian species diversity in sagebrush communities. This technique maintains large blocks of undisturbed sagebrush habitat.

Mechanical habitat management can be applied to Texas rangelands for quail management without harming bird communities if the treatments are carefully planned and applied in an appropriate manner and on areas where benefits will be maximized. Grassland birds in particular could benefit from mechanical habitat management if significant acreages of brush are reduced in favor of native herbaceous vegetation. This is an important consideration because grassland birds have declined more precipitously during the past 30 years than any other comparable avian guild in North America (Sauer, Hines, and Fallon 2002), and habitat improvement on Texas wintering grounds may be vital to reversing the declines of numerous species.

Small Mammals

Mechanical habitat manipulation does not appear to substantially impact rodent populations to the same extent it does bird populations. The reason is that rodent populations appear to recover quickly after the initial shock effects associated with the vegetation structure and composition changes resulting from mechanical habitat treatments. For instance, Powell (1968) reported that rodent densities were higher on root-plowed areas in South Texas than on untreated areas. Similarly,

Guthery, Anderson, and Lehmann (1979) reported that cotton rat densities were higher on South Texas root-plowed pastures than untreated areas because biomass of important grass species and forbs was greater on the treated areas. Furthermore, O'Meara et al. (1981) reported that small-mammal populations were 200–300 percent higher on pinyon-juniper rangeland in Colorado that had been chained 1, 8, and 15 years prior to their sampling operations. Fulbright and Guthery (1996) also noted that even though rodent populations may increase following mechanical brush clearing, the rodent community composition might also be altered.

Unlike rodents, lagomorphs may not prefer areas where mechanical brush clearing has occurred. Several studies have indicated that cottontail (*Sylvilagus audubonii*), black-tailed jackrabbit (*Lepus californicus*), and antelope jackrabbit (*L. alleni*) populations seemed more abundant on undisturbed areas than on partially cleared mesquite savanna, though one study indicated that cottontail populations increased as a result of brush-clearing operations.

Small-mammal communities do not appear to be as significantly impacted by mechanical habitat manipulation as are bird communities that inhabit rangelands. However, significant reductions in rodent species composition and diversity can be avoided if treated blocks are interspersed with undisturbed blocks of habitat (O'Meara et al. 1981; Germano, Hungerford, and Martin 1983; Fulbright and Guthery 1996).

Large Mammals

The majority of mechanical habitat management research devoted to large mammals inhabiting Texas rangelands has focused on determining the impacts that mechanical habitat manipulation has on white-tailed deer populations. Fulbright and Guthery (1996) recently concluded that mechanically removing extensive tracts of rangeland without maintaining adequate brush cover is one of the most harmful things a landowner can do to a white-tailed deer population. They argued that root-plowing is the most destructive mechanical technique that can be applied to deer habitat on both a short-term and long-term basis. In the short term, root-plowing significantly reduces browse as well as screening and thermal cover. Over the long term, browse diversity and abundance can be reduced in the absence of adequate availability and abundance of forbs.

Evidently, other mechanical treatment alternatives should be considered over root-plowing if white-tailed deer, as well as quails and other nongame birds and mammals, are a management concern. Roller-chopping and disking operations that leave 20–50 percent of the brush on a treated pasture will likely improve white-tailed deer populations.

Reducing brush cover to create openings where diverse forb populations can exist benefits white-tailed deer. However, root-plowing should probably be avoided in favor of other mechanical habitat management alternatives that do not reduce woody species composition and diversity to the extent that occurs in response to root-plowing. However, to maintain or improve deer numbers, it is probably more important to maintain sufficient undisturbed woody cover on mechanically treated areas than it is to select the proper mechanical methodology.

Although other large-mammal species are undoubtedly affected by mechanical habitat manipulation, research documenting these impacts is sparse compared to research completed for white-tailed deer. Species that are dependent on woody vegetation are more significantly impacted by brush-reduction operations than species that are more adaptable. The endangered ocelot (*Felis pardalis*) represents such a mammal because the persistence of viable breeding populations in the lower Rio Grande Valley of Texas is dependent on preservation of dense mixed-brush communities (Tewes and Schmidly 1987). Javelinas also require sufficient, dense brush cover to survive in the southwestern United States. For instance, Germano, Hungerford, and Martin (1983) reported that javelinas preferred undisturbed rangeland in southeastern Arizona over areas where brush was significantly reduced. Feral hogs, although they require woody escape and resting cover, do not appear to be negatively impacted by mechanical brush management so long as extensive expanses of brush are not removed from the landscape.

Grazing

Excessive grazing is one of the most significant problems confronting quail managers in Texas today (figure 23.2). However, ranchers and leaseholders are becoming more aware of the detrimental impacts that overgrazing has on quail populations. Stocking rates are therefore being reduced, and on some ranches, cattle are being removed altogether when management for quail is the top priority.

Because most Texas rangelands have been exposed to livestock overgrazing at some time during the past 150 years, the composition of herbaceous vegetation has changed over the same period of time on most of these rangelands. Landscapes that were once savannas or grasslands are now shrublands. Vertebrates that were adapted to grasslands have declined relative to populations of vertebrates that are better adapted to woody vegetation. Therefore, improved grazing management implemented to benefit quail populations will have a secondary benefit of improving habitats for vertebrates that are adapted to grasslands or savannas.

Most shrub-dependent species should not be negatively impacted by improvements in grazing management because shrublands will never be completely eradicated, and it would be counterproductive to remove woody species over large areas if optimum quail production is a management objective. Consequently, most nongame bird and wild mammal populations currently inhabiting Texas rangelands should benefit from improved grazing management, though responses will vary on a species-specific basis.

Nongame Birds

Grazing management applied in a manner that benefits quail populations will usually benefit nongame bird communities because grazing is applied in a conservative manner, emphasizing conservation of herbaceous cover. Therefore, few individual upland bird species would be negatively impacted under a grazing regime that consists of low stocking rates and significant rest periods on the shrub-dominated vegetation communities that predominate on Texas rangelands today. Moreover, numerous species display neutral responses to livestock grazing, and a few species respond positively. For example, Saab et al. (1995) recently reviewed the literature for several dozen bird species that inhabit rangelands in North America in an effort to determine each species' response to livestock grazing and then ranked responses as favorable, neutral, or negative. They found that of 34 Neotropical migrant species that breed in shrublands, 12 species responded favorably to grazing, 12 responded negatively, and 10 displayed no clear response. Grassland species were most sensitive to livestock grazing—only 8 species in the study responded favorably to grazing, whereas 17 were negatively impacted and 18 displayed a neutral response.

Clearly, livestock grazing impacts shrub-associated bird species to a lesser extent than grassland species. These trends are almost certainly apparent on Texas rangelands today. Recall that most Texas rangelands are now shrublands grazed primarily by cattle, although goat and, to a lesser extent, sheep production occurs in some areas, particularly in the Edwards Plateau ecoregion.

Many grazing operations continue to facilitate and increase brush infestations. Consequently, though some members of the shrub-associated bird guild may be negatively affected by excessive grazing—such as the curve-billed thrasher (*Toxostoma curvirostre*), verdin (*Auriparus flaviceps*), and cactus wren (*Campylorhynchus brunneicapillus*)—the olive sparrow, groove-billed ani (*Crotophaga sulcirostris*), long-billed thrasher (*T. longirostre*), common ground-dove, and northern cardinal (*Cardinalis cardinalis*) are more abundant today than they were 35 years ago. Therefore, some shrub-associated bird species certainly benefited as brush invaded Texas rangelands.

However, a decline in grassland bird species has occurred simultaneously to the increase in shrub-associated species during the past 35 years (Sauer et al. 2001). This decline almost certainly began as brush started to invade grasslands and savannas more than 150 years ago. For example, Peterjohn and Sauer (1999) analyzed Breeding Bird Survey (BBS) data collected between 1966 and 1996 and found that, as a group, grassland birds displayed a lower proportional increase than any other avian guild in North America. Furthermore, they reported that populations of 13 species of grassland birds had declined, whereas only 2 species demonstrated population increases over the 30-year period. Moreover, Knopf (1994) stated that the grassland bird decline has been remarkably consistent across geographic areas, compared to recent forest-obligate Neotropical migrant declines, which can vary considerably on a geographic basis (James, Wiedenfield, and McCullough 1992).

These declines in grassland species continue today and can be at least partially attributed to the overgrazing of savannas and grasslands by livestock (Smith 1940; Buttery and Shields 1975; Saab et al. 1995). Populations of Bell's vireos (*Vireo bellii*), Cassin's sparrows (*Aimophila cassinii*), dickcissels (*Spiza americana*), horned larks, grasshopper sparrows, lark buntings (*Calamospiza melanocorys*), lark sparrows, long-billed curlews (*Numenius americanus*), savannah sparrows (*Passerculus sandwichensis*), Sprague's pipits (*Anthus spragueii*), vesper sparrows, and western meadowlarks have all declined significantly in North America over the past 35 years. Furthermore, most of these species winter in Texas where habitat problems, including overgrazing, could be contributing to the observed declines (Vickery and Herkert 2001).

Few nongame bird species truly benefit from severe overgrazing that significantly reduces herbaceous cover, lowers shrub height and cover, and leaves a browse line among trees, because the structure and cover provided by grasses and shrubs are necessary for the survival of many rangeland bird species (Knopf 1994). Grazing, therefore, does not directly affect a bird community. Instead, livestock grazing alters the composition and structure of the plant community, indirectly impacting the bird community that depends on specific habitat types provided by the plant community (Bock and Webb 1984; Knopf 1994). Birds, therefore, respond to the impacts that livestock grazing has on the plant community, and the impacts of grazing on a plant community can vary tremendously from region to region and even site to site (Knopf 1994). Precipitation patterns (Bock and Webb 1984), soil types (Knopf 1994), stocking rates (Barnes et al. 1991), seasonality of grazing (Weins 1973), and types of grazing systems (Bryant, Guthery, and Webb 1982) all influence the effects of grazing on wildlife.

However, continuous heavy grazing on Texas rangelands generally reduces herbaceous cover, and if this type of grazing has been occurring for decades, particularly under high stocking rates, the composition of the herbaceous plant community has likely been significantly altered in a manner that is not conducive to maintenance of a diverse bird community. Buttery and Shields (1975) emphasized that the single most important thing range managers can do for rangeland birds is practice good grazing management. Similarly, Monson (1941) noted that when severely overgrazed rangeland in Arizona was placed under prograzing management, species abundance of the nongame bird community increased by almost 100 percent.

Caution is in order, however, when one evaluates the impact of livestock grazing on rangeland bird communities. Identifying individual species as indicators of livestock grazing pressure by labeling a species as an increaser or decreaser, as recommended by Ryder (1980), is useful for recovering populations of rare or endangered species or species of particular management concern (Knopf 1994). However, Knopf argued that efforts to quantify the impacts of livestock grazing on rangeland bird communities should not focus on individual species but on groups of birds. He noted that focusing on individual species as increasers or decreasers relative to grazing pressure ignores the dynamic nature of ecological processes. He emphasized that it is far more important to monitor the species composition of a bird community by defining "grazing response guilds," which are composed of a group of species that respond in a similar manner to grazing pressure, rather than focus on numbers of species or quantity, because the composition of a bird community oscillates dynamically in response to natural and artificial disturbances within a specific time frame. Bird community responses to livestock grazing are complex and are related not only to livestock grazing and other disturbances but also to rainfall patterns and physical characteristics of a site.

Soil type, for example, represents a physical characteristic of a site that has a very important influence on how birds will respond to livestock grazing (Knopf 1994). Indeed, Kantrud and Kologiski (1982) reported that the responses of most nongame bird species to livestock grazing appeared to depend a great deal on the effects that soil type and grazing intensity had on herbaceous vegetation. In addition, Baker and Guthery (1990) evaluated the impacts of soil texture and grazing intensity on the abundance of eastern meadowlarks (*Sturnella magna*) and mourning doves (*Zenaida macroura*) in South Texas. They found that meadowlark densities were higher on clay soils than on sandy-loam soils under moderate grazing intensities, whereas mourning dove densities were higher on sandy-loam soils under heavy grazing intensities.

Adding precipitation to the interaction between soil textures, grazing intensity, and seasonality of grazing further complicates the response of a single bird species to livestock grazing. Given the patchy nature of precipitation in South Texas, for example, bird communities occupying pastures composed of certain soils that receive moderate stocking rates and have experienced above-average rainfall could be more diverse and have higher species abundance than bird communities occupying pastures with similar soils and light stocking rates if the pasture received little rainfall.

The responses of rangeland bird species to livestock grazing appear to be influenced by site-specific variables such as soil texture, rainfall patterns, grazing intensity, and the season when grazing occurs, so the responses of a single species can be highly variable in space and time. Developing management decisions based on grazing response guilds would enable managers to create and maintain habitat conditions that benefit more of the bird community than a single species management approach.

Livestock grazing obviously impacts rangeland bird communities, but the responses of bird communities to grazing depend on grazing intensity, seasonality, soil-texture characteristics, and precipitation patterns of a management unit, together with other disturbances such as those generated by prescribed burning and/or mechanical habitat management. Responses of the bird community to grazing will also vary over time as specific habitat management treatments age and rainfall oscillates between drought and wet periods. But generally, livestock grazing management programs utilized to produce and maintain good quail populations will benefit nongame bird communities.

Small Mammals

Livestock grazing affects small-mammal populations, as it does nongame birds, by altering the species composition and structure of plant communities as well as the physical properties of the substrate on which vegetation is established. However, overgrazing generally simplifies small-mammal communities by reducing species diversity. Although a few species may increase in abundance, the majority of the species that compose rangeland small-mammal communities decline as grazing intensity reduces plant species diversity and herbaceous cover (Fagerstone, Lavoie, and Griffith 1980; Fagerstone and Ramey 1996).

Small mammals that appear to be negatively impacted by livestock grazing include cotton rats, antelope ground squirrels (*Ammospermophilus* spp.), harvest mice, wood rats, and most species of pocket mice (*Perognathus* spp.) because these species prefer heavy vegetative cover. Alternatively, populations of deer mice (*P. maniculatus*), kangaroo rats (*Dipodomys* spp.), hispid pocket mice (*P. hispidus*), silky pocket mice (*P. flavus*), and white-footed mice (*P. leucopus*) are apparently impacted little by grazing and may even benefit from overgrazing.

Lagomorphs represent the other class of small mammals occupying Texas rangelands that are impacted by livestock grazing. Black-tailed jackrabbits, eastern cottontails, and desert cottontails are the most common lagomorphs found in Texas. Unfortunately, little agreement exists among the researchers who have studied them in the Southwest about how grazing impacts populations of these species.

Black-tailed jackrabbits can tolerate overgrazing so long as important foods are not limited and except where a long history of overgrazing has resulted in dense thickets of brush, because jackrabbits typically prefer open habitats interspersed with low shrubs (Dunn, Chapman, and Marsh 1982). Like jackrabbits, cottontails appear to tolerate moderate grazing pressure, though populations apparently decline with severe overgrazing. Most likely, the impacts of livestock grazing on cottontails that inhabit rangelands vary with annual rainfall. In West Texas, cottontails are probably less tolerant of livestock grazing because the impacts of grazing on herbaceous plants is more severe than it is on the more mesic rangelands of the Edwards Plateau and the eastern Rio Grande Plains and Coastal Prairies.

Large Mammals

Like the other quail habitat management practices that have been discussed thus far, most of the grazing management wildlife research conducted in Texas has been devoted to determining how grazing impacts white-tailed deer populations. Grazing can impact these populations in either an indirect or direct manner.

Livestock can indirectly impact deer by altering the structure and composition of the plant community, which in turn impacts the thermal, screening, and escape cover required by deer populations. Severe overutilization of the herbaceous component of deer habitats not only limits food availability but also reduces screening and fawning cover. Moreover, if brush density and cover from the ground to about 1 meter (1.1 yard) aboveground is reduced, screening, resting, escape, and thermal cover may be negatively impacted. However, limited livestock disturbance can benefit deer by disturbing soil surfaces, thereby stimulating the germination of forbs. Nevertheless, on rangeland heavily stocked with livestock, cover resources important to deer can be rapidly reduced and then be maintained in poor condition for many years if pastures remain overstocked (figure 23.2).

Livestock directly impact deer populations by altering deer behavior and by direct competition for food and water. Reducing the presence of cattle in pastures by minimizing stocking rates and maximizing pasture rest reduces this direct impact.

Numerous other large, native wild mammals also inhabit Texas rangelands grazed by livestock. Unfortunately, little research has focused on how grazing impacts many of these mammal species in Texas. However, the life-history requirements are well documented for most of these animals, and research done elsewhere in North America illuminates how livestock grazing likely impacts these species in Texas.

Pronghorns clearly prefer open landscapes and therefore generally inhabit grassland or savanna ecosystems. Pronghorns continue to inhabit rangelands that are grazed by livestock in the Panhandle and Trans-Pecos regions of Texas. O'Gara and Yoakum (1992) estimated that 98 percent of pronghorn populations today share habitat with live-stock, yet pronghorn populations remain viable. Of course, pronghorns shared the North American prairies with bison (*Bison bison*) for thousands of years (O'Gara 1978), so they have been exposed to the grazing pressure of a large herbivore for a long period of time and obviously adapted to it in a successful manner.

Several studies have evaluated the impact of livestock grazing on pronghorns in various parts of the western United States, and the results of these studies generally indicate that pronghorn and livestock production are compatible because there is little dietary overlap between the two species. Nonetheless, excessive livestock grazing can have a detrimental impact on pronghorn populations by reducing fawning cover or by enhancing woody plant invasions of grasslands. Moreover, fences erected to contain livestock, particularly net-wire fences, can restrict pronghorn movements, thereby preventing animals from escaping predators or blizzards and from moving to ranges where food and water are more abundant (Yoakum, O'Gara, and Howard 1996).

Little research has been conducted to determine how livestock grazing impacts other large wild mammals that inhabit South Texas rangelands. Feral hogs are so adaptable and have such broad diets that it is unlikely that livestock grazing adversely affects their populations. Additionally, livestock unlikely impact javelina habitat; the brush invasion that began more than a century ago in South Texas as a result of livestock grazing probably increased the amount of javelina habitat in the region. Likewise, bobcats and ocelots may have benefited from brush invasions as well because dense woody cover became more available, although significant local declines in rodent and lagomorph populations due to overgrazing could reduce wild felid populations.

However, livestock grazing conducted in a manner that is beneficial to quail populations will probably benefit large-mammal, small-mammal, and native bird communities. A few bird and mammal species that prefer habitats created and maintained by heavy livestock grazing might suffer population declines in response to grazing management conducted to improve quail habitat, but the species diversity and abundance of native bird and mammal communities should improve as quail habitat improves.

Herbicides

Since the 1950s, various herbicides have been used to manage brush on Texas rangelands to increase forage production for livestock. Herbicides remain an attractive brush management alternative widely used today because they can be aerially applied to large areas in a few hours, whereas roller-chopping or chaining operations require days or weeks to improve a similar area. Prescribed burns are cheaper than herbicide applications and—like herbicide applications—can be accomplished in a few hours. However, woody plant mortality from fire is generally not as high as mortality resulting from herbicide treatments.

In addition, landowners often like to use herbicides because of the inherent flexibility that is associated with using them to manage woody vegetation. For example, herbicides have been developed to target specific plant species. Thus, a specific herbicide can be used alone to impact a specific plant species, unlike prescribed fire and some mechanical brush management techniques, or a combination of herbicides can be mixed and applied to target a broader spectrum of plants. Herbicides can also be scheduled and applied in precise patterns to increase the structural and species diversity of an area targeted for treatment. Vegetation responses to herbicide treatment can vary significantly from site to site depending on numerous factors, including soil types, plant community composition of the site treated, type(s) of herbicide applied, application rates, and time of year of application (Koerth 1996). It is therefore difficult to generalize about how herbicides will affect plant communities because individual treatment sites can differ from one another.

Texas landowners and quail managers have not used herbicides as extensively as roller-chopping, prescribed burning, or grazing to improve habitat for quails. Quail enthusiasts have been reluctant to utilize herbicides to manipulate vegetation for quails because in addition to killing shrubs, subshrubs and cactus, many herbicides also kill forbs, which make up a major portion of quail diets.

On King Ranch during the 1950s, bobwhites abandoned areas treated with herbicides in favor of adjacent untreated areas where sufficient food and thermal cover occurred (Lehmann 1984). Similarly, Beasom and Scifres (1977) reported that quail numbers declined on South Texas mixed-brush communities treated with herbicide, presumably because of high forb mortality, and quail numbers on treated areas remained low for two years. However, herbicides are unlikely to negatively impact quails and most other rangeland wildlife species because of the types of herbicides used today and the manner in which treatments are applied.

Nongame Birds

Koerth (1996) stated that herbicides have little direct impact on wildlife because many chemicals used to manage vegetation are nontoxic to most wildlife species. Herbicides kill plants by acting on specific enzymes that are not present in animals. Moreover, Koerth concluded that the most significant impact that herbicide treatment of plant communities has on wildlife is the manner in which herbicides affect cover and food. Several studies have provided convincing evidence that bird habitat requirements are shaped by floristics (Weins and Rotenberry 1981; Meents, Anderson, and Ohmart 1982; Rotenberry and Weins 1998). Therefore, the composition of a plant community and the densities and distributions of individual plant species, together with species relationships within a community, appear to play a significant role in habitat selection among birds.

Understanding the importance of floristics relative to how birds select habitats is important with regard to chemical manipulation of plant communities because herbicides are generally developed to target specific species or classes of plants. If an herbicide is used that targets a single or a few plant species, then the bird community is unlikely to be dramatically altered if the herbicide is applied properly.

However, if a particular bird species is dependent on attributes of a specific plant species or class of plants—such as quail and forbs—then herbicide application will likely elicit a negative response, at least on the treated area. For instance, where herbicides have been used to kill significant acreages of sagebrush, Brewer's sparrow populations decline because sagebrush provides essential nesting cover. However, herbicide management of woody vegetation often results in positive or neutral responses from bird communities.

The neutral or positive responses of bird communities to herbicide treatment of their habitats may be a result of the manner in which many ranchers use herbicides to manage rangeland vegetation today. Cattle ranchers not only use herbicides to increase forage production but also try to plan treatments in a manner that benefits wildlife because wildlife has become a valuable commodity. When herbicides are used to manage brush in Texas today, the chemicals are usually applied in patterns that impact a small portion of the targeted landscape, leaving a substantial amount of untreated refugia that can be used by birds that had previously used the treated habitat. Most species of birds can fly reasonable distances if required, so constraints of movements are usually not an impediment to birds. The inherent flexibility associated with applying herbicides permits landowners to manage vegetation with herbicides in a manner that, at worst, minimizes and, at best, substantially improves habitat for wildlife.

Koerth (1996) provided a detailed description of variable-rate-pattern (VRP) herbicide application methodology that has been used to enhance the habitat diversity of mixed-brush communities in South Texas. Scifres and Koerth (1986) developed VRP in an effort to maximize the value of mixed-brush plant communities for both cattle and wildlife. By varying the rate, pattern, and timing of tebuthiuron (N-[5-(1,1-dimethylethyl)-1.3,4-thiadiazol-2-yl]-N,N′-dimethylurea) application in one study and applying a triclopyr and picloram mixture in another study, they increased grass cover as well as the structural diversity of the plant community in experimental areas. Though forb populations were depressed on deeper soils at application rates that exceeded 2 kilograms/hectare (about 1 pound/acre), forb populations on shallow, gravelly sites were similar to those on untreated sites. Moreover, depressed forb populations recovered two to three years posttreatment and in some areas were more abundant than prior to treatment.

Koerth (1996) stated that treating mixed-brush communities with herbicide could reduce the plant complexity of these communities. Short-term acute declines of specific classes of plants or individual species can occur and may have consequences for animals that have an obligatory relationship with the plants that are negatively impacted. However, Koerth also stated that herbicide treatment of vegetation communities could increase community biodiversity over the long term. Though research on the subject is meager, most of the studies that have evaluated how herbicides impact rangeland birds seem to support Koerth's statement because most avian communities displayed no response to herbicide treatment of their habitats (Gruver and Guthery 1986; Nolte and Fulbright 1997) and some bird communities may have become more diverse and abundant (Schulz et al. 1992a, 1992b).

Small Mammals

Few studies have been conducted to determine how small mammals respond to herbicide treatment of rangeland vegetation communities in Texas. Koerth (1996) stated that populations of animals characterized by limited mobility and/or those with small home ranges are likely to decline in treated areas because it would be very difficult for them to move to suitable untreated habitat. Acute responses of vegetation to herbicide exposure, which can include defoliation of woody species and high forb mortality, would reduce food and cover for many small-mammal species, prompting population declines. Herbaceous habitat conditions may not improve for several weeks in the case of grasses to several months in the case of forbs, and woody cover and composition may be altered for years, particularly if the herbicide applied targets a broad spectrum of plants.

Populations of rodents that prefer woody cover, such as wood rats, decline in response to herbicide applications that significantly reduce shrub cover (Senzota 1986). However, many species of small mammals, such as cotton rats and cottontails, display neutral or positive response to herbicide treatment of vegetation communities because the post-treatment flush of herbaceous cover often improves habitat conditions for some species, whereas the posttreatment woody plant community continues to provide adequate habitat conditions for other species.

Applying herbicides in patterns that retain sufficient untreated habitat adjacent to treated areas may not negatively impact small-mammal populations because significant movements to unaffected habitat would not be required (Koerth 1996). Most herbicides, with the exception of picloram, do not kill every species of woody mast-producing plant or herbaceous seed-producing plant contacted, so food and cover supplies may not be impacted substantially. Forb and grass abundance and cover may increase in response to herbicide treatments because competitors are eliminated and opening woody canopies exposes understory vegetation to more solar radiation.

Large Mammals

As in other sections in this chapter, the majority of the research conducted to determine how herbicide treatment of Texas rangelands influences large mammals has focused on white-tailed deer. Koerth (1996) not only provides an excellent discussion about how white-tailed deer respond to herbicide treatment of their habitats but also details how herbicides can be used to improve deer habitat. He summarized studies indicating that herbicide applications can improve white-tailed deer habitat if appropriate individual or combinations of herbicides are used to target specific woody species and if they are applied in the appropriate manner. Specifically, he stated that herbicides can be used to improve a vegetative community in a manner that provides better cover and more diverse food resources of higher quality than those on similar untreated sites.

The initial response of white-tailed deer to herbicide treatment of their habitats is movement out of treated areas as a result of defoliation of cover plants and a reduction in browse and forbs. However, if herbicides are applied in patterns that leave a portion of the treated area unaffected, deer populations may not be adversely impacted for more than a few months.

Feral hogs, nilgai, and javelinas represent three additional large mammals that can be impacted by the application of herbicides on Texas rangelands. Feral hogs and nilgai are adaptable animals and can successfully utilize a broad range of habitat conditions. Therefore, treating woody plant communities with herbicide does not appear to negatively impact feral hog and nilgai populations. Conversely, javelina populations declined in response to herbicide treatment of woody plant communities because brush is an essential habitat requirement.

Pronghorns could also benefit from herbicide application to reduce brush infestations on West Texas and High Plains rangelands. However, like white-tailed deer, pronghorns might vacate treated areas in response to acute forb mortality that often accompanies the application. Nevertheless, pronghorns would likely return to treated areas as forbs recovered, and over the long term, pronghorn populations might even increase if posttreatment forb abundance and food availability increased in response to reduced competition from shrubs.

Predators would likely respond to herbicide treatment of rangeland habitats according to how prey populations respond to alteration of the treated vegetation community. If the small-mammal community is negatively impacted and rodent populations decline as a result of habitat deterioration, then bobcats and ocelots will be forced to move to habitats where small mammals are more plentiful. Coyotes, skunks, and raccoons, however, may not be forced to vacate treated habitats in response to small-mammal declines because they have broader food habits than felids. Most predator populations would remain unaffected by herbicide management of rangeland communities if block treatments are avoided in favor of treatment applications that retain some untreated areas or promote habitat diversity. Block treatments that result in a significant reduction in woody cover might prove harmful to bobcat and ocelot populations because of their affinity for brush. However, using herbicides to create a few small, strategic openings in mature brushland habitats occupied by ocelots, for example, might increase rodent populations and thus could benefit ocelots by increasing food abundance.

Quail Management in Forest Habitats

The Piney Woods of East Texas support widely scattered, low-density populations of bobwhites (chapter 9). Unlike the Rio Grande Plains and Coastal Prairies of South Texas and the Rolling Plains of northern Texas, where bobwhite distribution is for the most part continuous on rangelands, bobwhite distribution is fragmented in East Texas. The majority of self-sustaining, huntable bobwhite populations in the East Texas Piney Woods are restricted to public lands, such as national forests, or private timber corporations that maintain an open, parklike stand structure with prescribed fire (figure 23.3).

Bobwhites remain a popular game bird in East Texas, prompting some timber corporations to actively manage portions of their land for bobwhites in order to provide hunting opportunities for

Figure 23.3.
Longleaf and southern pines can provide excellent habitat for quail and other wildlife if maintained in an open, parklike condition with prescribed fire and mechanical hardwood control (top). Moderate (middle) and excessive (bottom) hardwood encroachment can severely restrict available habitat for quails and other wildlife that require open, parklike structure in southern pine forests.
Photos by Leonard A. Brennan

corporate executives and their guests. Similarly, federal forest managers recognize that hunters continue to be interested in upland bird hunting opportunities, so portions of national forests in East Texas are managed to support bobwhite populations.

More recently, the presence of the federally endangered red-cockaded woodpecker (*Picoides borealis*) in national forests has forced Forest Service administrators to initiate recovery actions that conserve and/or improve its habitat. These woodpeckers prefer open pine forests, so their habitat recovery benefits quail populations (Brennan, Cooper, et al. 1995). Therefore, relatively small, but ecologically significant portions of East Texas forests are currently being managed in a manner that improves and/or maintains habitat space for bobwhites. Besides bobwhites, many other nontarget wildlife species are impacted by the habitat improvement operations directed toward bobwhites and red-cockaded woodpeckers. The final sections summarize how nontarget wildlife populations respond to these habitat management operations.

Rosene (1969) noted that quail management in forests was probably first initiated by Native Americans when they established small plots to grow food crops and when they periodically burned forests to improve hunting opportunities. Quail habitat was later substantially improved by European settlers, who unwittingly began managing for quail in eastern and southeastern forests 150 to 200 years ago by simply clearing small parcels of land to raise crops and livestock (Rosene 1969). A patchwork of disturbed areas was therefore created within forests that prompted an increase in bobwhite populations east of the Mississippi River, but particularly in the southeastern United States. Primitive farming practices depleted the soil fertility on many of these small farms, and crop productivity declined, causing widespread abandonment (Stoddard 1931; Rosene 1969). Although quail carrying capacity declined in response to the reduced fertility of these small farms, quail populations nevertheless continued to persist on most of them well into the twentieth century.

Bobwhite habitat was further reduced when the lumber industry began to grow in the Southeast during the early 1900s. Commercial timber harvesting resulted in the loss of many of the longleaf pine ecosystems that provided superior habitat conditions for bobwhites. The resulting regeneration of hardwood thickets and elimination of human- and lightning-caused fires reduced nesting habitat and native food supplies for quail (figure 23.3).

These were the habitat conditions that, for the most part, confronted H. L. Stoddard when he started the first modern, comprehensive study to improve quail populations on hunting plantations in southern Georgia and the Panhandle of Florida during the 1920s. After spending almost a decade studying quail ecology and evaluating different management schemes, he and his colleagues developed bobwhite management protocols that significantly improved quail populations on plantations where he worked. Walter Rosene later acknowledged the valuable contributions made by Stoddard and then added management techniques, particularly with regard to silviculture, that further improved quail management in the Southeast. Both of these individuals contributed a great deal to the improved management of forests for quail. The management guidelines they developed are thoroughly described in their books (Stoddard 1931; Rosene 1969). Although our knowledge of bob-white ecology has increased over the intervening decades, enabling wildlife biologists to further refine and improve quail management, the methods developed by Stoddard (Engstrom and Baker 1995) and Rosene continue to be used throughout the Southeast today to improve and maintain habitat for bobwhites.

Impacts of Forest Management for Quail on Nontarget Wildlife

Though the management protocols developed by Stoddard (1931) and Rosene (1969) and later implemented on thousands of acres through-out the Southeast—including parts of East Texas—were designed to im-prove habitat for bobwhites, the resulting habitat improvements ben-efited an array of nontarget wildlife species. Engstrom and Baker (1995) indicated that the increased production of rare and endangered biota that has occurred in the Red Hills region of the Florida Panhandle and southeastern Georgia is an indirect product of the land management instituted by Stoddard 70 years ago.

Quail management in forests of the Southeast and East Texas has been refined and improved over the past 70 years. However, the basic quail management tenets developed by Stoddard (1931) and Rosene (1969), which coordinated application of prescribed fire, strategic plow-ing, and selective timber removal, are as relevant today as they were then. What has changed is that we have begun to recognize that quail management in forests also directly impacts a host of nontarget wildlife groups, particularly nongame birds and mammals, as well as herpto-fauna (reptiles and amphibians).

Generally, most nontarget wildlife groups have benefited when for-ests are managed for quails. However, anytime that vegetation com-munities are dramatically altered, at least a few species of fauna decline. Some of the inevitable trade-offs are summarized in the following sections.

Nongame Birds

Despite the popularity of bobwhites to hunters in the Southeast, from an ecological perspective, quail are no more important than other members of the vertebrate community that inhabit the same forest eco-systems. Habitat conditions that favor bobwhites in longleaf pine for-ests also favor an array of other vertebrate species. Many other birds are adapted to live in fire-dependent longleaf pine forests, and although pine forests in many areas of the Southeast were initially managed strictly for bobwhite production, other bird species benefited. For in-stance, it was recently discovered that red-cockaded woodpeckers, bob-whites, and numerous other bird species appeared to respond favor-ably to some of the same forest-thinning management actions used by Stoddard (1931) 70 years ago. Conversely, other vertebrates that are not adapted to live in fire-dependent forests will decline when thinning op-erations are used to maintain the open-forest conditions required by red-cockaded woodpeckers and bobwhites. Table 23.2 provides a sum-mary of responses of selected forest wildlife species to forest manage-ment practices used to improve quail habitat and can be consulted in relation to the following discussion.

Table 23.2.
Response(s) of Selected Forest Wildlife Species to Forest Management Practices Utilized to Improve Quail Habitat in Texas.

Source	State or region	Management practice	Species affected and response,[a] (+), (−), (n)
Brennan, Cooper, et al. (1995)	Mississippi	Mechanical operations and prescribed burning	American goldfinch (+), Carolina chickadee (+), Carolina wren (+), common grackle (+), northern cardinal (+), red-winged blackbird (+), rufous-sided towhee (+), white-throated sparrow (+), Bachman's sparrow (+), blue-grey gnatcatcher (+), common yellowthroat (+), white-breasted nuthatch (+), great-crested flycatcher (+), yellow-breasted chat (+), hooded warbler (−), wood thrush (−), least shrew (+), cotton rat (+), white-footed mouse (n), southeastern shrew (n), eastern harvest mouse (n)
Provencher, Gobris, and Brennan (2002)	Florida	Prescribed burning, herbicides, mechanical thinning	Bird community that prefers open habitat (+)
Provencher et al. (2002)	Florida	Prescribed burning, herbicides, mechanical thinning	Bachman's sparrow (+), red-cockaded woodpecker (+), northern cardinal (−), tufted titmouse (−), Carolina chickadee (−), northern bobwhite (+), American kestrel (+)
Senzota (1986)	Texas	Herbicides and prescribed burning	Cotton rat (+), wood rat (−)
White et al. (1999)	Southeast	Prescribed burning	Bird community (+)
Wilson, Masters, and Bukenhofer (1995)	Southeast	Mechanical thinning and prescribed burning	Eastern wood-pewee (+), prairie warbler (+), red-cockaded woodpecker (+), northern bobwhite (+)

[a] + = positive population response, − = negative population response, n = neutral.

Bird species that benefit from restoration of pine/grassland ecosystems and other forest-thinning management operations in the Southeast include the American goldfinch (*Carduelis tristis*), American kestrel (*Falco sparverius*), Bachman's sparrow, Carolina chickadee (*Poecile carolenensis*), Carolina wren (*Thryothorus ludovicianus*), common grackle (*Quiscalus quiscula*), common yellowthroat (*Geothlypis trichas*), eastern wood-pewee (*Contopus virens*), great crested flycatcher (*Myiarchus crinitus*), indigo bunting (*Passerina cyanea*), northern bobwhite, northern cardinal, prairie warbler (*Dendroica discolor*), red-cockaded woodpecker, red-winged blackbird (*Agelaius phoeniceus*), eastern towhee (*Pipilo erythrophthalmus*), white-breasted nuthatch (*Sitta carolinensis*), white-throated sparrow (*Zonotrichia albicollis*), and yellow-breasted chat (*Icteria virens*). Species that were less abundant in forests that had been restored included Carolina chickadee, hooded warblers (*Wilsonia citrina*), northern cardinal, tufted titmouse (*Baseolophus bicolor*), and wood thrush (*Hylocichla mustelina*). Clearly, restoring pine/grassland ecosystems benefits a host of bird species; however, populations of certain species, such as the Carolina chickadee and northern cardinal, decline if too much hardwood removal occurs.

Opening the midstory of most forests composed of pine species other than longleaf pine can improve habitat conditions sufficiently to enhance native bird communities; however, the bird community may not approach that typically supported by maintaining fire-dependent longleaf pine forests. For example, Repenning and Labisky (1985) evaluated how converting longleaf pine plantations to slash pine plantations in northern Florida impacted bird communities and reported that the breeding-bird community adapted to natural longleaf pine forests suffered long-term negative impacts. Aging and management actions improved the structural features of slash pine plantations by adding a shrub layer, which attracted breeding-bird species normally not found in longleaf pine forests. Nevertheless, the composition of breeding-bird communities supported by slash pine plantations did not resemble that found in longleaf pine forests.

Repenning and Labisky (1985) concluded that the short-term harvest rotations (less than 40 years) typically utilized on private pine plantations in the Southeast represent a threat to pineland bird communities. Nonetheless, recent research has demonstrated that pinelands can be restored and managed in a manner that provides habitat conditions that support a diverse avian community (Wilson, Masters, and Bukenhofer 1995; Provencher, Gobris, and Brennan 2002; Provencher et al. 2002). Consequently, active bobwhite management and the continued implementation of red-cockaded woodpecker recovery activities in East Texas should benefit nongame bird communities that inhabit the improved forests.

Small Mammals

Like the bird communities that inhabit East Texas pinelands, small-mammal communities are probably also impacted by quail management activities applied to pine forests. Furthermore, some small-mammal species likely increase in response to quail management as other species decline. For example, Brennan, Cooper, et al. (1995) reported that least shrews (*Cryptotis parva*) and hispid cotton rats seemed more abundant in loblolly pine forests on their Mississippi study areas that were managed for red-cockaded woodpeckers and, by association, bobwhites. White-footed mice were captured more frequently in unmanaged sites on one of their study areas, but on the other study area they were more frequently observed in red-cockaded woodpecker colonies. Similarly, eastern harvest mice and southeastern shrews (*Sorex longirostris*) were detected most frequently in managed areas on one study area but not on the other. Similarly, Senzota (1986) noted that cotton rat numbers increased on thick, wooded areas in Central Texas that had been treated with herbicide and then exposed to a prescribed burn two to four years posttreatment, whereas wood rat populations declined. Cotton rats prefer herbaceous habitats and wood rats prefer woody cover; therefore, cotton rat population increases and wood rat population declines were attributed to the improved herbaceous cover that resulted from the reduction in woody cover caused by the herbicide/prescribed fire treatments.

Large Mammals

Deer require appropriate food and cover to successfully survive and reproduce in sustainable numbers, so management practices that promote forb and deciduous browse production will benefit deer populations in East Texas pine forest just as they did in South Texas. Clearly, the tree-thinning, prescribed burning, and plowing advocated by Stoddard (1931) and Rosene (1969) for bobwhites, as well as the red-cockaded woodpecker habitat management currently being applied in southeastern pine forests (Wilson, Masters, and Bukenhofer 1995; Provencher, Gobris, and Brennan 2002), should create good habitat conditions for white-tailed deer.

Reducing midstory hardwoods with a combination of herbicides, cutting and girdling, and prescribed fire promotes herbaceous plant production, resulting in an increase in forb supplies and fawning cover, whereas brushy thickets protected to provide cover for quail would provide browse and hiding cover. Some food supplies could be lost if numbers of hardwood mast-producing species were significantly reduced in managed forests, but increased forb production and the browse provided by retention of brushy thickets would likely mitigate losses in mast availability. Moreover, most pine forests managed for quail in East Texas are also managed for deer, so deer habitat requirements would probably be more than adequate on pinelands managed for bobwhites. Pinelands managed for bobwhites and/or red-cockaded woodpeckers certainly provide better deer habitat than pinelands managed strictly for commercial softwood production.

In addition to white-tailed deer, feral hogs are probably the other most common large mammal that inhabits East Texas forests. As mentioned earlier, feral hogs are supremely adaptable animals, so improving pinelands for bobwhites and/or red-cockaded woodpeckers should not unduly impact feral hog populations. Increased herbaceous plant species diversity and abundance would benefit feral hogs by increasing root and tuber food supplies. Hardwood reduction would reduce mast resources, but the riparian areas and swamps that occur throughout pinelands managed for bobwhites and/or red-cockaded woodpeckers should provide sufficient mast as well as loafing and escape cover for hogs. However, conserving feral hogs is probably not a concern among individuals who own or manage land for quail in East Texas because of their perception that feral hogs destroy quail nests and ruin quail habitat.

Summary

Quail can be considered an economic keystone species in many parts of Texas. Their economic and social importance to landowners lies in the landowners' potential to derive substantially more income from leasing access for quail hunting than from raising livestock. Moreover, quail hunters have begun to purchase property that was formerly used for cattle or timber production, with the express purpose of maximizing quail production. A variety of habitat management techniques are being applied on these properties to create vegetation structure that provides usable habitat space for bobwhites. Land management for bobwhite production is fast becoming a reality throughout Texas. People who are interested in wildlife species that have habitat requirements similar to those of quails should embrace this development.

Webb and Guthery (1983) and Gruver and Guthery (1986) concluded that bobwhite habitat management applied to Texas rangelands also improved habitat for nongame birds. The research cited in this chapter also provides reasonably strong evidence that habitat management performed for quail production benefits both small- and large-mammal populations. Therefore, carefully planned quail habitat management that is applied in the appropriate manner will probably benefit native flora and fauna communities in most parts of Texas because quail management emphasizes maximizing habitat diversity. Self-sustaining nongame bird and small-mammal communities, as well as large wild-mammal populations, should all flourish on rangelands managed for quails. Bobwhites are grassland birds that require habitats composed of about 65–75 percent herbaceous habitat and 25–35 percent woody cover. The herbaceous plant community should be composed of a diversity of forbs and grasses that provide sufficient food as well as foraging, nesting, brooding, escape, and thermal cover. Similarly, the woody plant community should also be composed of a diversity of plants that provide additional food in the form of mast as well as thermal and escape cover. Woody cover should be interspersed throughout herbaceous plant communities in a manner that ensures that a quail does not have to move more than 60–80 meters (54–72 yards) to find woody cover. These vegetation conditions will provide habitat that generally supports diverse and abundant native bird and small-mammal communities, as well as healthy populations of predators and popular game mammals such as white-tailed deer, javelinas, and feral hogs.

Quail habitat requirements can be provided on rangelands by applying a number of habitat management techniques. Research has demonstrated that mechanical techniques such as roller-chopping and chaining, herbicide applications, and prescribed fire, as well as grazing, can all be utilized to provide good quail habitat conditions on rangelands. In fact, a combination of these techniques, such as roller-chopping followed by prescribed burning, or herbicide treatment followed by prescribed burning, will usually create and maintain better habitat conditions for quails than a single technique. Ranchers and quail managers therefore have a great deal of flexibility in choosing habitat management techniques that will provide the best quail habitat conditions for their individual operations. Fortunately, numerous research projects have indicated that most of the habitat improvement techniques utilized to improve landscapes for quails also benefit nontarget wildlife populations. Grassland birds in particular represent a declining avian guild that could benefit significantly as quail habitat management continues to increase on Texas rangelands.

Quail management in the forests of East Texas will also likely benefit nontarget wildlife populations. Recent research has demonstrated that midstory hardwood-removal techniques, such as thinning and girdling and herbicide application followed by prescribed burns ignited in the spring two to three years posttreatment, can be used to restore longleaf pine forests in a manner that benefits native bird populations. Other studies have shown that native wildlife populations can also benefit from efforts to improve pine forest composed of fast-growing species, though the composition and abundance of bird communities remain different from those of native bird communities of longleaf pine forests. Nevertheless, the commercial pine forests that dominate most of East Texas are capable of supporting diverse native fauna communities when they are managed for bobwhites. The local and regional abundance of numerous species of Neotropical migratory birds, which have been declining in recent years, could improve if more acreage in East Texas and the Southeast are managed for bobwhites. In addition, forest communities of small mammals, white-tailed deer, and feral hogs would also probably benefit from bobwhite management of pinelands.

Nontarget wildlife species that require woody cover would likely decline on rangelands and forests managed for quail production. Anytime that vegetation communities undergo dramatic alteration, populations of a few species suffer and decline. Trade-offs are inevitable and unavoidable. However, most of the bird and mammal species that decline as a result of quail management are species that responded positively to destructive land management practices that ruined the native rangeland and forest ecosystems in Texas. Restoring these ecosystems by applying habitat management that creates vegetation communities preferred by quails simultaneously encourages restoration of native fauna populations, generally resulting in a more diverse and abundant vertebrate community.

Most of the rangeland ecosystems in Texas that support or historically supported quail populations have deteriorated over the past 150 years as a result of overgrazing, exotic plant invasions, urbanization, and other disturbances. Similarly, the longleaf pine forests that once dominated the uplands of East Texas are now reduced to small, highly fragmented remnant stands. They have been replaced by commercial forests composed of fast-growing pine species managed in a manner that maximizes profits for timber companies at the expense of wildlife. Native bird and mammal abundance and diversity in these commercial forests are poor and generally remain in this condition as long as traditional silviculture is observed. Consequently, good quail management of rangelands and pinelands is a superior alternative to traditional land management practices because the vegetation communities created and maintained for quails support more abundant and diverse wildlife communities than do the overgrazed, brush- and exotic grass–infested pastures and intensively managed commercial pine plantations. The increasing popularity of quails in Texas represents a genuine benefit to nontarget wildlife species. As more of Texas is improved for quails, more of Texas will be improved for native wildlife.

The Science of Quail Management and the Management of Quail Science

24

Fred S. Guthery and Leonard A. Brennan

> There are in fact two things, science and opinion;
> the former begets knowledge, the latter ignorance.
> Hippocrates

The science of quail management and the management of quail science are issues that revolve around decisions. People make decisions to accomplish objectives. In the context here, the objectives are to elevate and stabilize quail populations, and the decisions involve focusing research on knowledge deficiencies so that we are better able to accomplish this.

Astrology, intuition, troupe allegiance, and scientific facts, among other sources, serve as bases for decisions. Despite inclinations of the glitterati, including former First Ladies, we doubt astrology will be helpful in managing the quails in American hinterlands. We are skeptical of intuition because it is a rectilinear leap of induction in a world that processes itself with curves and loop-the-loops. We admit to being upstanding members of various troupes and, as such, victims of groupthink—"it must be true if everybody in the group believes it is true." However, we have developed deep skepticism over herd-sanctioned knowledge because it is so often wrong when matched up with the findings of observational and experimental science.

We are left with scientific facts as a tautological basis for scientific management. This is regrettable, in a way, because some scientific facts come and go as trends do in pop music. Others come and go in the way of El Niño events—they disappear only to reappear years or decades later. A few have the staying power of Mozart's *Requiem*. It is around these types of pillars that we try to build a science of quail management.

Our purpose is to illustrate scientific approaches to elevating and stabilizing quail populations. We start with long-standing pillars of knowledge, which are at once the infrastructure from which management knowledge diverges and the constraints that bind management practice. We then delve into the current crop of facts, which we call management hypotheses. We address, in particular, hypotheses on harvest and habitat management. Finally, the preceding arguments lead naturally into the management of quail science, that is, into management of the programs that assist in getting rid of bad facts and establishing new ones for challenge via the scientific method. We will approach the management of quail science from a cultural perspective. This is necessary because successful management of quail science requires the interaction of several different human cultures, such as those of scientists, patrons, administrators, and hunters.

The Science of Quail Management: Pillars of Knowledge

The four topics that follow provide the knowledge-based context within which management decisions operate. These concepts are powerful, in that they seem to hold generally. Their power suggests that management action will have little impact if such action takes place in contradiction to the concepts. Put differently, management action may be folly if it is not in accord with these principles.

r-selection

Biologists somewhat arbitrarily classify animal species as *r*- or *K*-selected (MacArthur and Wilson 1967). The *r*-selected animals, for example, scaled quail (*Callipepla squamata*), tend to have low rates of survival and high rates of production, whereas the *K*-selected animals, for example, whooping cranes (*Grus americana*), tend to have high rates of survival and low rates of production. Either strategy may result in the persistence of populations.

The *r*-strategy that characterizes quails arose from some hundreds of thousands to millions of years of evolution, depending on the species (Gutiérrez 1993). Such traits are fixed in their genes and are not amenable to management. Thus, management simply has to accept high annual turnover rates in quail populations (e.g., 70–80 percent annual mortality, on average). It is estimated that bobwhites might experience mortality from senescence (old age) of 23–44 percent per annum if there were no losses to predators, hunters, and other factors (Guthery 2002:50). The management relevance is that there are distinctly limited expectations on what some practice, for example, predator suppression or reduced harvest, might accomplish in reducing annual turnover.

Two demographic processes in quail populations further dampen expectations. The first is competing risks, meaning there are many potential sources of mortality. Removing one risk tends to increase the power of competing risks. For example, removing raptors as a source of mortality would make quails not killed by raptors more vulnerable to other predators, harvest, accidents, weather catastrophes, and senescence. In general, by eliminating a mortality source for one quail, the manager saves less than one quail because of competing risks.

The second demographic process is density-dependent survival and reproduction (Errington 1945; Roseberry and Klimstra 1984). Given some fixed area, there is a tendency for low numbers of quails to survive at higher rates than high numbers. Likewise, there is a tendency for low-density breeding populations to be more productive on a per-capita basis than high-density breeding populations. Density-dependent mechanisms seem to operate in different seasons and on different parts of the birth-death cycle in different areas. However, they are a recognized population process, and they dampen management expectations. For example, reduction of a mortality source might invoke stronger density-dependent mortality, thus negating, to some degree, benefits accruing from removal of said source. Management that somehow reduced winter mortality, leading to a higher density of breeders, might be expected to reduce per-capita production because of density dependence in production.

Regardless of the density-dependent nature of production, which appears to be stronger in northern than in southern latitudes (Guthery 2002), quail populations have limited production potential in any breeding season. Age ratios, the number of juveniles/adult bird, provide an index of production. Average age ratios of bobwhites range from about 2.8 juveniles/adult in southern latitudes to more than 5 juveniles/

adult in northern latitudes (Guthery 2002:48). An age ratio of 7 juveniles/adult is improbable in any area. We would expect a bobwhite ratio this high in 91 of every 10,000 years in southern Illinois (derived from Roseberry and Klimstra 1984) and 26 of every 10,000 years in South Texas (derived from Lehmann 1984). This limited potential is due in no small part to a limited amount of time when environmental conditions are appropriate for reproduction in any breeding season.

The points of this discussion of quail demography are that demographic expectations operate within distinct boundaries for survival and production and that competing risks and density-dependent population processes dampen expectations of some response to management that alters survival-production schedules. If fall population abundance is the goal of management, then it is accurate to say that within bounds at this time unknown, it is possible (and perhaps probable) that management alteration of survival-production schedules will have no effect on the goal. The scientific quail manager recognizes and accepts these constraints.

Successional Affiliation

Grange (1949) was one of the first wildlife biologists to recognize that game birds are associated with stages of plant succession. The general concept holds for quails, but the optimal successional stage changes with the productivity of environments.

For example, northern bobwhites (*Colinus virginianus*) are termed, somewhat dogmatically, as lower successional species. This means they are adapted to some stage of succession that occurs within a few years of disturbance. If a forest in a rainy environment is clear-cut, bobwhites might thrive thereon for the first few years (appropriate successional stage) and then decline and disappear as dense hardwoods and, ultimately, mature trees take over the site. In forest environments bobwhites are definitely a lower successional species, and management for the birds implies maintenance of lower successional vegetation.

In semiarid environments, however, bobwhites fare better in mid- to higher successional stages (Spears et al. 1993). Even in relatively small regions such as South Texas, there is evidence of changing successional affiliation of bobwhites from, say, Corpus Christi to Carrizo Springs. As distance from the Gulf of Mexico increases, annual precipitation declines and temperatures during the breeding season increase (Guthery, Land, and Hall 2001). Because of the temperature-precipitation trend, the optimal succession stage trends from somewhat lower near the Gulf to somewhat higher farther from the Gulf.

There is, however, a common thread in the variable successional affiliations of quails. It is the structure (height, density, and dispersion of woody cover; height and density of herbaceous cover) of habitat that maximizes quail abundance. Whether one is on a southeastern plantation or a southwestern ranch, the habitat structure that favors bobwhites will be generally similar. Only the names of the plants will change. For example, little bluestem (*Schizachyrium scoparium*) in the Southwest becomes the structural homologue of broomsedge bluestem (*Andropogon virginicus*) in the Southeast (and vice versa).

Thus, the scientific manager recognizes that the successional affiliation of quails changes with the productivity (amount of rainfall, length of growing season, nature of soils) of the environment. The manager then manages for the successional stage that is consistent with the adaptations of the quail species under management, given site productivity.

Adaptive Plasticity

The breadth (north-south, east-west) of the North American distribution of quails that occur in Texas and the range of annual precipitation within occupied U.S. ranges (table 24.1) suggest that each species is adapted to a diverse set of biotic and climatic conditions. The northern bobwhite is especially remarkable. It occurs naturally from Canada to Central America and from eastern Colorado to the Atlantic Coast. Masked bobwhites (*C. v. ridgwayi*) occur in Sonora, Mexico, well west of eastern Colorado. The broad distributions connote the general plasticity of the species, as enhanced with adaptations to local conditions through subspeciation. More than 20 different subspecies have been described for the northern bobwhite (Brennan 1999).

The broad ranges also connote a good deal of adaptive plasticity at more local scales. This means there is a large set of habitat configurations that are suitable and, indeed, optimal, for a given quail species (Guthery 2002). We may deduce from the foregoing that search for a single set of optimal habitat features (properties of woody and herbaceous cover) is not practical for a widespread species such as the northern bobwhite, except insofar as that set might serve as a crude model for management. However, such constructs may have merit when addressed at a regional scale for a species with a relatively limited geographic distribution, such as the mountain quail (*Oreortyx pictus*) (Brennan, Block, and Gutiérrez et al. 1986; Brennan 1991b).

We may further deduce that within specified ranges of habitat properties, quails are irresponsive to changes in the properties (Guthery 1999a). For example, contrary to Leopold's (1933) conjecture, we would not expect quails to increase in proportion to the amount of "edge" in an area if "edge" were added to an area already fully usable (Guthery and Bingham 1992; Guthery 1997). We provide further details on these concepts in subsequent discussion of habitat management hypotheses.

Scientific management of quail habitat operates under the recognition that optimal habitat generally is a set, not an instance. Accordingly, the manager well schooled through study and experience recognizes when habitat is beyond improvement. "The value of habitat management has recognizable limits" (Guthery 2002:192).

Weather Influences

Variation in the weather is the primary arbiter of variation in quail abundance. In northern latitudes, bobwhites are vulnerable to winter

Table 24.1.
Approximate North American Ranges of Texas Quails and Annual Precipitation within Their U.S. Ranges

Species	Maximum breadth of range (km)		Annual precipitation (cm)	
	North-south	East-west	Min	Max
Northern bobwhite	4,195	3,170	~37.5	>125.0
Scaled quail	2,390	1,370	~25.0	~62.5
Gambel's quail	1,900	1,370	<25.0	~50.0
Montezuma quail	2,450	1,670	~25.0	>50.0

Source: Data for breadth of ranges from Johnsgard (1973).

mortality of up to 80 percent as a result of blizzards (Leopold 1937; Errington 1945). Likewise, Guthery has observed approximately 90 percent fall-spring mortality of bobwhites in the Texas Panhandle in association with the relatively severe winter of 2000–2001.

In more southerly latitudes in western quail range where winters are mild, weather variation during the breeding season explains a good deal of—but not all of—the variation in productivity and, hence, trends in abundance. Based on data in Rice et al. (1993: table 4), precipitation effectiveness (precipitation/evaporation) was two to three times stronger than a habitat index in explaining variation in fall density of bobwhites in southern Texas. Two weather factors seem to be important. A positive correlation between rainfall and production has long been recognized for scaled quail (Campbell et al. 1973), Gambel's quail (*Callipepla gambelii*) (Swank and Gallizioli 1954), Montezuma quail (*Cyrtonyx montezumae*) (Brown 1979), and northern bobwhites (Lehmann 1953; Kiel 1976). Recently, biologists have recognized that variation in production is best explained by consideration of rainfall and temperature. High temperatures may reduce the positive effects of rainfall for Gambel's quail (Heffelfinger et al. 1999) and bobwhites (Guthery et al. 2002). Further, cool temperatures can partially reverse the effects of drought. These constructs work well for explaining variation in quail production in arid and semiarid environments, but only explain about 25 percent of the annual variation in productivity and abundance in the humid southeast (Brennan et al. 1997). Likewise, precipitation effectiveness does not seem to explain variation in bobwhite abundance in the Gulf Prairies and Marshes of coastal Texas (Rice et al. 1993). Reid and Goodrum (1960) noted a similar relationship almost four decades earlier. Their figure 3 suggests greater than 25 percent variation in production explained by maximum temperatures; however, they did not provide statistical estimates of the actual parameters.

The scientific manager recognizes and essentially lives with the powerful influence of weather on quail dynamics. To a certain degree, the influence cannot be lessened through management because quails are vulnerable to thermal insult not only on the basis of their size and physiology but also on the basis of their adaptations to habitats that provide a weak shield against thermal insult. The impact of weather variation can be lessened, but not eliminated, through provision of adequate herbaceous and woody cover.

Management Hypotheses

The pillars of knowledge discussed previously provide a set of constraints within which the science of quail management operates. The constraints should not necessarily be regarded as immutable, because the history of Western science is replete with examples of the revision and replacement of knowledge regarded as formidable at one time. That history shows theories to be ephemeral, but they often leave traces of themselves when revised (Poincaré 1952). At this juncture, our theoretical understanding of demography, adaptations, and weather influences is worthy of greater confidence than our hypothetical understanding of management approaches. Nonetheless, scientific management operates under currently accepted hypotheses, including those detailed in the following sections.

Scientific management of the quail harvest operates at two scales: states and specific areas. Principles of harvest management differ between these scales, invoking confusion and contradiction in the minds of biologists and hunters alike.

At the state level, the matter of fundamental importance is the statewide trend in quail populations. If a population is nontrending (or trending upward), then harvest regulations (bag and possession limits, season length, shooting hours) are automatically justified. Note that trend must be viewed from the perspective of decades, not from the perspective of years. A population not trending over decades almost certainly will show large annual fluctuations.

A substantial body of data suggests that moderate changes in bag and possession limits and season length have minor to virtually nonexistent effects on the total annual harvest—and hence the breeding population—in a state. In Texas, for example, reducing the daily bag from 15 to 10 birds would affect only 3–5 percent of scaled quail or bobwhite hunters, in part because the most common daily take (44 percent of hunters) is 0 birds (Peterson 2001). Reducing the daily bag from 15 to 8 birds would reduce the statewide harvest by 27 percent for bobwhites and 15 percent for scaled quail. Season length is not particularly germane to the total state harvest because less than 44 percent of hunters hunt more than three days. Ironically, Peterson found that reduction in bag limits was regressive, meaning reduced bags put relatively more pressure on low populations and relatively less pressure on high populations—exactly the opposite of the desired effect. Moreover, hunting pressure is somewhat self-limiting because fewer hunters go afield during population lows and those who hunt spend fewer days hunting at lower than at higher population levels (Peterson and Perez 2000).

Scientifically, then, state game departments managing nontrending quail populations are justified in promulgating liberal, year-to-year consistent harvest regulations. Variation in regulations from time to time or from state to state generally represents political pressure rather than biological process.

States need not necessarily be concerned with the nuances of harvest management—additivity, compensation, sustained yield—germane to the taking of quails on specific areas. A reasonable goal of scientific harvest management on specific areas (ranch, farm, management area) is maximum sustained yield. Maximization involves understanding the interaction between natural and harvest mortality (questions of additivity and compensation) and the relation between breeding density and per-capita productivity in variable environments.

Whether harvest mortality is additive or compensatory is a longstanding (since about 1935) and somewhat quixotic bone of contention. Many biologists believe additivity means one bird lost from some future populations for each bird shot (1:1 additivity) and compensation means zero birds lost to the future for each bird shot (0:1 compensation). Whether either definition is accurate depends upon the passage of time. Over short time frames, harvest is expected to be 1:1 additive, whereas over long time frames, it is expected to be 0:1 compensatory. Neither of the limit concepts (1:1 additivity, 0:1 compensation) is particularly useful or realistic in scientific management of the harvest on specific areas.

Rather, we need to specify a time frame to address the nature of harvest mortality. The logical frame is fall to spring, because hunting takes place during fall-winter and breeding starts in spring. The nature of fall-spring harvest mortality has a probabilistic background that must be understood for scientific management. Total mortality (Q) may be defined under what is called the additive model of harvest mortality as

$$= V_o + K_o - V_oK_o,$$

where V_o = natural mortality rate in the absence of harvest mortality and K_o = harvest mortality rate in the absence of natural mortality. The latter variable cannot be determined, generally, because quail populations are expected to experience natural mortality. The product V_oK_o can be thought of as "birds shot that would have died anyway." The loss of these birds is not a deduction from the breeding population, so paradoxically, the additive model has a compensatory element.

The additive model also may be expressed as

$$Q = V_o + S_oK_o,$$

where S_o = the survival rate in the absence of harvest mortality. This manifestation of the additive model suggests that total mortality is proportional to harvest mortality and that each bird shot reduces the breeding population by the fraction S_o of 1 bird (S_o:1 additivity). For example, if survival in the absence of harvest mortality is expected to be 0.5 fall to spring, then the additive model predicts that the kill of 2 birds removes 1 bird from the breeding population (0.5:1 additivity).

Although the additive model serves as a theoretical background for harvest management, it is problematic because of the variable K_o, which is difficult but not impossible to estimate (Guthery 2002). A simple, yet more realistic model, derived from equations in Anderson and Burnham (1976) is

$$Q = V_o + (1 + b)K,$$

where b = a coefficient that ranges between -1 and <0 under the additive model of harvest and K = the harvest mortality rate in the presence of natural mortality. The coefficient b is estimable (Anderson and Burnham 1976) for a specific area if managers have maintained records on the annual fall-spring survival rates and the proportion of the population harvested.

There is mounting empirical evidence that the harvest of bobwhites is more additive than compensatory from fall to spring. In southern Illinois, the parameter b was estimated at -0.37 (Roseberry and Klimstra 1984:141), which suggests that, under the additive model, $1 + b = 0.63$ birds lost for each bird shot (0.63:1 additivity). The actual estimated relationship was 0.54 birds lost for each bird shot (0.54:1 additivity). In that 0:1 compensation requires $b = -1$, it is evident why Roseberry and Klimstra regarded harvest mortality as more additive than compensatory on their study area.

Elsewhere, similar findings have arisen (Baumgartner 1944a; Glading and Saarni 1944; Lehmann 1984; Robinette and Doerr 1993; Dixon et al. 1996; Guthery 2002:101). That is, fall-spring mortality of quails on specific areas tends to be additive (but not 1:1 additive, the chimerical limit of additivity!).

The point of this lengthy prologue is to demonstrate that harvest mortality of quails, from fall to spring, tends to add to natural mortality but not in a 1:1 fashion. This empirically demonstrated fact has to be dealt with in scientific harvest management on specific areas.

The basic idea of such management is to apply harvest in the presence of natural mortality such that a fall population is taken to a breeding population expected to be maximally productive (Guthery 2002). This requires an estimate of the preharvest population and knowledge of the relationship between breeding density and per-capita production; under the principle of inversity, low-density breeding populations are expected to be more productive per capita than high-density populations, but the relationship is nonlinear (Errington 1945; Roseberry and Klimstra 1984). An expedient is to take a population down to the point at which the average spring-fall increase leads to a desired fall density. Knowing the fall population objective and the desired breeding population, one calculates the total mortality (fall to spring) that will take the fall population to the breeding population objective:

$$Q = 1 - (\text{desired spring population/existing fall population}).$$

Then the harvest rate can be estimated (Guthery 2002) as

$$K = (1/a)[(Q - V_o)/(1 - V_o)],$$

where a is a theoretical coefficient. A value of $a = 1.05$ may be used as an approximation. Natural mortality in the absence of harvest can be placed at $V_o = 0.5$ as an approximation. See Guthery (2002:110–12) for further details and example calculations.

Because harvest mortality is more additive than compensatory from fall to spring does not necessarily imply it is additive from fall to fall. Density-dependent production can reverse the effects of additive harvest such that fall populations may remain similar among years, given variation associated with weather. But harvest rates cannot be extreme, or a population will decline despite density-dependent production. On large areas of quail habitat in Texas, a safe harvest rate is less than 30 percent of the fall population (Guthery et al. 2000). The prudent manager might reduce harvest to lower levels during population busts but exact harvests greater than 30 percent during population booms, consistent with the breeding population objective.

Thus, scientific management of the quail harvest at the state level is exercised with liberal and consistent annual regulations. On specific areas, the theory behind maximum sustained yield management is available for application should managers choose to manage the harvest under scientific protocols. This will entail annual records on fall density, spring density, and harvest (including unretrieved loss), perhaps augmented with banding data to better estimate harvest rates.

Habitat

Two competing hypotheses regarding the management of habitat for quails currently prevail. These are the habitat quality hypothesis and what we shall call the habitat quantity hypothesis. The latter is also known as the usable-space hypothesis and the space-time hypothesis (Guthery 1997, 2000).

Under the habitat quality hypothesis, quail abundance is presumed to increase with increases in variables such as habitat edge, cover type interspersion, forb diversity, food supplies, and other variables that provide some apparent measure of habitat quality. The quality hypothesis implicitly posits some minimum value for any quality feature, below which the existence of quails on an area is impossible, and some maximum value for quail response (an asymptote) because there is an upper limit on average quail density for any area (figure 24.1). The asymptote disproves the quality hypothesis over certain domains of inference. In other words, there are values for any quality feature above which no response from quails can be expected. Indeed, it is possible to imagine so much of a quality feature that mean quail abundance declines. Taking food as quality to the limit, for example, might mean we manage for corn and end up with no quails.

The habitat quantity hypothesis, on the contrary, says that mean abundance of quails on an area is proportional to the quantity of space-time on the area, within limits set by the area requirements of a viable population and maximum expected mean abundance (figure 24.2). Space-time can be thought of as the amount of usable cover—that fits quail adaptations—multiplied by the time it is available on an annual basis. For example, if an area had 500 hectares of usable cover available 365 days a year, the area would provide 182,500 hectare-days (451,000 acre-days) of space-time.

The concept of usable space is a key component of the habitat quantity hypothesis. Usable space is defined as an area supporting habitat that is consistent with the physiological, behavioral, and physical adaptations of quails (Guthery 1997). Usable space has infinitely many optimal configurations (Guthery 1999a, 2002) because of the adaptive plasticity of quails (see previous discussion), the interchanges of cover functions between woody and herbaceous components of habitat, and the flexibility of quails regarding time in activities (which makes different configurations of foraging and resting cover, for example, equally satisfactory because quails can trade time in movement or resting with little or no effect on survival).

Given usable space, there can be great variation in so-called habitat quality features that have no effect on quail abundance. For example, in fully usable space we could, within limits, add or subtract edge, food, and forb diversity or reduce or increase interspersion of cover types and there would be no effect on mean quail abundance.

The habitat quality hypothesis has been around since antiquity (e.g., food plots), whereas the habitat quantity hypothesis originated in the 1930s (Errington and Hamerstrom 1936). Lehmann (1984:189) expressed it directly: "To supply most of the needs of high populations of

Figure 24.1.
Graph portraying the habitat quality hypothesis for quail habitat management.

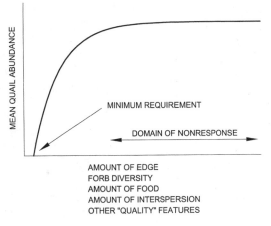

Figure 24.2.
Graph portraying the habitat quantity hypothesis for quail habitat management.

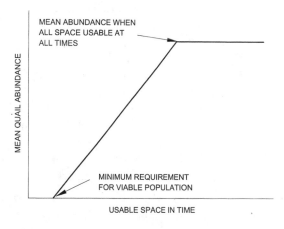

quail, they must be assured continuous [i.e., *full-time*] use of virtually every square foot of ground." Lehmann was talking about maximizing usable space in time.

Guthery (1997) formalized the quantity hypothesis and put it on a quantitative footing. He surveyed all of the management literature on bobwhites that he could find. The survey revealed that no quality practices (e.g., food, water, edge), as assessed in field experiments and reported in the literature, resulted in increased abundance. The only practices that increased abundance on particular areas were those that added suitable permanent cover (usable space) to the areas. Application of the quantity hypothesis in the Southeast recently resulted in a dramatic near-term increase in bobwhite abundance (Sisson, Stribling, and Mitchell 2002).

We have presented competing hypotheses—quality versus quantity—as underlying concepts for the management of quail habitat. We did not call them principles or theorems because at this juncture the superiority of one hypothesis over the other is not clearly demonstrated; moreover, we expect that some melding of the hypotheses may ultimately occur as thought and experiment continue in the future.

Despite ambiguity over the habitat quality and habitat quantity hypotheses, the weight of evidence at this juncture favors the quantity hypothesis. The quality hypothesis clearly breaks down in domains of nonresponse, which we suspect are fairly broad for some quality features. Scientific habitat management, therefore, involves the assessment of an area for usability, that is, the identification of usable space and space that is not usable or less than fully usable (usable only a portion of some time period). After a usable-space audit has been conducted, habitat management should focus on creating fully usable space where it is not available (making all areas habitable at all times: space-time saturation). The alteration of so-called quality features in the fully usable space on an area is not expected to increase quail abundance on the area. When an area is saturated with habitat space-time, further habitat management need only be directed at maintaining that saturation in the presence of ecological *succession*.

The Management of Quail Science

The idea that creative endeavors, either artistic or scientific, can be managed is in many ways counterintuitive. In the simplest sense, people create beautiful art or achieve dazzling scientific breakthroughs because they can. The creative intellectual processes that allow scientists to conceive breakthroughs, or artists to paint masterpieces, are complex (Beveridge 1957) and beyond the scope of this brief chapter. Despite the complex nature of factors that inspire people to create new knowledge via the scientific method, we believe that there are certain cultural factors that can, and should, be addressed and understood to foster scientific endeavor and creativity. This is especially true with respect to the management of quail science.

The Culture of Quails
Game birds in general, and quails in particular, have a cultural advantage over most other wildlife species. The root of this advantage is that many people who are passionate about hunting upland game birds, and

especially about hunting quails, are relatively wealthy. Many of these people are also extremely generous and eager to fund research that will result in management to elevate and stabilize quail populations. The landmark study of northern bobwhite life history (Stoddard 1931) was funded by a small group of wealthy quail hunting plantation owners who were concerned about declining quail numbers. Stoddard's work, and rapport with these plantation owners, eventually resulted in the founding and endowment of Tall Timbers Research Station in Tallahassee, Florida. Comparable passion for wildlife resources, and especially quails, has resulted in the programs and endowments that support the positions that each of us currently holds as university professors. Endowment funding is especially important for supporting long-term research initiatives, providing program stability, attracting and retaining productive personnel, and reducing—but not eliminating—the pressure to raise operating funds that are typically limited to short-term investigations. The donors have the satisfaction that their contributions to endowments will be used to support quail research in perpetuity.

However, the successful management of quail science requires more than just people with passion for quail hunting and a willingness to throw money at research whenever a real or perceived problem arises. The successful management of quail science is the result of a complex intersection—and interaction—among the disparate cultures of scientists, philanthropists, agencies, administrators, and hunters. The common element that binds these cultures is a passion, and fascination, for understanding the processes that influence populations of wild quails. All of these cultural elements fall under the aegis of conservation. It is safe to say that the scientists, philanthropists, administrators, and hunters who are interested in the management of quail science are conservationists.

Because of the common conservationist thread, there is often considerable overlap among subsets of the cultural groups that are necessary for successful quail science. For example, as scientists, we also share past membership in the administrative culture—Guthery as a former university department chair and Brennan as a former research director—and current membership in the hunting culture. However, because of various life circumstances, neither of us has ever, nor will ever, belong to the philanthropy culture. But it is the patronage of the philanthropic culture, which has broad overlap with the hunting culture, that provides the financial—and often political—support that is critical for us, and other scientists, to conduct quail science.

The role of resource management agencies is also extremely important to the management of quail science. Because quails are widely hunted resident game birds, state wildlife agencies have spent millions in quail research from Pittman-Robinson funds, general revenue, license fees, and so on. It would be an oversight not to consider these agencies an important aspect of quail culture. When public money is involved in supporting quail science, the political pressure from the hunting culture brought to bear on the administrative culture—typically a state wildlife agency—is usually necessary to make public funds available for quail science. Although hard data are not readily available, we suspect that over the years state resource agencies have spent many millions to support quail research.

The table upon which quail science rests is supported by four legs: people, money, land, and laboratory facilities. Credible science cannot be conducted in the absence of even one of these resources. The need for people and money is obvious. A field-oriented, graduate research project at a university typically costs between $30,000 and $120,000, depending on the nature of the project and the degree being sought. The interactions between land and laboratories are also especially important. Land is, of course, essential for conducting management experiments to test population responses, monitoring long-term trends of quail numbers, and carrying out many other aspects of research. Frequently, research hypotheses and the subsequent investigations to test them are inspired from the accumulation of observations of different landscapes and scales that biologists and scientists have made over time. Many other research questions can be answered only by using captive animals (i.e., physiological responses to environmental factors) or laboratory facilities (i.e., population genetics or effects of environmental contaminants).

The role of land—especially private land, although many of the same constructs apply to conducting research on public land—and the access provided to these lands for quail research are especially important for the progression and management of quail science. During most of the twentieth century, people who were passionate about funding quail research were also generous with respect to providing access to their private hunting lands for scientists to conduct quail research. If the scientists and landowners understand and can communicate about critical aspects of access, cooperation, and other mutual obligations—such as landowners understanding the importance of the scientific method and the need to maintain the integrity of control and treatment plots—then the management of quail science is usually successful (Brennan, Engstrom, et al. 1995). When critical elements of access, cooperation, and other important mutual obligations just noted are not understood, the scientific process is compromised and the relationship breaks down. Acrimony, hard feelings, and distrust can result.

Incentives for Successful Management of Quail Science

There are several important incentives that drive the cultural factors and influence the management of quail science.

Scientists

Although a successful scientist can enjoy a relatively comfortable living, the pursuit of wealth is seldom, if ever, a motivation for someone to embark on a scientific career. The incentives that drive and motivate a successful scientist are often intangible. For example, seeing the results of his or her scientific study in print is usually a thrill that gives a scientist satisfaction. The positive recognition, and reputation, that a scientist engenders among peers is also a major incentive that motivates many scientists. The institutionalized systems of promotion and tenure at universities are age-old mechanisms to assure that productive scientists are rewarded and nonproductive scientists are moved to other pursuits. A final intangible motivator, and a very important one to many scientists, is the search for the truths that have eluded us, the truths that condense and unify knowledge and that change the direction of thinking and research. These great truths distinguish the careers of but a handful of scientists, but the search for them is considered great fun by anybody who has ever sat down before a set of original data and devised strategies for analyzing and interpreting it.

Patrons
Lindberg (1992:181) correctly noted that "a flourishing scientific enterprise requires peace, prosperity, and patronage." Although it can be argued that philanthropy is often not completely charitable, it is interesting to consider some factors that inspire patronage in the context of the management of quail science. We believe that it is safe to assume that people who make large donations to support quail research do so because they have real concern about the quail resource and want to see this resource sustained in perpetuity. Of course, there is also the intersection between philanthropy and hunting. Many people are inspired to support research because they believe that such research will ultimately result in the stabilization and enhancement of the quail populations they hunt. There are myriad charitable causes that compete for the attention of patrons. The fact that numerous individual patrons have contributed hundreds of thousands, and in some cases millions, of dollars to support quail research is one of the most remarkable aspects of modern wildlife science.

Administrators
Administrators and other program leaders and directors have several unique incentives to manage quail science. First, effective program administration can result in successful scientific outcomes. It is one thing to conduct effective science but an entirely a different thing to lead and inspire successful science. Like scientists, programs also develop reputations. Second, effective administrators almost always leave some form of positive, programmatic legacy, and hence reputation, in their wake. Ineffective administrators, like unproductive scientists, nearly always fade to oblivion.

Hunters
Hunters have an obvious incentive to support the effective management of quail science. Their primary goal is the stabilization and elevation of quail numbers that have been addressed throughout this chapter. Hunters, when they work as a group, can also bring effective political pressure to bear when state wildlife agencies are reluctant to support either the science of quail management or the management of quail science.

When the cultures of hunting and philanthropy overlap, the effects on quail science, as mentioned previously, can be tremendous. An unfortunate disconnect exists, however, between political pressure from hunters and the ability of resource agencies to provide consistent high-quality quail hunting on public lands. This is one of the major quail management conundrums that has plagued the quail world for many decades. It may simply be that such management is impossible, although we tend to believe otherwise. With effective management of harvest, habitat space, and other factors, it should be possible, at least theoretically, to provide high-quality quail hunting experiences on private lands with at least some remaining potential for quail populations. Unfortunately, much of Texas and America exists under land uses that are incompatible with quails. It is not realistic to suppose that prevailing economies and cultures in such areas are going to change for the benefit of game birds.

Some aspects of our present-day economies have potential for using what we know about the science of quail management to stabilize and enhance quail numbers on public lands. For example, federal resource agencies lease land to ranchers for grazing. Why not instead lease land to people to hunt quails, especially if they are willing to outbid the cattle ranchers?

As the science of quail management and the management of quail science progress, innovative scientific and management constructs should be attempted to solve the problems that work against the stabilization and elevation of quail populations. We have pillars of knowledge that support the science of quail management. We have significant elements of culture that contribute to the management of quail science. Getting these factors to interact and overcome political roadblocks, such as the one noted in the previous paragraph, will be essential to keep space for quails on the landscape of twenty-first-century America.

The Future of Quail Hunting and Sustainability Science

25

Leonard A. Brennan

> Quail are grand-opera game.
> Leopold (1932)

> A thing is right when it tends to preserve the integrity, stability, and beauty of the biotic community. It is wrong when it tends otherwise.
> Leopold (1949)

Given the widespread and ongoing population declines that quails continue to face in Texas, it is important to consider what the future of quail hunting will be for the next generation. It may also be of value to examine how the future of quail hunting is related to emerging concepts of sustainability science. Thus, the purpose of this chapter is to identify the connections between these two topics, which at first glance may seem disparate but are actually closely connected.

"Quail are grand-opera game," as Aldo Leopold noted more than seven decades ago. Few, if any, hunting experiences compare with wing shooting into a covey rise of wild quails. Witnessing the explosive flight of a dozen birds in more than a dozen directions as they flush in front of a pointing dog is a major adrenaline rush. Then, put yourself on the ground next to the dog and somehow project, in a split second, past the adrenaline. Your goal is to focus on, and shoot at, one or two of the birds before they fly out of range. Indeed, this is grand opera whether the stage is rangeland, piney woods, or a fallow field border.

The grand-opera analogy for quail hunting is not limited to the hunting drama performed on the habitat stage. It is also an allusion to a rarefied experience that is affordable to a minority of people. There is also an element of elitism; quail hunting is a rarefied experience, much like grand opera, that is typically enjoyed by wealthy people. Nevertheless, I have seen wild quails make fools out of even the most elite of hunters. Grand opera can become grand comedy under the right circumstances.

The General Status of Hunting in Texas

Texans spend more than $1.7 billion per year on hunting and hunting-related activities. This has an economic multiplier effect of more than $3.6 billion (International Association of Fish and Wildlife Agencies 2002). This is the good news. The bad news is that Texas is losing 10,000–20,000 hunters per year (Brown et al. 2003). Of the approximately million people who buy hunting licenses in Texas, this means a 10–20 percent (100,000–200,000 people) decline in hunters over the next decade. These losses translate to both economic and political problems that threaten the North American model of wildlife conservation that has been supported by hunters for most of the past century (Mahoney 2002).

Fortunately, policy makers and agency administrators realize that hunting, as we know it in Texas, is in trouble and will require comprehensive strategic actions to sustain it (Brown et al. 2003).

Quail Hunting in Texas Today

The number of quail hunters in Texas has declined from more than 250,000 in 1988 to less than 140,000 in 1999 (Adams and Causey 2000). This represents an annual decline of 4.6 percent, which is approximately equal to the rate wild quail populations are declining in Texas. It is not just the quail populations that are declining in Texas but the quail hunters as well.

Youth Programs

The average age of Texans is 35 years, and the average age of Texas hunters is 42 years (Adams and Causey 2000). Texas hunters are aging faster than Texas citizens. Thus, it is clear that more young people must be recruited into the hunting community if hunting is to be sustained.

The Texas Wildlife Leadership Youth Brigades have a huge potential to educate young people about wildlife management and the North American model of wildlife conservation. These programs, especially the Bobwhite Brigade (Rollins, Steinbach, and Brown 2000), educate teenagers by using a creative mix of material on biology, ecology, and hunting-firearms safety (figure 25.1). Even though these programs are still relatively new (less than a decade), they have exposed more than 1,000 young Texans to wildlife and upland game-bird management and, over time, have the potential to positively influence tens and perhaps hundreds of thousands of young people. The Texas Wildlife Youth Leadership Brigades are model programs that should be adopted by other states. If these programs are successful in Texas, they have the potential to recruit a new generation of quail hunters.

Economic Incentives

It takes considerably more habitat to satisfy a quail hunter than a deer hunter. Forty acres and a tree stand provide a deer hunter the potential opportunity to harvest a trophy animal. Forty acres might provide one quail hunter with one or two coveys, if any. If these 40 acres are

Figure 25.1.
Teaching shotgun handling and safety to young people is essential for sustaining the future of quail hunting in Texas. Placing an inexperienced shooter in a two-sided wire "cage" helps assure that the gun movement will be constrained to 90 degrees and reduces the risk of accidents. Photo courtesy of Texas Wildlife Leadership Youth Brigades

isolated from other patches of quail habitat, they will probably provide zero quail for the hunter.

The current economic trends that relate to quail hunting are working, in some ways, at cross-purposes with respect to the future of quail hunting. We laud the record high prices that quail hunting leases now bring (in many South Texas places, greater than $30/hectare/year, or $12/acre/year; with another $12+/hectare/year, or $5+/acre/year, for grazing rights). These values, when compared to lease costs 30 years ago, have risen from about $10/hectare/year ($4/acre/year) (Jim McAllen, McAllen Ranch, pers. comm.). However, in a state such as Texas, in which 98 percent of the land is private, such steep economic prices limit access to grand-opera quail hunting to the wealthy few. The positive aspect is that quails are becoming an economic magnet that attracts dollars from wealthy urbanites to economically challenged rural communities. The negative aspect of this development is that blue-collar quail hunting is disappearing from the landscape.

Farm Bill Policy Economics

The intention of the federal Farm Bill is to provide economic incentives to achieve certain policy objectives. For more than a decade, a group of optimistic quail biologists, managers, and enthusiasts have held great hope that Farm Bill programs and associated incentives could play a major role at restoring quail population—and increasing hunting opportunities—on private lands. Whether Farm Bill incentives will work to become a major incentive that helps pay for quail management and restoration remains a yet-unproven hypothesis. Farm Bill incentives were a tremendous asset to successfully implementing the North American Waterfowl Management Plan. Will similar incentives eventually do the same for quails? I certainly hope so.

Taking the Pulse of Quail Experts

I conducted an informal survey of colleagues and acquaintances that I consider experts on various aspects of quail management. Some are expert hunters; others are expert biologists, researchers, managers, or administrators. I asked them to give me their thoughts on the future of quail hunting in Texas, at least for the next generation. I sought their opinions because I thought that my perspectives were somewhat limited and potentially biased.

In general, the quail experts I surveyed were more optimistic than I am with respect to the future of quail hunting. Was this difference simply my skeptical attitude compared to more generally optimistic colleagues? Or is it that I have been watching the declines continue for more than a decade on a continental scale (Brennan 1991a, 1993, 2002a)?

Many quail experts pointed to the new economics of quails compared to that of cattle and see this as a way of keeping large ranches and private landholdings intact. I concur, because even the best cattle operations struggle to net $10–$12/hectare/year ($4–$5/acre/year) when quail leases can bring in twice as much revenue, at least in South Texas. However, this development is causing some powerful cultural shifts. For example, it is anathema for independent cattle ranchers to cede land management decisions to city folks with dollars who want to pay to hunt quails. Or, as T. Boone Pickens recently stated, "These ranchers are going to have to realize, if they want to live on ranches, they're not in the livestock business any more. They're in the hospitality business. And that's a big change for a bunch of these guys" (Wethe 2003).

Managing Hunting Pressure

As quail hunting gets more expensive and the land base that supports wild quails shrinks, management of hunting pressure will become increasingly important. At least two chapters of this book address factors related to quantitatively (chapter 24) and qualitatively (chapter 20) managing hunting pressure. In the future, understanding elements of the hunter-covey interface (HCI) as a theoretical model for managing hunting pressure will increase in importance. Too often, opinion and anecdote prevail over data and objectivity when it comes to managing quail hunting pressure.

The theoretical basis for understanding HCI dynamics has been developed by Radomski and Guthery (2000) and refined by Guthery (2002). The core of HCI pertains to understanding how daily harvest mortality is related to the velocity of the hunt and the amount of area hunted. Basically, the faster you hunt and the more area you cover, the more birds you kill. This is intuitive to any quail hunter. However, the HCI models are tools that allow a quail manager to quantify and refine these relationships and achieve a specified density of breeding quails after the hunting season.

To test whether HCI models provide meaningful real-world results, we need data on the spatial aspects of quail hunting dynamics. Hardin (2003) equipped pointing dogs (figure 25.2) and quail hunting trucks with global positioning system (GPS) technology to obtain this spatial information on quail hunting (figure 25.3). Such information provides managers with data on the spatial extent of the hunts, allowing them to distribute hunting pressure evenly across a pasture and avoid revisiting the same area too many times during the season.

Figure 25.2.
Global positioning system (GPS) units on pointing dogs to determine the velocity and spatial extent of their hunt for testing the hunter-covey interface theory.
Photo by Jason B. Hardin

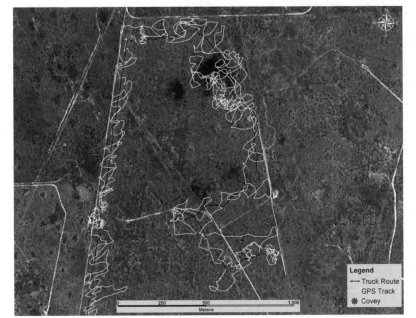

Figure 25.3.
Spatial coverage of a quail hunt in South Texas. By determining the velocity and spatial extent of quail hunts, managers can calibrate daily mortality and achieve a predetermined breeding-season population density.
Photo by Jason B. Hardin

What Is Sustainability Science?

The concept of sustainability in resource management has gained considerable traction during the past few years. Our expanding human population is threatening the sustainability of the ecosystems—and the goods and services these ecosystems provide—that support life on earth as we know it (Christensen et al. 1996). For example, ocean fisheries that were once considered inexhaustible are now impoverished from over-fishing. Vast areas of once-productive rangelands have been converted to desert from excessive grazing. Agricultural cropping, while producing more food than ever, demands ever-increasing inputs of fuels, fertilizer, and chemicals to maintain razor-thin profit margins. What are the limits to the ecosystems that sustain us?

Sustainability science builds on traditional, hypothesis-driven science by blending observational studies with GIS and remote sensing (Kates et al. 2001); developing place-based models of management strategies that may be extended to other systems and regions; and involving scientists, stakeholders, advocates, and citizens who will apply new information from scientific investigations to enhance stewardship of resources such as quails.

The concept of developing a scientific basis for the sustainable management of natural resources is gaining momentum (Kates et al. 2001). The emerging discipline of sustainability science provides a natural framework for organizing efforts to restore, sustain, and elevate populations of wild quails and grassland birds in Texas (table 25.1). The core questions of sustainability science are consistent with the philosophy that science and stewardship are the keystone concepts upon which quails, grassland birds, and the habitats that support them will be sustained through management.

Sustainability science is an approach to answering research questions by (1) spanning the range of spatial scales between on-the-ground resources and economic factors that influence them, (2) overcoming temporal inertia and implementing alternative management strate-

Table 25.1.
Core Questions of Sustainability Science and Their Relation to Restoring, Sustaining, and Elevating Quail and Grassland Birds in Texas

Sustainability science core question	Examples of quail and grassland bird conservation research, management, and education issues and opportunities
1. How can the dynamic interactions between nature and society—including lags and inertia—be better incorporated in emerging models and conceptualizations that integrate biological systems, human development, and sustainability?	Northern Bobwhite Conservation Initiative Texas Quail Conservation Initiative
2. How are long-term trends in environment and development, including consumption and population, reshaping nature and society in ways relevant to sustainability?	Economics of quail hunting in Texas Using GIS to track land-use changes
3. What determines the vulnerability or resilience of the ecological systems and human culture in particular places?	Quail nest predation and landscape ecology Hunter-covey interface study Impacts of exotic grasses on quails Landscape-scale assessment of vegetation condition and quail abundance
4. Can scientifically meaningful "limits" or "boundaries" be defined that would provide effective warning of conditions beyond which a system or resource would incur a significantly increased risk of serious degradation?	Landscape-scale assessment of vegetation condition and quail abundance Aflatoxin effects on quails and songbirds Impacts of exotic grasses Understanding impacts of weather and climate change
5. What systems of incentive structures—including markets, rules, norms, and scientific information—can most effectively improve social capacity to guide interactions between people and resources toward more sustainable trajectories?	Quantifying the economic value of quails Hunting Delivering true wildlife conservation benefits from federal Farm Bill Program incentives
6. How can today's operational systems for monitoring environmental conditions be integrated to provide useful guidance for efforts to promote sustainability?	Cooperative Quail Disease Survey Landscape-scale assessment of annual quail population productivity
7. How can today's relatively independent activities of research planning, monitoring, assessment, and decision support be better integrated into systems for adaptive management and societal learning?	All topics described in this book

Source: Kates et al. (2001).

gies, (3) embracing the functional complexity that often confounds our management of natural resources, and (4) recognizing the wide range of perspectives about what makes knowledge usable for sustaining a particular resource of interest (Kates et al. 2001), which in this case are populations of wild quails in Texas. The research described in table 25.1 is an essential step toward expanding and applying the unified scientific framework for the sustainable management of wild quails described in chapter 24 and by the Texas Quail Technical Support Committee (2003).

Quail Stewardship Management

Getting the general public to embrace a stewardship management philosophy is one of the major hurdles that must be overcome if the wild quail populations of Texas are to be sustained and elevated. Linking the concept of sustainability with the philosophy of stewardship will be essential for overcoming the cultural apathy and inertia that stand in the way of quail restoration in Texas. Bringing the concept of stewardship into the context of quail management is crucial to the successful conservation of these species. It is important because stewardship requires "a moral responsibility for the careful use of resources, especially with respect to the needs of a community or group" (Neufeldt and Guralnik 1997). Indeed, we have a moral responsibility to sustain and elevate populations of wild Texas quails to sustain the future of quail hunting. It would be wrong to do otherwise.

If the strategic plans outlined by Brown et al. (2003) and the Texas Quail Technical Support Committee (2003) are successful, then quail hunting in Texas will have a sustained future. If we are not successful at implementing these plans, important aspects of Texas wildlife culture and heritage will be lost to future Texans.

References

Abbott, C. W. 2003. Transplanting northern bobwhite (*Colinus virginianus*) in the Southern High Plains of Texas. Thesis, Texas Tech University, Lubbock.

Adams, C. E., and L. A. Causey. 2000. *The future of hunting in Texas*. College Station: Department of Wildlife and Fisheries Sciences, Texas A&M University.

Adams, N. E., Jr. 1978. The effects of cattle grazing on white-tailed deer distribution. Thesis, Texas A&I University–Kingsville.

Addison, E. M., and R. C. Anderson. 1969. A review of eyeworms of the genus *Oxyspirura* (Nematoda: Spiruroidea). *Wildlife Disease* 55:1–58.

Albers, R. P., and F. R. Gehlbach. 1990. Choices of feeding habitat by relict Montezuma quail in central Texas. *Wilson Bulletin* 102:300–308.

Allen, A. W. 1994. Conservation Reserve Program (CRP) benefits to wildlife: A national perspective. *Land and Water* 38:23–25.

Allen, A. W., B. S. Cade, and M. W. Vandever 2001. Effects of emergency haying on vegetative characteristics within selected Conservation Reserve Program fields in the northern Great Plains. *Journal of Soil and Water Conservation* 56:120–25.

Allen, C. R., R. S. Lutz ,and S. Demarais. 1993. What about fire ants and northern bobwhite? *Wildlife Society Bulletin* 21:349–51.

———. 1995. Red imported fire ant impacts on northern bobwhite populations. *Ecological Applications* 5:632–38.

Allen, C. R., R. S. Lutz, T. Lockley, S. A. Phillips, and S. Demarais. 2001. The non-indigenous ant, *Solenopsis invicta,* reduces loggerhead shrike and native insect abundance. *Journal of Agricultural and Urban Entomology* 18:249–59.

Allen, C. R., R. D. Willey, P. E. Myers, P. M. Horton, and J. Buffa. 2000. Impact of red imported fire ant infestation on northern bobwhite quail abundance trends in southeastern United States. *Journal of Agricultural and Urban Entomology* 17:43–51.

Allen, E. A. 1930. *Trichomonas* in quail. *Journal of Parasitology* 16:162.

Alley, W. M. 1984. The Palmer Drought Severity Index: Limitations and assumptions. *Journal of Climate and Applied Meteorology* 23:1100–1109.

Amin, O. M., and M. D. Dailey. 1998. Description of *Mediorhynchus papillosus* (Acanthocephala: Gigantorhynchidae) from a Colorado, USA, population, with a discussion of morphology and geographical variability. *Journal of the Helminthological Society of Washington* 65:189–200.

Anderson, D. R., and K. P. Burnham. 1976. *Population ecology of the mallard VI. The effect of exploitation on survival*. U.S. Department of the Interior, Fish and Wildlife Service, Resource Publication 128.

Anderson, E. W. 1969. Why proper grazing use? *Journal of Range Management* 22:361–63.

Anderson, R. M., and R. M. May. 1978. Regulation and stability of host-parasite population interactions. Vol. 1: Regulatory processes. *Journal of Animal Ecology* 47:219–47.

———. 1979. Population biology of infectious diseases: Part I. *Nature* 280:361–67.

Anderson, W. L. 1974. Scaled quail social organization and movements. Thesis, University of Arizona, Tucson.

———. 1978. Vocalizations of scaled quail. *Condor* 80:49–63.

Andrews, R., and R. Righter. 1992. *Colorado birds.* Denver, Colo.: Denver Museum of Natural History.

Anonymous. 1942. *The propriety of attempting to restore bobwhite quail in Texas by raising the quail in pens for release in the wild.* Austin: Texas Game, Fish, and Oyster Commission.

Anonymous. 1945a. Why Texas doesn't pen-raise quail. *Texas Game and Fish* 2:6–8, 14, 17.

———. 1945b. Why Texas doesn't pen-raise quail. *Texas Game and Fish* 3:6, 16.

Anonymous. 1948. Report of the joint committee on wildlife. The Wildlife Society and the Division of Biology and Agriculture, National Research Council. *The Wildlife Society Newsletter* (Winter).

Anonymous. 1970. *Tree regions of Texas.* Circular 75, Texas Forest Service, College Station.

Ar, A., and Y. Sidis. 2002. Nest microclimate during incubation. Pages 143–60 in D. C. Deeming, ed., *Avian incubation.* Oxford: Oxford University Press.

Archer, S., and F. E. Smeins. 1991. Ecosystem-level processes. Pages 109–39 in R. K. Heitschmidt and J. W. Smith, eds., *Grazing management and ecological perspective.* Portland, Ore.: Timber Press.

Arnold, L. A., and D. L. Drawe. 1979. Seasonal food habits of white-tailed deer in the South Texas Plains. *Journal of Range Management* 32:175–78.

Atkinson, C. T. 1999. Hemosporidiosis. Pages 193–99 in M. Friend and J. C. Franson, eds., *Field manual of wildlife diseases: General field procedures and diseases of birds.* Information and Technology Report 1999–001. Reston, Va.: U.S. Geological Survey, Biological Resources Division.

Ault, S. C. 1981. Food selection by scaled quail in northwest Texas. Thesis, Texas Tech University, Lubbock.

Ault, S. C., and F. A. Stormer. 1983. Seasonal food selection by scaled quail in northwest Texas. *Journal of Wildlife Management* 47:222–28.

Baccus, J. T. 2002. Impacts of game ranching on wildlife management in Texas. *Transactions of the North American Wildlife and Natural Resources Conference* 67:276–88.

Backs, S. E. 1982. An evaluation of releasing first generation (F_1) bobwhite quail produced from wild stock. *Pittman-Robertson Bulletin* 14:1–17.

Bailey, F. M. 1928. *Birds of New Mexico.* Santa Fe: New Mexico Game and Fish.

Bailey, J. A. 1984. *Principles of wildlife management.* New York: Wiley.

Bailey, R. G. 1995. *Descriptions of the ecoregions of the United States.* Miscellaneous Publication 1391. Washington, D.C.: U.S. Department of Agriculture, Forest Service.

———. 1998. Ecoregions: The ecosystem geography of the oceans and continents. New York: Springer-Verlag.

Bailey, V. 1905. Biological survey of Texas. *North American Fauna* 25:1–222.

Baker, D. L., and F. S. Guthery. 1990. Effects of continuous grazing on habitat and density of ground-foraging birds in South Texas. *Journal of Range Management* 43:2–5.

Baker, R. H. 1940. *Better quail shooting in east Texas.* Bulletin Number 20. Austin: Texas Game, Fish, and Oyster Commission.

———. 1999. Texas clamored for quail in the 1930's. *East Texas Historical Journal* 37:42–46.

Banks, R. L. 1970. An ecological study of scaled quail in southeastern New Mexico. Thesis, New Mexico State University, Las Cruces.

Bareiss, L. J., P. Schulz, and F. S. Guthery. 1986. Effects of short-duration and continuous grazing on bobwhite and wild turkey nesting. *Journal of Range Management* 39:259–60.

Barkley, R. C. 1972. Foods of scaled quail in southeastern New Mexico. Thesis, New Mexico State University, Las Cruces.

Barnes, T. G., R. K. Heitschmidt, and L. W. Varner. 1991. Wildlife. Pages 179–90 in R. K. Heitschmidt and J. W. Stuth, eds., *Grazing management: An ecological perspective.* Portland, Ore.: Timber Press.

Barnes, W. B. 1947. Is artificial propagation the answer? *Outdoor Indiana* 14, no. 2 (April): 8–10.

Bartlett, R. C. 1995. *Saving the best of Texas.* Austin: University of Texas Press.

Baru/s/, V. 1970. Studies of the nematode *Subulura suctoria. Folia Parasitol (Prague)* 17:191–99.

Bass, C. C. 1939. Observations on the specific cause and the nature of "quail disease" or ulcerative enteritis in quail. *Proceedings of the Society for Experimental Biology and Medicine* 42:377–80.

———. 1940. Specific cause and nature of ulcerative enteritis of quail. *Proceedings of the Society for Experimental Biology and Medicine* 46:250–52.

Baumgartner, F. M. 1944a. Bobwhite quail populations on hunted vs. protected areas. *Journal of Wildlife Management* 8:259–60.

———. 1944b. Dispersal and survival of game farm bobwhite quail in northcentral Oklahoma. *Journal of Wildlife Management* 8:112–18.

———. 1945. Management of bob-white on the oak-tall grass prairie: North central Oklahoma. *Transactions of the North American Wildlife Conference* 10:185–90.

———. 1946. Bobwhite food relations to land use in northcentral Oklahoma. *Proceedings and Transactions of the Texas Academy of Science* 29:234–39.

Baumgartner, F. M., M. J. Lewis, J. L. Steel, and J. E. Williams. 1952. Oklahoma bobwhite food relations. *Transactions of the North American Wildlife and Natural Resources Conference* 17:338–58.

Beasom, S. L. 1974. Intensive short-term predator removal as a game management tool. *Transactions of the North American Wildlife and Natural Resources Conference* 39:230–40.

Beasom, S. L., and C. J. Scifres. 1977. Population reactions of selected game species to aerial herbicide applications. *Journal of Range Management* 35:790–94.

Bendell, J. F. 1955. Disease as a control of a population of blue grouse, *Dendragapus obscurus fuliginosus* (Ridgway). *Canadian Journal of Zoology* 33:195–223.

Bendire, C. 1892. *Life histories of North American birds: With special reference to their breeding habits and eggs.* Special Bulletin Number 1. Washington, D.C.: Smithsonian Institution, U.S. National Museum.

Bennett, L. J. 1945. The pheasant in Pennsylvania and New Jersey. Pages 11–31 in W. L. McAtee, ed., *The ring-necked pheasant and its management in North America.* Washington, D.C.: American Wildlife Institute.

Bennitt, R. 1946. Report on a three year quail stocking experiment. *Missouri Conservationist* 7:10–11.

Bent, A. C. 1932. *Life histories of North American gallinaceous birds.* United States National Museum Bulletin 162. Washington D.C.: Smithsonian Institution.

Bentley, H. L. 1898. *Cattle ranges of the Southwest.* Bulletin 72. Washington, D.C.: USDA.

Berkhoff, H. A. 1985. *Clostridium colinum* sp. nov., nom. rev., the causative agent of ulcerative enteritis (quail disease) in quail, chickens, and pheasants. *International Journal of Systematic Bacteriology* 35:155–59.

Bermudez, A. J., L. L. Munger, and D. H. Ley. 1991. Pasteurellosis in bobwhite quail. *Avian Diseases* 35:618–20.

Best, L. B. 1972. First-year effects of sagebrush control on two sparrows. *Journal of Wildlife Management* 36:534–44.

Best, T. L., T. E. Garrison, and C. G. Schmitt. 1992. Ingestion of lead pellets by scaled quail (*Callipepla squamata*) and northern bobwhite (*Colinus virginianus*) in southeastern New Mexico. *Texas Journal of Science* 44:99–107.

Best, T. L., and R. A. Smart. 1985. Foods of scaled quail (*Callipepla squamata*) in southeastern New Mexico. *Texas Journal of Science* 37:155–62.

Beveridge, W. I. B. 1957. *The art of scientific investigation*. 3d ed. New York: Vintage Books.

Bidwell, T. G., S. R. Tully, A. D. Peoples, and R. E. Masters. 1991. *Habitat appraisal guide for bobwhite quail*. Oklahoma Cooperative Extension Service Circular E-904. Stillwater.

Bishop, R. A. 1964. The Mearns quail (*Cyrtonyx montezumae mearnsi*) in southern Arizona. Thesis, University of Arizona, Tucson.

Bishop, R. A., and C. R. Hungerford. 1965. Seasonal food selection of Arizona Mearns quail. *Journal of Wildlife Management* 29:813–19.

Black, H. L., and N. C. Frischknecht. 1971. *Relative abundance of mice on seeded sagebrush-grass range in relation to grazing*. USDA Forest Service, Research Note INT-147.

Blair, F. W. 1950. The biotic provinces of Texas. Texas Journal of Science 2:93–117.

Blodgett, B. J. 2002. Big ranch country productions: One-of-a-kind authentic ranch experiences. Big Ranch Country, Guthrie, Texas, USA.

Blankenship, L. H., R. E. Reed, and H. D. Irby. 1966. Pox in mourning doves and Gambel's quail in southern Arizona. Journal of Wildlife Management 30:253–257.

Bock, C. E., and J. H. Bock. 1992. Response of birds to wildfire in native versus exotic Arizona grasslands. *Southwestern Naturalist* 37:73–81.

Bock, C. E., and B. Webb. 1984. Birds as grazing indicator species in southeastern Arizona. *Journal of Wildlife Management* 48:1045–49.

Boggs, J. F., A. D. Peoples, R. L. Lochmiller, C. S. Elanganbam, and C. W. Qualls Jr. 1990. Occurrence and pathology of physaloperid larvae infections in bobwhite quail from western Oklahoma. Proceedings of the Oklahoma Academy of Science 70:29–312.

Bolen, E. 1998. *Ecology of North America*. New York: Wiley.

Borden, B. D. 1973. Characteristics of a scaled quail population in southeastern New Mexico. Thesis, New Mexico State University, Las Cruces.

Boren, J. C., R. L. Lochmiller, and D. M. Leslie Jr. 1996. Relation of serum and muscle free amino acids to dietary protein in the northern bobwhite. *Proceedings of the Oklahoma Academy of Science* 76:55–65.

Boren, J. C., R. L. Lochmiller, D. M. Leslie Jr., and D. M. Engle. 1993. Long-term effects of woody vegetation management on seasonal body condition of northern bobwhites. *Journal of Range Management* 46:520–23.

———. 1995. Amino acid concentrations in seeds of preferred forages of bobwhites. *Journal of Range Management* 48:141–44.

Bovey, R. W., S. K. Lehman, H. L. Morton, and J. R. Baur. 1969. Control of live oak in South Texas. *Journal of Range Management* 22:315–18.

Bozzo, J. A., S. L. Beasom, and T. E. Fulbright. 1992. Vegetation responses to two brush management practices in South Texas. *Journal of Range Management* 45:170–75.

Bradley, G. A., M. R. Shupe, C. Reggiardo, T. H. Noon, F. Lozanoalarcon, and E. J. Bicknell. 1994. Inclusion body hepatitis in Gambel's quail (*Callipepla gambelii*). *Journal of Wildlife Diseases* 30:281–84.

Brady, S. J., C. H. Flather, and K. E. Church. 1998. Range-wide declines of northern bobwhite (*Colinus virginianus*): Land use patterns and population trends. *Gibier Faune Sauvage* 15:413–31.

Brawn, J. D., S. K. Robinson, and F. R. Thompson. 2001. The role of disturbance in the ecology and conservation of birds. *Annual Review of Ecology and Systematics* 32:251–76.

Bray, W. L. 1901. The ecological relations of the vegetation of western Texas. *Botanical Gazette* 32:99–123.

———. 1904. *Forest resources of Texas.* Washington, D.C.: Bureau of Forestry, U.S. Department of Agriculture.

———. 1905. *Vegetation of the sotol country in Texas.* University of Texas Bulletin, Science Service no. 10. Austin.

Brennan, J. M. 1945a. Field investigations pertinent to Bullis fever: Preliminary report on the species of ticks and vertebrates occurring at Camp Bullis, Texas. *Texas Reports on Biology and Medicine* 3:112–21.

———. 1945b. Field investigations pertinent to Bullis fever: The Lone Star tick, *Amblyomma americanum* (Linnaeus, 1758)—notes and observations from Camp Bullis, Texas. *Texas Reports on Biology and Medicine* 3: 204–26.

Brennan, L. A. 1991a. How can we reverse the northern bobwhite population decline? *Wildlife Society Bulletin* 19:544–55.

———. 1991b. Regional tests of a mountain quail habitat model. *Northwestern Naturalist* 72:100–108.

———. 1993. Fire ants and northern bobwhites: A real problem or a red herring? *Wildlife Society Bulletin* 21:351–55.

———, ed. 1993. Strategic plan for quail management and research in the United States. *Proceedings of the National Quail Symposium* 3:160–69.

———. 1999. Northern bobwhite (*Colinus virginianus*). In A. Poole and F. Gill, eds., *The birds of North America, no. 397.* Washington, D.C.: The American Ornithologists' Union; Philadelphia: The Academy of Natural Sciences.

———. 2002a. A decade of progress, a decade of frustration. *Proceedings of the National Quail Symposium* 5: 230–32.

———. 2002b. Closing remarks: Pieces of the puzzle, circles in the stream. *Proceedings of the National Quail Symposium* 5:246–49.

Brennan, L. A., W. M. Block, and R. J. Gutiérrez. 1986. *Habitat use by mountain quail in northern California. Condor* 89:66–74.

Brennan, L. A., J. L. Cooper, K. E. Lucas, B. D. Leopold, and G. A. Hurst. 1995. Assessing the influence of red-cockaded woodpecker colony management on non-target forest vertebrates in loblolly pine forests of Mississippi: Study design and preliminary results. Pages 309–19 in D. L. Kulhavy, R. G. Hooper, and R. Costa, eds., *Red-cockaded woodpecker: Recovery, ecology, and management.* Nacogdoches, Tex.: College of Forestry, Stephen F. Austin University.

Brennan, L. A., R. T. Engstrom, S. M. Hermann, W. K. Moser, J. M. Lee, S. T. Lindemann, R. S. Fuller, and K. McGorty. 1995. Ecosystem management research on private lands: Access, cooperation, and obligations. Pages 109–23 in R. A. Williams, ed., *Forest ecosystem management in the Gulf Coastal Plain.* Rushton: School of Forestry, Louisiana Tech University.

Brennan, L. A., R. T. Engstrom, W. E. Palmer, S. M. Herman, G. A. Hurst, L. W. Burger, and C. L. Hardy. 1998. Whither wildlife without fire? *Transactions of the North American Wildlife and Natural Resources Conference* 63:402–14.

Brennan, L. A., W. Rosene, B. D. Leopold, and G. A. Hurst. 1997. *Population ecology of the northern bobwhite on the Groton Plantation, South Carolina: 1957–1990.* Miscellaneous Publication no. 10. Tallahassee, Fla.: Tall Timbers Research Station.

Bridges, A. S. 1999. Abundance of northern bobwhite and scaled quail in Texas: Influence of weather and land-cover change. Thesis, Texas A&M University, College Station.

Bridges, A. S., M. J. Peterson, N. J. Silvy, F. E. Smeins, and X. B. Wu. 2001. Differential influence of weather on regional quail abundance in Texas. *Journal of Wildlife Management* 65:10–18.

———. 2002. Landscape-scale land-cover change and long-term abundance of scaled quail and northern bobwhite in Texas. *Proceedings of the National Quail Symposium* 5:161–67.

Brill, C. J. 1941. Pen-raised versus wild-reared. *Southern Sportsman,* 24–25.

Bristow, K. D., and R. A. Ockenfels. 2000. *Effects of human activity and habitat conditions on Mearns' quail populations.* Federal Aid in Wildlife Restoration Project W-78-R. Phoenix: Arizona Game and Fish Department.

———. 2002. Brood season habitat selection by Montezuma quail in southeastern Arizona. *Proceedings of the National Quail Symposium* 5:111–16.

Brown, D. E. 1968. *Tortolita Owlhead quail management information.* Federal Aid Project W-53-R. Phoenix: Arizona Game and Fish Department.

———. 1969. *Scaled quail habitat evaluation.* Federal Aid in Wildlife Restoration Project W-53-R-19, Job 3. Phoenix: Arizona Game and Fish Department.

———. 1977. *Results of an attempt to determine the presence of Montezuma quail in the Chisos Mountains.* Report to U.S. National Park Service. Phoenix: Arizona Game and Fish Department.

———. 1979. Factors influencing reproductive success and population densities in Montezuma quail. *Journal of Wildlife Management* 43:522–26.

———. 1989. *Arizona game birds.* Tucson: University of Arizona Press.

Brown, D. E., and N. B. Carmony. 1991. *Gila monster: Facts and folklore of America's Aztec lizard.* Silver City, N.M.: High-Lonesome Books.

Brown, D. E., C. L. Cochran, and T. E. Waddell. 1977. *Scaled quail investigations.* Federal Aid in Wildlife Restoration Project W-53-R-27. Special Final Report. Phoenix: Arizona Game and Fish Department.

———. 1978. Using call-counts to predict hunting success for scaled quail. *Journal of Wildlife Management* 42:281–87.

Brown, D. E., and R. J. Gutiérrez. 1980. Sex ratios, sexual selection, and sexual dimorphism in quails. *Journal of Wildlife Management* 44:198–202.

Brown, D. E., J. C. Hagelin, M. Taylor, and J. Galloway. 1998. Gambel's quail (*Callipepla gambelii*). In A. Poole and F. Gill, eds., *The birds of North America, no. 321.* Washington, D.C.: American Ornithologists' Union; Philadelphia: The Birds of North America, Academy of Sciences.

Brown, H. 1900. Conditions governing bird life in Arizona. *Auk* 17:31–34.

Brown, J. H., and A. C. Gibson. 1983. *Biogeography.* St. Louis: Mosby.

Brown, R. D., K. L. Brown, D. K. Langford, G. L. Graham, M. E. Berger, D. Baxter, L. Cantu, and S. Lightfoot. 2003. *Preserving Texas' hunting heritage: A strategic plan for ensuring the future of hunting in Texas.* Austin: Texas Parks and Wildlife Department; College Station: Department of Wildlife and Fisheries Sciences, Texas A&M University.

Brown, R. L. 1976. *Mearns' quail census technique.* Federal Aid Project W-78-R-15, Work Plan 1, Job 1. Final Report. Phoenix: Arizona Game and Fish Department.

———. 1978. *An ecological study of Mearns' quail.* Federal Aid Project W-78-R-15, Work Plan 2, Job 1. Final Report. Phoenix: Arizona Game and Fish Department.

———. 1982. Effects of livestock grazing on Mearns quail in southeastern Arizona. *Journal of Range Management* 35:727–32.

Bryan, K. B. 2002. *Birds of the Trans-Pecos: A field checklist.* Austin: Natural Resources Program, Texas Parks and Wildlife Department.

Bryant, F. C., F. S. Guthery, and W. M. Webb. 1982. Grazing management in Texas and its impact on selected wildlife. Pages 94–112 in J. M. Peek and P. O. Dalke, eds., *Wildlife-livestock relationships symposium: Proceedings 10.* Moscow: Forestry, Wildlife, and Range Experiment Station, University of Idaho.

Bryant, F. C., M. M. Kothman, and L. B. Merrill. 1979. Diets of sheep, angora goats, Spanish goats and white-tailed deer under excellent range conditions. *Journal of Range Management* 32:412–17.

Buechner, B. K. 1950. An evaluation of restocking with pen-reared bobwhite. *Journal of Wildlife Management* 14:363–77.

Buechner, H. K. 1944. The range vegetation of Kerr County, Texas in relation to livestock and white-tailed deer. *American Midland Naturalist* 31:697–743.

Bump, G., R. W. Darrow, F. C. Edminster, and W. F. Crissey. 1947. *The ruffed grouse: Life history, propagation, management.* Buffalo, N.Y.: Holling Press.

Burd, J. S. 1989. Foods of scaled quail during prebreeding and breeding in Northwest Texas. Thesis, Texas Tech University, Lubbock.

Burger, L. D., L. W. Burger Jr., and J. Faaborg. 1994. Effects of prairie fragmentation on predation on artificial nests. *Journal of Wildlife Management* 58:249–54.

Burger, L. W., Jr., T. V. Dailey, E. W. Kurzejeski, and M. R. Ryan. 1995. Survival and cause-specific mortality of northern bobwhite in Missouri. *Journal of Wildlife Management* 59:401–10.

Burger, L. W., Jr., E. W. Kurzejeski, T. V. Dailey, and M. R. Ryan. 1990. Structural characteristics of vegetation in CRP fields in northern Missouri and their suitability as bobwhite habitat. *Transactions of the North American Wildlife and Natural Resources Conference* 55:74–83.

Burger, L. W., Jr., D. A. Miller, and R. I. Southwick. 1999. Economic impact of northern bobwhite hunting in the southeastern United States. *Wildlife Society Bulletin* 27:1010–18.

Burger, L. W., Jr., M. R. Ryan, T. V. Dailey, and E. W. Kurzejeski. 1995. Reproductive strategies, success, and mating systems of northern bobwhite in Missouri. *Journal of Wildlife Management* 59:417–26.

Burger, L. W., Jr., M. R. Ryan, E. W. Kurzejeski, and T. V. Dailey. 1994. Factors affecting the habitat value of Conservation Reserve Program lands for bobwhite in northern Missouri. Pages 103–19 in M. Dicks and M. Monson, eds., *Proceedings of the NC163 Post-CRP Land Use Conference.* Stillwater: Great Plains Agricultural Policy Center, Oklahoma State University.

Buttery, R. F.. and P. W. Shields. 1975. Range management practices and bird habitat values. Pages 183–89 in D. R. Smith, tech. coord., *Proceedings of the Symposium on Management of Forest and Range Habitats for Nongame Birds,* General Technical Report WO-1. Washington, D.C.: USDA Forest Service.

Cain, J. R., and S. L. Beasom. 1983. *A guide for aging scaled quail.* Bulletin 1447. College Station: Texas Agricultural Experiment Station.

Cain, J. R., S. L. Beasom, L. O. Rowland, and L. D. Rowe. 1982. The effects of varying dietary phosphorus on breeding bobwhites. *Journal of Wildlife Management* 46:1061–65.

Cain, J. R., and R. J. Lien. 1985. A model for drought inhibition of bobwhite quail (*Colinus virginianus*) reproductive systems. *Comparative Biochemistry and Physiology* 82A:925–30.

Cain, J. R., R. J. Lien, and S. L. Beasom. 1987. Phytoestrogen effects on reproductive performance of scaled quail. *Journal of Wildlife Management* 51:198–201.

Cain, J. R., D. S. Smith, R. J. Lien, J. W. Lee, and S. L. Beasom. 1982. Protein requirements of growing scaled quail. *Poultry Science* 61:1430.

Campbell, H. 1950. Quail picking up lead shot. *Journal of Wildlife Management* 14:243–44.

———. 1957. Fall foods of Gambel's quail (*Lophortyx gambelli*) in New Mexico. *Southwestern Naturalist* 3:122–28.

———. 1959. Experimental feeding of wild quail in New Mexico. *Southwestern Naturalist* 4:169–75.

———. 1960. An evaluation of gallinaceous guzzlers for quail in New Mexico. *Journal of Wildlife Management* 24:21–26.

———. 1968. Seasonal precipitation and scaled quail in eastern New Mexico. *Journal of Wildlife Management* 32:641–44.

Campbell, H., and B. K. Harris. 1965. Mass population dispersal and long-distance movements in scaled quail. *Journal of Wildlife Management* 29:801–805.

Campbell, H., and L. Lee. 1953. *Studies on quail malaria in New Mexico and notes on other aspects of quail populations.* Santa Fe: New Mexico Department of Game and Fish.

Campbell, H., D. K. Martin, P. E. Ferkovich, and B. K. Harris. 1973. Effects of hunting and some other environmental factors on scaled quail in New Mexico. *Wildlife Monograph* 34.

Campbell-Kissock, L., L. H. Blankenship, and J. W. Stewart. 1985. Plant and animal foods of bobwhite and scaled quail in southwest Texas. *Southwestern Naturalist* 30:543–53.

Campbell-Kissock, L., L. H. Blankenship, and L. D. White. 1984. Grazing management impacts on quail during drought in northern Rio Grande Plain, Texas. *Journal of Range Management* 37:442–46.

Capel, S., J. A. Crawford, R. J. Robel, L. W. Burger Jr., and N. W. Sotherton. 1993. Agricultural practices and pesticides. *Proceedings of the National Quail Symposium* 3:172–73.

Carr, J. T., Jr. 1969. *The climate and physiography of Texas.* Report 53. Austin: Texas Water Development Board.

Carter, P. S. 1995. Post-burn ecology of northern bobwhites in West Texas. Thesis, Angelo State University, San Angelo.

Carter, P. S., D. Rollins, and C. Scott. 2002. Initial effects of prescribed burning on survival and nesting success of northern bobwhites in west-central Texas. *Proceedings of the National Quail Symposium* 5:129–34.

Carter, W. T. 1931. *The soils of Texas.* College Station: Texas Agricultural Experiment Station, Texas A & M University.

Castrale, J. S. 1982. Effects of two sagebrush control methods on nongame birds. *Journal of Wildlife Management* 46:945–52.

Cearley, K. A., ed. 1999. *Preserving Texas' quail heritage into the 21st century.* San Angelo: Texas Agricultural Extension Service.

Chamberlain, E., R. D. Dbrobney, and T. V. Dailey. 2002. Winter macro- and microhabitat use of winter roost sites in central Missouri. *Proceedings of the National Quail Symposium* 5:140–45.

Chandler, A. C. 1935. A new genus and species of Subulurinae (nematodes). *Transactions of the American Microscopical Society* 54:33–35.

Chenault, T. P. 1940. The phenology of some bob-white food and cover plants in Brazos County, Texas. *Journal of Wildlife Management* 4:359–68.

Christensen, N. L., A. M. Bartuska, J. H. Brown, S. Carpenter, et al. 1996. The report of the Ecological Society of America committee on the scientific basis for ecosystem management. *Ecological Applications* 6:665–91.

Church, K. E., J. R. Sauer, and S. Droege. 1993. Population trends of quails in North America. *Proceedings of the National Quail Symposium* 3:44–55.

Clark, C. L. 1942. Annual restocking—game management or public relations? *Transactions of the North American Wildlife Conference* 7:179–84.

Clark, G. M. 1958. One new and one previously unreported species of nasal mite (Acarina, Speleognathidae) from North American birds. *Proceedings of the Helminthological Society of Washington* 25:78–86.

Clary, W. P., and R. C. Holmgren. 1981. Observations of pronghorn distribution in relation to sheep grazing on the Desert Experimental Range. Pages 581–92 in J. M. Peek and P. D. Dalke, eds., *Wildlife-livestock relationships symposium proceedings.* Moscow: Forestry, Wildlife and Range Experiment Station, University of Idaho.

Cleaveland, S., G. R. Hess, A. P. Dobson, M. K. Laurenson, H. I. McCallum, M. G. Roberts, and R. Woodroffe. 2002. The role of pathogens in biological conservation. Pages 139–50 in P. J. Hudson, A. Rizzoli, B. T. Grenfell, H. Heesterbeek, and A. P. Dobson, eds., *The ecology of wildlife diseases.* Oxford: Oxford University Press.

Cohen, W. E. 1986. Deer movement and habitat response to short-duration grazing. Thesis, Texas Tech University, Lubbock.

————, ed. 1993. *Proceedings of the Texas quail short course.* Corpus Christi: Texas Agricultural Extension Service.

————, ed. 1996. *Proceedings of the Texas quail short course II.* Corpus Christi: Texas Agricultural Extension Service.

Coleman, H. S. 1941. The food patch in bobwhite quail management in Brazos County, Texas. Thesis, Agricultural and Mechanical College of Texas, College Station.

Collias, N. E. 1960. An ecological and functional classification of animal sounds. Pages 368–91 in W. E. Lanyon and W. N. Tavolga, eds., *Animal sounds and communication.* Washington, D.C.: American Institute of Biological Sciences.

Committee of Inquiry on Grouse Disease. 1911. *The grouse in health and disease.* Vols. 1–2. London: Smith, Elder.

Conner, R. C., D. C. Rudolph, and J. R. Walters. 2001. *The red-cockaded woodpecker: Surviving in a fire-maintained ecosystem.* Austin: University of Texas Press.

Coon, D. W., and R. R. Fleet. 1970. *A review of the imported fire ant problem with special emphasis on the use of Mirex as a control agent.* College Station: Department of Wildlife Science, Texas A&M University.

Cooper, S. M., and T. F. Ginnett. 2000. Potential effects of supplemental feeding of deer on nest predation. *Wildlife Society Bulletin* 28:660–66.

Correll, D. S., and M. C. Johnston, 1970. *Manual of the vascular plants of Texas.* Renner: Texas Research Foundation.

Costello, D. F. 1969. *The prairie world: Plants and animals of the grassland sea.* New York: Crowell.

Cottle, H. J. 1931. Studies on the vegetation of southwestern Texas. *Ecology* 12: 105–55.

Coues, E. 1874. *Birds of the Northwest.* U.S. Geological Survey, Miscellaneous Publication no. 3. Washington, D.C.

Cowdry, A. E. 1983. *This land, this South.* Lexington: University Press of Kentucky.

Craig, T. M., B. Panigraphy, and R. S. Houston. 1980. Schistosomiasis in a scaled quail. *Journal of the American Veterinary Medical Association* 177:915–16.

Cram, E. B. 1929. Note on the life history of the gizzard worm of ruffed grouse and bobwhite quail. *Journal of Parasitology* 15:285–86.

————. 1930. Parasitism in game birds. *Transactions of the American Game Conference* 17:203–206.

————. 1931. *Developmental stages of some nematodes of the Spiruroidea parasite in poultry and game birds.* Technical Bulletin no. 227. Washington, D.C.: U.S. Department of Agriculture.

————. 1933. Observations on the life history of *Tetrameras pattersoni. Journal of Parasitology* 20:97–98.

Cram, E. B., M. F. Jones, and E. A. Allen. 1931. Internal parasites and parasitic diseases of the bobwhite. Pages 229–313 in H. L. Stoddard, ed., *The bobwhite quail: Its habits, preservation and increase.* New York: Scribner's.

Crim, L. A., and W. K. Seitz. 1972. Summer range and habitat preferences of bobwhite quail on a southern Iowa state game area. *Proceedings of the Iowa Academy of Science* 79:85–89.

Crouch, G. L. 1982. Wildlife on grazed and ungrazed bottomlands on the South Platte River, northeastern Colorado. Pages 186–97 in J. M. Peek and P. D. Dalke, eds., *Wildlife-livestock relationships symposium proceedings.* Moscow: Forestry, Wildlife, and Range Experiment Station, University of Idaho.

Cuckler, A. C., and J. E. Alicata. 1944. The life history of *Subulura brumpti,* a cecal nematode of poultry in Hawaii. *Transactions of the American Microscopical Society* 63:345–57.

Curtis, P. D., B. S. Mueller, P. D. Doerr, and C. F. Robinette. 1988. Seasonal survival of radio-marked northern bobwhite quail from hunted and non-hunted populations. *Proceedings of the International Biotelemetry Symposium* 10:263–75.

Curtis, P. D., B. S. Mueller, P. D. Doerr, C. R. Robinette, and T. DeVos. 1993. Potential polygamous breeding behavior in northern bobwhite. *Proceedings of the National Quail Symposium* 3:55–63.

Dabbert, C. B., R. L. Lochmiller, R. J. Morton, and K. C. Powell. 1996. A pathogenic challenge model for adult northern bobwhite (*Colinus virginianus*) using a vaccine strain of *Pasteurella multocida* type 3. *Avian Diseases* 40:99–102.

Dabbert, C. B., R. L. Lochmiller, and R. G. Teeter. 1996. Thermal stress influences clinical chemistry values of northern bobwhite (*Colinus virginianus*). *Comparative Haematology International* 6:120–22.

————. 1997. Effects of acute thermal stress on the immune system of northern bobwhite (*Colinus virginianus*). *Auk* 114:103–109.

Dabbert, C. B., R. L. Lochmiller, P. W. Waldroup, and R. G. Teeter. 1996. Examination of the dietary methionine requirements of breeding northern bobwhite, *Colinus virginianus. Poultry Science* 75:991–97.

Dabbert, C. B., S. R. Sheffield, and R. L. Lochmiller. 1996. Northern bobwhite egg hatchability and chick immunocompetence following field application of diazinon. *Environmental Contamination and Toxicology* 56:612–16.

Dancak, K., D. B. Pence, F. A. Stormer, and S. L. Beasom. 1982. Helminths of the scaled quail, *Callipepla squamata,* from northwest Texas. *Proceedings of the Helminthological Society of Washington* 49:144–46.

Davidson, W. R., G. L. Doster, and M. G. McGhee. 1978. Failure of *Heterakis bonasae* to transmit *Histomonas meleagridis. Avian Diseases* 22:627–32.

Davidson, W. R., F. E. Kellogg, and G. L. Doster. 1980. An epornitic of avian pox in wild bobwhite quail. *Journal of Wildlife Diseases* 16:293–98.

————. 1982a. An overview of disease and parasitism in southeastern bobwhite quail. *Proceedings of the National Quail Symposium* 2:57–63.

————. 1982b. Avian pox infections in southeastern bobwhites: Historical and recent information. *Proceedings of the National Quail Symposium* 2:64–68.

Davidson, W. R., F. E. Kellogg, G. L. Doster, and C. T. Moore. 1991. Ecology of helminth parasitism in bobwhites from northern Florida. *Journal of Wildlife Diseases* 27:185–205.

Davidson, W. R., and V. F. Nettles. 1997. *Field manual of wildlife diseases in the southeastern United States.* Southeastern Cooperative Wildlife Disease Study. Athens: College of Veterinary Medicine, University of Georgia.

Davidson, W. R., V. F. Nettles, C. E. Couvillion, and E. W. Howerth. 1985. Diseases diagnosed in wild turkeys (*Meleagris gallopavo*) of the southeastern United States. *Journal of Wildlife Diseases* 21:386–90.

Davis, B. D. 1979. *Effects of brush control on quail populations.* FA Report Series no. 19. Austin: Texas Parks and Wildlife Department.

Davis, C. A., R. C. Barkley, and W. C. Haussamen. 1975. Scaled quail foods in southeastern New Mexico. *Journal of Wildlife Management* 39:496–502.

Davis, L. W. 1993. *Weed seeds of the Great Plains.* Lawrence: University Press of Kansas.

Davis, R. B. 1970. *Survival of hatchery raised bobwhite quail.* Technical Series no. 4. Austin: Texas Parks and Wildlife Department.

DeArment, R. D. 1950. Evaluation of Payne County, Oklahoma farm lands and vegetation patterns for bobwhite quail. Thesis, Oklahoma State University, Stillwater.

Demarais, S., D. D. Everett, and M. L. Pons. 1987. Seasonal comparison of endoparasites of northern bobwhites from two types of habitat in southern Texas. *Journal of Wildlife Diseases* 23:256–60.

DeMaso, S. J. 1999. Effects of hunting on quail populations. Pages 37–43 in K. A. Cearley, ed., *Preserving Texas' quail heritage into the 21st century.* Abilene: Texas Agricultural Extension Service.

DeMaso S. J., F. S. Guthery, G. S. Spears, and S. M. Rice. 1992. Morning covey calls as an index of northern bobwhite density. *Wildlife Society Bulletin* 20:94–101.

DeMaso, S. J., W. P. Kuvlesky Jr., F. Hernández, and M. E. Berger, eds. 2002. *Quail V: Proceedings of the 5th national quail symposium.* Austin: Texas Parks and Wildlife Department.

DeMaso, S. J., E. S. Parry, S. A. Cox, and A. D. Peoples. 1998. Cause-specific mortality of northern bobwhites on an area with quail feeders in western Oklahoma. *Proceedings of the Annual Conference of Southeastern Fish and Wildlife Agencies* 52:359–66.

DeMaso, S. J., A. D. Peoples, S. A. Cox, and E. S. Parry. 1997. Survival of northern bobwhite chicks in western Oklahoma. *Journal of Wildlife Management* 61:846–53.

DeMaso, S. J., M. J. Peterson, J. R. Purvis, N. J. Silvy, and J. L. Cooke. 2002. A comparison of two quail abundance indices in Texas. *Proceedings of the National Quail Symposium* 5:206–12.

DeMaso, S. J., D. E. Townsend II, S. A. Cox, E. S. Parry, R. L. Lochmiller, and A. D. Peoples. 2002. The effects of quail feeders on northern bobwhite density in western Oklahoma. *Proceedings of the National Quail Symposium* 5:241–44.

Derdeyn, C. H. 1975. Manipulating central Oklahoma rangeland vegetation for bobwhite quail. Thesis, Oklahoma State University, Stillwater.

DeVos, T., and B. S. Mueller. 1993. Reproductive ecology of northern bobwhites in north Florida. *Proceedings of the National Quail Symposium* 3:83–90.

DeVos, T., and D. W. Speake. 1995. Effects of releasing pen-raised northern bobwhites on survival rates of wild populations of northern bobwhites. *Wildlife Society Bulletin* 23:267–73.

Diamond, D. D., and T. E. Fulbright. 1990. Contemporary plant communities of upland grasslands of the Coastal Plain. *Southwestern Nature* 35:385–92.

Diamond, D. D., and F. E. Smeins. 1984. Remnant grassland vegetation and ecological affinities of the Upper Coastal Prairie of Texas. *Southwestern Nature* 29:321–34.

Dice, L. R. 1943. *The biotic provinces of North America.* Ann Arbor: University of Michigan Press.

Dietz, D. R. 1999. Winter food habits and preferences of northern bobwhite in East Texas. Thesis, Stephen F. Austin State University, Nacogdoches.

Diggs, G., B. Lipscomb, R. O'Kennon, and L. Heagy. 1999. Shinner's & Mahler's illustrated flora of north central Texas. Fort Worth: Botanical Research Institute of Texas.

Dimmick, R. W. 1971. The influence of controlled burning on nesting patterns of bobwhite quail in west Tennessee. *Proceedings of the Annual Conference of the Southeastern Association of Fish and Wildlife Agencies* 25:149–155.

Dimmick, R. W., M. J. Gudlin, and D. F. McKenzie, eds. 2002. *The northern bobwhite conservation initiative: A report on the status of the northern bobwhite and a plan for recovery of the species.* Columbia, S.C.: Southeastern Association of Fish and Wildlife Agencies.

Dixon, J. R. 2002. *Amphibians and reptiles of Texas.* College Station: Texas A&M University Press.

Dixon, K. R., M. A. Horner, S. R. Anderson, W. D. Henriques, D. Durham, and R. J. Kendall. 1996. Northern bobwhite habitat use and survival on a South Carolina plantation during winter. *Wildlife Society Bulletin* 24:627–35.

Dobson, A. P., and P. J. Hudson. 1992. Regulation and stability of a free-living host-parasite system: *Trichostrongylus tenuis* in red grouse. Vol. 2: Population models. *Journal of Animal Ecology* 61:487–98.

Dodgen, H. D. 1945. *Annual report—Game, Fish, and Oyster Commission for the fiscal year 1944–45.* Austin: Texas Game, Fish and Oyster Commission.

Doerr, T. B. 1988. Effects of supplemental feeding on northern bobwhite populations in South Texas. Dissertation, Texas A&M University, College Station.

Doerr, T. B., and F. S. Guthery. 1983. Effects of tebuthiuron on lesser prairie-chicken habitat and foods. *Journal of Wildlife Management* 47:1138–42.

Doerr, T. B., and N. J. Silvy. 1987. Application of supplemental feeding for northern bobwhite management in South Texas. Pages 111–19 in L. D. White, T. R. Troxel, and J. M. Payne, eds., *International Ranchers Roundup*. College Station: Texas Agricultural Extension Service, Texas A&M University.

———. 2002. Effects of supplemental feeding on northern bobwhite populations in South Texas. *Proceedings of the National Quail Symposium* 5:233–40.

Dollar, W. M. 1969. Movement, survival and behavioral patterns of pen-raised bobwhite quail (*Colinus virginianus*, Linnaeus) on an established management area. Thesis, Auburn University, Auburn.

Doster, G. L., N. Wilson, and F. E. Kellogg. 1980. Ectoparasites collected from bobwhite quail in the southeastern United States. *Journal of Wildlife Diseases* 16:515–20.

Doty, J. B. 2003. Denning ecology and home ranges of two sympatric skunk species (*Mephitis mephitis* and *Spilogale gracilis*) in west-central Texas. Thesis, Angelo State University, San Angelo.

Doughty, R. W. 1983. *Wildlife and man in Texas*. College Station: Texas A&M University Press.

Drawe, D. L. 1968. Mid-summer diet of deer on the Welder Wildlife Refuge. *Journal of Range Management* 21:164–66.

———. 1991. *Influence of grazing on vegetation and cattle, 1983–1987.* Welder Wildlife Foundation Contribution B-11. Sinton, Texas.

Drew, M. L., W. L. Wigle, D. L. Graham, C. P. Griffin, N. J. Silvy, A. M. Fadly, and R. L. Witter. 1998. Reticuloendotheliosis in captive greater and Attwater's prairie chickens. *Journal of Wildlife Diseases* 34:783–91.

Duck, L. G., and J. B. Fletcher. 1943. A survey of the game and furbearing animals of Oklahoma. State Bulletin no. 3. Oklahoma City: Oklahoma Game and Fish Commission.

Dunn, J. P., J. A. Chapman, and R. E. Marsh. 1982. Jackrabbits (*Lepus californicus* and allies). Pages 124–45 in J. A. Chapman and G. A. Feldhamer, eds., *Wild mammals of North America*. Baltimore, Md.: Johns Hopkins University Press.

du Pratz, L. P. 1774. *The history of Louisiana*. Translated from the French by T. Beckett, 1975. Baton Rouge: Louisiana State University Press.

Durant, A. J., and E. R. Doll. 1941. *Ulcerative enteritis in quail*. Research Bulletin 325. Columbia: Agricultural Experiment Station, University of Missouri.

Duszynski, D. W., and R. J. Gutiérrez. 1981. The coccidia of quail in the United States. *Journal of Wildlife Diseases* 17:371–79.

DuVall, V. L. 1962. Burning and grazing increase herbage on slender bluestem range. *Journal of Range Management* 15:14–16.

DuVall, V. L., and N. E. Linnartz. 1967. Influences of grazing and fire on vegetation and soil of longleaf pine–bluestem range. *Journal of Range Management* 20:241–47.

Dyksterhuis, E. H. 1946. The vegetation of the Ft. Worth plains prairie. *Ecological Monographs* 1:1–29.

———. 1948. The vegetation of the western Cross Timbers. *Ecological Monographs* 18:326–76.

———. 1949. Condition and management of range land based on quantitative ecology. *Journal of Range Management* 2:114–15.

Edminster, F. C. 1954. American game birds of field and forest. New York: Scribner's.

Einarsen, A. S. 1945. The pheasant in the Pacific Northwest. Pages 254–74 in W. L. McAtee, ed., *The ring-necked pheasant and its management in North America*. Washington, D.C.: American Wildlife Institute.

Ellis, C. R., Jr., and A. W. Stokes. 1966. Vocalizations and behavior in captive Gambel's quail. *Condor* 68:72–80.

Ellis, J. A., W. R. Edwards, and K. P. Thomas. 1969. Responses of bobwhites to management in Illinois. *Journal of Wildlife Management* 33:749–62.

Ellis, J. E. 1970. A computer analysis of fawn survival in pronghorn antelope to water deprivation. Dissertation, University of California, Davis.

Ellsworth, D. L., J. L. Roseberry, and W. K. Klimstra. 1988. Biochemical genetics of wild, semi-wild, and game-farm northern bobwhites. *Journal of Wildlife Management* 52:138–44.

Elwell, H. M., H. A. Daniel, and F. A. Fenton. 1941. *The effects of burning pasture and woodland vegetation.* Oklahoma Agricultural Experiment Station, Bulletin B-247, Stillwater.

Emerson, K. C. 1948. Two new species of Mallophaga. *Journal of the Kansas Entomological Society* 21:137–38.

———. 1949a. A new species of Mallophaga from a partridge. *Entomological News* 60:116–17.

———. 1949b. Three new species of Mallophaga. *Journal of the Kansas Entomological Society* 22:75–78.

———. 1950. New species of *Goniodes. Journal of the Kansas Entomological Society* 23:120–26.

Engel-Wilson, R., and W. P. Kuvlesky Jr. 2002. Arizona quail: Species in jeopardy? *Proceedings of the National Quail Symposium* 5:1–7.

Engle, D. M., J. F. Stritzke, and F. T. McCollum. 1991. Vegetation management in the Cross Timbers: Response of understory vegetation to herbicides and burning. *Weed Technology* 5:406–10.

Engstrom, R. T., and W. W. Baker. 1995. Red-cockaded woodpeckers on Red Hills hunting plantations: Inventory, management and conservation. Pages 489–93 in D. L. Kulhavy, R. G. Hooper, and R. Costa, eds., *Red-cockaded woodpecker: Recovery, ecology, and management.* Nacogdoches, Tex.: College of Forestry, Stephen F. Austin University.

Errington, P. L. 1945. Some contributions of a fifteen-year local study of the northern bobwhite to a knowledge of population phenomena. *Ecological Monographs* 15:1–34.

Errington, P. L., and F. N. Hamerstrom Jr. 1936. The bob-white's winter territory. *Iowa Agricultural Experiment Station Research Bulletin* 201:302–443.

Eubanks, T. R., and R. W. Dimmick. 1974. Dietary patterns of bobwhite quail on Ames Plantation. Bulletin 534. Knoxville: Agricultural Experiment Station, University of Tennessee.

Evans, C. A. 1997. Reproductive biology of scaled quail in southern New Mexico. Thesis, New Mexico State University, Las Cruces.

Evans, C. A., and S. D. Schemnitz. 2000. Temperature and humidity relationships of scaled quail nests in southern New Mexico. *Proceedings of the National Quail Symposium* 4:116–18.

Fagerstone, K. A., G. K. Lavoie, and R. E. Griffith. 1980. Black-tailed jackrabbit diets and density on rangeland near agriculture crops. *Journal of Range Management* 33:229–33.

Fagerstone, K. A., and C. A. Ramey. 1996. Rodents and lagomorphs. Pages 83–132 in P. R. Krausman, ed., *Rangeland wildlife.* Denver, Colo.: The Society for Range Management.

Falvey, E. B. 1936. His majesty, the Mearns' quail. *Game Breeders and Sportsmen* 40:226–27, 241.

Fehrenbach, T. R. 1968. *Lone star: A history of Texas and the Texans.* New York: Collier Books.

Feldhamer, G. A. 1979. Vegetative and edaphic factors affecting abundance and distribution of small mountains in southeastern Oregon. *Great Basin Naturalist* 39:207–18.

Fenneman, N. M. 1938. *Physiography of the eastern United States.* New York: McGraw-Hill.

Fies, M. L., J. E. Fischer, and D. E. Steffen. 2000. Survival of game farm, F_1-wild progeny, and wild-relocated northern bobwhites using two release methods. *Proceedings of the Annual Conference of the Southeastern Association of Fish and Wildlife Agencies* 54:350–64.

Fischer, J. R. 1997. Cryptosporidiosis. Pages 295–96 in W. R. Davidson and V. F. Nettles, eds., *Field manual of wildlife diseases in the southeastern United States.* Southeastern Cooperative Wildlife Disease Study. Athens: College of Veterinary Medicine, University of Georgia.

Fitzgerald, S. M., and G. W. Tanner. 1992. Avian community response to fire and mechanical control shrub in south Florida. *Journal of Range Management* 45:396–400.

Forbes, A. R., C. B. Dabbert, R. B. Mitchell, and J. M. Mueller. 2002. Does habitat management for northern bobwhites benefit the red imported fire ant? *Proceedings of the National Quail Symposium* 5:135–39.

Ford, S. D. 1977. Range, distribution and habitat of the western harvest mouse, *Reithrodontyms megalotis,* in Indiana. *American Midland Naturalist* 98:422–32.

Forrester, D. J., J. K. Nayar, and M. D. Young. 1987. Natural infection of *Plasmodium hermani* in the northern bobwhite, *Colinus virginianus,* in Florida. *Journal of Parasitology* 73:865–66.

Forrester, N. D., F. S. Guthery, S. D. Kopp, and W. E. Cohen. 1998. Operative temperature reduces habitat space for northern bobwhites. *Journal of Wildlife Management* 62:1506–11.

Foster, J. H. 1917. The spread of timbered areas in Central Texas. *Journal of Forestry* 15:442–45.

Foster, W. C., ed. 1998. *The La Salle expedition to Texas: The journal of Henri Joutel, 1684–1687.* Austin: Texas State Historical Association, University of Texas.

Freehling, M., and J. Moore. 1993. Host specificity of *Trichostrongylus tenuis* from red grouse and northern bobwhites in experimental infections of northern bobwhites. *Journal of Parasitology* 79:538–41.

Friend, M., and J. C. Franson. 1999. Intestinal coccidiosis. Pages 99–109 in M. Friend and J. C. Franson, eds., *Field manual of wildlife diseases: General field procedures and diseases of birds.* Information and Technology Report 1999–001. Reston, Va.: U.S. Geological Survey, Biological Resources Division.

Friend, M., R. G. McLean, and F. J. Dein. 2001. Disease emergence in birds: Challenges for the twenty-first century. *Auk* 118: 290–303.

Frost, C. C. 1998. Presettlement fire frequency regimes of the United States: A first approximation. *Tall Timbers Fire Ecology Conference* 20:70–81.

Frost, J. 1999. An evaluation of short-term mesomammal control on nesting success and survival of northern bobwhites in west-central Texas. Thesis, Angelo State University, San Angelo.

Frye. O. E. 1942. The comparative survival of wild and pen-reared bobwhite in the field. *Transactions of the North American Wildlife Conference* 7:168–78.

———. 1954. Studies of automatic quail feeders in Florida. *Transactions of the North American Wildlife Conference* 19:298–315.

Fuertes, L. A. 1903. With the Mearns quail in southwestern Texas. *Condor* 5: 112–16.

Fuhlendorf, S. D., and D. M. Engle. 2001. Restoring heterogeneity of rangelands: Ecosystem management based on evolutionary grazing patterns. *BioScience* 51:625–32.

Fulbright, T. E., and S. L. Beasom. 1987. Long-term effects of mechanical treatments on white-tailed deer browse. *Wildlife Society Bulletin* 15:560–64.

Fulbright, T. E., and F. S. Guthery. 1996. Mechanical manipulation of plants. Pages 339–54 in P. R. Krausman, ed., *Rangeland wildlife.* Denver, Colo.: The Society for Range Management.

Gallagher, B. 1916. Epithelioma contagiosum of quail. *Journal of the American Veterinary Medical Association* 50:366–69.

Gallizioli, S. 1965. *Quail research in Arizona.* Federal Aid Project W-78-R. Phoenix: Arizona Game and Fish Department.

———. 1967. Sex and age differential vulnerability to trapping and shooting in Gambel quail. *Proceedings of the Western Association of State Game and Fish Commissions* 47:262–71.

Gallizioli, S., and W. Swank. 1958. The effects of hunting on Gambel quail populations. *Transactions of North American Wildlife Conference* 23:305–19.

Gallizioli, S., and P. M. Webb. 1958. *The influence of hunting upon quail populations.* Federal Aid Project W-78-R. Phoenix: Arizona Game and Fish Department.

———. 1961. *The influence of hunting upon quail populations.* Federal Aid Project W-78-R. Phoenix: Arizona Game and Fish Department.

Gamble, M. 1970. Conservation uses of weeping lovegrass. Pages 41–44 in R. L. Daltymple, ed., *Proceedings of the First Weeping Lovegrass Symposium.* Ardmore, Okla.: Noble Foundation.

Germano, D. J., R. Hungerford, and S. C. Martin. 1983. Response of selected wildlife species to the removal of mesquite from desert grassland. *Journal of Range Management* 36:309–11.

Gerstell, R. 1938. An analysis of the reported returns obtained from the release of 30,000 artificially propagated ringneck pheasants and bobwhite quail. *Transactions of the North American Wildlife Conference* 3:724–29.

Giuliano, W. M., C. R. Allen, R. S. Lutz, and S. Demarais. 1996. Effects of red imported fire ants on northern bobwhite chicks. *Journal of Wildlife Management* 60:309–13.

Giuliano, W. M., and R. S. Lutz. 1993. Quail and rain: What's the relationship? *Proceedings of the National Quail Symposium* 3:64–68.

Giuliano, W. M., R. S. Lutz, and R. Patiño. 1996. Reproductive responses of adult female northern bobwhite and scaled quail to nutritional stress. *Journal of Wildlife Management* 60:302–309.

———. 1999. Influence of rainfall on northern bobwhite and scaled quail abundance and breeding success. *Texas Journal of Science* 51:231–40.

Giuliano, W. M., R. Patiño, and R. S. Lutz. 1998. Comparative reproductive and physiological responses of northern bobwhite and scaled quail to water deprivation. *Comparative Biochemistry and Physiology A-Molecular and Integrative Physiology* 119:781–86.

Glading, B., and R. W. Saarni. 1944. Effect of hunting on a valley quail population. *California Fish and Game* 30:71–79.

Godfrey, C. L., C. R. Carter, and G. S. McKee. 1967. *Resource areas of Texas.* Bulletin 1070. College Station: Texas Agricultural Experiment Station, Texas A&M University.

Goetze, J. R. 1998. *The mammals of the Edwards Plateau, Texas. Special Publication of the Museum.* Lubbock: Texas Tech University Press.

Goldstein, D. L., and K. A. Nagy. 1985. Resource utilization by desert quail: Time and energy, food and water. *Ecology* 66:378–87.

Goodrum, P. D. 1949. Status of bobwhite quail in the United States. *Transactions of the North American Wildlife Conference* 14:359–69.

Goodrum, P. D., and V. H. Reid. 1954. Quail management on forested land. *Journal of Forestry* 52:518–20.

Goodwin, J. G., Jr., and C. R. Hungerford. 1977. *Habitat used by native Gambel's and scaled quail and released masked bobwhite quail in southern Arizona.* USDA Forest Service Research Paper RM-197. Fort Collins, Colo.: U.S. Department of Agriculture, Forest Service.

Goodwin, M. A. 1993. Adenovirus inclusion body ventriculitis in chickens and captive bobwhite quail (*Colinus virginianus*). *Avian Diseases* 37:568–71.

Gore, H. C., C. E. Holt, and J. C. Barron. 1971. Weight and age characteristics as criteria for harvest of bobwhites in north central Texas. *Proceedings of the Annual Conference of the Southeastern Association of Fish and Wildlife Agencies* 24:213–23.

Gore, H., and D. Wilson. 1987. *Bobwhite facts and fantasies.* Leaflet 9000–63. Austin: Texas Parks and Wildlife Department.

Gorsuch, D. M. 1934. Life history of the Gambel quail in Arizona. University of Arizona Bulletin 2:1–89.

Gould, F. W. 1962. *Texas plants—a checklist and ecological summary.* Publication MP-585. College Station: Texas Agricultural Experiment Station, The Agricultural and Mechanical College of Texas.

———. 1975a. *The grasses of Texas.* College Station: Texas A&M University Press.

———. 1975b. *Texas plants—a checklist and ecological summary.* Texas Agricultural Experiment Station Miscellaneous Publication 585–revision. College Station.

Gould, F. W., G. O. Hoffman, and C. A. Rechenthin. 1960. *Vegetational areas of Texas.* College Station: Texas Agricultural Experiment Station, Texas Agricultural Extension Service, and U. S. Department of Agriculture.

Grange, W. B. 1949. The way to game abundance. New York: Scribner's.

Grelen, H. E. 1978a. Winter and spring prescribed fires on Louisiana pine-bluestem range. *Proceedings of the International Rangeland Congress* 1:242–44.

———. 1978b. Forest grazing in the South. *Journal of Range Management* 31:244–50.

Griffing, J. P. 1972. Population characteristics and behavior of scaled quail in southeastern New Mexico. Thesis, New Mexico State University, Las Cruces.

Gross, A. O. 1925. Diseases of the ruffed grouse. *Auk* 62:423–31.

———. 1928. The heath hen. *Memoirs of the Boston Society of Natural History* 6:490–588.

———. 1931. Report of the New England ruffed grouse investigation and Wisconsin prairie chicken investigation. *Proceedings of the New England Game Conference* 3:44–49.

Grue, C. E. 1977. Classification, inventory, analysis, and evaluation of the breeding habitat of the mourning dove (*Zenaida macroura*) in Texas. Dissertation, Texas A&M University, College Station.

Gruver, B. J., and F. S. Guthery. 1986. Effects of brush control and game-bird management on nongame birds. *Journal of Range Management* 39:251–53.

Gullion, G. W. 1954. Management of Nevada's Gambel's quail resource. *Proceedings of the Western Association of State Game and Fish Commissions* 32:234–39.

———. 1956. Evidence of double-brooding in Gambel's quail. *Condor* 58:232–34.

———. 1957. Gambel quail disease and parasite investigations in Nevada. *American Midland Naturalist* 57:414–20.

———. 1958. The proximity effect of water distribution on desert small game populations. *Proceedings of the Western Association of State Game and Fish Commissions* 38:187–89.

———. 1960. The ecology of Gambel's quail in Nevada and the arid southwest. *Ecology* 41:518–36.

———. 1962. Organization and movements of coveys of a Gambel's quail population. *Condor* 64:402–15.

Guthery, F. S. 1986. *Beef, brush and bobwhites: Quail management in cattle country.* Kingsville: Caesar Kleberg Wildlife Research Institute Press, Texas A&I University.

———. 1995. Coyotes and upland gamebirds. Pages 104–107 in D. Rollins, C. Richardson, T. Blankenship, K. Cannon, and Scott E. Henke, eds., *Coyotes in the Southwest: A compendium of our knowledge.* San Angelo: Texas A&M Agriculture Extension Service.

———. 1996a. Conflicting opinions on harvest management: Why do they exist? Pages 41–48 in W. E. Cohen, ed., *Texas quail short course II: Proceed-*

ings of a second conference on quail management. Kingsville: Texas A&M University–Kingsville.

———. 1996b. Upland gamebirds. Pages 59–69 in P. R. Krausman, ed., *Rangeland wildlife.* Denver, Colo.: Society for Range Management.

———. 1997. A philosophy of habitat management for northern bobwhites. *Journal of Wildlife Management* 61:291–301.

———. 1999a. Slack in the configuration of habitat patches for northern bobwhites. *Journal of Wildlife Management* 63:245–50.

———. 1999b. The role of free water in bobwhite management. *Wildlife Society Bulletin* 27:538–42.

———. 2000. *On bobwhites.* College Station: Texas A&M University Press.

———. 2002. *The technology of bobwhite management: The theory behind the practice.* Ames: Iowa State University Press.

Guthery, F. S., T. E. Anderson, and V. W. Lehmann. 1979. Range rehabilitation enhances cotton rats in South Texas. *Journal of Range Management* 32:354–56.

Guthery, F. S., and S. L. Beasom. 1977. Responses of game and nongame wildlife to predator control in South Texas. *Journal of Range Management* 30:404–409.

Guthery, F. S., and R. L. Bingham. 1992. On Leopold's principle of edge. *Wildlife Society Bulletin* 20:340–44.

Guthery, F. S., M. C. Green, R. E. Masters, S. J. DeMaso, H. M. Wilson, and F. B. Steubing. 2001. Land cover and bobwhite abundance on Oklahoma farms and ranches. *Journal of Wildlife Management* 65:838–49.

Guthery, F. S., N. M. King, W. P. Kuvlesky Jr., S. DeStefano, S. A. Gall, and N. J. Silvy. 2001. Comparative habitat use by three quails in desert grassland. *Journal of Wildlife Management* 65:850–60.

Guthery, F. S., N. M. King, K. R. Nolte, W. P. Kuvlesky Jr., S. DeStefano, S. A. Gall, and N. J. Silvy. 2000. Comparative habitat ecology of Texas and masked bobwhites. *Journal of Wildlife Management* 64:407–20.

———. 2001. Comparative habitat ecology of masked bobwhites, scaled and Gambel's quail in southern Arizona. *Journal of Wildlife Management* 64:407–20.

Guthery, F. S., and N. E. Koerth. 1992. Substandard water intake and inhibition of bobwhite reproduction during drought. *Journal of Wildlife Management* 56:760–68.

Guthery, F. S., N. E. Koerth, and D. S. Smith. 1988. Reproduction of northern bobwhites in semiarid environments. *Journal of Wildlife Management* 52:144–49.

Guthery, F. S., and W. P. Kuvlesky Jr. 1998. The effect of multiple-brooding on age ratios of quail. *Journal of Wildlife Management* 62:540–49.

Guthery, F. S., C. L. Land, and B. W. Hall. 2001. Heat loads on reproducing bobwhites in the semiarid subtropics. *Journal of Wildlife Management* 65:111–17.

Guthery, F. S., and J. M. Lusk. 2004. Radiotelemetry studies: Are we radio-handicapping northern bobwhites? *Wildlife Society Bulletin* 32:194–201.

Guthery, F. S., J. M. Lusk, D. R. Synatzske, J. Gallagher, S. J. DeMaso, R. R. George, and M. J. Peterson. 2002. Weather and age ratios of northern bobwhites in South Texas. *Proceedings of the National Quail Symposium* 5:99–105.

Guthery, F. S., M. J. Peterson, and R. R. George. 2000. Viability of northern bobwhite populations. *Journal of Wildlife Management* 64:646–62.

Guthery F. S., M. J. Peterson, J. J. Lusk, M. J. Rabe, S. J. DeMaso, M. Sams, R. D. Applegate, and T. V. Dailey. 2004. Multi-state analysis of fixed, liberal regulations in quail harvest management. *Journal of Wildlife Management* 68:1104–13.

Guthery, F. S., and D. Rollins. 1997. Sculpting brush for upland gamebirds. Pages 68–72 in D. Rollins, D. N. Ueckert, and C. G. Brown, eds., *Brush sculp-*

tors: Symposium proceedings. San Angelo: Texas Agricultural Extension Service.

Guthery, F. S., T. E. Shupe, L. J. Bareiss, and C. E. Russell. 1987. Responses of selected plants to herbicide treatment of disturbed soil. *Wildlife Society Bulletin* 15:247–51.

Gutiérrez, R. J. 1993. Taxonomy and biogeography of New World quail. *Proceedings of the National Quail Symposium* 3:8–15.

Gutiérrez, R. J., R. M. Zink, and S. Y. Yang. 1983. Genetic variation, systematic, and biogeographic relationships of some galliform birds. *Auk* 100:33–47.

Hall, B. W. 1998. Habitat use by sympatric northern bobwhite and scaled quail in the western Rio Grande Plains. Thesis, Texas A&M University–Kingsville.

Halls, L. K., R. H. Hughes, R. S. Rummell, and B. L. Southwell. 1964. *Forage and cattle management in longleaf–slash pine forests.* Farmers' Bulletin no. 2199. Washington, D.C.: U.S. Department of Agriculture.

Hamilton, T. H. 1962. The habitats of the avifauna of the mesquite plains of Texas. *American Midland Naturalist* 76:85–105.

Hammerquist-Wilson, M. M., and J. A. Crawford. 1981. Response of bobwhites to cover changes within three grazing systems. *Journal of Range Management* 34:213–15.

———. 1987. Habitat selection by Texas bobwhites and chestnut-bellied scaled quail in South Texas. *Journal of Wildlife Management* 51:575–82.

Handley, C. O. 1931. Food of the young. Pages 159–65 in H. L. Stoddard, ed., *The bobwhite quail: Its habits, preservation and increase.* New York: Scribner's.

Hanley, T. A., and J. L. Page. 1982. Different effects of livestock use on habitat structure and rodent populations in Great Basin communities. *California Fish and Game* 68:160–74.

Hanselka, C. W. 2002. *Brush busters: How to take out tallowtrees.* Publication L-5416. College Station: Texas Cooperative Extension, Texas A&M University System.

Hanselka, C. W., and F. S. Guthery. 1991. *Bobwhite quail management in South Texas.* Publication B-5005. College Station: Texas Agricultural Extension Service, Texas A&M University.

Hansen, H. M., and F. S. Guthery. 2001. Calling behavior of bobwhite males and the call-count index. *Wildlife Society Bulletin* 29:145–52.

Hanson, H. G. 1947. Missing—56,434 bobwhites! *Oklahoma Game and Fish News* 3:20.

Hanson, W. R., and R. J. Miller. 1961. Edge types and abundance of bobwhites in southern Illinois. *Journal of Wildlife Management* 25:71–76.

Hardin, J. B. 2003. Spatial aspects of quail hunting on the Rio Grande Plain of Texas. Thesis, Texas A&M University–Kingsville.

Hart, D., and T. Mitchell. 1941. *Report of data and indications as of spring 1941 relative to the value of artificial stocking.* East Alton, Ill.: Game Restoration Department, Western Cartridge Company.

Hart, R. H. 1978. Stocking rate theory and its application to grazing on rangelands. Pages 547–50 in D. N. Hyder, ed., *Proceedings of the First International Rangeland Congress.* Denver, Colo.: Society for Range Management.

Harveson, L. A. 1995. Nutritional and physiological ecology of reproducing northern bobwhites in southern Texas. Thesis, Texas A&M University–Kingsville.

Harveson, L. A., P. M. Harveson, and C. Richardson. 2002. *Proceedings of the Trans-Pecos Wildlife Conference.* Alpine, Tex.: Sul Ross State University.

Hatch, D. E. 1975. Behavior and ecology of bobwhite (*Colinus virginianus*) and the scaled quail (*Callipepla squamata*) in their area of sympatry. Dissertation, University of Nebraska, Lincoln.

Hatch, S. L., K. N. Gandhi, and L. E. Brown. 1990. *Checklist of the vascular plants of Texas.* Publication MP-1655. College Station: Texas Agricultural Experiment Station, Texas A&M University.

Haussamen, W. C. 1974. Food habits of scaled quail in southeastern New Mexico. Thesis, New Mexico State University, Las Cruces.

Hawbecker, A. C. 1975. The biology of some desert-dwelling ground squirrels. Pages 277–303 in I. Prakash and P. K. Ghosh, eds., *Rodents in desert environments*. The Hague, Netherlands: Junk.

Hawkins, A. S. 1937. Winter feeding at Faville Grove, 1935–1937. *Journal of Wildlife Management* 1:62–69.

———. 1945. Bird life of the Texas Panhandle. *Panhandle-Plains Historical Review* 18:110–50.

Hays, K. B., M. Wagner, F. Smeins, and R. N. Wilkins. 2004. *Restoring native grasslands*. College Station: Texas Cooperative Extension, Texas A&M University System.

Heffelfinger, J. R., F. S. Guthery, R. J. Olding, C. L. Cochran Jr., and C. M. Mc-Mullen. 1999. Influence of precipitation timing and summer temperatures on reproduction of Gambel's quail. *Journal of Wildlife Management* 63:154–61.

Heffelfinger, J. R., and R. J. Olding. 2000. Montezuma quail management in Arizona. *Proceedings of the National Quail Symposium* 4:183–90.

Heirman, A. L., and H. A. Wright. 1973. Fire in medium fuels of East Texas. *Journal of Range Management* 26:331–35.

Hellickson, M., and A. Radomski. 1999. *Bobwhites of the Wild Horse Desert: Status of our knowledge*. Management Bulletin no. 4. Kingsville: Caesar Kleberg Wildlife Research Institute, Texas A&M University–Kingsville.

Henke, S. E, V. C. Gallardo, B. Martinez, and R. Bailey. 2001. Survey of aflatoxin concentrations in wild bird seed purchased in Texas. *Journal of Wildlife Diseases* 37:831–35.

Henshaw, H. W. 1875. Report upon the ornithological collections made in portions of Nevada, Utah, California, Colorado, New Mexico and Arizona during the years 1871, 1872, 1873 and 1874. Pages 131–507, 977–89, plates I–XV in G. M. Wheeler, *Report on the Geographic survey west of the 100th meridian*, vol. 5, chap. 3. Washington, D.C.: U.S. Government Printing Office.

Hensley, M. M. 1954. Ecological relations of the breeding bird population of the desert biome in Arizona. *Ecological Monographs* 24:185–207.

Henson, K. D. 2006. Species visitation at free-choice quail feeders in West Texas. Thesis, Texas A&M University, College Station.

Herman, C. M. 1963. Disease and infection in the Tetraonidae. *Journal of Wildlife Management* 27:850–55.

———. 1969. The impact of disease on wildlife populations. *BioScience* 19:321–30, 335.

Hernández, F. 1999. The value of prickly pear cactus as nesting cover for northern bobwhite. Dissertation, Texas A&M University–Kingsville, Kingsville, and Texas A&M University, College Station.

———. 2004. Characteristics of Montezuma quail populations and habitats at Elephant Mountain Wildlife Management Area, Texas. Thesis, Sul Ross State University, Alpine.

Hernández, F., F. S. Guthery, and W. P. Kuvlesky Jr. 2002. The legacy of bobwhite research in South Texas. *Journal of Wildlife Management* 66:1–18.

Hernández, F., L. A. Harveson, and C. Brewer. 2002a. Ecology and management of Montezuma quail. Pages 11–14 in L. A. Harveson, P. M. Harveson, and C. Richardson, eds., *Proceedings of the Trans-Pecos Wildlife Conference*. Alpine, Tex.: Sul Ross State University.

———. 2002b. Efficiency of line drives to locate Montezuma quail at Elephant Mountain Wildlife Management Area. *Proceedings of the National Quail Symposium* 5:117.

Hernández, F., S. E. Henke, N. J. Silvy, and D. Rollins. 2003. The use of prickly pear cactus as nesting cover for northern bobwhite. *Journal of Wildlife Management* 67:417–23.

Hernández, F., D. Rollins, and R. Cantu. 1997. Evaluating evidence to identify ground-nest predators in West Texas. *Wildlife Society Bulletin* 25:826–31.

Hernández, F., J. D. Vasquez, F. C. Bryant, A. A. Radomski, and R. Howard. 2002. Effects of Hurricane Bret on northern bobwhite survival in South Texas. *Proceedings of the National Quail Symposium* 5:87–90.

Hightower, B. G., V. W. Lehmann, and R. B. Eads. 1953. Ectoparasites from mammals and birds on a quail preserve. *Journal of Mammalogy* 34:268–71.

Hill, R. G. 1940. Some observations on farm game management cooperatives in Michigan. *Journal of Wildlife Management* 4:383–91.

Hodge, F. W., and T. H. Lewis, eds. 1984. *Spanish explorers in the southern United States, 1528–1543.* Austin: Texas State Historical Association, University of Texas.

Hoerr, F. J. 1997. Poisons and toxins: Mycotoxicoses. Pages 951–79 in B. W. Calnek, H. J. Barnes, C. W. Beard, L. R. McDougald, and Y. M. Saif, eds., *Diseases of poultry*, 10th ed. Ames: Iowa State University Press.

Hoffman, D. M. 1965. *The scaled quail in Colorado: Range, population status, and harvest.* Technical Publication no. 18. Denver: Colorado Game, Fish and Parks Department.

Holdermann, D. A. 1992. *Montezuma quail investigations.* Professional Services Contract 80–516–41–83. Santa Fe: New Mexico Game and Fish Department.

Holdermann, D. A., and C. E. Holdermann. 1993. Immature red-tailed hawk captures Montezuma quail. *New Mexico Ornithological Society Bulletin* 21:31–33.

Holdermann, D. A., and R. Holdermann. 1998. Some aspects of the ecology of yellow nutsedge, Gray's woodsorrel and pocket gophers in relation to Montezuma quail in the northern Sacramento Mountains, New Mexico. *New Mexico Ornithological Society Bulletin* 26:31.

Holechek, J. L., R. D. Pieper, and C. H. Herbel. 1998. *Range management: Principles and practices.* Upper Saddle River, N.J.: Prentice-Hall.

Holechek, J. L., R. Valdez, S. D. Schemnitz, R. D. Pieper, and C. A. Davis. 1982. Manipulation of grazing to improve or maintain wildlife habitat. *Wildlife Society Bulletin* 10:204–10.

Holman, E. O. 1961. Osteology of living and fossil New World quails. *Bulletin of the Florida State Museum* 6:131–233.

Homerstad, G. E., and K. L. Brown. 2001. *Comprehensive wildlife management planning guidelines for the Gulf Prairies and Marshes ecological region.* Austin: Private Lands Enhancement Program, Texas Parks and Wildlife Department.

Hon, L. T., D. J. Forrester, and L. E. Williams. 1978. Helminth acquisition by wild turkeys (*Meleagris gallopavo osceola*) in Florida. *Proceedings of the Helminthological Society of Washington* 45:211–18.

Hooker, W. A. 1909. Some host relations of ticks. *Journal of Economic Entomology* 2:251–57.

Howard, M. O. 1981. *Food habits and parasites of scaled quail in southeastern Pecos County, Texas.* Alpine, Tex.: Sul Ross State University.

Howard, R. 1994. Record keeping—a key to having more quail. Pages 59–64 in W. E. Cohen, ed., *Texas quail short course I: Proceedings of the first conference on quail management.* Kingsville: Texas A&M University–Kingsville.

———. 1996. Bobwhite quail harvest management: A ranch perspective. Pages 25–40 in W. E. Cohen, ed., *Texas quail short course II: Proceedings of a second conference on quail management.* Kingsville: Texas A&M University–Kingsville.

Howell, D., and B. Isaacs. 1988. Does CRP spell quail? *Quail Unlimited Magazine* 7 (3): 6–9, 34.

Hubby, T. E. 1926. *Annual report—Game, Fish and Oyster Commission for the fiscal year ending August 1926.* Austin: Texas Game, Fish and Oyster Commission.

Hudson, P. J. 1986. The effect of a parasitic nematode on the breeding production of red grouse. *Journal of Animal Ecology* 55:85–92.

———. 1992. *Grouse in space and time.* Fordingbridge, U.K.: Game Conservancy Trust.

Hudson, P. J., A. P. Dobson, and D. Newborn. 1985. Cyclic and non-cyclic populations of red grouse: A role for parasitism? Pages 77–89 in D. Rollinson and R. M. Anderson, eds., *Ecology and genetics of host-parasite interactions.* London: Academic Press.

———. 1992. Do parasites make prey vulnerable to predation?: Red grouse and parasites. *Journal of Animal Ecology* 61:681–92.

Hudson, P. J., A. P. Dobson, and D. Newborn. 1998. Prevention of population cycles by parasite removal. *Science* 282:2256–58.

Hudson, P. J., D. Newborn, and A. P. Dobson. 1992. Regulation and stability of a free-living host-parasite system: *Trichostrongylus tenuis* in red grouse. Vol. 1: Monitoring and parasite reduction experiments. *Journal of Animal Ecology* 61:477–86.

Hudson, P. J., A. P. Rizzoli, B. T., Grenfell, J. A. P. Heesterbeek, and A. P. Dobson. 2002. Ecology of wildlife diseases. Pages 1–5 in P. J. Hudson, A. Rizzoli, B. T. Grenfell, H. Heesterbeek, and A. P. Dobson, eds., *The ecology of wildlife diseases.* Oxford: Oxford University Press.

Huggler, T. E. 1987. *Quail hunting in America.* Harrisburg, Penn: Stackpole Books.

Hughes, J. M. 1993. Major vegetation regions and avian habitat use of Elephant Mountain Wildlife Management Area, Brewster County, Texas. Pages 83–97 in J. C. Barlow and D. J. Miller, eds., *Proceedings of fourth symposium on resources of the Chihuahuan Desert region.* Fort Davis, Tex.: Chihuahuan Desert Research Institute.

Hungerford, C. R. 1955. A preliminary evaluation of quail malaria in southern Arizona in relation to habitat and quail mortality. *Transactions of the North American Wildlife Conference* 20:209–19.

———. 1960a. The factors affecting the breeding of Gambel's quail *Lophortyx gambelii* in Arizona. Dissertation, University of Arizona, Tucson.

———. 1960b. Water requirements of Gambel's quail. *Transactions of the North American Wildlife and Natural Resources Conference* 25:231–40.

———. 1962. Adaptations shown in selection of food by Gambel's quail. *Condor* 64:213–19.

———. 1964. Vitamin A and productivity in Gambel's quail. *Journal of Wildlife Management* 28:141–47.

Hunt, J. L., and T. L. Best. 2001. Foods of scaled quail (*Callipepla squamata*) in southeastern New Mexico. *Texas Journal of Science* 53:147–56.

Hurst, G. A. 1972. Insects and bobwhite quail brood habitat management. *Proceedings of the National Bobwhite Quail Symposium* 1:65–82.

Hurst, G. A., L. W. Burger, and B. D. Leopold. 1996. Predation and galliform recruitment: An old issue revisited. *Transactions of the North American Wildlife and Natural Resource Conference* 61:62–76.

Inglis, J. M. 1964. *A history of vegetation on the Rio Grande Plain.* Texas Parks and Wildlife Department Bulletin no. 45. Austin.

International Association of Fish and Wildlife Agencies (IAFWA). 2002. *Economic importance of hunting in America.* Washington, D.C.: IAFWA.

Jack, S. W., and W. M. Reed. 1994. Experimental infection of bobwhite quail with Indiana-C adenovirus. *Avian Diseases* 38:325–28.

Jackson, A. S. 1942. Bobwhites and scaled quails in the lower plains. *Pittman-Robertson Quarterly* 2:220–21.

———. 1947. A bobwhite quail irruption in northwest Texas lower plains terminated by predation. *Transactions of the North American Wildlife and Natural Resources Conference* 12:511–19.

———. 1952. The bobwhite quail in relation to land management in the west-

ern Cross Timbers. Federal Aid Project 18-R. Final report. Austin: Texas Game, Fish and Oyster Commission.

———. 1962. A pattern to population oscillations of the bobwhite quail in the lower plains grazing ranges of northwest Texas. *Proceedings of the Southeastern Game and Fish Commissioners* 16:120–26.

———. 1969. *A handbook for bobwhite quail management in the West Texas Rolling Plains.* Bulletin no. 48. Austin: Texas Parks and Wildlife Department.

James, F. C., D. A. Wiedenfield, and C. E. McCullough. 1992. Trends in breeding populations of warblers: Declines in the southern highlands and increase in the lowlands. Pages 43–56 in J. M. Hagen III and D. W. Johnston, eds., *Ecology and conservation of neotropical migrant landbirds.* Washington, D.C.: Smithsonian Institution Press.

Jensen, J. K. 1925. Late nesting of scaled quail (*Callipepla squamata squamata*). *Auk* 42:129–30.

Jimenez, E., and M. R. Conover. 2001. Ecological approaches to reduce predation on ground-nesting gamebirds and their nests. *Wildlife Society Bulletin* 29:62–69.

Johnsgard, P. A. 1973. *Grouse and quails of North America.* Lincoln: University of Nebraska Press.

———. 1975. *North American game birds of upland and shoreline.* Lincoln: University of Nebraska Press.

———. 1988. *The quails, partridges, and francolins of the world.* New York: Oxford University Press.

Johnson, A. S. 1961. Antagonistic relationships between ants and wildlife with special reference to imported fire ants and bobwhite quail in the Southeast. *Proceedings of the Annual Conference of the Southeastern Association of Game and Fish Commissioners* 15:88–107.

Johnson, D. B., and F. S. Guthery. 1988. Loafing coverts used by northern bobwhites in subtropical environments. *Journal of Wildlife Management* 52:464–69.

Johnson, D. B., F. S. Guthery, and A. R. Kane. 1990. Attributes of whistling posts used by northern bobwhites (*Colinus virginianus*). *Southwestern Naturalist* 35:229–31.

Johnson, K. H., and C. E. Braun. 1999. Viability and conservation of an exploited sage grouse population. *Conservation Biology* 13:77–84.

Johnston, M. C. 1963. Past and present grasslands of southern Texas and northeastern Mexico. *Ecology* 44:456–66.

Jones, J. K., Jr., D. M. Armstrong, and J. R. Choate. 1985. *Guide to mammals of the Plains States.* Lincoln: University of Nebraska Press.

Joseph, J., M. Collins, J. Holechek, R. Valdez, and R. Steiner. 2003. Conservative and moderate grazing effects on Chihuahuan Desert wildlife sightings. *Western North American Naturalist* 63:43–49.

Judd, S. D. 1905. *The bobwhite and other quails of the United States in their economic relations.* Bureau of Biological Survey Bulletin no. 21. Washington, D.C.: U.S. Department of Agriculture.

Jurries, R. W. 1979. *Attwater's prairie chicken.* Federal Aid Series no. 18. Austin: Texas Parks and Wildlife Department.

Kabat, C., and D. R. Thompson. 1963. *Wisconsin quail, 1834–1962: Population dynamics and habitat management.* Wisconsin Conservation Department Technical Bulletin no. 30. Madison.

Kane, A. H. 1988. Effects of management on bobwhite habitat and density in southern Texas. Thesis, Texas A&M University–Kingsville.

Kantrud, H. A., and R. L. Kologiski. 1982. Effects of soils and grazing on breeding birds of uncultivated upland grasslands of the northern Great Plains. Wildlife Research Report no. 15. Washington, D.C.: USDI Fish & Wildlife Service.

Karunamoorthy, G., D. J. Chellappa, and R. Anandan. 1994. The life history of

Subulura brumpti in the beetle *Alphitobius diaperinus. Indian Veterinary Journal* 71:12–15.

Kassinis, N. I., and F. S. Guthery. 1996. Flight behavior of northern bobwhites. *Journal of Wildlife Management* 60:581–85.

Kates, R. W., W. C. Clark, R. Correl, J. M. Hall, C. C. Jaeger, et al. 2001. Sustainability science. *Science* 292: 641–42.

Kaufman, D. W., E. J. Finck, and G. A. Kaufman. 1990. Small mammals and grassland fires. Pages 46–80 in S. L. Collins and L. L. Wallace, eds., *Fire in North American tall grass prairie.* Norman: University of Oklahoma Press.

Keeler, J. E. 1959. *Quail feeder study.* Alabama Department of Conservation, Wildlife Restoration Project W-32-R. Final Report, 1953–57. Montgomery.

Kellogg, F. E., and J. P. Calpin. 1971. Checklist of parasites and diseases reported from bobwhite quail. *Avian Diseases* 15:704–15.

Kellogg, F. E., and G. L. Doster. 1972. Diseases and parasites of the bobwhite. *Proceedings of the National Bobwhite Quail Symposium* 1:233–67.

Kellogg, F. E., and A. K. Prestwood. 1968. Gastrointestinal helminths from wild and pen-raised bobwhites. *Journal of Wildlife Management* 32:468–75.

Kelso, L. H. 1937. Food of the scaled quail (preliminary report). Bulletin 21. Washington, D.C.: U.S. Department of Agricultural, Biological Survey.

Kiel, W. H., Jr. 1976. Bobwhite quail population characteristics and management implications in South Texas. *Transactions of the North American Wildlife and Natural Resources Conference* 41:407–20.

King, D. J., S. R. Pursglove, and W. R. Davidson. 1981. Adenovirus isolation and serology from wild bobwhite quail (*Colinus virginianus*). *Avian Diseases* 25:678–82.

King, N. M. 1998. Habitat use by endangered masked bobwhites and other quail on the Buenos Aires National Wildlife Refuge, Arizona. Thesis, University of Arizona, Tucson.

Klimstra, W. D., and J. L. Roseberry. 1975. Nesting ecology of the bobwhite in southern Illinois. *Wildlife Monograph* 41:1–37.

Klimstra, W. D., and V. C. Ziccardi. 1963. Night-roosting habitat of bobwhites. *Journal of Wildlife Management* 27:202–14.

Knopf, F. L. 1994. Avian assemblages on altered grasslands. *Studies in Avian Biology* 15: 247–57.

Knopf, F. L., and R. W. Cannon. 1982. Structural resilience of a willow riparian community to change in grazing practices. Pages 198–207 in J. M. Peek and P. D. Dalke, eds., *Wildlife-livestock relationships symposium proceedings.* Moscow: Forestry, Wildlife and Range Experiment Station, University of Idaho.

Koerth, B. H. 1996. Chemical manipulation of plants. Pages 321–35 in P. R. Krausman, ed., *Rangeland wildlife.* Denver, Colo.: Society for Range Management.

Koerth, N. E., and F. S. Guthery. 1987. Body fat levels of northern bobwhite in South Texas. *Journal of Wildlife Management* 51: 194–97.

———. 1991. Water restriction effects on northern bobwhite reproduction. *Journal of Wildlife Management* 55:132–37.

Koerth, B., W. P. Kuvlesky Jr., and J. Payne. 1991. *Sexing and aging the northern bobwhite.* Leaflet 2455. College Station: Texas Agricultural Extension Service.

Koerth, B. H., J. L. Mutz, and J. C. Segers. 1986. Availability of bobwhite foods after burning of Pan American balsamscale. *Wildlife Society Bulletin* 14:146–50.

Komar, N., S. Langevin, S. Hinten, N. Nemeth, E. Edwards, D. Hettler, B. Davis, R. Bowen, and M. Bunning. 2003. Experimental infection of North American birds with the New York 1999 strain of West Nile virus. *Emerging Infectious Diseases* 9:311–22.

Kopp, S. D., F. S. Guthery, N. D. Forrester, and W. E. Cohen. 1998. Habitat selection modeling for northern bobwhites on subtropical rangeland. *Journal of Wildlife Management* 62:884–95.

Kozicky, E. L. 1987. *Hunting preserves for sport or profit.* Kingsville: Caesar Kleberg Wildlife Research Institute Press, Texas A&I University–Kingsville.

Kozicky, E. L., and J. Madson. 1966. *Shooting preserve management: The Nilo System.* East Alton, Ill.: Winchester Western Press.

Kuvlesky, W. P., Jr., T. Fulbright, and R. Engel-Wilson. 2002. The impact of invasive exotic grasses on quail in the southwestern United States. *Proceedings of the National Quail Symposium* 5:118–28.

Kuvlesky, W. P., Jr., S. A. Gall, S. J. Dobrott, S. Tolley, F. S. Guthery, S. A. De-Stefano, N. King, K. R. Nolte, N. J. Silvy, J. C. Lewis, G. Gee, R. Engel-Wilson, and G. Camou-Lourdes. 2000. The status of endangered masked bobwhite recovery in the United States and Mexico. *Proceedings of the National Quail Symposium* 4:42–57.

Labov, J. B. 1977. Phytoestrogens and mammalian reproduction. *Comparative Biochemistry and Physiology* 57 (A): 3–9.

Lack, D. 1954. *The natural regulation of animal numbers.* London: Oxford University Press.

Laing, J. D. 2003. Creating northern bobwhite habitat: Converting an abandoned pasture from bermudagrass to native grasses and forbs. Thesis, Stephen F. Austin State University, Nacogdoches.

Landers, J. L., and B. S. Mueller. 1986. *Bobwhite quail management: A habitat approach.* Tallahassee, Fla.: Quail Unlimited and Tall Timbers Research Station.

Lawson, L. L. 1950. *Quail research and investigation in southern Arizona.* Federal Aid Project W-40-R-2. Phoenix: Arizona Game and Fish Department.

Lay, D. W. 1940. *Bob-white populations as affected by woodlot management in eastern Texas.* College Station: Division of Wildlife Research and Texas Cooperative Wildlife Research Unit, Agricultural and Mechanical College of Texas.

———. 1952. *Bobwhite quail in relation to land management in pine woodland type.* Federal Aid Project 20-R. Final Report. Austin: Texas Game and Fish Commission.

———. 1954. *Quail management handbook for East Texas.* Bulletin no. 34. Austin: Texas Game and Fish Commission.

———. 1965. *Quail management handbook for East Texas (revised).* Bulletin no. 34. Austin: Texas Parks and Wildlife Department.

Lay, D. W., and H. R. Siegler. 1937. The blue jay as a link between acorns and quail. *Transactions of the North American Wildlife Conference* 2:579–81.

Lay, D. W., and W. P. Taylor. 1943. Wildlife aspects of cutover pine woodlands in East Texas. *Journal of Forestry* 41:446–48.

Lee, L. 1948. Fall and winter food of the bobwhite quail in Oklahoma. Thesis, Oklahoma State University, Stillwater.

Lehmann, V. W. 1937a. *Increase quail by improving their habitat.* Austin: Texas Game, Fish and Oyster Commission.

———. 1937b. Quail and cover on three Central Texas farms. *Transactions of the North American Wildlife Conference* 2:570–74.

———. 1939. *Habitat improvements for quail: Tested methods of raising quail in their native territories by providing suitable food and cover.* Bulletin no. 17. Austin: Texas Game, Fish and Oyster Commission.

———. 1941. *Attwater's prairie chicken, its life history and management.* North American Fauna 57. Washington, D.C.: U.S. Government Printing Office.

———. 1946a. Bobwhite quail reproduction in southwestern Texas. *Journal of Wildlife Management* 10:124–36.

———. 1946b. Mobility of bobwhite quail in southwestern Texas. *Journal of Wildlife Management* 10:124–37.

———. 1953. Bobwhite population fluctuations and vitamin A. *Transactions of the North American Wildlife Conference* 18:199–246.

———. 1965. Fire in the range of Attwater's prairie chicken. *Tall Timbers Fire Ecology Conference Proceedings* 4:127–43.

———. 1969. *Forgotten legions.* El Paso: Texas Western Press.

———. 1976. Bob-whites of the brush country. *The American Field* (December): 766–69.

———. 1984. *The Bobwhite in the Rio Grande Plain of Texas.* College Station: Texas A&M University Press.

Lehmann, V. W., and H. Ward. 1941. Some plants valuable to quail in southwestern Texas. *Journal of Wildlife Management* 5:131–35.

Leopold, A. 1929. Report on a game survey of Mississippi. Unpublished report. Jackson: Mississippi Department of Wildlife, Fisheries, and Parks.

———. 1931. *Report on a game survey of the north central states.* Madison, Wis.: Democrat Printing.

———. 1932. The river of the mother of God, and other essays by Aldo Leopold. Unpublished manuscript referenced in S. L. Flader and J. B. Callicott, *The river of the mother of god.* Madison: University of Wisconsin Press.

———. 1933. *Game management.* New York: Scribner's.

———. 1937. The effect of the winter of 1935–36 on Wisconsin quail. *American Midland Naturalist* 18:408–16.

———. 1939. The farmer as a conservationist. *American Forests* 45:6, 294, 299, 316, 323.

———. 1940. History of the Riley Game Cooperative. *Journal of Wildlife Management* 4:291–302.

———. 1949. *A Sand County almanac.* Oxford: Oxford University Press.

———. 1959. *The wildlife of Mexico: The game birds and mammals.* Berkeley: University of California Press.

———. 1978. Wildlife in a prodigal society. *Transactions of the North American Wildlife and Natural Resources Conference* 43:5–10.

Leopold, A. S., M. Erwin, J. Oh, and B. Browning. 1976. Phytoestrogens: Adverse effects on reproduction in California quail. *Science* 191:98–100.

Leopold, A. S., R. J. Gutiérrez, and M. T. Bronson. 1981. *North American game birds and mammals.* New York: Scribner's.

Leopold, A. S., and R. A. McCabe. 1957. Natural history of Montezuma quail in Mexico. *Condor* 59:3–26.

Lerich, S. P. 2002. Nesting ecology of scaled quail at Elephant Mountain Wildlife Management Area, Brewster County, Texas. Thesis, Sul Ross State University, Alpine.

Levine, P. P., and F. C. Goble. 1947. Parasitism and disease. Pages 401–42 in G. Bump, R. W. Darrow, F. C. Edminster, and W. F. Crissey, eds., *The ruffed grouse: Life history, propagation, management.* Buffalo, N.Y.: Holling Press.

Levy, S. H., J. J. Levy, and R. A. Bishop. 1966. Use of tape recorded quail calls during the breeding season. *Journal of Wildlife Management* 30:426–28.

Lewis, C. E., and T. J. Harshbarger. 1986. Burning and grazing effects on bobwhite foods in the southeastern coastal plain. *Wildlife Society Bulletin* 14:455–59.

Leyva-Espinosa, R. I. 2000. Use of broad-scale data to assess changes of scaled quail population in Texas. Dissertation, Texas Tech University, Lubbock.

Ligon, J. S. 1927. *Wildlife of New Mexico: Its conservation and management.* Santa Fe: New Mexico Game and Fish.

———. 1961. *New Mexico birds and where to find them.* Albuquerque: University of New Mexico Press.

Lindberg, D. C. 1992. *The beginnings of Western science.* Chicago: University of Chicago Press.

Linex, R. G. 1999. Key plants for quail in the Rolling Plains. Pages 12–14 in K. A.

Cearley, ed., *Preserving Texas' quail heritage into the 21st century.* San Angelo: Texas Agricultural Extension Service.

Liu, X., R. M. Whiting Jr., B. S. Mueller, D. S. Parsons, and D. R. Dietz. 2000. Survival and causes of mortality of relocated and resident bobwhites in East Texas. *Proceedings of the National Quail Symposium* 4:119–24.

Liu, X., R. M. Whiting Jr., D. S. Parsons, and D. R. Dietz. 1996. Habitat preferences of relocated and resident northern bobwhite in eastern Texas. *Proceedings of the Annual Conference of the Southeastern Association of Fish and Wildlife Agencies* 50:632–43.

———. 2002. Movement patterns of resident and relocated northern bobwhites in East Texas. *Proceedings of the National Quail Symposium* 5:168–72.

Lloyd, W. 1887. Birds of Tom Green and Concho counties, Texas. *Auk* 4:181–93, 289–99.

Lochmiller, R. L., J. F. Boggs, S. T. McMurry, D. M. Leslie Jr., and D. M. Engle, et al. 1991. Responses of cottontail rabbit populations to herbicide and fire applications on Cross Timbers rangelands. *Journal of Range Management* 44:150–55.

Lockwood, M. W. 2001. *Birds of the Texas Hill Country.* Austin: University of Texas Press.

Lund, E. E., and A. M. Chute. 1972. Reciprocal responses of eight species of galliform birds and three parasites: *Heterakis gallinarum, Histomonas meleagridis,* and *Parahistomonas wenrichi. Journal of Parasitology* 58:940–45.

———. 1974. The reproductive potential of *Heterakis gallinarum* in various species of galliform birds: Implications for survival of *H. gallinarum* and *Histomonas meleagridis* to recent times. *International Journal for Parasitology* 4:453–61.

Lusk, J. M., F. S. Guthery, and S. J. DeMaso. 2002. A neural network model for predicting bobwhite quail abundance in the Rolling Red Plains of Oklahoma. Pages 345–55 in J. M. Scott, P. J. Heglund, M. Morrison, M. Raphael, J. Haufler, and B. Wall, eds., *Predicting species occurrences: Issues of scale and accuracy.* Covello, Calif.: Island Press.

Lusk, J. M., F. S. Guthery, R. R. George, M. J. Peterson, and S. J. DeMaso. 2002. Relative abundance of bobwhites in relation to weather and land use. *Journal of Wildlife Management* 66:1040–51.

Lutz, S., G. Valentine, S. Nelle, D. Rollins, C. Coffman, and G. Miller. 1994. *Wildlife habitat management on former CRP lands.* Management Note 15. Lubbock: Department of Range and Wildlife Management, Texas Tech University.

Lyons, E. K. 2002. Effects of short-term predator control on nesting success and survival of northern bobwhites (*Colinus virginianus*). Thesis, Angelo State University, San Angelo.

MacArthur, R. H., and E. O. Wilson. 1967. *The theory of island biogeography.* Princeton, N.J.: Princeton University Press.

McCall, G. A. 1852. Some remarks on the habits of birds met with in western Texas, between San Antonio and the Rio Grande, and in New Mexico; with descriptions of several species believed to have been hitherto undescribed. *Academy of Natural Sciences of Philadelphia* 5:213–24.

McCauley, C. A. H. 1877. Notes on the ornithology of the region about the source of the Red River of Texas, from observations made during the exploration conducted by Lieut. E. H. Ruffner, Corps. of Engineers, U.S.A. Bulletin of the U.S. Geological Survey, Territory 3, no. 3. In K. D. Seyffert and T. L. Baker, editors. *Panhandle-Plains Historical Review* 61:25–88.

McDonald, A. P., ed. 1969. *Hurrah for Texas: The diary of Adolphus Sterne, 1838–1851.* Waco, Tex.: Texian Press.

McGinty, A. M., J. F. Cadenhead, W. Hamilton, C. W. Hanselka, D. N. Ueckert, and S. G. Whisenant. 2000. *Chemical weed and brush control suggestions for rangeland.* Bulletin 1499. College Station: Texas Agricultural Extension Service.

McGinty, A. M., and D. N. Ueckert. 1995. *Brush busters—how to beat mesquite.* Publication L-5144. College Station: Texas Agricultural Extension Service.

McGinty, A. M., and L. D. White. 1998. *Range monitoring with photo points.* Leaflet 5216. College Station: Texas Agricultural Extension Service.

McGregor, E. A. 1917. Eight new Mallophaga of the genus *Lipeurus* from North American birds. *Psyche* 24:105–17.

MacGregor, W. G., and M. Inlay. 1951. Observations on failure of Gambel's quail to breed. *California Fish and Game* 37:218–19.

McLendon, T. 1991. Preliminary description of the vegetation of South Texas exclusive of coastal saline zones. *Texas Journal of Science* 43:13–32.

McMillan, I. I. 1964. Annual population changes in California quail. *Journal of Wildlife Management* 28:702–11.

MacNamara, L. G. 1936. Farmer-sportsman cooperatives. *Transactions of the North American Wildlife Conference* 2:275–79.

McNay, M. E., and B. W. O'Gara. 1981. Cattle-pronghorn interactions during the fawning season in northwestern Nevada. Pages 593–606 in J. M. Peek and P. D. Dalke, eds., *Wildlife-livestock relationships symposium proceedings.* Moscow: Forestry, Wildlife and Range Experiment Station, University of Idaho.

McWilliams, W. H., and R. G. Lord. 1988. *Forest resources of East Texas.* U.S. Forest Service Resource Bulletin SO-136.

Mahoney, S. P. 2002. Keynote address: Ideas, landscapes, and conservation's new frontier. *Proceedings of the National Quail Symposium* 5:45–47.

Maple, D. P., and N. J. Silvy. 1988. Recovery and economics of pen-reared bobwhites in north-central Texas. *Proceedings of the Annual Conference of the Southeastern Association of Fish and Wildlife Agencies* 42:329–32.

Marsden, H. M. 1961. Natural longevity record for a bobwhite. *Auk* 78:94.

Marsden, H. M., and T. S. Baskett. 1958. Annual mortality in a banded bobwhite population. *Journal of Wildlife Management* 22:414–19.

Martin, A. C., and W. D. Barclay. 1961. *Seed identification manual.* Berkeley: University of California Press.

Maxwell, R. S., and R. D. Baker. 1983. *Sawdust empire.* College Station: Texas A&M University Press.

May, I. M., Jr. 1981. *Overton-agricultural research and education in northeast Texas.* College Station: Texas Agricultural Experiment Station.

May, R. M., and R. M. Anderson. 1978. Regulation and stability of host-parasite population interactions. Vol. 2: Destabilizing processes. *Journal of Animal Ecology* 47:249–67.

Medina, A. L. 1988. Diets of scaled quail in southern Arizona. *Journal of Wildlife Management* 52:753–57.

Meeker, J. O. 1981. Interactions between pronghorn antelope and feral horses in northwestern Nevada. Pages 573–80 in J. M. Peek and P. D. Dalke, eds., *Wildlife-livestock relationships symposium proceedings.* Moscow: Forestry, Wildlife and Range Experiment Station, University of Idaho.

Meents, J. K., B. W. Anderson, and R. D. Ohmart. 1982. Vegetation relationships and food of sage sparrows wintering in honey mesquite habitat. *Wilson Bulletin* 94:129–38.

Meinzer, W. P., and R. Sasser. 1997. *Texas quail.* Dallas: Collectors Covey.

Merrill, L. B., J. G. Teer, and O. C. Wallmo. 1957. Reaction of deer populations to grazing practices. *Texas Agricultural Program Report* 3:10–12.

Miller, L. 1943. Notes on the Mearns quail. *Condor* 45:104–109.

Mix, K., W. P. Kuvlesky Jr., and L. E. Drawe. 2003. *The impacts of summer prescribed fires on the vegetation, avian and invertebrate communities of the Welder Wildlife Refuge.* Rob and Bessie Welder Wildlife Refuge Annual Report. Sinton, Tex.

Monson, G. 1941. The effect of revegetation on small bird populations in Arizona. *Journal of Wildlife Management* 5:395–97.

Morris, J. M. 1997. *El Llano Estacado: Exploration and imagination on the High Plains of Texas and New Mexico, 1536–1860.* Austin: Texas State Historical Association.

Morris, M. J. 1957. Evaluation of plants suitable for bobwhite habitat management in central Oklahoma. Dissertation, Oklahoma State University, Stillwater.

Moss, R., A. Watson, and R. Parr. 1996. Experimental prevention of a population cycle in red grouse. *Ecology* 77:1512–30.

Moulton, M. P. 1978. Small mammal associations in grazed versus ungrazed cottonwood riparian woodland in eastern Colorado. Pages 133–40 in W. D. Graul and S. J. Bissell, eds., *Lowland river and stream habitat in Colorado: A symposium.* Denver: Colorado Chapter of The Wildlife Society and Colorado Audubon Council.

Mueller, B. S. 1984. Final report: An evaluation of releasing pen-raised quail in the fall. *Quail Unlimited Magazine* 2:6–8, 26.

Mueller, B. S., and J. B. Atkinson. 1985. The first year report: Post-fire mortality study. *Proceedings of the 1985 Tall Timbers Game Bird Seminar,* Tall Timbers Research Station, Tallahassee, Fla.

Mueller, B. S., J. B. Atkinson Jr., and T. DeVos. 1988. Mortality of radio-tagged and unmarked northern bobwhite quail. *Proceedings of the 10th International Symposium on Biotelemetry,* Fayetteville, Ark.

Mueller, B. S., W. R. Davidson, and J. B. Atkinson Jr. 1993. Survival of northern bobwhite infected with avian pox. *Proceedings of the National Quail Symposium* 3:79–82.

Mueller, J. M., C. B. Dabbert, S. Demarais, and A. R. Forbes. 1999. Northern bobwhite chick mortality caused by red imported fire ants. *Journal of Wildlife Management* 63:1291–98.

Murphy, D. A., and T. S. Baskett. 1952. Bobwhite mobility in central Missouri. *Journal of Wildlife Management* 16:498–510.

Murphy, P. A. 1976. *East Texas forests: Status and trends.* U.S. Forest Service Resource Bulletin SO-61. Washington, D.C.

Mutz, J. L., C. J. Scifres, D. L. Drawe, T. W. Box, and R. E. Whitson. 1978. *Range vegetation after mechanical brush treatment on the Coastal Prairie.* Texas Agricultural Experiment Station Bulletin 1191. College Station.

Myers, S. D. 1965. *O. W. Williams' stories from the Big Bend.* Monograph no. 10. El Paso: Texas Western College.

National Oceanic and Atmospheric Administration. 2003a. *Local climatological data: Annual summary with comparative data.* Washington, D.C.: NOAA.

———. 2003b. Lubbock precipitation from 1911–present. http://www.srh.noaa .gov/lub/climate/LBB_Climate/precipdata/Precipdata.htm (accessed May 11, 2005).

National Research Council. 1977. *Nutrient requirements of poultry.* 7th ed. Washington, D.C.: National Academy of Sciences.

Natural Resources Conservation Service (NRCS). 1997. *Resource data and concerns: Zone 1.* Austin: USDA NRCS.

Nedbal, M. A., R. L. Honeycutt, S. G. Evans, R. M. Whiting Jr., and D. R. Dietz. 1997. Northern bobwhite restocking in East Texas: A genetic assessment. *Journal of Wildlife Management* 61:854–63.

Nelle, S. 2002. Ranching in the desert. Pages 81–87 in L. A. Harveson, P. M. Harveson, and C. Richardson, eds., *Proceedings of the Trans-Pecos Wildlife Conference.* Alpine, Tex.: Sul Ross State University.

Nelson, T., J. L. Holechek, R. Valdez, and M. Cardenas. 1997. Wildlife numbers on late and mid seral Chihuahuan Desert rangelands. *Journal of Range Management* 50:593–99.

Nestler, R. B. 1946. Vitamin A, vital factor in the survival of bobwhites. *Transactions of the North American Wildlife Conference* 11:176–95.

Nestler, R. B., W. W. Bailey, and H. E. McClure. 1942. Protein requirements of bobwhite quail chicks for survival, growth and efficiency of feed utilization. *Journal of Wildlife Management* 6:185–93.

Nestler, R. B., and A. L. Nelson. 1942. The industrial aspects of pheasants and quail propagation in North America for 1939–1940. *Transactions of the North American Wildlife Conference* 7:115–30.

Nestler, R. B., and A. T. Studholme. 1945. The future of pen-reared quail in post-war restocking programs. *Pennsylvania Game News* 16:26–27.

Neufeldt, A., and D. B. Guralnik. 1997. *Webster's New World College Dictionary.* New York: Macmillan.

Newton, I. 1993. Predation and limitation of bird numbers. Pages 143–98 in D. M. Power, ed., *Current ornithology.* New York: Plenum Press.

Nolte, K. R., and T. E. Fulbright. 1997. Plant, small mammal and avian diversity following control of honey mesquite. *Journal of Range Management* 50:205–12.

Oakley, M. J., D. L. Bounds, T. A. Mollett, and E. C. Soutiere. 2002. Survival and home range estimates of pen-raised northern bobwhites in buffer strip and non-buffer strip habitats. *Proceedings of the National Quail Symposium* 5:74–80.

Oberheu, D. G., and C. B. Dabbert. 2001a. Aflatoxin contamination in supplemental and wild foods of northern bobwhite. *Ecotoxicology* 10:125–29.

———. 2001b. Aflatoxin production in supplemental feeders provided for northern bobwhite in Texas and Oklahoma. *Journal of Wildlife Diseases* 37:475–80.

———. 2001c. Exposure of game birds to ochratoxin A through supplemental feeds. *Journal of Zoo and Wildlife Medicine* 32:136–38.

Oberholser, H. C. 1974. *The bird life of Texas.* Vol. 2. Austin: University of Texas Press

O'Connor, J. 1936. Mystery quail: Hunting the least known of our native quail. *Field and Stream,* March, 24, 25, 72–74.

———. 1945. *Hunting in the Southwest.* New York: Knopf.

O'Gara, B. W. 1978. *Antilocapra americana. Mammalian Species* 90:1–7.

O'Gara, B. W., and J. D. Yoakum, eds. 1992. Pronghorn management guides. *Proceedings of the 15th Biennial Pronghorn Antelope Workshop,* Rock Springs, Wyo.

Oklahoma Department of Wildlife Conservation. 1992. *Bobwhite quail in Oklahoma.* Stillwater: Oklahoma Department of Wildlife Conservation.

O'Meara, T. E., J. B. Haufler, L. H. Stelter, and J. G. Nagy. 1981. Nongame wildlife responses to chaining of pinyon-juniper woodlands. *Journal of Wildlife Management* 45:381–89.

Orton, R. B. 1969. *Climates of the states—Texas.* Washington, D.C.: Environmental Data Service, U.S. Department of Commerce.

Osborne, D. A., B. J. Frawley, and H. P. Weeks. 1997. Effects of radio tags on captive northern bobwhite (*Colinus virginianus*) body composition and survival. *American Midland Naturalist* 137:213–24.

Overmire, T. G. 1963. The effects of grazing upon habitat utilization of dickcissel (*Spiza americana*) and Bell's vireo (*Vireo bellii*) in northcentral Oklahoma. Thesis, Oklahoma State University, Stillwater.

Paisley, C. 1968. *From cotton to quail.* Gainesville: University of Florida Press.

Palmer, E. J. 1920. The canyon flora of the Edwards Plateau of Texas. *Journal of Arnold Arboretum* 1:233–39.

Palmer, W. C. 1965. *Meteorological drought.* Weather Bureau Research Paper no. 45. Washington, D.C.: U.S. Department of Commerce.

Parmalee, P. W. 1952a. Contribution to the ecology of bobwhite quail in the post oak region of Texas. Dissertation, Agricultural and Mechanical College of Texas, College Station.

———. 1952b. Ecto- and endoparasites of the bobwhite: Their numbers, species, and possible importance in the health and vigor of quail. *Transactions of the North American Wildlife Conference* 17:174–88.

———. 1953a. Food and cover relationships of the bobwhite quail in east-central Texas. *Ecology* 34:758–70.

———. 1953b. Food habits of the feral house cat in east-central Texas. *Journal of Wildlife Management* 17:375–76.

———. 1953c. Hunting pressure and its effect on bobwhite quail populations in east-central Texas. *Journal of Wildlife Management* 17:341–45.

———. 1954. Food habits of the great horned owl and barn owl in East Texas. *Auk* 71:469–70.

———. 1955. Some factors affecting nesting success of the bobwhite quail in east-central Texas. *American Midland Naturalist* 53:45–55.

Parmalee, P. W., and M. A. Price. 1953. *Brücellia illustris* (Kellogg) and other ectoparasites from the bobwhite quail in Texas. *Journal of Parasitology* 39:222–23.

Parsons, D. S., R. M. Whiting Jr., X. Liu, and D. R. Dietz. 2000. Food plot use by juvenile northern bobwhites in East Texas. *Proceedings of the National Quail Symposium* 4:71–74.

Parsons, D. S., R. M. Whiting Jr., X. Liu, B. S. Mueller, and S. L. Cook. 2000. Reproduction of relocated and resident northern bobwhites in East Texas. *Proceedings of the National Quail Symposium* 4:132–36.

Pedersen, E. K. 1994. Impact of the red imported fire ant on newly-hatched northern bobwhite. Thesis, Texas A&M University, College Station.

Pedersen, E. K., W. E. Grant, and M. T. Longnecker. 1996. Effects of red imported fire ants on newly-hatched northern bobwhite. *Journal of Wildlife Management* 60:164–69.

Peebles, E. D., J. D. Cheaney, K. M. Vaughn, M. A. Latour, T. W. Smith, R. L. Haynes, and C. R. Boyle. 1996. Changes in gonadal weights, serum lipids, and glucose during maturation in the juvenile northern bobwhite quail (*Colinus virginianus*). *Poultry Science* 75:1411–16.

Pence, D. B. 1972. The genus *Oxyspirura* (Nematoda: Thelaziidae) from birds in Louisiana. *Proceedings of the Helminthological Society of Washington* 39:23–28.

———. 1975. Eyeworms (Nematoda: Thelaziidae) from West Texas quail. *Proceedings of the Helminthological Society of Washington* 42:181–83.

Pence, D. B., J. T. Murphy, F. S. Guthery, and T. B. Doerr. 1983. Indications of seasonal variation in the helminth fauna of the lesser prairie chicken, *Tympanuchus pallidicinctus* (Ridgway) (Tetraonidae), from northwestern Texas. *Proceedings of the Helminthological Society of Washington* 50:345–47.

Pence, D. B., and D. L. Sell. 1979. Helminths of the lesser prairie chicken, *Tympanuchus pallidicintus* (Ridgway) (Tetraonidae), from the Texas Panhandle. *Proceedings of the Helminthological Society of Washington* 46:146–49.

Pence, D. B., V. E. Young, and F. S. Guthery. 1980. Helminths of the ring-necked pheasant, *Phasianus colchicus* (Gmelin) (Phasianidae), from the Texas Panhandle. *Proceedings of the Helminthological Society of Washington* 47:144–47.

Peoples, A. D. 1992. Production, utilization and nutritional value of supplemental feed to northern bobwhites in western Oklahoma. Thesis, Oklahoma State University, Stillwater.

Peoples, A. D., S. J. DeMaso, S. A. Cox, and E. S. Parry. 1996. Bobwhite reproductive strategies in western Oklahoma. *Proceedings of the Texas Quail Short Course* 2:1–6.

Peoples, A. D., R. L. Lochmiller, D. M. Leslie Jr., and D. M. Engle. 1994. Producing northern bobwhite food on sandy soils in semiarid mixed prairies. *Wildlife Society Bulletin* 22:204–11.

Perez, M., S. E. Henke, and A. M. Fedynich. 2001. Detection of aflatoxin-contaminated grain by three granivorous bird species. *Journal of Wildlife Diseases* 37:358–61.

Perez, R. M. 1996. Survival and movement behavior of captive-raised and wild northern bobwhite quail in the coastal sand plain of Texas. Thesis, Southwest Texas University, San Marcos.

Perez, R. M., J. F. Gallagher, and M. C. Frisbie. 2002. Fine scale influence of weather on northern bobwhite abundance, breeding success, and harvest. *Proceedings of the National Quail Symposium* 5:106–10.

Perez, R. M., D. E. Wilson, and K. D. Gruen. 2002. Survival and flight characteristics of captive-reared and wild northern bobwhite in southern Texas. *Proceedings of the National Quail Symposium* 5:81–85.

Persson, O., and P. Ohrstrom. 1989. A new avian mating system: Ambisexual polygamy in the penduline tit *Remiz pendulinus. Ornis Scandinavica* 20:105–11.

Peterjohn, B. G., and J. R. Sauer. 1999. Population status of North American grassland birds. *Studies in Avian Biology* 19:27–44.

Peterson, M. J. 1991a. The Wildlife Society publications are appropriate outlets for the results of host-parasite interaction studies. *Wildlife Society Bulletin* 19:360–69.

———. 1991b. Wildlife parasitism, science, and management policy. *Journal of Wildlife Management* 55:782–89.

———. 1996. The endangered Attwater's prairie chicken and an analysis of prairie grouse helminthic endoparasitism. *Ecography* 19:424–31.

———. 1999. Quail management in Texas: A rational approach. Pages 124–31 in K. A. Cearley, ed., *Preserving Texas' quail heritage into the 21st century.* Abilene: Texas Agricultural Extension Service.

———. 2001. Northern bobwhite and scaled quail abundance and hunting regulation: A Texas example. *Journal of Wildlife Management* 65:828–37.

Peterson, M. J., R. Aguirre, P. J. Ferro, D. A. Jones, T. A. Lawyer, M. N. Peterson, and N. J. Silvy. 2002. Infectious disease survey of Rio Grande wild turkeys in the Edwards Plateau of Texas. *Journal of Wildlife Diseases* 38:826–33.

Peterson, M. J., D. F. Cowman, M. R. Krohn, R. D. Brown, and A. Vedlitz. 2000. *Private lands stewardship and conservation: Symposium report.* College Station: Center for Public Leadership Studies, George Bush School of Government and Public Service and Institute of Renewable Natural Resources, College of Agriculture and Life Sciences, Texas A&M University System.

Peterson, M. J., P. J. Ferro, M. N. Peterson, R. Sullivan, B. E. Toole, and N. J. Silvy. 2002. Infectious disease survey of lesser prairie chickens in the northern Rolling Plains of Texas. *Journal of Wildlife Diseases* 38:834–39.

Peterson, M. J., and R. M. Perez. 2000. Is quail hunting self regulatory? Northern bobwhite and scaled quail abundance and quail hunting in Texas. *Proceedings of the National Quail Symposium* 4:85–91.

Peterson, M. J., J. R. Purvis, J. R. Lichtenfels, T. M. Craig, N. O. Dronen Jr., and N. J. Silvy. 1998. Serologic and parasitologic survey of the endangered Attwater's prairie chicken. *Journal of Wildlife Diseases* 34:137–44.

Peterson, M. J., X. B. Wu, and P. Rho. 2002. Rangewide trends in land use and northern bobwhite abundance: An exploratory analysis. *Proceedings of the National Quail Symposium* 5:35–44.

Pleasant, G. D. 2003. Nesting ecology, health and survival of the scaled quail in the Southern High Plains of Texas. Thesis, Texas Tech University, Lubbock.

Pleasant, G. D., C. B. Dabbert, and R. B. Mitchell. 2003. Evaluation of the moisture-facilitated nest depredation hypothesis in a semiarid environment. *Wilson Bulletin* 115:344–47.

Poincaré, H. 1952. *Science and hypotheses.* New York: Dover Publications.

Pollock, K. H., C. T. Moore, W. R. Davidson, F. E. Kellogg, and G. L. Doster. 1989. Survival rates of bobwhite quail based on band recovery analyses. *Journal of Wildlife Management* 53:1–6.

Pollock, K. H., S. R. Winterstein, C. M. Bunck, and P. D. Curtis. 1989. Survival analysis in telemetry studies: The staggered entry design. *Journal of Wildlife Management* 53:7–15.

Porter S. D., A. Bhatkar, R. Mulder, S. B. Vinson, and J. D. Clair. 1991. Distribution and density of polygyne fire ants (Hymenoptera: Formicidae) in Texas. *Journal of Economic Entomology* 84:866–74.

Porter, S. D., and D. A. Savignano. 1990. Invasion of polygyne fire ants decimates native ants and disrupts arthropod community. *Ecology* 71:2095–2106.

Potts, G. R. 1986. *The partridge: Pesticides, predation and conservation.* London: Collins.

Potts, G. R., A. S. Tapper, and P. J. Hudson. 1984. Population fluctuations in red grouse: Analysis of bag records and a simulation model. *Journal of Animal Ecology* 53:21–36.

Pough, R. H. 1948. The arguments against the annual stocking of already inhabited coverts with artificially reared game birds. *Transactions of the North American Wildlife Conference* 13:228–35.

Powell, A. M. 1998. *Trees and shrubs of the Trans-Pecos and adjacent areas.* Austin: University of Texas Press.

———. 2000. *Grasses of the Trans-Pecos and adjacent areas.* Marathon, Tex.: Iron Mountain Press.

Powell, J. 1968. Rodent numbers on different brush control treatments in South Texas. *Texas Journal of Science* 20:69–76.

Prasad, N. L. N. S., and F. S. Guthery. 1986. Drinking by northern bobwhite in Texas. *Wilson Bulletin* 98:485–86.

Provencher, L., N. M. Gobris, and L. A. Brennan. 2002. Effects of hardwood reduction on winter birds in northwest Florida longleaf pine sandhill forests. *Auk* 119:71–87.

Provencher, L., N. W. Gobris, L. A. Brennan, D. L. Gordon, and J. L. Hardesty. 2002. Breeding bird response to midstory hardwood reduction in Florida sandhill longleaf pine forests. *Journal of Wildlife Management* 66:641–61.

Puckett, K. M., W. E. Palmer, P. T. Bromley, J. R. Anderson, and T. L. Sharpe. 2000. Effects of filter strips on habitat use and home range of northern bobwhites on Alligator River National Wildlife Refuge. *Proceedings of the National Quail Symposium* 4:26–31.

Purvis, J. R. 1995. Implications of Canada, snow, and white-fronted geese and northern bobwhite as disease reservoirs for the Attwater's prairie-chicken. Thesis, Texas A&M University, College Station.

Purvis, J. R., M. J. Peterson, N. O. Dronen, J. R. Lichtenfels, and N. J. Silvy. 1998. Northern bobwhites as disease indicators for the endangered Attwater's prairie chicken. *Journal of Wildlife Diseases* 34:348–54.

Pyrah, D. B., and H. E. Jorgenson. 1974. *Effects of ecological changes induced by sagebrush control techniques on nongame birds.* Job Progress Report W-7.2, November, 35–42. Helena: Montana Fish and Game Department.

Quist, C. F., D. I. Bounous, J. V. Kilburn, V. F. Nettles, and R. D. Wyatt. 2000. The effect of dietary aflatoxin on wild turkey poults. *Journal of Wildlife Diseases* 36:436–44.

Radomski, A. A. 1999. Physiological ecology of northern bobwhite reproduction. Dissertation, Texas A&M University–Kingsville and Texas A&M University, College Station.

Radomski, A. A., and F. S. Guthery. 2000. Theory of the hunter-covey interface. *Proceedings of the National Quail Symposium* 4:78–81.

Raitt, R. J., and R. D. Ohmart. 1966. Annual cycle of reproduction and molt in Gambel's quail of the Rio Grande Valley, southern New Mexico. *Condor* 68:541–61.

———. 1968. Sex and age ratios in Gambel's quail of the Rio Grande Valley, southern New Mexico. *Southwestern Naturalist* 13:27–34.

Ramos, M. G., ed. 1997. *Texas almanac.* College Station: Texas A&M University Press.

Ramsey, C. W., and M. J. Shult. 1984. *Bobwhite food development.* Leaflet 1665. College Station: Texas Agricultural Extension Service.

Reid, R. R. 1977. Correlation of habitat parameters and whistle-count densities of bobwhite (*Colinus virginianus*) and scaled quail (*Callipepla squamata*) in Texas. Thesis, Texas A&M University, College Station.

Reid, R. R., C. E. Grue, and N. J. Silvy. 1978. Breeding habitat of the bobwhite in Texas. *Proceedings of the Annual Conference of the Southeastern Association of Fish and Wildlife Agencies* 31:62–71.

———. 1979. Competition between bobwhite and scaled quail for habitat in Texas. *Proceedings of the Annual Conference of the Southeastern Association of Fish and Wildlife Agencies* 33:146–53.

———. 1993. Habitat requirements of breeding scaled quail in Texas. *Proceedings of the National Quail Symposium* 3:137–42.

Reid, V. H. 1953. Multiple land use: Timber, cattle, and bobwhite quail. *Transactions of the North American Wildlife Conference* 18:412–20.

Reid, V. H., and P. D. Goodrum. 1959. *Final progress report: Bobwhite quail on southern pine land.* Denver, Colo.: Branch of Wildlife Research, U.S. Fish and Wildlife Service.

———. 1960. Bobwhite quail: A product of longleaf pine forests. *Transactions of the North American Wildlife Conference* 25:241–52.

———. 1979. Winter feeding habits of quail in longleaf-slash pine habitat. U.S. Fish and Wildlife Service, Special Scientific Report—Wildlife no. 220. Denver, Colo.

Reisen, W. K., H. D. Lothrop, R. E. Chiles, R. Cusack, E. G. N. Green, Y. Fang, and M. Kensington. 2002. Persistence and amplification of St. Louis encephalitis virus in the Coachella Valley of California, 2000–2001. *Journal of Medical Entomology* 39:793–805.

Reisen, W. K., J. O. Lundstrom, T. W. Scott, B. F. Eldridge, R. E. Chiles, R. Cusack, V. M. Martinez, H. D. Lothrop, B. Gutiérrez, S. E. Wright, K. Boyce, and B. R. Hill. 2000. Patterns of avian seroprevalence to western equine encephalomyelitis and Saint Louis encephalitis viruses in California, USA. *Journal of Medical Entomology* 37:507–27.

Renwald, J. D., H. A. Wright, and J. T. Flinders. 1978. Effect of prescribed fire on bobwhite quail habitat in the Rolling Plains of Texas. *Journal of Range Management* 31:65–69.

Repenning, R. W., and R. F. Labisky. 1985. Effects of even-age timber management on bird communities of the longleaf pine forests in northern Florida. *Journal of Wildlife Management* 49:1088–98.

Reynolds, M. C., and P. R. Krausman. 1998. Effects of winter burning on birds in mesquite grassland. *Wildlife Society Bulletin* 26:867–76.

Rho, P. 2003. GIS-based multiple-scale study on scaled quail. Dissertation, Texas A&M University, College Station.

Rhyne, M. Z. 1998. Optimization of wildlife and recreation earnings for private landowners. Thesis, Texas A&M University–Kingsville.

Rice, S. M., F. S. Guthery, G. S. Spears, S. J. DeMaso, and B. H. Koerth. 1993. A precipitation-habitat model for northern bobwhites on semiarid rangeland. *Journal of Wildlife Management* 57:92–102.

Rickard, L. G. 1985. Proventricular lesions associated with natural and experimental infections of *Dispharynx nasuta* (Nematoda: Acuariidae). *Canadian Journal of Zoology* 63:2663–68.

Riggs, R. A., S. C. Bunting, and S. E. Daniels. 1996. Prescribed fire. Pages 295–319 in P. R. Krausman, ed., *Rangeland wildlife.* Denver, Colo.: The Society for Range Management.

Riskind, D. H., and A. G. Davis. 1975. Prairie management and restoration in the state parks of Texas. Pages 369–73 in M. K. Wali, ed., *Prairie: A multiple view.* Grand Forks: University of North Dakota Press.

Riskind, D. H., and D. D. Diamond. 1988. An introduction to environments and vegetation. Pages 1–16 in B. Amos and F. R. Gehlbach, eds., *Edwards Plateau vegetation.* Waco, Tex.: Baylor University Press.

Ritter, G. D., D. H. Ley, M. Levy, J. Guy, and H. J. Barnes. 1986. Intestinal cryptosporidiosis and reovirus isolation from bobwhite quail (*Colinus virginianus*) with enteritis. *Avian Diseases* 30:603–608.

Robel, R. J. 1993. Symposium wrap-up: What is missing? *Proceedings of the National Quail Symposium* 3:156–58.

Robertson, P. A., and A. A. Rosenburg. 1988. Harvesting gamebirds. Pages 177–201 in P. J. Hudson and M. R. W. Rands, eds., *Ecology and management of gamebirds*. Palo Alto, Calif.: BSP Professional Books.

Robertson, T. E., and T. W. Box. 1969. Interseeding sideoats grama on the Texas High Plains. *Journal of Range Management* 22:243–45.

Robinette, C. F., and P. D. Doerr. 1993. Survival of northern bobwhite on hunted and nonhunted study areas in the North Carolina sandhills. *Proceedings of the National Quail Symposium* 3:74–78.

Robles, J. T., S. I. Zibron, G. D. M. Martinez, C. Z. Hernandez, F. C. Sanchez, and L. A. T. Arambula. 2002. Population density of Montezuma quail (*Cyrtonyx montezumae*) in the northeastern region of the State of Mexico, Mexico. *Mexico Veterinarian* 33:255–63.

Rollins, D. 1980. Comparative ecology of bobwhite and scaled quail in mesquite grassland habitats. Thesis, Southwestern Oklahoma State University, Weatherford.

———. 1981. Diets of sympatric bobwhite and scaled quail in Oklahoma. *Proceedings of the Annual Conference of the Southeastern Association of Game and Fish Agencies* 35:239–48.

———. 1991. Creating your own reference seed collection. *Quail Unlimited Magazine* 10 (6): 63.

———. 1997a. Applied landscaping: A primer for brush sculptors. Pages 127–32 in D. Rollins, D. N. Ueckert, and C. G. Brown, eds., *Brush sculptors: Symposium proceedings*. San Angelo: Texas Agricultural Extension Service.

———. 1997b. Half-cutting mesquite trees to enhance loafing cover for quail. Page 149 in D. Rollins, D. N. Ueckert, and C. G. Brown, eds., *Brush sculptors: Symposium proceedings*. San Angelo: Texas Agricultural Extension Service.

———. 1999a. Is there a place for predator control in quail management? Pages 45–48 in K. A. Cearley, ed., *Preserving Texas' quail heritage into the 21st century: Symposium Proceedings*. College Station: Texas A&M University Agricultural Extension Service and Department of Wildlife and Fisheries Sciences, Texas A&M University System.

———. 1999b. *Key seed-producing plants for quail*. Color poster L-5083. College Station: Texas Cooperative Extension.

———. 2000. Status, ecology and management of scaled quail in West Texas. *Proceedings of the National Quail Symposium* 4:165–72.

———. 2002. Sustaining the "quail wave" in the southern Great Plains. *Proceedings of the National Quail Symposium* 5:48–56.

Rollins, D., F. C. Bryant, D. D. Waid, and L. C. Bradley. 1988. Deer response to brush management in Central Texas. *Wildlife Society Bulletin* 16:277–84.

Rollins, D., and J. F. Cadenhead 1995. *Woody plants for wildlife of the Rolling Plains*. Color Poster L-5064. College Station: Texas Cooperative Extension Service.

Rollins, D., and J. P. Carroll. 2001. Impacts of predation on northern bobwhite and scaled quail. *Wildlife Society Bulletin* 29:39–51.

Rollins, D., F. S. Guthery, and C. Richardson. 1993. Managing stocking rates to achieve wildlife goals. Pages 63–72 in J. R. Cox and J. F. Cadenhead, eds., *Managing livestock stocking rates on rangeland*. College Station: Texas Agricultural Extension Service.

Rollins, D., and L. Hysmith. 1997. *Upland game birds of Texas*. Color poster L-5186. College Station: Texas Cooperative Extension Service.

Rollins, D., D. W. Steinbach, and C. G. Brown. 2000. The Bobwhite Brigade: An innovative approach to wildlife extension education. *Proceedings of the National Quail Symposium* 4:227–31.

Rollins, D., D. N. Ueckert, and C. G. Brown, eds., 1997. *Brush sculptors: Symposium proceedings*. San Angelo: Texas Agricultural Extension Service.

Roseberry, J. L. 1974. Relationships between selected population phenomena and annual bobwhite age ratios. *Journal of Wildlife Management* 38:665–73.

Roseberry, J. L., and L. M. David. 1994. The Conservation Reserve Program and northern bobwhite population trends in Illinois. *Transactions of the Illinois State Academy of Science* 87:61–70.

Roseberry, J. L., D. L. Ellsworth, and W. D. Klimstra. 1987. Comparative post-release behavior and survival of wild, semi-wild, and game farm bobwhites. *Wildlife Society Bulletin* 15:449–55.

Roseberry, J. L., and W. D. Klimstra. 1984. *Population ecology of the bobwhite.* Carbondale: Southern Illinois University Press.

Roseberry, J. L., and S. D. Sudkamp. 1998. Assessing the suitability of landscapes for northern bobwhite. *Journal of Wildlife Management* 62:895–902.

Rosene, W. 1969. The bobwhite quail—its life and management. New Brunswick, N.J.: Rutgers University Press.

Rosene, W., and J. D. Freeman. 1988. *A guide to and culture of flowering plants and their seed important to bobwhite quail.* Augusta, Ga.: Morris Communications Corporation.

Rosene, W., and D. W. Lay. 1963. Disappearance and visibility of quail remains. *Journal of Wildlife Management* 27:139–42.

Rosson, J. F. 2000. *Forest resources of East Texas, 1992.* U.S. Forest Service Resource Bulletin SRS 53. Washington, D.C.

Rotenberry, J. T., and J. A. Weins. 1998. Foraging patch selection by shrubsteppe sparrows. *Ecology* 79:1160–73.

Ruff, M. D. 1985. Life cycle and biology of *Eimeria lettyae* Sp. N. (Protozoa: Eimeriidae) from the northern bobwhite, *Colinus virginianus* (L.). *Journal of Wildlife Diseases* 21:361–70.

Ruff, M. D., and R. A. Norton. 1997. Nematodes and acanthocephalans. Pages 815–50 in B. W. Calnek, H. J. Barnes, C. W. Beard, L. R. McDougald, and Y. M. Saif, eds., *Diseases of poultry,* 10th ed. Ames: Iowa State University Press.

Ruff, M. D., and G. C. Wilkins. 1987. Pathogenicity of *Eimeria lettyae* Ruff, 1985 in the northern bobwhite (*Colinus virginianus* L.). *Journal of Wildlife Diseases* 23:121–26.

Russell, P. 1931. New Mexico's scaled quail investigations. *Proceedings of the American Game Conference* 18:226–29.

———. 1932. The scaled quail in New Mexico. Thesis, University of New Mexico, Albuquerque.

Ruthven, D. C., III., E. C. Hellgren, and S. L. Beasom. 1994. Effects of root plowing on deer condition, population status and diet. *Journal of Wildlife Management* 58:59–69.

Ryan, M. R., L. W. Burger, and E. W. Kurzejeski. 1998. The impact of CRP on avian wildlife: A review. *Journal of Production Agriculture* 11:61–66.

Ryder, R. A. 1980. Effects of grazing on bird habitats. Pages 51–66 in R. M. DeGraff and N. G. Tilghman, comps., *Management of western forests and grasslands for nongame birds.* USDA Forest Service, General Technical Report, INT-86. Ogden, Utah: Intermountain Forest and Range Experiment Station.

Saab, V. A., C. E. Bock, T. D. Rich, and D. S. Dobkin. 1995. Livestock grazing effects in western North America. Pages 311–53 in T. E. Martin and D. M. Finch, eds., *Ecology and management of neotropical migratory birds.* New York: Oxford University Press.

Saiwana, L. L. 1990. Range condition effects on scaled quail in southcentral New Mexico. Dissertation, New Mexico State University, Las Cruces.

Saiwana, L., J. L. Holechek, A. Tembo, R. Valdez, and M. Cardenas. 1998. Scaled quail use of different seral stages in the Chihuahuan Desert. *Journal of Wildlife Management* 62:550–56.

Sauer, J. R., J. E. Hines, and J. Fallon. 2002. *The North American Breeding Bird*

Survey: Results and analysis 1966–2001. Version 2002.1. Laurel, Md.: USGS Patuxent Wildlife Research Center.

Sawyer, P. E. 1973. Habitat use by scaled quail and other birds in southeastern New Mexico. Thesis, New Mexico State University, Las Cruces.

Schemnitz, S. D. 1961. *Ecology of the scaled quail in the Oklahoma Panhandle.* Wildlife Monograph 8.

———. 1964. Comparative ecology of bobwhite and scaled quail in the Oklahoma panhandle. *American Midland Naturalist* 71:429–33.

———. 1994. Scaled quail (*Callipepla squamata*). In A. Poole and F. Gill, eds., *The birds of North America, no. 106.* Washington, D.C.: The American Ornithologists' Union; Philadelphia: The Academy of Natural Sciences.

Schemnitz, S. D., J. L. Dye, and M. Cardenas. 1997. *Fall and winter foods of scaled and Gambel's quail in southwestern New Mexico.* New Mexico Agricultural Experiment Station Bulletin 777. Las Cruces: New Mexico State University.

Schmidly, D. J. 2002. *Texas natural history: A century of change.* Lubbock: Texas Tech University Press.

Schmidly, D. J., and C. O. Martin. 1997. *The mammals of Trans-Pecos Texas: Including Big Bend National Park and Guadalupe Mountains National Park.* College Station: Texas A&M University Press.

Schmidt, G. D., and R. E. Kuntz. 1977. Revision of *Mediorhynchus* Van Cleave 1916 (Acanthocephala) with a key to species. *Journal of Parasitology* 63:500–507.

Schroeder, R. L. 1985. *Habitat suitability models: Northern bobwhite.* U.S. Fish and Wildlife Service Biological Report 82 (10.104). Washington, D.C.

Schulz, C. A., D. M. Leslie, R. L. Lochmiller, and D. M. Engle. 1992a. Autumn and winter bird populations in herbicide-treated Cross Timbers in Oklahoma. *American Midland Naturalist* 127:215–23.

———. 1992b. Herbicide effects on Cross Timbers breeding birds. *Journal of Range Management* 45:407–11.

Scifres, C. J. 1975. Fall application of herbicides improves Macartney rose-infested coastal prairie rangelands. *Journal of Wildlife Management* 28:483–86.

———. 1980. *Brush management: Principles and practices for Texas and the Southwest.* College Station: Texas A&M University Press.

Scifres, C. J., and W. T. Hamilton. 1993. *Prescribed burning for brushland management: The South Texas example.* College Station: Texas A&M University Press.

Scifres, C. J., and B. H. Koerth. 1986. Habitat alterations in mixed brush from variable rate herbicide patterns. *Wildlife Society Bulletin* 14:345–56.

Scifres, C. J., and J. L. Mutz. 1978. Herbaceous vegetation changes following applications of tebuthiuron for brush control. *Journal of Range Management* 31:375–78.

Scott, T. G. 1985. *Bobwhite thesaurus.* Edgefield, S.C.: International Quail Foundation.

Scriber, J. M., and F. Slansky Jr. 1981. The nutritional ecology of immature insects. *Annual Review of Entomology* 26:183–211.

Sellards, E. H., W. S. Adkins, and F. B. Plummer. 1932. *The geology of Texas.* Vol. 1: *Stratigraphy.* University of Texas Bulletin 3232. Austin.

Senzota, R. B. M. 1986. Effects of prescribed burning on a small mammal community in Post Oak Savannah, Texas. Dissertation, Texas A&M University, College Station.

Sermons, W. O., and D. W. Speake. 1987. Production of second broods by northern bobwhites. *Wilson Bulletin* 99:285–86.

Serventy, D. L. 1971. Biology of desert birds. Pages 287–339 in D. S. Farner and J. R. King, eds., *Avian biology,* vol. 1. New York: Academic Press.

Seyffert, K. D. 2001. *Birds of the Texas Panhandle: Their status, distribution, and history.* College Station: Texas A&M University Press.

Sharp, J. S. 1992. *Regional outlook: High Plains.* Austin: Comptroller of Public Accounts, State of Texas.

Shaw, J. L. 1990. Effects of the caecal nematode *Trichostrongylus tenuis* on egg-laying by captive red grouse. *Research in Veterinary Science* 48:59–63.

Shipley, D. A. 1911. "Grouse disease"—strongylosis: Part I—the threadworms. Pages 207–18 in *Committee of Inquiry on Grouse Disease, The grouse in health and disease,* vol. 1. London: Smith, Elder.

Shupe, T. E., F. S. Guthery, and R. L. Bingham. 1990. Vulnerability of bobwhite sex and age classes to harvest. *Wildlife Society Bulletin* 18:24–26.

Silvy, N. J. 1993. *Supplemental feeding application of northern bobwhite in South Texas.* Cd. Victoria, Tamulipas, Mexico: V Symposium Internacional de Memoria, Facultad de Agronomia, Universidad Autonoma de Tamaulipas.

———. 1999. Predator management: A counterpoint. Pages 49–52 in K. A. Cearley, ed., *Preserving Texas' quail heritage into the 21st century: Symposium proceedings.* College Station: Texas Agricultural Extension Service and Department of Wildlife and Fisheries Sciences, Texas A&M University System.

Silvy, N. J., M. J. Peterson, J. R. Purvis, and A. S. Bridges. 2000. Relationships of fur market conditions to Texas quail populations. *Proceedings of the Annual Conference of the Southeastern Association of Fish and Wildlife Agencies* 54:266–73.

Simon, F. 1940. The parasites of the sage grouse, *Centrocercus urophasianus. University of Wyoming Publications* 7:77–100.

Simpson, R. C. 1976. *Certain aspects of the bobwhite quail's life history and population dynamics in southwest Georgia.* Game and Fish Division Technical Bulletin WL 1. Atlanta: Georgia Department National Resources.

Sims, P. L., and P. G. Risser. 2000. Grasslands. Pages 323–56 in M. G. Barbour and W. D. Billings, eds., *North American terrestrial vegetation,* 2d ed. Cambridge: Cambridge University Press.

Sisson, D. C., D. W. Speake, and H. L. Stribling. 2000. Survival of northern bobwhites on areas with and without liberated bobwhites. *Proceedings of the National Quail Symposium* 4:92–94.

Sisson, D. C., H. L. Stribling, and S. D. Mitchell. 2002. Northern bobwhite population response to intensive modification of a farm landscape in middle Georgia. *Proceedings of the National Quail Symposium* 5:160.

Sisson, D. C., H. L. Stribling, and D. W. Speake. 2000. Effects of supplemental feeding on home range size and survival of northern bobwhites in south Georgia. *Proceedings of the National Quail Symposium* 4:128–31.

Sitton, T. 1995. *Backwoodsmen: Stockmen and hunters along a Big Thicket river valley.* Norman: University of Oklahoma Press.

Slater, S. C. 1996. An evaluation of prickly pear (*Opuntia* spp.) as a predator deterrent in nest site selection by northern bobwhite (*Colinus virginianus*). Thesis, Angelo State University, San Angelo.

Slater, S. C., D. Rollins, R. C. Dowler, and C. B. Scott. 2001. *Opuntia:* A "prickly paradigm" for quail management in west-central Texas. *Wildlife Society Bulletin* 29:713–19.

Smeins, F. E. 1980. Natural role of fire on the Edwards Plateau. Pages 4–16 in L. D. White, ed., *Prescribed burning on the Edwards Plateau of Texas.* College Station: Texas Agriculture Extension Service, Texas A&M University.

Smeins, F. E., D. D. Diamond, and C. W. Hanselka. 1991. Coastal Prairie. Pages 269–90 in R. T. Coupland, ed., *Natural grassland: Introduction and western hemisphere.* Amsterdam: Elsevier.

Smeins, F. E., and R. D. Slack. 1982. *Fundamentals of ecology laboratory manual.* Dubuque, Iowa: Kendall-Hunt.

Smith, A. P. 1917. Some birds of the Davis Mountains, Texas. *Condor* 19:161–65.

Smith, C. C. 1940. The effect of overgrazing and erosion upon the biota of the mixed grass prairie of Oklahoma. *Ecology* 21:381–97.

Smith, D. S., and J. R. Cain. 1984. Criteria for age classification of juvenile scaled quail. *Journal of Wildlife Management* 48:187–91.

Smith, G., J. L. Holechek, and M. Cardenas. 1996. Wildlife numbers on excellent and good condition Chihuahuan Desert rangelands: An observation. *Journal of Range Management* 49:489–93.

Smith, R. H., and S. Gallizioli. 1965. Predicting hunter success by means of a spring call count of Gambel's quail. *Journal of Wildlife Management* 29: 806–13.

Sneed, K., and G. Jones. 1950. A preliminary study of coccidiosis in Oklahoma quail. *Journal of Wildlife Management* 14:169–74.

Snyder, W. D. 1967. *Experimental habitat improvement for scaled quail.* Technical Publication no. 19. Denver: Colorado Game, Fish and Parks Department.

Soil Survey Staff. 1981. *Land resource regions and major land resource areas of the United States.* Agriculture Handbook 296, rev. ed. Washington, D.C.: U.S. Department of Agriculture, Soil Conservation Service.

Sorola, S. K. 1986. *Investigation of Mearns' quail distribution.* Texas Parks and Wildlife Department Final Report Project W-108-R-9. Austin.

Sowls, L. K. 1960. Results of a banding study of Gambel's quail in southern Arizona. *Journal of Wildlife Management* 24:185–90.

Speake, D. W. 1967. Effects of controlled burning on bobwhite quail populations and habitat on an experimental area in the Alabama Piedmont. *Proceedings of the Annual Southeastern Association of Game and Fish Commissioners* 20:19–32.

Spears, G. S., F. S. Guthery, S. M. Rice, S. J. DeMaso, and B. Zaiglin. 1993. Optimum seral stage for northern bobwhites as influenced by site productivity. *Journal of Wildlife Management* 57:805–11.

Springs, A. J., Jr. 1952. *Relation of bobwhite quail to mesquite grassland type.* FA Report Series no. 9. Austin: Texas Game and Fish Commission.

Stabler, R. M., and N. J. Kitzmiller. 1976. *Plasmodium* (Giovannolaia) *pedioecetii* from gallinaceous birds of Colorado. *Journal of Parasitology* 62:539–44.

Stabler, R. M., N. J. Kitzmiller, and C. E. Braun. 1974. Hematozoa from Colorado birds. IV. Galliformes. *Journal of Parasitology* 60:536–37.

Staller, E. L. 2001. Identifying predators and fates of northern bobwhite nests using miniature video cameras. Thesis, University of Georgia, Athens.

Stamp, N. E., and R. D. Ohmart. 1978. Resource utilization by desert rodents in the lower Sonoran desert. *Ecology* 59:700–707.

Stanford, J. W. 1976. Keys to the vascular plants of the Texas Edwards Plateau and adjacent areas. Brownwood, Tex.: Published by author.

Stangl, F. B., Jr., T. S. Schafer, J. R. Goetz, and W. Pinchak. 1992. Opportunistic use of modified and disturbed habitat by the Texas kangaroo rat (*Dipodomys elator*). *Texas Journal of Science* 44:25–35.

Steen, M. O. 1948. Shall we improve habitat or stock for wildlife? *Outdoor America* 13:4–10.

Steenburgh, W. F., and P. L. Warren. 1977. *Ecological investigations of natural community status at Organ Pipe National Monument.* Cooperative National Park Research Study Unit, Technical Report 3:1–152. Tucson: University of Arizona.

Sterling, K. B. 1989. Builders of the U.S. Biological Survey, 1885–1930. *Journal of Forest History* 33:180–87.

Stiles, J. H., and R. H. Jones. 1998. Distribution of the red imported fire ant, *Solenopsis invicta,* in road and powerline habitats. *Landscape Ecology* 13:335–46.

Stoddard, H. L. 1931. *The bobwhite quail: Its habits, preservation and increase.* New York: Scribner's.

Stokes, A. W. 1967. Behavior of the bobwhite, *Colinus virginianus. Auk* 84:1–33.

Stormer, F. A. 1981. *Characteristics of scaled quail loafing coverts in northwest Texas.* USDA Forest Service Research Note. RM-395. Fort Collins, Colo.: U.S. Department of Agriculture, Forest Service.

———. 1984. Night-roosting habitat of scaled quail. *Journal of Wildlife Management* 48:191–97.

Stransky, J. J. 1971. *Managing for quail and timber in longleaf pine forests.* Texas Forestry Paper no. 9. Nacogdoches, Tex.: School of Forestry, Stephen F. Austin State University.

Strecker, J. K. 1912. The birds of Texas, an annotated check-list. *Baylor University Bulletin* 25:1–69.

———. 1930. Field notes on western Texas birds. Pages 3–14 in *Contributions from Baylor University Museum,* pt. 1, vol. 22.

Stritzke, J. F., D. M. Engle, J. T. McCollum. 1991. Vegetation management in the Cross Timbers: Response of woody vegetation to herbicides and burning. *Weed Technology* 5:400–405.

Stromberg, M. R. 1990. Habitat, movements and roost characteristics of Montezuma quail in southeastern Arizona. *Condor* 92:229–36.

———. 2000. Montezuma quail (*Cyrtonyx montezumae*). In A. Poole and F. Gill, eds., *The birds of North America, no. 524.* Philadelphia: The Birds of North America.

Suchy, W. J., and R. J. Munkel. 1993. Breeding strategies of the northern bobwhite in marginal habitat. *Proceedings of the National Quail Symposium* 3:69–73.

———. 2000. Survival rates for northern bobwhites on two areas with different levels of harvest. *Proceedings of the National Quail Symposium* 4:140–46.

Swank, W. G. 1956. *Quail no. 5–56.* Game Bulletin. Phoenix: Arizona Game and Fish Department.

Swank, W. G., and S. Gallizioli. 1954. The influence of hunting and of rainfall upon Gambel's quail populations. *Transactions of North American Wildlife and Natural Resources Conference* 19:283–96.

Swarth, H. S. 1909. Distribution and molt of the Mearns quail. *Condor* 11:39–43.

Tanner, G. W., J. M. Inglis, and L. H. Blankenship. 1978. Acute impact of herbicide strip treatment on mixed-brush white-tailed deer habitat on the northern Rio Grande Plain. *Journal of Range Management* 31:386–91.

Tapia, R. J., Z. S. Ibarra, M. G. D. Mendoza, H. C. Zaragoza, and L. A. A. Tarango. 2002. Densidad poblacional de la cordorni Montezuma (*Cyrtonyx montezumae*) en la region noroeste del estado de Mexico, Mexico. *Mexico Veterinarian* 33:255–63.

Tarrant, B. 2002. Ecology and management of Gambel's quail in Texas. Pages 9–10 in L. A. Harveson, P. M. Harveson, and C. Richardson, eds., *Proceedings of the Trans-Pecos Wildlife Conference.* Alpine, Tex.: Sul Ross State University.

Taylor, J. D., II, L. W. Burger Jr., S. W. Manley, and L. A. Brennan. 2000. Seasonal survival and cause-specific mortality of northern bobwhites in Mississippi. *Proceedings of the National Quail Symposium* 4:103–107.

Taylor, J. S. 1991. Aspects of northern bobwhite reproductive biology in South Texas. Thesis, Texas A&I University, Kingsville.

Taylor, J. S., K. E. Church, and D. H. Rusch. 1999. Microhabitat selection by nesting and brood-rearing northern bobwhite in Kansas. *Journal of Wildlife Management* 63:686–94.

Taylor, J. S., K. E. Church, D. H. Rusch, and J. R. Cary. 1999. Macrohabitat effects on summer survival, movements, and clutch success of northern bobwhites in Kansas. *Journal of Wildlife Management* 63:675–85.

Taylor, J. S., and F. S. Guthery. 1994. Components of northern bobwhite brood habitat in southern Texas. *Southwestern Naturalist* 39:73–77.

Taylor, R. B., J. Rutledge, and J. G. Herrera. 1997. *A field guide to common South Texas shrubs.* Austin: Texas Parks and Wildlife Department Press.

Taylor, T. T. 1989. White-tailed deer response to habitat attributes in the Rio Grande Plains of South Texas. Dissertation, Texas A&M University, College Station.

Taylor, W. P., ed. 1956. *The deer of North America.* Harrisburg, Penn.: Stackpole.

Taylor, W. P., C. T. Vorhies, and J. B. Lister. 1935. The relation of jackrabbits to grazing in southern Arizona. *Journal of Forestry* 33:490–98.

Teel, P. D., S. W. Hopkins, W. A. Donahue, and O. F. Strey. 1998. Population dynamics of immature *Amblyomma maculatum* (Acari: Ixodidae) and other ectoparasites on meadowlarks and northern bobwhite quail resident to the Coastal Prairie of Texas. *Journal of Medical Entomology* 35:483–88.

Teer, J. G. 1996. The white-tailed deer: Natural history and management. Pages 193–210 in P. R. Krausman, ed., *Rangeland wildlife*. Denver, Colo.: The Society for Range Management.

Tewes, M. E. 1982. Response of selected vertebrate populations to burning of gulf cordgrass. Thesis, Texas A&M University, College Station.

Tewes, M. E., J. M. Mock, and J. H. Young. 2002. Bobcat predation on quail, birds, and mesomammals. *Proceedings of the National Quail Symposium* 5:65–70.

Tewes, M. E., and D. J. Schmidly. 1987. The neotropical felids: Jaguar, ocelot, margay and jaguarundi. Pages 703–705 in M. Novak, J. Baker, M. E. Obbard, and B. Mulloch, eds., *Wild furbearer management and conservation in North America*. Ottawa, Ontario, Canada: Ontario Ministry of Natural Resources.

Texas Game, Fish and Oyster Commission. 1945. *Principal game birds and mammals of Texas*. Austin: Von Boeckmann-Jones.

Texas Parks and Wildlife Department. 2002. *Land and water resources conservation and recreation plan*. Austin: Texas Parks and Wildlife Department.

Texas Quail Technical Support Committee. 2003. *Texas quail conservation initiative*. Austin: Texas Parks and Wildlife Department.

Texas State Data Center. 2001. *Projections of the population of Texas and counties in Texas by age, sex and race/ethnicity for 2000–2040*. College Station: Texas A&M University.

Tharp, J. E. 1971. A study of scaled and bobwhite quail with special emphasis on habitat requirements and brush control. Thesis, Texas Tech University, Lubbock.

Thogmartin, W. E., J. L. Roseberry, and A. Woolf. 2002. Cyclicity in northern bobwhites: A time analytic review of the evidence. *Proceedings of the National Quail Symposium* 5:192–200.

Thomas, J. W. 1959. *White-tailed deer populations*. Progress Report, Pittman-Robertson Project, W-62-R-6, Job 6. Austin: Texas Game, Fish and Oyster Commission.

Thompson, B. C. 1993. A successful Gambel's quail nest in a suburban areas. *Southwestern Naturalist* 38:174–75.

Thompson, C., and S. E. Henke. 2000. Effect of climate and type of storage container on aflatoxin production in corn and its associated risks to wildlife species. *Journal of Wildlife Diseases* 36:172–79.

Thornthwaite, C. W. 1948. An approach toward a rational classification of climate. *Geographical Review* 38:55–94.

Tolleson, D., D. Rollins, W. E. Pinchak, and L. J. Hunt. 1995. Feral hogs in the Rolling Plains of Texas: Perspectives, problems, and potential. *Great Plains Wildlife Damage Management Control Workshop* 12:124–28.

Tompkins, D. M., and M. Begon. 1999. Parasites can regulate wildlife populations. *Parasitology Today* 15:311–13.

Tompkins, D. M., A. P. Dobson, P. Arneberg, M. E. Begon, I. M. Cattadori, J. V. Greenman, J. A. P. Heesterbeek, P. J. Hudson, D. Newborn, A. Pugliese, A. P. Rizzoli, R. Rosà, F. Rosso, and K. Wilson. 2002. Parasites and host population dynamics. Pages 45–62 in P. J. Hudson, A. Rizzoli, B. T. Grenfell, H. Heesterbeek, and A. P. Dobson, eds., *The ecology of wildlife diseases*. Oxford: Oxford University Press.

Townsend, D. E., III, R. L. Lochmiller, S. J. DeMaso, D. M. Leslie, A. D. Peoples, S. A. Cox, and E. S. Parry. 1999. Using supplemental food and its influence on survival of northern bobwhite (*Colinus virginianus*). *Wildlife Society Bulletin* 27:1074–81.

Townsend, D. E., II, R. E. Masters, R. L. Lochmiller, D. M. Leslie Jr., S. J. DeMaso, and A. D. Peoples. 2001. Characteristics of nest sites of northern bobwhites in western Oklahoma. *Journal of Range Management* 54:260–64.

Travis, B. V. 1938. Fire ant problem in the Southeast with special reference to quail. *Transactions of the North American Wildlife Conference* 3:705–708.

Trefethen, J. B. 1975. *An American crusade for wildlife.* New York: Winchester Press.

Tripathy, D. N., and W. M. Reed. 1997. Pox. Pages 643–59 in B. W. Calnek, H. J. Barnes, C. W. Beard, L. R. McDougald, and Y. M. Saif, eds., *Diseases of poultry,*10th ed. Ames: Iowa State University Press.

Trippensee, R. E. 1948. *Wildlife management: Upland game and general principles.* New York: McGraw-Hill.

Tschinkel, W. R. 1988. Distribution of fire ants *Solenopsis invicta* and *S. geminata* (Hymenoptera: Formicidae) in northern Florida in relation to habitat and disturbance. *Annals of the Entomological Society of America* 81:76–81.

Tucker, W. J. 1934. *Annual report—Game, Fish and Oyster Commission for the fiscal year 1933–34.* Austin: Texas Game, Fish and Oyster Commission.

———. 1937. *Annual report—Game, Fish and Oyster Commission for the fiscal year 1936–37.* Austin: Texas Game, Fish and Oyster Commission.

———. 1938. *Annual report—Game, Fish and Oyster Commission for the fiscal year 1937–38.* Austin: Texas Game, Fish and Oyster Commission.

———. 1939. *Annual report—Game, Fish and Oyster Commission for the fiscal year 1938–39.* Austin: Texas Game, Fish and Oyster Commission.

———. 1940. *Annual report—Game, Fish and Oyster Commission for the fiscal year 1939–40.* Austin: Texas Game, Fish and Oyster Commission.

———. 1941. *Annual report—Game, Fish and Oyster Commission for the fiscal year 1940–41.* Austin: Texas Game, Fish and Oyster Commission.

Turner, D. 1999. Food plots for wildlife. Pages 59–62 in K.A. Cearley, ed., *Preserving Texas' quail heritage into the 21st century.* San Angelo: Texas Agricultural Extension Service.

Ueckert, D. N., J. L. Peterson, R. L. Potter, J. D. Whipple, and M. W. Wagner. 1988. Managing prickly pear with herbicides and fire. Pages 10–15 in *Research reports: Sheep and goat, wool and mohair.* Consolidated Progress Report 4565–4591. San Angelo: Texas Agricultural Experiment Station.

U.S. Fish and Wildlife Service. 2002. 2001 national survey of fishing, hunting and wildlife-associated activities. Shepardstown, W.Va.: National Conservation Training Center Publication Unit.

Uzzell, P. B., T. D. Moore, and O. C. Wallmo. 1953. *Quail in Texas.* Progress Report, Pittman-Robertson Project, W-62-R-6, Job 1. Austin: Texas Game, Fish and Oyster Commission.

Vallentine, J. F. 1989. *Range development and improvements.* San Diego, Calif.: Academic Press.

Vance, D. R., and J. A. Ellis. 1972. Bobwhite populations and hunting on Illinois public hunting areas. *Proceedings of the National Quail Symposium* 1:165–74.

Van't Hul, J. T., R. S. Lutz, and N. E. Mathews. 1997. Impact of prescribed burning on vegetation and bird abundance at Matagorda Island, Texas. *Journal of Range Management* 50:346–50.

Van Tyne, J., and G. M. Sutton. 1937. *The birds of Brewster County, Texas.* Miscellaneous Publications no. 37. Ann Arbor: Museum of Zoology, University of Michigan.

Vega, J. H., and J. H. Rappole. 1994. Effects of scrub mechanical management on the nongame bird community in the Rio Grande Plains of Texas. *Wildlife Society Bulletin* 22:165–71.

Venard, C. 1933. Helminths and coccidia from Ohio bobwhite. *Journal of Parasitology* 19:205–208.

Vermeire, L. T., R. B. Mitchell, S. D. Fuhlendorf, and R. L. Gillen. 2004. Patch burning affects grazing distribution. *Journal of Range Management* 57:248–52.

Vickery, P. D., and J. R. Herkert. 2001. Recent advances in grassland bird research: Where do we go from here? *Auk* 118:11–15.

Vinson, S. B., and A. A. Sorenson. 1986. *Imported fire ants: Life history and impact.* Austin: Texas Department of Agriculture.

Vleck, C. M. 2002. Hormonal control of incubation behavior. Pages 54–62 in D. C. Deeming, ed., *Avian incubation: Behaviour, environment, and evolution.* Oxford: Oxford University Press.

Vorhies, C. T. 1928. Do southwestern quail require water? *American Naturalist* 62:446–52.

Vucetich, J. A., and T. A. Waite. 1999. Erosion of heterozygosity in fluctuating populations. *Conservation Biology* 13:860–68.

Wadsworth, K. G., and R. E. McCabe. 1996. *Issues and problems in predation management to enhance avian recruitment.* Logan, Utah: Berryman Institute.

Wagner, M., F. Smeins, B. Hays, and S. Whisenant. 2003. *Pastures for upland birds: Restoration of native plants in bermudagrass pastures.* College Station: Texas Cooperative Extension, Texas A&M University System.

Walker, L. C. 1991. *The southern forest: A chronicle.* Austin: University of Texas Press.

Walker, L. C., and G. L. Collier. 1969. *Geography of the southern forest region.* Bulletin 18. Nacogdoches, Tex.: School of Forestry, Stephen F. Austin State University.

Wallmo, O. C. 1954. Nesting of Mearns quail in southeastern Arizona. *Condor* 56:125–28.

———. 1956. *Ecology of scaled quail in West Texas.* Austin: Texas Game and Fish Commission.

———. 1957. Ecology of scaled quail in West Texas. Dissertation, Agricultural and Mechanical College of Texas, College Station.

Wallmo, O. C., and P. B. Uzzell. 1958. Ecological and social problems in quail management in West Texas. *Transactions of the North American Wildlife Conference* 23:320–28.

Walsh, P. B. 1985. Habitat use and population fluctuations of white-tailed deer at the La Copita Research Area, Jim Wells County, Texas. Thesis, Texas A&M University, College Station.

Ward, J. W. 1945. Parasite studies of quail. *Journal of Parasitology* 31 (Supplement): 23.

Warner, S. R. 1940. *Some quail food plants of southeastern Texas.* College Station: Division of Wildlife Research, Texas Agricultural Experiment Station, Agricultural and Mechanical College of Texas.

Warnock, B. H. 1970. *Wildflowers of the Big Bend Country, Texas.* Alpine, Tex.: Sul Ross State University.

———. 1974. *Wildflowers of the Guadalupe Mountains and the sand dune country, Texas.* Alpine, Tex.: Sul Ross State University.

———. 1977. *Wildflowers of the Davis Mountains and the Marathon Basin, Texas.* Alpine, Tex.: Sul Ross State University.

Warnock, B. J., and L. Loomis. 2002. Was the Trans-Pecos a grassland? Past, present, and potential. Pages 94–97 in L. A. Harveson, P. M. Harveson, and C. Richardson, eds., *Proceedings of the Trans-Pecos Wildlife Conference.* Alpine, Tex.: Sul Ross State University.

Watson, H., D. L. Lee, and P. J. Hudson. 1987. The effect of *Trichostrongylus tenuis* on the caecal mucosa of young, old and anthelmintic-treated wild red grouse, *Lagopus lagopus scoticus. Parasitology* 94:405–11.

Wauer, R. 1973. *Report on harlequin quail release, Big Bend National Park, Texas.* Big Bend National Park, Tex.

———. 1996. *A field guide to the birds of Big Bend.* Houston: Gulf.

Webb, W. M., and F. S. Guthery. 1982. Response of bobwhite to habitat management in northwest Texas. *Wildlife Society Bulletin* 10:142–46.

———. 1983. Response of wildlife food plants to spring disking of mesquite rangeland in northwest Texas. *Journal of Range Management* 36:351–53.

Webb, L. G., and F. P. Nelson. 1972. Recovery data from pen-raised quail released before and during the hunting season. *Proceedings of the Annual Conference of the Southeastern Association of Game and Fish Commissioners* 25:140–47.

Webster, J. D. 1944. A new cestode from the bob-white. *Transactions of the American Microscopical Society* 63:44–45.

———. 1947. Helminths from the bob-white in Texas, with descriptions of two new cestodes. *Transactions of the American Microscopical Society* 65:339–43.

———. 1948. A new acanthocephalan from the bob-white. *Journal of Parasitology* 34:84–86.

———. 1951. Additional notes on the helminth parasites of the bob-white in Texas. *Journal of Parasitology* 37:322–23.

Webster, J. D., and C. J. Addis. 1945. Helminths from the bob-white quail in Texas. *Journal of Parasitology* 31:286–87.

Weins, J. A. 1973. Patterns and process in grassland bird communities. *Ecological Monographs* 43:237–70.

Weins, J. A., and J. T. Rotenberry 1981. Habitat associations and community structure of birds in shrubsteppe environments. *Ecological Monographs* 51:21–41.

Welty, J. C., and L. Baptista. 1988. *The life of birds.* San Francisco: Saunders College Publishing.

Weniger, D. 1988. Vegetation before 1860. Pages 17–24 in B. Amos and F. R. Gehlbach, eds., *Edwards Plateau vegetation.* Waco, Tex.: Baylor University Press.

Wethe, D. 2003. A takeover artist's new target is land. *New York Times,* October 5, BU-5.

Wetmore, P. W. 1941. Blood parasites of birds of the District of Columbia and Patuxent Research Refuge vicinity. *Journal of Parasitology* 27:379–93.

White, D. H., B. R. Chapman, J. H. Brunjes IV, R. V. Raftovich Jr., and J. T. Segenack. 1999. Abundance and reproductive success of songbirds in burned and unburned pine forests of the Georgia Piedmont. *Journal of Field Ornithology* 70:414–24.

White, L. D., and C. W. Hanselka. 1989. *Prescribed range burning in Texas.* Texas Agricultural Extension Service Bulletin B-1310. College Station.

Whiting, R. M., Jr. 1978. Avian diversity in various age pine forests in East Texas. Dissertation, Texas A&M University, College Station.

Wickliff, E. L. 1932. Game research in Ohio. *Transactions of the American Game Conference* 19:351–61.

Wiedemann, H. T. 1997. Factors to consider when sculpting brush: Mechanical treatment options. Pages 88–95 in D. Rollins, D. N. Ueckert, and C. G. Brown, eds., *Brush sculptors: Symposium proceedings.* San Angelo: Texas Agricultural Extension Service.

Wilkins, N., R. D. Brown, R. J. Conner, J. Engle, C. Gilliland, A. Hays, R. D. Slack, and D. W. Steinbach. 2000. *Fragmented lands: Changing land ownership in Texas.* Publication MKT-3443. College Station: Texas Cooperative Extension, Texas A&M University.

Wilkins, N., A. Hays, D. Kubenka, D. Steinbach, W. Grant, E. Gonzalez, M. Kjelland, and J. Shackelford. 2003. *Texas rural land: Trends and conservation implications for the 21st century.* Publication B-6134. College Station: Texas Cooperative Extension, Texas A&M University System, Texas A&M University.

Wilkins, R. N. 1987. Influence of grazing management on population attributes, habitats, and habitat selection of bobwhites in South Texas. Thesis, Texas A&M University, College Station.

Williams, C. K., W. R. Davidson, R. S. Lutz, and R. D. Applegate. 2000. Health status of northern bobwhite quail (*Colinus virginianus*) in eastern Kansas. *Avian Diseases* 44:953–56.

Williams, C. K., R. S. Lutz, R. D. Applegate, and D. H. Rusch. 2000. Habitat use and survival of northern bobwhite (*Colinus virginianus*) in cropland and rangeland ecosystems during the hunting season. *Canadian Journal of Zoology—Revue Canadienne De Zoologie* 78:1562–66.

Williams, E. S., M. W. Miller, T. J. Kreeger, R. H. Kahn, and E. T. Thorne. 2002. Chronic wasting disease of deer and elk: A review with recommendations for management. *Journal of Wildlife Management* 66:551–63.

Williamson, S., L. W. Burger, S. Demarais, and M. Chamberlain. 2002. Effects of northern bobwhite habitat management practices on red imported fire ants. *Proceedings of the National Quail Symposium* 5:151–55.

Wilson, A. D., and G. J. Tupper. 1982. Concepts and factors applicable to the measurement of range condition. *Journal of Range Management* 35:684–89.

Wilson, C. W., R. E. Masters, and G. A. Bukenhofer. 1995. Breeding bird response to pine-grassland community restoration for red-cockaded woodpeckers. *Journal of Wildlife Management* 59:56–67.

Wilson, D. E., and N. J. Silvy. 1988. Impact of the imported fire ants on birds. Pages 70–74 in Sportsmen Conservationists of Texas, eds., *Proceedings of the governor's conference on the imported fire ant: Assessment and recommendations.* Austin: Sportsmen Conservationists of Texas.

Wilson, E. A., and A. S. Leslie. 1911. Grouse disease. Pages 185–206 in *Committee of Inquiry on Grouse Disease, The grouse in health and disease,* vol. 1. London: Smith.

Wilson, M. H. 1984. Comparative ecology of bobwhite and scaled quail in southern Texas. Dissertation, Oregon State University, Corvallis.

Wilson, M. H., and J. A. Crawford. 1979. Response of bobwhites to controlled burning in South Texas. *Wildlife Society Bulletin* 7:53–56.

———. 1987. Habitat selection by Texas bobwhites and chestnut-bellied scaled quail in South Texas. *Journal of Wildlife Management* 51:575–82.

———. 1988. Poxvirus in scaled quail and prevalences of poxvirus-like lesions in northern bobwhites and scaled quail from Texas. *Journal of Wildlife Diseases* 24:360–63.

Wiseman, D. S. 1977. Habitat use, food habits, and response to bird dog field trials on northeastern Oklahoma rangeland. Thesis, Oklahoma State University, Stillwater.

Wiseman, D. S., and J. C. Lewis. 1981. Bobwhite use of habitat in tallgrass rangeland. *Wildlife Society Bulletin* 9:248–55.

Wiseman, J. S. 1959. The genera of Mallophaga of North America north of Mexico with special reference to Texas species. Dissertation, Agricultural and Mechanical College of Texas, College Station.

———. 1968. A previously undescribed species of *Menacanthus* (Mallophaga: Menoponidae) from bobwhite quail. *Journal of the Kansas Entomological Society* 41:57–60.

Wood, J. E. 1952. The ecology of furbearers in the upland Post Oak region of eastern Texas. Dissertation, Agricultural and Mechanical College of Texas, College Station.

Wood, K. N., F. S. Guthery, and N. E. Koerth. 1986. Spring-summer nutrition and condition of northern bobwhites in South Texas. *Journal of Wildlife Management* 50:84–88.

Wood, S. F., and C. M. Herman. 1943. The occurrence of blood parasites in birds from southwestern United States. *Journal of Parasitology* 29:187–96.

Wright, H. A., and A. W. Bailey. 1982. *Fire ecology: United States and southern Canada.* New York: Wiley.

Wrinkle, J. 2002. Does fire have a role in the Chihuahuan Desert? Pages 98–100 in L. A. Harveson, P. M. Harveson, and C. Richardson, eds., *Proceedings of the Trans-Pecos Wildlife Conference.* Alpine, Tex.: Sul Ross State University.

Yoakum, J. D., B. W. O'Gara, and V. W. Howard Jr. 1996. Pronghorn on western rangelands. Pages 211–26 in P. R. Krausman, ed., *Rangeland wildlife.* Denver, Colo.: The Society for Range Management.

Contributors

Ty H. Allen
Department of Natural Resource and
Wildlife Management
Sul Ross State University
Alpine, Texas 79832

John Baccus
Department of Biology
Texas State University
San Marcos, Texas 78666

Leonard A. Brennan
Caesar Kleberg Wildlife Research
Institute
Texas A&M University–Kingsville
Kingsville, Texas 78363

Fred C. Bryant
Caesar Kleberg Wildlife Research
Institute
Texas A&M University–Kingsville
Kingsville, Texas 78363

J. Richard Conner
Department of Agricultural
Economics
Texas A&M University
College Station, Texas 77843

Jerry Cooke
Texas Parks and Wildlife Department
Austin, Texas 78744

C. Brad Dabbert
Department of Range, Fisheries, and
Wildlife Management
Texas Tech University
Lubbock, Texas 79409

Stephen J. DeMaso
Texas Parks and Wildlife Department
Austin, Texas 78744

James Dillard
Texas Parks and Wildlife Department
Mineral Wells, Texas 76068

Jack C. Eitniear
Department of Biology
Texas State University
San Marcos, Texas 78666

Fred S. Guthery
Department of Natural Resource
Management
Oklahoma State University
Stillwater, Oklahoma 74808

Jason B. Hardin
Audubon Texas
901 South MoPac
Austin, Texas 78746

Louis A. Harveson
Department of Natural Resource and
Wildlife Management
Sul Ross State University
Alpine, Texas 79832

Fidel Hernández
Caesar Kleberg Wildlife Research
Institute
Texas A&M University–Kingsville
Kingsville, Texas 78363

Froylan Hernández
Department of Natural Resource and
Wildlife Management
Sul Ross State University
Alpine, Texas 79832

Michael D. Hobson
Texas Parks and Wildlife Department
Alpine, Texas 79830

Dave A. Holdermann
Department of Natural Resource and
Wildlife Management
Sul Ross State University
Alpine, Texas 79832

Ronnie Howard
San Tomas Hunting Camp
Encino, Texas 78353

William P. Kuvlesky Jr.
Caesar Kleberg Wildlife Research
Institute
Texas A&M University–Kingsville
Kingsville, Texas 78363

Duane R. Lucia
Department of Range, Fisheries, and
Wildlife Management
Texas Tech University
Lubbock, Texas 79409

Robert B. Mitchell
Department of Range, Fisheries, and
Wildlife Management
Texas Tech University
Lubbock, Texas 79409

James M. Mueller
Department of Natural Resource and
Wildlife Management
Sul Ross State University
Alpine, Texas 79832

Robert Perez
Texas Parks and Wildlife Department
LaVernia, Texas 78121

Markus J. Peterson
Department of Fisheries and
Wildlife Sciences and Center
for Public Leadership Studies
George Bush School of Government
and Public Service
Texas A&M University
College Station, Texas 77843

Dale Rollins
Texas A&M University Extension
Service
San Angelo, Texas 76901

Nova J. Silvy
Department of Fisheries and Wildlife
Sciences
Texas A&M University
College Station, Texas 77842

Shane Whisenant
Department of Fisheries and Wildlife
Sciences
Texas A&M University
College Station, Texas 77842

R. Montague Whiting Jr.
Arthur Temple College of Forestry
Stephen F. Austin State University
Nacogdoches, Texas 75962

M. Shane Whitley
Department of Natural Resource and
Wildlife Management
Sul Ross State University
Alpine, Texas 79832

Index

491

Index

ISBN-13: 978-1-58544-503-5
ISBN-10: 1-58544-503-7